Personal Writings

The Personal Writings of
Samuel Roskelley

———•••———

*A Line-by-line Transcription
of the Surviving Manuscripts
and Published Renditions*

with an introduction and afterword by

Richard L. Saunders

Caramon Press

2018

Licensed under a Creative Commons 4.0 CC BY NC license (Attribution, Non Commercial)

Cover images: Samuel Roskelley collection, P0013, Utah State Univ. Special Collections.
          Logan, Utah, ca.1872 (from a stereograph print).
       Map: *History of a Valley: Cache Valley, Utah and Idaho,* ed. Joel E. Ricks (Cache Valley
          Centennial Commission, 1956).

Roskelley, Samuel, 1837–1914.

     The personal writings of Samuel Roskelley : a line-by-line transcription of the surviving manuscripts and published renditions / with an introduction and afterword by Richard L. Saunders. — s.l. : Caramon Press, 2018.
     xii, 387p. ; 29cm.
     ISBN-13: 978-0-9627804-5-5

  1. Cache Valley (Utah and Idaho) -- History -- Sources. 2. Smithfield (Utah) -- History -- Sources. 3. Logan Temple (Utah). 4. Mormons -- Diaries. 5. Mormon Church -- Cache Valley (Utah and Idaho). 6. Frontier and pioneer life -- Utah. 7. Roskelly family. I. title. II. Saunders, Richard L., 1963- .

Contents

Introduction   *vii*
   Richard L. Saunders

Untitled Autobiography   *1*
   Early life in Devonport, England
   Westward emigration, 1853

Journal 1   *15*
   Eastward travel, 1856
   British Mission (Wales), 1856–1857

Journal 2   *31*
   British Mission (Wales), 1857
   Post-mission life, 1857–ca.1860

Journal [3]   *69*
   Eastward travel, 1880
   British Mission (London), 1880

Journal 4   *109*
   British Mission (London), 1880–1881

Journal 5   *143*
   St George mission, 1883–1884
   Cache Valley, 1884–1887

Journal [6]   *249*
   Cache Valley, 1888–1901

Journal [7]   *367*
   Cache Valley, 1901–1910

Autobiographical notes
   A Faith-promoting Incident   *385*
   A Visit from the Spirit World   *393*

Afterword   *395*

Introduction

Richard L. Saunders

For Twenty years I successfully dodged my second great-grandfather, Samuel Roskelley. He had loomed large in my upbringing; my mother is the oldest daughter of R. Welling Roskelley, an institution at Utah State University whose name held clout and opened doors. Our family was much closer to the Roskelley side of the family than the Saunders side. My uncle, mom's only brother, lived on a city farm lot that had been Samuel's city property in Smithfield, in a house built by one of Samuel's younger sons. My grandfather owned and farmed (and I hauled sprinkler pipe and sprayed corn) on the last of working Roskelley farm properties in the fields west of town. I grew up with grandpa's stories of his own grandfather, and a host of other Roskelley and Smithfield stories. I heard his family stories, including his recollection of meeting his grandfather as a very young child.

In the early 1980s I began college at Utah State University as a third-generation Aggie, working with manuscript material the library's Special Collections unit where Samuel's papers had been donated to the university in 1955 as virtually its first manuscript collection. The collection contained two diaries and a number of other papers and records. Working in Special Collections under A. J. Simmonds I encountered Samuel Roskelley in a different capacity, as a figure who loomed large in local history. More than once I sat in the stacks and simply leafed through the two journals that were housed there. I heard rumors that he had kept other diaries but no one I knew had seen them for years nor had any idea what had happened to them, other than they were certainly scattered among his other descendants. I saw the transcript, but the fact that the original documents were not all in one place, available for everyone, bothered me as a professional Special Collections librarian and as a Roskelley descendant.

Finally, in 2014 our family returned to Utah. In a single afternoon I repented sufficiently to quit stalling and get to work regathering what could be found. That decision has sustained me for four years as doors and windows into the family past began opening immediately. The project became a personal quest that involved me re-learning what many in the family already knew.

Samuel Roskelley and His Journals

Samuel was an irregular diarist. He kept diaries of routine activity during his two proselyting missions, but when not on a mission he recorded entries only during a relatively brief period of his late adulthood that corresponds roughly to his service as Recorder for the Logan Temple. His final diary ends abruptly in the front of a volume and middle of a page several years before his passing. Several statements scattered through the diaries suggest that he wrote his diary entries weekly or biweekly rather than daily, backtracking in time and memory to catch up when he could.

Samuel retained his own diaries, of course, but others in the family must have known about them. At Samuel's passing his papers, photographs, and diaries were distributed among interested family members. No one knows how the distribution is made or precisely what was scattered, but it likely involved all seven diaries, dozens of photographs (many belonging to his wives), and at least one scrapbook. In my heart of hearts, I hope that the diaries exit quietly in the hands of family members and that owners of those materials will eventually see fit to donate them to USU so that Samuel's work may be re-gathered for the benefit of all his descendants, not just the lucky few who have them in hand.

We have Samuel's personal writing because at different times across the past century sections were brought to the family in different forms and for different purposes. The present transcription and publication project has benefited and drawn from the work of many predecessors. I may have done the lion's share of the typing to get things into digital form, but it was possible only because of the good offices of other folks in years gone by. If you are unaware, here is a brief summary of the formats that Samuel's writing exists in other than the manuscripts themselves, not all of which are presently accessible.

Mortensen transcript Around 1945, Cache County clerk and Roskelley granddaughter Lula R. Mortensen had access to all seven of the diaries and the duplication equipment of the time: a manual typewriter and carbon paper. transcribed all seven in the 1940s. This had been done on a manual typewriter, which allowed duplicates to be made at the same time, but also limited the number of copies. Try as I might, I could not locate any of those transcripts. Finally in my explorations I noticed a transcript of journal 3 existing in the Samuel Roskelley papers, which I conclude is very likely the sole remainder of Mortensen's hard work. All other Mortensen transcripts have since disappeared from public knowledge.

Genealogical Society of Utah microfilm In 1954 an organizing committee under Dr. Joel Ricks announced plans to publish a centennial history of Cache Valley. A public call was made for families of the valley's settlers to bring family papers to light to inform the history. Samuel's son Richard Roskelley and his son (my grandfather) R. Welling Roskelley persuaded a unknown number of family members to allow material in their hands to be microfilmed by the Genealogical Society of Utah. Made in 1954, the microfilm (which has since been transferred to the Church History Library collections) included diaries 1, 3, 5, and 7, and a genealogical table of his family members made by Samuel himself. Since at least 2014 it has been digitally available through the Church History Library, the historical arm of the Church of Jesus Christ of Latter-day Saints.

Samuel Roskelley collections I've mentioned the collection at USU. On New Year's Day of 1955, Samuel's birthday, the Roskelleys jointly donated a collection of Samuel Roskelley material to Utah State University. It was the first donation of unpublished papers made to the school. The collection included two of the diaries on the GSU microfilm (journals 5 and 7), but included two additional diaries (2 and 6) that had not been microfilmed. The microfilm and family gift to USU provided descendants with access to five of Samuel's diaries.

The Roskelley Organ On the heels of the donation to USU, in 1955 the family organization began publishing a family magazine. Its first issue (maybe two issues) reproduced Samuel's autobiography from a Mortensen transcript made years earlier. We can be profoundly grateful that the newsletter/ magazine chose to do so, for even by that date Samuel's handwritten manuscript itself had disappeared. With the manuscript gone, the newsletter publication is the earliest rendition of the autobiography available.

Killpack transcript Though it is undated, this is the format with which most family members will know Samuel Roskelley's personal writing, both the autobiography and the diaries. When I visited with her she could not recall clearly whether she had made typescript four decades earlier from the original diaries or a carbon of the Mortensen typescripts. It doesn't matter, really. Produced on a typewriter during the United States' Bicentennial celebration in 1976, Mrs. Killpack's edited compilation of Samuel's writing was the first reasonably complete gathering of Samuel's work ever made available. The photocopied pages also reproduced a group of portraits of Samuel, photos of his wives' homes, a long section of Samuel's autobiography, and extracts from Samuel's diaries. Copies are available through the family and now the Church History Library.

A Devonport Boy Comes to America As I started nosing around a couple of years ago, it was clear that the family needed a founding myth (*myth* as in *origin story*, not *a made up tale*), the story of how a poor English kid ended up in northern Utah. In 2015 I finally pulled myself together to publish an edited version of Samuel's autobiography with notes. That it did not sell well was irrelevant—it was explicitly a project I hoped would spark attention and flush the missing diaries out of the woodwork. Pushing that project to completion finally allowed me to put down into text what I knew about Samuel, to challenge what I did not know, and to correct what I though we knew. As I was exploring source material to edit the autobiography, I stumbled across a digital collection of the incredible 1856–1862 Ordnance Survey maps of

Devonport. I realized that the ten-feet-to-the-mile maps provided an opportunity to look down at exactly the city that Samuel knew, something I have never had an opportunity to do as an historian or as a genealogist. The detail is incredible. One can see the street lamps, the corner hydrants, the mews and alleyways of the mid-Victorian city. I took the opportunity to plot the city and the Latter-day Saints that Samuel would have known on a companion map to the autobiography titled *Samuel Roskelley's Devonport*. I made mistakes on the first version of that map, partly because the low-resolution digital images did not allow me to read street addresses with great accuracy. A fortunate opportunity to see and handle original Ordnance Survey maps in the British Library and National Archives in 2017 allowed me to correct the residential placements.

As you can see, this publication is only the latest of a long list of good works wrought by family members in preserving the family record. As I began my own rediscovery of Roskelley family history, I made the acquaintance of a number of Roskelley relatives either in person or digitally. During those pleasant interactions a number of Samuel's things came back to light: the ambrotype photograph of his parents, the photoprint of him as a 19-year-old missionary, several letters and other documents, but most importantly, the remaining missing manuscript diaries, journals 2, 4, and 6. Suddenly, all seven diaries were available again, five of them the original manuscripts. The Roskelley papers at USU were beginning to enlarge after years of neglect, too, as the custodians of three diaries first made careful digital copies for sharing and then donated them to USU, where they rejoined the others.

With the missing manuscripts' return to accessibility, it did not take long for my professional heart to turn back to the project that I had long wanted to pursue: a biography of Samuel Roskelley, for no other reason than there was not one. To do that, I really needed access to the diaries. Digital technology solved that problem quickly and easily, sparing me a lot of trips to Logan.

As an historian and collegiate librarian I am well aware that many of the rising generation do not read handwriting well at all. My fear was that though Samuel's personal writing had resurfaced, it was quite possible that even easily accessible in digital form, his latest descendants would not care because they could not connect with him or read his writing. So, here you are folks—a complete line-by-line transcript of Samuel Roskelley's diaries in clear, easily read print. I don't know that I'll ever get to the biography, but I am now comfortable that Samuel will live again in a modern format accessible to those carrying his genes into coming generations.

Transcribing the Diaries

Transcription is a precise but inexact art. Accommodations and compromises must always be made when rendering handwriting and handwritten pages with typed characters. Readers should know first off that the volume is organized roughly chronologically, with the autobiography first but with the two autobiographical stories at the end. The "Faith Promoting Incident" might reasonably have been inserted chronologically between journals 5 and 6, but—whatever. I am doing this as insurance against the possibility that I might never complete editing or the biography.

This volume reproduces as best I can a line-by-line transcription of the manuscript diaries, without editing, clarification, or exposition—basically no corrections, no notes, no context, just the straight stuff. Things got a bit complicated with the tabulations pasted on the pages, but everything should be shown in order from top of the page to the bottom. Some caveats are merited, however:

- The pages of the five manuscript diaries now in the Samuel Roskelley collection at Utah State Univ. were numbered in pencil to allow matching the transcription easily against page locations in the originals. In these transcripts the now-numbered pages are identified by the numbers given in braces. For the two diaries that exist only as microfilm and digital copies, I've used the image number of a downloaded PDF file as reckoning points, so instead of numbered pages you are given the image numbers. This isn't perfect but it is the best that can be done until the two manuscript volumes again come to light.
- I have made every effort to confirm and represent Samuel's spelling quirks as he set them down, but I am sure that my typing did not set down every word correctly. Mea culpa; I tried.

- Initial capitals represent a real problem and Samuel's habits of mixing lower case and capital letters make for odd reading in a typescript. He regularly used a large lower-case *s* or *m* in the position of an initial capital, and sometimes used an upper-case *S* for no reason at all. I preserved those uses as regularly as possible Capital *K* was used virtually anywhere the letter appeared, even in the middle of words; that is an example of where I simply used the correct lower-case letter.
- Samuel's manuscript insertions to his own diary texts are indicated by an /opening and closing solidus\ around the inserted text, as shown in this sentence; the characters and words between them occupy the line above and are shown for reading sense.
- Transcriptions of text that span two-page spreads indicate the fold's place in the line by inserting a *pipe character* (|) in the transcription to mark the place of the book's fold.
- Indecipherable words are marked thus: [---]. There are not many.
- Most blank lines left in the manuscript diaries are eliminated in the transcript to save space.
- Space in this publication is saved where possible by setting the transcription in double columns, with the page transcriptions separated clearly by a line.

All of the published versions of Samuel's autobiographical manuscripts were incomplete at the time they were transcribed by Lula Mortensen around 1945, and when they were published in the mid-century family newsletter. The place of the missing leaves are indicated where known. The incomplete autobiography may or may not have included the two stories at the end of this volume, but since they were published separately, separate they remain. From length of the published version of the "Visit," its full manuscript was probably four or five pages; at the time Mrs. Mortensen transcribed it around 1945 the first leaf (two pages) had disappeared, leaving modern readers to pick up in the middle of Samuel's account. This vision would have happened some time after 1871 and perhaps before Samuel was asked to serve as Recorder for the Logan Temple in 1884, but at this point there is no way to tell for sure unless we can identify the C. L. Olsen whose demise he refers to. The three autobiographical texts are simply set as straight text, making no effort to maintain line breaks.

No, there is no index. I want the complete diaries to get into your hands quickly and will opt not to produce an index. If I ever manage to complete an edited version or biography, an index will be part of the project on which I will lavish attention. Until then you are encouraged to read often enough that you can get a sense of Samuel's record-keeping and activities.

Share this transcript as widely as you would like, in any format you find convenient. I want the families' founder and his times to be known and appreciated by his descendants.

Samuel Roskelley

Since this volume begins with an autobiography there is little use in restating what Samuel himself records. The autobiography with careful notes about the family and its background is available in a separate volume. It is helpful, however, to fill in some blanks that Samuel fails to document.

Samuel Roskelley was born 1 January 1837 in Devonport, England, the youngest son of Thomas and Ann Kitt Roskelley. His autobiography fails to note that the family originated at least three hundred years earlier in St Keverne parish, at the extreme southeastern tip of Cornwall. Following his emigration to Utah Territory in 1854, Samuel made a living as farmer in the southern half of the Cache Valley. This well-watered space was well-known to a generation of fur traders. By the time Samuel settled there permanently in 1862, the eastern slope of the valley floor was becoming a patchwork of cultivated fields. Large reaches on the west provided pasturage for cattle.

Samuel Roskelley was, like many of his church and time, married plurally. This fact and the complications which it multiplied on his famil(ies), suffuses his diaries. Though Samuel was relatively successful as a farmer, his diaries document how comparatively little he worked his own properties, relying heavily on a succession of "hired men" to do much of the routine farm labor while he worked steadily as Recorder. Though the cramped handwriting of his diaries belies it, Samuel wrote a fine hand. As temple Recorder in a day before typewriters, clerical handwriting was essential for recordkeeping.

Employment in the temple ended in 1910, shortly after his diary was discontinued. It is possible that Samuel felt a diary was no longer necessary. He retired to Smithfield (if a farmer ever retires), and passed away at home of natural causes in 1914.

Principals Named in the Diaries

Since these are personal writings, the diaries provide comparatively little context about the people named. A table of Samuel's principle family members mentioned in the diaries is included for context. Individuals who are not family probably have enough detail to explain their relationship to Samuel.

Wives:
- Rebecca Hendricks Watson Roskelley (2 November 1835 – 11 May 1880)
- Mary Roberts Roskelley (22 November 1843 – 20 January 1927)
- [Mary Florence Kelsey Roskelley (4 March 1851 – 18 or 25 January 1868) *never mentioned*]
- Mary Jane Rigby Roskelley (28 June 1857 – 28 July 1949)
- Margaret Rigby Roskelley (12 February 1864 – 20 January 1918)
- Sarah Maud Burton Roskelley (1 or 4 October 1861 – 24 September 1932)

Children:
- James Roskelley (1865–1919), Rebecca's son
- Joseph Roskelley (1868–1951), Rebecca's son
- Mary Roskelley (1870–1942), Mary's daughter
- William Hendricks Roskelley (1866–1948), Rebecca's son
- Zina Young Roskelley Hyde (1862–1881), Rebecca's daughter

Richard L. Saunders
Cedar City, October 2018

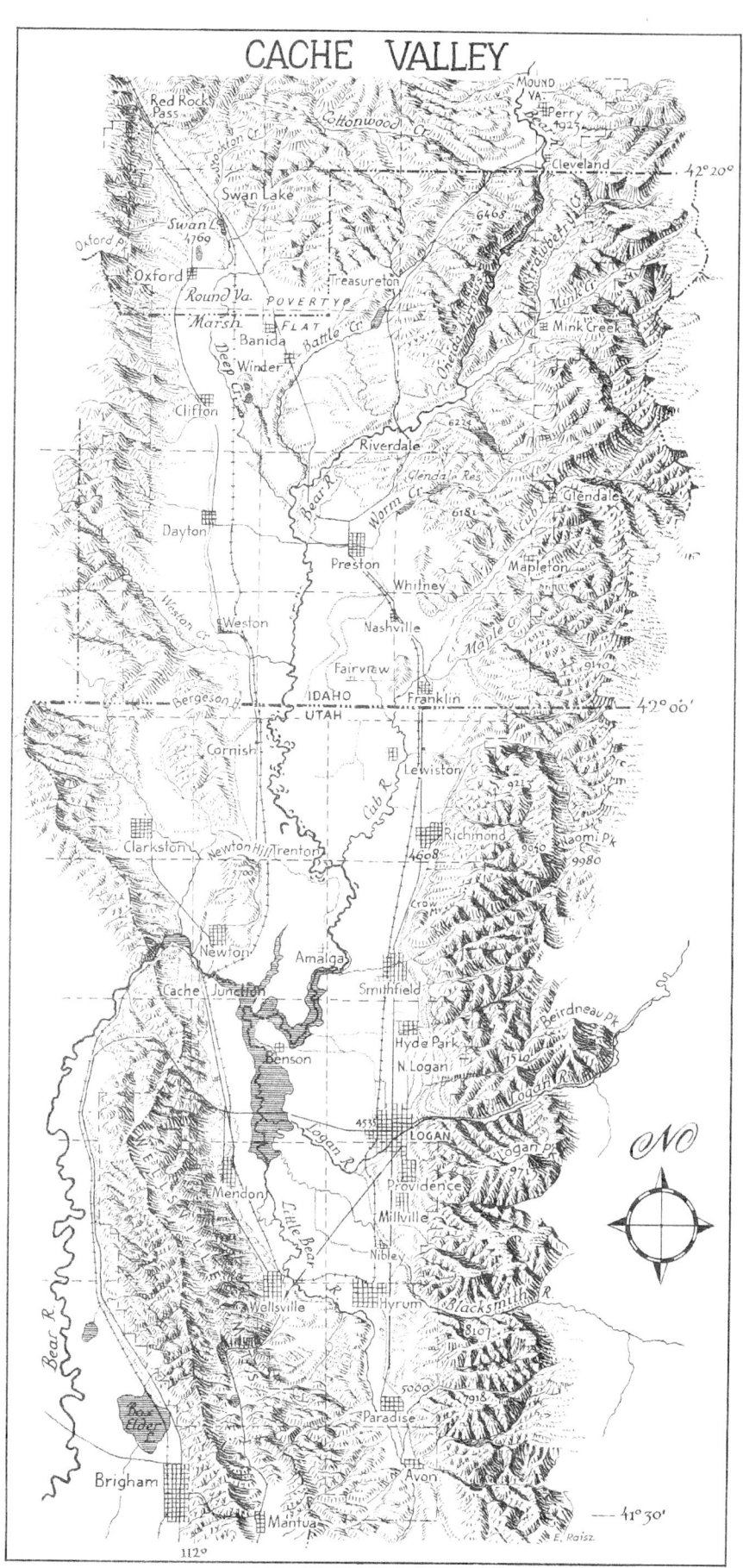

[Untitled Autobiography]

ca.1888

Having Spent most of my life as a member of the Church of Jesus Christ of Latter-day Saints, I feel prompted to write a few items of my history for the perusal of my family and those that may be interested; and that my testimony may remain with those it may concern regarding the work of God revealed and organized through the Prophet Joseph Smith in this, the last dispensation of the fullness of times. As the Lord in His mercy saw fit to bring me to a knowledge of His work in the days of my youth and by His merciful providence has kept me from turning my back upon His kingdom and people. I owe Him all I have and am, because He has over-ruled all things during my life for my good, and has given me the testimony of His spirit more or less according to my faithfulness to Him thru life.

Samuel Roskelley was born 1 January 1837 in Morris Square, Devonport, Devon, England, being the 6th and youngest child of Thomas and Ann Kitt Roskelley. The family consisted of Richard, Thomas, John Joseph, Jane (now Mrs. Williams), William Henry, and Samuel. My parents were born and spent their youth in the county of Cornwall in the parish and neighborhood of St. Germans, removing to Devonport, the place of my birth, a few years after they were married. And although in but moderate circumstances, they gave their children a good common school education which they considered as good a Legacy as they could bestow upon them. Being Baptists by profession, the children were all taught in the faith and belief of that denomination by Sabbath School and church teachings, and I being the youngest in the family was subject to more strict discipline than the older children. Although being religiously inclined in my childhood I could readily understand that there was quite a difference between the teachings of my Sabbath School teachers and the teachings of the New Testament, consequently when I was about 11 or 12 years old I used to ponder over these differences and frequently wish that I could have lived in the days when the Savior and His Apostles lived on the earth, little realizing I was living in the "dispensation of the fullness of times."

When nearly 14 years old, my father desired to apprentice me to learn a trade. Opportunities were given annually to young men to learn trades in Her Majesty's Dock Yards and my father did all in his power to get me a position there, but his application was too late and his efforts to bind me an apprentice was a failure. The cause can be readily seen now, for the Lord wanted me somewhere else. While of tender years, I became associated with a number of youths about my own age and older, whose habits and examples were of a pernicious character and to some extent I fell a prey to their evil influence, but there was a spirit with me that held me in check and many times have I felt the

---

Manuscript presently unlocated, but transcribed by Lula Mortensen ca.1945; this is a transcript of its first publication in *The Roskelley Organ* 1, no.1–2 (1955): 2–19.

remorse that follows wrong doing when the good Spirit would chide me for my acts. Notably I remember walking along a street with my companions who would swear and drink and were habituated to other vices. One of the boys annoyed me and I made use of an expression using a vulgar word that made my hair almost stand on end. I was so shocked at my own words that I stood still for a moment as if paralyzed and looked around to see if anyone was near me or heard me. I felt so ashamed of my expression that it made a lasting impression upon my mind and I have never permitted myself to swear or use bad language since.

When I was near 14 years old the members of the Maurice Square Baptist chapel were quite exercised over the question of "Open" and "Close" Communion, upon which they seemed about equally divided—my parents and other members of the family took quite a prominent part in the discussion which finally divided the flock—causing many bitter feelings—this led me to believe that other sects were as good and sincere in their worship as the Baptists and I asked and obtained my father's consent to go to other places of worship on Sunday evenings. I visited and heard the services of the Methodists, Catholics, Ranters, Episcopalians and other sects but did not feel at home with any of them. If I had a preference it was for the last-named sect because they seemed to teach as good doctrine as the rest and their singing was superb, but my youthful companions and their examples held quite a sway over me and I more or less fell into the snares they laid for me, much to the regret of my parents and family associates. But the eye of the Lord was over me and His spirit chided me in my silent reflection and He wonderfully plucked me from the path I was walking and gave me work in another direction.

While walking the streets of my native town during the month of November, 1850, I heard some singing in a hall above some stables—it attracted my attention because it seemed to have a peculiar "ring" to it, I had never heard before. I stepped up the stairway and listened with delight much to the annoyance of my companions, who, after making some unkind and vulgar remarks about me and the singing, went away and left me. I remained until the song was ended much impressed with the words and the tune. In passing the same place in about two weeks later (This place proved to be the Latter-day Saints' Granby Street meeting room, Devonport) I was again attracted with the singing. This time my companions left me thinking I would follow them, but I did not. I remained until the singing was over and heard remarks made by several persons bearing testimonies to the Gospel revealed in our day and the Priesthood brought to earth by an angel. This sounded strange to me but not inconsistent. I pondered over it for several days, told my father what I had heard, and asked him what he thought of such things. But he made light of it saying it was some of the false prophets that scripture said should arise. But I resolved to go again at an early date and hear more. Within a few days a lady acquaintance, a Sunday school companion of my sister, named Maria Kicks, came to my mother's to visit my sister and to help her with the dressmaking business. She was much afflicted with rheumatism, and having heard of a people called Latter Day Saints who believed in Laying hands on the sick after the Scriptures pattern, she induced my mother to send for one of the elders of the church to visit and take tea one afternoon, and explain the doctrines of this faith. I overheard all that was said by the elder on one side and my mother, sister, and Miss Kicks on the other, and understood that the doctrines he advocated, although scriptural, were unpopular and were not well received by my mother and sister, but they sank deep within me altho I was not permitted to say a word. But learning where the elders preached on Sunday evening I lost no opportunity to go to meeting and took note of all references made to the Bible doctrine, I afterwards read and found correct. Altho but a boy I was deeply impressed with the sermon preached by elder Wm. G. Mills and left the meeting feeling if any sect were true, these people had the true Gospel, if Scriptural evidence were any proof. My former companions no more possessed any influence over me. I cared no longer for their society. I had found something more congenial. And when the following Thursday evening came I wended my way to the place where I had previously heard such delightful singing. Altho services had already commenced, I found a seat and was enraptured with the service during the evening. It was a testimony meeting and truly the Spirit ran from heart to heart, for all seemed eager to testify that they knew this to be the work of the Lord revealed through Joseph Smith the Prophet. I was a silent listener to these testimonies and the beautiful songs interspersed, and to the exhortations of some of the elders. Near the close of the meeting my thoughts were many and I firmly believed what I had heard them testify to. After the meeting closed the usual salutations and hand-shaking among saints took place and I marveled, for I had never seen such freedom and affection for each other exhibited among any other sect I had visited. All seemed so kind to each other and I could not help but look on with astonishment and, I might say, delight. In wending my way toward the head of the stairway to make my exit I encountered the president of the branch (Elder Nichols) who asked me how I liked the meeting. I answered him "pretty well" or something to that effect, then he raised his hand and placed it on my head, said in a voice loud enough for all persons nearby to hear, "Young man, I prophecy in the name of Jesus Christ that you will become a Mormon elder and preach the Gospel in its fullness."

The action and prophecy of Elder Nichols was so unexpected to me and sent such a thrill through me that for a moment I felt quite perplexed, for there was such a strange feeling ran through me at the time. But I quickly recovered myself and turning to him I looked what I could not say, for I was dumbfounded, but I thought you foolish man, what do you know about me or my future, as I am an entire stranger to you in every respect? Little did I know that the spirit of Prophecy was restored to earth and this people I was with possessed it. I felt that with this people I was more at home than anywhere else, and I desired to unite with them, but I felt sure my parents would not give consent by the manner I had heard them express themselves. And just how to do I could not tell, as I was a minor and my parents had the right to control me by law. But I prayed to my Heavenly Father in the depths of my heart that He would forgive me all my sins and if it was right for me to be baptized for the remission of my sins to open up, for the impression remained with me to be baptized at an early date. Learning from the traveling elder (James Caffall) that the ordinance of baptism was to be administered to some applicants soon, I resolved to be one of the party if possible. Succeeding in getting a bundle of clothing to be baptized in, I found the party among whom was Elder Wm. G. Mills, James Caffall, and a few sisters with a lady candidate for baptism. We left Mutton Cove, Devonport, in a boat and crossed the Tamar River after dark on a very pleasant evening (for the season of the year), and arrived at Barn Pool near Mount Edgcombe, on the west side of the river in about 45 minutes, and after the usual change of raiment and prayer I was baptized by Elder James Caffall, Wednesday, 3 December 1851, and afterwards witnessed the baptism of the other candidates. I felt, no coming out of the water an inward satisfaction that I had done right, for I realized God's approval was upon me and much enjoyed the society and company of my newly made friends in the gospel—for in their fellowship I felt a contentment and satisfaction I could feel nowhere else. Little did I dream while with the Saints on that memorable occasion, and feeling that I had eventually entered into a new life, that such a storm was gathering and would break upon me in such a short time, for after bidding the Saints good-night and going to my home I found my father and some of the other members of the family eating supper, which, tho so late in the evening, was customary. My father, looking up, asked me where I had been till so late an hour? Altho it was not unusually late for me to be out, I answered I had been with some friends, but my mother taking up the subject answered, "I know where he has been! He's been to Barn Pool and been baptized by the Mormons, I know he has." Whether my mother's imagination had been aroused by seeing my hair glistening in the light of the candle, through being wet with the sea water, or whether an inspiration from an evil source caused her to know where I had been I do not know, but her statement had an effect I never saw produced in the family before. There was no more supper eaten that night and it was the only time in my life I ever saw my father give way to passion without restraint, that I remember of, but on this occasion, his voice together with my mother's, sister, and brothers mingled and co-mingled till it was hard to tell which was loudest in denouncing the Mormons and their youngest son and brother who, Mother said, she knew had been baptized. Father walked the floor, white as a sheet and shaking his clenched fist in my face said, "If I had known you were going to Barns Pool to be baptized by these Mormons I would have sunk the boat if I had been drowned myself." This was poor encouragement for a young convert to Mormonism and especially one so young in years. Not-with-standing all the threats and abuse I kept still and said nothing, considering it unwise to retaliate. I shortly went to bed but not to sleep, for the circumstances of the previous day and evening were of such a nature that sleep had fled from my eyelids, for I rejoiced that the Lord had led me to the Truth. No better outward evidences could I ask for than to see the manifestations of anger on the part of my parents and the family, under the influence of the power of the evil one. But I had resolved to serve the Lord at all costs, hence the more consistent I tried to live to the spirit of my religion the more embittered the family seemed to be toward me. I attended the Baptist Sabbath School as usual on the following Sabbath but excused myself early in the afternoon and went to the Saints' meeting at Heydens rooms, Devonport and was confirmed a member of the church by elder William G. Mills 7 December 1851. I rejoiced to hear the testimonies of the Saints and the teachings of the elders from this time forth and I gradually withdrew from the Baptist Sunday School and meetings and became more fervently attached to the Saints and took comfort in their meetings, God strengthening my faith and adding testimony to testimony of the divinity of His work until my heart was fully satisfied of its divine character. But so many thorns beset my path I doubted my own ability to withstand all the trials that met me. But God gave me strength according to my day and time, for which I gave him thanks—the elders and Saints knowing my situation would encourage me and I received much strength through their kind words and took much comfort in their company.

While learning the principles of the Everlasting Gospel through the teachings of the Elders and reading the Books of the Church, things grew worse at home. My people would gather as sweet morsels every bad story told against the Saints and their bitterness became more pronounced against my religion and consequently against me because of the sect I had chosen to unite my destinies with. I was looked upon as the blacksheep of my family and told that I had brought all the trouble upon them because of my persistence in doing as I pleased and would not be controlled. My company was undesirable and the sooner I changed my faith or withdrew from the family, the more pleased it would be. I was of the same opinion, as my home had been a very unpleasant one since the night I was baptized. I found employment with Brother William G. Burton—he being a member of the church and knowing my circumstances, gave me a home at his house where I assisted in helping in the bake house and doing such things as I was capable of doing until an opening presented itself for me to teach school as the Saints held meetings. My school was very successful considering I had so little experience previously. During the time I taught school I boarded most of the time with sister Matilda Hooper (now Hall) a member of the church and a widow.

Receives the Priesthood

My promptness at meetings, etc., soon gained the confidence of the Priesthood of the Branch and I was ordained to the office of Deacon January 8, 1852 by elder Wm. G. Mills, which calling I endeavored to magnify not-with-standing the influences brought to bear against me, for God had given me a testimony of the truth of his work and I felt I would be ungrateful to Him if I did not devote my whole life to His service. At a conference of the Saints held at Heydens Rooms, Devonport, Sunday, December 19, 1852, I was called and ordained a Priest by Elder John Chislett and took pleasure in accompanying the Elders to the villages in the country and assisting in the services—bearing testimony of the truths revealed through the Prophet Joseph Smith and sustaining the Elders in preaching the Gospel to the people. I used to take delight in going to Salt Ash with Elder James Caffall, who was a traveling elder in Devonport District of the Land's End Conference, and to him I owe much for explaining many principles of the Everlasting Gospel, although he has since apostatized and left the church. June rolled rapidly away.

Opportunity to Go to Zion

In my association with the Saints and becoming acquainted with the principles of the gospel and as the Spring of 1853 approached, the privilege was given by the Presidency of the European Mission for the Lands End Conference to send one person to Zion by the perpetual Emigration fund. Greatly to my astonishment and joy I was the one selected. No tongue nor pen can describe the feelings I had when notified by them of the fact that I had the privilege of going to Zion. Such a sudden change of circumstances, from bitter persecution to comparative peace. To travel and be in company with the saints, whose society I loved so well. Going to the gathering place of the people of God to be taught by prophets and apostles and learn of the ways of the Lord seemed to move my feelings to a higher plane, for I felt it would be among the happiest days of my life to leave kindred, friends, and Babylon behind me.

Being a minor—but 16 years old—and out of respect for my parents I concluded to tell them of my good fortune and that soon the Atlantic Ocean would separate us and perhaps "Absence would make the heart grow fonder." I never once dreamed that they would object to my leaving the country, and thus cause them no further pain through my wayward course in becoming a follower of the doctrine taught by the prophet Joseph Smith and the Mormons; but alas! I was doomed to meet more disappointment. I had carefully selected the time and place to tell my parents and family the—to me good news. When I had done so, my father passionately said "you shall not go, and if you succeed in leaving this town (Devonport) and get to Liverpool I will follow and put you in prison, for you are a minor and under my control according to law." I replied coolly, "I know I am a minor and under your control and you can put me in prison, but you can't keep me there always and whenever I am released from prison I'll go to Zion and you can't hinder me, so you might as well save all the trouble and let me go now, seeing it will cost you nothing." My bold answer rather cooled my father's anger for the time.

My troubles were not yet over altho I had little time to prepare for the journey awaiting me. The Evil One had set his eye upon me and made calculations to stop me from enjoying my anticipations, for I was taken violently sick with fevers. Going home to my parents I took to my bed and my mother seemed to think she would have the privilege to carry out her threat made at the time I told the family I had an opportunity of going to Zion—Viz: "That she would rather bury me than I should go off to America with these Mormons." The family Doctor was called, pronouncing it Very Violent Attack of Fever and left directions I must be watched constantly and medicine given me regularly, kept perfectly quiet. No one to see me but the persons attending me—I heard it all—low as I was, but I thought, "Old fellow, God is the greatest and I am going to Zion and you might as well keep your medicine in the Drug store." For notwithstanding all inducements I would not take a particle of medicine, altho the doctor called regularly and so did I call upon my people to send for the Elders of the Church, but there I lay for several days and nights, helpless—exhausted, burning up with fever, pleading to have the Elders sent for.

After several days and seeing no improvement, but rather getting worse, my people consented for the Elders to come and see me one evening. I was so thankful, they seemed like Angels. I had not seen a Latter Day Saint for some time, some of the Elders had called at the home but were informed that the Doctor said it was dangerous for anyone but my nurses to see me and were consequently denied. They brought oil and in the presence of my mother, who remained to see the administration as she said I could get no worse by being administered to. They anointed me profusely and then laid their hands on my head and rebuked the fever and promised me I should live and go to Zion and realize my hopes, but my mother, heaving a sigh and shaking her head said, "That will never be." Thanks to my Heavenly Father, the disease left me and I went to sleep quietly and slept all night, the first sleep for many nights.

I awoke in the morning feeling better and heard my attendants whispering to each other "He's better. He's slept all night—he's taken none of the medicine the Doctor left. There must be something with these Mormons after all for there is such a change in him." I took nourishment for the first time in many days, asked for my clothing, as I began to feel it was time to move and get ready to go to Zion. I expected each mail would bring my notification to be in Liverpool at a stated period. My clothing were refused me but were promised if I continued to mend and get stronger, I might sit up in a few days. I watched my chance when my attendant left the room and I crawled to the wardrobe and got my pants. After several trials and several rests, I succeeded in getting them on and was part way down stairs when I met the nurse coming up with some refreshments. She screamed—I sat down, took my time and after a while succeeded in getting to the room down stairs to the utter astonishment of mother and the family, who the night previous had been expecting to carry me before long to the bone yard. I was there, a living monument of Gods mercy and the power of faith through the ordinance of the Gospel, for no medicine had passed my lips and they could not but acknowledge some superior power had saved my life and raised me up from the very verge of death.

To their credit be it written their opposition was broken, for as I gradually grew stronger and the words of the Elders who administered to me rang in my ears "You shall live and go to Zion" inspired me with confidence and I began gathering articles necessary for the journey. Seeing my determination in the matter, my father, mother, and the family did what they could to give me a comfortable fitout.

Ordained an Elder

In due time the "notification" to be in Liverpool to sail on the Packet Ship *Falcon*, Captain Wade, on Saturday 26 March 1853, came to hand. My heart leaped high with expectation when I read the letter, for I looked upon it as a High Honor to be selected under such circumstances to go to Zion and mingle with the saints of God. At a Priesthood meeting held in the Granby Rooms, Devonport, about the 16th of March 1853, I was called and ordained an Elder by the elders of that branch, Elder Joseph Hall being mouth. Receiving a certificate of good standing and with the blessings of the Saints, whom I had learned to love, my parents accompanied me to the railway station at Plymouth. After repeated solicitations I promised them that if I did not "like it" when I got to America I would write and let them know. I bid them an affectionate good bye.

Arriving at Bristol in the evening I fortunately found some Saints who intended starting for Liverpool the next morning to sail in the same ship as myself and, being invited to accompany them, I gladly remained over night [with them] for the sake of company. I was unused to traveling and my trip from Plymouth to Bristol had been somewhat lonesome as I knew no one on the cars. Arriving at Liverpool and reporting myself at No. 42 Islington, I was instructed about getting the necessary "Tins" and an outfit for a sea voyage. This completed and the Saints on board to the number of several hundred, under the presidency of Elder John Bagnall of London and councilors.

Sails for Zion

The good ship Falcon was towed out of her dock and set sail on Saturday, 26 March 1853. I was 16 years, 2 months and 26 days old, leaving home, friends, kindred and everything that was near and dear to me on earth, to follow the Lord and obey His commands. Not a soul on board had I ever met before in my life except a few I had accompanied from Bristol but a few days since, but I rejoiced and praised the Lord for His mercies to me in bringing about my deliverance from Babylon and sang with many of the Saints on board:

> *The gallant ship is under way*
> *To bear me off to sea*
> *And yonder floats the streamers gay*
> *That says she waits for me.*
> *'Tis not for treasures that are hid,*
> *In mountain or in dell,*
> *'Tis not for joys like these I bid*
> *My native land Farewell.*

After a voyage of 7 weeks and 2 days without any unusual incident we landed at New Orleans, La, U. S. America. Cloth having been provided England, many of us spent our leisure time on the ship making tents for the use of the Company while crossing the plains. I thus learned to sew with needle and palm. [We] ascended the Grand Old Mississippi River on one of those large, magnificent Steamboats common on that River, to Keokuk, Iowa, the outfitting point of the Mormon Emigrants. Spring of 1853. With a few other young men I was assigned the duty of herding cattle for several weeks, opposite the famed city of Nauvoo. I crossed the river and spent several hours in looking among the ruins left by the mob who sacked the city and drove the Saints out, also destroying the once-Magnificent Temple built by the hands of Gods chosen people. There was but little of the walls standing of that once blessed ediface and but few houses inhabited. It seemed to be a "deserted City," where once the feet of Holy Men and women had trod and evidences of thrift and industry were seen on every hand. Now all was silent as the grave and all I saw that gave evidence of life was a few women passing in and out of the house and curling smoke from a few of the chimneys.

Appleton M. Harmons Company

Our company being organized—Appleton M. Harmon was appointed Captain and we set out to cross the state of Iowa, but no pen can describe the starting. Thirteen or fourteen of the teams were composed of young wild steers with perhaps one yoke of partly broke cattle to each wagon. Teamsters composed of men fresh from cotton factories and workshops—many of whom had never seen two animals with a yoke on their necks before arriving at the campground at Keokuk. They knew as much about Gee and Haw as the unbroken steers in the team. In using a whip, such teamsters would as frequently strike themselves as the animal they were aiming at. Plank roads were frequent and sometimes of considerable length, bridging large and deep sloughs and ponds of stagnant water. While passing over these roads, herders would be placed each side of the teams. This in many instances would do more to frighten than keep the team straight, consequently many of the teams made a wild run for the sloughs to gain freedom, running over their herders and into water and mud half way up their sides, tipping over wagons, breaking bows, tongues, and ruining the contents of the wagons with mud and water while the united yelling of woa from the teamsters and herders frightened the cattle until they would get so badly tangled up with turned yokes and the chains around their legs and horns that an axe in the hand of an experienced man would have to be used to cut the bows and free the cattle from death by drowning. Then accusations from teamsters of herders or both, would follow in quick succession and while wading from knee deep to half way up to the armpits in mud and sluch would be forgotten for the time being and war of words unbecoming Saints—indulged in. Thus on our road to Zion we had the privilege of learning the art of self-government if we would improve it. As night came on, Camp was formed on as dry a place as could be found near a creek and the cattle unchained from each other, would be turned out to feed after a colored string of some sort had been tied around the horses or the yoke by the green teamsters so he might know his cattle when driven up in the morning. Wood and water brought to Camp and the skill of a green factory girl as also the English house wife would be tested in frying bacon and slap-jacks for the mess. (usually of 10 persons) Burnt fingers, scorched hair, tired limbs and more tired throats of the men who lay around the fire stretched upon the ground to get a little ease for their aching limbs, or drying their clothes after wading through the sloughs and mud, closed the days' labors after prayer and the setting of the guard for the night. Matters improved day by day as the teamsters and cattle knew each other better.

Becomes Teamster in Stewarts Freight Company

Arriving at Council Bluffs 3 July 1853, we crossed the Missippi river in a ferry boat and wended our way toward the setting sun. Nothing of particular interest occurred with me until a little over two weeks before arriving at Fort Laramie. Our train overtook a freight train of goods under captain Andrew Jackson Stewart, of Springville, Utah. He was crippled for lack of teamsters and asked our captain for help, promising liberal wages to those who would then engage to drive teams for him to Utah. A few were selected—myself among the number, to help drive these teams. Captain Harmon's train passed forward leaving Captain Stewart to follow. I remained with his train until it passed Fort Laramie. When looking in my satchel I discovered to my dismay that the best of my clothing was gone, I supposed by some of the teamsters who left the train at Laramie because of the abuse from Captain Stewart. The train becoming shorthanded through these teamsters leaving the train at Laramie, greater burdens were placed upon those remaining until it became almost unbearable and I told the Captain I could not stand it. He answered I'd have to stand it or leave the train, which latter alternative he thought I had not the courage to do. But waiting until morning I put a little bread in my pockets, my carpet sack in my blankets and told him I wanted something for my services rendered. He was (non plussed). He thought to disuade me from leaving his train and said he could not pay me till he got to Utah. But I had made up my mind that I might as well die in an attempt to overtake Captain Harmon's company as to be killed by overwork and buried like a dog by Captain Stewart and his train hands. Being an Englishman, those claiming American birth took every opportunity to impose upon me and I was tired of it.

Alone on the Vast Plains

I had no idea of the road or how far Captain Harmon's train was in advance of me but had idea I could probable reach it in about a days forced travel. I set out with my pack over my shoulder as best I could with a light heart as I considered I was exchanging oppression for freedom. As the sun became warmer I began to walk slower, for my pack became heavier each mile I traveled. The train behind me was soon lost sight of and my loneliness aided my anxiety to reach the train I desired. Crossing a stream of water on coming to the bank of the Platte River I would sit down on my pack, wish it was lighter, soak my hard bread in the water, kneel down and ask the Father to guide my footsteps aright, then with tired limbs press forward on my journey. I watched the sun in its decline in the west, eagerly straining every nerve of my eyes to discover, if possible, the curling smoke of a camp fire or some signs of life on those vast plains, but my efforts were fruitless. Occasionally on the road I had picked up a buffalo skull or shoulder blade that the beating storms of years had bleached white, with something like the following written upon it in pencil. "Captain H. C. Wheelock's company passed here at [blank] o'clock A.M. on the [blank] day of August 1853" "All well." "Captain Appleton Harmon's company camped three miles East of this point last night and buried 2 emigrants [blank] day of August, 1853." But these signboards were of little value to me as I did not know the day of the month. For in the train I had been with, Sunday was unknown. I scarcely knew for certain what day of the week it was.

Alone—Night and the Howling Wolves

Night drew nigh apace, I was tired, very tired, footsore, and my poor shoulders ached beyond measure carrying my pack. What should I do? Travel as long as I could drag a foot, or lie down and take a rest till the morning? Prudence suggested that I rest somewhere—I looked around. All seemed cheerless. I saw about 1/2 mile distant a ledge of rocks on a little rising bluff, and resolved to get there if possible, which I accomplished just as it became dark. I found a projecting ledge of rock and mechanically unrolled my bundle and laid down, not knowing whether I should ever rise again. Entirely alone—many miles from any human being that I knew of. I queried to myself, "is this what I left parents, kindred, and friends for, to die alone on these almost trackless plains—and be eaten by wolves and wild beasts who may gather around my carcass and fight over the possessions of a fragment of my remains?" This thought was intensified by hearing the howling wolves not far from me. The picture of my once pleasant home and its inmates around the festive board gave my almost famished stomach and gnawing vitals but little comfort. The recollection of most of the acts of my life came before me in quick succession and I seemingly was in the presence of God. The last I knew I was praying to be preserved that I might go to Zion and live with the Saints of God. I must have slept an hour or two and when I awoke I felt much refreshed although my bed was a ledge of rock and not as comfortable as some beds. I turned over many times before morning—my cogitations and peculiar situation kept me awake, but I had the satisfaction of hearing the howling of the wolves farther away than when I lay down to rest. I resolved to proceed on my journey as soon as I could see my way in the morning, for I felt that the Lord would grant me my desires and the desires of the Elders before leaving England would be realized—Viz: "I should go to the land of Zion."

Sundown—Sights Capt. Harmon's Co.

I arose with the dawn of day and gathered up my bundle and hobbled along as best I could, wondering what would be the results of the coming day. When I came to the water I sat down, soaked my remaining crust, ate thankfully—washed my feet and proceeded on my way, praying and hoping that deliverance would come and give me the opportunity of again mingling with Saints and friends. When near sun-down, with blistered feet and aching limbs, I came upon the camp nestled on the bank of the Platte River. My friends were surprised to see me and asked many questions, which I postponed answering until I got something to eat, which was forthcoming. The Captain, learning I was in camp, came to see me and asked me how I got along with Captain Stewart and why I came back to his camp? I told him how I had been treated during my stay and of my adventure in returning to his camp and what I had passed through coming from one camp to the other, afoot and alone. He seemed pleased I had courage enough to do as I had done, and told me he was glad I had got back again—but the strain, physically and mentally had been too much for me. I had over-done myself and has sown the germs of sickness in my system, for when I went to my quarters to rest, I seemed on fire throughout my entire system and the fever seemed to be eating me up.

Next morning I started with the camp, assisting in whatever I was called upon to do by the Captain of Ten, but it seemed the train traveled too fast, for it halted at noon and the cattle were turned out to graze before I caught up with it. But as I staggered into the camp it happened I sat down, or rather fell down, on the tongue of Captain Harmon's wagon and there fainted from nervous prostration. Sister Hulda Barnes (Captain Harmon's sister) came to me with others and applied such restoratives as were at hand, but I was too sick to realize much. She however nursed me tenderly as a son and after a few days I was able to be around again, feeling very thankful for the kindness I had received at the hands of so good a woman—for she seemed to spare me no pains to give me every comfort in her power.

As we got into Black Hills the weather became cooler and my health better. The scenery along the road became more varied the farther west we traveled and consequently the more pleasure I took. I have neglected to mention Bro. George Taylor from Nottingham Conference, England whom I first met in the Bachelors Hall on board ship. A friendship grew up between us of a lasting character. We spent many hours on the ship and crossing the plains, walking, singing, and discoursing together, and whenever we could be—were bed-fellows.

Short Rations

After leaving the sweetwater river, our provisions got short and we were put on short allowance until we met some teams with provisions from Utah, and the nearer we approached the Valleys, the more teams they were expecting to meet in the emigrant trains. With what pleasure I have looked upon seeing the reunion of husbands, wives and children and bosom friends, meeting each other on those dreary plains after having been absent from each other in many cases for years—but under those sunburned faces and necks—those ragged clothes—those rough exteriors, beat hearts that had courage to forsake father and mother, house and lands, husbands, wives, children, and friends for the gospel's sake and surmount trials of the most severe character to build up a Zion under the direction of a living priesthood guided by Him who shapes the destinies of all who trust in Him. Green River, Fort Bridger passed, all were getting anxious to see the far-famed valleys of Utah, and many were the speculations indulged in relation to the future.

Bird's Eye View of Salt Lake Valley

The summits of the big and little mountains reached, the "bird's eye view" of the Western side of Salt Lake Valley looked lovely beyond description. The captain told us we might get into the city the next day if no accidents occurred.

Arrived in Zion Sunday, October 16, 1853

In crossing the bench from the mouth of Emigration canyon to the Bluff east of the city, our eyes were feasted with the sublime sight we had desired so long to see and as we caught a view of the City the throbbing of our hearts increased and our anticipations were realized—the promise of the elders at Devonport fulfilled—"I had come to Zion.' We camped on the 16th Ward square Salt Lake City—Sunday 16 October 1853, a little west of the place where now stands the Deseret University. Friends met friends and took them from the camp ground to their homes. By night over half the company was gone. By Monday night but few were left on the camp ground and I began to wonder where I should go and what I should do to find a home. A brother that came from Devonport was living in the Nineteenth Ward. I found him but he could give me no employment.

Friends for Everyone Except Me

The people of the camp seemingly all had friends to go to but me. I did not seem to have any. I seemed to be a stranger in a strange land. Perhaps my outward appearance was so repulsive that no one felt disposed to offer me a home or place to stay till I could find employment. I certainly was a sad looking sight, for I owned no clothing but an extra shirt, except what I stood upright in, [and] that I had worn nearly all the time since I left England. It was so filled with dust and dirt, had been torn, patched, and mended, was sewed and re-sewed while upon my body, that I could not get it off my person. It was about skin-tight and I dare not stoop and had to sit down very carefully for fear of exposing my nakedness. All this came about through my clothing having been stolen at Laramie. Notwithstanding, I thanked the Lord for His kindness and mercies to me in giving me the privilege of coming to Zion. I felt my lot a hard one as I knew no one to unburden my feelings to or ask advice from, but I knew God was my friend, and I laid my case before Him feeling that He would open up my way for good.

Later, Monday evening I met one of the brethren of our camp who told me he had got work as a carpenter and invited me to go with him the next morning as he thought I could get employment. I did so but had not been at work long when Bro. Nelson Spafford of Springville, Utah Co., drove up with a team and wagon and inquired for a young man that came in with the last company of emigrants and had no home. I heard him and spoke to him. He scanned me from head to foot thinking no doubt, I was a hard looking subject. He said he had been recommended by some friend of his to find me as he was called on a mission to Fort Supply and wanted someone to stay with his family through the winter. He lived some sixty miles south and if I wanted to go with him and stay the winter he would give me a home and plenty to eat if I would do his work and look after his family. I thought it would be the best step I could take and told him I would do the best I could for him. The brother I was working with thought it the best and I got into the wagon and started for Springville without further ceremony, arriving there on the evening of the next day. Seeing my pityable condition for clothing he gave me some of his partially worn clothing, as at that time clothing of any kind was very scarce and high priced. I was strange to every kind of work done in this country and whatever I went at I made hard work of it and it took me all my time to get the wood, milk the cows and do the chores for sister Spafford and her child. Bro. Spafford soon left for his field of missionary labor and I thought I had an immense labor on my hands of caring for his wife and child. I had to work an ox team on shares to get the wood, but the winter passed very pleasantly. I made many acquaintances and friends among the rest was Bp. Aaron Johnson who used to speak of me as "That young English man at Spafford's". When spring came Bro. Spafford came home and could do his own work so I was no longer needed by him. I felt impressed to go to Salt Lake City.

$5.00 A Month and Board

I got an opportunity to ride with one of the brethren and went directly to President Young's and saw him and asked for work, told him who I was, where I came from and what I had been doing since my arrival in Utah etc. He seemed favorably impressed and gave me work at $5.00 a month with board and lodging with Bro. Hamilton G. Park. The first article I drew for pay was a pair of Buckskin pants. That meant nearly three months wages. In dry weather they would come about half way between my ankles and knees and in wet weather, would flippity flop on the side walk every step I took. I intended no reflection on Pres. Young or the pants in thus describing them, but to show the scarcity of clothing in the Spring of 1854. We used to think in those days that a man who was the owner of a pair of "American" (cloth) pants was exceedingly well off, while the man who was fortunate enough to own a suit of Buckskin was prepared for society or meetings or the dance, and need not fear tearing them up while at his daily labor. I think about the 4th June 1854 was the first time I ever saw Prest. Young. At the time I applied for work. I was deeply impressed with the man—a prophet of God! a Seer and Revelator. I looked upon him almost with awe, he was the man of all men I desired to become acquainted with—and I suppose that was the reason I was so bold in going to ask him for work, for my usual diffidence would have led me in any other direction. I boarded with Bro. H. G. Park for about two months and worked with him making road in City Creek Canyon, sawing wood, and about anything that was to be done. With a recommend from Pres. Brigham Young I received my endowments in August 1854. A blessing I had

[missing sheet, two pages]

My wages were increased to $15.00 a month and board, I did not continue to drive team long as the President was finishing the Lion House and he set me to cleaning up and preparing the rooms for occupancy. I helped his families to move into their new quarters about the last of November 1855. The President boarded half of his time in the Lion House and when not there it devolved on me to call the family together and pray with them and to ask blessings at the table, etc. This used to be a hard task for me, diffident as I was, and many times I should have shrunk from it had it not been duty.

As winter approached, the President sent all his teams and men, except me, to Cottonwood canyon to work for the winter while he went to Fillmore as governor of the territory to attend the Legislation. Before leaving he met me and told me to continue living in the Lion House and take care of his families, as I was the only man he was leaving around his premises, except the clerks in the office. I thanked him for the confidence he reposed in me and told him I would do the best I could. He started for Fillmore first day of December 1855. Four of his wives and their children lived in the house and it took me all my time to do what was required of me.

Measles

After the President had been gone a few weeks the measles broke out among the children and we had a serious time. Nine were down at one time. It seemed that the Evil One had his own way, for as we would administer to one of the children in one of the rooms it would get much better, but those we had just been administering to would get much worse. For five weeks I never took my clothes off except to change my underclothing, and all the sleep I would be able to get was when so much exhausted I could go no longer, administering so much day and night took all the vitality out of me. Often when I would take my hands off the sick child I would rest with exhaustion. I fasted much to benefit the sick and pled with God to restore them to health. Clara Decker Young's Jeddie was very sick and I exercised myself over him very much, but after a lingering illness of several weeks his spirit left its body to go to a better place on 11 January, 1856. I believe I mourned over it as much as I ever did over one of my own, for I loved the child dearly. I am sure sister Clara felt I was devoted to her child's interests and remembered me with gratitude. Many years afterwards in a letter written by her to a valued friend of mine, in referring to the circumstances of the winter of 1855-6 she says "And as my mind turns to these trying scenes there is no one that claim my thanks and gratitude more than Samuel Roskelley." As the winter passed away, the family got better. When the President returned home about the last of January 1856, things began to assume a brighter look. It has been a gloomy winter. I remember that while conversing with sister Clara after the death of her darling, the question of having faith in God was spoken of—she said "It has been a severe trial of my faith to lose my child in the absence of its father—my husband—but it has taught me a lesson to rely upon the Lord more and my husband less, for I do not know but I have thought too much of my Brigham." I write this as a lesson to my own dear family—not to expose Sister Clara's private feelings as expressed to me in all confidence.

Famine

During the Spring and Summer the famine for breadstuff was very severe—as the grasshoppers had cleaned the fields two previous years to an alarming extent and flour had run up to fabulus figures, entirely out of reach of the poor. The President had succeeded in buying a few loads of flour from Bro. Reese and stored it away. He did not reduce his force of work hands, but counting noses, reduced all dependent upon him to half pound of flour per day. Out of that, much would be given away daily to the poor, who would call and the family would divide and many times the box would be scraped for some poor mother who represented that her children were hungry. Perhaps half an hour afterward it would be scraped again for some other poor soul under similar circumstances. The flour box always yielded a little every time it was scraped for the poor. Thus have I seen the goodness of God and the faith of Brigham Young and his family manifested in helping the poor, for when the famine was at its worst stage, President Young said at the table his family was sitting at, "I wish every poor soul who has no bread was here to sit down and eat till they were satisfied," for the family had not eaten more than half that was put on the table for their use at that meal under the ration system. Many of the Saints in Utah suffered for want of bread during those hard times. Many resorted to pig weeds, thistle roots, mustard leaves, and every kind of vegetable, mixing [it] with bran or shorts for food, but no one died of starvation that I am aware of.

Being one of the 18th Ward teachers I was kept busy in connection with the 70s meetings and prayer circle meetings in the Old Tabernacle and my time was fully occupied with duties of various kinds. While preaching in the old tabernacle one Sunday afternoon President Young said he had a set of men around him that were incompetent to make a living for themselves and he could not drive them away so he had to provide for them. This expression struck me with much force and I thought—Pres. Young you shall not have the opportunity of saying that much about me very long." For altho but nineteen years old I felt I could dig for myself, and I knew I could under ordinary circumstances make my own living.

In May 1856 I Met Rebecca Hendricks

In a short time afterward (I think perhaps in May 1856) I met Rebecca Hendricks for the first time. She was then what is known as a grass widow. Her husband having left her in the Spring of 1855 to go east on a mission but never returned to her and her child. Our acquaintance ripened into friendship and love for each other of which I shall write more hereafter.

During the summer of 1856 I spent most of the time in the Lion House—being acquainted with the family and affairs—I took particular pains never to mention anything I saw or heard, but treasured it up, thinking that if it ever was my privilege to have more than one wife I would have some valuable lessons laid away in my memory to draw upon. But alas! all mortals err—for I have never yet seen the place in my experience that one of these lessons fitted. It has all been new ground to me or I have new to the ground.

To supply the Public works and the citizens of Salt Lake City with lumber the President with others had made a road at great expense to the upper basin in Big Cottonwood canyon and built several mills for making lumber, and desiring an Out, he invited a large number of the Saints to join him in celebrating the 24, July, 1856 at the lake in Big Cottonwood.

July 24th Celebration

Brigham Young personally gave me an invitation to accompany a portion of his family, who he also had invited. I looked upon it as a great honor, as I was nobody and did not expect such distinguished favors. When about to start, I found he had made provisions for me to ride in a carriage with some of the family and go free from care and responsibility. I enjoyed this outing very much and the society more—for the meetings held were of the best character and I felt thankful for the privilege of the good association.

Age 19 Called on a Mission

During the next week, in August 1856, one evening after the workmen had all gone home, I stood looking into the street from the porch over the Lion of the Lion House, when suddenly I felt someone's arm around my shoulders and neck. Turning my face I discovered it to be Pres. Young. Said he—calling me by name—"I think you had better go on a mission." As soon as I could recover from my surprise I answered, I don't know what you want to send me on a mission for. I don't know anything. He answered—I'll risk you in that matter. You have not been so attentive to every meeting you could get to in the Tabernacle in the ward and quorum and prayer circle for nothing and

[manuscript page 31 missing]

pay it up on my return to Utah, which I said I was willing to do. But Pres. Young spoke up and said he would not ask me for my note altho he was satisfied I would return to Utah alright, but in consideration of service I had rendered to him and his family he would make me a present of the amount and square the account. This I considered very generous and I thanked him warmly for his kindness—wished him goodbye with many of my old associates, who had gathered around.

Leaves for Mission

After receiving his blessing I got into my cart and Bro. George Taylor and I started for Emigration canyon to overtake the missionary company who had started 2 days ahead under the Captaincy of Apostle Parley P. Pratt. I have not power to portray my feelings in leaving the family of Pres. Young. It was felt more keenly by me than my leaving the home of my parents. For I thought much of the family and I believe they thought much of me.

We overtook the Missionary camp the 3rd day after leaving Salt Lake City and soon got acquainted with the members of the camp. Our trip was quite pleasant as we would meet the trains of emigrants pulling hand carts occasionally—although it was heart aching to see the last of the company so far away from Utah, so late in the season. At Independence Rock we met Apostle F. D. Richards, Jos. A. Young, Charles W. Penrose, D. C. Dunbar and quite a number of the European Missionaries returning to Utah. We camped all night with them and spent a very pleasant evening chatting, singing, etc. Bro. Dunbar was sick in bed but at our solicitations got up and leaned against a wagon wheel and sung—Oh Ye Mountains High and several soul stirring songs of Zion. The two missionary companies, one going to the nations and the other returning from their labors, reluctantly parted the next morning, resuming their journey after bidding each other "good bye" with well wishes and expressions of good desires for each other's welfare.

We met the last company of emigrants near Chimney Rock with hand carts heavily loaded, during the latter part of October, when they ought to have been in the valley. When near Fort Kearney, all our company were short of flour as it was scarce there, but we bought some crackers and buffalo meat dried by Indians, which served us until we reached Florence, once Winter Quarters. Although we went on very short rations for several days. Arriving at Florence where many of the Saints lived. The President of the branch quartered the elders with the Saints. Bro. Geo. Taylor and I were sent to Bro. Alexander Pyper's to stop, and we enjoyed ourselves highly. We were fortunate enough in selling our teams for cash, enough to pay our way to Liverpool by being economical. Some of the other elders were not quite as fortunate in selling their teams but borrowed money to proceed on their journey—which we did in a few days by taking passage down the Missouri River for St. Louis on board the "Red Cloud" steam boat and arriving at St. Louis with out accident. We were quartered among the Saints for a few days—spending the Sabbath and going to Saints meetings under the presidency of Apostle Erastus Snow.

(supplement to manuscript page 32)

I cannot omit an incident that occurred in President Young's office about 2 weeks previous to my starting on my mission. I had been aware for some time that President Young had desired Apostle Parley P. Pratt to go and visit the churches in the Eastern States during the winter of 1856-7 and also given his sanction for sister Marion McLean Pratt to go to the fronteer with him. He to go on East for the winter, and she to go to New Orleans, her former home, and if possible obtain her children—as she had taught school in President Young's family for some time, she was well acquainted with me and had desired the President to instruct me to put my team with Apostle P. P. Pratt's team and carriage and be teamster for him and her. Also accompany her in trying to get her children to the frontiers so she could get them to Utah the following spring. I had overheard her talking with the President about it and as I had no love for her—but a decided dislike—I made up my mind I would not do as she desired unless positively commanded. Although if Bro. Pratt had been going alone I should have taken it as a pleasure to have waited on him. But that woman—well I did not want to wait upon her on no terms.

One afternoon the office was full of clerks and others, I went in to see President about getting a team for Bro. George Taylor and I to cross the plains with, and after making arrangements about the animals, President Young said he would like me to hitch to Bro. Parley's carriage and go with him. I expressed my feelings about the matter by saying I was willing to do anything for Bro. Parley but I preferred to travel with Bro. Taylor and let sister Pratt wait on herself. The

President let the matter drop and matters were arranged as I desired much to my satisfaction. As I did not have to go to New Orleans nor have anything to do with the McLean children. The obtaining of them thru the efforts of Sister Pratt and one of our missionary company Elder James Cammell, cost Apostle Parley P. Pratt his life in the Spring of 1857. I have always been thankful my mission took me in another direction.

Set Sail November 26, 1856

[*msp.34*] Friday 14 Nov. 1856 we left St. Louis, Mo. on the Terra Haute R.R. After a number of delays, at Albany N.Y. at 5 A.M. on the 18th Nov. remaining at Albany, seeing all we could through the day and starting at 6 P.M. on one of those magnificent steam boats plying between New York and Albany on the Hudson River. Our voyage was made without accident, landing at New York City at 7 A.M. on Wednesday, 19 Nov. We found the Mormon office Apostle John Taylor not being at home, Elder T. B. H. Stenhouse did the honors and treated us very kindly. During the day I wrote a letter for publication in the "Mormon" descriptive of our trip from Utah and with elders visited many points of interest in New York. With six other elders engaged 2nd cabin passage for Liverpool on board ship Thornton. My companions were elders George Taylor, Ezra T. Clark, Charles Hubbard, S. F. Neslin, George Gates, and Elder Bevin. Leaving the dock, was towed to Horse Shoe Bend Tuesday, 25 Nov., and on Wed. 26th 1856 weighed anchor and put to sea. The waves being quite choppy, wind increasing, I found my berth the best place for several days for our voyage was a very rough one in consequence of frequent gales and heavy seas, running mountains high. We were—in the language of the Apostles of Old, In perils by sea for the waves seemed determined to break up the ship—on one occasion it broke in the gally door, tearing through the partition and carrying everything it had loosened overboard. Elder George Taylor was in the Galley at the time, cooking. The waves took him off his feet and jammed him under the large stove or he would have gone overboard. On one occasion a heavy wave struck the corner of our cabin and crushed it so that the water came in to the depth of many inches, wetting all our clothes and making us very uncomfortable. At the same time all the sails we had up were blown to shreds and our good ship left to the mercy of

[end of printed memoir; end of transcript]

Manuscript was incomplete when transcribed ca.1945;
past this point the published version reproduced the relevant entries from Journal 1

Journal [1]

14 November 1856 – 31 March 1857

{001}* [*2-page spread, or back-front covers*]
| [*illegible line*]
| 86
| Colliers Row
| Grange
[*mostly illegible*] | Journal
Isaac Scofield | 1.
    Prest | S. Roskelley
Hobbs |

{002}
diseased Lungs
[---] of a teaspoonful
[---] [---] mixed with
[*illegible line*]

13qt Beer
2 basin [---] Malt
1 oz Hops
1/2 lb Treacle
2 oz Herbs Acramony
boil all together
[---] strain thru a [---]

{003}
[---]lotte
  [---]
    [---]
Yellow Jaundice
2^d alicor [---]
Alicsor of propria[---]
2tablespoonful a day
Severe [---] stitch
Tincture of [---] [---]
2teaspoonfulls [---]
to bed and ½ a [---] [---]

Manuscript presently unlocated, but microfilmed September 1954 by Utah Genealogical Society (now MS 8239, Church History Library, Salt Lake City), microfilm digitized ca.2014; line-by-line transcription follows digital image number

* Right-hand or *recto* pages typically carry odd page numbers since 1 numbers the first page of a book; in this file the initial image has either a spread (2 pages) or the front/back covers, but it is also missing a frame between images 007 and 008, so in the current digital file (July 2018) the numbering is off, making *verso* pages odd-numbered and right or *recto* pages even-numbered. To correct this, a place holder has been added to the transcript to force pages to number two-page spreads correctly. Sorry for the confusion.

{004–005}

| Tune Patrick was a Gentleman

1 The Prophet | Joseph Smith

Joseph Smith was a poor man born | ~~all the people~~ /every body\ knows
He always payed his tailors bills or he | [*stricken*] had no clothes
Sometimes he'd gloves upon his hands | you might well suppose
A nice clean collar 'round his neck | and shoes to line his toes
Yet Joseph was a prophet | of these modern times

2

Joseph Smith was a prophet true | that all the saints do know
That God had surely called him | that all his works do throw [show?]
He told the wicked of their faults | which made them hate him sore
And never would they rest again | 'till Joseph was no more
Chorus

3

He had a brother Hyrum called | who loved him as his life
He always stood by Joseph's side | in mobs, in peace, or strife
He to for the oppresed would pray | and righteousness he'd teach
To know if these were inspi | ring you should just have heard them
Chorus

{006–007}

5

They loved each other in their lives | and together fell in death
They loved their children and their | wives, blessed them till their [---] [---]
They loved the Saints and died for | them tis the wicked whom they hate
So to satisfy a mobbing crew this was | a prophets fate
Chorus

6

Some wicked men accused them of | treason and the like
So to appease their hellish rage | this awfull blow they strike
They pleged their very faith to him | that he should be kept safe
Then in cold blood they butchered him | so now the truth you have
Chorus

{008} [*frame (verso page) missing from scanned file*]

{009} [*was 008 in digital file, all numbers advanced one to account for missing frame/page*]

Ps I copy of the note to Pres Wilms
There is a failure somewhere
in the book agents I have
complaints all through the
branches some are charged
too much others are charged
for what they never get
and some get their parcels
and others do not, if it
is a ~~failure~~ mistake it
happens pretty often
JS

{*cross-written on 009*}

works your ~~light~~ will show
In whome we've s[---] put our trust will
may it then be proved
During our checquered life on earth to be
Made a friend in heaven
Ever than let us p[---] all that's real & good

{010}
~~D. Jones } Comic song~~
~~[---] Hicc[---]~~
~~Recite comic~~
Ann Reese } Hail to the
W. Roper } 255 hymn
~~John Thomas~~
~~/ Sing [---] [---]~~
~~Benj Allen~~
~~Recitation com~~
~~Choir catak~~
~~M Vaughn } [---] [---]~~
~~D Carter } Life is a~~
~~D Jones } Vapour~~
~~W. Roper } Comic song~~
~~William Peters }~~

{011}
~~Nessesary to all P[---] and~~
~~Say we ask thee~~

{012}
[---]ssy Drudge 2 hyms
        ~~270 Page~~
        138
W. Roper }
Ann Rese } Comic song

~~W. Roper } Ri[---]~~
            ~~[---]~~
~~[---] [---]~~
        ~~Recitation~~
~~Ellen Roper }~~
~~Anne Rese } Hymn~~
~~Agnese Reese }~~
~~Job Griffen } [---]~~
        Comic
~~[---] [---] T[---]~~
    ~~} [---]~~

{013}
Davy Jones   {Hymns
                    { [---] No
                    { 251
John Gold
~~Rcit   Sentimental~~
1 Song   Do
~~A Dialogue between~~
~~a Parson and Nany~~

~~Penlan by N [---]rrle~~
~~Miss Jacobs~~
~~Married Jester~~
~~1 Song Sent~~
2 Ann Reeses
1 Hymn 2 ~~R[---] Sent~~
1 weed
~~James Abrams 1 [---] Wels~~
~~Clerk Authors~~

{014}
Friday Novr 14th we left St
L bound for New York by Terra
Haute RR at nine o'clock in
the morning cost 22 Dollars--
I had a great many delays
on the road
Tuesday 18th arrived at Albany
at 5 AM and took steam Boat
for New York at 6 PM
Wednesday 19th Arrived in
New York at 7 A.M. with
Bro George Taylor and S. F. Norton
found the Mormon office and
saw Bro T. B. H. Stenhouse, Bro
John Taylor not being in town.
wrote a letter by request
for publication in the

{015}
Mormon
Thursday 20th President John
Taylor arrived from Connecticut
we had an agreeable visit
with him
Friday 21st Went with Bro
Dulin to engage our passage
on Board Ship Thornton for
20 Dollars each for 2nd cabin
passage
Saturday 22nd Took our
baggage on board and secured
our berths in the afternoon
went to the Museum to see
Genl Tom Thumb at Presid
ent Taylors expense
Sunday 23rd Went to meeting

{016}
of the New York Branch and

spoke for the first time
heard an excellent address
from President Taylor in the
evening
Monday 24th Hauled out into
the river from No. 38 Pier East
River send a letter to Eld^r
T. B. H. Stenhouse stating the
numbers of missionaries where
from and where bound also
of our clearance—the numbers
so as 7, all for England—
~~the numbers was~~ we lay
hear all night preparing
for sea and to get seamen
Tuesday 25th Tow boat

{017}
came alongside and towed us
into the Horseshoe could
not sail because of contrary
winds—felt a slight sick
ness on account of the rolling
of the ship—provisions dealt
out by the carpenter
Wednesday 26th Had a little
conversation with the first
mate upon the system of
government in Utah, he
said he wished to bring back
a load of Saints on
this vessel. I asked him
why—he said because we
have no trouble with them
they are clean and take
{018}   November
care of themselves—the
carpenter confirmed this
statement and said he
would rather have 1000
Saints aboard than 30 Irish
people. I was much pleased
with the assertion. in the
afternoon the wind changed
and at high Tide we hoisted
the anchor and bore out
to sea with gallant hearts
to do our masters will.
Thursday, Friday and Saturday
felt sick and kept my berth

most all the time.
Sunday 30th Sudden squalls
from the N.W. all day and

{019}
at night increased into a
gale my pen or tongue is
inadequate to give a des
cription of a storm at sea but
never the less I will give
some faint idea. The
Chronomiter had given
indications of the approach
of the storm beforehand
and the captain taking
the precaution ordered
every sail to be furled
excepting fore and main top
sails and those were to be
lose reefed and as night
came on so the storm in
creased until it seemed

{020}
as though the surrounding
elements were all combined
to destroy our little barque.
The wind howled furiously
through the Rigging and the
angry waves would wash
over and break on the deck
as though it thought
our barque was an
intruder upon its sur
face. We called upon
our father to preserve us
he answered that he would
and that not a hair of
our heads should be
hurt which was ver-
ified in truth, for while

{021}
the sea was washing over
our decks and tearing
everything loose and on
one occasion broke the
gally door away and the
door of the adjoining cabin

carrying everything before
it through a partition
of the cabins and on to the
other side of the ship yet
heavier seas broke upon
our little cabin and it broke
not although the water
found its way through
sometimes but no one
could tell where during
the night the mate thought

{022}
it might possibly ease the
vessels straining so much
by shifting the sails a
little all hands were called
but few could be found most were
so afraid that they hid
themselves and I could not
blame them for no one
could stand on deck
without being in danger
of being washed overboard
except they were tied or had hold of
something that was solid
but by considerable cursing and
swearing on the part of
{023}
   Dec^r
the mates, a sufficient
number of men were
collected to trim the
sails and our Barque
sent schudding along
before the wind almost
like a feather on the
surface of the water.
After 3 days and nights
of this storm the weather
broke up into frequent squalls
until the night of ~~the~~
Thursday 4th Dec Wind
very high ~~so rough that~~
~~they hove the ship~~
~~about to be~~

{024}
Friday 5th ~~Wind~~ /Sea rises\ so
high they hove the ship
to under closereefed

main topsail about
4 oclock this morning
wind blows a perfect hurracane
Saturday 6 continued hove
to all day until 4 oclock
this Evening weather modera
ted and we set a few
sails again.
Sunday, Monday, and Tuesday.
heavy squalls. Squalls continued
until Friday 12th At which
time the squalls agreed
to collect in Lat 47° 6″

{025}
Long 20° 30' to have a
down right shindig to
commemorate the
embarkation of George
Taylor & Samuel Roskell
ey from Salt Lake
City /3 months since\ the spree to
commence at 2 oclock
presicely the time of
Embarkation of said
Persons from said place
and it appeared as if
all the devils of the
infernal regions were
let loose upon us and
each one tried to raise
his wave the highest.

{026}
   Dec^r
Awful indeed was the
sight—the sea run
mountains high and the
wind blew so furiously
that no one could stand
against it except they had
hold of something fast
They hove the vessel to
directly the gale commenced
but the wind blew so bad
that it blew the main
topsail to pieces--but we
raised another sail which
kept her to the wind and about
sundown the hurricane

broke--during the storm
I was on the Poop deck
{027}
with the Captain and
helped him to take a
reef in the spanksail
and raise it to the wind
we conversed freely
upon Mormonism for
he loves the Mormons—
he said he would rather
take Mormons for half
the price across the atlantic
he said he never saw the
sea run higher in his
life than during this
hurracane he asked me once
what I thought of it
I told him I thought

{028}
like the Sailor said
if the Lord would forgive
me this time I would not
get on the sea again until
I was forced to—he said
he thought that was not
in accordance with my
faith which I readily
owned up he is a noble
fellow I like him much
The storm and the tempest rage
fearful the grand
And our brave little barque
rides the sea
But a little while more and we'll be
on the land
Where from perils of shipwreck
we're free.

{029}
Saturday 13th Sunday 14th
Frequent Squalls from the N.W.
Monday 15th Be called the finest
day we have had on board.
Tuesday 16th Wednesday 17th Pleasant
weather.
Thursday 18th almost reached
Holy Head in the Irish channel
contrary winds forced us to
tack considerably and
Friday 19th off Holy Head at
4 oclock took a pilot on board
at 9 and landed on
the dock at Liverpool at
1/2 Past ten oclock A.M. on
Saturday 20th Well and in
Good Spirits and felt to

{030}
 Dec^r
thank my father in Heaven
for a safe passage across
the mighty Deep visited
Pres. O Pratt at the office
and borrowed 2£ to take
me to my fields of labors
which I found was in
Wales under the direction
of Pres Daniel Davies
Monday visited Bro. Pratt
and took train for Plymouth
to pay a visit to my folks
The train arriving at Plymouth
at 8 oclock in the evening and I
went to see my parents and

{031}
visit the Saints. all were
glad to see me
Wednesday 24th Preached at
Plymouth on the practical
duties of the Saints.
Thursday with my Parents
Saturday visited Sister
Knight and broke up the
contract made 4 years
previous I told her she
was at liberty to marry
when she pleased but
that I considered I was under
no further obligations to
her as I lived 3 1/2 years
single on her account and
she broke the contract by

{032}
 Dec^r
being cutt of the church

Sunday 28 Preached at
Plymouth in the Afternoon
and at Devonport in the
Evening among whom were
my Parents, Brother & sister
A good spirit prevailed
Monday 29th Fasted then
a council meeting at D'port
and the brethren gave me
eight shillings to assist me
on my way to my field of
labour
Wednesday 31st Last Evening
Elder Thomas Sargent Knight
died after a severe
Illness of long duration

{033}
      Jan^y
I administered to him
and he found relief
from his pain he [---]
me just before I left
he died a good saint
Thursday Jan 1th Spent most
of the day with my Parents.
The Evening at the Churches
S. School party My Birthday
~~Resejated~~ Received 8s of
Elder W. Burton as a donation
from the Plymouth Branch
I spoke a little on the
government and tra[---]
children and Blessed the
whole Congregation in the
name of Jesus Christ

{034}
      Jan^y
felt well
Friday 2nd I left Plymouth
For Bristol en Route from Wales
My Parents have treated me
kindly while I have been in
D'port and I felt to Bless them
In the name of Israels God
Saturday 3rd rote a letter to Eld^s
Job Rishell & George Taylor on
business was arrested by a Po
liceman for Passing a base

2^s pice—
Sunday 4th Attended & assisted
Conference and spoke to the
Saints in the Afternoon
Monday 5th Attended a meeting
of the Saints at the Rooms

{035}
in the Evening we had a
Glorious time all felt well
A Glorious [---] was given
All felt to [---] [---] [---]
Tuesday 6th Went to Cardiff
Staid all night with Bro
Williams President of the
Conference
Wednesday 7th Arrived at
Swansea [---] Bro Daniels
at the office was warmly
received—rote Several letters
to various persons
Made the office Home
Preached on Sunday at Swansea
And left there with John Davis
President of Swansea Conference

{036}
Tuesday Jany 13th wrote
Several Branches in the Confer
ence preached some and got back
to Swansea again on Saturday 17th
Met the Presidency and received
my appointment to travel in the
Monmouthshire, ~~Glamorganshire~~ /Breconshire\
And Eastern District of Glamorganshire
Sunday 18th Attended the Western
Glamorgan Conference had 7 bully
B'hoys there and had a good
time
Monday Proceeded to Cardiff
to meet Bro Williams and attend
my future field of Labour
Tuesday Jan 20th Attended District
Conference at Cardiff and

{037}
Bro Williams made appointment
for me during the week
Wednesday 21st Went to Newbrige (Glam)
and attended a district council

Slept at Sisters Wilkins and Roderick
Felt first rate they made me
very comfortable and /Thursday 22nd\ attended a
saints meeting in the Evening
Instructed the Saints Generally
Friday 23rd Returned to Cardiff
and went to Llandaff Preached
in the Evening & a good Congregation
of Saints and returned to Cardiff
Sunday 25th Went to [---]
with Bro Pugh had a good time
came to Cardiff to Sleep
Monday 26th According to Appointment

{038}
January
of President Daniels I took
train to Merthyr Tydfil
Tuesday 27th Went to Tredegar
in Monmouthshire to labor
under Eldr Benjamin Evans
Wednesday 28th Visited several
Branches in company with Bro
Evans
Thursday 29th Preached at Machen
Sister Cingner opposed Plurality
and consequently would not go to
the Valley I prophesied in the
name of Jesus Christ that
she would be glad to go there
[---]
Friday 30th Motioned that the
[---] branch fall away

{039}
Feby
into nothingness that they give
up there present chapel and
that the saints increase in
this place and occupy it and
grow to a large branch of the
Church seconded by David
B. Evans and carried by show
of hands
Saturday 31st Went to [---] district
met a [---] very much [---] [---]
no letters stopped over
Sunday 1st [---] on [---] [---]
Monday 2th Returned to Tredegar
and remained there untill

Thursday 5th went to Ebbw Vale
or Peng-ea
Friday 6th Went to the ~~Blaina~~
      Blaina

{040}
had a good time preaching
and counselling the Priesthood and
Saints
Feby 10th Went to Ebby Vale to a
District Council
Feby 11th Attended a Council
at Tredegar
Thursday 12th Preached at [blank]
victuals and returned to
Sir Howy to sleep
Friday 13th Preached at Blew
fort Returned to Sirhowy
Sunday 15th Went to the
Blaina Met with Presidents
Miller and Evans
Monday 16th Held council With
Presidents Miller & Evans in Nantyglo

{041}
and in the Evening went into
Breckonshire to Labour under
Eldr John Thomas
Tuesday 17th Preached at Bren
Mawr
Wednesday 18th Went to Gilwern
Preached to a good Congregation
Thursday 19th Preached at
Black Rock told the people
to repent and do better.
Friday 20th Went to the Blaina
to see if my clothes were finished
returned to Black Rock in the
Evening
Saturday 21st Went to Tredegar
instead of Breckon as it
rained very much and prevented

{042}
Feb 7
me from carrying out my former
intentions
Sunday. Preached twice againsts
a very bad influence.

Monday 23rd Went to the Blaina Met in council and spoke to the Priesthood upon the necessity of Living their religion
Friday 24th Went to Black Rock, Breckonshire, met in council exhorted the Priesthood to live by every word that proceedeth out of the mouth of God.
Wednesday 25th Preached at the Bliana and showed the Saints what influence inclined them to do wrong.

{043}
March
Thursday 26th Went to Tredegar exhorted the saints to live their religion and do right.
Friday 27th Went to North Tredegar and exhorted the Saints to live by every word that proceeded out of the mouth of God.
Sunday 1st March Went to Risca Preached reformation and in the Evening preach Gospel Restored.
Monday 2nd Went to Mach Preached to a good Congregation
Tuesday 3rd Went to Flower de Luce held council a Bad influence prevailed

{044}
Wednesday 4th Went to Tredegar
Thursday 5th Spoke to the Saints on Practical Mormonism exhorted them to live their religion
Saturday 7th Went to Black Rock, Breconshire
Sunday 8th Held a council at Black Rock Eldr Wm Emmitt opposed several principles I discussed with him for upwards of 2 hours and answered him satisfactorally but would not acknowledge the Priesthood and was counsequently suspended until he should see his error

{045}
Monday 9th Went to the Blaina Held Council showed them they must not covenant before God if they did not mean to carry it out.
Tuesday 10th Held council at Penny Cas and then went to Sirhowy
Wednesday 11th Went to Merthyr Tidfile and thence to Abardare held a council Meeting and Preached
Thursday 12th went to Swansea to attend a large council of Elders Held at the Udgord Seion office

{046}
March
under the Presidency of President E. T. Benson We all stated our feelings and were well provided we fasted and prayed and the things were set right that were wrong and in the Evening we had the prevalage of renewing our Covenants before the Lord by baptism, was reconfirmed by Eldr James Taylor
Friday 13th Fasted and met in Council at 9 'clock had a good time, was appointed to Preside over the Cardiff

{047}
District of the East Glamorgan Conference
Saturday 14th Accompanied President Evans and Ashby to my new field of Labour.
Sunday 15th Spoke of the

Saints in the Forenoon and
Bore my testimony to the
work in the Afternoon.
Monday 16th Went to White
Church and thence to Llandaff
and held Meeting
Tuesday 17th Council Meeting
at Cardiff was voted in President
of the Cardiff and Newbridge
Districts.
Wednesday 18th Went to New

{048}
      March
Bridge to District Council
Preached reformation the Spirit
of God working with the
people
Thursday March 19th Went
with Brother Evan Richard[?]
to Llanfabon held a
meeting the Priesthood
felt well
Friday 20th Went to Flower
d luce
Saturday 21st Returned
to Newbridge
Sunday 22nd Held Saints
Meeting Fasted and Prayed
and Preached Reformation
Baptized 7 of the Priest

{049}
hood in the Evening
Monday 23rd Went to
Concert in Treforrest
held for the Benifit
of the Mormon Choir.
Tuesday 24th Accompanied
Eldr Evan Richards to
Cumsebren held Saints
meeting had such a severe
cold could not speak hardly
but managed to talk a
little—all felt well—
Wednesday 25th Went
to Newbridge, Pintyrch
afterwards and held a
meeting
Thursday 26th Went to Cardiff

{050}
met President Miller and at
his request accompanied him
to Llandaff Preached to the
Saints
Friday 27th Went to Ely in
the morning and thence
to White Church had a good
time 2 were baptized
and all felt well.
Saturday 28th Returned to
Cardiff
Sunday 29th Spoke to the
Saints three times and
felt first rate
Monday 30th visited
with Captain William Stevens
and in the evening attended

{051}
a baptism of the Cardiff
Branch 17 Babtized
Tuesday 31st Attended a
District Council in Cardiff
Ordained several to the
Priesthood
        Journal 2nd

{052} [illegible]

{053}
[Pencilled tallies and figures headed "Rebap"; looks like two- and three-letter abbreviations for branch locations together w/ numbers (people?)]

{054–055}
      Do They Miss Me | at Home
Do they miss me at home do | they miss me
[?] be an assurance most | dear
To know that this moment | some love one
Was saying I wish he was | here
To know that the groupe | by the fire side
Are thinking on me as | I roam
Oh! yes t'would be Joy | beyond measure
to know that they miss | at home
their twilight approaches | the season
That ever is sacred to song
Does some one repeat my | name over
And say that I tarry so | long

or is there a chord in the | music
That is missed when I | am away
[---] a chord in each heart | that awakeneth
A regret at my wearisome | stay

{056–057}
Do they set me a chair at | the table
When evenings home pleasure | are nigh
And the candles are lit in | the parlour
and the stars in the cabin | azure sky
When hearty good nights are | repeated
and all lay them down for | to sleep
Do they think on me | absent and waft me
A whispered good night | when they weep

Do they miss me at home | do they miss me
At morning at noon or | at night
Or lingers a gloomy shade | round them
That only my preasance can | light
Are joys less invitingly | welcome
Or pleasures less held than | before
Because one is missed fro | m their circle
And because I am with | them no more

{058–059}
      Reply | to Former
We miss thee at home yes | we miss thee
Since the hours we bid | thee adieu
And prayers have encir | cled they pathway
From anxious hearts loving | and true
That the Saviour would | guide and protect you
So far from the loved | ones you roam
And whisper when'ere thou | art saddened
They miss they all miss | thee at home
When daylight awakens | us from slumber
We catch from its lips | the first kiss
And wish in a wander - | ing zepher
To be wafted to him whom | we miss.
When we have Joined the | home circles
We still place thee a | vacant chair
In each eye rolls a gath | ering tear drops
For him who we want | to be there

{060–061}
The shadows of evening | are falling
O where is the wanderer | snow
The breeze that floats | lightly around me
Perchance may soon | visit his Brow
Oh! bear on this bosom | a message

oh! when will the wan | -derer come
The heart has grown | sad and dejected
We miss Thee All | miss thee at Home

{062–063}
      The Martyrs
I came to the spot where | [*missing*]rtyrs lay
And painsively stood by | [*missing*][---]
When in a low whisper | [*missing*]ard something
                              say
How sweetly we sleep here | alone

When told by the Saviour to | publish on earth
The pure testimony again |
With hearts of rejoicing we | gladly went forth
Enduring all things for | his name

We Wandered as exiles and | pilgrims on earth
To publish salvation abroad |
Endeavoring the trump of | the gospel to blow
Preparing a people for God |

And when among stranger | in prison we lay
And promised protection | by law

{064}
A lawless band [*missing*] | [*leaf may be missing*]
And our bodies do [*missing*] |

Go tell to our bretherin [*missing*] |
To weep not for Joseph though |
Nor Hyrum for Jesus through |
Has safely conducted us home |

The tempest may rage and |
And gathering storms may |
Yet calm and serene and |
He has safely conducted us |

{065}
      On"
up the heart
/life\ ~~runn~~eth impart
or gave to man
[---]th to scan
   Love on

of Youth
and to truth
lurk in smiling guise

[---] from our eyes
   Love on

age
fills up the page
drop the tear
gin by year
   Love on

{066–067}
Love on
Love on in Lifes declining | age
When youthful and mature | becomes the sage
Threescore and ten may | number out our day
But still [---] /on\ until | we pass away
    Love on | Love on
      | Hannah King

      Tune Mary Blan |
Love is the fulfilling of the Law |
Oh let me love how drear | a blight
Would cloud life's rugged | way
Did not that star of heaven's | own light
Shed down one sunny ray |
Oh let me love how bleak | would be
The sunniest day of earth |
Did not that essance breath | in me
Which hath a heavenly | birth

{068–069}
    Chorus
For God is love and love is | heaven
And friendship is of life the | wine
Oh give me this immortal | leaven
To raise this soul of mine |

Oh let me love the darksome | day
that dawns on mortals here |
Illumed by loves inspiring | ray
Would still my pathway cheer |
Oh let me love some kindred | soul
Endewed with heavens own | light
Oh god my wayward heart | controle
And guide my mind aright |
    Chorus
But let me love erase the | dross
That clings to earthly love |

{070–071}
And may thy love all mine | engross
In blissful realms above |
But while my home is on | the earth
My spirit in the will
One Bright basis in the [---] | dearth
Grant to thy feeble child |
    Chorus | Hannah King

Song | Tune 'It'll never do to give it up so"
Come raise my muse a cheerful | lay
[---] we pass o'er lifes rugged way
Let us invoke the aid of son
To cheer us as we pass along
    Chorus
Owe life was made for happiness |
    And not for sorrow and [---] |

{072}
We'll bless our God for daily bread
And all the bounties earth has spread
And for that bright prolific ray
Emitted by the King of day
    Chorus
We'll bless him for the book of health
That mine of sweetest richest wealth
And ne'er forget whenever we bend
To ~~thank~~ /praise\ him for the faithful friend
    Chorus
We'll bless him for the home's we share
And all the wealth we've hoarded there
For parents, Brothers, Sisters wives
With promise of eternal lives
    Chorus
We'll bless him for this peaceful [---]
Where truth and virtue doeth [---]

{073}
That in from babylonish guile
Where peace looks down with Godlike smile
    Chorus
We'll bless him no historic page
Enrolled on names in its past age
But that we live in days or bright
[---] by the gospel light
    Chorus
Revealed by Joseph firm and true
By Brigham and by Heber too
And Bro Grants respected names

As on our hearts bit warm a claim
Chorus
To love them men needs no command
We do uphold them heart and hand

Our presidential head we bear
Before the Lord in dayly prayer
Chorus

{074–075}
God bless his people everywhere |
His spirit may they ever share |
And then they'l Know by day and | night
Whater's betide them all is right |
    Chorus | Hannah King
    Tune "Reva | May"
O once I dwelt in Babylon in | darkness and in dread
For I could see that some dark | clouds were hanging oer my head
But soon the Mormon sun burst | forth dispersed those clouds of jet,
And I became a working bee | in the hive of Deseret.

When I began the truth to scan | kind friends their warnings gave
They straight condemned the Mormon | plan and tried poor me to save
They raved persuaded me to quit | the poor deluded set
But I became a working bee | in the hive of Deseret.

{076–077}
Enlightens part of this dark earth | and onward upward flows
I read marked and learned and did di | gest the plan which Joseph taught
For of all plans it is the best the | one that Jesus brought
And from my heart I blessed the day | I first the Mormons Met
And glad became a working bee | in the hive of Deseret.

Thanks to our King the stone rolls | forth the kingdom lives and grows
And saints go forth | and spread the Gospel net
Returning with fresh working bees | for the hive of Deseret

While discord reigns throughout the | earth proud nations rush to war
And famine pestilence and strife | extend form shore to shore
All Mormon hearts united are | on peace their minds are set
No drones nor discord plague the | bees in the hive of Deseret

When Brigham speaks the Saints | give ear they work with hand and heart
And by hard knocks the kingdom rear | and cheerfully impart

{078–079}
Abundantly of earthly goods and | Grudge no nor regret
The have become good working bees | in the hive of deseret

Both old and young and grave and g | ay from every sect have fled
They've found the straight and | narrow way and follow Christ their head
By day and night to keep his laws | their hearts are fondly set

And praise his name they're wor | king bees in the hive of Deseret.

And from my heart I now invite | each wanderer in the earth
To come and prove the joys I sing and | gain celestial birth
Ere Satan by his wiles beguile | and catch you in his net
May you become good working | bees in the hive of Deseret.

———

Hark the prophet is calling | he roars from the west
Come saints let's our journey persue
Arouse arouse from your slumber
And to Zion repair
     Chorus

{080–081}
To the Vale then lets a | way then
With our hearts full | of joy

See the Elders are | waiting
An ready to start |
To escort us safe over | the plains
All dangers their sca | ing
We've nothing to fear |

Let us Journey toget | her
And always retain |
Our integrity firm to | the end
And whatever we do |
Let to Zion perdue

Soon the wide spread | ing praries
Where the Buffalo ro | am

{082–083}
Shall rejoice in its | splendor and pride
With its vines and its | figtrees
Our spirits shall cheer |
May
~~May~~ we all reach in | safety
The home of the Blest |
Where industry will | reap its reward
Then we'l shout Hall | ujah
To our Father Jehovah |

———

    Tune – Ivy | Green
The Mormons are the happiest lot | that can in the world be found
They have often been Killed but are | lively yet & flourishing all around
The living wonder of the age | these Mormons seem to be
Their deeds will shine on histories | page through all eternities
  Then hail my boys for | ever hail
  Let truth and liberty | prevail

{084–085}
Their Independence is as great | as their principles are grand
No wonder then that they create | such [---] throughout the land
The error of ages and systems of men | they scatter into the brieze
They'll own no earthly creeds again | but believe just what they Please
      For Mormon creeds are | short and bright
      and all are [---] in | this do right

But o what trouble they're giving | the world in trying to put them [---]
They come with gospel banners unfirled | and [---] they gain renown
By [---] hypocrits grand and [---] | at as they headed their mobs from hell
But you see the Mormons are not dea | d yet but seem to be doing well
      They're gathering home | to their Mountain hive
      Where by industry st | ill they thrive

But stand the [---] our p[---] | friends with holy zeal inspired
Kind [---] his Judgments sa[---] | ds and done what we descried

{086–087}
[*illegible line*] | failed this spreading faith to stop
[*illegible line*] | revailed and crickets have done their
      How the Grasshoppers jump | and the crickets hop
      As they wage their war on | Mormon crops

But the Mormons now and ever pray | Good Lord stretch forth thy hand
[---] cricketts and locust keep away | from this our favoured land
[---] may [---] [---] ever be with | Gentile locust curst
For of all the crickets you'll agree | the Gentiles are the worst
      For Gentile crickets [---] | [---] eat the lives
      And houses of Mormons | and their wives

But the Crickets are gone and | the Mormons live by faith in a right /[---]\
And to Gentiles they would kindly give | the hurt to Keep away
For should they pay then [---] [---] | they will most surely find
The Mormons will themselves [---] | in against crickets of every kind
      Then go it yet scoffers for | slander is cheep
      The Mormons will laugh | while their enemies weep

{088–089} [*duplicates 086–087*]
{090–091} [*duplicates 084–085*]
{092–093} [*duplicates 082–083*]
{094–095} [*duplicates 080–081*]
{096–097} [*duplicates 078–079*]
{098–099} [*duplicates 076–077*]
{100–101} [*duplicates 074–075*]
{102} [*duplicates 072*]
{103} [*duplicates 073*]

[*end of digital file; end of transcript*]

Journal 2

1 April 1857 – 20 September 1858, 1859–1874

{free front endleaf recto}
No 2 Journal
Commencing April 1st
1857.

Samuel Roskelley
Elder in the Church
of Jesus Christ of
Latter-day-Saints.

{free front endleaf verso}
[blank]

{page 1}*
[columns of figures; no diary text]

{2}
Wednesday
April 1st Went from Cardiff to
Twynerodyn and held a council
of Elders I intended to go to
Pendylon but the Weather
prevented me–
Thursday 2nd Held a Saints
Meeting at Twynerodyn
Friday 3rd Went to Cog Branch
Preached at Scily had a council
meeting afterwards and disposed
of some petty cases
Saturday 4th Went to Cardiff
Sunday 5th Preached in the
morning at Cardiff in the
Afternoon at Landaf and
at cardiff in the Evening
Monday 6th Went to Newbridge
held a prayer meeting
Tuesday 7th Went to Tyla-
coch held a meeting, a good

{3}
Spirit prevailed and I
preached a good sermon
to gentiles showing that their
faith was not grounded upon
Knowledge and that they did
not Know the Bible was true
Wednesday 8th Preached in
the Cymmer Branche Eldr
Evan Richards translated
it into Welch a good spirit
prevailed and I cam to
Newbridge the same night
Thursday 9th Went to Llanfabon
I preached to the saints being

Samuel Roskelley papers, MS 65, Utah State Univ. Special Collections. Page numbers were added to recto pages of the manuscript to simplify matching the transcription to the document. They are given in this transcription between braces.

full of the Holy Ghost– several
brethren testified that they
Knew I was a servant
of god for even my tough
seemed to fill them with
the Holy Ghost

{4}
April
Friday 10th "Good Friday" Went to
Newbridge and attended the
opening of a meeting house
of the "Christian Bretheren"
after once the preacher
caught my eye he would
not look at me again at
the close of the meeting they
made a collection. I told
the collector I was an American
minister traveling without
purse or scrip and he need
not look for anything form
me at which he turned
away very abruptly
Saturday 11th Visited the
Saints in Newbridge
Sunday 12th Went to Treforrest
spoke 3 times in connection
with President W. Miller and

{5}
April
had a few gentiles to here
Monday 13th Went to Cardiff
and visited all the Saints in
their houses in that Branch
and made some alterations
in in the council meetings.
And the Branch meetings
Bless sister Leattia Thomas and on
Sunday 19th Went to Whitchurch
to a camp meeting Preached
in the morning opposite the
Baptist Chapel and in the
afternoon in the Saints
meeting and in the Evening
opposite the ministers house

and returned to cardiff.
Monday 20th Went Treforest
thence to Newbridge and held
a prayer meeting.
Tuesday 21st Went to Cumsabrin

{6}
April
held a saint meeting
Wedneday 22nd Returned to Newbridge
and preached to the Saints
Thursday 23rd Visited the Saints in Newbridge and went to Treforest and Preached
in the evening
Friday 24nd Went to Cardiff and
remained until
Sunday 26th Went to Pendurylon
with President Miller and roused
the feelings of the Saints and
returned to cardiff in the
Evening
Monday 27th Went to Pentyrch
Branch preached to the Saints
Tuesday 28th Went to Cardiff /to district
Council\ and on
my way called at Whitchurch
and Llandaff
Wednesday 29th Went to Newbridge
to district Council and this

{7}
May
day received an appointment from
Liverpool to Preside over the
Cardiff Conference felt to call
upon the Lord to help me to
carry out the duties incumbet
upon me.
Thursday 30th Went to Llanfabon
and preached in the Evening
felt first rate— Called Br
William Lewis to the Office
of Elder and Daniel Isaac
to the office of Deacon.
Friday May 1st Went to Flower
de Luce and in the Evening
went to Githlagar and preached

not a very good attendance
slept at Llanfabon at Bro Isaac
Saturday 2nd Went to Newbridge
and on the way heard the Coko [cuckoo?]
for the first time for the season

{8}
  May
Went to Treforest and returned
to Newbridge to slepp at the
old sisters
Sunday 3rd Went to Gill-le-galed
and preached, the people had
hearts like stone an old apostate gave me a shilling, in the
afternoon went to Tilla-coch
a few of the Bosses turned out
the people were not very plenty
in the Evening went to Cwm-
sabris a good influence was
felt until one of the Bretheren
began to talk Welch and the
People began to disperse, the
principles were taught in plain
ness and faithfull testamonies
bourn in English and Welch
Monday 4th Went to Newbridge
and thence to Treforest

{9}
  May
and held a Prayer meeting
and Rebaptized Brother
Francis Gibbon – Slept at Bro
Wm Gibbon's
Tuesday 5th Went to Cardiff
and thence to Llandaff
and Preached and back
to Cardiff again Stayed
at Bro [---] Evans
Wednesday 6th Went to Pon-
dylon and on the road
attacted with Fits. I had
3 struggles, the second time
it overcame me and pros
trated me on the road
for upward of half and hour

when I arrived at the
meeting place I had to
go to bed instead Of Preach
Slept at Bro John Johns.

{10}
Thursday 7th Felt a little better and went to
Twin-
erodyn and Preached
slept at Bro Jacob Thomas
Friday 8th Went to Cog and
Scilly and Prached a little
while I did not feel well in
body slept at Bro
Saturday 9th Went to Cardiff
and remained over
Sunday 10th Spoke 4 times
during the day and enjoyed a good spirit
Monday 11th In Cardiff felt
Sick, went to Prayer Meeting
in the Evening
Tuesday 12th In Cardiff felt
a little better attended council
Meeting
Wednesday 13th Went to Newbridge

{11}
  May
to district Council slept
at the Old sisters ~~and took~~
Thursday 14th Took breakfast
with Sister Mary Williams
and Went to Cardiff to a
Branch Council to devide
the villages between the
Branches.
Remained in Cardiff until
Sunday 15th Went to Penterch
and preached 4 times in
vilages around there and
returned to Cardiff in the
evening to an attentive congregation
Monday 18th Went to Newbridge
and attended the Prayer
Meeting
Tuesday 19th Went to Cwm-

sabra slept at Brother Samuel

{12}
May
Hornsby's.
Wednesday 20th Returned to
The Cummyr, counseled Eld^r
William Thomas to move his
Family to the Cumsabra Dist^c
to establish a branch there
Preached at the Cummyr
Elder Evan Richards translated
it into Welch, came to New
bridge to sleep at the old
Sisters.
Thursday 21st Went to Treforest
to Preach Counseled with
William Davis and told him
if he could make his a/c's
straight with his creditors
I was willing for him to go
to America so far as I was
concerned, slept at Bro
William Gibbon's.

{13}
May
Friday 22nd Went to Merthyr
and thence to Tredegar the
Folks felt glad to see me
Slept at Bro Benjamin Evans
Saturday 23rd Went to Merthyr
met with President Miller and
Sunday 24th Attended Conference
and Felt well I spoke twice
Monday 25th /Got a License signed at
Merthyr\ Went to Cardiff
attended Prayer meeting and
on Tuesday 26th District Council
and spoke to some length on reformation
rebuked anyone teaching who
had not reformed
/Went to the Editor of the Cardiff &\
Wednesday 27th Went to New
/Merthyr [---] to get a piece published\
Bridge District Council slept at
/in answer to Judge Drummond's report but

could not\
Sister W Daviss and counseled
with W. Davis about going to the
States
Thursday 28th Went to Llanfabon

{14}
June
Branch and Preached to the
Saints. Preached Reformation
Slept at Brother Isaac's
Friday 29th Went to Flower-de-luce
and thence to Crumline and then
to the Blina slept at Brother
Thomas Jones
Saturday 30th Went to Black
Rock to visit Elder John Thomas
and came back to the Bliana
to Bro Thomas Jones
Sunday 31st Went to Nantyglo
to the Monmouthshire Conference
I preached twice and stayed all
night at Brother Thomas Reese
Monday 1st Jun Attended a
concert at Nantyglo to raise
means to gather to Buy Prest
James Taylor a watch — had a
Good time and went to Tredegar

{15}
Slept at Bro Evans
Tuesday 2nd Went to Merthyr
and Bought Books for Book
Agent and Conference Accounts
for the Cardiff Conference
Wednesday 3rd Went to Cardiff
and attended a Saints
meeting
Thursday 4th In Cardiff making
up accounts and writing letters
Attended the Cardiff Branch
Council taught the Brethren
to Keep the Commandments
of the Lord
Friday 5th In Cardiff in
the Meeting Room in the after
noon and a man by the name

of William Ellis came into
the room and began to abuse
the saints and said they acted

{16}
June
dishonestly with him. I did not
appear to take much notice of
him as he was more than half
drunk but he caught me by
the collar of the Coat and
forcibly ejected me from the
room. we went to the Separinten
dant of Police and he told us we
had better proceed any further with the case as we
could not get any satisfaction
for it in consequence of not
having any legal claim to the
room—
Saturday 6th Visiting and
writing in cardiff and attended
a Conference Council in Cardiff
and Prepared the Organization of
Conference Bissiness to come
before the Conference on

{17}
June
Sunday 7th Conference Organized
in Cardiff Good instructions
given and the Saints felt
well
Monday 8th Set the Conference
Books in Order, Wrote to the
offices to devide the Debt and
books in the next Quarters
Accounts and Attended Prayer
Meeting in Cardiff
Tuesday 9th Remained in Cardiff
and studied
Wednesday 10th Went to Llandaff
and tried the case Evan
Avery @ wife in connexion with
my two counsellors— we settled
the case that all should
be restored to proper standing

by making acknowledgements
which was done accordingly

{18}
June
Thursday 11th Went to Canton
and visited the Saints and
then wen to Twinrodyn and
held Saint Meeting. I spoke
of the Saints being necesi
ated to live by all the
commandments of God as
the time was come for the
downfall of Wickedness and
corruption, and old Gentleman
a stranger—said at the close
of the meeting that I had
spoken very plain and he
was glad he had come to
meeting
Friday 12th Went to Cardiff
and remained until
Sunday 14th Went to Cog Bran
ch—for company with my
councellors and preached

{19}
June
at Danys Powis and at
Caticston—not very good attend
ance. Returned to Cardiff in
the Evening
Monday 15th Went to Penarth
by the politeness of Sister
Mary Wride in a Pheaton
accompanied by Prest Miller
Sister Wride & Hannah Salmon
enjoyed myself first rate
Tuesday 16th Went to Newbridge
and thence to Cumsabra and
held a saints meeting
Wednesday 17th Went to Pentrya
and held a Saints meeting
and ordained Brother Jenkins
a Priest

Thursday 18th Whent [sic] to Treforest
and held a Saints Meeting all
felt well

{20} [whole page crossed out]
Thursday 11th Went to Canton
and visited the Saints and
thence to Twinrodyn preached
in the Evening
Friday 12th Returned to
Cardiff and in the Evening
attended the Singing Class
Saturday and talked with
Elder John Oliver about he's
mission to the Gentiles—I
counseled him not to
get married nor set his mind
on the Girls until he was
told to do so
Saturday 13th Remained in Cardiff

{21}
   June
Friday 19th Visited the Saints
in Newbridge and Treforest
Saturday 20th Visited the Sick
in Newbridge and then went
to Llanfabon—slept at Bro
Jonathan Isaac's
Sunday 21st Preached at
Quakers Yard— it rained and
we had to quit—Preached
at Nelson and Gill-la-gar
the people were very scarce
and those that did attend
felt ill of the truth
Monday 22nd Went to Newbridge
and thence to Whitchurch and
attended a prayer meeting
Tuesday 23rd Went to Llandaff
and thence to Cardiff and
held District Council—the
representations showed that

{22}
   June
the people are angry and
sought to hurt is if they
could—
Wednesday 24th Went to
Pendylon visited the saints
as there was no meeting on
account that the Bretheren
were in the Hay fields until
late
Thursday 25th Went to
Pentyrch and thence to Teforest
and attended to the Saint
meeting—Mr Francis
Croshaw an Iron Manufacturer
of treforest the employer of
Bro Wm Gibbon has shut up
the works and offers Bro Wm
the privilege of still working
for him providing he will
renounce Mormonism and

{23}
   June
never speak to a Latter-day Saint
upon pain of instant dismissal
and have 10 shillings per week
untill he can suit himself
I told Br William that I
should tell Mr Crowshaw
<u>to kiss my foot</u>
Friday 26th Went to Cardiff
my feet were blistered with
walking so much and I re-
mained in Cardiff until
Sunday 28th Went to
Twinrodin and thence to St
Nicholas—Bro David Pugh spoke
and the policeman asked him
for his Authority—he could not
produce any and then he asked
me for mine as I had been
preaching, after a while I showed
it to him—he said the law would

{24}
July
not protect me as I was more
than five miles from the place
where the Licence was signed
he took our names and said
Mr Bruce was determined to
prosecute—I told him to
crack down—Returned to Cardiff—
Monday 29th West Cardiff
Writing and fixing up accounts
until
Wednesday 1st Went to Cogin
Danys Powas, and visited the
Sick and the President of the
Branch and Returned to Cardiff
in the Evening
Thursday 2nd in Cardiff writing
until
Friday 3rd Went to Llandaff
thence to Whitchurch thence to
Newbridge District council

{25}
July
Saturday 4th Went to Treforest
and visited the saints and in
the Evening baptized 3 Persons
in the River Taff
Sunday 5th Went to Newbridge
and Preached in the open air
in the morning, held a Saint
meeting in the Afternoon and
preached twice again in the
Evening
Monday 6th Visited the Saints
in Treforest & Newbridge
Attended a Prayer Meeting
in Treforest and afterwards
baptized 5 Persons in the
Taff River
Tuesday 7th Went to Cumsabra
and slept at Bro [---] Howsleys
and preached at Gill-legalled
good attention

{26}
July
Wednesday 8th Went to the
Cummer and preached with Bro
Henry Harris had a good mee
ting—and went to Newbridge to sleep
Thursday 9th Went to Treforest
and thence to Cardiff and
attended a Branch conference
Friday 10th in Cardiff and
remained until
Tuesday 14th Went to Newport
to see Bro Wm Davies off to America
returned to Cardiff the same night
Wednesday 15th Went to Pentyrch
and attended a Saints meeting
Thursday 16th Went to Merthyr via
Treforest & Newbridge and settled
up the divisions of conference Books
and some other affairs that
were to be attended to
Friday 17th Went to Newbridge

{27}
July
Saturday 18th Went to Pentyrch
to settle up the Book agents
affairs–
Sunday 19th Went to Pendnoylon
Settled the Book agents accounts
and held Saint meeting and
Preached out doors to a small
but attentive congregation
Monday 20th Went to Twynrodyn
Settled the book agents affairs
there and then went to cardiff
to sleep
Tuesday 21st Was in Cardiff
attending to general business and
attended District council and
remained in Cardiff until
Friday 24th Went to Devonport
to visit my Relatives–
Saturday 25th Visited my
Brothers Richard & John and their

{28}
July
wives. Went to Barnpool the
place I was baptized and
picked Limpits & Periwinkils
Sunday 26th Went to Plymouth
and spoke in the afternoon and
Preached at Devonport in the
Evening and my father was
present
Monday 27th Went fishing with
my Brother and afterward went
to the Park with Bro Yeats & Bro
& Sister Wood of Plymouth and
Sister Elizabeth Wyatt & E. E.
Knight
Tuesday 28th Went to the
Plymouth Breakwater and then
to woody hedge and spent the
day with My Brother R^d &
John And their wives & my sister
Jane—returned to Plymouth

{29}
August
in the evening and thence to
Devonport and spoke to the
saints
Wednesday 29th Went to
Tideford and spent the day
with Uncle William Roskelley
Returned in the Evening
Thursday 30th Left Devonport and
went to Bristol on my way back
to my field of Labour Slept
at the Bristol Conference house
Friday 31st Went to Cardiff in
the Ely Steam Boat and thence
to Newbridge and held District
Council—had a good meeting
slept at William Davis's
Saturday 1st Visited the saints
in Treforest and returned to
Cardiff—Slept at my
Lodgings

{30}
August
Sunday 2nd Started in the morning
for Landaff to Examine the
P. Fund & Book agents Accounts
and disposed of that matter
and whent from thence to
Whitchurch to accomplish
the same purpose which
I did—Met with the Saints
in the Afternoon and held
a Saints Meeting—I spoke
upon the necessity of saints
living their religion to be able
to receive the blessings to
be imparted to them hereafter
/returned to cardiff to sleep\
Monday 3rd was making up a/c's
all day pertaining to the conference
Tuesday 4th Do Do Do
Wednesday 5th Made out an
Estimate of Conference Expenditures
for two months Ending Aug 6th

{31}
fore President Daniels in Swansea
I found I had used about
10 shillings per week—Entered
it upon my tithing account
Book—Went to the Peir to
Meet the Bretheren from
Bristol Elders Asa Calkin
and Robert F Neslin—went
to Meeting in the Evening Elders
Neslen & Calkins addressed
the assembly a good spirit
prevailed all was peace and
quietness
Thursday 6th Went to the
Railway Station to see the
bretheren off and went to my
Lodgins and wrote several
letters of various persons
~~Friday 7th At home in Cardiff writing~~

{32}
August
Dedicated and Set apart Elders Henry Watts and William Lewis to Travel and Preach the Gospel to the Gentiles and the started on their missions.
Friday 7th Saturday 8th At home writing for Book Agent
Sunday 9th Went to Treforest and examined the Book agency and Penny Fund a/c and attended a saints meeting and thence to Newbridge and examined the Books–
Monday 10th Went to the Cymmer Branch and Examined the Books–
Tuesday 11th Went to the Cumsabra Branch and examined their Books and

{33}
August
Held a Meeting a good influence pervated thro the assembly and on Wednesday 12th I returned to Newbridge and and [sic] stayed over night–
Thursday 13th Went to Llanfabon Branch and held a meeting & few saints at meeting
Friday 14th Went from Llanfabon to Newbridge thense to Treforest thence to Pentyrch and examined the Books and thence to Llandaff to see the sick Saints—found them better and thence to Cardiff—
Saturday 15th In Cardiff Reading and Writing and

{34}
Making up accounts
Sunday 16th Remained in Cardiff and spoke to the saints 3 times—had a good time
Monday 17th & Tuesday 18th In Cardiff attending to Bisiness pertaining to the Financial affairs of the Conference—
Wednesday 19th Went to Whitchurch and stayd over night.
Thursday 20 Went to Llandaff thence to Ely and thence to Pendoylon and thence to Twynrodyn and stayd over night—
Friday 21st Went to Dynas Powis and thence to Crogin and thence to Cardiff
Saturday 22nd ~~Went~~ was

{35}
to Cardiff writing and settled to take the Book agency from Brother Evan Richards
Sunday 23rd Went to Whitchurch and thence to Pentyrch and thence to Cardiff—
Monday 24th In Cardiff posting books and moving conference stock from Brother E. Richard's to my Lodgings—
Tuesday 25th Attended to some business in Cardiff and went to Whitchurch via Llandaff and stayed over night at Bro Littons.
Wednesday 26th Went to Treforest and thence to Newbridge and Went to see Sister Catherine Jones who was very, very sick, by request
5-11

{36}
August

sat up with her in connexion
with some of the Saints—some
of the Gentiles came to visit her
but they soon walked off again
feeling that the "company" did
not suit them, Sister Catherine
died about 2 O'Clock in the
morning and thus died one
of the Best Saints in the
British Isles. She died
as quiet a child going to
sleep
Thursday 27th Visited the
Saints in Newbridge and in
the Evening Preached a short
sermon to them
Friday 28th Visited the
Saints in Treforest and in
the Evening went to Newbridge
and attended a district council

{37}
August

Saturday 29th Went to treforest
and attended the burial of
Sister Catherine Jones and then
went to Cardiff
Sunday 30th Went to Twinyrodyn
and thence to [blank] and then
Back to [blank] and preached
both places to Gentiles – the people
Hissed and Laughd and Scoffed &
Mocked us most abominable—I returned
to Cardiff the Same night
Monday 31st At home in Cardiff
writing and making up accounts
Tuesday September 1st Went to
Llandaff thence to Whitchurch and
thence to Pentyrch talked in
the families of the Saints
Wednesday 2nd Went to
Pendylon and thence to Penforth
Powr and thence to Twynyrodyn

{38}
September

And Preached to the Saints
a good spirit was manifested
Thursday 3rd Went to Denys Powis
and thence to Cog and thence
to Cardiff—visited Saints by the way
Friday 4th Went to Merthyr
to find out what stock I was
to retain in Cardiff as conference
Stock
Saturday 5th Returned to Cardiff
after I had transacted the business
I went upon
Sunday 6th Went to Llandaff
and whent around that district
and preached to the gentiles
and afterwards came back to
Llandaff and Preached to the
Saints. – we all felt well
returned to cardiff and spoke
in the Evening

{39}
September

Monday 7th At home writing and
in the Evening went to Whitchurch
and staid over night
Tuesday 8th Took 1/2 past 9 Oclock
train for Newbridge—stayd at Bro
Matthews and then Whent to Cumsebra
Stayd at the house of Bro J R Morgan
during the Evening Mr William
Thomas and his wife quarrled
very much and Sister Morgans
had a fit—I administered to her
and then got up directly
it rained very much during the
latter part of my journey—
Wednesday 9th Returned to
Newbridge and visited the saints
and went to Treforest to stay
over night at Sister Davis's
Thursday 10th Very Poorly—went
to Llanfabon and Preached—Bro

{40}
September
Evan Richards translated—the
Saints felt well
Friday 11th Went to Flower-d-
luce and stayd at Bro Frasure's
the folks felt well to see me
in the [sic] went to see the Monster
Bridge called [blank]
in company with Elders Richards
and Frasure
Saturday 12th Went to Llanfabon
and thence to Inclive top and
took the 2o.clock train for
Newbridge—stayd at Bro
Matthews a little while and
then went to treforest to visit
the Saints and then went to
Cardiff
Sunday 13th Staid in Cardiff
all day and preached to
Saints and Sinners

{41}
Monday 14th In Cardiff
Packing up Books and divided
the Stock and writing to make
the ~~stock~~ accounts straight
Tuesday 15th I was writing
nearly all day and ruling
my penny fund Book and in
the Evening I attended the
Cardiff District Council
A good spirit prevailed
and the bretheren manifested their determination to
sustain me as the Penny
fund Treasurer
Wednesday 16th Went to
Notify the Saints in Cardiff
that Elder Calkin would preach
this Evening and went to the
Train Station to meet Elder Asa
Calkins—Attended the meeting

{42}
September
in the Evening and addressed
the saints for some time was
followed by Eldrs Calkin and
Miller—the Saints felt well
Thursday 17th Went out walking
in the morning with Bro Miller &
Calkin and in the afternoon took
train for Llandaff Station and
went to Whitchurch—Stayd
over night with Bro Litson's
dreamed a curious dream
about Bro F. F. Neslen
Friday 18th Went to Bro
Selmans and thence To Bro
Wride's and thence to Pentyrch
to Bro John A Lewis's and stayd
over night
Saturday 19th Wrote several
letters in the Morning and
went to see Sister Mary

{43}
Wilkins and in the Afternoon
went to Treforest–
Sunday 20th Went to Cumsebra
and organized the branch by
appointing John R. Morgan
President—held a saint
meeting in the Afternoon an [sic]
a prayer meeting in the
Evening—Stayd at Br S
Hornsby
Monday 21st Went to Treforest
via Newbridge—felt very
unwell went to Sister
Davis's and lay on the bed
Tuesday 22nd Went to Cardiff
and Stayd over night
Wednesday 23rd Went to
Twynyrodyn and held Saint
Meeting—Slept at Bro Luke
Bezzants

{44}
September
Thursday 24th Went to Denys
Powis and thence to Cogg and
thence to Cardiff and attended
the Council Meeting
Friday 25th Went to Newbridge
District Council—Had a
good meeting—Slept at
Treforest—
Saturday 26th Went to Pentyrch
and stay^d over night at Bro
J. A Lewis's intended to go to
Pendoylon next day but wether prevailed
Sunday 27th Went to Cardiff
and Packed up the Books
in the morning, in in the [sic]
Afternoon and Evening went
to meeting heard Bro Calkin
Preach After Meeting went
with Sister Mary Wride
to her Uncle's—Strawson

{45}
the Surveyor—the folks were
full of the Devil and the
old man had not common
deacensy—Mary spoke upon
the Principles of Life and salvation and tried to get me
to speak too but I would not
and at last she asked me
why I would not speak—I
told her the reason was—I
knew I was not welcome in
that house and consequently
if I told the greatest truths
ever revealed to man (Just
at this moment the old man
burst forth) I would not
believe you, I would not believe a word of it!! afterwards
the son ~~asked~~ said with a
long sigh—We shall not see

{46}
(September
God till we get to heaven ! !
I turned to him and asked if
he thought we should then
to which he made but lite
reply—After I came away
the Old man told Mary that
she was welcome there at any
time but never more to bring
me there and I presume to
say he will have his request
granted—
Monday 28th the Day fixed
for a Pic-Nick Party but
in consequence of the Rain
we did not go out until the
Afternoon when we went and
had a good frolic—I
played Rounders—slept
at Bro Selmans—
Tuesday 29th Went again to

{47}
October
the Pic-Nick and had a good
time—all things went off
well and all were perfectly
satisfied except the Gentiles
who looked on and they were
full of the Devil and would
like to do us an injury but
they couldn't come it—
Stay^d at Bro Selmans all
night
~~Tuesday~~ /Wednesday\ 30th Went to Cardiff
and attended to the Saints
meeting
Thursday 1st October Went to
Newbridge and thence to Treforest
and held Saint Meeting—
the Spirit of God was there
in abundance
Friday 2nd Wend to Llanfabon
and visited the Saints and

{48}
Returned to Newbridge to the
Saints meeting in the Evening
a good spirit prevailed
Saturday 3rd Rained all
day—I wrote some letters
Posted my Journal and in
the Evening went to visit the
Saints
Sunday 4th Went to the Cummer
and Visited some of the Saints
Among whome was Bro John
Richards who was an apostate
which has been brought on
by unbelief and lack of
faith—Attended the saints
meeting at 2 Oclock and
talked to the Saints upon
the Principle of Obedience
and Unity—Preached
out of Doors to a rather

{49}
thin Congregation and then
returned to Treforest
Monday 5th Went to Cardiff
Tuesday 6th in Cardiff
writing and making up
accounts
Wednesday 7th Went to
Pentyrch and thence to
Pendoyloyn and held a
saint meeting at 2 Oclock
all felt well and thence
to Twynyrodyn and slept
over night
Thursday 8th Went to
Cardiff and thence to
Whitchurch and attended
a Saints Meeting—Stayd
over night
Friday 9th Went to Newbridg
and expected to meet

{50}
October
Bros Enock Reese and
Rd G. Evans according to
appointment but those
Brethren not coming I
had to fulfil the ap-
pointment and occupy
the time in the meeting
the Lord blessed me with
his spirit and the saints
rejoiced–
Saturday 10th Returned to
Cardiff and attened
a General Conference
Council in the Evening
found the conditions of
the Conference pretty
good—learned that
the Emigration to the
States was stopped and
that another point of

{51}
October
outfit would have to be
made before the emigration
could recommence
Sunday 11th Attended our
conference all day—transacted
the Business in the forenoon
and in the evening bore testamony
to what had been said and
further proposed that if
the People of this land
hated the saints so bad
Why not Fast and Pray
and get up a subscription
fund and send them all
to Salt lake also that
the British Army in
India had rejected the
gospel and Judgments had
come in consequence

{52}
October
Monday 12th Went to
Newport to see president Wm
Miller start on his Journey
returned to Cardiff and wrote
some letters and transacted
some business and attended
meeting in the Evening and
remained making up the
Book Agency & Taking Stock
&c &c until
Wednesday 13th Went to Llandaff
and Ely and held Meeting in Company
with Elder Enoch Reese—had a
good meeting Bro Reese Preached—
returned to Cardiff to sleep
Thursday 15th Went to Whitchurch
after visiting some of the Saints
in Cardiff and held a Saint
Meeting after which Bro Reese
Preached a good discourse

{53}
Friday 15~~6~~th Visited the Saints
in the Morning and in the
Afternoon went to Pentyrch
with Bro Reese—held meeting
in the Evening in Bro Jno A
Lewis's house—Elder Reese
Preached and Bro Lewis
interpreted
Saturday 16~~7~~th Went to
Llantrissaint Station with
Bro Reese and proceeded by
the 2 Oclock Train to Swansea
arrived at 1/4 to 4—Met
Bros Taylor & Evans at the
Station and went to Prest
Daniels's and transacted
some business concerning
the P. Fund and Paying
for the Books out of the
Tithing

{54}
October
Sunday 18 Attended the Swansea
Conference, by Request, all day
had a good time spoke a
little in the Evening to a good
congregation
Monday 19th Went to Merthyr
with Elder George Rowley to
transact some busines
with Bro H. Harries—he
was not at home—came on
to Treforest on foot slept
at Sister Wm Davies's
Tuesday 20th Went to Cumsebra
with Bro Rowley held meeting
at Bro Hornsby's Bro Rowley
spoke at some length and
I followed spoke upon the
Saviour's Prophesy on the
Mount and Elder Richards
interpreted—went to the

{55}
October
water to witness a rebaptism
slept at Bro Hornsby's
Wednesday 21st Went to
Newbridge to Bro Thos Davies,
Treforest & Newbridge Branches
were met together and Elder
George Rowley Preached followed
by Myself and I taught,
Plainly that the kingdom of
God was established and
about to roll—quoted
the scripture to answer
Thursday 22nd Went to
Cardiff and Packed up
the Books—Visited some of
the Saints and wrote some
Friday 23rd At home Preparing
the Penny Fund for A/c's—wrote
several letters—send a duplic-
ate of the 4 last months

{56}
October
expences to Swansea and
Went to Newbridge with the
Evening Train to Attend Newbridge
District Council Meeting
had a good meeting and
I told the Presidents of Branches
not to Preach any more to the
Gentiles except by request no
distribute any more tracts but
turn their whole attention to
the house of Israel—to do away with
Sunday morning Preaching
meetings and let <u>all</u> the officers
turn out to visit the Saints on
Sunday Morning and take
care of them as a sheppard
would of a flock of sheep
Saturday 24th Took trains for
Cardiff with Bro Rowley

{57}
Sunday 25th Attended Meeting
in Cardiff three times Preached
to the Saints and we had a
good meeting day the holy spirit
was Poured out copiously upon
all present—in the Evening
several Gentiles came into
the Meeting but it was
hard work to preach to the
Gentiles as the word had
been given for us to turn our
attention to the house of Israel
Monday 26th Attended the
Funeral of Sister Jane Chugg
who died on Friday 23rd and
heard the Episcopalian Priest
go through the Hypocrytical
cerimony and after it was
over I said a few words to
the Living and told them the

{58}
Llandaff
only way to be saved—all
passed off in Quietness and in
the Evening I returned to Cantoh
and attended Prayer Meeting
in the House of Brother Chugg
after the Saints had got through
Elder G. Rowley occupied a short
time followed by myself and
all passed of well returned
to Cardiff to sleep
Tuesday 27th Went to Pentyrch
with Elder G. Rowley and had
a first rate meeting
Wednesday 28th Went to Penday-
lon saw some of the Saints
and feeling rather sick
in consequence of having
taken a cold I went on
to Twynrodyn—left Bro
Rowley at Pentyrch—he could

{59}
October
not walk because of a gathering on his heel—
Thursday 29th Went to Denys
Powis and feeling sick still
I went on to Cardiff where
I was very sick all night
wit sore throat and chest
Friday 30th Was in Bed
all day excepting an hour or
two in the evening when I felt
a little better
Saturday 31st Continued to
get a little better and I
ventured to go down to far
as Elder S. Shepton to transact some business in the
Evening—a few Saints called
to see me in the Evening
Sunday 1st November Went
to Whitchurch and met with

{60}
November
the Whitchurch and Pentyrch
Branches and had a good
meeting booth Afternoon and Evening
I preached as long as my lungs
would allow me both times
Monday 2nd Went to Cardiff
and Pack^d up the books for the
branches and in the Evening
went with Elders George Rowley &
Samuel Evans to see a Figure of
the Human Being (moddeled in
wax) dissected—it was a
very interesting sight
Tuesday 3rd Went to Treforest
and wrote in the Evening—slept
at Sister Davis'es
Wednesday 4th Visited the
Saints at Treforest and attended
a Saints Meeting held at Bro
Thomas Davies, Chair Works,

{61}
November
had a good time, on the
Thursday 5th went to Llanfabon
and held a saint meeting we
had a good time—preached
on the Deliverance of Gods people
Friday 6th Went to Newbridge
and treforest and held a singing
school at Sister Davis's
Saturday 7th Went to Cardiff
and in the afternoon went to Whitchurch and thence to Llandaff
to carry the Books—returned
to Cardiff to sleep
Sunday 8th Went to Twynrodyn
in company with Elders Rowley
Pubh, Evans & Capt Stephens
the Cogg & Llandaff Branches
met with the Twynrodyn
Branch and we had a
good day I spoke afternoon

{62}
November
and Evening returned in the
Evening to Cardiff
Monday 9th Went on board the
two Sisters and dined with
Captain Stephens and afterwards
pack^d up the Books for the
branches—attended prayer
meeting in the evening.
Tuesday 10th Visited some of
the Saints in Cardiff—according to appointment went to Bro
Pughs to take dinner. Bro Pugh
was not at home and sister
Pugh said Bro Pugh was not
coming home to dinner and consequently she had not prepared
any dinner—I took it as a
<u>broad hint</u> and walked off
and got Dinner at Bro Glades
and supper at Bo Edwards

{63}
November
in the Evening went to District
Council—but few present
but we had a good meeting
Wednesday 11th after settling
some business in Cardiff
went to Cogg with Bro Rowley
and then went to Scillery to
see Sister James and then went
to Cawson and Preached to
the Saints and some Gentiles
who were present two of whome
said they would be baptiszed
pretty soon—slept at Bro
Glovers
Thursday 12th Went to
Cogg and thence to Twnyrodyn
and visited the Saints and
from thence to Pentforth[---]
and Place to Pendoylon
and preached at the house

{64}
November
of Bro David Roderick—slept
at Bro Wm Evans–(so cold all
night could not sleep)
Friday 13th Went to Pentyrch
visited with Bro Lewis & family
and stayd over night with
them
Saturday 14th Went to
Treforest and thence to Newbridge
to see the President of the Branch
and thence to Merthyr to see
Prest Taylor according to his
request—met with him at
Br. Harris's and settled the
Bisness I was called upon
slept with Prest Taylor
Sunday 15th Went to Newbridge
and held a meeting
5 Branches met had a
Splendid time and no mstake [sic]

{65}
November
slept at Sister Davis's at
Treforest
Monday 16th Went to
Cardiff—packed up the
books—made out Eldrs Millers
and Calkins Expenditures while
in the Confce—returned to
Treforest by the Evening Train—slept
at Brother Littons
Tuesday 17th Went to Cumsebra
the Saints did not meet as
usual because of the darkness
of the night—had a little
conversation upon the deliverance
of Zion with Bro Saml Hornsby
Wednesday 18th Went up the
dingle and visited the Saints
settled a difficulty between the
Sisters and returned to Treforest
to sleep–

{66}
Nov
Thursday 19th Went to Llanfabon
and Held Meeting Bro Rowley
and myself preached—had a
good time Slept at Bro Jonh Isaacs
Friday 20th Went to Newbridge
and held District Council
and went to Treforest to sleep
Saturday 21st Went to Pentyrch
and visited with the Saints
Sunday 22nd Went to Pendylon and held a meeting—had
a good time—I spoke on the
gathering of the Saints—went
to Cardiff with some of the
Brethern and thence to Whitchurch and stayd all night
Monday 23rd Went to Cardiff
and Packed up the Books
and attended a prayer meeting
in the Evening

{67}
Nov
Tuesday 24th In Cardiff
writing and making up a/cs
Wednesday 25th Went to
Cogg and thence to Dynas Powis
and thence to Twnyrodyn and
Talked with the bretherent on
the deliverance of the Poor
from these lands
Thursday 26th Went to Dynas
Powis and Cogg and Preached and
returned to Dynas Powis to Sleep
Friday 27th Went to Cardiff
and Posted my Journals—Sent
Elder Rowley to Visit the Saints
in the Upper District and stir
them up in their duties–
Recd information from Prest
D. Daniles that the Valley
boys were going home in the
spring

{68}
Nov
and that we were required to ~~make~~/raise\
donations from the Saints. Eld
Reese arrived from Merthyr
and we talked over the prospects
of Going home—
Saturday 28th Was in Cardiff
Visited many of the Saints with
Elder Reese in the Evening
several of the Bretheren came
up to see us
Sunday 29th Went to Canton
in the Morning to visit the
Saints and returned to Cardiff
to Attend the afternoon Meeting
We had a good Meeting
Elder Reese and myself
spoke—Evening a good
many strangers present
Elder Reese Preached
Monday 30th In Cardiff

{69}
Nov-Decr
visited the Saints and
attending to business and
In the Evening Attended a
Special District Council in
Cardiff to Ask the Bretheren
for Assistance to help the
Valley Bretheren to go home
The holy Ghost rested upon
the Meeting and the Bretheren
subscribed liberally 43£
subscribed in Council—
Tuesday 1st December—Went
to Newbridge and thence to
Cwmsaebra and held a meeting
the Saints felt well and
I put the Emigration of the
Elders before them and
there was 3£10s10d raised
the Bretheren all felt well
and wished us "Gods speed"

{70}
Dec
Wednesday 2nd Went to Newbridge
and attended a "Special" District
Council the Holy Spirit did
its work by inspiring the Brethren
to do their duty and they did
subscribe liberally towards
our going home and May
God Bless them for Blessing
us £22-2-6 was subscribed
in Council
Thursday 3rd Was in Treforest
writing and visiting the Saints
attended the Meeting in the Evening
The Treforest & Newbridge Branches
met together Elders Reese & Rowley
and Myself spoke slept at
Bro Litsons—
Friday 4th Went to Rhydfelyn
and thence to Pentyrch—only
a few Saints met and I talked

{71}
December
to them by the Fireside for
about 2 hours and the folks
felt first rate—
Saturday 5th Went to Cardiff
and wrote and read—
Sunday 6th Went to Newbridge
by the Morning train and met
Elders Reese & Rowley they and
I held a meeting at Bro Thos
Matthews the Newbridge &
Treforest & Cymmer Branches
met together and we had
a good time all day.
Monday 7th Came to Cardiff
with Eldrs Reese and Rowley
and Packd up the books
and attended a meeting in the
Rooms Elder Reese spoke at some
length, and we had a good
meeting

{72}
December
Tuesday 8th in Cardiff–
dined at Bro John Bladdons with
Elders Reese & Rowley and went
around the docks and called
at Sister Glades and went to
Bro Robert Liddiards to Tea and
then Attended a district council
meeting in Cardiff–
Wednesday 9th Went to Merthyr
with the Morning Train with
Bro Reese to meet Prest Daniels
to have a settlement of the "Penny
Fund" settled the Business and
Prest Daniels requested me to
Accompany Prest Harries to
Abardare and talk to the
Bretheren about the best
course to pursue in refferance
to the Strike among the Colliers
I attended meeting in Aberdare

{73}
December
and did as I was requested–
slept at Bro Bodin's
Thursday 10th talked with the
bretheren in the morning and
took the 1 Oclock train to
Taffs Well and then went
to the Graig Farm to Bro Wrides
but on the way called to see
Sister Hughs—Called at Bro
Wrides and conversed with Mrs
& Mr Wride Senr upon the
principles of the Gospel the old
lady seemed quite pleased and
I think she will soon yeild obedience
to it—In the evening attended a
saint Meeting at Whitchurch and
had a good time—slept at
Bro Sheppards
Friday 11th Went to Cardiff
and met Bro Rowley and thence

{74}
December
to Ely to visit the Saints and
thence to Llandaff and held a
saint Meeting a good feeling
prevailed I spoke at some length
on the redemption of Zion and
was followed by Bro Rowley–
returned to Cardiff to sleep–
Saturday 12th In Cardiff all
day writing making up the
Penny Fund a/c's in the Evening
went to Whitchurch with Sister
Ann Wride had a long conversation
with Bro Sheppard about his
Branch
Sunday 13th In Cardiff did
not feel well in the Afternoon
but Preached in the Evening on
the setting up of the Latter day
Kingdom and what it was to
accomplish

{75}
December
Monday 14th was in Cardiff
visited some Saints wrote and
made up some Penny fund a/cs
and spent the Evening with
Sisters Thomas Elizabeth–
Tuesday 15th Went to Treforest
and thence to Pentyrch
and held meeting—I spoke upon
the necessity of self Goverment
in All the Saints in order that
they may bring about the
purposes of the Almighty
Wednesday 16th Went to the
Cymmer Branch with Elder
George Rowley held a saint
meeting and I spoke upon
the necessity of the faithfully
of the Saints that they may
Join links with their fore-

{76}
fathers and also stand as
Saviours upon Mount Zion to
those who have died without
the Gospel
Thursday 17th Went to Llanfabon
and held a Saint Meeting — I
spoke upon the test that
would come upon the Saints
in the Mountains and
brought up the parable
of Jesus to prove that
five would be wise and
five foolish — slept at
Bro Jonth Isaac's–
Fri 18th Went to Newbridge
and held a District Council
Meeting the Spirit of god was
with us and I told the Bretheren
what course to take with those
persons that are slacking

{77}
     December
back in the work — all seper-
ated in Peace and harmony
slept at Sister Davie's and
on Saturday 19th Went to visit
the Saints at Treforest & Rhydfelyn and thence to Cardiff
and met some of the Bretheren
at my Lodgings–
Sunday 20th Went to Pentyrch
and met Brother George Rowley
and Evan Ricahrds and
held meeting and the spirit
of God was poured out upon
us, about one O'clock we
started for Pendoylon and met
with the Saints in that
place had a good meeting
and came on so far as
Twinyrodyn to Sleep at Bro
Jacob Thomas's.

{78}
     December
Monday 21st Visited the Saints
in Twnyrodyn and in the
Evening held meeting Elders
Rowley & Richards spoke and
I followed — splendid meeting
Tuesday 22nd Went to see
Sister Mary Ricahrds and
Gave her council to go with
her Grandmother and do as she
wanted, she promised to do so,
went from thens to Cogg and
tood dinner and thence to
Cardiff to make arrangements
to receive Pres^t Calkins–
Wednesday 23rd Went to Sister
Liddiards to take dinner
with Pres^t Calkins and
continued with him until
the Evening — went to Meeting
several of the Branches met

{79}
and we had a good time
the spirit of God was with us
Thursday 24th Went to the Railway Station to see President
Calkins off after having enjoyed
his Society for a few hours
very Comfortably at home
writing till Evening when Sister
Mary Wride came in according
to My invitation to prepare
a few Nick-Nacks for the
following day — after this
was done I went to the
Circus with her — nothing
but the riding worth seeing
Friday 25th <u>Christmas day</u>
Got up Early in the morning and
went to the Roman Catholic
Chapel with Sister
Mary Wride — The Priest was at the

{80}
December
Alter with a Garment on his
back having a large Cross worked
upon it which looked very
hansome—he stood with his
back to the Congregation
nearly all the time making
long Prayers—Bowing and Kneeling
very often and sometimes he
would turn around to the
Congregation and make the
sign of the Cross on his face
all the Prayers were in
Latin and consequently we
were Just as wise when we
went in as when we came out
as to what was being said
and as to Learning any principle
of Righteousness by seeing what
we did was out of the Question
and how the people can be

{81}
satisfied with what they
see and hear I have no Idea
but as the old saying is–
"Where Ignorance is bliss
'tis folley to be wise" and
so I suppose they think so,
came home about 1/2 Past 8
and Sister Mary got my Breakfast
and we Prepared to receive
the Bretheren & sisters who
I had Invited to spend Christmas
with me they were Brothers
George Rowley, Evan Richards &
Barry Wride and Sisters Mary
Wride & Ann Wride, Margeret
Jenkins, Ann Selman & Hannah
Selman they Came in about
1 O'clock, and we spent the
day very Comfortably together
in Singing, Dancing and Merry

{82}
December
making of all Discriptions
We broke up about 1/2 past
8 in the Evening and all felt
quite satisfied with the days
enjoyment.
Saturday 26th At home writing
all day—in the Evening Elders
Pugh & Hancock came in to
see me also Sister Elizth
Thomas—
Sunday 27th Attended the
meeting in the afternoon in
Cardiff—Elder John Evans
Thought that the Saints had
Got dead because they did
not speak in tongues as they
did 10 years ago—I showed
the Saints that they were
more awake to their duties
now than they ever were

{83}
December
and that they enjoyed more
of the Holy Ghost the Comforter
and that I did not want the
Saints to speak in tongues
but Cultivate the spirit of
Wisdom and Understanding,
in the intermission went to
Bro Watt's Caton to take
tea and Returned to Cardiff
to Speak in the Evening
Monday 28th Was in Cardiff
visiting the Saints and Writing
at home
Tuesday 29th Went to Treforest
and thence to Cwmsaebra
and held a meeting the
spirit of God was Poured
our upon us after Meeting
we were treated to some
Blackberry wine made

{83}
December
by Sister Elizabeth Hornsby
and as much Christmas
Cake as we wished—we
had a good time and enjoyed
ourselves for a few hours
together—Bro Samuel Hornsby
Presented me with a Knapsack
for the Purpose of Packing
across the Plains for which
I feel Thankfull and ask
God to bless him–
Wednesday 30th Went to Newbridge
and held meeting I spoke
at some Lengths on the Trials
that awaited the Saints
and showed them what they
would have to pass through
in order to get into the Celestial
Kingdom of God–
Thursday 31st Went to

{85}
Jany 1858
Rhydfelyn and visited the saints
and then went to Pentyrch
and thence to Whitchurch
and held a meeting I spoke
to the saints upon the principles
of Salvation and said that
Every one was at Liberty to
Get what degree of Glory they
were inclined to work for
Friday 1st January 1858 Went to
Cardiff—and had a few Saints
at my Lodgings to enjoy ourselves
to commemorate My Birth-day
we had a first rate time of
it
Saturday 2nd Was in Cardiff
writing and making up accounts
Sunday 3rd Went to Llandaff
to attend a Saints Meeting and
had a good time—returned

{86}
Jany
to Cardiff in the Evening
and spoke in the Room to
several Strangers present—
Monday 4th & Tuesday 5th
Was in Cardiff writing and
making up a/c's for my successor and attended a prayer
meeting in Canton on Monday
Evening and Tuesday Evening
a District Council in Cardiff
as I had heard some rumor that
some of the Saints were not satisfied
with my course I called
upon the Bretheren to state
their feelings—the most of
them did and a good feeling
prevailed as some of the brethen
almost felt to petition
the presidency to let me stay
with them a year Longer

{87}
Jany
Wednesday 6th Went to Coggin
to Preach with Elders Rowley
& E Richards—had a good
meeting—
Thursday 7th Returned home
by way of Twnyrodyn & Ely
and Called to see and visit
with the Saints.
Friday 8th & Saturday 9th Was in
Cardiff writing and making
up a/c's preparitory to my
successor taking Charge
Sunday 10th Went to Pentyrch
to settle a difficulty between
Evan A Lewis and his wife
who had been quarreling.
failed in the attempt.
Also went to Whitchurch
to settle a difficulty there
but failed also went

{88}
        Jany
to Cardiff to sleep.
Monday 11th Tuesday 12th Wednes
day 13th Tursday 14th Was in
Cardiff with the Elders and
spent a good time.
Friday 15th Went to Newport with
Elder Enoch Reese who had
Started for the Valley Came
Back by the 1/2 Past 8 Oclock
Train A.M and in the Evening
went to Newbridge to Attend
District Council with Bro
E D Miles, my successor, had
a good meeting–
Saturday 16h Went to Cardiff
via Whitchurch with Bro
Miles and settled up and
turned over the a/c's to Bro
Miles My Successor

{89}
        Jany
Sunday 17th was in Cardiff
to Meeting in the Afternoon
and voted Bro E D. Miles be
My Successor—carried
unanimas—In the Evening
At home making up a/cs
Monday 18th Went to Bristol
on my way to London to Visit My
Brothers William & Richard
met with Brother Wm Bramhall
of Springville that I used to
know when I lived there we had
a chat on old times and he
took me to the Railway Station
and I started by the 10/h\-30/m\am
train for paddington Station
and arrived at paddington
Station at 5/h\-55/m\P. M and
was met by my Brother Richard who Conducted me to his

{90}
        Jany
house and after taking Supper
we went to Madme Tausauds
wax works where I enjoyed
myself very much—the Wax
Figures looked much like
life and in many instances
one would take them for
life—Slept at my Brothers
Tuesday 19th Went to Shepperton
15 miles from London With my
/on my way visited Hamton Court palace and
                                        the\
brother R— and /\ spent, the day
at my Sister in laws Sisters house
and in the Evening an old
Parson (the Parish Pastor) came
in to enquire of the health
of the Family and in the
Course of Conversating he
asked me where I came
form At first I gave him
an evasive answer but that

{91}
        Jany
did not suit so he asked me
more minutely and I gave
him a straightforward answer
that I was a Mormon and Came
from Utah that sent the
Devil in him and a right
good time he had for he
Called me anything but a
Gentleman and as he was
going out of the Door I told
him that it was a good
Job for him that he was
not in my house or he
would go out quicker than
he came in and at the same
time thanked him for the
compliment he gave me
(Why I evaded giving him a
straightforward answer at first
was because I did not want

{92}
Jany
to Make a noise in a strangers
house—the folks in the house
took my Part and said that
the Parson acted very ungentle
manly in the course he persued
towards me—I slept at a
public house
~~Wednesday 20th~~ Thursday 21st Went to the
Feltham Railway station with
a donkey Cart and Went
so far as Kew at which
place we Changed Carriages
for the London Terminus
in the Evening went to Drury
Lane Theatre and then went
to see my Brother William
and then Went to Ashleys
Amph-Theatre and saw
some horesemanship which
was followed by Dr Christhy

{93}
Pantomime—Returned to my
Br Rds with My Brothers
Rd & William whose I had
not been in Company with
together for many years
~~Thursday 21st~~
Wednesday 20th Spent the
Day in riding around to
several County Villages
and writing a few Letters to
the Bretheren—slept at a
public as before mentioned
Friday 22nd Went in the
Morning to see the Public
Buildings—St Pauls Cath-
edral & Royal Exchange—
General Post office—Lord
/called at the Depot\
Mayors Mansion &c /\ &c
/and Saw Bros Ross and Harrison|
in the Afternoon went down
the Thames River to see

{94}
Jany
the Monster Ship "Leviathan"
Proceeded so far as Greenwich
visited the hospital, the
Picture gallery & Chapel
and returned to London by
Railway in the Evening
Went to the Polytechnic and
was much amused with
the Evenings Entertainment
it was splendid—Dissolving
and panoramic Views was
the most of it—
Saturday 23rd In the
morning went to the House of
Lords and Commons in the
British Parliament and was
honoured with a seat in the
Latter house went from there
to Westminster Abbey and
saw many of the Tombs

{95}
Jany
of Departed "heroes" and viewed
the Carriage of the Prince
of Prussia but did not
get to see him as he was
traveling so fast—In the
Evening I went to (Concert Room)
Where all the nobs of London
assemble and also visited another
Concert Room where all the
Theives & Whores assemble
the Contrast between the
fitting up of the Rooms was
great but the Spirit
Manifested was of the Same
Class.
Sunday 24th Went in the
Morning to the "Foundling Church"
and saw & heard the Singing
of an immence number of
Children it was Splendid

{96}
Jany
a Sermon Preached by
A Revd Devine from the Words
of Jesus "Sufficient for the
day is the Evil Thereof"
in the evening went to
Saints Meeting and then took
a walk with my Brothers
Monday 25th Went in the
Morning to St James's Palace
to try to see the Prossession
of the Princess Royal of
England and Frederick
William of Prussia who
were to be Married that
day—I saw the Carriages
of a Great Many Lords & Dukes
& Bishops of the English
Aristocracy but I did not
get to see Royalty as they
did not pass that way—

{97}
Jany
in the Afternoon I went to the
Great Globe in Leiscester Square
and heard a Lecture on the
"Laying Down of the Electric
Telegraph Cable around the
World" and also saw a Diorama-
a on India and heard a
Lecture on the Same Subject
Saw a great many likenesses
of Notable Individuals through
the Earth. In the Evening
went to see the Illuminations
through the City in Celebration
of the Marriage of the
Princess Royal and Frederick
Prince of Prussia—the
Illuminations were splendid
principally of Gass, and
for the first time in my life
got into a London Mob

{98}
Jany
Tuesday 26th Went to the
City to see My Brother
Richards Establishment and
the various Departments in
the Drapery Business carried
on there and went from there
to the Crystal Palace and
spent a few hours in viewing
the various Curiosaties
to be seen at that Exebition
the Building itself is
built exclusively of Iron
and Glass and Certainly is
a splendid place.
In the Evening went to the
Colliseaum with My Brother
Richard and viewd the Scene
of London by Moonlight which
is a painted View of London
giving a view of it by

{99}
Jany
Moonlight—it is very grand
saw also the Dessolving Views
of various parts of London
in the 16th century and the
City of Lisbon before & after
the Earthquake &c &c
Wednesday 27th Left Paddington
Station at 7:20/A.M.\ and arrived at
Bristol at 2 P.M and Went
to See Bro Hannam the Pres^t
of the South Conf^{ce} and had a
little Conversation with him went
on Board the Packet for Cardiff
at 4 OClock and arrived about
1/2 past 6 glad to get home
to the house of a Saint once
more although My Brothers
treated me with every kind of
respect yet they were not
in possession of the spirit

{100}
~~Feby~~ Jany
of God and this is the
main spring to all happiness
and without it I can have
none, I am perfectly /satisfied\ with the
sights to be seen in old Bablyon
I have seen enough and now
I want to leave it entirely
and this Evening I received a
notification to be in Liverpool
on the 12th preparatory to
Sailing on the 13th, this Accord.
ing to the desires of my heart
and although I leave many
Saints behind whome I love
near & Dear by the Gospel
ties yet I ask God to protect
them and Bless them for Ever
and for Ever. In the Evening
I went to Meeting and did
a little at preaching—

{101}
~~Feby~~ Jany
Thursday 28th this morning
I recd a note from Bro James
Taylor and in accordance
with its instructions I
went immediately to Whitchurch
to see Bro Rowley—met him
there an then returned
against to meeting—I occupied
a considerable portion of the
time—
Friday 29th Went to Cardiff
Wrote some Letters and dictated
one for Bro Rowley and
attended meeting (Rehersal)
at the room which was
for the getting up of a Farewell
Concert for me—
Saturday 30th Was in Cardiff
writing and visiting the Saints
and attended to some business

{102}
Feby
Sunday 31st Went to Pendoylon
with Bro Hugh for take a Fare
well of the Saints had a good
meeting ~~the Saints~~ and they all
expressed their sorrow at my
departure and testified to my
having done all in my power
to assist them to gain their
Exaltation in the Kingdom of
heaven—came back to
Twinerodyn and wished the
Saints Good bye and thence
to Llandaff and held meeting
and wished the saints good
bye there—all wished me
Gods speed—
Monday Feby 1st Went to
Treforest and Newbridge and
thence to Cumseabra and held
a saint meeting a good

{103}
Feby
spirit prevailed and we had
a good time—the Saints
all felt to bless me but
their means were very limited
as the work was very slow
and they felt sorry to part
Bro and Sister Hornsby Especially
Tuesday 2nd Went to Cardiff
and attended a District Council
Meeting I spoke on the Policy
I had persued while I had
been here and what I had
labored to accomplish &c
&c and I Kne the Lord had
blessed my labors &c &c
and I hoped to do right all
the time—I blessed them in
the name of the Lord
Wednesday 3rd Went to Pentyrch
and visited the Saints there

{104}
Feby
for the last time and
Returned to Cardiff on
Thursday 4th by way of
Bro Wrides Parents—I called
there to say good bye to the
old folks Drank a glass
of Wine and gave the Following
toast—I wish the next
time I see you you may be
good, firm, Mormons and
may I soon meet your
daughters in the Vallies of
the Mountains—in the
Evening went to a Concert in
the room and had a good
time, it was got up as a
farewell to me—During
the Entertainment I was
presented with a splendid
ring to Keep me in remembrance

{105}
Feby
of the Saints in the Cardiff
Conference—with this
injunction That I must not
Part with it upon no
Consideration except for
bread—
Friday 5th Went to Whitchurch
and had a party in the
Evening at Bro Selmans—
we had a good time—Sister
Ann Wride presented me
with a splendid purse and
Sister Amelia Hughs with
a muffler for which I
gave my sincere Thanks
Saturday 6th In Cardiff—
writing and arranging my
papers
Sunday 7th attended meeting in
Cardiff twice and spoke

{106}
Feb
both times, to the Saints
and Sinners in the Evening
Monday 8th At Cardiff packing
up my affairs and Sister
Mary Write was marking them
I enjoyed this day very much
with sister Mary and I told
her when she came home if
she chose to come to my
house she should be welcome
to have share of anything
that I have, in the Evening
whent Visiting the Saints
Tuesday 9th wnd in the Morning
with Sister M Write to get
her likeness put in my
ring and then visited the
Saints and in the Evening
/Saw Sister Wride start home\
went to Canton to Meeting
had a first rate time

{107}
Feby
Wednesday 10th Packed up my
traps and went to Newbridge
to prepare to start, In the
Evening went to Meeting
Newbridge, Treforest, & Cymmer
Branches met together
Sister Margaret Jenkins came
from Pentyrch to assist in
getting my traps ready and
we staid up about all
night preparing and packing
and on thursday morning
I had about all ready at
Sister Sarah Davis's
Thursday 11th Started from
treforest to Llanfabon and
preached to the Saints and
had a good time *the Saint* [smeared]
the Saints expressed their mind
in reference to me and felt

{108}
     Feb
/Bros Thos Reese gave me a double barreled pistol & accoutrements.\
first rate /\ Slept with Bro Evan Richards at Bro Jonathan Isaacs and on
Friday 12th Started to Liverpool form Llancaich and overtook Bros Danils—B Evans R. G Evans & several others and arrived in Liverpool at 1/2 Past 7 P. M and went to Ths Powells to ~~Liberty~~ Lodge–
Saturday 13th Was in Liverpool buying a few traps and went to the Office to see the bretheren. And got my passage Paper and 5£ in Cash to pay my expenses to Iowa City—In the Evening went to the Circus and saw some good riding.

{109}
     Feby
Sunday 14th Went to Meeting at the Royal Assembly Rooms– in the Morning and evening and heard the Returning Missionaries speak of their various fields of Labour and their feelings on being released to go home /office and got a rifle to take through to the valley for the church & fast\
Monday 15th Went to the /\ Bramley More Docks with my Luggage and put them on Board the Ship "Empire" and selected my berth in a Cabin with Bro Daniels & others—Bro George Taylor my partner as usual and slept on Board for the first time
Tuesday 16th Went on shore in the Morning to buy some

{110}
     Feby
Breat & Butter &c &c and about 12 Oclock the ship went through the Docks and was hauled out of the Docks into the River I wrote a note to Bro Saml Evans of Cardiff and another to Sister Mary Wride and send them by Bro Benjn Evans ashore—fixing up my Bath on board and getting things lashed.
Wednesday 17th Was fixing up a Board for comfort and Convenience and was got pretty well fixed up— /could not go to sea in consequence of fog\
Thursday 18th Passed The Doctor and Government Inspector and lashed up several Boxes &c &c

{111}
     Feby.
~~Saturday~~ /Friday\ The Tug Boat came alongside about nine Oclock and we commenced to heave anchor—left our moorings in the River Mersey at a 1/4 past 10 O'Clock and bid farewell to my native Land once more with feelings of Joy and Gratitude to My Father in heaven for the privelage of receiving and obeying the Everlasting Gospel and of having received the Priesthood and having been honoured with the previlage of a Mission of Life and Salvation to the Inhabitants of these Lands and that the call is now come to go home I feel glad of the Privelage of going to the Bosom of the Church

{112}
   Feby
once more and enjoying the
society of the Prophets of God
I Know that I have done my
duty in these Lands and been
faithful in the discharge
thereof and I feel Free from
the Blood of these I have
Laboured amongst and I Know
My Garments are Clean
Saturday 20th Off the North
Coast of Ireland and saw the
the Land for the Last time on
this side of the atlantic—
Wind Fare—Bro Daniels
appointed President of our Cabin
of 8 persons & I his councellor
—was preparing dinner and
was taken sick and had to
go to bed and remained there
until

{113}
   Feby
Monday 22nd got up on
deck to get Fresh air once
more but was so weak I could
hardly walk or stand on
my legs—obliged to go to bed
and have a good puke again
felt awful bad—never
felt worse from sickness
in my life—
Tuesdays 23rd Wednesday 24th
continued to get better and
stronger—wind pretty high
in the Evening of Wednesday
had a gale of Wind—hove
to till
Thursday 25th Put up a
few Sails again in the Evening
with a pretty good brieze almost
on our Course—all well and /first rate\
Board except a few suffering

{114}
   March
from seasickness—getting
better myself and able
to get around again a little
agreed to be cook for 6 of our
men in No 8 Cabin during
our sea voyage.—Nothing of
any consequence occurred except on Mondday Evening the
1st of February /March\ a sudden
gust of Wind carried away
the Flying Jib & Main top-
mast staysails.
Tuesday 2nd Almost becalmed
wind—from East but very
light—wind continued
favourable and all went
well with us until
Thursday Evening 4th when
Iceburghs were discovered
over our right Bow and Ice

{115}
   March
all around the Ship—the ship was
put on the back track and run in
a S.E. Course till daylight when we
were again clear of those Monsters of
the deep and gain resumed our course
for the west—
Friday 5th Cleared the Great Bank
off Newfoundland at Noon and at
dusk the Brieze carried away our
stunsail Boom
Sunday 7th hove in sight of
Sabels Island and the wind not
being favourable we had to tack
and in the Evening again run
in sight of the Breakers on the
Ld Island and about ship again
winds continued contrary until
Monday 15th when we once
more job a fare wind for our
destined port, I had a great

{116}
March
impression upon my mind that I should have to return to the old Country to labour for another Year, I suppose time will tell the tales.
Wednesday 17h Hove in sight of Long Island about 1 O Clock P.M and the sight of land did our eyes good and filled our hearts with Joy
Thursday 18th Came in sight of Fire Island Lighthouse in the afternoon and Kept tacking in Consequence of adverse winds until the Pilot Came on board at 10 O' Clock P.M
Friday 19th A tug boat hitched on to us in horseshoe bay this morning about 9 O'Clock and having passed the Examination of the Doctor opposite the Hospital we

{117}
March–
dropp'd Anchor opposite Castle Gardens at 1 O'Clock P.M. and soon had our Luggage Examined by the Custom House Officers and passed the Officers at the Gardens and was again Landed on the Land of my adoption the Land of Joseph after a passage of 28 days from Liverpool—
The following is a List of My Companions on Board the "Empire"
[blank]

{118}
[blank]

{119}
March
all the above names marked V are returning Missionaries going home by order of Prest Brigham Young
We are the last company of Missionaries starting from England and we leave the Gentiles to their fate now and pray God to Protect and Bless all the Saints left in the Old Country and give them a speedy deliverance from the Yolk of Bondage.
Was met by Judge Dulin at the gardens and conducted to Walkers boarding house where I remained till
Saturday 20th Went to Williams burgh with Bros George Taylor and Martin Littlewood and stayed at the

{120}
March
house of Brother George Stone and Sisters Mary Cantle and was very comfortably entertained by them Went to the Post Office and got a letter from Sister Mary Wride–
Sunday 21st Wend to meeting in the afternoon and enjoyed myself well the meeting was held in the 7th ward in the evening finished a letter to Bro Saml Evans of Cardiff
Monday 22nd Attended a meeting of the missionaries at Mr Walkers to consult on the best policy of Going West and come to the conclusion that nothing could be done till Bro W I Appleby arrives, finished a letter to my sister Jane
Tuesday 23th Attended a meeting at Bro Miles's in John St and met Bro W. I. Appleby there and got

{121}
council to Break up all boxes and put everything in carpet Bags or something of the Kind we were allowed 50lbs each paid 13$ each for our passages and went in the afternoon to the New York & Erie R R depo and packed away all necessary luggage in my Trunk and a Bag so that all George and I had did not exceed 100lbs and put what we did not actually need

in Georges Box and took it to Bro
Stones in Williamsburgh I
left several articals of Value — my
Fine Cloth Coat and a Sheep skin
Coat and several other articles;
Wednesday 24th Left New York City
ab 1/2 Past Eight and crossed the River
and got on Board a 3rd class car
behind a luggage Train and arrived
at Dunkirk on

{122}
March
Thursday 25th at 3 Oclock P.M
and started again at 1/2 Past 6 after having
partook of a good meal and got
considerably refreshed and arrived at
Cleaveland on
Friday 26th at 1/2 past 7 Oclock
A.M. and Changed carrs and started
again by 1/2 past 8 and arrived at Toledo
at 8 in the Evening and changed cars
and was again in motion at 1/2
past 9 Oclock and this time had
no fire in the car and a miserable
poor Car at that, made a bed on
the floor of the car with Bro G Taylor &
W. S. Muir my head & Bones ached
in the morning pretty bad. arrived
at Chicago at 11 O'Clock P.M. on
Saturday 27th and got lodging at
the Rock Island Tavern and talked
and conversed with persons boarding there

{123}
March
upon all Kinds of subjects and heard all
Kinds of opinions upon Utah and her
present difficulties (pro&Con) no one
surmising that we were what we
are
Sunday 28th Started at 1/2 Past 8 by
Express from Chicago and arrived in
Burlington Iowa on
Monday 29th where we expected to meet
with G. G. Snider and others but to our
dismay we were informed they were

gone nearly a week we did not
know what course then to persue but by
consulting together we came to the conclusion to stay awhile in Burlington and see
if anyone of Responsibility would come
in this we were gratified by the appearance
of Bros H. S. Eldridge & H. C. Haight on
Friday 2nd April who told us to get to
Florence N. T. the best way we could.

{124}
April
not having much means left I borrowed
$10.00 and no boat coming down the
River I did not start for St Louis
until Monday 5th when we engaged
a passage on board the "Anne Whittle"
and arrived in St Louis on Wednesday
morning 7th and found out the Office
and took our luggage there and remained
there until
Tuesday 13th when by the Kind assistance
of Eldr Coward we engaged a passage
on board the "Omaha" for Florence at
the reduced price of $4.00 Per head
there were 50 exclusive of Children under
the presidency of Elder. James Taylor the
Company is Composed of about 20 Returning
missionaries and the balance are
Saints Going to Nebraska to Settle the
officers of the Boat are very kind and
accomodating to us and we have their

{125}
April
fullest confidence as I did the Bissiness
of the Company with the Clerks I was
treated with marked civility
Friday 23rd Arrived in Florence in
safety after a passage of 10 days and found
that several of the boys were here and
ready to start but our company (the European Missionaries) were received with the
same word that they got everywhere else
viz that nobody Knew anything about
the arrangements made for us or rather
there were any or not. we were told to

hold on here until some word was
received from Bro. H. C. Haight.
During our stay I slept at Bro
Thomas Stephens who made me just
as comfortable as they could but they
could not Board us and the Saints
being poor we were reduced to great
Extremity and had but little food

{126}
May
Bro Joseph W. Young & Company arrived
from Fort Desmoins on Friday the 30th
and the Company rolled out of Florence
so far as 2 Mile Grove on Saturday
May 12st and I rolled out and joined
the Camp on Sunday 2nd Inst and
while on Guard at Midnight the
Horses Stampeeded and we had the
pleasure of an uncomfortable night
ride on horseback
Monday 3rd Found the horses this
morning and rolled out as far as
Elk Horn and camped, nothing of
interest transpired except that I was
appointed Cook to No 3 Mess untill I
arrived at Monroe on Friday 7th
and found some friends Bro James Keati
and Elizabeth his sister who made me
comfortable &c &c
Saturday 8th Went to Genoa and

{127}
June
joined the Camp again and attended
a camp meeting and voted to leave
the Expressmens luggage
Monday 10th Was assisting to put
the waggons &c over the Loup Fork
River. Was standing and wading
in the river most all day
Tuesday 11th Started from the
Loup Fork River Several things
of note transpired but I could not
get time to Keep my journal in consequ-
-ence of hard traveling but I hope to get it
from the Clerk of the Company.

Monday 22nd June arrived in Great
Salt Lake City about 9 O'Clock in the
Morning in company with Elders
Bernard Snow & John L. Smith, we left
the Camp on the devide West of Weber
at 1/2 past 8 at night an walked ~~in~~
into the City several hours ahead of the

{128}
June
Express sent form Camp. took break-
-fast at the Globe by the politeness of
Bro David Candlin — in the Evening
the Train arrived all right
Tuesday 23rd Started for Provo City
the Quarters of the Presidency
Wednesday 24th Arrived in Provo
City and sat the President /Brigham Young\
who
invited me to go and see his family
and told me to loaf around untill I
got rested
Thursday 25th Went to Springville to
see my old Sweetheart Sister Rebecca
Hendricks and deliver a letter to
Sister Calkins from her husband
Saturday 27th Went to Spring Creek with
L. D. Young to drive sheep to his herd
Ground at the point of the West
mountain and went to driving teem
for Prest B. Young untill Bro Geo

{129}
July
Taylor and I agreed to run the Prest.
Thrashing Machine in Provo — terms
1/4 of the profits
Monday 19th Started for the City
Thursday 22nd Had the great
pleasure of taking Sister Rebecca Hendr-
-icks to wife at the Sealing Room over
the Presidents Office — Prest B. Young
officiated —
Tuesday 27th Started for Provo
with my Wife and her Boy to
Fulfill my engagement at the
Thrashing Machine — arrived

on Wednesday 28th did not have
a great deal of work to do for 2
or 3 Weeks but did a considerable
amount of fixing up around the
machine—nothing of interest
transpired untill the Man (Joseph Alpine)
went and wilfully lied about us to Bishop

{130}
September
E. D. Woolley who write me a letter stating
that if when the machine did not pay us
for our labour for running we were at
liberty to settle up and quit and I
having nothing in particular to do my
partner George Taylor went to the City
to see Bro Woolley—
Tuesday 12th Bro Woolley arrived and
measured
up the Grain and found we had 20 1/2 bushells
of Wheat coming to us for 2 1/2 Month Work
without /giving\ us the privalege of a larger
share
of the profits he let the Machine to other
men for 1/2 the profits
Wednesday 20th Moved to my wife's fathers
house in the City with the calculation to
remain there during winter—worked for
the interest of the family in getting wood and
cleaning stables &c &c boarded with the old
folks and not doing much through the
cold weather

{131}
Jany 1859
January 1st Spent the forenoon at home
and the Afternoon on the mountains hunting
my Father-in-laws cattle—tried to get lumber
several times to work up to pay up my
tithing but without success and not having
anything else to pay with was obliged to
let my tithing stand over for a while.
Bro Wm Vannoy and myself bought a
shingle and lath machine of Geo Nebuker
and [blank] Knowlton Senr situated on N
Mill Creek price $400.00.
Hauled the machine down to

Bro Vannoy's shop to repair it
Called on by Bro Joseph Scofield
to stand guard at ~~the~~ President
Youngs every Thursday night
February [blank]
Worked on the machine once
in a while the weather being cold
could not do much

{132}
February. March-April
Went up to the mill but the snow
was so deep could not do anything
March — Went up to the Mill
and commenced clearing away the
snow so as to go to repairing but
the weather was so unfavorable
that we could not do much
April – Attended Conference and
set out 42 Peach and several
apple and currant Trees wich my
Father-in-law let me have on my
wifes City lot
The latter part of this month
the weather moderated considerable
and we worked on the Mill most
of the time
Friday 22nd My Wife confined with
a daughter—had a very hard
time and my poverty would not
allow me the nessesaries for

{133}
April-May
such an occasion without
borrowing and this I was obliged
to do.
May—Fixing up the mill
June—Commenced sawing shingles
and hired a man to help us.
Sunday 12th Blessed my daughter
and called her after her
Mother Rebecca—
July 4th Bought 2 Yolk of
Cattle in Coy [i.e., county] paid $66 per Yolk.
Friday 22nd Sawd Shingles and
used up the last logs that had

/Been\ brought to the Mill in consequence of the water Failing.
August—Went to the Kanyon
and hauled timber too make
pumps—made several
but they did not sell
well and consequently I

{134}
1859   Fall & Winter
quit the Business.
October—I agreed with
Bro. Enoch Reese to run his
Shingle Machine in South
Mill Creek Kanyon—went
and worked on the mill
with 2 hired hands for 4
weeks and upwards when the
Snow fell so deep that I
had to quit the Kanyon thru
the negligence of W. A.
Kiffoil– Mr E. Reese's
partner in not furnishing
lumber and boarding up
the mill according to
agreement
Dec^r— Concluded in
connection with the Ballance
of the family to move to
Cache Valley and get

{135}
        Spring & Summer 1860.
a farm—
Jany & Feby worked ~~on~~
~~on~~ with Bro Wm Vannoy in
getting up a Saw mill to
work by horse power which we
accomplished
April 18th 1860 Left G. S
L City for Cache Valley with
my family—And arrived
at the Old fort Richmond
on the 28th—took up a
20 acre Lot broke up 12
acres and sowed to wheat
which the Grasshoppers

swept clean Set our
Saw in motion with the
horsepower and sawed 3
or 4 thousand feet of Lumber
for various folks and then
concluded to put it up by

{136}
1860.   Summer & Fall.
Water power in the Kanyon.
We consulted with Bro A
Walton and agreed to take
him as partner or thirdman
Aug 8th Commenced work
on the Water Mill and worked
off and on at it as Circumstan
ces would permit—
October 7th My wife was
Confined with a Daughter
    "   20th I blessed
it and called it Charlotte
1862 My wife was confined
March 18th with a Daughter
which we named After our
old acquaintance and
friend Zina Young.
        After a severe sickness
and much anxiety on our
parts our beloved and

{137}
lovely child Charlotte
died of Scarlet Fever on
the 2nd day of August 1862
at which time I was unable
to do anything in consequence
of having my Thumb, Fore &
Third Fingers cut badly with
Waltons Circular Saw which
laid me up for 3 months
acted as Clerk for Bp
Marriner W. Merrill from
Oct 1861 to Dec 1st 1862.
and as Chorister of the
/Richmond\ Ward from May 1860 to
Dec 1862 during which time
the Richmond Choir gained great

Noteriety and was published
as being the most accomplished
choir in the Territory outside
of G. S. L. City

{138}
Nov 30th 1862 Was called
upon by Prests E. T. Benson and
P. Maughan (by advice of Prest
B. Young) to Act as Bishop at
Smithfield in place of John G
Smith and was ordained
and set apart the same
day.
  Visited the Settlement
(Smithfield) on Sundays and
Thursday Evenings to attend
meetings &c &c called and
organized the Teachers Quorum
Dec 7th 1862 & bought
the Fort Improvements of
the Late Bishop John G
Smith on the 19th Dec
Jany 21st 1863 moved
my family to Smithfield
and the few days foll

{139}
  1863.
-owing was fixing up the
house I moved into
Jany 29th Commenced to
Settle Tithing—had all
the a/cs of 1860-1 to fix
up previous to settling
with the Bretheren "
Feby 24th got through settling
Tithing in Smithfield and
" 25th went to Logan with
Bro Geo Barber who acted as
my clerk during this /years\ Settlement
and settled with the Logan
Office—all that I had
done was satisfactorily
received by Prest P. Maughan
March 23rd Motioned by
Prest E. T. Benson that I

should be the Major of this
Smithfield Battallion

{140}
  March 1863
which was re/a\dily voted
for by the Bretheren of the
Battallion, Calld Bro
Geor Barber to Act as my
adjutant—Bro D. C. Thom
as Capt of the A Company
and Alonzo P. Raymond
Capt of the 2nd or B Compy
Was instructed in the drill by
major McDonal Rush
My Wife Rebecca Had a Son
Born August 11th 1863 /3' oClock in th
morning\
blessed it on Sep 20th and called
his name Samuel After myself

{141}
  1865
Continued to act as Major
until fall of 1865 when in Consequence
of ill. Health I resigned in favor
Geo Barber ~~And at the reorgan
ization of the Millitia of Cache
County I was Elected as Chaplin
of the Cache Military Brigade~~

was Elected Director and Subsequ
ently Prest of Logan & Richmond
Canal Company

{142}
  1870
Eleted Prest of Smithfield Coop
Mercantile Association Jan 20th
1870

Elected Mayor Smithfield City
May 23rd 1870

Elected Supt of Common Schools
for Cache County Aug 7th 1870

by 2691 votes

Elected Chaplin Cache of Brigade
of ~~Cache~~ Military District Sep 28th
1870

{143}
　　　　1871
Elected Secty Pro Tem at the
organization of the Utah Northern
Rail Road Company

Elected a director of the Utah
Northern Rail Road Company
　　　　1871

{144}
　　　　1872
Re Elected Prest Smithfield Coop
Merchantile Association Jan 20th 1872
Commenced my contract to Build Culvert
under Cottonwood Hollow fill on Utah N.R
Road May 3rd 1872.
ReElected Mayor of Smithfield
May 20th 1872
Commenced contract to fill Cottonwood
Hollow fill U.N.R.R.　　　1872
And finished to the satisfaction of said
Company　　　1872
　　It contains 48000 yards Earth work
Re Elected Supt Common Schools
for Cache Co Aug 1872

Re-Elected director Utah Northern Rail
Road Aug　　1872

{145}
　　　　1873
Re Elected Prest of Smithfield
Coop Inst January 20th 1873.

Re Elected Director Utah Northern
Rail Road Aug [blank] 1872.

　　　　1874
Re Elected Prest Smithfield Coop
Institution Jan 20th 1874

[*succeeding pages after 187 are blank, include
account records, calculations, and notes not
transcribed, with the following exceptions*]

{196}
Smithfield Friday
Nov 13th 1863
　The following Bretheren helped
me on my house
Thos G Winn　Ezekiel Hopkins Jun
[blank] Miles　John Boyce
Wm Ainscough　David Weeks
Joseph McCraken　Thos Pilgrim
and William Coleman furnished
a team to haul away dirt

On Friday 27th the following
Bretheren helped
Joseph Horton　George Dean
Daniel Collett

　　　{222–223}
　　Come unto me too long has been thine | absence
　　Too long my heart has called for thee in V | ain
　　Oh when that kiss was given me at pa | rting
　　Didst thou not mean to come to me | again

　　When thy warm hand closed in my | trembling fingers
　　When hey dear voice uttered that | low "good bye"
　　Thy kiss gave me comfort and and the hop | e of meeting
　　Again ere long kept down this Yearning | cry

But now it riseth – loud and wild an|d fearful
I cannot hush its strong and bitter | tone
The Wailing call for what hath long | been wantting
Oh ! come and bring me peace | mine own

[*remaining accounts not transcribed*]

[*end of Journal 2; end of transcript*]

Journal [3]

8 March 1880 – 19 September 1881

{front pastedown} not microfilmed

{front endleaf recto} not microfilmed

{front endleaf verso} not microfilmed

{001}
1880
With Pleasure I Samuel Roskelley,
record that after settling Tithing with
the saints of smithfield Ward. Cache
County Utah. Territory, year Ending
Dec 31st 1879. by request of stake
President Wm B. Preston I assisted in
the general making up of the Tithing
settlement for the Entire Stake at Logan
in Connexion with Bros George L. Farrell
and Francis Gunnell which occup
ied most of the time till Early spring
in 1880.
on March 9th I received the
following letter. viz.,   Salt Lake City
Elder Samuel Roskelley \   March 8th 1880.
            Smithfield /   Dear Brother
Your name has been suggested and
accepted as a missionary to Europe
The work of the Lord is progressing in the
nations, and faithful, Energetic Elders are
needed in the ministry to promulgate the
everlasting gospel. openings for doing good
selected for this mission; should there
be no reasonable obstacles to hinder you
appearing in numerous directions
Yourself with others, having been
{002}
         Mch 10th 1880.

from going. we should be pleased to
have you make your arrangements to start
at as early a date as April Conference
Please let us Know at your Earliest
convenience, what your feelings are with
regard to this call.
Your Brother in the gospel
John Taylor.
My surprise was unbounded as I had
received no intimation heretofore about
the matter from any authority. I com=
municated the Contents of the letter to
Rebecca, my wife and sat down
and wrote the following.
Smithfield   Cache County, Utah.
March 10th 1880.
President John Taylor \
Salt Lake City, Utah. /   Dear Brother
Yours of March 8th requesting me
to prepare for a mission to Europe is

Manuscript presently unlocated, but microfilmed September 1954 by Utah Genealogical Society, microfilm available as MS 8239, Church History Library, Salt Lake City; microfilm digitized ca.2014; line-by-line transcription follows digital image number.

at Hand. I do not recollect saying "No"
to the requests of those in authority, and
trust I shall always be found willing
to comply with their requirements.
I hope to be prepared to report "Ready
at april Conference. I will work to
that End. Praying God to bless you

{003}
for Ever.   your Brother in the gospel
Samuel Roskelley.
from this date I made Every arrangement
I possibly could to prepare for the trip and
spent days and days straightening the
City affairs and making deeds conveying
city lots from City Corporate authorities to the in=
=dividuals the property belonged to. arranged
best I could to have my farming carried
on by the Boys (my sons). I drew up
an agreement with Bro A. P. Welchman
to take care of my nursery and the
garden at home. giving him a portion
of the proceeds for his labor upon the
same. I arranged the sale of my
portion of the steam saw Mill owned
by Bro. W^m T Vannoy as I was yet owing him for
a portion of the amount I bargained to pay
him for the share I bought in it in the
spring of 1879.
<u>Sunday April 11th 1880</u>
President Moses Thatcher. Wm B. Preston
and C. O. Card attended Sunday afternoon
meeting and all spoke quite feelingly about
my going away. Prest. Preston made the
remark that if any of the Saints had any

{004}
difficulty with the neighbors they
could not settle. that should be brought
before a bishops Court. now is a good
time to do so as your Bishop is going
on a mission for a while. and you will
have no bishop till he returns to make
any appeal to, from this remark I
felt quite confident that I should not
be removed or rather supplanted by
some one else.
   I ought to mention the Excellent

surprise dinner and Entertainment
gotten up by the relief society. and
the many good and heartfelt Expressions
of good feelings Expressed by Men & Women
on the occasion. the most Excellent din
=ner and large number interested by
gathering at the schoolhouse on the
happy occasion. My wives all present
as also my Dear daughters Rebecca &
Zina. <u>I appointed Bro. Morehead my agent
       Monday April 12th 1880.</u>
Went to the farm and bid Mary and the
Children good bye. bringing Mary to
town with me and a number of my
friends gathered into my house

{005}
to say goodbye. I bade adieu to my
family. My dear ones and rode to the
Railway station. where many of my
friends had gathered to see me start.
God Bless them all. Bp Merrill on
the Train. talked freely. at Logan
Bro Geo Thatcher, Supt of the U & N
R. R. Kindly gave me a pass to Ogden
Bro. G. L. Farrell and his Wife Lotta
met me at the station and wished me
Gods speed. saw Frank Gunnell on
the Road at Mendon. arrived at
Ogden and put up at Bro & Sister
Jos Hall's and spent a pleasant Even
=ing. Morning came. breakfast I
went to station to get my ticket
and finding a number of missionaries
I asked Bro John Reeves to request
Union Pacific Conductor to let Mor=
=mon Missionaries have a car for
themselves which was granted.
Here we got acquainted. left Ogden
10.30 a. M. Weber River Very High.
Bp. Thos X Smith of Logan and I had
agreed to "chum" ate our dinner
together. and having no organization a
little party of the Bretheren came and asked
me if I would consent to call the brethren
together to organize a Company. I did as
requested and we met at 5 P. M. in
the Union Pacific Rail Road 1st class car
No 31. following are the names of the company.

1. Samuel Roskelley
2. Thomas C. Griggs
3. Thomas X. Smith
4. John Donaldson
5. Jesse West
6. Thomas Maycock
7. Robert Kewley
8. Edward King
9. John Evans
10. Joseph Orton
11. Wm C. Parkinson
12. Edward Kay
13. David R. Davies
14. Robert L. Fishburn
15. Newton Farr
16. Lorenzo Farr
18. Simon Christensen
19. J. I. Jensen
20. Ole C. Tellesfsen
21. A. G. Johnson
22. N. O. Anderson
23. Hans Madson
24. C. P. Warnick
25. C. H. Lundberg
26. H. J. Christiansen
27. Lars K Larsen
28. John Christensen
29. Ulrich Stauffer
30. C. C. Schramm
31. John Alder
32. George L. Graehl Jr.

Wm. M. Palmer	(US)
Jos. W. Burt	(US)
B. H. Roberts	(US)

Thomas Jackson (US)
John Francom. on a visit to his relatives
in London.

{007}
on Motion that I was unanimously Elected to
be president of the Company and Elder Thomas
C. Grigg /of Salt Lake City\ 1st and Bp Thomas X.
                                         Smith of
Logan Cache County 2nd councillor. Elder John
Donaldson of Mendon. Cache Co. secretary.
after the organization I addressed the company
a few minutes. about 7 we had passed

Evanston, Wyoming at which point I met Bp W
                                       /G\ Burton
and Wife and Daughter and they presented me
a large pound cake and 2 loaves of Bread
for the Journey Eastward -- and Calling
the Company together we sang Come all ye
sons of God &c. Praise to the Man. The Spirit
of God &c Oh say What is Truth. addresses
were made by Bro Palmer. T. C. Griggs &
myself upon the nature of the mission
we were Engaged in. I my Councillor
T. C. Griggs Captain of the Guard. to arrange
the night watches &c
Wednesday, April 14th 1880 UPRR
Daybreak found us at Rawlins and Fort Steele
and wind blowing furiously and Very Cold.
Night Passed pretty Comfortably. with Bp Thos X
Smith Covered up in a blanket. Jogging along
very nicely with lots of Thoughts and reflections
passed and took a good View of Dale Creek

{008}
Bridge also sheerman Station the highest
point the R. R passes over the black Hills
ead books. chatted & got acquainted with
the brethren, and Enjoyed ourselves much.
singing, prayers & speeches Morning & Evening
Pile up Luggage to sleep.
    Thursday April 15th 1880. UPRR Co.
New Conductor woke us up Early asking for
Tickets. all the tickets held by Clk of
Company (John Donaldson) beautiful sight
miles of Prairie on fire. again sleep.
got a Wash. Council Meeting prayers etc.
get up a programme for daily meetings, some
talk bear testimony, some boys Confess their
negligence of duties while at home and
now see where they missed it got up a
Collection for Bro Palmer to aid him ($32⁵⁰)
saw a man and woman plowing. Mutual Imp
=rovement meeting at 10. subject of Baptism.
arrived at Council bluffs at 6 P. M. late
for the trains going East Farr Brothers like
rowdy boys want to go-as-you-please. I saw the
supt. of Chicago & Northern R R and secured
a car for our use. and got a good one, prayers
and fix luggage & bed. slept pretty well on
wheels. Friday April 16th 1880 C & N W. R R

{009}
Cold. disagreeable Morning. Raining & blowing.
train
late and running Very fast. washed in a fire
bucket. breakfast. fruit. singing & Prayers. Mut=
=ual at 10 at which Lord Dunmure and
several others Gentlemen were present and seemed
much interested, in changing cars to make up
a lighter train left some of my papers behind
arrived at Chicago about 4 P. M. /here Elder Burt
left the company.\ and
was introduced to Supt C. Ft W. & P. R. R.
who I had telegraphed to have a Car at
our disposal. he treated us Kindly. he paid
for us on the Parmalee omnibuss to his
line and we got a good car all to ourselves
we telegraphed from this point to Bro Stains
at New York to meet us on Sunday morning.
Weather Very Gloomy. left Chicago at 6 P. M.
Enjoying supper by telegraph ahead. rode
along lake shore at great speed. all Enjoyed
the good supper provided /which had previously
Engaged by telegraph.\ Guards Mounted
/at each door of cars\ Prayers, Farr Boys with more
money than Wits
raised a question about /the\ Holy Ghost. which
was ably
answered by several of the party present. the high
rate of speed on this train prevented anyone
unused to such travel obtaining a great deal
of sleep. but Bro Thos X. Smith and I took cat
naps and rested a little.

{010}
Pittsburg, Fort Wayne and Chicago R. R.
Saturday, April 17, 1880. our Rail Road
Car presented a buisy scene as each awoke
and put me in mind of what the scene will be
on the Morning of the Resurrection then more Eyes
will be open to behold the dawn of a glad & Joy=
=ous morning than the Kisses of this beautiful
morning sun greets.. beautiful country, got a
wash in a lard bucket. called the company toge=
=ther in the center of car and sung – prayers. and
Eat our morning meal from our lunch buckets
prepared by our loved ones at home. arrived
at Pittsburg about noon. while travelling down
the banks of the susqueannah River I recalled with
Joy, the [stricken] many Revelations God has given

to the
Prophet Joseph on that River. at my request our
car was put on the train going Eastward, altho it
is usual to change cars at this place. did not
have any Mutual Meeting to day as we would be
subject to repeated annoyance of persons travelling
this our, car from one End of train to the other.
ordered
supper for the company, by telegraph at altoona at
the Rain Road dining saloon. and Enjoyed the
beautiful scenery around the Catskill Mountains
on the Horse shoe bend. some of the finest scenery I Ever saw in my life. did Justice to
supper. gave instructions to the guards about
seeing no strangers remained in our car. toward
Morning a nigger came into the car and the
Conductor followed him and asked him. Do
You belong to this Company? Yes sah! was the
immediate
reply. the conductor passed on and the nigger also
slipped out.   Sunday April 18th 1881.
on cars between Philidelphia and New York Cities
all hands up Early. after a rapid ride through the
night. Prayers. thanking our heavenly father for
care while passing over the R Roads &c arrived at
New York City at 6 a M.. Met Brother W^m C.
Stains as per telegram from Chicago. and he

{011}
conducted us across the river to the Stevens
House, Washed, wrote, breakfast and general
clean=
=up. Walked around Battery point and some 10
of us went over to Brooklyn and and Elders
T. X. Smith. T. C. Griggs John Donaldson and I got
seats in the Tabernacle of the Eloquent, popular
preacher, /Rev. H. W. Beecher\ Choir sung an
anthem. Prayer by an
assistant Minister, Mr. Beecher read 19th chap
Luke – all the Congregation then sung then a
text from John. sermon from notes on the
Love of God. Alluded to the Heathen Chince,
and Indian and Negro question. spoke of the
question now prevailing at West Point
about the Whittaker Case and defended
the Colored Cadet. Whittaker. prayer, Con=
=gregational Singing. took lunch at Resturant
and met Elder W.C. Stains at Elder Bywaters the
Prest of New York Branch. thence to the Latter-

day-Saints Meetings, Most of the [stricken] Elders from
Utah speaking to the small number of saints pres=
=ent. took train to Greenwood Cemetry – lovely
spot for the last resting place for the dead
strolled around till tired seeing the many inter=
=esting and lovely monuments and tombs there
Erected in memory of departed dead. back to
New York,– hungry & cold,. lunch at Restaurant
went to Telegraph office and sent message to
Prest. John Taylor at Salt Lake City stating that
our Missionary Company had arrived at New York
safely and should proceed on our Journey by Steam
ship "Arizona" on Tuesday next – Met Elder Gronway
Parry from Pensylvania that had received instructions
from Prest John Taylor after laboring in Pensylvania
for 6 months to Join a Missionary Company and
proceed to England. he Joined us accordingly.
<u>Stevens House Monday, April 19th 1881</u>.
Wrote home to my dear Family. went with Elder
stains to office of the Guion Steam Ship Company
the agent Mr. [blank] treated me Very Kindly
said he could only provide 2nd class berths for 20
passengers out of our company. but after I had
talked to him he concluded to turn the ships offices
and stewards out of their cabins to accommodate us

[separate sheet pasted on page]
and reduced our fare from 40 Dollars to 30
Each. and gave me as the President of the Com=
=pany and my Councillors T.C. Griggs and Thos X
smith and the Clerk John Donnaldson a 1st
class cabin between us with 1st Class accom=
=odations and made me this statement. our

{012}
and reduced our fare from 40 Dollars to 30
Each. and gave me as the President of the Com=
=pany and my Councillors T.C. Griggs and Thos X
smith and the Clerk John Donnaldson a 1st
class cabin between us with 1st Class accom=
=odations and made me this statement. our
company have never lost a Vessel that has had
Latter day. Saints on Board. We always think that
when one of our ships leaves a port with any of
the Latter-day. Saints on board she is as sure to
arrive at her destination as she sails. again
we consider that Latter-day-Saints on our ships
are better than an insurance – this coming unsolicited
from the lips of a person caring nothing for our Prin
=ciples made a deep impression on our minds.
Paid 990 Dollars for 33 full fares, and Exchanged
American for English money. Called a council
meeting of the brethren at Room 72 Stevens house
and arranged about going on board. Committees
to take care of baggage. buy Fruit and necessit-
=ies for all the company. Gloomy. Cold and raining.
6 of us took Elevated Rail Road to Central
Park. beautiful park – took Carriage Ride
around park – Visited menagerie and muse-
=um. Meterological department – dinner at a
Restaurant. Very long on Tram Car – saw docks
shipping &c and Visited with the bretheren and pre=
=paring for going aboard ship tomorrow.
<u>Stevens House New York. Tuesday, April 20th</u>
after breakfast packed up traps and getting all
ready for ship life. paid Hotel bill and with some
15 of the bretheren took train for dock and saw our
luggage on board of the ship Arizona. Mr. [blank]
came and he lotted off the best berths to the
Elders. all perfectly satisfied, splendid ship. good
officers – Then went to the gangway and watched the
Various persons Come aboard. quite a feast to look
at the great Variety of faces and watch Eagerness
sticking out – Very few Calm and dispassionate
at ½ past one. Whistle blew. we backed out of dock
and in a short time were fairly under way. a tug
boat followed us some distance with the friends of
a young british officer on board of our boat. They
singing – Waving handkerchiefs & calling out Good

{013}
[same as 009]

[not visible on microfilm or scan; from Lula Mortensen transcript:]
bye to Jo. With all of our crew and post of the
passengers would join in calling out good-by. It set
in to rain some time before the passengers lost

sight of the little tug boat and raining

{014}
constantly for a length of time. At 4 PM
the Pilot left us and the Weather seemed
to clear up a little much to our satisfaction
in going by the store room of the steward I noticed
that they have Every luxury the heart could desire
seemingly. Turtles. Lobsters. Wines & Every other
nicety. we settled up amongst us for the
fruit &c brought on board. Beautiful Moon=
=light Evening. some seasick. our accommodations
were all we could ask for. good room. Washing
accommodations. Beds and light Excellent. in our
cabin were My two Councillors Elders Thomas
C. Griggs and Thomas X Smith and the Company
clerk. John Donnaldson and myself -- had prayer.
Good bye land. the steady working of the Engines
indicate that the good ship is progressing
finely with her load of precious freight.
good night to all at home -- and Oh God
the Father of a humanity Kindly care for
thy servant and all on board the good
ship Arizona and cause the Winds & waves
to be propitious that we may reach our
destination and honorably fill our respect=
=tive missions that we may have thy
approval. bless all we have left behind
with joy & peace.
S.S. Arizona. Wednesday, April 21st 1880.
Up Early clear and fine. Water Everywhere,
a little nauseaus. rather queer. looked
around ship. Beautiful in construction. Every,
=thing complete. Steer by steam. bring Every thing
from below by steam. 69 furnaces. 120 tons
coal. boat 440 feet long. spoke to another ship
some of the steerage passengers are Very
                    boisterous
and hard on the Mormons. Think they know it all
but they don't. night feel very unsettled.
S.S. Arizona, Thursday, April 22nd 1880.

[015; sheet pasted on page]
Wind raised. Sea Rougher this Morning. I
feel quite sick – go to bed. can't go to the
table all day. this sea sickness takes all
the tuck out of a fellow, and I fancy bed
is the best place. The 2nd Cabin passengers
hold a concert tonight.
S.S. Arizona, Friday, apl 23rd, 1880.
Sick. so Sick. foggy this morning but warm
after it cleared off go on deck a little
While but glad to get back with help and
lie down again – head all of a whirl. Turned
foggy and cold. whistle blowing at intervals
making a horrible noise can't bear to hear
it. it sounds so lonesome.
S.S. Arizona, Saturday, apl 24th 1880.
I feel a little better can crawl around a
little and see folks. Pleasant but cool on
Deck. ship (steam) Rhineland from Antwerp
to N. York passes very close. 2nd Cabin passengers
held a concert? and such an affair!
S.S. Arizona, Sunday, apl 25th 1880.
Better to day. service on board in the grand
saloon at 10 a.M. but got there too late to
be admitted but several boys got together
in the 2nd Cabin dining room and had a good
sing. Mind filled with reflections about home
and folks. felt a little better till.
    Wednesday, April 28th 1880.
a beautiful morning. all seemed astir.
great Expectations of seeing land soon and
all Eyes turned towards "Old Ireland." at
1.30 P.M. Land appeared tho dimly on our
port and all were delighted to see land
once more. We raised a collection for a
poor woman in the steerage who was in Very
bad circumstances. arrived off Queenstown
at 6.45. and boarded by a tug boat. stopped
about 45 Minutes transferring mails (over
300 Sacks) and passengers. the sight of land

{016}
[same as 009]

{017}
together with the Villages and Churches with their
tall steeples & spires made one think of my
early youth and many pleasant memories
connected therewith. We passed fleets of
fishing boats and Vessels of almost all
grades and descriptions, some bound in,
others outward. but we felt thankful
to our father in heaven with a heart
full of Gratitude for sparing our
lives to cross the Ocean the 4th time

and the second time as a messenger
of life and salvation to the sons of
men.
[rest of page blank]

{018}
       1880 Thursday
April 29th Morning, first thing before
breakfast went on Deck and had a
good view of the Welsh Coast, about
breakfast time passed Holy head light
house and was able to get a good
View of it in consequence of running
so close to the land. passed numerous
steam ships and sail Vessels of
all sizes sailing up and down the
Channel. arrived at the mouth
of the Mersey River at one O'clock
and shortly after the tug boat with
Custom house officers came along side
and in the boat was Prest Budge
of the British Mission together with
Elders John Nicholson & Francis Cope
of the Liverpool office. we were
pleased to see them as we were greeted
heartily by them and and welcomed to the
shores of Great Brittan.
    We landed and Passed the
Custom house offices after some little
waiting occasioned by the Exceeding
formality of the Custom House officers
and about 1/2 past 2 Oclock we had
started our Baggage to the office.

{019}
       April 29th 1880.
altogether by a drayman sending
2 of our members with the dray
to care for the baggage paying 4 pence Each
       arriving at the office. 42
Islington we met a cordial Welcome
and after settling up some business among
ourselves and went to the Camden Hotel
to sleep with all the missionaries for Great
Brittan. the 11 going to Denmark and
Norway went to another Hotel and also the 4
for German Mission to another Hotel.
Met all the Missionaries of our Company
at the Office 42 Islington in Evening. Prest. W^m
Budge Presiding, Prest Budge Elder John Ni
=cholson myself & Bp Thos X Smith were the
speakers – had good meeting – good councils
given the Elders.
       April 30th 1880 Friday.
Paid 1^s 5^d for Breakfast at the Camden Hotel
slept with Bp Thomas X. Smith – went to the
office at 42 Islington and Received our
appointments from Prest Wm Budge the
Prest. of the European Mission. I was appointed
to Labor in the London Conference

{020}
       1880.
and with Prest Budge went Every
hour or two to the Rail Road stations
to see some of our party leave for
their fields of labor. in the Evening
I by request of Prest Budge went to
the Liverpool Plunge bath and re=
=baptized Bros Newton and Lorenzo
Farr of Ogden City they have requested
a rebaptism at my hands – they
were afterwards re Confirmed at the
office No 42 Islington by Bros Budge
and John Nicholson.
    Saturday, May 1st 1880
Bros Lyman Martineau of Logan and
Henry Dixon and Vickers of the Liverpool
Conference came in from their fields to Visit the
missionary company Just arrived from Zion Many
of our company had already gone to their appoint=
=ments but those remaining were glad to see these
bretheren and have their company in Visiting the
sights in Liverpool. as a company of 15 saints had
unexpectedly arrived from Iceland on their way to
Utah the bretheren connected with 42 Islington
were very buisy and could not go with us

{021}
       1880
to show us around and this day is a gala
day in Liverpool. at an Early hour several of us
missionaries got a good standing place at the
St Georges Hall where many thousands of Persons
were gathered to see sights, and we were not
disappointed. Firemen in Uniform with band,

then Horses & Carts belonging to Liverpool
corporation
then private horses & Vehicles, Brewers Horses
and
carts and Drays followed by the Horses of the
London and North Western Rail Way Comp^y fixed
up with Every possible care and trapping. Ribbons,
gold & silver Lace. Braiding and decoration concei
=vable. the greatest and beautiful lot of Horses
I ever saw in my life – never saw anything to
compare with it – in the afternoon went with the
Brethern viz Thos X Smith. Dixon. Martineau.
Kewley
Evans. Parry. Vickers to the museum & gallery
of arts, and had an Excellent time well repaid
for time & Trouble and in the Evening with
Elders Thos X Smith and Evans & Parry went to
see the Wax Works, getting home at night Excee
=dingly tired and leg Weary.

{022}
1880 Sunday May 2nd
In the morning, With Prest Budge. Elders
Nicholson
Cope. T.X. Smith. Parry and Evans attended
Meeting
at saints assembly rooms, Elder T X Smith. Evans
Parry. Roskelley & Budge speakers, took dinner
at Mission House 42 Islington and with same
Elders held meeting at [blank] Park. the President
of Liverpool Branch preached an Excellent dis=
=course on the 1st principles of the Gospel. I
followed with testamony – quite a spirit of
opposition manifested. Evening met again
with saints and a number of Strangers at
the Saints assembly rooms. Elder John Nicholson
preaching a masterly sermon on the necessity of
authority to preach the Gospel. by request
I followed bearing testamony to the divinity
of Joseph Smiths Mission and after our War=
ning will Come the Warnings of Thunders.
Earthquakes &c &c. the spirit of God was
poured. out upon us. to a great degree
between meetings I visited with the breathern
in the Liverpool Office Viz Elders Budge. Cope
and Nicholson.
Monday. May 3rd 1880.
Went to the Lime street station to see Elders
Evans & Parry off to their field of Labor in

{023}
Wales. then none of our Company of Missionaries
were remaining in Liverpool but Elder Thos X
Smith and Myself – I went to the Office 42
Islington and bought a Book of Mormon. Doctrine
and Covenants. Hymn Book. Voice of Warning
and Key to Theology, and at 9-15 left Lime St.
station Liverpool in Company with Elder Thos
X Smith after bidding Prest Budge and John
Nicholson good bye I for the London Confer=
=Ence and Bro Smith for the Nottingham
Conference. and traveling with me as far as
Rugby. I arrived at London viz 10 Dorset
Street Bride Street. Liverpool Road, Islington, N.
at 2-30 and after a little trouble found the
address of the Conference President and Judge
my disappointment on finding he had Just left
to be gone some weeks – I was here left in
a quandary as to my course to persons. and
feeling this Keenly I took the opportunity to Kneel
down and ask the Lord to remove from my
mind and feelings Every feeling of dispondancy
which was done and in about an hour after
who should come but The President of the Confer
=ence Elder George H. Taylor accompanied by
Elder
George Griggs my councillor in the Presidency
of the Missionary Company, also Elder W. W.
Willis
of Bountiful. Davis County, Utah, The President
of the conference has here 2 Rooms, and Keeps

{024}
1880. Tuesday May 4th
batch. they brought some bread home with them
and putting on the tea Kettle. Made a little tea
and some Bread and butter Constituted our
Evening Meal (dinner to me as I had nothing
to Eat since breakfast at Liverpool). after Tea
Elders Taylor and Griggs washed up dishes
and put up table cloth composed of a folded
newspaper as tho they were used to it.
In the Evening we walked about 1 1/2 Miles to
a rail Road station ~~and~~ (Highgate) and Rode
to Dalston Junction and walked to Sister Todd's
house to hold meeting with the saints at Old
ford Branch. Elder Griggs and myself were
the speakers, and after meeting Visited with
the saints, then returned to Dorset Street to

sleep with Prest. Geo. H. Taylor. ,

Tuesday May 4th 1880.
after our Morning meal like that of last
Evening I visited with Prest G H Taylor for some
time talking about the affairs of the Church
generally, wrote a letter home. and in the
afternoon went out to a restaurant and got some
dinner and wrote a letter to my family and one to
P. T. Morehead – in the Evening went with Prest
Taylor
and W. W. Willie to visit some saints in the
Clerken=
=well Branch and returned home about 11 O'Clock

{025}
Wednesday, May 5th 1880.
after breakfast assisted Prest. Taylor to fix up
his Stars & Journals and mail them to the saints
in the Various parts of the Conference, received
this morning 3 Very welcome letters being the first
news I have received from Home since I left
there 1 letter from Thos Hillyard, 1 from Sons
Samuel &
James & Zina – With Elder Taylor I went to try
and find my brother Richard. but after quite
a long search I found the Business house
of his former Employers Messers Bradbury & Co
who
said he had left their Employ something over a
year
his present address being Mount Edgecombe
House, 23 Burlington Place, Eastbourne, Eng.
I wrote him a note stating I was in England
and would call upon him at an early date
also Wrote a letter to A R.Wright about
our account of Books and forwarded it to
Bro W. C. Stains as I did not Know Bro
Wrights address. in the afternoon went with
Bro Taylor Visiting some saints and took Tea
with a family named Farnes a relative of
the families Farnes at Logan, then went
to the meeting of the saints of the Whitechapel

Branch. /I occupied the time\ the Church Clock
struck 11 P.M
when we got into the street where the house
is situated that we reside at and I was
very tired and soon went to bed.

{026}
1880 Thursday, May 6th
This morning I went with Elder W. W. Willie to
a Brother Wells. at 15 Wade Street. East dock
Road. Poplar. London and ordered a suit of
Black Clothes to cost $^{lb}4^{10sh}$ I paid him
2£ in advance the balance to be paid when
I get the clothes in a week from Nors. on
Returning to the Conference House I met Elder
William Driver of Ogden City who is Especting
to go home soon as he has been here a little
over a year, in the afternoon I wrote.
and with Elder G. H Taylor and W. W. Willie
went to take tea and talk a short time with
Bro and Sister William Driver of Ogden at
the room they have rented for the season
they have been here living a portion of the time
spent in this Country.   In the Evening in Company
with the Same Elders I went to the saints Meeting
place 42 Penton St. Penteville and heard some
Excellent
songs and recitations from the sunday school
children of that and other Branches of the
Church in London, and well Entertained with
recitations of the articles of our faith singly
from 5 Girls, after these Recitations Elder Willie
gave as Vivid description of the Manners and
customs of Indians in Utah, much to the
amusement of the Children. during these Exercises
I was Enquired for form outside and on

{027}
1880
going to the door found my Brother Richard and
My sister Jane's Eldest son samuel who had hun
=ted me up. his daughter in Eastbourne having
received my note written to her Father the day
before but her father (My Brother) being in London
she telegraphed him of my being here giving
my address, I Excused myself from the Sunday
school party and went with them to the lodging
place of my nephew samuel; with Whom Richard
was staying at the time and had quite a
Visit till 1/2 past 12 O'clock when I returned to
the Conference House promising to renew the Visit
again soon. I am very glad to have this found
some of my Kindred.

Friday, May 7th 1880.
Wrote up my Journal and Copied addresses

in the morning and sent off 2 packages of
photos from Bp David James. one for
Mr Wm H. Pennington, Holt Terrace
    Cronkeyslaw, Rochdale England
also Mr William James
    Lindley Street, Castlefields
    Shrewsbury England
at noon went to see my Brother
Richard at 43 Offord Road
    Barnsbury, London. N.

{028}
    May 1880
and ate dinner with Richard and afterward accom=
=panied him to see many of his friends in Various parts of London where he Introduced me
to quite a number of his friends in well to do
circumstances. we are well treated in Every
instance – Richard saying to me before
starting out "Where I am welcome, you are
as my Brother" My Brother Richard having
recently lost his wife by Dropsey and having
only 1 son in the Cape of Good Hope, and one
daughter, now living with him, both Children
by his first wife who died in 1858 – he feels
sadly afflicted and Very dispondant, and has
since I met him repeatedly solicited me to
come to his home at East bourne and stay as
long as I liked and he would make me
welcome. In the evening my nephew Samuel
Williams hunted us up and accompanied us
in Visiting till a late hour when I returned
to the Conference house and stayed chatting with
Prest Geo H. Taylor till Early Morning.
    Saturday, May 8th 1880
Left conference house soon as breakfast was
over and Bro Taylor accompanying me to High
=bridge station and took train for Brad Street
and walked to Cannon Ville Station and took

{029}
    Saturday May 1880
another train for Waterloo Station arriving there
5 minutes too late to catch train at 9 o'clock
for Southamption, and had to wait till 11.20
as I had been appointed by President Geo H.
Taylor to labor in the district and under the
direction of Elder Burningham who comes
from Bountiful, Davis County, Utah the ticket
agent told me the train did not stop at St
Denny's and I bought a Through ticket for
Southampton arriving at 1.40 p m. and took the
returning train for St Denny's about 2 1/2 miles
from Southampton, I found but little difficulty
to find friends at the House where Elder
                           Burningham
was stopping viz Bro Bailey, Lurline Cottage,
Cedar Road, Bevoir (Beaver) town, Southampton,
sister Bailey had Kindly prepared dinner Expecting
me on the former train, but not finding me comes
by it had partially given me up, but made me
Very welcome when I did come, In the Evening
with Bro Burningham and some of the Saints I
visited Southamption visiting some saints who live
there. stayed and slept at the above address with
Elder Burningham.
    Sunday, May 9th 1880.
Wrote up Journal &c in forenoon. and went
with some Elders to Visit Cemetery which

{030}
    Sunday May 9th 1880.
was Very much to be admired. In afternoon
met with Saints as also in the Evening in
their usual meeting place and preached
to them on Both occasions. Elder Burning-
=ham followed both times and we had a
season of refreshings. as usual with Bro
Burningham, stayed at the house of Bro
and Sister Bailey and Enjoyed ourselves
very much.
    Monday, May 10th 1880.
Spent part of Morning writing letters
posting Journal &c and balance of day
spent travelling Visiting several old mem=
=bers of the Church that have been slack in
attending their Meetings and other duties for
some time past. as usual slept at Sister baileys
    Tuesday, May 11th 1880.
With Elder James Burningham visited many old
members of the Church in the suburbs and in
                           South
=ampton some of which have been on the back
                           ground
for some time past – I think our Visit did much
good as some of these old members promised
to renew their Covenants by rebaptism.

{031}
Wednesday May 12th 1880
Wrote to Sister Jane's son Samuel R Williams
London. stating that I should be in London on
the 29th inst, and would stay with him if
all was well for a few days also wrote
to my Bro Richard that if all is well
I should Endeavor to Visit him some time
the first week in June. afterwards walked
to Bro Quinton. Satchel. Hambell. about
7 Miles from Southampton. they gave us a supper
Bed and Breakfast on

Thursday May 13th 1880.
With Bro Burningham I walked to Farh=
=am and Rode on R Road to Gosport Road and
then Walked to Brother Wilkes, 35 Chapel
View, Kingston Road, Landport,
Portsmouth, this is about 15 Miles from
Satchel, Hambell. Bro. Simms is the
President of the Portsmouth Branch.
but we did not go to See him, to day being
so Very tired from walking so far and not being
used to it. Slept in the house of Bro Wilkes.

Friday May 14th 1880.
With Elder James Burningham visited a number
of the Saints of this Branch Encouraging them.
also wrote a letter home to Wife Mary also one
to Bro sharp, and in reply to my letter to

{032}
Friday May 14th 1880.
my sister Jane I received the following answer:
2 Dock Wall St Davenport May 13th 1880
My Dear Brother   My heart is too full to be

Expressed at the idea of Meeting you again on
                                    Earth.
I fell I could almost wish our dear parents
back again to Join with us in that pleasure
but I dare not. Excuse my not Saying much
hoping to see you soon. My family and husband
and myself all unite in fondest love,
    Your Sister Jane.
In the Evening went to the place occupied
by the parties calling themselves the Salvation
Army – and when bellowing, shouting and Cry=
=ing out to the top of their Voices. Glory to God &
Bless the Lord &c &c we got perfectly dis=
=gusted and left.

Saturday, May 15th 1880.
With Bro. Burningham Visited some saints and
parties that had been cut off the Church
who treated us Kindly and promised to
Come to meeting tomorrow (Sunday.)
one Sister named Chambers we spent
some time with. Considered herself very
greatly injured by the members of the
portsmouth Branch and talked to us
with a spirit of Self Justification.

{033}
Sunday May 16th 1880.
with Elders Burningham and Wilkes we
visited the Saints at Gosport and invited them
to the meeting – in afternoon & Evening held
                                    Meeting
with the Saints of the Portsmouth Branch and
I talked about 30 Minutes in the forenoon
and took all the Evening meeting talking
about the administration of the sacrament
and necessity of Putting away hard feelings
from our heart & &c. Quoted largely
from Revelations on 155 and 255 pages
of old Edition of Doc & Cov. Visited
Sister Chambers and took tea with
her and found her son and
daughter in quite bad condition

Monday, May 17th
With Bro Burningham left Portsmouth
Bro Wilkes going with us 2 Miles
and Walked to Busham a distance
of 16 or 17 Miles. Wind & dust
right against us and Stopped
at the house of Bro & Sister Wallace
who treated us Very Kindly – in Even=
=ing visited a Mr White who has
a Brother living at Mill Creek, Utah
and bore testimony to him of this
Gospel. saw Pochester Castle said to have

{034}
1880
been 2000 years before Christ.
    Tuesday May 18th 1880
Elder Burningham and self went to Visit a
Family of Saints at /old\ Fishbourne Called
                                    Charles Rid=

=dett, The Brother is afflicted but the wife and the Children are good and feel and look well. then went to Visit a family at Port Field named Gambrell and Met a Sister to Elder George Batt of Logan that had been baptized some time Since and Elder Burningham and myself confirmed her a Member of the Church I being mouth, we also found a /Grand\daughter of Bro & Sister Gambrell believing and after talking to her sometime she Expressed a desire to be baptized but on asking her Mother if she Could her mother would not Consent, but I pray god to open her way to be a member of the this Church. We passed thro' Chichister and Saw its old Cathedral built in 1006. and called on a Sister Mathews whose husband is not in the Church at New Fishbourne and Visited and Comforted her all we could. wrote a letter to Prest Woodruff and did not get to bed till 2 O'clock Wednes-
=day morning having Wrote my letter to Bro Woodruff
after Visiting Sister Wallace and her Mother all the Evening till 2 O'clock. God blessing

{035}
1880.
our Visit.
Wednesday May 19th
Returned to day to Portsmouth, felling tired and weary from our Much walking, and spent the Evening at Bro Wilkes's house
Thursday May 20th
With Bro Burningham walked to Gosport and took dinner with Bro and Sister Newman and then went to the house of a Mrs Urry a friend of Brother Burningham who once belonged to the Church but waved in her faith and left the Church and married a gentile he died a short time since. she treated us Very Kindly gave us tea and asked us to call again.
Evening held a Very interesting meeting at Prest Simms House of the Members of Portsmouth Branch I spoke about 40 minutes.
slept at Bro. Wilkes .

Friday May 21st
Walked to Farcham station about 18 Miles and rode to Southampton.

{036}
Friday May 21st 1880.
getting to Bro Baileys about 6 Oclock Completely tired out and went right to bed to rest.
Saturday May 22nd 1880.
Wrote a Letter to Mary Jane and one to Daughter Rebecca. posted my Journal etc. and went Visiting with the saints in the Evening.
Sunday May 23rd 1880.
With Elder Burningham went to Bro Powells to dinner and there met Elder Stephens who had lately arrived from the Valley, his home being at Payson, Utah County, and we all attended meeting at the Saints Meeting place in the afternoon and Evening, rejoicing much in the Spirit of the Gospel made manifest. I spoke in connexion with the other of the Bretheren in the afternoon and occupied nearly all the evening speaking to the Saints.
Monday May 24th 1880.
Elder Burningham Visited the persons that had promised to be ready to be baptized and found 8 who said they were ready – we went to the Baths and

{037}
1880.
arranged to get them for the baptisms of the persons hereafter named. this being the Queen Victoria's birth day we went to the Battery on the Quay and Viewed the artillery men fire the Royal Salute and in the Evening repaired to the Baths from Sister Randall's and felt glad to accompany my fellow creatures to make Covenants with god. I spoke to the company about 15 minutes on the Importance of the Covenant &c following are the names-
~~Eliza Metcher~~ Baptized by Elder James Burningham
Eliza Metcher Confirmed by Samuel Roskelley .
William Esau Bailey Confirmed by William Coles

Jacob Ralph Bailey " " Edward Stephens
Henry Clark (rebaptized) " " Edward Stevens,
Francis Tracy Bailey (rebaptized) " James
                                                            Burningham
Francis Tracy Bailey ordained Deacon by Samuel
Roskelley. we returned to Sister Randall's
to confirm the above persons and all felt
well and Enjoyed themselves well.
      Tuesday May 25th 1880.
We started from Southampton this
afternoon having been writing letters &c
all Morning and walked to Bishop Stoke
accompanied by Bro. Randall and Sisters

{038}
      May 25th 1880.
May and [blank] Bailey were they left
us and returned to Southampton. we
took train for Dunbridge and then walked
to Mrs Batts the Mother of Elder George
Batt now President of the New Zealand
Mission. Mrs. Batt is not in the Church
but feels well toward us and we slept
at her house and she treated us Kindly
Keeping her up till late at night talk-
=ing to her. Mrs Batt lives at Houghton.
      May 26th 1880. Wednesday
We walked today to Winchester about
13 Miles making me very tired and
it being Very Warm it affected me Very
much – took dinner about 2 Oclock at
Bro & Sister Burgoz's I got a letter here
from Home by Zina telling me of Wife Mary
having a fine boy on May 4th all Well. I
was rejoiced to receive the same as I
had been anxious for some time. got the
heels of my Boots fixed here and Slept
at Bro & Sister Gamblin and had a
good nights rest very glad being so
tired. Bro & Sister Bergon were pre
=paring to Start to Utah the 5th of June next

{039}
      Thursday May 27th 1880.
Left Winchester after Breakfast Walking
thro New Alresford to Old Alresford and
with Elder Burningham ate Dinner at Bro
Henry Rampton's brother's who treated us Very

Kindly. we afterwards walked to a place
called Upper Wield and put up at the house
of a Gentile called James Giles who treated
us Very Kindly giving us good supper, Bed &
Breakfast. we preached Mormonism to them
and their daughter. I think with some Effects
on them praying god to give the seed sown
a good soil to grow upon.
      Friday. May 28th 1.880
Elder B. and self walked to Newton Common
and called upon a Sister Blake
and she pressed us to Eat some Bread
and Cheese which we did, Visiting with her
and singing a few hymns and I prayed
in her house and afterwards walked
to alton and get on a train and
rode to [stricken]/Farmham\ and after hunting
                                    some
time found [stricken] /Charles Rampton\ and
                                        stayed
a Brother to Elder Henry Rampton who is
a watch maker on the Main street. we bore
our testamony to him and his wife and then

{040}
      Friday May 28th 1880.
found an Uncle & his Wife of Elder Burning=
=ham and bore a faithful testamony to
them. after which went about 1 1/2 Miles to
Cop Bridge to meet a Sister H. M. Goodhall
who Elder Burningham had Baptized some
little time previous and we then walked
back into the town and to the Park and sat
down and Sang and preached to her of the
good things of God revealed in these latter
days. at 7 O'clock took train for Suberton
and after some hunting found Elder Thos Finch
and family and remained there all
night the good wife fixed us a bed or
a Lounge & some Chairs making us Comfortable.
      Saturday May 29th 1880.
Took trains for London arriving at Waterlooe
station at 10' O'clock and stopping at
Bro /Wm\ Stoneman's No 30 Earl St. Finsbury.
Wilson Street. London. near Broad Street
Station and took dinner then went
to Conference House found letters from
My sons James and Thomas and also
from Frank sharp dated May 11th bringing

me the mournful tidings that Rebecca
Hendricks the Wife of my youth died

{041}
　　　Saturday May 29th 1880.
that morning at 16 minutes past 6. this
to me was indeed sad news for it seem=
=ed to me that no greater calamity could
befall me than the Loss of My Dear
Wife. nevertheless not my will, but thine O
Lord be done. I sat down and wrote to
mine & Rebecca's children to let Rebecca's
things. House & affairs all remain and
not allow them to be scattered. In
the Evening with Elder Geo H. Taylor Prest
of the London Conference went to Highbridge
Station to Meet Prest William Budge
from Liverpool and then walked with
him about 2 1/2 miles to his Lodgings and
after supper returned to the Conference
House sleeping with Prest Taylor.
Sunday May 30th 1880.
This is the day for the London Conference
held at Orsons Assembly Rooms 23
New Road. Commercial Road. London E.
Meeting at 10-30 and 2-30 and 6-30 and
out door Meetings at Street Corners,
dividing the Elders in 2 lots making
2 Meetings. Elder Garner Prest of the
Whitechapel Branch Presiding at the
Meeting I went to. I took part in the

{042}
　　　Sunday May 30th 1880.
meeting – after we had commenced our
Meeting the salvation army commenced
singing about a hundred yards from
us to commence a Meeting. I spoke
about 30 minutes at the afternoon
Meeting on the continuation of the auth=
=ority of the Priesthood. – We had a splen=
=did conference.
Monday May 31st 1880.
Wrote at the office in fore noon and
on the solicitation of Elder Taylor I went
to Sister Keep's　No 20 Gifford Street
Calidonia Rd \London N./ the Mother-in-law of
　　　　　　　　　　　　　　　　　Elder

John Nicholson Prest Budge. Nicholson
Taylor. Griggs and self taking dinner
and supper and all being well
Satisfied. returning to the office to
sleep.
Tuesday Jun 1st 1880
Wrote to My Children at home and
went to EUston station to see Prest
Budge start to Birmingham and
in the afternoon with Elder Jos Bentley
of St George started to Visit the saints
in his District took train at

{043}
London Bridge Station for Horley and
slept at Bro. Mansbridge who made
us comfortable.
Wednesday Jun 2nd 180
Walked with Elder Bentley to
St Johns about 17 Miles and stayed
at Bro Millers who made us Very
comfortable – held a meeting out of
doors about 30 listeners. Elders
Bentley & I preached. about 20 Minutes
Each and I then went into the midst
of the congregation and invited them to ask
any Questions they wished to but little
conversation could be got out of them.
Bro Miller's address is Timothy Miller
1 Albermarle Terrace. Newport Road
St Johns. Burgess Hill. Sussex.
Thursday Jun 3 180
took train from Keymer Junction.
Burgess Hill to Eastborne to see my
Brother Richard, arriving at Eastborne
at 10-49. Met at station by my Brother
and taken home by him to his house
Mount Edgcombe House. 23 Burlington
Place. Eastborne. Sussex. I felt quit

{044}
　　　Thursday June 3rd 1880.
at home with him and his dear dau=
=ghter Anne and after dinner wrote
up Journal and a note to S. R. Williams
making an apoligy for not calling upon
him while in London also wrote a letter to
Bro G L Farrell, was introduced to several

of My Brothers acquaintances and had much
liberty in conversing with them. and walked
and talked with them and My Brother and
his daughter in a very agreeable manner.
Friday June 4th 1880.
with my own Brother Richard and his dau=
=ghter Annie Visiting and introducing the prin=
=ciples of the Gospel. Both seeming to Vie with
Each other in their Kind attentions to me. Annie
Would play on the piano and Sing for my ben-
-efit for hours. walked to Beachey Head with
Bro Richard.
Saturday June 5th 1880
still with my Bro Richard. & wrote to Bro
G. L. Farrell and my sons Samuel & James
and recd a letter from Bro Francis Sharp
and one from my daughter Rebecca and
and Son-in-Law Thomas Hillyard telling me
that Elder George L. Farrell of Logan had
been appointed by President M. Thatcher

{045}
June 5th 1880.
and Wm B. Preston to succeed me ~~an~~ as the
Bishop of smithfield Ward of which Ward
I had been Bishop since November 1862
up to May 16th 1880. no one can describe
my feelings on receipt of this news as I had
received no intention of the change, but a
number of Intimations to the contrary from
my presiding officers. but in this as Well
as all other matters connected with my
Varied and Very singular Experience since
joining myself to the Latter-day Saints I am
only led to one Conclusion that. "all things
shall work together for the good of them
that love the Lord", and I trust I may
prove Eventually to be one of that number.
I had thought that the death of my Wife
Rebecca was an Exceedingly hard blow but
this second blow in the Same Week seemed
more than I could bear, and this only by
the Lord's Kind assistance of his Blessed
spirit and influence, in answer to prayer,
that I am able to put or ~~maintain~~/Keep\ a
smile on my face or maintain the dignity of
an Elder of the Church in the Company and
Society of those that Know not God or his
Gospel, I ~~went~~ occupied a beautiful Bed

with Excellent pillows but my head was

{046}
Sunday June 6th 1880.
Sleepless. and many reflections of a car=
=eer of nearly 30 years of many vicitudes
passed through my mind before morning
dawned and a short nap helped to rest my
aching head.
Sunday June 6th 1880
ate Breakfast Early with Brother Richard
and his daughter Annie by their Kindness
makes me feel to ask god to bless them with
Eyes to see the Gospel of Jesus Christ in its
true light and have power to Embrace the
same. I bed them adieu promising to
again Visit them after a while leaving
Eastborne at 7.32 a M and arriving at
Brighton at 8.54 a.m. and was met at
the Station by a Bro John Mitchell the
President of the Brighton Branch. who took
me to his Mothers House No 4 Spa Street
Brighton. Met with Saints (16 in all) at
the House of Mr Hyrum Mitchell No 85
Spa Street Brighton neither him nor his wife
being Members of the Church. Elder Jos C
Bentley and myself occupied the time and
held another meeting in the Evening and had
a pretty good attendance of the Saints.,
at which I occupied most of the time. then
walked 4 miles (which we had done

{047}
June 6th 1880.
twice before today) to Bro Brown's house No
7 West Street Port Slade by Sea. to sleep.
  Monday June 7th 1880
at Bro & Sister Browns Writing Journal and
letters to Various persons occupying all
day. in the Evening by appointment met
at Bro Mitchells about 2 1/2 miles from
Brighton the President of Brighton Branch
and Elder Bentley and some other saints
had proceeded to the Sea side to find
a suitable place to baptize a young man
and little Girl. after hunting around some
time we found a good place in the river as
the sea was too Rough for our purposes. I add=

=ressed the candidates for baptism some time
Explaining the nature of the Covenant they were
taking upon them &c. Elder Bentley prayed and
Elder John Mitchell the Prest of the Brighton
Branch
baptized them. I confirmed the young man
Harry Robbins and Elder Bentley Confirmed
the girl Lucy Mitchell, we afterwards walked
back to Port Slade to sleep at the house of Bro
Brown it being late at night when we
arrived.
Tuesday June 8th 1880
With Elder Bentley I walked thro Fisher gate

{048}
Tuesday June 8th 1880.
Southwick and Shoreham on our way to
visit a Brother & Sister Grimes at Findon.
arriving there after Walking about 12 Miles
and spent the time in the late afternoon
Writing and sudying. the wind and Very
Cold disagreeable weather prevented our holding
an out door Meeting as we had contemplated.
we Enjoyed ourselves in Visiting Brother and
sister Grimes and they having a son in Mic=
=higan I gave them the address of the
some Elders in that state. we administered to
Bro Grimes for his health.
Wednesday June 9th 1880.
Elder Bentley and myself returned today
to Port Slade and after resting a while
went to the House of the Prest of Brighton
Branch (Elder John Mitchell) and took
tea and by invitation of some of the Bretheren
went to the Brighton aquarium. where
is gathered all Kinds of fishes from the
smallest blubber to the porpose and Cali=
=fornia Sea Lion /and seal of the north\ some of
the most beau=
=tiful Kinds I Ever saw, and many Kinds
I never did see before. also some Bycical
riders who were Experts and did their work
Exceedingly Well. the best Bycical riding
I Ever saw. we went back to Bro. Browns

{049}
at Port Slade to Sleep making our travel this
day on foot about 20 miles, the most I have walked
anydayyetandmakingme extremelytired.
Thursday June 10th 1880
With Elder Bentley started from Port Slade and
Called on Bro Mills and No. 4 Spa Street and
on Sister Hider at Patcham. Near Preston. Brighton
and Visited her a short time and proceeded
to St Johns Burgess-hill. getting there nearly
night and Very tired having traveled about
16 miles. Visiting Bro Miller and family.
Friday June 11th 1880
Changed my clothing, and Bro Bentley got his
shoes repaired and started for Isfield to
Visit the family of Bro and Sister R. Withers who
take care of a farm /Green farm.\ etc. they Seem
thrifty, good.
people and we stayed over night leaving there
in the morning of
Saturday June 12th 1880
We traveled to Clapper Heathfield. and
found. a Brother James Reed whos wife and
family are not in the Church. but they
treated us very Kindly and we stayed over
night. next day being sunday.

{050}
Sunday June 13th 1880.
and being 2 months since I left Ogden Utah
to proceed in my mission to preach the gos-
=pel and oh! what changes have taken
place since I left home, in my affairs
and family at home, but relying upon
the promise of God viz "all things shall
work together for the good of those that love
the Lord" I feel to put my trust in
him and ask him for strength.
after Breakfast Elder bentley and I
went to Healthfield and notified the En=
=tire Village that we would preach on the
green by the Post Office at 1/2 past 10 O'Clock
but after passing around from door to door
to notify them not a single soul came to the
place appointed for meeting. we remained for
1/2 and hour after the time appointed still no one
came. we lifted our voices in supplication to
God to accept our feeble Effort in this matter
tho' unsuccessful, and returned to Clapper to
the House of Bro James Reed and took
dinner. Bro. Reed had circulated a notice
that we would preach at this house in the

afternoon at 3 o'clock and about 20 persons met and Elder Jos Bentley and I occupied the time Explaining the doctrines of the Church a good feeling prevailed and the spirit of

{051}
the Lord was poured out upon speakers and Congregation and two persons after meeting said they should like to be baptized Soon. the lady of the house gave us some tea, and requested us to come again soon and stay longer. we then walked 10 miles to sister Winchesters BrownBread Street, Ashburnham and found letters from home dated May 22nd and May 24th bringing me news of Mary Jane's confinement with a boy on Saturday May 22nd all right and with thankfulness I received this news stayed and Slept at Sister Winchesters all night tho her husband is not in the church

Monday June 14th 1880
Wrote letters to H. A. Watson and Daughters Zina & Rebecca and rested

Tuesday June 15th 1880
With Bro Bentley I went to See Bro & Sister Vietler and thence to Bray's Hill to See Bro & Sister Honeysett and thence to Sister Isteds a sister to Sister Honeysett that lives in the alms house at ashburnam Estate and from there to Catsfield to Visit Bro & Sister Guy and family – they are very Poor but good in spirit and rejoice

{052}
in the latter day work, Back to Sister Winchesters at Ashburnam – Rained all day.

Wednesday June 16th 1880
left Sister Winchesters in the Morning and traveled to Sister Whatman's at Gotam near Broad Oak near Brede. it rained nearly all day, making roads very muddy and hard walking.

Thursday June 17th 1880
went from Gotam to Northiam to Visit Brother & Sister Elphic. a gardener to Frewing Esqr. took us around the Garden & Lawn which was Exceedingly well Kept we took dinner with Bro. Elphic and then started and walked to Bodiam to visit a

Mr Gurr who has a brother at Payson Utah Co. Utah. and then walked back to Sister Whatman's at Gotam. it rained all day and we walked about 20 miles making me Very tired.

Friday June 18th 1880
Returned to Sister Winchesters at Brown Bread Street. ashburnam and wrote some letters in the Evening. Bro Bentley going to Windmill Hill and gave out some tracts and preached to a congre= =gation that some Local preachers had

{053}
1880.
been preaching to. giving him a good opportu= =nity to talk to the people.

Saturday June 19th 1880.
With Bro Bentley walked to the House of Bro James Reed at Clapper and got there in time to write a few letters in the Evening. and Visit with the family after a tiresome walk thru the day.

Sunday June 20th 1880
Went to Visit some families named Briggs & Brooks at [blank] about 5 or 6 miles from Clapper and finding them all at the house of Briggs's I set to and gave them a good preach for about an hour the Ladies had been to our meetings at Clapper and acknowledged our doctrines to be true but did not obey because their husbands were not favorable. and this gave us a good chance. all persons acknowledging our argu= =ments were inanswerable. in the afternoon we walked to Clapper and held meeting at the house of Bro J. Reed. about 15 strangers present, and we were much pleased to see them. I first read Prest Taylor's sermon on the 7th of December 1879 in the 14th Ward Meeting House

{054}
Sunday June 20th 1880.
in Salt Lake City and then preached to them about an hour and Bro Bentley 25 minutes. a Mrs Wilmshurst told her feelings to me that she would gladly obey but her hus=

=band was a drunkard and had abused her
because of her desire to follow the Church,
we also found there were 5 women in the
meeting already for Baptism except
for their husbands.   held an out door
meeting at the green at Heathfield in the
Evening. we notifying the people as we went
through the Village, this time the devil
stirred up all the youths in the Village to
come and make a noise but while Elder
Bentley was preaching I tried to Keep them
still and while I preached they Kept pretty
still. we returned to Clapper to sleep

  Monday June 21st 1880
Elder B. and I walked from Clapper to
Uckfield and stayed at Bro & Sister
Brunsden. he a stone mason. but had
not succeeded in getting to Join. had been
in the Church some 30 years. rained most
of the day

  Tuesday June 22nd 1880
Elder B. and I walked to Isfield to Bro

{055}
Withers and took dinner and from thence to
St John's Burgess hill it having rained all
day and roads being Very bad made us very
tired. in the Evening with Elder Bentley and
Elder Miller we blessed a granddaughter of Elder
Miller and called its name Mary Jane
Miller daughter of John and Ann Fields Miller
I was mouth. baby was 6 weeks old

  Wednesday June 23rd 1880
With Elder Bentley walked to Port Slade by Sea
to the House of Brother Brown. who treated us
Very Kindly. and stayed over night but called
at Bro Mitchells and went to the Brick Yard
and got information about making Brick
went to Sleep at Bro Browns at Port slade ~~to sleep~~

  Thursday June 24th 1880
Walked to Brighton and took train for East-
-bourne at 1/2 past one leaving Elder Bentley
at Brighton. and remained at East=
=bourne at the House of My Brother Richard and his daughter Annie trying to
instill the principles of the Gospel into
them writing Letters and Visiting Various places
of interest around Eastbourne, old castles, &c

till   Tuesday June 29th 1880.

{056}
  Tuesday June 29th 1880
after Bearing my testamony &c after dinner I
bid them adieu. Bro Richard going to the
Rail Way station with me and I took a ticket
for Berwick and walked on the road to Chel=
=vington to the House of Brother Benjm Guy
Church Farm. Chelvington, near Hawkherst.
Sussex,, and Met Elder Jos C. Bentley again
and in the Evening We both preached at an out
    door
meeting at Ripe about 30 persons present and Very
    good
attention paid. and preached a good sermon after
meeting by answering questions &c &c. slept at
Bro & Sister Guys.

  Wednesday June 30th 1880
Walked with Elder Bentley to Plumpton
and then took R.R to Keymer Junction and then
walked to Bro Millers at St Johns. Burgess
Hill. and stayed over night

  Thursday July 1st 1880
with Elder Bentley walked to Bro & Sister
Mansbridge at Horley and took tea
then took train to London Bridge arriving at 1/4
to nine P.M. Walked ot Broad Street R. R.
Station and found Brother & Sister Stoneman
at No 30 Earl Street. Finsbury. Wilson Street
and took supper. then took the Blue
train to Liverpool Road and arrived at the

{057}
  Friday July 2nd 1880.
Conference house about 1/4 to 11. Prest G. H.
    Taylor
arrived from North London Branch about 1/2
past 11 O'clock I having walked 398 miles since
starting out of London June 1st 1880 having
gone form London Just one month

  Friday July 2nd 1880
after Breakfast took a good bath at the
Bath house, and spent the forenoon Visiting
Prest G. H. Taylor, and in the afternoon
wrote letters. and Evening with Prest Taylor
went to see Bro Farnes of Whitechapel Branch
to arrange about his going to Utah. returned

to Conference House.
    Saturday July 3rd 1880
Wrote at Conference house in forenoon and
Visited my nephew S.R. Williams in afternoon
and with him met my sister Jane at the
Waterloo station for the first time in 22 years
and she having her daughter Annie with
her. and Samuel R. Williams. and My Sister
Jane and her daughter Annie and myself
took train for Eastbourne in the Evening arriving
there at 1/2 past nine met at the Station
by Brother Richard and Welcomed at his
home by his daughter Annie.

{058}
    Sunday July 4th 1880
spent the day Visiting My Relations and tal=
=King over old times and telling them my
Experience in Mormonism adding my testi=
=mony to my Experience in Mormonism.
    Monday July 5th 1880
With S. R Williams left Eastbourne at
7:45 for London and found at the Conference
Prest G H. Taylor, W. W. Willie, Thos Griggs,
James Burningham, and J. C. Bentley and spent
the day with them at the Conference house Prest
Taylor provided us a good dinner and we clubbed
together and purchased all the strawberries
milk and Sugar we could Eat and had a loyal
time. and in the afternoon we went to Primrose
Hill and the Zoological Gardens and saw
almost all Kinds of animals and fish the
world produces wild and tame, and in
the Evening in Company with Elders Willie,
                              Bentley,
and Griggs went to Old ford to meeting and
had a good time. returned to Conference
House to sleep.
    Tuesday July 6th 1880
at Conference House all day writing letters
and assisting Prest Taylor about writing
addresses on Star Wrappers. In Evening

{059}
with Elder James Rampton went to Bro & Sister
Crosse's in Pleasant Place and met Elders Willie
Burningham. Griggs and spent a couple of hours
with the saints quite agreeably. and returned
to Conference house to Sleep.
    Wednesday July 7th 180
Prest G H. Taylor started this morning to
Burningham to Meet Prest Budge in an=
swer to a telegram from him. I was
occupied all forenoon making up
packages of Stars and Mailing same
and in afternoon called on my nephew at 140
Leadenall Street, and cashed a cheque for Prest
Taylor at City Bank for 31£ – and took tea at
Bro Stoneman's and went with Elders Stevens
Bentley & Riggs to meeting of Saints at White-
chapel branch of the church. and retu
=rned to Conference House to sleep.
    Thursday July 8th 1880
With Prest Taylor and Elders Bentley.
Stevens. Burningham and Willie went to
Housten Street Station to wish Bro Henry
Rampton start for home and did some
business at the office till 4 O'clock
when I started for Faversham in Kent

{060}
    Thursday July 8th 1880.
arriving there at 7+20 and met at the R R.
Station by Elder Edward King and Brother
Alfred Millgate and went to the Meeting
of the saints, a good Spirit prevailing
I spoke 3/4 of an hour Elder King following
and after meeting When to the house of
Bro & Sister Baker to sleep.
    Friday July 9th 1880
Called upon Several of the saints in
the morning and in the afternoon went
to Stalisfield to arrange for a Meeting on
Sunday next and sister Jane Clifford
having company were were to go on
to Wood-Side Green and ate supper at
sister steadman's and afterwards went
to Bro & Sister Neaves to sleep and took
Breakfast, they treated us very Kindly.
    Saturday July 10th 1880
Elder King and myself went to Marden
Beech via Headcom and stopped at
the House of Mr. Walker. Mrs Walker
having previously notified Elder King that
she would be baptized when he or an Elder
came that way again, and we found her
in the same mind and after we had talked

{061}
Saturday July 10th 1880 .
to her Husband. he also made up his mind to
be baptized and about 1/2 past 11 We had the
Unspeakable pleasure of adding 2 Members
to the Church by Baptism. Elder Edward King
officiating. witnessed by Myself and Sister M
Mary Ann Chiel and having walked and
sung and talked so much in one day
I was Exceedingly tired and retired to
bed after Midnight and got up at
an early hour.
Sunday July 11th 1880
our new Brother Stephen Walker and his
Wife Sister Ellen Susan Walker had hired
a horse and Van to take Elder King and
myself to Stalisfield to meeting and
taking sister Chiel also We all set out
from Marden Beech at 7 o'clock/a m\ and
arrived at Stalisfield about 1 O'clock
P.M. finding the Majority of the Saints
from Faversham and Wood Side Green
assembled with the Saints at Stalisfield
with Prest G. H. Taylor and met in Bro &
Sister Ciffords barn.* some strangers being
present. Prest Taylor. myself & Elder king occ=
=upying the afternoon and some Gentiles try=
=ing to annoy us by throwing Rocks on the
Roof of our Meeting place while I was
* I confirmed Sister Ellen Walker on the above
named day

{062}
Sunday July 11th 1880.
talking. The Evening Meeting was occupied
by My talking of the progressive duties of
saints in teaching their children and
setting good Examples &c &c and the
necessities of saints having no hard fee=
=lings against Each other. /& Prest Taylor on
gathering\ the saints
returned to their Homes feeling refreshed
in their spirits and that they had been
blessed in their days meetings. Elder
(Prest) G H Taylor and myself remained
at Bro Cliffords. over night to talk to
Bro & Sister Clifford about gathering to
Utah with the saints and left them on

Monday July 12th 1880.
arriving at Faversham in time for the
train to take Prest Taylor to London and
I to Sittingbourne to Meet Elder King and
go with him on a preaching tour thro'
Kent./County\ stopped at Bro Willis Simons.
No [blank] High Street Sittingbourne, for the
night and wrote some letters and visited some
people claiming to be saints.
Tuesday July 13th 1880
Elder King and I walked to New Brompton
and could not find any of the people at

{063}
July 14th 1880.
home that we wished to find and had to
hire a Bed at a Lodging house – we visited
a Woman in the afternoon that had been baptized
into the Church in Childhood who treated us very
Kind.
Wednesday July 14th 1880
We called upon a Mrs. Hammond who had
relatives in Utah, and she treated us Very Kind
getting good breakfast for us &c and at 12+15
we started from Gillingham Pier by a steam
packet for Sheerness and found some of the
Saints not at home. called on a Mrs. Barber
No 18 Cavour Street. Miletown. Sheerness.
She is a firm believer in our doctrines but
her husband has prohibited her being
baptized. but she liked the Elders to call
on her. at 4-30 we took a steam boat
for Southend and Reached the house of
Brother & Sister Camper in the Evening and
sat up late talking of the doctrines of the
church.
Thursday July 15th 1880
started at 9 O.clock and reached the
house of Sister Gardner, Smiths Farm
Hockley. husband not in the Church. 2
daughters & 3 sons do. do. Good woman
held in bondage. but all the family

{064}
Friday July 16th 1880.
treated us Very Kindly and gave us a
good dinner. and in the afternoon crossed
the Crouch River where we took a good

Bathe and then pushed on to the House
of Brother & Sister Green and their daughter
and had a good nights rest after talking
and administering to Sister Green who
was sick from Rhumatism and other
deseases. and slept at their house.
 Friday July 16th 1880.
We Walked to Hatfield Peverel and took
dinner with sister Hawkes & family and then
walked to Braintree. Visited Bro Hedges
and Bro & Sister Saddler, stopping over night
with Bro Hedges at ~~get~~
 Saturday July 17th 1880
got up at 5 O'Clock and walked 12 miles to
Chelmsford and took train for London at 10-46
arriving at the office at 1 O'clock P.M finding
Prest Taylor gone from home, and being Very tired
I took possession and Wrote to Wife Mary and in
the Evening I had some of the Bretheren call
at the office and we Enjoyed a Very Enjoy=
=able chat till a late hour and I retired
to bed Very tired.

{065}
 Sunday July 18th 1880
according to previous arrangement went to Bro
Stonemans house to breakfast and studied the
Bible the rest of the forenoon. went to the Swan
Pier above London Bridge and took steam Boat
with Bro Stoneman for Woolwich to meet with
the saints and on the way met Elder E. King.
at Stonewall Pier and on landing at Wool
=wich proceeded to house of Bro Purser and
there found out that the Meeting house had
been given up for some weeks and no mee=
=ting of the Saints had been held Since.
we Visited several of the saints and then
returned by Boat to London Bridge having
spent the day and seemingly profitless.
 Monday July 19th 1880
after Breakfast went to 43 Offord Road
and found My Sister Jane and her daughter
Annie and by her solicitation went with
her to the Zological Gardens and from there
to Mrs Coper and the daughter of a Mrs Elizabeth
Rowley who nursed my mother when I was
born, and took Great interest in my well
-fare for years afterward. the nurse is
dead and Mrs. Cooper is 74 years old

and cryed like a child to see me and
said she could recognize my features as

{066}
 Tuesday July 20th 1880.
a Roskelley. in the Evening I went to Old
ford to attend meeting. with Elder E. King
and had a good meeting.
 Tuesday 20th 1880
Met My sister Jane and her daughter Annie
and went to St Pancrast R. R. Station. took
train for Tottenham and spent the day with
a Mrs & Mr Purver, 50 Tilson Road. Lans=
=down Road. High Cross. Tottenham N.
Mrs Purver is the only sister of George Williams
the Husband of My only sister Jane R. Williams
and their only daughter and her husband
lives with them. Returned to Conference house
and found Prest Geo H. Taylor and Elder
Peter Reid the Prest of the Newcastle on Tyne
Conference Just Returned from a Visit to
France.
 Wednesday July 21 1880
spent the day with the bretheren at the office
and writing Letters &c. and with the two
Presidents of Conferences went to Meeting at
the Saints Meeting House in Whitechapel Bra-
=nch. Prest Peter Reid preached. and we
had a good meeting.

{067}
 Thursday Jul 22nd 1880.
Went with Prest Peter Reid to Kings Cross station
         to
see him start to his field of Labor viz Newcastle=
=on=tine and then I returned and With My
Sister Jane and Daughter annie went from London
Bridge R.R. Station to Christial Palace at Syd=
=Enham and returned in the Evening and left
them at nephew S.R. Williams's place in the
City and afterwards I walked to the Meeting
house of the North London Branch. 42 Penton
Street. Pentonville. where I preached to the
strangers and Saints present and had a good
meeting.
 Friday July 23rd 1880.
Spent the Entire day with my sister and her
daughter annie. Visiting the British Museum

Containing all Manner of Interesting specim=
=Ens of Birds Beasts & Fish. Sculpture. Pain=
tings, ancient Relicts of ancient work and
many things to instruct those seeking inform=
=ation. and Joined by my nephew Samuel
R. Williams I visited the Royal Polytechnek
in the Evening Enjoyed the many Grant Sigh=
=ts and interesting curiosities to be seen there
in Sculpture. Machinery. Diving Bell. Tight
Rope Walking. Theatrical Performances where one
person does all the talking and the rest the
acting, and liquid fire falling and a

{068}
     Saturday July 24th 1880.
thousand and one things I cannot here mention
that is of great interest /to\ those that Visit the
institution. and being well repaid for my
time through the day I return to the Confer-
=Ence house tired and find an advanced
Copy of the "star" from Liverpool awaiting my
arrival releasing Elder Geo H. Taylor from
the Presidency of the London Conference to
return home and appointing me his succes=
=sor. Praying that an increased portion of
the spirit of God may rest upon me to
Enable me to perform the duties of the new
Calling I went to Bed.Contemplating the
Many preperations being made in the sett=
=lements of the saints in Utah to celebrate
the 24th of July 1880.
     Saturday July 24th 1880.
Wrote Letters. Studying &c until late afternoon
went to Visit a person desirous to be baptized
into the Church and after tea with him and
his wife went to Visit my Sister Jane and
She with annie & Samuel R and myself
walked through some of the Principle Streets
in London and saw a saturday Evening
among the buisy population of Porrer classes
of London and the immense throngs that go

{069}
     Sunday July 25th 1880.
shopping on Saturday Evening purchasing for the
usual sunday (Englishmans) dinner and
it is indeed difficult to concieve how so
many persons get a living and the immense

trafic of Wagons & Vans. Drays. Cabs & omnibus-
=ses have to waits one for the other to move on
under the direction of a Policeman. I got home
to Conference House Very late in the Evening
     Sunday July 25th 1880
With Prest G H. Taylor visited the sunday
School of the North London Branch in forenoon
and took dinner at Bro Crosse's and then
went to Visit the Saints at Lambeth Branch
I occupied 40 Minutes and on Sitting down
a brother named Marsh jumped up and decl=
=ared he saw angels in the Room and Extending
his right hand partially slowly moved
toward the stand seeming to feeling for some=
=thing until he came to Elder S. F. Ball the
President of Lambeth branch when placing
his right hand on Brother Ball he uttered
a blessing in strange and disconnected
speech showing that no good influence pervaded
his mind. he then sat down on the Seat of
the Priesthood alongside of Elder Ball trem=
=bling in a fearful Manner. /President Tayor\ after
                        meeting
occupied 20 Minutes and briefly cautioned the
                        brother that he was led
by a wrong spirit and must repent.   after Meeting

{070}
we returned ~~to~~ via London Bridge to Brother
Stonemans and took tea and thence to 42
Penton Street. Pentonville. the meeting place
of the North London Branch and Happy was
I to See My sister Jane and her daughter
annie and Son Samuel and Wallace and
a Young Man friend came to Meeting upon
a request I had made of them the day
before. Prest G.H. Taylor preached a good
discourse on the first principles of the
gospel and the carrying the gospel into the
spirit World &c   I followed with testamony
pertaining to the restoration of the gospel in
this our day thro Prophet & apostles &c
as it was anciently. went home with Samuel
and Jenny and took supper returning to the
Conference house late.
     Monday July 26th 1880.
Visited My Sister in the morning, wrote and
studied in the afternoon and with Prest G.
H Taylor Went to Old Ford to meeting in the

Evening. I occupied about 30 Minutes
    Tuesday July 27th 1880.
according to agreement met my sister and
neice annie in the Morning and took tickets

{071}
    Tuesday July 27th 1880.
at the Holloway R. R. station for the alexander
Palace and spent the Whole day sight seeing
and then did not see a tithe of what was
to be seen as we were constantly Employed
following up the programme looking at Conjur=
=Ers. Theaters. Dancers Little Red Riding Hood
Concerts. Grand Organ Performances. Circuses
&c Winding up with a Concert on the Lakes
of a Most Magnificent description. the Lakes
and Walkers &c being lit up with thousands
of Chinese lanterns of all Kinds and tints
and colors and suspended over all was a
most magnificent Electric Light changing
night into day. it was nearly midnight
when I got to the Conference house.

    Wednesday July 28th 1880.
after Breakfast addressed the packages
of Stars to the subscribers and went with
My sister Jane & Neice annie to the Holban
Viaduct and saw them start off to sheerness
I then returned to the office and with Prest
Taylor and went Visiting some saints in the
Whitechapel Branch and attended the White=
=chapel Branch Meeting and had a good time
returning to Bro stonemans to supper. In the
Meeting I blessed a girl Baby of Bro Hallett. And
    also
administered to it for its health.

{072}
    Thursday July 29th 1880.
assisted by Prest Taylor to make out some star
and Book accounts and forward them to the
persons owing them and in the afternoon went
to the saints houses opposite the foundling
Hospital and Examined a great Number of Very
Curious and ancient Coins and curiosities
the Coins dating back to Contantines reign
shortly after the savious death. these
were in the possession of Sister Godfry who's
husband died out of the church but took
great delight in collecting old coins &c
    Went to the North London branch to Meet
the saints in meeting, and had an Excellent
time in a testimony Meeting
    Friday July 30th 1880.
With Prest Taylor in the office making
out accounts in order to settle up the
Star and Book business of the conference
and in the Evening went to the agricultu=
=ral Hall by invitation to see the Mohawk
Minstrels and had quite an Enjoyable time
    Saturday July 31st 1880.
assisted to make out a/cs and Wrote to Prest W
    Woodruff
and aunt Zina Young at Salt Lake City and in the
    Evening
Prest Taylor & I walked to Notting Hill Via Hyde
    Park

{073}
and the albert Memorial and Kensington Gardens
taking tea at Elder Balls. the President of of the [sic]
Lambeth Branch and then Proceeding to the
    Serpentine
River in Hyde Park and Baptized a Man named
    George
Cook witnesses Prest G. H. taylor. – Balls and
got to Conference house late and found a man and
his Wife from Sheerness waiting for us and we
    gave
them our bed and we took the floor.
    Sunday August 1st 1880.
attended General Priesthood Meeting at the
L.D. Saints Meeting place 42 Penton St. Pentonville
about 55 present and had an Excellent time
I was mount in ordaining Wm Stoneman to the
office of an Elder. Attended meeting at Whitech
=aple Branch Prest Taylor and I the Speakers. and
between meetings /in the Hall\ held meeting in the
    Streets I and
Brother Loveday the Speakers, and in the Evening
held another Meeting in the Hall. Prest Taylor
and I being Speakers. After Meeting walked
with Bro Taylor to Old ford to administer to
Old Sister Todd and then to conference House
as usual Very tired.
    Monday August 2nd 1880.
Being a general holiday tho' the land

Elder Taylor and I went to Visit the Presid=
=Ency of the North London Branch and Met

{074}
the President at the office and went to his house
with him and Visited him and his family and
took dinner with him and then we visited
his 1st Councillor. and his family and spent
the Evening with them returning home late as
Usual
    Tuesday Aug 3rd 1880.
as Usual Employed in the Office receiving
instructions about the duties I was assuming,
and late in the afternoon I started for the
London Bridge R. R. Station to attend a
Meeting of the Saints at Deptford at the
House of Bro Reed, altho there were
but few present we had an Excellent
Meeting. I Visited a few of the saints
at their homes and returned to the Confer=
=Ence house late in the Evening.

    Wednesday aug 4th 1880.
Wrote the Star addresses for Weekly
star, & the Journals, and did the mail-
-ing for the 1st time and received form
Prest Taylor the Cash Box with £5.1.9 in
Cash and did the purchasing of stamps
and materials for Office use and other
things after this date. With Bro Taylor
took tea at a Coffee shop at Dalston

{075}
Junction and then took train to Shoreditch and
walked to the Whitechapel Meeting house to the
saints meeting. Returned to Conference house
to sleep as usual.
    Thursday aug 5th 1880
Wrote letters till the mail closed at 4 O'
Clock. To Wife Mary and Thomas and a General
Letter to Rebecca and the family. and in the
afternoon with Bro Taylor went to sister Pierces
to take tea and I parted with him and Met
Prest Ball at Blackfriars Bridge and accomp
anied him to Clappham Common and Saw
him baptize 6 Persons for the remission of
their sins, returning to Dorset Street by way
of Westminister Bridge and Under Ground R

R to Kings Cross.
    Friday aug 6th 1880.
Writing and studying till afternoon late
some saints came in to Visit us and in the
Evening Bro Taylor walked to High bury Vale
to Visit a family of French people we had not
before seen named Vinceage. received letters from
home.   Saturday aug 7th 1880
Wrote to Elders King and Griggs also also to Bro
                                  Geo
Barber and a. P. Welchman at home, and
in afternoon Elder Taylor and I took a bath and
he went to Wiltshire to Visit Elder Willey

{076}
and I studied the Scriptures. In the
Evening I was invited by Bro Crackles to take
tea and spent some hours with his nephew
discussing Mormonism and he seems of an
                                Enquiring
turn of mind.
    Sunday august 8th 1880.
Went to North London Branch sabbath school, and
with Elder Joseph Maines to Dinner and thence to
Lambeth Branch and preached on the principles
of Forgiveness and the sacrament of the Lords.
Supper. and Returned to North London to Evening
Meeting. Elder [blank] occupied 25 minutes and
I occupied 35 Minutes to a good congregation
of Saints and a good sprinkling of strangers.
Went to Bro Cross's and took supper, and returned
to Conference house late
    Monday august 9th 1880.
occupied the forenoon writing letters and
posting accounts forwarding letters to Elders
&c. and Elder E. B. Snow arrived on his way to
Southampton o Preside and after Dinner He & I
                                  went
to Victoria Park and saw the Beautiful Grounds
and Gardens there laid out so nicely that it
seems almost like Heaven on Earth so far as
these things are concerned. and in the Evening
Elder snow and I attended meeting of the saints

{077}
at Old ford at the House of sister Todd.
we administered to sister Pipkin for her health
and she afterward stood up and Expressed her

gratitude for the Healing power restored.
Elder Burningham & Stevens returned to
Conference House late the
Evening
 Tuesday august 10th 1880.
Wrote and Visited with Elders. Viz Prest
Taylor. Snow. Burningham and Stevens. and
in afternoon with Elders Snow and Burningham
Visited Bro and sister Stoneman and took
tea with them and in the Evening went to
Thames Embankment between Blackfriars
and Westminster Bridges and saw the Emban=
=Kment lit up with the Electric light and
saw Cleopatra' Needle on the bank of
the Thames and returned to London Bridge
by a River Steam Boat down the Thames River
and thense home. to Conference House
 Wednesday aug 11th 1880.
Forenoon wrote addresses on stars and mailed
them and afternoon with Elders Burningham and
Snow went to see Westminster Abby and old Bui=
=lding devoted to the Monument of Illustrious
personages who have obtained celebrity and
been buried in the Vaults of this ancient Church
it has an immense amount of imposing sculpture

{078}
work on the tombs and most Excellent
workmanship. stepped into the House of Parli=
ment and took tea with Bro & Sister stoneman
several Brethern and sisters being present,
and proceeded to the Whitechapel Branch to
hold meeting. Elders Stevens. Snow. Burningham
and I being the speakers. on returning to
the Conference house found Elder Joseph Mathews
President of the Welsh Conference. and spent a
few hours with him about my old missionary
labor in the Welsh missionary labor
 Thursday august 12th 1880.
Writing letters and answering correspondence
with the Elders. till Evening went to the
Meeting at North London Branch and met
there Prests G H. Taylor and Joseph Mathews
speakers were self. and Prest Mathews and
Taylor.
 Friday august 13th 1880.
With Prests Taylor and Mathews went to
Billingsgate fish market and saw fish
of all Kinds by the Wagon load and thence

we past the Column. With 310 steps high.
and by the moat of the Tower of London
and the Mint and the Custom House and
thence through some of the great thorough=

{079}
=fares of the Great City of London and turned
into a Jew store and bought six shillings worth
of shells to send home. In the evening we all
Visited the Caledonian Cattle Market were alm=
=ost Everything is proffered for Sale Excepting
~~Meat~~
Meat and Vegetables, it is a remarkable place
Horses of all Kind and Qualities are here
offered for sale.
 Saturday aug 14th 1880.
With Presidents G. H. Taylor and Joseph Mathews
stated out to See sights, traveling through Grays
Inn Road. Holborn. New Oxford and oxford
Streets
to Hyde Park and Kensington Gardens to the
albert Memorial. and Royal albert Hall and
hence to the South Kensington Museum and with
the gorgious displays in the shop windows on
Holborn Street and Oxford Street was a full
feast to the mind and Eyes but again the
Eye could find something new in the albert
Memorial for it is of Elaborate Design
and Workmanship but the Museum Excells
Everything of the Kind I could imagine, here
you find the Old Engines first constructed
to run on the English Rail Roads. The "Rocket,"
"Puffing Billy" and, and with modles of all Kinds
of ships and Ship gear and Machinery. harbor
defences. Boats. Reapers & Mowers, steam Engines
P[---]ps, steam Hammers. Furniture old and

{080}
 Saturday aug 14th 1880.
Unsick in design and workmanship. Castings of
all Kinds and patterns. ancient and Modern,
and sculpture work of the Highest order and
among the lot that attracted my attention
was 2 sleeping babes folded in Each others
arms cut in White Marble, the most life like
of anything of the Kind I Ever saw. and. was
simply superb. the Paintings in oil and water
Color was Magnificent to behold and in almost

Endless Variety, ancient and Modern. and in one Room was castings in Plaster of some of the Masterpieces of art on Various Memorial Columns and Triumphal arches thro the nations. China Ware and other ware and ancient Relics dug from the Ruins of Troy and Pompee together with the Furniture and articles of domestic use now and anciently used by the people of European nations as well as the asiatics, in fact the Eye and mind cannot contain the immense store of wealth and information given by this sight, of this feast to the mind. in the Evening Prest Taylor treated me and Elder Mathews to a Visit to the Haserly Minstrils at her Majesty's Theatre. and it certainly was a grand success at showing up Negro life in years ago in the

{081}
Southern States of America. The Singing was sup=erb .and the dancing and Merry making all that could be asked for. We all returned to Conference House having Enjoyed our trip Hughly. a tired and I hope wiser lot of men.

Sunday aug 15th 1880.
spent Morning Reading &c and in after=noon Visited Whitechapel Branch in com==any with Bro Blanchard, and I preached on the Blessing of Children and their being Baptized at 8 Years old and the responsab==ility of Parents in reaching their children the doctrine of the Church. in the Evening I attended Meeting in the North London Branch and preached on the History of the Church. giving a few items of its rise and Progress.

Monday aug 16th 1880
Went with Elder Mathews in the Morning to see the Celebrated Tower of London and after waiting in a long row of Impatient people we got our durn and under the guidance of a Tower servant generally Known as a "Beef Eater" passed through the principal portions of this famous Tower. Visiting the Great archway. Traitors Gate

{082}
the Statues and Wepons of War of ancient Monar-=chs and instruments of torture and death, the. axe & Block used in the beheading of several of the old Kings and Queens of this realm. the citidel within the tower with about 800 soldiers Constantly in it and all the warlike instruments of war of a great nation with 108 Thousand stand of arms of the most improved patterns. ready for immediate use. Visited the room where the state prisoners have been confined viz Tyreseil Philip Howard. John Dudly, Dr John Store. William Rawe. Edmund Poole. Lady Jane Gray and Many other persons, above all the sights is the Crown of Queen Victoria. and said to be Worth 5 Million Dollars. the Gold Plate, Maces, and the other Gold articles within the Iron Cage is said to contain property to the Value of 15 Million Dollars . Afternoon wrote and Evening Visited Mrs Whitfield at Dalston. and then went to Meeting at Sister Todd's in company with Prest Taylor.

Tuesday aug 17th 1880
Tuesday. spent the day writing and in the Evening went to See Brother & Sister Cook to Know if they intended to go to Utah this season. took tea with them and

{083}
afterward went to Madam Tusaud's Wax works and Enjoyed the Evening Very much. Wednesday august 18th 1880.
Elder Jos Mathews. Prest of the Welsh Con--ference bid us adiew this Morning for Wales; Stars arrived and I sent them out to subscribers. and then wrote letters to all the travelling Elders. and attend Meeting with prest Taylor at Whitechapel

Thursday august 19th 1880.
Forenoon wrote letters to Various Persons at Home about Land and other Matters and in the /afternoon\ Worked at my compendium and
in
the Eveing attended meeting at North London Branch with Prest Taylor and for the first time met Elder Mark Beezer from Kaysville from Kaysville. [sic] Utah. now travelling Elder in the Bristol conference.

Friday aug 20th 1880.
Wrote all forenoon and in the afternoon
With Prest Taylor went to Notting Hill and
spent the afternoon with Elder Henry
Garner Prest of the Whitechapel Branch
and in the Evening we went to Visit Bro
and sister Dow and family. and get acquainted

{084}
Saturday august 21st 1880.
Morning Went to the town (City) to attend
to some business shopping Books fo the
Liverpool office to Bro Batt. in New
Zeland and wrote in the Evening. and
studied Scripture till late
Sunday august 22nd 1880.
With Prest Taylor and Self Visited the
Headquarters
of the Salvation Army for this Country, at
Whitechap
=el and had much regret at finding persons
professing to be God worshippers acting more
like maniacs than sane persons in their so
called worship. attended our Whitechapel
Branch Council meeting and afternoon Meeting
and Spoke and also Evening Meeting and spoke
35 Minutes and Prest Taylor spoke 65 Minutes
this being Prest Taylors farewell discourse to
the saints in this branch most all the saints
present belonged to the branch . held an open
air meeting between meetings in the hall
Preaching by Elder Garner and Myself
Monday aug 23rd 1880.
Went to Town to purchase paper. Envelope &c
to send stars to Subscribers, and wrote letters
in afternoon went with Prest Taylor to Old
Ford. took tea at Sister Todds and held Meeting

{085}
Prest Taylor and I occscupied the time. Elders
B. S. Young (son of BY Junr) and W.B. Parkinson
of Morgan came to London to see sights and take
an out before going to Utah.
Tuesday august 24th 1880..
Wrote all forenoon, and recd Explanation
of Book a/c's of Conference, and accepted
the Book and a/c as it was stated. And
in the Evening went to See the family of

Bro & Sister Hill. Homerton. and Contin=
=ued till a late hour – they Expect to go to
Utah this Season.
Wednesday aug 25th 1880.
Having an invitation to accompany the
North London sunday School to Hampton
Court Palace. I accepted, and rode in
a Large Van with the President of the
Branch (Bro Cornell) and 27 Others to
Bushey Park and took dinner and thence
to Hampton Court gardens and saw the foun=
=tains playing and walked over the beauti
=fully laid out grounds. saw a grape
Vine covering 2200 ft of trellis thickly
with foliage, 112 years old, and has
bourn this year 1250 Bunches of grapes
went form room to Room Examining the
Excellent paintings &c and then Visited

{086}
the celebrated Maize, and found my way
into and out of it, and then back to the
Park and took tea. then took a boat Row
with 17 others on the Thames, and started
home in the Van at 1/4 Past 7 OClock.
arriving about 11 O'Clock and found Elder
Kinkey had arrived to do London for
a few days from Berlin where he had
been imprisoned and banished for preaching
the Gospel.
Thursday august 26th
after writing up my correspondence
I went with Elder Kinkey to see the sig=
=hts and Evening went to North London
Branch to Meeting and Elder Kinkey related
his arrest. Imprisonment and Expulsion
from Germany followed by Elder M. Beezer
and Prest Taylor.
Friday august 27th
writing up correspondence all forenoon
and with Elder W. B. Parkinson went to Visit
some Relatives of his but did not find them
then With Prest Taylor I went to Lambeth to
hunt up a Sister Gibbs and also Bro & Sister
Brown about Emigration Matters. Evening
Wrote a letter home.

{087}
Saturday august 28th 1880.
With Prest Taylor went to see the House of Lords and audience Room, and other rooms. pertaining to the British Parliment and then to the Horse Guards, and Nelson Square and then through the National art Gallery and saw some of the best Prod= =ductions of Paintings I Ever saw. wrote in the afternoon and a number of Bretheren came to see us in the Evening at the Conf= =Erence House

Sunday august 29th 1880.
at home all Morning, with the Bretheren at the office ad in afternoon with Elder Taylor. B. S. Young. W. B. Parkinson. W. W Willey. And had had an Excellent Meetings both forenoon and afternoon and Crowded house full in Evening and all felt Well listning to the testamony of Elder Taylor.

Monday august 30th 1880.
Elder W. B. Parkinson left this Morning for Bir= =mingham. Elders King & Griggs arrived from their Districts, and by Invitation prest Taylor and Elder B. S. Young and I took dinner at Bro Cornell's and went to Hoborn Viaduct to transact some Business together, and in the Evening Went to Old Ford to Meeting as is usual on Monday Evening.

{088}
Tuesday aug 301st 1880.
With prest Taylor arringing our Con[ference] business through the day and in the Evening Visited Sister Keep and spent an agreeable Evening.
Elder Burningham arrived from Southampton.

Wednesday sep 1st 1880.
The following Elders met at the office viz. G H. Taylor. S Roskelley. J. C. Bentley. W. W. Willey. Jas Burningham. T. C. Griggs. Edward King Mark Beezer. Edward stephens. & S. B. Young and Enjoyed ourselves much in signing & Chatting. took tea at Sister & Bro stonemans and all attended meeting at Whitechapel at night.

Thursday Sep 2nd 1880.
arranging for a meeting and surprise party this Evening at North London favor Prest G H. Taylor this being the last Evening he will be in London. With Bro Taylor I went to sister Godfrey's to tea and then to the Meeting place, and all had assembled and prepared Cake and fruit &c and a large Testimonial recounting the Labors of Bro Taylor and the Travelling Elders brought a beautiful albium and put their photos and the photos of the Branch Presidents in it and presented it with their best wishes. Elder B. S. Young went to Lpool in the forenoon

{089}
Friday sep 3rd 1880.
This being the day for Elder Taylor and the saints to leave London for Liverpool on their Way home we assembled at the Euston station at ½ past 10 and 11' 22 saints started for Zion. With Joy and gladness I met George Williams my brother-in-law in the afternoon and went to Mr Greens Office in Fenchurch St and paid them £2.3.2 as per order of Prest Budge. With G. W. Visited the albert Memorial and returned to the office and wrote in the Evening. Weather hot & Sultry.

Saturday. Sep 4th 1880.
This Morning. Elders Griggs. Bentley. Burning= =ham. Stevens. Willey and I took train for Alexandia Palace to spend the day and considered the day well spent in hearing Professor Holden's lecture on slight of hand, and Esquiterian performances and horse= =manship. singing and performances on the Great organ. also Theater playing Paul Pry, and the finest display of Fruit I have seen in England. . .In the Evening Excellent singing and Band Playing on the Lakes Ill= =uminated by thousands of little lamps of Various Colors and Electric lights saw the Large Balloons inflated and assend with 3 men in car.

{090}
Sund.ay september 5th 1880.
In Company with Elders Griggs and King I held 3 meetings at Lambeth after the General Monthly priesthood meeting

at North London in the Morning Making
4 Meetings and preaching 4 times – 3 in
and 1 out of doors.

    Monday Sept. 6th 1880
at home at the Conference House in Meeting
with the Traveling Elders and in the Evening
with Elder Bentley. Willey. Burningham &
stevens attended Meeting at Old ford
and had a good Meeting.

    Tuesday September 7th 1880.
 Making up conference a/co. and re=
=arranging star List. as a number of the
Saints had Emigrated that had been taking
the stars formerly. Elder Burningham & Stevens
                           started
for Southampton Con. and Willey & King for
                       Deptford & Woolwich.

    Wednesday September 8th 1880
Elder Bentley and I made up stars and sent
them off to Weekly and By. Weekly Subscribers,
and completed Weekly list, Went to the
Meeting at Whitechapel Branch in the
Evening and had a good meeting – nearly
all present bearing testamony to gods Works.

{091}
    Thursday Sep 9th 1880.
Cleaning up office in the Morning, and fixing
up Conference a/cs. and worked at it all
afternoon. Evening attended Meeting at
North London Branch and had a good
time in a testamony Meeting

    Friday Sep 10th 1880
Entering P. E. a/cs on Ledger and writing
correspondance all day

    Saturday Sep 11th 1880
Writing home in forenoon and Making
up a/c's in the afternoon and Evening
Elder Griggs came back from Visiting his
friends in Norwich. I spent the Evening
writing till 9 O'clock when Elder Stephen
Tucker arrived straight from Salt Lake City and
we continued Visiting with him till a late
hour.

    Sunday Sep 12th 1880 .
Elders Griggs, Cornell and I took train
for Greys to Meet with the saints and we
had a pleasant time in Meeting with them
in the afternoon and Evening returning home
at night feeling that the Lord has blessed
us largely in Visiting and talking with
the saints.

{093}
    Monday September 13th 1880
at the Office writing up the accounts and went
to Old Ford and accompanied Sister Eliza Todd
to Wellesden Junction to start her off to Liv=
=erpool and in the Evening Went to Old ford
with Elder Willey to meeting and Preached.

    Tuesday. Sep 14th 1880
Making up Monthly accounts to send to
Liverpool. Elders Willie and Bentley started
for the Brighton District and was left
alone at the Conference house. I labored faithfully
                              to
make up the accounts and get the Books all
straight belonging to the Conference and get to
understand them Correctly.

    Wednesday sep 15th 1880.
Recd star parcel and Sent off Weekly star
to subscribers and worked at Books and
attended usual Meeting at Whitechapel
Branch getting home late.

    Thursday sep 16th 1880.
spent forenoon Reading Scripture, afternoon
writing home, and Evening at. North London Bra=
=nch with the saints.

    Friday sep 17th 1880.
posting a/cs and Visiting with Elder Tucker
and in the afternoon took train at Kings
Cross and got out at Latimer Road and

{093}
went to Visit Elder Garner at Notting Hill
and in Evening went to Visit Elder Balls.
arranging with those Presidents of Branches
about the Meetings at Victoria Park on Sun=
=day Next.

    Saturday sep 18th 1880.
 Writing and Making up a/cs at the
office Elder T. C Griggs arrived from Fav
ersham to do the Conference Business till
I return form Devonshire. Elder Tucker also
at Conference House and had good times

shatting all the time I could spare from books.

    sunday sep 19th 1880
With Elders Griggs and Tucker went to the North London Branch sunday School in the Morning and took train to Victoria Park after Eating dinner at Bro George Cross's. attending a Camp Meeting well attended and presided over ~~by~~ in the afternoon by President Corn= =nell of the North London Branch. He Elders Parsons. T. C. Griggs and I was the speakers. and had a good time, a good spirit prevailing. went home to Bro Hills at Homartown to Tea with Elders Tucker and Garner. and

returned again to the Park and held

{094}
another Meeting under the Presidency of President Garnet of Whitechapel, we had an Excellent Meeting of saints and Strangers. all seeming to feel quite well. Elders Garner, Tucker. T. C. Griggs and I were the speakers. after Meeting took train and arrived at the North Lonton Meeting in time to speak a short time before the Meeting Closed. thus Ended one of the favorable days for preaching that I Very much Enjoyed.

{095}
    Letters Received 1880.
on Dec 4th from Zina Y. Hyde Hyde Park dated Nov 17

"	" "	Mary Jane Roskelley	Smithfd	"	" "
"	6th	Joseph Hall	Ogden	"	" 17
"	13	Rebecca Hillyard	Smithfd	"	" 28
"	"	B. Morris Young	Box Elder	"	" "
"	"	Silvester Lowe	Clarkston	"	" 29
"	20.	Mary Roskelley	Smithfield	"	" 28
"	"	Thos J. Lutz	"		" 28
"	21	Mary Jane Roskelley	"		Dec 3
"	25	Preston L. Morehead	"		" 2
"	27	Joseph Newbold	"		" 5
"	29	Seth Langton	"		" 11
"	"	Geo L. Farrell	"		" 9
"	31	Zina Y. Hyde	"		" 12
"	"	Samuel Roskelley Jr			"
Jan	2nd	Mary Roskelley			"
		James Roskelley			"
Jan	2nd	Book Marker from Rebecca			"
"	"	Aunt Zina Young			14
"	"	Mary Jane & Williams			"
"	"	Bro Welchman			6
"	8	Daughter Rebecca			20th
"	8	Joseph Roskelley			"
		Mary Roskelley			"
"	12	Mary Jane Roskelley			Dec 24

    See Writing Paper
    Jan 15th 1881

{096}
　　　　Letters sent home

Sep	17th	to Zina Y Hyde	from	London
"	"	" M. J. Roskelley	"	"
"	24th	" M. J. Roskelley	"	Devonport
Oct	2nd	" Mary Roskelley	"	London
"	9th	Mary Jane Roskelley	"	London
	14th	Jos Hall Ogden	"	London
	16th	G. L. Farrell		London
	"	Mary Roskelley		London
"	20	Aunt Zina	"	"
"	"	Prest Woodruff	"	"
"	23	" Mary Jane	"	"
"	"	Joseph Hall ogden	"	"
"	29	Mary Roskelley	"	"
"	"	Samuel Roskelley Jnr	"	"
"	"	Rebecca R Hillyard	"	"
"	30th	Zina Y Hyde	"	"
Nov	11	Mary Jane	"	"
"	"	James Roskelley	"	"
"	13	Mary Roskelley	"	"
"	18	Rebecca Hillyard	"	London
"	"	Frank Gunnell	"	"
"	20	William Roskelley	"	London
"	"	Joseph Roskelley	"	"
"	"	Daughter Mary	"	"
"	25	Mary Jane Roskelley	"	"
"	"	Zina Hyde	"	"
Dec	9th	Mary Roskelley	"	"
"	"	G. L. Farrell	"	"
"	18th	Mary Jane Roskelley	"	"
"	25th	Rebecca Hillyard	"	"
		Mary Roskelley	"	"
	"	Wm Brown Salt Lake City	"	
"	30th	Samuel Roskelley Junr	"	"
"	"	Thomas Hillyard	"	"
"	"	William Roskelley	"	"
"	"	Mary Jane Roskelley	"	"
"	"	Sylvester Lowe	"	"
"	"	also Missletoe to Bro Welchman	"	"
1881 Jan 6		Zina Y. Hyde	"	"
		S. Roskelley Junr	"	"
"	8	-----P. T. Moorehead & James Roskelley		
		F. Sharp & Mary Roskelley		

{097}
[blank recto]

{098}

Letters sent Home from Jan ~~15th~~ \15/ 1881.

Dated	Place Written	Who to.
Jan 15	London	Mary Jane Roskelley.
" 22	do	Mary Roskelley
" "	"	Prest W. Woodruff
" 25	"	Grandma Hendricks, Sent her Pat Blessing
" 29	"	Rebecca H. Sent her Pat Blessing
" "	"	Seth Langston
29 "		Mary Jane Roskelley
" "	"	Relief Society
Feby 5	"	/ Mary Roskelley
" "	"	\ Zina Y. Hyde Sent her Pat blessing
" 8	"	Thos Hillyard & Pvte
" "	"	F. Sharp & on Land
" 12	"	T.H Paper 60& 85&
" "	"	Mary Jane Roskelley
" "	"	P. T Morehead
" 17	"	Don Hyde
" 18	"	sister M. A. Hymas.
" 19	"	Mary Roskelley
" "	"	Samuel Roskelley Jnr
" 26	"	Mary Jane Roskelley
" "	"	L. O. Littlefield
" 28	"	T. Hillyard Paper 1^{60}
Mch 3	"	Rebecca Hillyard
" "	"	Bp. W. F. Rigby
" 5	"	Mary Roskelley
" "	"	Geo L. Farrell
" "	"	Jos Hill. D. Weeks & Hansen
" 12	"	Mary Jane Roskelley James R
" "	"	T. Hillyard Paper 60&
" 15	"	Geo H Taylor
" 15	"	James Roskelley Paper & 3. Hankercf
" 18	"	Samuel Roskelley " " do
" "	"	Mary Roskelley Paper " do
" 19	"	Mary Roskelley
" "	"	Joseph Newbold.
" 22	"	Samuel Roskelley
" "	"	William Roskelley
" "	"	Joseph Roskelley
" "	"	Mary Roskelley Jnr
" 25	"	H. a Watson [---] Pat Blessings
" 26	"	Mary Jane Roskelley
" "	"	Prentis T. Morehead
" "	"	Harrison a Thomas
" "	"	Mary Jane Roskelley Papers & Slk Hank
Mch 31	------------------	Mary Roskelley
" "	------------------	Rebecca Hillyard
" "	------------------	Zina D. Young

apl 11 ----------------- mary Jane Roskelley
" 12 ----------------- Thomas Hillyard
" 19 Eastbourne H. a. Thomas
                       Mary Roskelley
                       Samuel Roskelly Jnr
                       ~~William Roskelley~~
                       Joseph Hale

{099}
Letters Rec^d from Jan 8th 1880.

Place Written	Date written	Who From	Date rec^d
Smithfd US.	Jan 10. 1881	Thos Hillyard	Feby 1st 1880
"	" 11 "	H a Watson	" " "
"	" 9 "	Mary Roskelley	" 1 "
"	" 2	Zina Hyde	" 1 "
"	" "	James Roskelley	" 1 "
San Antonio	" 9	John Barker	" 2 "
Smithfield	" 14	Jos Hill	" 2 "
"	" 15	a. P. Walchman	" 2 "
"	" 17	Mary Senr	" 4 "
"	" "	" Jnr	" 4 "
"	" "	Joseph & William "	4 "
"	" 16	F. Sharp	" 4 "
"	" "	Sister Jones	" " "
"	" 20	Mary Jane	" 7 "
"	" 22	H. a Thomas	" 8 "
"	" 24	Jane Moler	" 15 "
"	" "	Geo Barber	" 15 "
"	" 26	G. L. Farrell	" 16
"	" 28	G. L. Farrell	" 16
"	" "	Sylvester Lowe	" 16
"	" 31	Don C Hyde	" 21
"	Feby 5	Mary Roskelley	" 22
"	"	Mary Junr	" "
"	" 12	Bp Rigby	" 27th
"	" "	Sister Williams	" "
"	" "	David Weeks & Jos Hill	" "
"	" 14	W. W. Woodruff	Mch 1st
"	" 16	Samuel Roskelley Jr	" 5
"	" "	William Roskelley	" "
"	" 13	Mary Jane Roskelley	" "
"	" 14	Thomas Hillyard	" 9th
"	" 25	Jos. Newbold	" 14
"	" 25	Mary Roskelley	" 19th
"	" 28	G. L. Farrell	" 22nd
"	Mch 1	Samuel Roskelley	" 22
"	" 5	Preston T. Morehead	" 23rd
Ogden	" 5	Joseph Hall	" 28th

Salt Lake City	" 6	Aunt Zina Young	" 29
Smithfd	" 10	Mary Roskelley (Photos)	" 30th
"	" "	Mary Jane Roskelley (Photos)	" "
"	" 12	adeline Barber	apl 4
Hyde Park	" 12	Don C. Hyde	" "
Smithfd	" "	Mary Jane Roskelley	" "
"	" "	Mary Roskelley (Photo)	apl 6th
"	" 30	Mary Jane --------	" 14th
"	" "	Thomas Hillyard	" "
Logan	apl 1	Samuel Junr	" 16th
Smithfield	" "	James Roskelley	" 17th
"	" "	Mary Junr	" "
"	" "	William	" "

{100}
Letters Sent Home from April 19th 1881

Dated	Place Written	Who to
apl 23rd	London	/ George Barber | Thos. J. Lutz \ John McCarthy
" 26	London	/ Mary Jane Roskelley | Silvest Lowe \ Bro Brown (Ham[---])
" 30	London	/ James Roskelley | William and Joseph Roskelley \ George L Farrell
May 3rd	London	/ Mary Roskelley \ Don C. Hyde
May 10	London	/ Mary Jane Roskelley \ Elizabeth Harris
" 12	"	| Papers to H a Watson | do all the Boys
" 17	London	/ Mary Roskelley | Zina Y Williams \ John Nicholson
" 21	London	Mary Jane Roskelley Preston T. Morehead
June 4	London	| Mary Roskelley | Bp Rigby
" 11	London	-------Mary Jane Roskelley David James
" 18	London	Mary Roskelley Rebecca Hillyard (Papers)

{101}
Letters Recd form home from

Place Written	Date Written	Who from	Date Received
Evanston Wyo	apl 8	W. G. Burton	apl 25
Market Lake I.	" 9	Sylvester Lowe	" 25
Smithfield	" 9	Mary Jane Roskelley	" "
do	" 10	Mary Roskelley	May 2nd
"	" "	Joseph Roskelley	" "
"	" 19	Mary Jane Roskelley	" 7
"	" 24	Mary Roskelley	" 14
"	" 15	Mary Jane	" 5th
"	" 12	Bp Rigby	" 3rd
Salt Lake City	" 14	David James	" 6th
Smithfield	" 24	G L. Farrell	" 11th
"	" 26	Mary Senr \ Mary Junr | Joseph /	" 13th
"	" "	Mary Jane Roskelley	" "
"	Jun 1st	Rebecca Hillyard	" 18th

{102}
Letters Received.   1880

Date		Who from	Place	Date dated
Sep 16th	from	Zina Y. Hyde	Hyde Park dated	Aug 29
" 17	from	Mary Jane Roskelley	Smithf	" "
" "	"	Silveste Lowe	"	" "
" "	"	a.S anderson	"	" "
" 24	"	Thomas Roskelley	"	" 21
" "	"	Mary Roskelley Jur	"	" 21
" "	"	Wife Mary Roskelley	"	" 29
" 27	"	Thomas Hillyard	"	" 30
" "	"	H. J. Petersen	"	Sep 2
" 29	"	L.O. Littlefield	"	" "
" "	"	a. P. Welchman	"	" 6
Oct 2	"	W. T. Vannoy	Bever Kayn "	" 10
" 3	"	Rebecca Hillyard	Smithfd	Sep 14
" 5	"	Bp Rigby	Beaver	" 12
" 9	"	Zina Y Hyde	Hyde Park	" 20
" 18	"	Rebecca Hillyard	Smithfd	" 29
" "	"	F Sharp Mary Jane	"	" 29
" "	"	Zina Y. Hyde	Hyde Park	" 29
" 20	"	Mary Roskelly	Smithfd	Oct 3
" "		Miss Batt	do	" 3
" 26		Thomas Hillyard	do	" 10
" 26	"	Rebecca do	"	" 10
Nov 1		M Jane Roskelley	Smithfd	" 13
" 9		Joseph Hall	Ogden	" 19
" 12th		Rebecca R. Hillyard	Smithfield	25
" "		Geo H. Taylor	"	"

" 15th	"	Thomas Hillyard	"		27
" "	"	Mary Roskelly	"		29
" 18	"	Zina Y. Hyde	Hyde Park	"	31
" 20	"	Mary Jane	Smithfield	Nov	1st
" 22	"	Bp W. F. Rigby	Newton	Oct	5
" 30	"	Mary Roskelly Senr	Smithfd	Nov	12
" "	"	" Junr	"	"	11
"		Jos Roskelley		"	14
Dec 3rd		W. W. Woodruff	Salt Lake City	"	15th

{103}

Letters sent home /Since\ June 30th 1880.

from London to	W.T Vannoy	Beaver	July	2nd
" "	W. D. Hendricks	do	"	"
" "	Mary Jane	Smithfid	"	5
" "	Rebecca & Jun	"	"	5
" "	Brother John R	Devonport	"	8th
" "	Mary Roskelley	Smithfield	"	21st
" "	S Roskelley Jur	Smithfield	"	21st
" "	Mary Jane Roskelley	"		23rd
" "	G L. Farrell	Logan	—	24th
" "	Geo Barber	"	—	24th
" "	Drusilla Hendricks	Richmond	"	24th
" "	Prest Woodruff	Salt Lake City	"	31st
" "	Aunt Zina Young	Salt Lake City	"	31
" "	Mary Roskelley	Smithfield	Aug	5th
" "	Thomas Roskelley	"	"	"
" "	Rebecca H(General)	"	"	"
" "	George Barber "	"	"	7th
" "	a P. Welchman "	"	"	9th
" "	Mary Jane Roskelley	"	"	12th
" "	Joseph Roskelley	Smithfield	"	12th
" "	William Roskelley	"	"	12th
" "	Zina Hyde "	"	"`	12th
" "	Mary Jane Roskelley	"	"	19th
" "	Francis Sharp "	"	"	19th
" "	Bp Rigby Beaver Kanyon		"	19th
" "	Bp Rigby "	"	"	24
" "	Wm T VanNoy	"	"	24
" "	Mary Roskelley	Smithfield	"	28
" "	Zina Hyde	Hyde Park	"	31
" "	Rebecca Hillyard	Smithfield	"	"
" "	Mary Jane	"	Sep	4
" "	James Roskelley		"	4
" "	Mary Roskelley		"	9
" "	Rebecca Hillyard ------------			9
" "	P.T. Morehead ------------			11
" "	W. T Vannoy	Beaver	-----	11
" "	H. a. Watson	Beaver	-----	10

{104}

Letters Received 1880.   from June 30

Date		From	Place	Date sent
July 2nd	from	Rebecca Hillyard	Smithfield	June 15
"	"	P. T Morehead	"	" 12
"	"	G. L. Farrell	Logan	" 15
" 4	"	Zina Hyde	Hyde Park	" 16
" 8	"	Aunt Zina Young	Salt Lake City	" 20
" "	"	A. Geo Barber Junr	[---]	July 6th
" "	"	Francis Sharp	Smithfield	June 23rd
" 14	"	Mary Jane	Smithfield	" 22nd
" 16	"	Mary	Smithfield	" 26th
" "	"	James	Smithfield	" "
" 17	"	G. L. Farrell	Smithfield	" 29th
" "	"	Willie Farrell	Logan	" "
" "	"	Daughter Rebecca	Smithfield	" 28th
" "	"	Brother John	Devonport	July 16th
" 20th	"	Zina Hyde	Hyde Park	" 5
" 24th	"	Thomas Hillyard	Smithfield	" 6
" "	"	Rebecca R Hillyard	Smithfield	" 6
" 27th		Mary Jane Roskelley	Smithfield	" 10
Aug 2nd	from	G. L. Farrell	Smithfield	" 12
"		son Willey	Smithfield	" 15
" "	"	daughter Rebecca	Smithfield	" 15
" 2nd	"	George Barber	Logan	" 16
" 10	"	Zina D. Hyde	Hyde Park	" 26
" 13	"	Mary Roskelley	Smithfield	" 28
" "	"	Joseph "	"	" 28
" "	"	Thomas "	"	" 28
" "	"	Rebecca Hillyard	"	" 27
" "	"	Thomas Hillyard	"	" 15
" "	"	Samuel Roskelley	"	" 11
" 19	"	Zina Y. Hyde	Hyde Park	Aug 2nd
" 23	"	Zina Y. Hyde	"	" 7th
" "	"	Rebecca Hillyard	Smithfield	6th
		Apostle W Woodruff	Salt Lake city	Aug 11th
" "	"	James Roskelley		Aug 8th
Sep 6		Francis Sharp	------------	" 18th
" "	"	Geo L. Farell	------------	" 18th
" "		John McCarthy	------------	" 18

{105}

Letters sent 1880

from [---] apl 28 to Rebecca & family to Queenstown
From Lpool Apl 30th   to   "   Rebecca & family
  "   ~~Lpool May~~ 2nd   "   G. Barber Jur
  "   London " 4th   "   Rebecca & family
  "   [---] May 5th   "   A.r Wright thro W. C Stains.
  "   Southampton   10   "   Sister Jane   Devonport.
  "   Southampton   12   "   Bro Richard   Eastbourne

"	"	12	"	Nephew S. R Williams London
"	Burnham May	18	"	Prest Woodruff Salt Lake City
"	Southampton	22	"	Mary Jane Smithfield
"	"	"	Daughter Rebecca	"
"	London May	29	"	Smithfield
"	June 1st		Mary Jane Smithfield	
"	Eastbourne		3rd	Nephew S. R. Williams London
	Eastbourne		4th	G. L. Farrell Logan
"	"	5th	sons samuel & James Smithfd	
"	"	5th	Thomas Maycock derby	
"	Brighton		7th	Prest G H Taylor London
"	"	"	Jas Burningham London	
"	"	"	Thos X Smith Nottingham	
"	"	"	a. G Barber Norwich	
"	"	"	Richard Roskelley Eastbourne	
"	Ashburnham	14	Zina " Smithfield	
			Rebecca " "	
			H. a. Watters Cub Hill	
"	Ashburnham	18	Mary Smithfield	
	"	9	Mary Jane "	
"	Uckfield	21	Bp Rigby Newton	
"	Clapper	20	Bro G[---] Findon	
	Uckfield	21	Prest G. H Taylor London	
	Eastbourne	26	" Southampton	
	"	"	T X Smith Nottingham	
	"	"	J. C. Bentley Brighton	
	"	"	John Donnaldson Stockton[---]	
	"	28	/ Mary \	
			| Thos Hillyard | Smithfield	
			\T. Lowe /	

{106}

Letters Recd. 1880

May	4th	from	Thos Hillyard	Smithfield	dated apl [---]
"	"	"	son Samuel	"	" 2
"	"	"	daughter Zina	"	" "
"	"	"	son James	"	" "
"	8	"	Geo Barber Junr Sprowston Norwich	" " 7	
"	7	"	seth a Langton	Sontag Va.	Apl 6th 1880
"	13	"	Francis Sharp	Smithfield	Apl 25th
"	14	"	Sister Jane	Devonport	May 12
"	22	"	Mary Jane	Smithfield	Apl 29
"	"	"	Mary	"	" "
	"	"	Rebecca Hillyard	"	" "
"	26	"	Zina R. Hyde	"	May 4th
"	29	"	F. Sharp	"	" 11
"	"	"	James & Thomas	"	" 9th
"	30	"	Geo Y Smith	"	" 12 "
"	"	"	Geo Barber	"	" 12th

"	30	"	Thomas Maycock	Birmingham	"	29th
June	~~30~~1	"	Geo L Farrell	Logan	May	12th
"	4	"	Bp Rigby	Newton	"	14th
"	4	"	Thos & Rebecca Hillyard	Smithfd	"	17
"	"	"	Bro F. Sharp	"		16
	"	---	H. a Watson.	"		14
"	6		Thomas X Smith	Nottingham	June	4
"	"	"	a. G. Barber	Norwich	"	4
"	"	"	S. R. Williams	London	"	5th
"	8		daughter Zina	Hyde Park	May	19th
"	13		daughter Rebecca	Smithfield	"	24th
	13		wife Mary Jane.	"	"	22nd
"	15		Sylvester Lowe.	"	"	14 & 28th
"	"		James Burningham	Southampton	June	13th
"	"		Richard Roskelley	Eastbourne	"	12th
"	"		Edward Stevens	Southampton		"
"	23		a. P. Welshman	Smithfield	May	12
"	24		G. H. Taylor	London	June	16
"	"		T. X. Smith	Nottingham	"	"
"	"		John Donaldsen	Stocktown.[---]	"	17.
"	28	"	T. Hillyard and \ Rebecca Hillyard/	Smithfield	"	8th
"	"		J. C Bentley	Brighton	"	28th
"	30		W. Woodruff	Salt Lake City		24th
	"		Mary Jane	Smithfield		10
	"		John Barker	Newton	"	12

{107}
    Photos Sent 1880   Mis photo
Bp Rigby   Aug 24th sent
Mary   Fath. Roberts Oct 2nd
M. Jane   Sep 4th   R T Morehead " 9th
Rebecca " 9th T C Griggs   " 9th
Zina   " 15   Sister Cross
Jos Hall Oct 14   Bro Hill
                       Bro Burningham
                       John Nicholson
                       Frank Gunnell.

     Paper & sent
Oct 9 Penny Illustrated   Joseph
"   "   "   Thomas
" 12 Graphic James
                     and 2 pocket Kerchiefs to Catherine
"   "   Devonport Independent   Zina Hyde
               also Views of Devonport
"   "   WJSansfor's Papers from australia
               and View of Devonport to Rebecca
" 18   Judy & 1 HKchf to   Mary Jr

	"		Pictoral paper " Willie
	"	19	Graphic & Hkchfs Sam¹ Jr.
	Nov 11		Daily to --------- Mary

{108}
[*loose paper, inserted*]
Names and Date of Birth
of Samuel Roskelley and
<u>Mary Roberts's Children</u>

Names	Day	Month	Year	Remarks
Ann Jane		Dec	1866	Died same day
Thomas	27	Dec	1867	
Mary	10	March	1870	
Catherine	31	Oct	1872	
Hannah	13	Jan	1876	
Richard	4	May	1880	

{109}
[*loose paper, inserted*]
Ginger Beer
3 Pounds of Sugar
1/4 Pound of old ginger
1 Lemon
1/4 Pound of Sherbert
1/4 oz Tartaric acid
4 Gallons of water. Well bruise the ginger
put into the water cold and boil for 10 minutes
pour it on the sugar lemon sherbert & acid boiling
hot=.

[*end of journal 3; end of transcript*]

Journal [4]

20 September 1880 – 22 April 1881

{front paste-down}
Samuel Roskelley
10 Dorset St Bride St
Liverpool Road
Islington, London, N
September 18th
1880

{free endleaf recto/verso}
[missing]

{page 1}*
      Monday Sep 20th 1880
At 1/2 past 7 started from Conference
House in Company with Elder T C
Griggs and called at S R Williams's
45 Offord St and thence to Kings
Cross R R Station by Under Ground R.R.
To Perade St Station and thence to the
Paddington Station on the Great Western
RR taking a ticket (Returns) for
Plymouth and having the Company.
Samuel Roskelly Williams and Wallace
George Williams (sons of my Sister Jane) arr
=iving at Devonport at 4-15 P.M. and met
at the Station by my Brother John Joseph and
also Brother in law George Williams who had
got leave of abstance from their Employment

once and meet us and getting on a
buss for Devonport arrived there about
5 P.M. in passing thru the town of
Plymouth. Stonehouse and Devonport
Recognized many places and things I
Knew in the days of my youth and

{2}
alighting from the Buss proceeded to the
House of my Sister Jane No 2 Dock
Wall St and did Justice to a hearty
dinner prepared by My sister in a
good old fashioned manner. After
a while Brother John and his Wife Charlotte
Pinkham came in and spent The
Evening and I accepted the Kind in=
vitation of My Brother to sleep at
his house and make it my partial
home while at Devonport and accom
=panied them home and staid all
night, being very comfortable.
      Tuesday Sep 21st 1880.
With Samuel R Williams Wallace
& Thomas William (my sisters child)
I visited H.M Gun Wharf and
went through the shops, armory with some
45 thousand small arms of the
Martini-Henri Pattern and also saw
cannon & Mortars for ship and

Samuel Roskelley papers, MS 65, Utah State Univ. Special Collections. This version is a line-by-line transcription of the manuscript. Page numbers were added to recto (right hand) pages of the volume to simplify matching the transcription to the document. They are given in this transcription between braces. The names and records noted as written in pencil on p.{86}–{91}, {92}–{103} are the notes cited on p.{15}.

{3}
land forces of small and large sizes
the object being 25 ton armstrong
battery guns and the smallest being
Quarter deck brass 4 Pounder guns
and the ammunition to suit it. Also
saw a Gatling gun which being
quite a new thing to me I took quite
an interest in, and Enjoyed its sight
also cranes worked by Steam-power
for hoisting light and heavy weight
up to 30 tons by steam and on
the whole I Enjoyed my Visit. in the
afternoon I accompanied my Sister
to Princess Square Plymouth, to see
an own cousin of mine, a son of
my Mother's sister named Henry
Croft and returned to Devonport
and Spent Evening with friends. Going
to Stoke and sleeping as usual at
my Brother John's home remaining talk;
to John & Charlotte till nearly 1 Oclock
in the morning.

{4}
   Wednesday Sep 22th 1880
This day Brother John Roskelley obt-
-ained a pass from the office. and I &
my sisters Boys Met at the Dock Yard
Gates and by influence of my Brothers
friends in the Various departments we
were permitted to Visit the Ropery
and seeing its construction in detail
from preparing the hemp, tarring it
and manufacturing it into cable Ropes
we then went into the Back building
sheds seeing all Kinds of boats from
steam launches to Canvas boats
including life boats also saw the
model of the [blank] gun and how
it was placed on ship board to
protect the ships from torpedo
boats-- we then proceeded to the Iron
screw steamer Implacable, having
Iron sides about 20 inches thick
and carrying 17 Large armstrong

{5}
18 ton guns carrying a solid conical
chilled pointed shot of 100 pounds Each
propeled by 50^{lbs} powder at Each
charge. we also visited the Various
parts of the monster Ship carrying
800 men as a crew. and all the
implements of modern warfare.
Engine for almost Everything to save
manual labor. And immense ma=
=chinery for the driving of her
immense Screw Propeller. the
Torpedo (Fish) and the gearing
was a matter of no little interest
to me as it was the first I
had seen and Each torpedo is
said to Cost $2,500^{00}. We next
Visited the Galvanizing Works
and saw Iron for Ship use
being galvanized in detail. We
next went thro the celebrated tun=
=nel connecting the Gun wharf and
Keyham dock yard with the

{6}
Devonport Dock Yard and Visited
the Ships on the immense dry
docks & floating docks the cas=
=soons for retaining water in the
docks and floating Iron docks
and lifts for docking and raising
ships of all sizes to repair
their bottoms. And all the nes
=sesay apperations to lift 100 ton
guns in and out such ships
we Visited the immense works
for the repairs of the steam
Engines and screw propellers of
these monsters of the sea
and saw Marine Engine Cilyn
ders that I could walk through
with stove pipe hat on upright
being repaired, and all Kinds of
macheniry and modern improvements
truly to represent the great Nation
we are now in. I went back
to Sister Janes to dinner and did

{7}
Justice to the meal and in the Evening
sat and gave John, Jane & her
Husband an idea of our land Matters
in our territory.

Thursday September 23rd 1880
Remained at John's House till 10 O'
clock. Then walked over the government
ramparts and hights overlooking the
town and went to the Ragland Barr=
=acks to see the Scots Fusileers Ex=
=ercise and from there to devonport to
my Sisters Residence and thence in the
afternoon in Company with my Brother
John, and Nephews Samuel; Emma, Wallace
and Thomas to Mount EdgeComb park
Visiting by the way the Barn Pool where
I was baptized into the Church also
the Battery at Picklcome, an immense
Fortress and thence around on the hights
of Maker to the Earl of Mount Edge
Come's house and thence home again for
the Evening and to Brother Johns to sleep.

{8}
Friday Sep 24th 1880.
Started in the morning visiting the
town and some objects of interest
near by and in the afternoon Bro
John and I went to Stonehouse and
Visited the Marine Barracks. The
Mill Bay Docks and Merchant ship-
-ping. and Plymouth Hole, and
Barbican, thence to the ~~Borsen~~ /Stadden\
Hights and got a soldier to pilot
us around the Borsand Fort and the
immense fortification and thence
we went to Staddon Fort with
its heavy 25 ton guns and the
Improved Mon/creith carriage & platform\ ~~gun~~
fixed so men
can load behind a fortification and
fire the gun by reflectors and they
be protected by the walls and Em=
=bankment of concrete from 5 to
8 ft thick covered with Earth to
great depty. and all the subtranius
passages to other citadile and

{9}
forts, this was a day well spent.
so far as sight seeing was concer-
-Ened.
Saturday Sep 25th 1880
Bro John & I took train to St. German
to find Aunt Alice Buttars but on
arriving there could not see her
as she had gone to Visit her
Daughter Ann at another town
but found Alice Ough a grand
daughter of this Aunt Alice
Butters. Visited St Germans ~~paris~~
parish Church yard and saw the
graves of Grandfather Joseph & Grand
mother Mary Roskelley, it being placed
on his grave stone <u>Skellen</u> by a
mistake. and also Great Uncle
William and Aunt Mary (his wife)
Roskelley, (he the Waterloo Soldier) also
William Butters the Husband of our
Aunt Alice Butters our fathers sister
and in the afternoon Visited the

{10}
Justly celebrated Saltash Bridge
and in the Evening I visited the
Plymouth hoe and the Drakes
Island and its immense fortifi
=cation and I was surprised to
see the great Changes in the fortification
of the Town and its surroundings and
forts Erected by the Government.
returned to Devonport to Sister Janes
house and in the Evening my Brother
Richard arrived from Eastborne
and we spent a very Plesent time
together till bed times – sleeping
at Brother John's house.
Sunday Sep 26 1880
In forenoon with Bro Richard
and Brother-in law Geo Williams
and his son Samuel R. I went to
Hope Chapel and heard Mr John
Haddie preach—from the Text
"Continue in prayer" which remark

{11}
were to me a parcel of nonsense.
And we 3 Brothers and John's Wife
Charlott Pinkham all ate dinner
at my Sister's house together and
had a very comfortable time together
thro the afternoon. In the Evening I
with Bro Richard John & George
Williams and his son Thomas went to

the Latter day Saints Meeting at
Haydens Room. Fore Street Devonport
and the Saints rejoiced to see me
as I being an old member of
this Branch. A Brother Charles Wade
48 Pembroke St. Devonport is the new
President of the Branch and a Brother
from Ogden Utah also as a travelling
Elder and Visiting here now. he preach
=Ed about 20 Minutes and I occupied
about an hour bearing testimony to
the fact that God had revealed his
gospel tho Jos Smith in these latter
days. as usual my Brothers attacked

{12}
me regarding my faith and I defended
my views.
      Monday Sep 27th 1880.
With My Brothers Richard. and John
and his Wife Charlotte also Samuel R.
Emma. Geo Wallace. and Thomas Williams
we hired a boat and going to the
place of my first Baptism into
the Church of J.C. of Latter-day Saints
=viz Barn Pool we went to the
Break Water. I climbed up to the
cape in the East End and to the
light in the Lighthouse on the
West End and saw the beautiful
light and its workings and life
saving aparatus, sailed under the
British War Ship Cleopatra and
out side the Breakwater
      Tuesday Sep 28th 1880.
Fixed in the morning at Johns
house and Richard, John, & Wife

{13}
Charlotte, Sister Jane, and Samuel & niece
Ball, Wallace and Thomas. also a
Mr. Trescott, (sister Jane's daughter
Anne's Young Man) and got a Boat
under Richmond Walk and went to
Barn pool and had an Enjoyable
time in Cooking dinner and Eating
the same in pick-nick fashion
and thence proceeded to the Coast
on the other side of the sound under
Woody hedge and building a fire

prepared tea and had a most Ex=
=cellent time in partaking a meal
on the sands. but our Joy was
seemingly come to an End for that
day, as a fog came over both sea
and land. So dense that we could
not see the length of the boat
ahead of us and pushing off
from the shore we proceeded
as we supposed to plymouth but
must have turned quite around

{14}
and found ourselves against a bouy
to which we considered it safest
to moor ourselves till the fog lif=
=ted-- in about 1/2 an hour we
heard an anchor of a vessel drop
and Voices a short distance from
us, and on Enquiry found it to
be a fishing Vessel of large size
and being invited by the captain
we proceeded in the direction of
the Voice as the Captain repeated
=ly called to us to guide us
by the sound of his Voice. on
arrival at his boat we found
it a large size boat and got
aboard of it and got some food
and were quite comfortable in the
Cabin. The fog lifted and we on
board the fishing boat landed
at the Barbican pier. Plymouth
about 1 O'Clock A.M. Getting
home some time after 2 O Clock

{15}
A. M on
      Wednesday Sep 29th 1880.
feeling thankful for the preservation
of our lives up to this present
      We started with Richard,
Samuel W. & Wallace W and I
in the Morning to plymouth
and got out boat and brought
it home to its owner and thence
proceeded to Minheniot to Visit
our own Aunt Alice (My fathers
only surviving sister) now living
with her daughter and son-in-

=law George and Ann Butters Ough
and their family– from whom I
received a good many items of
the history of her father. (My Grandfather)
of which I took notes. We all ate
tea together – A sumptious repast -
in commemoration of the Event of so
many of the family being together and
returned to Devonport late in the

{16}
Evening, John and Charlotte and I
sat for hours talking before I was
to bed, about our feelings one tow=
=ard the other and Expressing Joh
at this Eventful Meeting. I gave
John a nice copy of the Book
of Mormon, well bound and he
gave me a fine picture of the
Harbor's of Plymouth & Devonport
and the Towns of Devonport, Stone=
=house and Plymouth also a very
nice Walking Cane.

Thursday Sep 30th.
Richard and I took Early break
=fast and bidding John and Charlott
good Bye went to Devonport and
saw Sister Jane. Went to Mr Worley's
/a\ Shoemaker in Clowance Street.
Devonport to see about some bus=
=iness about the Hall family at
Ogden, Utah. Also called upon

{17}
Bro Wade 48 Pembrooke St, the Pres
of the Devonport Branch, and with
others of the Saints spent a very
agreeable time for a couple of
hours and returned to My sister Janes
and found a Brother W. H. Sheppard
from Beaver, Utah waiting my
arrival. I ate dinner with sister
Jane and bidding all good bye
starting for London my field of
Labor. Elder Sheppard proffering
to accompany me to Plymouth
to see me off, on the Way Bro
Sheppard introduced a matter of
his being healed of his feet

sweating and his body & feet stin
King, attributing it to his having
found out (as I supposed) some
new process of washing them, but
he refuses to tell me the secret
as he called it, and I am quite
astonished to hear him say that

{18}
he intended to Sail for New Orleans
U.S. America in About 2 weeks. I
naturally asked him if he was relea
=sed to return home- he answered he would
write to Prest Budge and ask for his release
as he felt his family affairs needed him at
home. A short time afterward he said
he did not Expect to get home to Ogden
till about a year from next May.
I saw there was something wrong
with him but the Train starting I left
him with a feeling that I did not
feel satisfied with his labors. I
left Plymouth at 3-15 P.M and arrived
at Paddington. London at 10-49 P.M
and taking London Underground R. R.
arrived at Kings Cross at 11-5 and
was met there by Elder T. C. Griggs
of the North London Branch who bid
me Welcome, and I was glad to see
them again

{19}
Friday Oct 1st 1880.
the accumulation of matters of
Business and letter requiring answers
took me all day to straighten out
ready to be attended to, in the
Evening I went to Waterloo Station
in Company of Elder T. C. Griggs and
Met My nephew Wallace Williams
who arrived from Devonport.
Oct 2nd 1880 Sautrday,
Writing most of the day, answering corr=
=espondents and in Evening went to
Notting hill to see Prests Ball of the
Lambeth Branch and Prest Garner of the
Whitechapel Branch on Emigration
Business. on Returning to the office
I found Elder W. W. Willey had arrived
from Sussex and we were also favored

with the Company of Elders Heber J. Romney
Charles F. Wilcox and E. H. LeCheminant
straight from Salt Lake City and appointed

{20}
to labor in this Conference and we
had an Excellent visit till Early morn
=ing with them – glad to hear from Zion

Sunday Oct 3rd 1880.
This /is\ our Monthly Priesthood Meeting to-
=day at 42 Penton St Pentonville and
a glorious good meeting we had, 6
Elders from Utah, and a house most
full of other Bretheren of all grades
of Priesthood.--arranged for a genl
Conference of the London Conference on
Sunday Oct 31st and a great number
of other items of interest. I devided
the Elders around to the Various Branch
in London for the day-- I with Elder
Wilcox attended the meetings at
North London Branch, and in the af=
=ternoon I attended the Baptism of
B. A Seamans and afterward confir=
-med him a member of the Church.

{21}
Monday Oct 4th 1880.
In the Office all day talking to the
new comers. giving advice and my
Experience to them. about clothing, tra=
=cts. & tracting &c &c. in the Evening
Elders Willey, Wilcox and I attended
meeting at Old Ford, returning about
11 P.M.
Tuesday Oct 5th 1880.
Again taking opportunity of talking
to the Elders in the morning, and spent
the Afternoon Writing and posting my
Conference books, Elders Willey &
Wilcox started for the Beds & Books
district and Elder Griggs and I went
to Deptford and held Meeting at the
house of Elder Josiah Reed, Elder G.
and I talked to the Saints Sister An=
=geline Cross came to the office. in the
afternoon with Elder Le Cheminant
and brought a tart for us of her
own making.

{22}
Wednesday Oct 6th 1880.
Fixing up Conference accounts in the
Morning. Prest Cornell of North London
Branch and Elder Cotterel came in
and Visited most of the afternoon on
Emigration Business, Elder G. and I
went to Bro Stonemans to tea and
thence to Whitechapel Branch
to Meeting. I talked to the saints.

Thursday Oct 7th 1880.
I wrote at the office while Elder G
=riggs went to London Bg Station with
Elder H. J. Romney starting him for
Sussex to meet Elder Jos Bentley
to labor with him. In the afternoon
I went to Waterlooe Station with
Elder Le Chimant to start him
for Southampton on his way to the
Islands of Jersey & Gurney to labor
in that District of Country. I went
to North London Branch to the

{23}
meeting and had a good meeting.
Friday Oct 8th 1880.
Fasted. I wrote till afternoon
and in the afternoon I went to
Woolwich. Held meeting at the hose
of Bro Blackmore and had a good
Meeting-- but few Present, division
seems to have split them asunder,
went to the house of Bro Jackson and
administered to their sick child.
and then returned to London, Elders
King & tucker returned from Kent
Saturday Oct 9th 1880.
Visited with Elders King & Griggs &
Tucker all forenoon. relating my
Experience &c and afternoon I
worked posting up books, till bed
time.
Sunday Oct 10th 1880.
Elder Griggs & I went to Lambeth
to the Spurgeon Tabernacle and
heard Mr Spurgeon discourse on

{24}
the Text found 5th Chapter and 1st

part of the 2nd Verse- Mr Spurgeon is
a gifted man in flow of Language
and conception of Ideas, and is fond
of Comparisons, in his sermon made
several remarks to the indolent
Clergymen and tho' plain in his man=
=ner yet very attractive in his ad=
=dress which makes him notorious.
the Singing is Congregational- no
Music instruments. the preacher
giving out Each verse as the Con-
-gregation sing them. ate dinner at
a coffee House, and went to the
Lambeth meeting, Elder Griggs &
I talked to an appreciative aud=
=ience, we then administered to
a sick sister and made the
acquaintance of a Bro & Sister Jack-
=son of Monmouth now here on a
Visit. and went to the House of Bro
and Sister [Brown/Bronson] and administered

{25}
to their daughter Emma who is
sick with a fever- took tea there
and proceeded to North London Branch
and found on Arrival /a\ Bro Hill from
Whitechapel preaching and bearing
his testimony before Saints and Many
strangers. He being going to Zion on
the next ship Oct 23rd. I followed
with testamony, the meeting being
one of Interest to all present.
Administered to a Brother and
Sister after Meeting for the recovery
of their health.
        Monday Oct 11th 1880
At office all forenoon writing up
Journal and letters to Bretheren.
several Bretheren called to see us on
Emigration Business. in the Evening
I went to Old Ford to meeting as usual
and met Elder James Burningham from
the Southampton Conference. had a
good meeting. I preached. 11 Persons

{26}
present. I confirmed a man named
William Hale who had been re=
=baptized last Evening by Elder King

on the Isle of Dogg. got home late.
Bro Stoneman gave me 15 pounds on his E a/c.
        Tuesday Oct 12th 1880.
Six month from home this morning.
In the morning attending to the bus=
=iness of Monthly reports &c Elder
J. Burningham came in to pay us a
Visit and he and I went to Notting
hill to See Prests Garner & ball
on matters about the coming Confer=
=ence meeting. Printing Bills &c
        Wednesday Oct 13th 1880.
finished up our ~~quarterly~~ /monthly\ report
and sent it to Liverpool with 30
pounds sterling. and with Elder
T. C. Griggs went to take tea with
Bro & Sister Stoneman and thence
to Whitechapel Branch Meeting

{27}
Elder Griggs and I preached and
I staid to singing meeting.
        Thursday October 14th 1880
Writing, answering correspondence
with Elders &c and Elder T. C.
Griggs and I attended meeting
of North London Branch. in the
Evening after going to Bro Stonem=
=ans to arrange with him to take 2 of
Bro Gamblin's children to Utah. I
spoke at the meeting on the
celestial law of god. reading from
the Book of Doctrine and Covenants
        Friday Oct 15th 1880.
as usual spent most of the day
in the office writing and booking
a/cs &c. in the afternoon late Bro
Griggs and I went to Caledonia Mar=
=ket and while there I purchased
Cassels. pictorial Bible. at a

{28}
Very low price 5 shillings—about 30
shillings below Cost. I prize it
very much. and in the Evening I
went to Homerton to Visit Bro J
Hill's family but did not find
him at home.
        Saturday Oct 16th 1880.
Cleaned up our hose, with

Elder T. C. Griggs and Elder C. E
Brain came in from Bristol
Conference and We visited a
good long time. Wrote a letters
to Elder G. L. Farrell and Wife
Mary and in Evening walked to
Aryel seeing signs on the Holl=
=oway Road returning on the Liv=
=erpool Road.
      Sunday Oct 17 180.
Elder T. C. Griggs and I went to
St Pauls Cathedral at 1/2 past
10 O Clock to attend the morning ser=

{29}
=vices of Pomp and show and outward
form of an Empty carcase. Everything
in this Magnificent building
was superb and Grand.. Organ. Priests, sing=
=ing by Boys and men, with beautiful
Voices. the chanting was Excellent.
I sat under the great dome in
a chair looking with amaizement
at the ponderous building and
the magnificent workmanship upon
it. A priest read the prayers in
a low monotone, the Choir chanted
the response another priest read the
Lessons Viz Dan 3rd Chapter also
2 Chap of 1st Epis to Thessalonians
and another Priest read a sermon
from the Text Mathew. 18 Chap 14 Vers
during the services about 1/2 past 11
A.M. a London fog came over the city
and so Enveloped the Cathedral that
we could scarcely see Each other
in the Building it was so dark, and

{30}
the gas was lit so we saw the
interior of the Building by gass
light at Mid-day as well as
daylight but the form and pomp
is surprising, we went to Sister
Farises at Whitechapel to get Din-
-ner and thence to the Whitechapel
Meeting- Elder Griggs and I occupied
the time in speaking and he went
to North London Branch to Evening
meeting. I remained at Whitechap=

=el and held our door services
and used part of the time with
Elder Clark the rest also met
with opposition in an old gray
headed man saying he was
Daniel the Prophet. we maintained
our ground and held our meeting
and retired to the meeting hall
in good time to hold our Evening
services at 1/2 past 6. Elder
Hooton and I occupied the time

{31}
I took up 70 minutes.
      Monday Oct 18th 1880.
Good news from home, 4 letters
from Kind friends that remember
their pa. Wrote letters to corres=
=pondents and posted Journal
till Evening. Elder T. C. Griggs filled
my appointment at Old Ford and
/I went to Clappam Common with Prest\
~~I wrote a letter to Prest Woodruff~~
/Ball of Lambeth to baptize 2. a young man and a
                      young\
~~at Salt Lake City~~. woman
      Tuesday Oct 19th 1880.
Elder J. T Griggs /and I\ were in the
office all day arranging our Em=
=igration matters and answering
correspondence with the Elders &c
till Evening Elder Griggs went to Dept
=ford to hold meeting and I wrote a
letter to Prest W. Woodruff and aunt
Zina.

{32}
      Wednesday Ot 20th 1880.
In the Office writing &c till after=
=noon and then went to Bro Stonemans
to assist him to Pack up his traps and
thence to Whitechapel to meeting and
had a good meeting. I spoke part of the
time, the Bretheren going to Zion occupied
the balance. Elder E. E. Brain occupied
the balance of the time after Visiting
part of the day with us at the Office
      Thursday Oct 21st 1880.
Prest Budge sent me word to get
one Person to go by P. E. Fund form

this Conference /by tomorrows train\ and after visiting
some of the Saints, and Walking and
riding till I was tired I got
Bro Wm Brown of Lambeth to prom=
=ise he would accept the offer.
and after getting back to the office
I wrote till Evening- Bro Wilkes &
Son James came in from Portsmouth

{33}
and staid all night. Went to
North London meeting and afterward
went to Waterloo Bridge R. R. Station to
Meet Bro Gambling and 2 Children from
Winchester. and returned home Very
tired.
      Friday Oct 22nd 1880.
I was stirring early in the morning
and sent Elder Griggs to the R. R.
Station at Liverpool Street to meet
Sister & Brother Wager and others at
and Early hour, and a company
of 40 Saints left Euston Station
for Zion all feeling well to thus
have the privelage to go. I went
to Wellsden Junction with them
and returned in the afternoon
to the Conf House and wrote,
then went to Sister Cross's to spend
the Evening with Elder Griggs, sister
Cross getting Supper for us.

{34}
Fasted to day before the Lord, asking
the Lord to restore to health my
son Thomas who I learned by letter was
sick. I wrote up my Journal and
at 5-12 I started from Ludgate
Hill Station for Faversham, arriving
at Faversham at 7-35 P.M. Met at
the R. R. Station by Elders King and
Tucker who took me to the House of
Bro & Sister Baker and to my surprize
the most of the Bretheren and
Sisters of Faversham were here gath
=ered here [erased] to bid me welcome and
sit down to a well spread table
filled with Lifes Comforts. After
partaking sumptiously they asked

me to talk about the Duties of Rel=
=ief Societies which I did, showing
that their duties were not only to assist
the Temporally poor but also the
spiritually Poor- Talking also about

{35}
the benefits of associating themselves
together to mutually improve each other in
good language. Cultivating good thoughts
and Ideas and impressing others with true
womanly dignity and spirit to do and
accomplish good results for the benefit of
mankind. As a late hour we dism=
=issed our meeting. I staying at Bro
Millgates over night
      Sunday Oct 24th 1880
Held a Priesthood Meeting at 1/2 past
10 A.M. And recd reports from Traveling
District Elders and Branch President and
gave such instruction as was prompted
to my mind by the spirit of God.
Held Sacrament Meeting at 1/2 past
2 Oclock, and Evening meeting at
1/2 past 6 at which I occupied most
of the time and blessed with a goodly
portion of Gods spirit I preached
the Gospel, and what to do to be saved.
to attentive Congregations. all feeling
and Expressing themselves pleased at
the End of the days services, and test=
=ifying to the goodness of God and his
manifestations to us that day.
      Monday Oct 25th 1880
with Elders King and Tucker met at
Bro Milgates house to organize a

{36}
relief Society. the sisters present chose
Sister Ann Cornford as President
and sister Ellen Stringer and Sister /Mary\
Millgate Councillors also Sister
Harriett Steadman Secretary and Sister
Jane Baker Treasurer. assisted by
the Elders mentioned I set these good
Sisters apart and going to bro Stevens
to Dinner, and then to Stallisfield to
Bro & Sister Cliffords. 10 miles Walk and
took tea. Good Bread & Butter of Sister
Cliffords own make. And then Walked

to Wood Side Green 4 miles and held
Meeting and Organized A Branch of the
Church with Elder Willis Simons as
President, William Steadman 1st Councillor
Harry Hampshire to be ordained an Elder and
2nd Councellor John Neeves Secretary.
Stephen Walker to be ordained a Teacher
Alfred Steadman to be ordained a Teacher
John Skeer to be ordained a Deacon
Charles Loftus Neaves to be ordained a Deacon
I ordained ~~William Steadman~~ /Harry Hampshire\
 an Elder
and ~~Stephen Walker~~ /Alfred Steadman\ a Teacher
 and
Charles Loftus Neeves A Deacon and set
apart Jas Neeves as superintendent
of sabbath schools and sister Neeves
his Wife as a teacher and this organized
as sunday school. And all this was
done after partaking the hospitality of
of the good saints of this branch who
had Kindly provided a sumptuous tea

{37}
at the house Bro & Sister Hampshire.
On our arrival. And all had met, as
one family. I got to bed at Bro Neives
in the Small hours in the morning
with Elders Kind and Tucker in the
same bed to Keep each other warm
 Tuesday Oct 26th 1880.
It rained furiously but we started
and arrived at Settingbourne about
1/2 past 4 Oclock. Notified Elder Willis
Simons of his appointment as President
 of Wood Side Green Branch and set
him apart as such and after getting
tea and something to Eat I took train for
London arrising Very late in the Evening
found that Elder Griggs had gone to
Deptford to attend Meeting and had
not yet got back.
 Wednesday Oct 27th 1880.
In the office answering correspondents and
arringing for places for the Elders to stay dur-
=ing Conference as we somewhat Expect
more help form Zion. In the Evening Elders
Griggs and I went to Whitechapel and
held meeting and staid till after
meeting and had a singing Meeting
preparing for the Conference.

 Thursday Oct 28th 1880.
At Office fixing up correspondence
as usual till Evening and attended
North London Branch Meeting and
had a good time in Singing and
preparing for Conference. Elders Willey
and Wilcox arrived from Bucks & Wilts

{38}
District and stopped at the office
night.
 Friday Oct 29th 1880.
getting the statistical and financial
reports ready for Conference. in the
afternoon With Elders Willey, Willcox
and Griggs I sent to the Caledonian
Market and bought a pair of
glass vases. and in the Evening
I was at home writing and
making up my Journal. and chat
=ting with the Elders. Elders King
and Tucker came in from the
Kent and Essex district and Elder
Rommey from the Brighton and Sussex
District. preparitory for Conference on
Sunday next. I visited with the Bretheren
tho the Evening and getting their Reports
 Saturday Oct 30th 1880.
Went visiting part of the day with
some of the Elders. And wrote a letter
Home to Zion. And in the Evening met Elder
C. W. Stayner & Wife from the Liverpool
Office who had come to represent the

{39}
President of the Mission.
 Sunday Oct 31st 1880
London Conference Meetings at Orsons
Assembly Rooms. New Road. Commercial
Road. ~~N~~. this day at 10.3 & 2.30 & 6.30;
Elders present from Utah 9. Presidents of
Branches 12. Elders in whole Conference 103
Priests 41. Teacher 16, Deacons 26. Members
751. Total officers & men 937. Baptized in 5
months past 440 Emigrated (souls) 123. Recd
from the Saints Tithing £136.12.4 1/2, on I.E.
Deposits £79.15.6. Book Monies £50 14.7. Relief
Societies 3. Sunday Schools 2. Names of
Utah Elders present Charles Stayer. Samuel
Roskelley. W. W. Willey. Jos c. Bentley. Thos C. Griggs

Edward King. Stephen Tucker. Chas F. Wilcox
Heber J. Romney; belong to London Conference
but not present because of distance Elder
E. A. Le Cheminant. good meetings. and
the Spirit of the Lord poured out upon
the Speakers & hearers – in the Evening Elder
C. W. Stayner occupied the whole of the time
talking 89 minutes to an appreciative
audience of between 400 & 500 persons.
After meeting the Elders met at Bro
Cross's house and sung for an hour
and at 1/2 past ten I left and went
to the place of Boarding of my nephew
S. R. Williams at 43 Offord Road and there
met my niece Annie Williams and her
sweetheart and sat talking to the three
persons until 3 O'clock on Monday
morning. bearing testimony of the glorious
truths revealed from God thro Jos Smith

{40}
  Monday Nov 1st 1880.
Went to Sister Godfrey's to see Bro and
Sister Stayner and after some talk. I
returned to the office to arrange with
Elder J. C. Bentley to attend meeting at
Oldford, and I returned to Sister Cross's
and took tea in Company with the rest
of the Elders, and spent the Evening with
them till late.
  Tuesday Nov 2nd 1880.
Went to Sister Godfreys and chatted with
Bro & Sister Stayner and went to Euston R. R.
Station to meet Valley Elders from Liverpl
Expected to arrive, but could not find
them. Returned to the office and at 5 Oclk
the Elders viz Moroni F. Brown and Frank
H. Snow and Shortly afterward. Elder and
Sister Stayner arrived and all the Elders
sat down to tea together. paper (Brown)
tablecloth & all. we all then went
to the Conference Concert which was well
attended and well performed. and spoke
at close.   Elder stayner spoke to Elders | at
                                          Conference house
  Wednesday Nov 3rd 1880
With Bro and Sister Stayner at Sister
Godfrey's at 11'O'Clock and took Buss
at Gray's Inn Road for Angel and
the train for Dalston, and found Miss
Whitfield and Visited her all of us

bearing testimony of the Restoration of the
Gospel, &c. thence from Dalston to
Barnsbury by R. R. and thence to Kings
Cross. by Buss. thence to Lattimer

{41}
Road by Metripoliton R R over which
there were conveyed as passengers in the
year 1877 – 56.175.753 persons
  " 1878 – 58.807.033   "
  " 1879 – 60.743.553   "
going to Bro Garners to get Dinner & tea
together, and thence to Baker Street by
RR. and saw Madam Tusaud's wax
works. leaving there for Kings Cross
at 1/4 to 10 P. M.
  Thursday Nov 4th 1880.
With Elder & Sister Stayner went to Visit
Sister Cross and bidding them good bye
went to the office and held meeting
with Elders Willey, Griggs, Bettey
Tucker. King. Wilcox. Romney Snow
and Brown. instructing them in
the duties of Elders of Israel and
attended meeting with all the Elders
at North London all testifying with
many of the London Saints of the
restoration of the Gospel. in these latter
day &c and a season of Rejoicing.
  Friday Nov 5th 1880.
Receiving a letter from Prest Wm Budge
requesting me to attend the Conference at
Southampton on Sunday Nov 7th as he would
not be able to do so as he had contemplated.
I started from Waterloo Station at 11.20 AM
arriving at St Denney's near Southampton at
1.40. P.M. proceeding to the Conference house
and met Sister Baily and afterwards Prest
Jackson and Elders Jas Burningham all of
the Southampton Conference. and all seemed
glad to see me. I remained at the house

{42}
chatting with Prest Jackson and Enjoyed
myself much in his Company.
  Saturday Nov 6th 1880.
With the Elders of the Conference Visited
several points of interest in Southampton
and Enjoyed myself much in the
Company of the Elders and Saints.

Sunday Nov 7th 1880.
This is the Conference day of the South=
=ampton Conference. At 10.45. Meeting
called to order by Prest Jackson. 22 persons
present. And as I had been advertized
on large placards all through the town
I felt Exceedingly small and more
than once lifted my heart in fervant
prayer to God for his Blessings to
attend me. The Morning services were
an Exhibit of the Financial affairs of
the Conference. Voting on the Authorities &c
took dinner at Conference House and by the
request of Prest Jackson I occupied the whole
of the Afternoon, 80 minutes, relating Experience
in the Gospel and bearing testimony to its truths.
in the Evening I occupied 45 minutes, and Prest
Jackson 37 minutes to an attentive audience
of Saints and Gentiles. after Meeting I had
quite an argument with an Infidel but
he went away saying he felt glad to have
met me, and should come to the meetings
of the Latter-day Saints again. After
meeting many of the Saints met at the
House of Sister Bailey and Enjoyed ourselves
in the conversation and singing—I taught
them the tune of "Arise My Soul arise."

{43}
Monday Nov 8th 1880.
Recd Notice from Liverpool that the
Islands of Guernsey & Jersey were attached to
the Southampton Conference from this date
being detatched from the London Conference
from this date—Councilled and talked
with Prest Jackson & Elders Burningham and
Stevens most of the day—Evening went to
the Saints meeting Hall and with the
Saints of this Branch and some from the
Portsmouth Branch had a good Social
Party-- Singing. Reciting and speaking pieces
till a late hour.
Tuesday Nov 9th 1880.
Started from Bro Bailey's (Conference
houses) at 6-45 A.M accompanied by Prest
Jackson & Elders Burningham and Stevens of the
Southampton Conference and young Sister Bailey
to the St Deneys R.R. Station leaving there
at 7.5 A M for London. having Enjoyed a
good time with my Southampton friends in
my Visit to them.-- Arriving at Waterloo

at 9.45. and on arriving at our Rooms in
Dorset Street found Elder T. C. Griggs and a
number of Letters awaiting an answer.
After reading the same I went with Elder
Griggs to Moregate Street to see the
procession of the Lord Mayor of London
and in doing so felt the Effect of being
in a London Mob with its swaying-rest=
=less, mass of humanity-rushing and ser=
=ging like the Waves of the Sea. Tens of
thousands of people was on View of the
"Lord Mayors Show" and a "show" it was
I got up on the hind End of a Wagon
but only got sight of the rear of the
procession-- We proceeded to Ludgate
Hill and by dint of much Effort got

{44}
a 4th rate position and saw the great
procession of a "Lord Mayor of London" going
to Westminster Abby to take the Oath
of Office. The Bands and magnificent dis=
=play of Guilt was something grand. It
would take too much time to describe it in
detail but clip the following from the Telegraph
Daily Newspaper of today.
   [folded clipping "Lord Mayor's Day," The Daily
   Telegraph (London, England), 9 November 1880
   pasted to the remainder of the page]

{45}
Wednesday Nov 10th 1880.
At the office assisting Elder Griggs to
make out Bills for Stars and Journals
to Send out to the subscribers. this occupied
the whole day till it was time to go to the
Whitechapel Branch Meeting-few Saints
met– Some testified and Elder Griggs &
I occupied the time talking to the Saints
a little circumstance took place which
caused anoyance for a short time. Elder
Griggs had the weeks supply of stars for the
Whitechapel and Lambeth Branches and
getting out of the R.R. Train at Shoreditch
forgot the Stars leaving them in the R. R.
carriage on the seat. we had not left the
station long before the discovery was made
and Elder T. C. Griggs returned and walked
and rode some considerable distance but
failed to find the parcel but Solicited the

officers of the R. R. Company to continue the
search and finally succeeded in getting the
parcel much to our Joy as it would be
hard to replace so many stars.

Thursday Nov 11th 1880.
Writing letters to Prest A Carrington and others
and was Highly gratified to greet and
meet Elders Joseph A Jennings and
John H. White from Salt Lake City who
had been assigned to Labor in this Conf-
=Erence. this making us 14 Elders from
Utah. in this Conference. in the Evening
we all went to Prest Balls at Notting
=hill-gate and met ~~Bro~~ Prest Garner
and proceeded to the Royal Albert Hall
and paid 1 shilling for a "standing" seat
to list to one thousand singers and
players accompanied by the immense
organ of that Building. in an Oritorio

{46}
of "Judas Maccabeus" led or con=
=ducted by Mr Barnly & organist
Dr Stenier. An orchestra of 100 Perf=
=ormers including the Band of the
Coldstream Guards.. about 7000 persons
comprised the audience. the Young
Ladies wore White dresses with Pink
Sashes over Right Shoulder on the Right
of the Organ, and blue sashes over the
left shoulder on the left of the organ..
the Men sitting behind Each company
of Ladies.– 350 ladies & 450 Gents
composed the Chorus. It was the
grandest piece of singing I Ever heard
and my feeble pen fails to find words
to describe its grandure.

Friday November 12th 1880.
7 months today I left Smithfield for
this Mission. May god grant it they
be a profitable one to me in Every
respect.—making up my monthly
report for October all day at the
office, and got it mailed in the
Evening about dark. I wrote a letter
to Elders King & Tucker notifying them
of the change about to take place
in the decision of their district. and
at 9 Oclock the postman brought me
a letter from my daughter Rebecca
announcing the death of my son Thomas

on the 25th of October 1880. at 12.40
P.M.—though not unexpected—for
my dreams have fully warned me

{47}
for some time past of a change in
my family affairs yet the blow can only
be borne up by me by the aid and
assistance of gods good spirit and
comforting influence, which I cannot
but acknowledge I feel that I have
with me.

Saturday Nov 13th 1880.
Morning Writing to Elders. Afternoon
I wrote a letter of Condolence to My Dear
wife Mary feeling at the same time I should
like to get a share from some Kind friend and
Especially from the Holy Spirit of Promise,
in the Evening I walked to the City and
with Elders Griggs. J. A. Jennings and J. H
White Purchased some books to send home
Viz a Cassell Family Bible—13 shillings
Paleys Theology 1s Foxes Martyrs 3s3d Watts
Logic 6d Prince of the House of David 1s5d
Josephus 2s3d History of England 4 Vol £1.3.0
Cassells History of U.States. 3 Vol 10s and my
Esteemed friend Thos C. Griggs presented
me with Spurgeons Word "The Ploughman"
called at Bro & Sister Cross's and got
Supper and sung a few hymns. getting
home late.

Sunday Nov 14th 1880.
Elders Griggs. Jennings. White and I
Went to The Catholic Church at Moorfields
near Broad St Station and paid 1d for admission
but not getting a good seat we left and got
into the Church by another door and paid
6d to get a good seat and saw the Priests
at the alter going through the forms and
ceremonies of the Catholic Religion and
Blessing the Bread and Wine and making

{48}
it as one of the Priests Expressed it
pat of the Sacred heart of Jesus, it
took 4 Priests. 4 assistants and 9 Boys
and youths to perform the ceremony and
wave the Incence cup, and ring the
bell. prayers in Latin. Preaching in
English by a Pretty Good Preacher. who

also gave out notice that certain persons
would be prayed out of Pergitory on
the Various days of the Week at that
church. the Priests would not cross
the Church. Enter or leave their Seats
without looking to the crucifix and bowing
in passing the font Dip their fin=
=gers into the font and cross themselves
The Church is Beautifully fitted
up some Excellent paintings and
sculpture work of Jesus on the Cross
with the wound in his side and blood
settled in under the nails of his hands
and toes. Also may pictures of his
carrying the Cross to Calvary. falling
down 3 times and Roman soldiers
scourging him with thorns & cords &c,
with Elder J H White I took dinner
at Cross's and attended meeting
at North London and talked about
20 minutes. Elder J. H W made his
maiden speech. Evening spoke about
20 minutes. Elder Wells of Whitechapel
and Elder J H. White occupied the rest
of the time. Good full house.

Monday Nov 14th 1880
Wrote and made up accounts all
day till Evening when I went to
Sister Todds, with Elder White. had a
good meeting. I had a bad cold

{49}
received a letter from Wife Mary and
one from Bro Hillyard giving more
full account of the death and burial
of my Son Thomas. Elders T C Griggs
and Jos A. Jennings started off for
Kent to Labor in the lower End of
that County.

Tuesday Nov 16th 1880
Wrote and making up Star accounts till
Evening when I went to Notting-Hill-Gate
and called upon Prest Ball and took tea and
also chatted about his Branch affairs
then went to Visit Brother and Sister Dow
and Enjoyed myself well in their com
=pany returning to 10 Dorset St late.

Wednesday Nov 17th 1880
Mailing weekly and By-Weekly Stars
and Journal and Sending Bill to those
owing for same. Elder John H. White
started for Essex to travel with Elder
Stephen Tucker at 5-37 from Highbury
R.R. Station. I held meeting at
Whitechapel and preached nearly
all the meeting time-- Slept alone
at the office.

Thursday Nov 18~~17~~th 1880.
At Home at Conf^{ce} House filling orders
for Books posting accounts and writing letters
till Meeting time. Attended meeting at
North London Branch few present in Consequence
of so Stormy a night. My fast day--
had a good time all alone, received
a letter from Zina my daughter and
containing a likeness of My Dear Wife
Rebecca. Sent letters home to Rebecca
~~My~~ Daughter and also Bro. F. Gunnell,

{50}
Friday Nov 19th 1880.
I wrote all day as usual answering
correspondence and in the afternoon late
took a buss for St Pauls cathedral square
and bought a small American stove
which with the pipe I paid 30 shillings
for and had 2 shillings left for fitting
up the stove in the house. I went in the
Evening to Sister Godfrey's and took tea and
read part of "The Vision and other Revelations from
the Doctrine & Covenants showing the degree
of Glory and those that inhabit thereon.

Saturday Nov 20th 1880.
As I awoke in the Morning it seemed as tho'
some one said to me "You'll loose another one
of your family" and it seemed to make quite
an impression on my mind all day. I
wrote, and Elder King came in from Essex
to wait for his partner. Our stove came
in but too late for us to put it up today
Worte letters home to my sons William and
Joseph and daughter Mary. Spent Evening in
Testifying to Bro Crackels nephew. that the Gospel
is restored

Sunday Nov 21st 1880
At Con House with Elders Edward King advi=
=sing for the best good of his (The Upper part
of Kent District) He going to Whitechappel
and I going to Lambeth to hold meeting with
the Saints. we had most Excellent meeting
non but Saints met in the afternoon and I
talked. occupying the whole time reading

Extracts from Doc & Covenants and bible on the Celestial and Terrestrial Glories. In the Evening between meetings Prest Ball & I went to look at a nice Hall with the View of renting the same for a meeting place for the Saints. not finding the man at home we took his address with the View of writing to him. At the meeting in the Evening Prest Ball occupied most of the time on 1st Principles

{51}
I followed occupying about 40 minutes to an Excellent congregation, with quite a number of Strangers and a good Spirit returned home late. to Conference House

Monday Nov 22nd 1880
Wrote to all the Elders in the field Except in Kent and Herts & Bucks in answer to letters from them, and posted up some few accounts and attended meeting at old ford. had a pretty good congregation of Saints only

Tuesday Nov 23rd 1880.
I was as usual writing all day. That I could do so. In company with Elders King went to St Pancras R. R Station and met Elders George and [blank] String==fellow who had come from Nottingham to day. to Labor in this Conference. they went to see sights with Elder King as I had work in the office to do. and putting up my little Heating Stove.

Wednesday Nov 24th
All forenoon cleaning up the Mess caused by cutting the hole in the Chimney. for the Stove pipe last Evening and it took me all the afternoon to write the addresses and get off the Stars. Evening. went to Whitechapel Branch to Meeting and occupied most of the time-- had a terrable cold and cough

~~Thursday Nov 25th~~
Elders King and [blank] Stringfellow started for the Upper part of the Kent District and Elder George Stringfellow for Brighton District

Thursday Nov 25th
Receiving word from Prest Carrington that he would arrive here in London on his way to Brighton. I went to sister Godfreys to seek a place for him

{52}
to stay over night and succeeded in arranging the matter with Sister Godfrey, it being fast day. I being about 1/2 sick and Sister Godfrey made me stop to dinner about 3. OClock. went home and wrote till meeting time and attended meeting at North London Branch. I presided as none of the presidency were present. had an Excellent meeting.

Friday Nov 26th 1880
I wrote to several persons in the Morning and went to the picture makers in City road to get my dear wife Rebeccas Likeness Copied. Also my dear son Thomas's ordered a dozen of Each. Went to Euston R. R. Station and met Prest Carrington and with him went to Sister Godfrey's and took supper and Visited with him till 11 OClock and arranged to keep him in London and vicinity a week. Enjoyed my Visit very much.

Saturday Nov 27th 1880.
I wrote this morning, to all the Elders in the Conference except the 3 at Brighton to come to London to attend the meeting on Sunday Dec 5th also wrote to the presidents of Branches to arrange to tell the people about a meeting to be held through the week. and took dinner at Sister Godfreys and took buss to London Bridge with Prest Carrington and thence to Brighton by B & London R. R. arriving at Brighton at 4.50 and was met by the Elders Bentley- Stringfellow & Romney. and [ ] took train for Port Slade by Sea. where Prest Carrington staid at Bro Brown and the rest of us scattered away to the Saints. Elder Jos Bently & I staid at Bro Mitchells about 3 miles from Brighton

{53}
Sunday Nov 28th 1880
with Prest A. Carrington & Elders Bentley, Romney and George Stringfellow proceeded to Temperance Hall
Brighton to hold District meeting and and [sic] com==menced by Reports from Prest of Branch John Mitchell of Brighton followed by Elder Jos Bentley &. Heber Romney with reports of their

Districts. Also Elder G. Stringfellow & myself.
in the forenoon. and in the afternoon
[blank]

Monday Nov 29th 1880.
I went with Elder Bentley and got Prest
Carrington from Port Slade by Sea and Went
to Brighton and with Eler Stringfellow added
to our company we went to the Brighton aquarium
to see the fish. sea lion & seals &c and
had a splendid time — after which Prest
C and I went to R R & booked to Southampton
starting at 1 OClock and arriving at 4.20.
and met with the saints at their hall under
the Presidency of Prest W. W. Jackson who had
sent the Town Crier around the Town to notify
the inhabitants of the fact that Albert Carrington
one of the Twelve Apostles of the Church of Jesus
Christ of Latter-day-Saints would preach at the
Latter-day-Saint Hall. About 12 or 15 persons
not connected with the church, together with

{54}
the Saints of the Southampton Branch were
present and had a splendid meeting. Prest
A Carrington occupying all the Evening- 1 1/4
hours — I being mouth in prayer, I wrote a synop=
=sis of his sermon. Slept at Sister Bailey's
in Bed with Prest Jackson and one of Bro Bailey's
sons.

Tuesday Nov 30th 1880.
Prest Carrington and I booked form St. Denneys
Southampton, to Havant and thence to Eastbourne
to Visit my Brother Richard and his daughter
Annie arriving at 2-38- found my Brother
and neice had arranged for our comfort. Much
conversation between my Brother and Prest Carr.
=ing as myself and music and singing Excellent
in the morning visited Bro Barkers sister Mrs
Smeath and promised to call again at no
very distant date-- My Brother Richard
piloted us around to the house of Mr & Mrs
Smeath and Prest Carrington had a good chat
with her. – . Staid all night together with
Prest Carrington at my Brothers house and
had a most Excellent time chatting to=
=gether in a most comfortable way. On
the principles of the Gospel.

Wednesday December 1st 1880
With Prest Carrington and Brother Richard
I took a stroll around Eastbourne and the
promenade along the sea beach. And left

for London at 12-25 bidding good Bye to [ ]
neice Annie and Bro Richard, and Prest
C telling me his Experience all the way
along the Road the time slipped along so
rapidly I was allmost in London before
I knew it at 4.40 and took buss from
London Bridge for Commercial Road and
Visited Sister Farnes. and thence to

{55}
the White Chapel Meeting where a nice
congregation of Saints and a few Strangers
were assembled.. Prest Carrington preached
an Excellent discourse on the subject of the
gathering and necessity of the saints helping them=
=selves to Emigrate

Thursday Dec 2nd 1880.
at the office doing Business till 4 P.M.
went to Sister Godfreys to visit Prest Carrington
and with him went to Sister Crosses and tool tea
thence to the Pentonville Meeting house and Pres
Carrington addressed a very good audience for
an hour and a half on very many of the
principles of the Gospel. Elder Willey same in
with Elder F. S[ ]

Friday Dec 3rd 1880.
Prest C came to 10 Dorset st and visit us and
ate supper with us and he and Elders Willey,
Butler & I went to Lambeth to meeting and had
an Excellent time.. getting home very late
I forgot to state yesterday that I got lost in
a London fog straying from 2 1/2 to 3 hours from
one place to another

Saturday Dec 4th 1880.
Elders came in from the Districts for a
meeting tomorrow. I was Visiting with them
most of the day — slept at night with Elder
Griggs at Sister Godfrey's when Prest Carrington
is stopping, and visited with him, Elders White
and Tucker and Griggs and Jennings came in from
district

Sunday Dec 5th 1880.
Met at 42 Penton Street Pentonville.
London. N. for Priesthood Meeting at 10-30
Present. Apostle Albert Carrington.. Prest of Euro=
=pean mission, Samuel Roskelley. Prest of. and
Thomas C. Griggs Jos C. Bentley. W. W. Willey
Edwd
King. Stephen Tucker. [blank] Wilcox. M. F. Frown
Frank Snow. W. H. White. [blank] Stringfellow
Jos A. Jennings.. forenoon occupied by the

Elders reporting their ~~Branches~~ /Districts\ and
                                  Prests of the
Branches their Branches and had an
Excellent good meeting. went to Sister

{56}
Godfreys and meeting again at 2.30
when the balance of the Elders occupied about
1/2 the time and Prest Carrington the other
half in a very interesting and profitable
address to the saints showing the Joys
the Saints Experienced in their association
together and the many blessings they Enjoyed
and passed above these outside the church
=took tea at Sister Godfreys and again
to meeting Prest C Preached one hour and a half
to a full house, the people listened attentively
and both saints and strangers said they
Enjoyed it Very much. slept at Sister Godfreys
       Monday Dec 6th 1880
went to the office and chatted with the
Elders there assembled about the Various
Questions and Circumstances arising in
their fields of Labor. spent the Balance
of the day with Prest C at Sister Godfreys
and Sister Crosses.. slept at Sister Godfreys
       Tuesday Dec 7th 1880
went with Prest C and other Elders to
the Agricultural Hall. Islington and
then to the office and had a good talk
with some of the Bretheren leaving for
their fields of Labor and then to sister
Godfreys and wen to Euston Station
with Prest C and saw him start for
Liverpool by the 2.45 train from Liverpool
returned to the office and posted up
accounts.
       Wednesday Dec 8th 1880.
In the morning I arranged and sent
off Stars to Weekly subscribers. and
attended meeting with Elders Bentley,
Willey & Tucker at Whitechapel. Each one
of us speaking a short time. to a small

{57}
but very attentive congregation of the Saints
we administers to sick sister Walker
and ordained Samuel Spillsman a Deacon
in the Church. I being mount in the ord=
=ination.

       Thursday Dec 9th 1880.
Elders Bentley. Willey & Tucker went to
W[*blotted out*] Woolwich to see the Dockyard and
the arsnel and I remained at the office
to Write home to family & friends. and late
in the afternoon I arranged my affairs &
went to Sister Godfreys and saw that the mail
matter sent to Prest Carrington was retuned
to Liverpool to him. And thence Sister Godfrey
went to the North London Branch Meeting and
had an Excellent time in testimony meeting
Elders from Utah present. W. W. Willey. J. C Bentley
S. Tucker. J.H. White & J.A. Jennings. Adminis=
=tered to a sick Brother.
       Friday De 10th 1880
after arranging some correspondance
Bro Bentley & I copied some Book
and Star accounts on the Ledger and I
went to the agricultural Hall to see
the ~~all~~ Smithfield Club Cattle Show.
including Sheep & pigs and agricultural
machinary of a great Variety of Kinds.
saw some of the fattest animals I Ever
did see. some seemed to pant for Breath
they were so fat. saw the Steer of Mr
J.J. Colman 3 years 7 months. 2W & 2 days old
cross shorthorn bull and aberdeenshire cow weight
20 cwt. 1 gr 23lbs and drew prizes amounting
to 1100 Dollars saw some Excellent sheep
of Various Kinds—too fat to thrive, the Scottish
mountain Sheep took 1st prize, they are
a close compact. Well made Sheep, close
fine wool not very long. Pigs 7 months old
weighing over 200lbs of the Berkshire
Breed no nose to amount to anything.
in the Evening I wrote part of a letter
for Publication in the Star.

{58}
       Saturday Dec 11th 1880.
Wrote Letters to Correspondents and finished
my Letter No 2 for the Millennial Star. giving
a description of the trip and Speeches of Prest
Carrington at Brighton Southampton. Eastb=
=ourne, and the London Meetings. In the
Evening I went to see Prest Ball at Notting
Hill gate.
       Sunday Dec 12th 1880.
Ate Dinner at Sister Farnes's of Whitecha=
=ple and meeting (Sacrament) at Whitechapel
Branch. had Testimony Meeting and all

spoke well. I spoke 15 minutes. and in
the Evening Elder W. W. Willey spoke 30
minutes and I 45 minutes to a pretty
good congregation of People.

Monday Dec 13th 1880.
With Elder J. C. Bentley at the office
writing letters and commenced my gen=
ological record so as to gether up
all the information I can regarding
my dead friends. With Elder W. Willey
attended meeting at old ford and
had a very nice time. Elder Willey
spoke about 20 minutes and I about
40 minutes to an attentive congregation

Tuesday Dec 14th 1880.
Made up my monthly report for the
Liverpool Office. and with Elder Bentley
went to Br Coles to tea and he took us
to a Mr Toole and his wife that used to
know me and the saints at Devonport many
years ago. we talked over old times and our
old acquaintances. Visited 2 families
of saints and had an Enjoyable time
with them.

{59}
Wednesday Dec 15th 1880.
Copied my monthly report and sent it
to Liverpool and assisted Bro Bentley to
get off the weekly & By-Weekly Stars to the
Subscribers and attended meeting at
White Chapel Branch with a few saints
had a good little meeting. Elder W
W. Willey occupied 30 minutes and I foll
=owed about the same length of time.

Thursday Dec 16th 1880
wrote some letters and mailed Some
Books to Elder Wilcox and went to
St. Pauls Church Yard to get stove pipe
Elbow fixed and then went to Lambeth
to take sister Brown a letter from
her husband in the Valley. thence
went to North London to meeting and
had a good meeting.

Friday Dec 17th 1880.
I wrote part of a letter to Bro Hall
of Ogden and assorted some old Mil
Stars all day for the purpose of getting
a few Volumes to take home with me
Elder Farmer called to See & Talk with me.

Saturday Dec 18th 1880.
Assorting Stars all day till Evening
Elder Bentley and I went to see Sister
Toole at 9 Landfield Street. Rendlesham
Road. Clapton. Also 4 Mansfield Road
Maitland park N.W.. she and her husband
were much acquainted with me in my
youthful days in Devonport. she treated
us very Kindly.,

Sunday Dec 19th 1880.
Went to Bro F S Ball's At Notting Hill gate
and got Dinner Met Elder Steven Tucker
there, and the three of us proceeded to ~~No~~
Lambeth to Meeting. I spoke about 30 Minu
=tes in the afternoon and about 40 minutes
in the Evening. Elder Farmer came into the Meetg

{60}
Monday Dec 20th 1880.
At the Office making up accounts till
Evening when I went to see and Visit
Sisters Godfrey and her Neice and had
an Excellent time with them. I believe
the neice will Soon ready for the
waters of Baptism.

Tuesday Dec 21st 1880.
at the office writing letters to the
Elders till late in the Afternoon and
took train to Dalston to P. Office and then to
Old Ford. With our clothes and took tea
with sister Todd and family. Elder Griggs
came in from Kent to-day.

Wednesday. Dec 22nd 1880.
At the office arranging stars till the
Evening when I attended the Whitechapel
meeting. Elder Willey & I and Prest Garner
spoke to the saints Present

Thursday Dec 23rd 1880.
After writing up our correspondence
with the Elders I took a walk with
Elder T. C. Griggs thro' some of the principle
Streets of the City to see the display they
were putting forth for Christmas and
went in to Bro Cross's to get some tea
and then to the north London meeting.
had an Excellent meeting, Time occupied
by Elders Bentley, self, king and Griggs &
Elder Ball from Lambeth. Bro Bentley
left before the meeting was out to go to
the Baths to Baptize a couple of
Women. /I went home and took supper with Sister
Godfrey.\

Friday Dec 24th 1880.
Wrote a Letter to Bro Geo H. Taylor
at Salt Lake City and Elder King and
I walked with Bro Griggs to London

{61}
Bridge R. R Station to see him start
to Brighton to spend the Christmas with
his Relatives living there. I then
went to the office and wrote to my wife
Mary in the Evening. this is Christmas
Eve. I received from the Photographers
5 Pictures of my own and 4 of Rebecca
and 6 of Thomas. I spent the Evening at
the office writing letters.
Saturday Dec 25th Christmas
Elder E. King and I by Invitation spent the day
with Sister Ann Godfrey and her niece. Enjoying
a Most Excellent Dinner and tea and Supper
and during the day I wrote up the names &
ages of Sister Godfreys dead friends for her to
take to Zion. Slept at her house
Sunday Dec 26th 1880.
attended Sunday School at North London Branch
and Branch Council Meeting. and took dinner at
Bro Shill's and meeting again in afternoon. took
tea with the Bro & Sister Cross and had a long
arrangement with a gentleman friend and he
came to the meeting in the Evening and listened
with many other Strangers. Elder E. Adams
and I occupied the Evening. I occupied an
hour in the Morning and 70 minutes in the
Evening Meeting. Slept at Sister Godfreys.
Monday Dec 27th 1880.
left Sister Godfreys at 1 O'Clock and taking the
metripolitan R. R. for Bro Garner's at Notting Hill
with Elder W. W. Willey ate Dinner and went
to Bro Dows to Supper and meeting Elder Batty
and Bro Garner & Ball we all went to the albert
hall and Enjoyed ourselves Hugely listening
to Handel's "Messiah" sung by 1000 voices,
to and immense congregation. it was an
Enjoyable treat altho I had to stand all
the time.
Tuesday Dec 28th 1880.
at the office all day Writing letters to make
up for holidays. Elder King started for Kent
and Elder Tucker for Lambeth District.

{62}
Wednesday Dec 29th 1880.
at the office Writing till Evening when I attended
the Whitechapel Branch Meeting and had a
very good meeting. and spoke 40 minutes.
Thursday Dec 30th 1880.
Attended ~~Mee~~ to the office Business and in
the Evening I attended the North London Branch
meeting and had a very good time in the Shape
of a Concert and Singing and reciting party. Elder
A. G. Basher arrived from the Norwich Conference
Friday Dec 31st 1880.
In the morning I finished up my correspondence
and in the Evening I took train form London Bg.
R. R. Station for Eastbourne- being accompanied
to the Station by Elder T. C Griggs who with
the usual festive greeting mutually wished Each
other Happy New Year. started from station at
7.50 arriving at Eastborne at 9.45. and meeting
with a cordial reception by my Bro Richard
and having received an invitation from him to
spend
my 44th Birthday with him and his friends at
Eastbourne. I was well provided with the best
of Food and Comfort and cared for by my Brother
&
his dear Daughter who Kindly cared for my
comfort
and happiness. I remained here till Wednesday
Jany 5th during which time I did all I could to
Explain to them the principles of the Gospel and get
them
to understand the true plan of Salvation. I pleaded
with my Brother Richard to obey the gospel and
take
the place at the Head of the Roskelley Family that
was justly his by birthright. but if he would not
I did not want him to find fault in the future
with some one that would do so. and he prom-
=ised he would not, I spent a very pleasant
time with my friends till
Wednesday Jan 5th 1881.
when bidding my friends good bye I took train for
Brighton with the purpose of meeting Elders
String=
=fellow & Romney, but found they had gone to
Burgess Hill about an hour before I arrived, I took
train for London Bridge arriving at 10.36. P.M.
getting
to the office at 1/2 past 11. O.Clock. with the
Bretheren

{63}
very glad to meet me- lots of letters waiting for
answers.
    Thursday Jan 6th 1881.
Recd quite a number of Bretheren & Sisters called
to Express the Complements of the Season. I was
writing letters till meeting time and with Elders
Bentley. Griggs. King. R. H. Stringfellow & Barber I attended
the North London Meeting and had quite an Enjoyable
time. Elders Barber & I stayed at Sister Godfreys
all night.
    Friday Jan 7th 1881.
attended to the Business of the Office and
by invitation I accompanied Elder Bentley to see
Sister Gearry and commenced a Geanological
Record for her.
    Saturday Jan 8th 1881.
As usual attended to the office Business
and wrote home to friends and family
    Sunday January 9th 1881.
Attended monthly Priesthood meeting at North London
Branch and had a Splendid time. ate dinner
with Elder A. G. Barber at Bro & Sister Cross's in the
afternoon Bro Barber Preached and did well – he
seems to have improved very much in his manner
of Expression &c. Evening Elder Bentley occupied
40 minutes. Elder Barber 20 Minutes and I 17 m==inutes and had an excellent meeting. quite a
number of Strangers present.
    Monday Jan 10th 1881.
arranged today with Elder Willey to go to the
Channel Islands and see and visit Elder
LeChaminant – he starts from here on Saturday
next on his visit. Elder Tucker called today.
attended meeting with Elder Willey ~~and~~
at Old Ford and arranged with Elder Griggs
to succeed him as Travelling Elder in the
Whitechapel District had a good meeting.
Had a good talk with a Lady after meeting.
she said she Expected to be Baptized soon
    Tuesday Jan 11th 1881.
~~at the office all~~ With Elder A. G. Barber
Visited the Rotunda at Woolwich. containing
all Kinds & classes of guns from the 64 pounder
cannons to the smallest pistols, also Indian
arrows & tomahawks-Knives. plans of noted forts &
fortresses. gun carriages for all Kinds of arms and

{64}
ammunition. Sections of War & transport
Ships and Iron targets showing the impression
made on it by the various Kinds of guns &
Balls fired at different ranges. the whole
being of Very great interest. in the afternoon
Escorted by Bro Blackmore of the Woolwich
Branch we Visited the Woolwich arsnell
where the guns & ammunition of all Kinds and
discription for both Naval & Military are made
for the discription of what we saw and the
4. 100 ton guns beside the great amount of
80 ton guns now in process of construction. as
also the Steam hammer capable of striking a
blow of 1000 tons. See the book Warlike Wool==wich. /attended a party of Bro Woods friends with
a Bro A. G
Barber\   Wednesday Jan 12th 1881.
at work in the Office till time for the
meeting at Whitechapel, had good meeting
Prest Garner. Elders Willey and I were the speakers
    Thursday jan 13th 1881.
at the office at work till Evening Meeting
at North London. general Testamony meeting
and had a good time. I spoke 20 minutes
    Friday Jan 14th 1881.
Fast day. Elder Bentley and I fasted and prayed
and worked in the office till late afternoon
I walked to see sister Godfrey's and she wished
me to stop & take tea with her. which I did
after which I met Elders Griggs & Willey and
went to Drury Lane Theatre Royal to see the Panto==mime, and was very much delighted with the sight,
in the magnificent scenery. gorgiousness of the
Dresses & attirements and Excellent appointments
of the Stage. Mother Goose was performed and
it was a grand success. the final scene was
the finest of the Kind I Ever saw. and with such
display of lights and apparatus it produced an
Exceedingly grand Effect beautiful to behold and
Representing Fairy Land. Elder T. C. Grigs and
I slept at Sister Godfreys.

{65}
    Saturday. Jan 15th 1881.
With Elder Griggs I walked to Waterlooe Bg
R R Station to see Elder Willey off to Southampton
on his way to the Channel Islands but did not
get there in time to see the train start. but
returned to the office and Wrote, and answered

my correspondants. Brother and Sister Shill
stayed at the office. as they had no place to
go to.
 Sunday January 16th 1881.
In the morning with Elder Bentley I went
to the North London Meeting Room and org=
=anized a mutual Improvement association
Elder Jos C. Bentley from Utah as Prest
and Alfred Cross and sister ~~Sarah Thoroughgood~~
        /Alice Croskell\
councillors. Richard Crackles Secretary
and Edith Cornell asst Secty. Alfred Cross
Treasurer. 11 Members Enrolled. took dinner
at Bro and Sister Cross's and took train at Snow
Hill for Eliphant & Castle and walked from
there to Lambeth meeting Hall. a good number of
saints assembled and had a good time
together in partaking he sacrament and they
testafying to their Knowledge of the Gospel
being Revealed in this our day and age of the
world, I bore testamony to the truth and
occupied some 20 minutes. Prest Ball &
I was invited to take tea by a Gentleman
that attended our meeting and we had a
very interesting Conversation on the Gospel
and its ordinances. I preached in the Evening
about 90 minutes to an attentive congregation
of Saints and 3 strangers and had good free=
=dom of speech. Our Weslean teatotal
friend that invited us home to tea seemed to
Enjoy himself very well. Went home with
Elder Ball and stayed all night returning to
the office on
 Monday Jan 17th 1881.
after answering my correspondents. I went
to meeting at Old Ford and had a nice little
meeting of a dozen persons. I talked 1/2 and
hour. 2 strangers present who Expressed

{66}
belief in our principles and Expected to be
baptized at an Early date.
 Tuesday Jan 18th 1881.
I wrote and arranged some of the Conf=
=erence financial accounts all day.
 Wednesday Jan 19th 1881.
at work all day on financial a/cs
of the Conference—no starts came. it
stormed furiously yesterday and today,
snow fell and drifted quite deep in
London and other places- stopping trains
in all directions train cars ceased. and
all Kinds of vehicles quit running for 2
days. telegraph lines were prostrated
and mails delayed such a storm has
not been Known in England for many. many
years
 Thursday Jan 20th 1881.
The day opens much brighter. stars came
and with Bro Bentley's aid I got them off
and attended North London Meeting in the
Evening. and spoke 20 minutes at a testimony
meeting. went home and staid all night
at Sister Godfreys. * * *
 Friday Jan 21st 1881.
at the office writing all day and Evening
Elders King & R. H. Stringfellow came in from
        Essex
 Saturday jan 22nd 1881.
at the office all day writing. to Wife Mary &
to President W. Woodruff at Salt Lake city. Utah.
Elders R H. Stringfellow started from London Bg
R R Station for Brighton at 4 PM ~~and~~ to Join his
Uncle Elder George Stringfellow. and Labor there.

* * * after Elder Bentley and I were prepared for
meeting. Bro Crackles sent his little boy to ask us to
        come
and administer to him. we went and found him in a
        very
bad State having fallen out of a Van on his hip and
        back
and hurt him self very bad. we anointed and
        blessed him
and prayed God to heal him and on Sunday he was
well and attended meeting and bore testimony to
        Gods N[---]

{67}
 Sunday Jan 23rd 1881.
With Elders Griggs & Bentley attended the
Young M&Y.L. Mutual Improvement Society at
        Pen=
=tonville in the Morning and assisted in the
Completion of the organization viz Alfred J Cross
and Alice Crackles as councillors to Prest Jos
C Bentley. after the Program was through with
I spoke upon the benefits of such organizations
and with Elder T. C. Griggs went to sister E
Farnes at Whitechapel to dinner and to
the Whitechapel to meeting in the afternoon
and Evening. I spoke about 1/2 and hour in
the afternoon congregation and went with

Elder Griggs to sleep at Prest Garners getting back to the office on

Monday Jan 24th 1881.
Walked from Prest Garners to Broad Oak R R. Station and took train for Kings Cross arriving at 10 Dorset St about 2 O'clock answerd some of our correspondant and With Elder T.. C Griggs went to Old ford to meeting. had a good little meeting after which I talked to Mrs Gill who has attended our meeting for some weeks and told me she believed our prin= =ciples.

Tuesday Jan 25th 1881.
Worked on the Tithing accounts up to Dec 31st 1880 all day and did not finish them

Wednesday Jan 26th 1881.
helped Bro Bentley to make up the stars and Journals to post and went to sister Farnes Mile End Road to get an Emigration Receipt. and attended the meeting at White= =chapel. spoke about 3/4 of an hour.

Thursday Jan 27th 1881
at the office writing. Elder H. J. Romney arrived from the South District and he and Elder J. C. Bentley and I went to the North London Meeting and Each one Spoke for a short time and I went home with Sister Godfrey and staid at her house all night.

{68}
Friday Jan 28th 1881.
after writing some letters &c till Evening and got Elder H. J. Romney to help me to clean and compile some volumes of Mill Stars for Binding

Saturday Jan 29th 1881
As usual I had quite a number of letters to write and among the rest some to write home to my family. in the Evening I went to Lattimer Road and saw Prest H. Garner's family and also called on sister Dow's family and administered to her little Son and called on Bro & Sister Ball and met Elders Tucker and T. C. Griggs there also. administered to Bro Ball. And returned to 10 Dorset Street.

Sunday Jan 30th 1881.
Went to London Bridge Rail Road Station with Elder H. J. Romney he going to Woolwich to meet Elder King. I went to Lambeth Branch to Meeting and occupied the whole time in the afternoon. About 90 minutes, I proceeded to North London in the Evening and had a good meeting there also. Elder J C. Bentley & I occupying the Evening. The Lord blessing us with speech. staid at Sister Godfrey's all night

Monday Jan 31st 1881.
Attended to the correspondence. Elders Wood, King and Romney called on me. In the Evening I went to Old Ford to meeting and had an Excellent time. Mrs Gell who had attended our meetings for some time told me she was converted and would "cast her lot with the people if they were wrong."

Tuesday Feby 1st 1881.
with Elder Bentley at the office all day writing, in the Evening a Mr Squires a blind man called on me to ask some questions about our faith and went away seemingly and saying he was well satisfied with the interview.

{69}
Wednesday Feby 2nd 1881.
In the office making up star lists and Mailing to subscribers till Evening—I went to Whitechapel to meeting and had a good meeting. quite a number there-- I talked about 25 minutes. On my road home I saw a brass Band outside a fine Gin Palace. ~~"Daughter of Zion."~~ and their playing in good style "Daughter of Zion" recd letters from home on arrival at Confer House which made me feel well.

Thursday Feby 3rd 1881.
I worked in the office till afternoon tho' feeling quite unlike work thro' having taken cold in the afternoon I went to Sister Godfreys to Dinner and then took her to meeting at Pentonville and had a good meeting I spoke about 15 minutes. had a testimony meeting

Friday Feby 4th 1881.
Worked in the office all forenoon,, and went with Elder Wood to his Brother at Goode Road to Dinner and I talked to him and his wife about Utah affairs. and then went with Elder Wood and his Brother and another Gent to the House of ~~Commons~~ Parliment. went into the house of Lords while some of the business was being done some cases being tried and appeal before the Lord Chancillor but did not have the privelage of going into the house of Commons as the day before 35 Irish members were Expelled from

the house for cause—obstructive--and
there being much Excitement the gal=
=lery of the House of Commons was filled
with Spectators and listeners and many
were unable to obtain admission.

Saturday Feby 5th 1881.
At the office all day writing up the
accounts of the Conference and preparing
sheets for Liverpool

{70}
Sunday Feby 6th 1881.
Took breakfast with Bro & Sister Crackle.
and attended monthly Priesthood Meeting at
Penton St. Hall and had an Excellent time,
a season of rejoicing, went to Bro & Sister
Crosses to Dinner and attended testimony
meeting at North London Branch in the Evening
Bore my Testimony to the Saints. took tea at
Bro Crackles with a number of Saints and
some Strangers and had a good time in
talking & Singing with them. Attend Evening
meeting. Elder W. Wood brought some of
his relatives to meeting. I talked 1 hour
on the Gospel Restored. Elders Bently &
Wood also spoke. saints & strangers seemed
to feel well and Expressed themselves well
Satisfied.. administered to Elder Wood after
the forenoon services as he had met a Very
bad injury to his ankle by spraining it and
it was very painful. he felt better after
the administration. I also ordained
Bro Wm Blackmore an Elder in the
Woolwich Branch.

Monday Feby 7th 1881.
Made up Quarterly financial Report
to Dec 31st 1880 and sent to Liverpool
and went to Old ford to meeting. And
had an Excellent meeting.

Tuesday Feby 8th 1881.
Elder Bentley and I worked in the
office copying up all our last years
Tithing a/cs and getting them straight
on the Book to be Kept in the office. and wrote
some letters, to some of the Bretheren.

Wednesday Feby 9th 1881.
With Elder Bentley in the office Mailed
stars & Journals to Weekly & Semi Weekly
subscribers and afterwards went to the
Whitechapel Branch Meeting. I spoke about
20 minutes.

{71}
Thursday Feby 10th 1881
Fast day. spent a few hours in study and
reflection and met Elder Bentley at Bro Crosses
and Proceeded to Houses of Parliment with ticket
from Bro E. Adams. In consequence of so many
seeking admission, the ballot was as usual
resorted to and Elder Bentley was the fortunate
one and I the Unfortunate. On coming out
I met Elder T. C. Griggs in the large hall who
informed me that he had stood outside at the
gate Expecting to see me and policemen had come
and ordered him and all strangers inside the
house. we supposed because of the present
unsettled state of Irish troubles, the Govern=
=ment seem to be using Every precaution – we
taking the locks off the guns in the armories where
stores of guns are Kept and also doubling and
threbling the usual number of Guards around
arsenals and magazines of war materials
Surely mens hearts are failing them for fear.
Elder Griggs and I walked to Sister Godfreys
and took tea with her– Elder Bentley came
in afterward. Elder Griggs went to Kingston
bathes to baptize 4 or 5 persons from Whitechapel
and I and Elder Bentley to North London Meeting
and had a good testamoney meeting.

Friday Feby 11th 1881.
at the office making up accounts and
writing letters to various parties, till afternoon
when I went to E. M. Greene & Co. fenchurch St
city. to pay freight on a box of Books from
Liverpool office to Elder Batt in New Zealand
but the steam Ship does not start till the
16 inst so I did not pay the bill. I called
at the House of Elder Woods Brother in Goswell
Road and spent from 1/2 past 4 till 1/2 past
11 P.M. conversing and singing with Elder Wood
and his Brother & Brother's Wife and a Miss
Campbell, all seemed much interested and
gave Evidence of Enlightenment by the good
spirit of God. I left them feeling well.

{72}
Saturday Feby 12th 1881
Withe Elder Bentley fixing up accounts of the
stars and other things, and I wrote to Wife Mary
Jane also P. T. Morehead and in the Evening
I left Paddingtong R. R. Station at 6.40
for Newberry and arriving at 8:25. and was

met at the Station by Elder /CF\ Wilcox and /AF\ Brown
and a number of the Saints and took pleasure
in Visiting with them. till late bed time.
Sleep at the house of a Stranger who had
Kindly consented to accommodate me

Sunday Feb 13th 1881.

Met at the house of Sister Herbert in the
Forenoon and proceeded to Bro Elijah Whornham and
took dinner and thence to House of Sister Her=
=bert and held a meeting. Elders C. F. Wilcox and
M. F. Brown administered the Sacrament to
the Saints of Newbury, and the saints from
the Cheelvy Branch all assembled at New=
=bury. some of the Saints took the opportunity
to bear their testamony to the restoration of the
gospel. and Elder George Pocock spoke in Tongues
and Elder C. F. Wilcox interpreted the Same viz
Be yea also ready for the Son of Man Commeth
~~when~~ /in an hour that\ ye Know not of. I spoke for
65 minutes
to an attentive congregation and in the Evening
held meeting at the house of bro Elijah Whor=
=nham. I occupied the whole time. the Congre=
=gation listening attentively to a discourse of
70 minutes. After ~~meeting~~ Preaching I had
the pleasure of Organizing a Branch of the
chruch to be Known as the Newbury Branch
with Elijah Whornham President. and William
Wheeler 1st Councillor and Ashley Fisher second
Councillor. I ordained Elijah Whornham and
Ashley Fisher to the office of Elders in the Church
and set them apart to their offices and afterward
went with Elders C. F. Wilcox and M. F. ~~Wilcox~~ Brown
to the River Thames and was delighted to
behold Elder Wilcox baptize George Herbert,
Albert Taylor and Thomas Whornham and we
all repaired to the House of Sister Herbert and
Confirmed them I being mouth over Bro Herbert.

{73}

Monday Feby 14th 1881.

I slept at the house of the Stranger who told
me this morning that I was welcome to all
the Kindness she had rendered, we called
at Bro Wheeler and set him apart as the
Councillor of Bro Whornham, and took a few
minutes with Bro Whornham introducing him
in the duties of his office and calling and
took train for Hungerford and passed a house
where lives a Mrs Nash a Sister to the wife
of Bros Thomas Smith and Henry Watts of
Smithfield Cache County, Utah. and walked
to Ramsbury putting up at the House
of Elder George Chowles. the Presiding Elder
here. sister Chowles is a woman that does not
appreciate this life very much. And I don't think
she appreciates the company of the Elders very much
and old Couple named Wilmott living close by and
being somewhat acquainted with the Elders came
in and invited us to take tea which she provided
comfortably for us. We held a meeting at Bro Chowles
house at which the saints and some strangers were
present. I talked 70 minutes to a much interested
congregation. we talked to a Bro Gooderman that
had been a member of the church for many years
and had been acquainted with Bro Thomas Smith
and Joseph and Henry Watts of Smithfield (my home)
and I learned some little about their relatives, but
did not get time to go see them., Elder Wilcox
and Brown and I slept at Mr & Mrs Wilmott and
on + **Tuesday Feby 15th 1881** +
Elders Wilcox, Brown & I started for ~~Cadley~~ /Torrants\ Farm
Cadley. Wilts   Calling at a Beer house named
The Red Lion Inn at axford at I heard that a
neice of Bro Joseph and Henry Watts of Smithfield
was living there. I found 2 girls named Watts were
living there but they did not Know the men
I referred to. It was pouring Rain all day but
we went on to Marlborough. to the House of Bro
Solomon Stone. here I received a letter from
Sister Jane Nolen. informing me of the
Death of my dear and loving daughter Zina.
who died Jan 24th 1881 at 2 O.Clock P.M.

{74}
having given birth to a male child at
12 Oclock-- she did not live to see her
infant. My feelings are beyond descr=
iption, but the Father who Knows all things
is abundantly able to sustain me in
this, another heavy affliction. What will my
poor Children do for someone they love?
Mother gone. Father gone, and now the loved
sister of the family also gone! Father,

comfort my poor grief stricken family and
bind and heal up their broken hearts I pray
thee in the name of Jesus Christ Amen.
With Elders C. F. Wilcox and M. F. Brown
I proceeded to Cadley. stopping and
holding meeting at the house of Bro John
Spackman. A number of Saints and 2
strangers came to meeting. I had a good
liberty and talked 75 minutes. The saints
seemed to be rejoiced but not so with
the strangers. Slept 3 in a bed as before,
the saints have been very Kind and good
to me. and I feel to say god Bless them.
for Ever. Received letters from Bro G L. Far=
rell from Logan. Cache Co Utah Confirming
my dear daughters death.

 Wednesday. ~~July~~ 16th 1881. Feby
Walked to savenack on the Great Western
R. R. and was accompanied by Elders W & B.
and took train for Paddington Station
arriving at 3.40.P.M and arriving at the
office 10 Dorset St at 1/2 past 5. found Br
Bentley & Frank Snow there and had a
good chat. Elder John Howard came in
also after a little while, and after supper
we all went to a concert at the White
=chapel Branch. all passed off very
pleasant and agreeable. got home again
about 1 A.M.

 Thursday ~~July~~ /Feby\ 17th 1881. +
sent my monthly Report for January to
Liverpool and wrote a letter to Don C
Hyde the Husband of my dear deceased

{75}
daughter. And answered a number of letters
on Conference business. It being fast day
Elder Bentley and I implored the Blessings
of our father in Heaven on our labors and
on our families at home in Utah-- in the
Evening I went to the North London Meeting Room
and had an Excellent Meeting Elders Frank
Snow, T. C. Griggs. J. C. Bentley. John Howard and I
spoke. Elder Griggs & I went to Sister Godfreys
and administered to her. she being quite sick
with a severe Cold.

 Friday Feby 18th 1881.
at the office writing till 5 OClock then
went to see the Brother of Elder Wood at
No 3 Goswell Road and had an Excellent
visit with them and Miss Campbell. in
investigating the Doctrines of our Church.

 Saturday Feby 19th 1881
Went to meet Prest W. W Jackson at the
Waterlooe R R. Station. He did not arrive
till 2.10 P.M and When He & I got back
to 10 Dorset St we found to our glad surprise
Elder David James from Salt Lake City
What a glad and Joyous meeting! We
spent the Evening at Sister Crosse's

 Sunday Feby 20th 1881
With David James. W. W. Jackson. & T.C. Griggs
I went in the morning to Hear Rev C. H Spurgeon
who read from the Bible for the lesson from 6th
chap Luke 12 verse to End, and Preached from
Luke 6 Chap & 32 verse after meeting Elders
T. C Griggs & W.W Jackson went to Whitechapel
Branch and Elder David James & I to Lambeth,
Bro James preached and I bore testamony, we then
went to North London in the Evening, and had
a full house of saints and attentive listeners
who were addressed by Elder David James
and W. W. Jackson.

 Monday & Tuesday Feby 21st & 22nd 1881
With Elders James & Jackson I went Visiting
sights. Viz. Houses of Parliment, Westminster
Cathedral at which place I attended the
Church service. the subway under the Thames

{76}
London Bridge, Tower of London, and Many
other points of Interest and Value, Elders J. H. White
and J A Jennings returned from their Visiting in Wales

 Wednesday July 23rd 1881.
With Bro Bentley mailed the stars
~~& Inv~~ to Subscribers and in Evening took Elders James,
Jackson, White & Jennings to Mad Tausauds Wax
works. Elders King & Romney came in & Elder Shaw started out.

 Thursday. Feby 24th 1881.
With Elders Jackson & James I went to the Woolwich
Rotunda in the forenoon, and the Arsnel in the Afternoon
and meeting in the Evening at North London. had a
good testimony Meeting

 Friday Feby 25th 1881
Wrote letters till afternoon and then I again made

and Effort to gain admission to the House of
                                    Commons
after waiting from 3 Oclock till 1/4 past 6 I at
last got the privelage of a look for the first
time of my life at the House in Session and
heard speaches from Lord George Hamilton
and Messrs Labouchere, Foster, Cowan and
other Irish members. tonight was passed
the famous "Coercion Irish Bill by 220
against 38. Elders C T. Wilcox & M F. Brown
                                        arrived.

Saturday Feby 26th 1881
attended meeting at Whitechapel all day
in Company with Elders David James. T. C. Griggs
and the presidents of North London and Lambeth
                                        Branch
and had Excellent meetings. I addressed the
assembly on both occasions afternoon & Evening.

Monday Feby 28th 1881.
Wrote letters till afternoon, took a bath. and went
to Old Ford to meeting and had a good visit
with our good sister Gell and a number of the
Saints.

{77}
Tuesday Mch 1st 1881.
Wrote and fixed up my accounts and visited
the St Pauls Cathedral with Elder David
James & his Brother. Going as high up as the
golds Gallery 542 steps from the Street,
went through the Whispering gallery and
heard the whispering from one side to
the other and climbed up and down
stairs so much and stood ground loo=
=king at the Statues that I was very
tired. in the afternoon I called at
Mr John Woods and chatted with them for
an hour-- his wife and himself treated me very
Kindly but they seemingly don't go much on
                                    Mormonism
In the Evening Sisters Call & Edwards called on
me and chatted. also sister Margaret Geary
came and paid the money for her Emigration to
Utah.

Wednesday Mch 2nd 1881.
Wrote and talked with Elders Wilcox and
Brown about the affairs in their district
and went to the meeting of the Whitechapel
Branch in the Evening. had a testamony mee=
=ting and I with the rest bore testamony of
the work of God. help to fix up the Stars.

Thursday Mch 3rd 1881.
Wrote to several Elders in the Morning, and
a letter to Bp Rigby & daughter Rebecca, and
attended North London Branch Meeting in
the Evening. had a good testamony Meeting
I occupied 15 minutes in talking to the
saints. I went and staid at Sister Godfreys
all night. she treated me very kindly.

Friday. Mch 4th 1881.
Wrote letters and attended to considerable
business at the office. --Elders Wilcox and Brown
started into their districts and Elder James
Wallace came from the Liverpool office
to Visit friends last Evening-- Elders Bentley
& I visited a Mrs Long & Mrs Nicholson
and took tea with them Explaining some
of the principles of the Gospel. called at
Bro & Sister Cross's after and spent an hour or two.

{78}
Saturday Mch 5th 1881
Wrote letters home and to others. Elders
Jennings & White started to Kent this P.M
several Bretheren and sisters called at the office
this Evening and spent the Evening chatting.

Sunday Mch 6th 1881.
attended the monthly Priesthood Meeting at
North London Meeting Room and had a very
good representation. Arranged for London Conf=
=Erence to be held at Orsons Assembly rooms
New Road. Whitechapel. E Sunday. April 3rd
1881. and a Concert the following Monday
Evening at Albion Hall. Moregate Street.
in the afternoon I attended meeting at the
Lambeth Branch and in the Evening at North
London. I spoke most of the time in the
afternoon and about 15 minutes in the Evening
as Elder David James occupied most of
the time in the Evening. Ordained William Crack=
=kles an Elder after the Priesthood Meeting.

Monday March 7th 1881.
Wrote Letters in the Morning and took a
pair of /my\ Garments to Elder Wood's Brother
to send to Elder Wood as he only had one
Pair and wanted to change. I had quite
a talk with a Mr & Mrs Wood and Miss
Campbell on Religious Matters. and though
they are favorably impressed with Mormonism
they are not willing to accept Mormonism
yet. ~~Tuesday March 8th 1881.~~
in the Evening I went to meeting at Old Ford

had an Excellent Meeting. I spoke
nearly an hour.
    Tuesday March 8th 1881.
I visited Bro Wells at poplar.and Sister Todd
about the Emigration of her grand-daughter.and
sent home some seeds. and wrote letters
in the Evening.
    Wednesday March 9th 1881.
helped about sending off stars to Weekly
and By Weekly correspondents. read a letter
from Thomas Hillyard and bringing me news of

{79}
my daughters Rebeccas Confinement with a son
on saturday. Feby 12th this is my second Grand
son and I pray God my father to bless these my
children & childrens children, and may I live
to see them and assist in their development
as Heirs to a crown and Kingdom in our fathers
mansions in the Evening attended the Meeting
at Whitechapel Branch and had a good
meeting. I spoke 20 minutes
    Thursday Mch 10th 1881.
Worked in the office all day at the Monthly
accounts and writing letters. till Evening
when I attended the North London Branch
Meeting and had an Excellent testamony
meeting. bore my testamony to the gospel.
    Friday March 11th 1881.
Spent the day with Elder David James in
going about the City of London. seeing sights
and he bought some silks and other things
at Mrs Kings at Hobborn Viaduct. And Elders
King and Romney came in from Essex and
we in Company will Bro Bentley went to see
Bro James off to Wolverton after spending
nearly 3 Weeks in London. where we Enjoyed
his visit right well. He started from
Easton station at 5.15.P.M
    Saturday Mch 12th 1881.
Elder George Stringfellow came in from
Sussex in the morning feeling well. And
Elder King left for Grays in Essex, went
to St Pancras Station and met Elder W. C
Dunbar from Scotland. who came to make
London a visit. I spent the day writing &
sent my monthly Report for Feby to Liverpool
    Sunday March 13th 1881.
Elder H. J. Romney left this morning for
Grays Essex to attend the council meeting
of that Branch of the Church. Elders Stringfellow

and Bentley & I met Elder Dunbar at the
Mutual improvement Meeting at 11 a.m.
Elder Stringfellow and I ate dinner at Bro
Crackells and proceeded to the Whitechapel
Branch where we preached and I returned
to the North London Branch and I met Elders

{80}
Dunbar & Bentley in the Evening. Elder
Dunbar & I occupied the time in the
Evening-- I confirmed sister Ester Wilkes
a member of the church and sister sarah
Woodcock and Ella Woodcock were also
confirmed at the same time and place
at Whitechapel.
    Monday March 14th 1881.
With Elder George H. Stringfellow and W. C
Dunbar I visited the Towers of London. the Crown
Jewels Room, ancient Armor Room. Political
                              prisons
Room. Martin-henry Rifle Room. Containing 60M
stand of arms. going into the Lower Crypt
the place where the poorer=Class of Prisoners used
to be confined in dungeons. we next took a
walk through the Tunnel or Subway for
Pedestrians under the Thames, coming out
on the Bourough side and walked back over
London Bridge. took steam boat up the
River to Cleopatra's Needle. thence to the
Sommerset house meeting Elder Jos Bentley
here I left and went to Highbury and took
train for ~~Kings~~ Grays and spent the Evening
with the saints Keeping the 71st Birthday of
Bro [Benee/Bence] and I talked to the saints for
about 3/4 of an hour. leaving them about 1/2 past
9 OClock feeling Well. having had an Enjoy=
=able time returning to No 10 Dorset St
    Tuesday March 15th 1881.
Elder George Stringfellow left for Nottingham on a
                                visit
Forenoon in the Office Writing and posting a/cs
Elder Tucker & White came in at Noon, and I
arranged for them to go to Lambeth and Labor
and they started off. I visited Elder Dunbar
at Sister Crosses in the Evening and found
Elder White at home quite comfortable and
cosy at Sister Crosses. Had a good Visit with
Elder Dunbar. He slept with me at the office
    Wednesday March 16th 1881.
Spent the day at office till Evening. I went
to see sister Farnes and her baby, and found them

quite comfortable. attended the Relief Society

{81}
concert of the Whitechapel Branch and had quite
and Enjoyable time.

Thursday March 17th 1881.
In office all morning writing to correspond=
=ents &c. and in the Evening in Company
with Elder D. C. Dunbar went by invitation
of Bro Ephraim Adams to the House of Com=
=mons and Joined the Company. viz
[unidentified clipping "Railway to Wimbledon-common" pasted on page]
Elders S Roskelley & D. C Dunbar attended
the above named meeting and his Courtesy of
Mr. Broadhurst. MP. Got a special permit
to visit the House of Commons then in Session.
Heard a large number of the members of
the parliament speak on the army supply
bill before the Vote was taken.

Friday March 18th 1881.
at the office all day writing letter to
various persons and making out blanks
for the statistical report at our coming
conference. and in the Evening Elder Bentley
and I went to the Agricultural Hall to see the
show of Domestic Labor saving machinery of
almost all Kinds. together with children from
Industrial schools. carrying on their various trade
of Carpenter work. tailoring. and other branches
also Blind Men and Women making brushes

{82}
by hand. And splitting wood and other indus=
=trial pursuits. also saw many Kinds of
Labor saving machinery. Elder Dunbar left for
Norwich

Saturday March 19th 1881.
Spent the forenoon with the saints and chatted
with them, taking a walk through the park of
a Gengleman Close by with Bro F Snow and Bro
Swainston. Held a meeting at the House of
Bro Swanston Elder Manlove Presidiing. I
talked to the saints. and after meeting I or=
=ganized a Relief Society. appointing Sister
Mary Swanston president, and Sister sophia
Waller Secratery of the same. Elder Frank
Snow and I accompanied by sevearl of the saints
waling part of the distance, went to Hemel
Hempstead, and Met with Bro William Sills &
Family. slept at sister Childs House and
went to Bro Sells to dinner he is an acquaintance
with
Bro & sister smith and the Poacock family at
Smithfield Cache Co. Utah.. walked to Boxwood Sta
=tion and took train for Wolverton in Bucks, and
we arrived at 6O'Clock P.M. and were Kindly gree
=ted by Bro Smith and his family. Preached to the
family all Evening.

Tuesday March 22nd 1881
I visited Bro Smiths family till 2.8. P.M. when
I left Wolverton for London arriving at Highbury
at 5 O'clock and found Elder Bentley at the office
and a lot of Letters waiting for me to answer.

{83}
Wednesday March 23rd 1881.
at the Office all day till Evening I went to the
Whitechapel Branch to a testimony Meeting. I
spoke
20 Minutes. Assisted to send off Stars and Journals

Thursday March 24th 1881.
at the office all day with Elders Griggs & J. C
Bentley preparing statistical statements for the
Conference. in the Evening went to Sister Godfreys
and took his Books that I had send for her
and attended the meeting of the Committee who
were preparing the amusements for the Conference
and were occupied all the Evening

Friday March 25th 1881.
at the office Writing all morning, and in the
Evening I went to see Miss Campbell at Mr
Woods and had a good chat with her on the
principles of our faith she seems to be satisf
=ied about the 1st principles of our belief
but has strong traditions to overcome and
I pray God to help her to do so for I fully
believe her and Ephraimite. Elder Dunbar left today
for Nottingham

Saturday March 26th 1881.
In the morning I went to the Jewish
synagog and saw their manner of worship
and noticed a great similarity between
their singing and that of our american Indian
tho men sit on the ground floor with hats
on and a sort of White shawl over their
shoulders hanging down at the Ends at
their sides. The women go in the galley
and it has a high lattice, work so the
women have to peep thro it. Some little boys
behind the priests chant a sort of Chorus at

Intervals to the prayers and laws read by the priests. these boys are taking from and returning the laws and parchments rolled upon the sticks from the desk to the stand come to the priest who put his right hand on the front and top of the hat or cap of the boy as a sort of blessing. I thought strange to see the seeing indifference to the services going on. I took train to see Bro Wells about my clothes being made, and then returned to

{84}
the office, found Elder John H. White – he had been at Grays since last Wednesday and came to London to day. I wrote letters home and with Elder T. C. Griggs and Jos C Bentley I accepted and invitation from Sister Emily Keep to spend the Evening with her at her Moth =ers in commemoration of her 21st Birth day and we had a very pleasant time.
Sunday March 27th 1881.
attended the Mutual Improvement meeting at north London in the Morning and got dinner at Bro Crosses and Proceeded to Lambeth and attended
Lambeth Branch Council Meeting and Spoke to the Bretheren about saving means for Emigration and attended afternoon meeting and spoke to the saints about living to Enjoy the good Spirit in this Country so they can take it to Zion with them, took tea at sister Bro Br[---]'s, and preached 40 Minutes in the Evening – a good influence prevailing. Elders John H. White went to Woolwich to attend meeting.
Monday March 28th 1881.
In the office writing letters till Evening when I attended the meetings at Sister Todds and had a good fellowship meeting I talked about 40 minutes. I sent Miss Campbell a letter answering the question was the Gospel preached to the Children of Israel? and an invitation to attend our Conference on April 3rd
Tuesday March 29th 1881.
We worked in the office all day and Evening till nine O'clock when I proceeded to the Pentonv= =ille Baths in Company with Elders Tucker & Bent= =ley and Bro Crackels and Baptized the foll- =owing named persons Ann Dennis age 54. William Lodge age about 47. Emily Andrew age 21 Mary Elizabeth Aistrup

aged 14 Montague Walter Cornell aged 9. Several sisters came to attend the baptisms and had a good time. all felt well .

{85}
Wednesday March 30th 1881.
I went to see Bro Wells at Poplar about my Clothes for Conference and called on Sister Todd to. Know about some Porters Emigrating. and then went to Notting Hill to see if sister Dow could accommodate some of the Elders with a bed during the Conference. /I confirmed Mary Elizabeth Aistrup for Mem =er of the Church.\ Friday April 1st 1881.
Elders White and Romney came in from Essex. Elders Wilcox and Brown came in from their districts and all the Elders came in to this office and Enjoyed themselves well.

Saturday April 2nd 1881.
With much satisfaction I chatted with the Elders coming into London from their Districts as Each came to the office to report, with Elders Wilcox and Brown and Prest Jackson I went to Euston station and met President Albert Carrington at 7. 30 on arrival from Liverpool and proceeded to Sister Godfreys to stay for the night. Chatting by the way and remaining till a late hour when I and Bro Jackson went to the office to Sleep and ~~in the evening I~~
Sunday April 3rd 1881
London Conference was held at Orsons Assembly Rooms, New Road, Commercial Road. London, E. and I went to all 3 of the meetings a partial report of which is in the Star and added hereto. we had a Most Enjoyable time, and full Meetings. I think over 500 persons were present Sunday Evening of 1/2 of which were Strangers,

{86}
Monday April 4th 1881.
with the Elders belonging to the Conference
[Pencilled at left fore edge: Isaac]   I went and got a group likeness taken
and all were present but Elder Willey who had not come in from the Channel

Islands, In the afternoon most of the Elders and I went to the Natural Art Gallery and had a book look at the pictures and in company with Prest. Carrington I went to our Conference concert at Albion Hall and Presided as Chairman, during the Eatin[?] Concert. all went off well and all seemed to Enjoy themselves.

Tuesday April 5th 1881.
spent part of the day at the office and with Prest Carrington started from Holborn Viaduct Rail Way Station at 4/15 arriving at Faversham Kent. At 5 47. were met at the station by Elders King and J. A. Jennings. held meeting with the Saints, and returned to London, arriving at London at Midnight. Stopped at Sister Godfreys. Wednesday April 6th 1881.
spent most all of the day with President Carrington at Sister Godfrey's having an Exceeding good Visit with him. in the Evening he & I visited the Crosses and spent a few hours with them and returned to Sister Godfreys to sleep

Thursday April 7th 1881.
spent most of the Day Visiting with Prest Carrington at Sister Godfreys and saw Elder Oscar F. Hunter off for Nottingham to his Conference. feeling Well. spent Evening in Meeting at North London Branch and spoke about 35 minutes and returned to Sister Godfreys to Sleep.

Friday April 8th 1881.
With Elder Jos C. Bentley went to Euston Station to See Prest Carrington start for Liverpool at 10.10 A.M. Feeling first rate. having had a good Visit to the London Conference. In the Evening

{87}
Elder Bentley & I went to Prest Cornells to talk about the Meeting house business.
[Pencilled at gutter, left: John] Saturday April 9th 1881.
spent the day at the office writing. Except hunting up some persons going to Emigrate by the ship on April 16th 1881. Bro Willey arrived from Jersey. Sunday April 10th 1881.
With Elders Bentley & Willey went to North London Mutual I. Association Meeting and thence to Prest Garners at Lattimers Road and thence to Prest Balls at Notting Hill gate and with him to Lambeth Meeting and spoke to the Congregation over an hour. and Confirmed into the Church, William Hodges and Emily Andrews and after doing some business with some members going to Utah I took buss and arrived at the Whitechapel meeting during 2nd singing. and occupied 75 minutes to an attentive audience of saints and a number of strangers.

Monday April 11th 1881
In the office Writing till Evening when I went to Old Ford as usual to meeting and had a good time with the Saints. Elders Willey, Griggs, Wallace and I spoke, I about 30 minutes these Old ford Meetings are becoming quite interesting. several called on me through the day to arrange about their Emigration Matters.

Tuesday April 12th 1881.
spent the day writing to Various persons and I went to hunt up sister Brown and Sister Evans to arrange about their Emigration to Utah. I sent to Utah by Sister Selina Evans 4 Vols of History of England, for myself and a silk dress for Bro David James. and I sent by Sisters Margaret Geary. 1 apocraphy, 3 Vols Rollins Sacred History for Myself and a Silk dress pattern for Bro David James

Wednesday April 13th 1881
Writing in the office all day till Evening I attended Whitechapel Branch meeting and had a very good meeting. Elder Willey spoke.

{88}
Thursday April 14th 1881.
[Pencilled, circled at left page fore edge: Edward] At the office till afternoon making up monthly a/c for the Liverpool office. Afternoon Elder Willey and I went and took tea with Sister Godfrey and in the Evening attended meeting at north London Branch. I spoke 20 minutes and went to the office and worked on my Emigration a/c's till 1/2 past 2 A.M. When elder W. W. Willey and I went to High Holborn to see my nephew Saml R. Williams and got some Medicine for Elder Willey to prevent Sea sickness, we then went to Sister Godfreys to tea and the old Lady made us comfortable. I to day rec'd letters from Home bringing news of the Death of Sister Drusilla Doris Hendricks the Esteemed mother of my dear

wife Rebecca – I afterwards attended meeting at north London Branch and had an Excellent meeting, Elders W. W. Willey and Thos C. Griggs were the Speakers. I Engaged the services of Elder T. C. Griggs and with him & Elder Bentley I worked and made out my Emigration a/c for the present Comp==any and did not get to bed till 1/2 past 2 A.M. Very tired.

Friday April 15th 1881.
Met the Saints going to Liverpool to Embark for Utah at Euston Station at 9 A.M and after arranging for their Tickets &c had the Pleasure to Bid adieu to 29 London saints and 3 from Southampton. Giving Charge of the little Compy to Elder W. W Willey also the money and the papers pertaining to them and also my monthly report and money for March. Many saints and strangers assembled to see the Saints off. proceeded to office and wrote some letters and in the afternoon with Elder Bentley & Griggs I took dinner at Sister Godfreys thence I went with Elder Griggs to the Royal Albert Hall and heard the Messiah: Most magnificently rendered, Returned with Elder Griggs to Bro & Sister Ames of Whitechaple to stay over night and had a very good Breakfast, on

{89}
[Pencilled, circled, on left gutter: William] Saturday April 16th 1881.
I started with Elder TC Griggs for Brighton from Whitechapel at 8.40 A.M. Changing several times on the way and arriving at Brighton at a little after 2.O'Clock and were met at the Sta==tion by Elders George and R H Stringfellow and a Samuel Bantock formerly Prest of the North London Branch. I went with Elder Griggs to see his cousin and Mr. Brooks her husband and we were treated very Kindly by them and afterward met the Elders Stringfellow and while standg in the street talking were much surprised at see Elders King & Jennings from Kent walking up street from Kent we went to Bantocks to tea. and the sight was not pleasurable to appointed a time to meet John Mitchell the Prest of the Brighton Branch but he failed to come to time. so I did not see him. I went with Elder Griggs to Sleep at Mr Brooks

and had a good nights rest.
Sunday Apl 17th 1881.
after Breakfast had a pleasant sing & chat with Mr Brooks & wife who are some little interested in Mormonism and at 1/2 past 10 OClock met in a Branch coun=cil meeting with Elders George & R. H Stringfellow and T. C Griggs, King, and Jennings from Utah and 6 or 7 members of the priesthood of Brighton ~~Branch~~ Branch. all talked freely and I gave a state==ment of the relative positions of Presidents of conference, District, & Branches &c and gave a relation of the financial affairs of the branch. con==cluded to support the Prest of Branch (John Mitchell) with 2 Councillors and releive him of the financial cares, Ate Dinner with Elder Geo Stringfellow at the house of Bro George Reed. Afternoon sacrament meeting. Elder King. Jennings. &c the saints spoke and we had a good time. I talked about 1/2 and hour on the practical duties of saints. Evening I occu=pied about 20 minutes. Elder Griggs preached for an hour to a small but appreciative audience. I ordained George Reed an Elder and set him apart as 1st Councillor to Prest John Mitchell.

{90}
[Pencilled, circled at left fore edge: Joseph] Monday April 18th 1881
arose Early and prepared for seeing the Volunteer review of the Volunteers of England and sat them march to Quarters after their arrival by train in Brighton. With Elder Griggs I went to the common near Brighton and had an Excellent sights at the review of 25 thousand Volunteers, a sham battle 26 cannon. stood close to the commanding general and staff. the Duke of Cambridge and Prince the Duke of Connaught. Gen Sir Arthur Woolsey and other distingu==ished generals. Well satisfied with my trip I returned to the house of Mr Brooks and found a letter from my son William the day being very pleasant over head we got into the Excellent position at an early hour on the Line of the Defense and Viewed the proceedings of the Battle. Skirmishers were thrown out and

followed by the main army with good
Effect. The wind arose and filled the
air and covered spectators & Soldiers with
dust from the chalky roads. Making it
very unpleasant in the after part of the
day – we retuned to Brighton and went
up and got tea and left for Eastborne at
8.30 P.M arriving in a compartment of
a 1st class R.R. Carriage with 17 persons
in it at 10 O Clock. and proceeded to
the house of my brother, was welcomed
by him and his daughter Annie.

<u>Tuesday Apl 19th 1881.</u>
spent a very Pleasant day walking & Writing
letters home to Wife Mary, also Son
Samuel, Jos Hall & Harrison A Thomas, and
my Brother being sick with Rheumatism
spent a part of the time Visiting with him
in his Bed Room and in the Evening I spent
very pleasantly in listening to my neice play
the piano at Elder Griggs & I was with

{91}
[*Pencilled at top of page, divided from diary text by double line:*
Nancy or Ann   See St. Germans
Register]   her a number of pieces of
music We recd word of the Death of Be[---]d

<u>Wednesday April 20th 1881.</u>
after breakfast Elder Griggs walked around
the martello tower. Wind blowing hard and quite
cold.. My Niece Annie played several pieces of
music at the Piano after our Return to the House
My Brother being a little better was up and
going around again – but not well. Taking leave
of my dear relatives once more, Elder Griggs and
I left Eastbourne at 1.5.8 arriving at Brighton at
2.58 and Visited Elder Griggs relatives till 5
O'clock. we went to the Brighton R R. Station and
met Elders George and Richard H. Stringfellow and
chatted with them till 610 P.M. when the train
started for London. again I rode under the
River Thames this the celebrated Thames Tunnel

and arrived at Whitechapel branch during the
                                            meeting
and talked to the Saints about 20 minutes. and I
felt quite at home again among the saints in London

<u>Thursday April 20th 1881.</u>
The accumulation of Letters and Business at
the office during my abstance to the south . .

Coasts was heavy and I wrote all day and finished
up my list of P. E. Receipts wanted from the Lpool
Office after ~~the north~~ attending the North London
Meeting, where I spoke to the saints. for 20
minutes, and confirmed Miss Sophia Campbell
a member of the church. I was assisted by
Elders Jos C. Bentley and George Cross. Elders
                                            White
and W. Words started for the Norwich Conference

<u>Friday Apl 22nd 1881.</u>
Wrote all day in the office. in the Evening
I went to the Photographers and got a dozen
likenesses of myself for distribution among the
Elders of the Conference. then went to Ludgate Cir=
=cus to a firm of Frenologists and got a Chart
of my head so as to compare in the future means
spent the Evening at Bro & Sister Cross's talking
about their Emigration to Utah

{92}
Joseph and Mary Hambly's
family   S.R.'s Grandfather & Mother
buried at St Germans

{93}
Mary Roskelley ~~Curch~~
Sammels and wife of John
Sambells of St Germans
(Supposed)
Mary died at Germans, buried St
Germans church
        Children
Elizabeth Sambells Aggott (at Stonehouse)
year in 1880)
Joseph died in Russian War
John Sambells (died young)
William at Downderry
*Mary Ann /Sambells Farthing\ married a Soldier
Jane   died

Ask Elizabeth Hackett about
Fathers death or my Sister Jane

Elizabeth Sambells Aggett
    31 Cremyll St
    Stonehouse Mr Diospl

{94}
Ann   See next page

tho this is proper

Ann Butters Ough, daughter
of William and Alice Roskelley
Butters and the Wife George Ough
Alice Clotilda [stricken word] /Ough\ born
Aug 10th 1859
Alfred George /Ough\ born Feby 18th 1861
Maud Mary Ough born Sep or Oct 1863
George Harrington Ough born
Apl 24th 1866.
Rebecca Haszon Ough born
19 Feby 1868
   [crosswritten vertically:]
   All Born in the
   Parish of
   Minheniott Cornwall

{95}
~~Elizabeth~~ Thomas

{96}
~~Thomas~~ Elizabeth Roskelley
Hansford wife of Job Hansford
both died in Australia. Ask
Walter Hansford.

Walter   in australia
Harriett   now Mrs Parker
     of Australia
Emily-- died in Australia

Ann Couch Long
6 Park Street. Weymouth
   Dorset
*Geo Couch, Coast guard Station
   Keyston. Mr. Litll Champlin
     Sussex

{97}
died in Torpoint union, buried at St Germans
Ann Roskelley Married a man
named John Couch
died in St Germans and buried St Germans
Elizabeth (married, dont Know who)
Jane (Married a Soldier and she died
   abroad – left 2 children
Ann Married a butcher at Weymouth
Henry. died at Jersey of Small pox

John – is in America with / 2 Marys children
                     \ 1 Elizabeth do
Mary (died in Gurnsey)
Isaac died a drunkard in Torpint
Deborah in Australia <u>McCelland</u>
*George coast guard
Frederick in Devonport can tell all
Mary Couch daughter of the above
John and Ann Roskelley Couch
born at Nackers, Cornwall on
Feby 24th 1823

{98}
Alice Roskelley /Collins\ Butters
Bort at Landrake Nov 19. 1804
Wife of William Butters
She is living at St Germans
he is buried at St Germans
he came from Rickle, St Germans
Richard Butters bor St Martin
Cornwall, Dies at Woolrich. about July
1863   born 1827 Jun 17th
Anne Butters born Dec 19th 1830,
married George Ough of Minheniot. Cornwall

William born Apr   1843
(supposed) died at 5 years old

Alice Collins. and old maid
Aunt Alice's great aunt died
St Stephs Cornwall

{99}
<u>youngest daughter of Jos & Mary--</u>
Aung Jane Roskelley married
a Wm Giddlecome, who died
in Gurnsey Dec 6th 1853
aged 55 years
She afterwards married a
Man named John Delamare
who died also at Guernsey
April 3rd 1865 aged 84
years (he was a Cooper or barr
=el (maker for Powder Works)
buried in the Arsnel Cemetry
{100}
    From St Germans Church yard
In Memory of <u>Ellen Sharp</u> who died
Oct 10th 1856 aged 6 years
Also William who died Oct 12th

1856. aged 4 years
Also Nicholas who died Oct 23rd
1856. aged 10 months.
the above were children of
Nicholas & Hannah Sharp of
the <u>Country of Northumberland</u>

{101}
    from Plymouth Cemetrys
Ann Kitt wife of Thomas
Roskelley died Mch 6th 1859
aged 62 years
Also Thomas Roskelly Husband
died Sep 28th 1876 aged 80 years
also Lydia daughter of George
& Jane Roskelly Williams died
Dec 2nd 1875 aged 13 1/2 years
all died at Devonport Devon

{102}
    mems from St Germans
Church yard
Joseph Skellen (Roskelley)
  who died May 18th 1857 at St Germans

  aged 91 years (our Grandfather)
also Mary Hambly   wife
of Joseph Roskelley who died
at St Germans Apl 9th 1832
    aged 68 years
also William Butters of St Germans
who died at St Germans July 13th
1870 aged 71 years
also William Roskelley of tideford
Parish of St Germans who died Apl
27th 1864 aged 83 years
also Mary   wife of above
who died Nov 6th 1849 aged 66

{103}
James /Friends\ Glencoves of Devonport
Died Sep 29th 1867 aged
68 years ask Sister Jane
or John about this if it is
James or Josiah

{104}
[blank]

[end of journal 4; end of transcript]

Journal [5]

1 January 1883 – 1 January 1888

{cover}
Diary
From 1 Jan. 1883
to 1 Jan 1888

{front pastedown}
[blank]

{free endleaf recto: *pasted on page*}
```
            / Male Names page 2
2 Quire  | Female do      "   30
            \ Sealings do   "   64

            / Male Names page 2
3 Quire  | Female do      "   50
            \ Sealings do   "  106

            / Male Names page 2
4 Quire  | Female do      "   66
            \ Sealings do   "  140
```

{free endleaf verso}
[blank]

{unruled page recto}
Charles Ora Card

Samuel Roskelley's
 Diary
Commencing 1 Jan 1883.

{unruled page verso}
[blank]

{page 1}

<u>January 1st, 1883 (Monday) Birthday.</u>
Spent the Day very agreeably with my co-missionaries at
our rented house. Received several callers, who congratulated
me on the Eventful day. Accepted an invitation to take
supper with Bro M. F. Farnsworth the Recorder at the Temple.
and spent the Evening there also.

Samuel Roskelley papers, MS 65, Utah State Univ. Special Collections. The volume was microfilmed in September 1954 by the Utah Genealogical Society; microfilm now available as MS 8239, Church History Library, Salt Lake City. The microfilm was digitized ca.2014 and is publicly available through the website. This version is a line-by-line transcription of the manuscript. Page numbers were added to recto (right hand) pages of the volume to simplify matching the transcription to the document. They are given in this transcription between braces. The transcript is not set in double columns because of longer line lengths in the manuscript and to accommodate the tabulations interspersed through the transcript.

Tuesday 2 Jan 1883
Spent at the Temple, calling names for Baptism at the
font and in assisting to confirm.
Wednesday 3 Jan
I was Endowed for my brother William Henry Roskelley. assisting
before and afterward at the records as usual.
Thursday & Friday 4 & 5 Jan
Assisted to record as usual
Saturday 6 Jan 1883
Copying the Adoption Record.
Sunday 7 Jan 1883.
Attended Sunday School in the 14th Ward (Tabernacle)
was called upon by Supt Morris to assist in administering
the Sacrament to the Children also to teach a class of
pupils in the New testament. Attended meeting in
the Tabernacle in Afternoon, and spent evening with wife
Margaret visiting Father Samuel Turnbow at
the House of his daughter Sophronia Ellen Leonard
Turnbow Carter. Bro Turnbow related his visions to
us of his visits to the Spirit world and testified in the
strongest language of his great desire to once more
get back to that place of happiness and joy.
The ~~coming~~ week was spent in the temple at the
recorders desk and becoming more familiar with the
records and copying them.
Sunday 14 Jan 1883.
President McAllister invited my wife Margaret and
I to go to the Clara Settlement, in company with him and
Elder Farnsworth. We did so, and had a good meeting
administered to Bishop M. Ensign also some
other sick brethren, and learned that some 40 children
had been stricken down with measles and feaver
the 24 hours before. It seems to be quite a sick turn.
Monday 15 Jan 1883
I received a letter from Prest W. Woodruff thru
Bro Bleak asking me to remain in St George for a time
and more thoroughly qualify myself with the Books of
the Temple. I wrote an answer that I would stay
as long as was thought fit.
I passed the week at the Recorders
labor and desk doing my duty to the best of my
skill and ability.

{2}
Sunday 21 Jan 1883
I attended meeting at St George Tabernacle. Pres E Snow
had returned a few days previous from a trip to old
Mexico and Southern Arizona in Company with Apostle Moses
Thatch, C. Layton, J. H. Martineau & others, and preached all
the afternoon. giving a glowing account of the Country and

the facilities for a livelihood, and Stated that the location had been selected for a settlement of the Saints and we would have to look in that direction for a Refuge for some of the Gods people while the storm of Persecution from the United States swept over the Saints in this nation. he spoke very comforting to those who had been called to mourn the loss of dead Relatives the last month.

I spent the week as usual at the Temple. I learned by letters from home that on the 20th inst my wife Mary Roberts Roskelley was blessed with a girl baby which blessing I thank my heavenly father for.

Sunday 28 January 1883.
I borrowed Bro Jas Batteys Horse and buggy and my wife Margaret and I went to Washington Ward and visted the sabbath School. a good School, and well attended. I spoke a litt while to the Children. Prest McAllister and Bro M T Farnswroth and I attended the meeting and we all spoke about 20 minutes each Elders Moroni Snow & John E. Pace also took some time talking to the Saints

Monday 29 Jan 1883
Elder N C Edlefsen and wife and sisters Ansie Poppleton 3 of the Missionaries from Cache Valley Stake took the Morning Stage for the north on the way home having completed their missions in the St George Temple. I continued my labors in the Temple as Usual through the week

On Friday 2nd Feby 1883
Bro Moore & wife and my wife and I broke up houskeeping at the Romney house and we returned the Borrowed dishes and Furniture, paying $5.00 for Rent of furniture $5.00 to Bro Mahonri Snow for 1 months Rent of House and $40.00 to Wolley Lund & Judd for 4 months Rend of House. Bro & Sister Moore moved for a few days to Board with Sister Cottam and my wife and I took Board and Lodgings with Br. M. F Farnsworth and Family. taking supper the first meal.

Saturday 3 Feby 1883. <u>Priesthood Meeting</u>
Pres Snow present. He desired those desiring to move from this district of country to not go until they had done all the work they could in the Temple for themselves and their Kindred dead. that they might be approved of God, he also bore Testimony that the Prophet Joseph

{3}
Smith stated in Nauvoo that the work of redeeming the Dead rested upon the Elders of this Church and God would require it at their hands. Elders let us think of this great responsibility and ask our heavenly father to give us power and strength to do so acceptably in his Sight

Sunday 4 February 1883
on Invitation of Prest McAllister, he and I Visited Price City and held meeting and had a good time.

the place is a small one but the people seem to be
well united, happy and prosperous. I talked 45 mts
    attended my usual work in the Temple until
Friday Feb 9th I went to the Temple and took the Morning
Record as usual and at 10 O'clock with Prest McAllister
Elder Samuel Miles, Sister Hallam Worthen, with Bro George
Worthen, for teamsters, we started for Toquerville, by way of
Harrisvill Leeds, Grapevine Springs to Toquerville, arrived at
6 o'clock, Prest McAllister and I were kindly entertained by
the Bishop William Bringhurst who provided us with a good
bed and food this as a place of Rare surrounding. About
50 inhabitants, almost every family has their orchard and
vineyard and generally speaking good houses. Altho' a
long distance to haul timber and lumber to build up
the Settlement, held meeting here, fair attendance and
people paid good attention, time occupied by Prest
McAllister. Elder Samuel Miles and Myself about equally.
[written vertically in gutter]
    Wednesday 7th inst Bro Moore & his
    Wife Started for home. having
    been honorably released
[journal text]
        Saturday 10th Feby 1883
our Party left Toquerville about 1/2 past 8A.M. crossing
the Verkin River a stream about 2 Rods wide and perhaps
average 1 foot deep at this Season of the year. passing up
through Nephi's Twist. A series of Washes where the
floods have made deep gorges in the Mountain Sides, and
left Room Sufficient for a wagon in the Bottom of the
wash, and /when\ the wash is not wide enough dug roads are
made to accommodate teams, this Twist is so called
because of its continuous curvature for hardly 2
Rods of straight road can be found in any part of
the Wash, the Rocky Road and Sand alternate till Virgin
City is Reached a distances of [blank] miles from Toquerville
Virgin is Situated on the North Side of the Rio Virgen River
on a sand bank filled with excellent orchards and
Vineyards. Stopping to feed the team and get some dinner
at Bishop Parkers. After Dinner we rolled out passing
Duncan's Retreat 3 miles, and Grafton on the South
side of the River And Reaching Rockville at 6P.M.
being 9 miles from Virgin City, a Stringtown of about
35 or 40 Families with good soil for raising the best
Kind of Fruit and Shade trees, containing good orchards and
Vineyards and many good Improvements, Situated on the
North Bank of the Rio Virgin River, the People seem to
be happy and Prosperous. And having to pass over many
miles of tedious, rough, dugroad, it would seem that
persons who settle in these Isolated places would not want to
pass over the road to other Settlements very often. We were
the Guests of Bishop Smith and his wife Lizzie who was the
wife of Asa Calkin during his lifetime. We held a

{4}
meeting in the School House at 7 O'clock, Bro Miles and I
/and Prest McAllister\
occupying the time. Bro McAllister and I slept together,
after administring to a sick girl suffering from Pain in
her side

   Sunday 11 February 1883.
Held meeting at 10 O'clock, the people gathering in from
Grafton, Shonesburg and Hillsdale, and filed the house to
overflowing. Bro Miles and I occupied the time in the forenoon
and Prest McAllister in the Afternoon—I opened the meeting. And after meeting
I assisted Prest McAllister to set apart Bro /Cyrus M.\ Jennings as a High Prest and as
2nd Councillor to Bp Smith of the Rockville Ward. As soon as meeting was
over We got into our wagon and Bid Adieu to our friends traveled 9 miles
to Virgen City, putting up at Bp Parkers for the night. attended a meeting
at the "Order House and had a good meeting. Bro Miles, Myself and
Prest McAllister were the Speakers. the people seemed to feel well and
enjoy the Visit. After Meeting we went and administered to Sister
Jeppson, the Mother of Bro Jeppsen that killed Hunt a few weeks
since while Jeppson was defending himself against Hunt, we took
some Brine and pie with the old lady , and then went to the House of
Sister (wife of Samuel W. Richards) and heard some Excellent singing and
organ music. Retiring to Bed at a late hour

   Monday 12 Feb 1883.
I went with Pres M cAllister to the house of Sister [blank] and took a
good Breakfast of Ham and Eggs. and we left Virgen City ab 1/2 past
Eight O'Clock arriving at Leeds at 1/2 past 12 Taking dinner with Bro
Wilkinson and family—the Gentleman had over 1000 Gallons of Wine
in his Cellar which we can testify is a good article. We walked
over much of the Land between Virgen and Leeds and also between
Leeds and St George—leaving Leeds at 2 O'Clock and arrived at St
George at 1/2 past 6 OClock P.M. pleased and gratified with our trip and
visit with the Saints in the Settlements of the Rio Virgen River.

   Tuesday 13 Feby 1883
Attend at the Temple. and alternated with Recorder M F Farnsworth
calling names at the font for Baptisms. 1260 were Baptized for
making a good days work, as we did not quit till we lit
lam to see to read the names.

   Wednesday, Thursday & Friday 14,15,16 Feb.
Worked at the Recording in the Temple as usual and spent 20 00 for Board
at Lodgings at Farnsworths <u>Saturday Feb 17th 1883</u>
I spent the whole day in the Temple copying the Adoption Record.

   Sunday 18th Feb 1883
Wrote several Letters in the forenoon . And attended meeting at the Tab-
-ernacle at 2 P.M. I was called upon by Prest E Snow and I spoke about
30 Minutes. Prest Snow followed on the propisies of Ezekiel, showing that
the Valley of Dry Bones referred to are a portion of the house of Israel
and are persons who would be officiated for in the temples of God by
the living and administer the ordinances of redemption for them.
I spent the evening with wife Margaret at Bro & Sister Cottams. And
had a very pleasant time

Monday 19 Feb 1883.
Spent the day at the Temple copying the Adoption Records.
Tuesday 20 Feb 1883.
Baptismal day. 1163 Baptized. I called names alternately with Recorder
M. F. Farnsworth
Wednesday. Thursday and Friday
I took Record on Female Side for Endowments in the Morning
and assisted at the Desk up Stairs till all the Company

{5}
were through and then copied on the Adoption Record
Saturday 24 Feb 1883.
At the Temple all day copying on the Adoption Record.
Sunday 25 Feb 1883
Attended Meeting in the Tabernackle at 2 P.M Elder Jacob Gates Spoke and
was followed by Apostle Erastus Snow asking if the Parents were neglecful
of their sons and daughters or Where are our Sons and Daughters? and
Why not at Meeting? he taught us how Parents should govern their Children
and draw and attract them to them by Exercising the attributes of the
Diety. In the Evening with wife Margaret attended meeting at the
1st Ward School House, by invitation I occupied all the time.
Monday 26 Feb 1883.
I worked all day copying up the Adoption Record, and
wrote letters to wife Mary and Son William
Tuesday 27th Feby 1883
Baptismal day, 808 were baptized for to day, I called names
at the font alternative with the Recorder.
Wednesday 28th 1883
I copied on the Adoption Record as usual after the
usual daily routine.
Thursday 1 March 1883.
Prest Wilford Woodruff's Birth day 76 years old today,
18 men were Endowed for his dead friends and I had
the followind Dead women sealed to me. My wife Mar-
-garet Standing proxy for them- Emma from my own
Record and Permelia Pierce Polly Pierce, Jerusha Pierce,
Hannah Williams, Flora L. Pierce, Leona E. Pierce and
Martha Williams, the latter 7 are Relatives of Bro
Moses Franklin Farnsworth's and he gave them to me.
I omitted to mention that on Monday last I was
invited with Wife Margaret to Dine at Elder Joseph
Cotton's, he being one of the Company of Missionaries
for Gt Britton who Closed the continent and the Sea
in my Company in April 1880. Prest Erastus Snow
and wife and his daughter Artemesia was at Bro
Coton's and took Dinner and afterwards gave us
some good instruction regarding the condition of
the Dead.   Friday & Saturday 2&3 March.
At the Usual Work of Recording, and copied up all the work
of Adoptions and Sealing Children to Parents to date having
commensed /at\ Jan 5th 1882 /date\ and Copied 139 pages or about 4500

names.   Sunday 4 March 1883.
Attended meeting at the Tabernacle in the Afternoon and at
the 1st Ward School House in the Evening. Bro Jas G. Bleak preached
in the Evening.   Monday 5 March
I am appointed P. this week so I spent the day studying.
          Tuesday 6 March 1883
Baptismal day. 569 were baptised for today for the dead
3 first. 2 Renual of Cov. 3 for Health. I was mouth in prayer
this morning at the opening Exercises at the Temple. This
Evening I paid Bro F. Farnsworth $10.00 to apply on account
of our Board and lodgings

{6}
          Wednesday 7 March 1883.
Took the Part of P. today and then assisted at the desk after
the company was all through. And being invited I went with Prest
McAllister and Recorder Farnsworth to the top of the Tower of the
Temple, got outside and the View is delightful. Cottonwood trees
just budding into leaf. Almond and Apricot trees Just filling into
Bloom.   Thursday 9th Friday 9th Mch 1883.
          Took the part of P. and the Lord Blessed me in my labor.
          Saturday 10 Mch 1883.
I wrote all day as 2nd Asst Record and in the Evening I
purchased the 1st 4 Vols of Millenial Stars and Vols 19. 20 & 21.
paid $15.00 cash for them to Sister Marcette Calkins. wife of Brother
Asa Calkin.   Sunday 11 March 1883.
Wife Margaret & I attended 1st Ward Sunday School and Joined
Bible Class and afterwards spoke to the Children about 10 Minutes
and in the afternoon attended meeting at the Tabernacle and
heard Bo Goudy Heryave and Prest McArthur speak, took supper with
Bro Wm H Thompson and family and went home and read our new
papers.   Monday 12 Mch 1883.
I copied at the 2nd Ant Record and in the Evening I packed
and lashed up our trunk, and bed and bed clothing to send home
I called with my wife on Brother Samuel Turnbow to wish him
good bye as he intends to start off tomorrow for his home in
Salt Lake City. He has been here several months and successfully
labored in the Temple for dead friends and I have formed quite an
attachment for him.
          Tuesday 13 Mch 1883.
I read names at the Font, alternating with Recorder Farnsworth
and confirmed 111.--I called names, Bro N. H Jensen
baptized and M. F Farnsworth confirmed 163 in 40 minutes
spent the Evening at Bro Cottams.
          Wednesday 14 Mch 1883
The usual routine, and copied on the 2nd Antg Record
and Spent the evening with my wife Margaret and Bro & Sister
Alder and Bro & Sister Jensen with Prest J. D. T. McAllister
and his families. And had a good Pleasant time
          Thursday 15th 1883.
Today after the usual routine, I copied up the 2nd

annointing record to date. and with wife Maggie I
spent the Evening at Bro James G. Bleaks in company with
Prest J.D. T. McAlliser and wife, and Bp David H. Cannon &
wife—Sister Baker played the organ and we had a good time
   Friday. 16th 1883.
My last day in the Temple. The Temple record shows
I have put in 152 days, work in the Temple and my wife
Margaret has put in 86 days work I helped take the
morning record and much of the work for adoptions and
Sealings &c for top stairs. And Prest McAllister gave
me the Following dated St George Temple 16 Mch 1883
Presidents John Taylor and Wilford Woodruff. Dear Brethern
as Elder Samuel Roskelley is about to return home, We
cheerfully give him this letter of commendation. During

{7}
his labors here, He has applied himself Diligently in the
parts assigned him, and in the Recorders department, for
Baptisms Endowments Sealings, Adoptions and Anointings.
His wife Mar/a\gret R has been faithful, and is full prepared for Temple labor. Praying our Father to bless them in
all the labors of life, With Kind regards I am your
brother in the Gospel. John D. T. McAllister.
I greatly esteem the foregoing letter of commendation
coming from the President in charge of the Temple, and I know
and have the Satisfaction that I have done my duty faithfully
and am quite Satisfied with my own labors, and not
withstanding I want to see and associate with my dear
family at home, I leave the Temple and my associates these
with many regrets. This Evenings mail brought me
a letter from my Son Wm containing $25.00 from Preston T.
Morehead of Smithfield.
   Saturday 17 March 1883.
Attended Quarterly Conference of St George Stake. Prest J. D. T.
McAllister presiding, (See Report). After Afternoon Meeting
Margaret & I took supper at Bro Wm M Thompsons, with his family
Elder Jas G Bleak and wife being present. Elder Bleak gave
us a rehersal of his trip visiting Zunas. Pampas. And other
Indian Tribes in Arizona which much interested us. we
afterward went to the Amature Theatre given in aid of the
1st St. George Sabbath School.
   Sunday 18th March 1883.
attended Conference (See Report).
   [clipping pasted to page (newspaper unknown)]

St. George Stake Confer-
ence.

 The St. George Stake
Conference was held on the
18th of March, 1883.
 President John D. T. McAllister
presiding.
 This conference was attended [by]
an unusually large number of the
Saints from the settlements com-
posing the St. George Stake.
 Of the General Authorities of the
Church, we were favored with the

presence of our old time President and wise counselor Apostle Erastus Snow, and with that of Presidents Henry Harriman and Jacob Gates, of the Presidency of the Seventies. These, each and all, administered to us the good word of God according to the dignity of their holy callings in the Priesthood.

Besides these, the speakers were, Presidents McAllister, Eyring and McArthur; Bishops Robert Knell, Geo. H. Crosby, Edward Bunker, Jr., Fred'k W. Jones, Marius Ensign, Charles N. Smith, Marcus Funk and Nephi R. Fawcett; also Elders Samuel Roskelley, Moroni Snow, Adolphus R. Whitehead and John C. Naile.

Every one of the Nineteen Ward of the Stake was represented by the presence of the Bishop or other officer.

The reports of the spiritual, statistical ad financial condition of the Wards, Relief Societies, Sabbath Schools, Primaries and other organizations were very full and very good. The General and the Stake, Ward and Branch Authorities were heartily voted for, and without one dissentient vote.

We had a very instructive and refreshing time together, and, although some of this Stake of no railroads and very rough wagon roads, have had to come a hundred miles to Conference, they express themselves as amply rewarded by being partakers of the spirit and counsel present in our gatherings.

James G. Bleak, [c/sc]
Stake Clerk.

{8}

<u>Monday 19th March 1883.</u>
My wife Margaret and I took stage at 7 A.M. After taking a very affectionate leave of our St George friends and amid many hearty responses to the "God Bless You" from my fellow laborer Bro M F. Farnsworth we left St George and our Many good kind friends, also the Holy Temple where we had passed so many happy days fulfilling our Mission We arrived at Silver Reef at 12.15 and started again at 2 P.M. traveling all night and the next day Reached Milford the Terminus of the Utah Central R.R. At 3:15 PM. On <u>Tuesday 20 March 1883</u> and took train at 6.10 the same evening arriving at Salt Lake City at 10 A.. on <u>Wednesday 21 Mch</u> Stopping at Bro and Sister Edward King in the 15th Wd I went to the Historians Office and found Prest Woodruff & Apostle Teasdale and was welcomed by them and answered their many questions before going to Prest John Taylors offices. I afterwards went to See Prest Taylor and found him and his Councillors Prests Geo Q Cannon & Jos F Smith attending to some business with the celebr-ated Phil Robinson who had written So many favorable letters in behalf of our people, was invited and took dinner with Prest Taylor at the Gardo House Prest Geo Q Cannon and L. John Nuttall and Prest Taylors family being also present. The conversation was both Pleasant and instruc-tive, I afterward saw Apostle Franklin D. Richards and

agreed to meet him on the next morning to talk over the
ordinances administered in the Temple at St George. In
the Afternoon I visited Bro A R. Wright and Sister Evan
M. Greene and her son-in-law and Daughter Lula, in
E King and a number of my London Conference Friends.
Slept at Kings.

Thursday 22 March 1883.

Met Apostle F. D. Richards at the Historians office according to appointment and answered such questions
about the Temple ordinances and the Administration
Thereof as he asked till 1/2 past 2 Oclock. Then met
Prest W. Woodruff and went to his house and took dinner
with him and his wife Phebe and had a long chat.
Was Escorted by him to the U.C.R.R. Depot. My wife
Margaret being escorted by Sister King. Took the
UC. Train for Ogden at 3.40 and after arriving at Ogden
called on Bro Joseph Hall and family and took Supper
with them after which We took U&W.RR for the north
arriving at Smithfield at 11.40. P.M. I found my wife
Mary Jane and family well, as also my Wife Mary &
her family.

{9}

Friday 23rd March 1883

Took a good survey of my farm and its surroundings
and visited with my family-several of the folks of Smithfield
called to see and talk with me.

Saturday 24 March 1883.

Several Bretheren going to Logan invited me to go also,
I went with my Son-in-law Bro Thomas Hilliard and had
a good visit with Supt C.O. Card of the Temp Construc=
tion and with him went through the Building and
I was delighted with the progress and class of work
being done, altho it will yet take months to complete
it. ready for Ordinance work. had a good visit
with the Stake Presidency. W. B. Preston, M. W. Merrill
and C.O. Card, and greeted with "welcome home" form
members of the Bretheren & Sisters. Lavina Rigby came
home with me. Sunday 25 March 1883.
The Stake Presidency met at Smithfield and held a
meeting with the Saints in the Afternoon, I also spoke
about 15 minutes, and occupied the whole of the Evening
in Speaking to the Saints on the Subject of the Redemption
of the dead and work of the Temple. and all seemed
well pleased.   Monday, Tuesday & Wednesday 26.27.28 Mch
I trimmed Trees and Set out and fixed trees where
the Winter had Killed the old ones.

Thursday 29th March

I worked all my Trees in the nursery and farm,
my Wife Margaret and her Sister Lavina Went to Newton
with my Son Joseph and my Team.

Friday 30th Mch
My Sons James. William and Joseph and I cleaned
out the Ditches North and East of the Lots in town.
Saturday 31st Mch
Put in Peas at the farm and in town, in the Afternoon
attended the Annual Meeting of the Primary Association Sister M
A Williams Presiding. Sister Adaline Barber of the Stake
Presidency was also there and Spoke to the children. After the
Meeting some 15 or 20 Persons came to my house and brought their
Picknick and set table Containing many good things and
said they had long waited for the opportunity to catch
me and were now pleased to have the opportunity to
see and converse with me for a time it was truly
a genuine surprise. We spent the evening in Very
pleasant conversation on the ordinances administered
in the Temple for the Living and the dead.
Sunday 1st April.
This Morning Bro Wm T Vannoy called on me and rode
with me to Logan, I having an appointment to preach at 2.Oc
Prest W. B. Preston Presiding. I spoke to a large and very atten
=tive congregation for 75 minutes and returned home
in the evening.

{10}
Monday. Tuesday. Wednesday. Thursday. 2.3.4.5 Apr
I worked part of the time on farm, with nursery
and in the Gardens planting Seeds and Trees &c
Friday 6 Apr 1883
Worked Setting trees with my Sons and in the
Evening Sold 5 yearlings and calves to Lars Torelsen fr
$57.00 Cash.
Saturday 7 Apl 1883
left Smithfield on the 3.20 AM train for Salt Lake City
to attend Conference arrived at City at 11.00 and went to
Temple Block met a great many old and new friends
and attended the Afternoon meeting Elders M. Thatcher
and G. Teasdale spoke, attended Priesthood meeting at
the Assembly Hall. Prests John Taylor and Jos F. Smith spoke
giving good advice to Presiding officers in the Church.
I paid Thos E Ricks $25.00 on account of Interest due
for money invested in Logan and Smithfield Canal
Company also Paid Joseph Bentley 25.00 for money
I had borrowed from him at St George.
Sunday 8 Apl
Attended meetings til 1/2 past 3P.M. When I left
the Meeting while Prest John Taylor was speaking and
took the 3.40 P.M train for the north arriving home at
11.40 P.M. Monday 9 Apl
Planted and trimmed trees and wrote some.
Tuesday 10 Apl
Went to Newton to get my wife Margaret who

had been visiting her relatives for several days
Roads very muddy and bad found folks well
and glad to see me

   Wednesday 11 April

Returned home with Wife Margaret-it Snowed
or rained all the way home and we got quite wet.
Went to farm at night

   Thursday 12 April

Fixed tongue on Horse Cultivator, and Borrowed
16 Bu 27^{lbs} Seed Wheat from Bro Robt Meikle to
Sow, promising 75 cts per bushel for it to be paid to
the Coop Store to his Credit.

   Friday 13 April

I borrowed 648 lbs = 18 Bu 18^{lb} Seed Oats from
Royal Tidwell at 2^{cts} per pound and spent the day
planting currant and Raspberry bushes,

   Saturday 14 Apl

attended Priesthood Meeting at Logan and had
a conversation with Prest Wm B Preston about matters
pertaining to our Quorum of High Priests. Paid Brother
E Ricks $25^{00} making a total of $50^{00} interest on the
money I borrowed for the Logan and Smithfield canal
met many old friends who congratulated me on
my return from St George. Went through the Temple

{11}

   <u>Sunday 15 April 1883.</u>

Spent the morning reading, and attended the ward
afternoon meeting and spoke about 3/4 of an hour.
with my wife Mary I went to Father Hugh Roberts and
made out the record of his Children to be sealed
to him and his wife.

   <u>Monday 16 April 1883.</u>

Bp. W. F Rigby came from Beaver Canon Saw Mill
this morning 's early train and I spent the Forenoon
with him about the affairs of Vannoy & Co and its
present and future prospects. Went as far as my meadow
and measured off a ton of Hay. for Bro Sheen for $7^{00}
and wrote several letters to friends.

   <u>Tuesday 17 Apl 1883.</u>

   And reminder of the Week
I spend planting trees at my farm and at the nursery
and doing such as seemed to be necessary to add
a little comfort to the Household

   <u>Sunday 22 April 1883.</u>

My daughter Rebecca's Birthday. Myself and fam
=ily spent the afternoon and ate dinner with her and
her husband and spent a very agreeable time.

   <u>Monday night 23rd Apl 1883.</u>

Will be remembered by the inhabitants of
Cache Valley. about 10 Oclock P.M the Wind com=

=menced to blow furiously and Kept it up all
night and all day Tuesday 24 April. During
a great amount of damage to fences, Barns,
new buildings and rail way &c &c
The balance of the week I worked in making
repairs where the wind had done damage.
and I also helped in the transplanting of trees
to my nursery.

Sunday 29th April

In company with my councillor Bro George Barber
attended meeting with members of the High Priests
Quorum in Smithfield Ward. I talked to the
Bretheren over an hour on the several duties
of High Priests, was followed by Bro Barber and
then Bp Farrell. in the Afternoon I went with
my son James to Hyde Park and talked 40
minutes to a very attentive audience, and
afterward went with the High Priests of that
Ward and talked about 30 minutes on the
duties of H.P. Celestial Marriage and preparing
for duty among the Lamanites as well as all
the duties requires as a quorum and as
individuals.

{12}
Spent the week gardening, working in the nursery
and fixing up generally. had storming weather
and cannot do much out of doors, putting in
some potatoes at the farm and in town, on Thur
=sday   On Friday night 4th ~~April~~ May
I met the 11.40 P.M. Passenger train at the
Smithfield Station and met Prest Wilford Woodruff
and escorted him home to his house and on

Saturday 5 May 1883

I took Prest Woodruff and my wife Margaret and
my son James to the Logan Quarterly Conference and
had much satisfaction listening to the Teaching of the
Visiting apostles & Prophets— in the Evening in
Company with Prests John Taylor, Cannon. Woodruff
and several of the Quorum of the 12 I visited the
the temple. And am very pleased with the progress
made on the Building. Came home to Smithfield
the same Evening bringing Prest Wodruff. Bp and
Sisiter Sarah Rigby, my wife Margaret and Son James

Sunday 6 May 1883.

Went to the Logan Quarterly Conference taking
the same persons I took home last Evening. had
a good day. Called on Prests J Taylor & G Q Cannon
in company with my councillors F Gunnell and Sis
Barker and presented a list of names of Elders
from Smithfield, Hyrum & Wellsville recommended

by the Bishops for ordination into the High Priest
Quorum, Prest Taylor expressed his willing-
=ness to have these Brethren ordained and Said
he wanted the H.P. Quorum of this stake filled
up from the Elders Quorums of good active [---]
bright young men to train them for Bishop's and
Councillors, Prests of Stakes and other imp-
=portant positions of Presidency. High councillors
&c. At Prest W. B. Preston's request to select a man
from my Quorum to fill the position of High-
=Councillor in this stake of Zion. I recommended
Bro Wm G. Burton to fill this important office
Prest Woodruff returned to Smithfield this
evening with Prest Angus M Cannon Prest of Salt
Lake Stake of Zion and held meeting with the
Saints of Smithfield, had a good meeting.

   Monday 7 May
spent the day at the nursery.
   Wednesday 9th May
Spent the forenoon administering to the sick
and sowed Carrots in the afternoon in the
nursery.

{13}
   <u>Thursday 10th 1883.</u>
sowed Marigold Wostzels and Beets at the
garden of the farm.
   <u>Friday 11th 1883.</u>
My Sons James and William went to Logan and
cleaned out the proportion of side hill ditch of the
Logan and Richmond Canal -- I sowed seed
and commenced to make a land Roller and
worked at the same on Saturday.
   <u>Sunday 13 May 1883</u>
I went to Logan with Bro Abel Smart and
attended a High Priest's Quorum Conference
in the Upper Room of the Tabernacle, at
ten O'Clock A.M. Apostle Moses Thatcher
and Prest Wm B. Preston were present, many
subjects of importance were laid before the
members of the Quorum and all seemed
pleased with the meeting. Also attended
the afternoon sacremental meeting. Bro
Wilcken a returned missionary from Mexico
Bp Wm Maughan. Apostle M Thatcher and
Prest Wm B. Preston were the Speakers. I
returned to Smithfield with Bro A Sinost
and F. Sharp how we spend a very profitable day
   <u>Monday 14 May 1883.</u>
spent at the farm also Tuesday 15th May.
   <u>Wednesday 16th May</u>

Edward Hansen the County Survey came along
laying off the Logan and Smithfield Canal and I
commenced work on it with 1 span of horses
[---] yoke Cattle, and 5 men and worked on it
till Saturday night.

Sunday 20th May

I took Bro George Barbers team from Smithfield
and with my wife Margaret went to Logan and
took up Bro Geo Barber and his wife Emma
and went to Hyrum holding meeting with the High
Priests of Hyrum, Wellsville. Paradise and Millville
Comprising the Southern district of Cache Stake. I
talked to the Bretheren on the duties of the High
Priests and explained the various calls that
we are more recently called upon to fill, and
the keeping of the proper Records of their forefathers
&c &c. took dinner with Bro hansen and I atte-
=nded the sacrament meeting of the Saints and I talked
to them for 75 minutes on Temple Labor and its
Blessings. had an excellent time, returning
home I called on Bro Chas O Dunn at Millville

{14}
and administered to him. He was suffering from
a sore leg. During the following week I worked on
my farm garden and Water Ditches.
The following list of names having been approved
by Prest John Taylor and Wm B. Preston were presented
to the Quorum for acceptance at Hyrum to be ordained
High Priests Lars Olesen, ~~Peter~~

     Peter Olsen   Ordained by S Roskelly
     Isaac Stevens " " Geo Barber
     Neils Petersen " " S Roskelly
     Kanute Halversen " " Geo Barber
     Hans I Johnson " " S Roskelley
     Han Iversen
     Christian Petersen "
     George Jensen
     Ola Ellefsen " " Geo Barber
     Ola Neilsen " "
     Fred^k Olsen " " S Roskelley

[*written vertically up the column of names:* Ordained on | Sunday 20 May | 1883.]

Sunday 27th May 1883.

I rode to Richmond with Brother Abel Smart and
attended a High Priests Quorum meeting at 11 O'Clock
the settlement of this northern district were well
represented. Prest M.W. Merrill and Prest L.H. Hatch of
the Eastern Arizona Stake were present and gave good
Council to the Bretheren

The following names having been properly
approved from the Smithfield Ward were accepted for

ordination as High Priests and were ordained
> Robert Nelsen ordained by S. Roskelley
> Nicholas Hendrickson " " M. W. Merrill
> Abel Smart " " Geo. Barber

I returned home in the afternoon and visited with my family.

I spent the week as usual on my farm and garden. till Thursday, attended the funeral of Fanny E. daughter of Alfred and Mary Chambers and spoke about 40 minutes. And on <u>Saturday June 2nd</u> I went to Logan and attended Priesthood Meeting of this Stake of Zion and attended some business returning home in the Evening

<u>Sunday 3rd June 1883.</u>

Wrote some letters in the forenoon and attended Ward meetings in the Afternoon and ordained Bro Ola Olson a High Priest—he having been recommended by Bp [---] and approved by the Presidency &c. I worked at my papers in the Evening.

<u>Monday 4th June 1883.</u>

I went to Logan and conversed with Bp Thomas X. Smith, B. F. Cummings, & Prest. Moses Thatcher and received their unqualified promise of any aid they could render me in furnishing Genealogical Records for Saints.

{15}

<u>Thursday 7 June 1883.</u>

attended fast meeting and assisted to confirm a number of young folks into the church, and blessed a number of Children and a number of Bottles of oil &c and continued to work on my farm through the week till <u>Saturday 9 June 1883.</u> I went to Logan and filed a claim before the Water Commission ers of this Cache County for secondary Rights to water of Birch Creek and Primary Right to 2/3 of the water of Dry Canyon

<u>Sunday 10 Jun 1883</u>

I called on Abel Smart who accompanied me to Newton and held meeting at 1/2 past 10, and ~~then~~ I preached about 50 minutes, got dinner at Pb Rigby's and went to Clarkston to Ward Meeting and talked to them 20 minutes . For supper at Bp Jardine's and retur =ned to Newton and held a high Priests meeting and talked 30 minutes then rode home to Smithfield arriving about 1/2 past 9. P.M. having spent a very interesting and profitable day.

<u>Monday 11 June 1883.</u>

I arranged my business as best I could and took the midnight train from Smithfield for Beaver Canon arriving there on Tuesday at noon, discussing the situation of the firm of Van Noy and Co for several days while I was posting up the Books of the firm

so we could send statements of accounts to those
that were owing us, we finally concluded to
value the property and each man handle his
own Share and be responsible for his portion of
the firms liabilities. The property all told was
valued at $24820^{82} being divided among
the 5 shareholders in 6 parts of $4136^{80} each
share. Bp W. F. Rigby asked me to throw my
property with his and form a co-partnership
which I did, he agreeing to take the Star Mill
and run it and deliver all the lumber sawed
at that mill for $8^{50} at Beaver Canon for
the Season, we also agreed to Hire a man
and deliver all our lumber to him and let
him sell and divide the proceeds proportion
=ately. I came home, arriving at noon

Sunday July 1st so tired that
I rested all the afternoon. Visited my dau
=ghter Rebecca in the Evening and administered
to her as she was very poorly in health.

Monday July 2nd 1882.
Visited the farm in the morning and then
watered the Lots in town, also attended
the meeting of the County Water Commissioners
and was granted a Primary right to Water
from Summit & Birch Creek for City Lots and
Nursery Lots. And the 20 acre medow.

{16}
During the week I Visited Bp Thos X Smith at
Logan and got his Lumber accounts with the firm
of Van Noy and Co. preparatory to making a
settlement with him. And worked at my garden
plowing and hoeing weeds. Attended Monthly
Priesthood Meeting at Logan on Saturday 7 July
and on

Sunday 8 July 1883.
In company with Bro Abel Stuart I held
meeting with the High Priests at Logan and had a
very good meeting arranging with the members that
3 or 4 should deliver a short Lecture each Meeting
hereafter.--Returned to Smithfield Prest George
Barber coming with us and attended the ward.
Afternoon meeting.—Prests M. W. Merrill and Chas
O. Card meeting with us in the Bowery
My Son James commenced cutting the Lucerne in
the South field on Tuesday 10 July and my Son
Hyram came from Lewiston saying he had no hay this
year so I rented the cutting and hauling of the
Lucerne patch to him giving him 5 Loads for his
Labor. My son's & I worked on the farm & garden

and the Logan Canal through the week till
      Sunday 15th July 1883.
Bro Abel Stuart, Francis Sharp & I went to Wellsville
to attend High Priests District Meetings In Company
with Bp. W. H. Maughan and the Bretheren from Smithfield
I attended the Sabbath school at 10 O'clock and spoke
to the Children, attended High Priests District
meeting at the New Rock School house at 10 O'clock.
The High Priests of Wellsville, Hyrum & Paradise
were well represented. I gave general instruct
=ions on the duties of High Priests and other matters of a general Nature. Took dinner with
my councillor Francis Gunnell Attended the
Afternoon Ward meeting. The following names were
presented to the people for their acceptance and
were ordained by Bp. W H Maughan, Francis
Gunnell & myself.

Robert Leatham by F. G.   W^m S Poppleton by S. R.
Chas Bailey   " W H.M   Walter Glenn   " S R
W. L Walters   " W. H. M William Haslem " S R
W. P. Deakin   " FG.   Richard Brenchley " S.R
James Parks   " S.R.   David Keer   " F G.
Ephraim Shaw " WHM   John Deakin   " S. R
John Redford   " W.H.M.

{17}
Robt Crowshaw and John Glenn were also
sustained by Vote of the people to be ordained
High Priests but they were not present and
were not ordained. I took supper with
Sister Eckersley and her daughters, and
Visited an old friend Sister Mary Selman
Nunnerley and partook of a dish of Ice Cream
which was very nice and cool. We left
Wellsville at 1/2 past Six arriving at Smithfield about
1/2 past nine. Very tired having spent
a very pleasant and profitable day and
seemingly much enjoyed by all interested
and returned home late in the Evening.
And spent much of the following week in fixing
and preparing my harvesting machine so as to
be prepared for the approaching harvest now getting
white for the sickle.
      Friday 20 July 1883.
I started my harvester in some Volunteer
wheat in the old South field and it worked
very well. My son James took charge of it
and run it to cut my grain afterward.
      Sunday 22 July 188.3.
In company with Bros Barber. Sharp and
Smart. with the last named persons team I.

visited and attended meeting at Franklin
at their Regular Ward Meeting at 2 P.M.
and afterwards attended a District High
Priests Meeting Smithfield. Richmond, Franklin
and Preston ward were represented and a good
spirit prevailed all seemed to feel well
I occupied about 40 minutes at the ward
meeting and the most of the time at the
Quorum Meeting.
Spent the week at the farm shocking up
wheat, watering, hoeing & till Friday 4 August
I hired James [Juchan] and his Brother and team
and hauled and stacked the fall wheat having
21 Loads in all.

Saturday 5 July 1883.
Attended Quarterly Conference at Logan
Prests W. Woodruff and Erastus Snow were
the only persons from Salt Lake City of the Church
authorities, both spoke and several of the Bishops
reported their wards.

Attended fast meeting on Thursday 3 Aug
and assisted in Blessing a number of Children
and confirming 18 or 20 persons and administering to

{18}
several that were sick.

<u>Sunday 5 August 1883.</u>
Went to Logan to Conference and took the
place of Brother Jas Leishman, the clerk of the Con=
=ference for the forenoon as his family were
sick. Prest W. Woodruff Preached on the object
of building Temples and the class of
work performed in them, a sermon
replete with instruction to the saints.
Prest E. Snow preached in afternoon on
a variety of topics. suited to the times we
live in. My wives Mary Jane and Margaret
were at the 2 days meetings; after the
meetings were over we went to the Temple and
went through it Visiting all the rooms.
Prest W. Woodruff spent the week at Smithfield
resting and recuperating, and I had a num
=ber of pleasant chats with him, and with
him laid hands on a number of sick, blessing
them. Abel Smart's machine threshed
our fall and Volunteer Wheat on Tuesday
Aug 7th I had 441 1/2 Bu Machine measured
I sold 104 Bu 50 lbs to pay up Crop Store
debt and hauled the rest to Logan Central
Mills and Sold for Cash got 80cts per Bu
for all of it. Paid Thos Richardson $21[25]

and W. Douglas 19^{74} in Cash to square up
my store debts, with them for goods bought by
my family what I was at St George. last
winter, and paid several little debts also

        Sunday 12 August 1883.

Bro Abel Smart took Prest W. Woodruff and
my wives Mary and Margaret and myself
to Logan. Prests J Taylor Geo Q Cannon and
Jos F Smith and W. Woodruff with Bp Sheets & L.
John Nuttall. being Present, had some most
Glorious meetings. Excellent teachings filled
with Vitality and Wisdom. on United Order
grading the Priesthood, and giving temple
blessings according to worthiness and
many Kindred doctrines & spent the week on the
farm and moving the fence on Town City lot between me
and Bro Farrell – moved it 9 feet north of the line Bro
Farrell agreeing to make a fence 9 feet South of the line

{19}
of the city lots so we may have a lane 18 feet wide
between us to get into our corralls &c

        Sunday 19 August 1883.

Our High Priests Meeting today at Hyrum—but Bro Abel
Smart by some means failed to come to time and I went
to Hyde Park with my own team to meeting and occupied
a portion of the time. and fixed fences at farm,
and Cradled 2 1/2 acres oats at the nursery and helped to
bind them.

        Sunday 26 Aug 1883.

Attended meeting at Richmond – good congregation – and had
a good time generally, Bro A Smart and F Sharp went with me
had a good meeting. Thrashed on Tuesday with Bro Harrison
with Thomas's Machine had 16 1/2 Bu Barley, 216 Bu Wheat, 273 Bu
oats, Wednesday took a load of wheat to Logan Mills, to
sell for Cash—Thursday, went to Lewiston and bought a
load of seed wheat from Isaac Bills, stayed at James Bain=
bridge and contracted with him to bore a well on his land.

        Sunday 2nd Sep 1883.

Spent the day at home and went to Meeting at Smithfield
my councillor Bro George Barber spoke as he is about to
leave on Tuesday next for England, on private business
spent the week in fixing my machine for Well Boring and
fixing around the farm

        Sunday 9th September 1883.

I attended the district meeting of the Quorum at Logan –
had a good meeting – on Proper recommend I ordained Bro
Hyrum Ricks a member of the Quorum. I afterward
attended regular afternoon meeting at the tabernacle.
W. W. Taylor, Don C. Young & Bro Orson Whitney were the
speakers – met Prests W. B. Preston and apostle Moses Thatcher

for the first time after their return from their Northern trip
among the Indians. Returned Home in the Evening with my
wives Mary Jane & Margaret with whom I had spent
the Evening previous at their fathers at Newton—and the
same day at Logan, and worked on my well boring
machinery during the week making a trip or two to Logan to
get Blacksmithing & mechanical labor for it and com=
=menced Boring a well for my daughter Rebecca on
Wednesday Afternoon and used 3 hands, on Friday
used 4 hands and quit early in the afternoon as
I came to a bed of washed sand and fine gravel
that could not get to stay in the augur to bring
out of the well. Millie & Thurson Hall arrived on the 13th
from Ogden.   <u>Sunday 16 Sep 1883.</u>
With Bro Abel Smart I went to Wellsville to Hold a
district meeting taking my wife Mary Jane and Thursa
Hall to Logan to Visit Bro & Sister W. G. Burton on the
way, we had a good time and good meeting I spoke at
the High Priests Meeting also at the afternoon Ward
meetings to the Saints and all seemed to feel well
got home late and found my wife Margaret had
gone to Newton having been hastily asked there
by the death of her Brother William's only son William
the father being now on a mission to the Southern States

{20}
spent the week following experimenting with my
well augur boring a well for my daughter Reb=
=ecca Hillyard. <u>Sunday 23 Sep 1883</u>
With Bro Abel Smart and Francis Sharp I went
to Richmond and took dinner with Bro Thomas
Moore the Ward teacher of the High Priests Quorum
and thence to Franklin and attended the Dist-
=rict Meeting of the Quorum, 5 Wards were
represented, and had a good time, also atten-
=ded the general ward meeting, and preached
to the saints and all seemed to Enjoy the meeting well
I arrived home about 9 P.M.
Fixed my machinery for Boring wells as best I could
and started to Lewiston to bore a well for Bro James Bain
bridge on Wednesday 26 Sep and on Friday got down
to sand and found that my augur would not hold and
bring up quick sand so I went to Logan on Saturday
and ordered a quick sand augur at the UO. Foundry
        <u>Sunday 30 Sep 1883</u>
I was at home and spent the day with my family
and enjoyed it very much. Attended the ward meeting
councillor Preston T. Morehead presiding with others I
spoke about 20 minutes on the Marriage covenant
for time and all eternity. The week following was
very stormy and my sons and I stripped the sugar

cane and topped it preparitory to cutting and hauling
to the mill. On Thursday 4 October I took the Passenger
train going to Ogden and stayed at Bro Joseph Halls
over night found Bro Thos E Ricks on the train and
paid him $50^{00} interest on the money borrowed on the
Logan & Smithfield Canal a/c. Took U. C train to
Salt Lake City next Morning and attended every day
and every evening meeting during the 3 days conference and
had a general good time meeting many old and
highly valued friends and old acquaintances and
started on my journey home from Salt Lake City at
1/2 past 5 O'clock P.M. arriving at 2 A.M. Monday
morning. had a very enjoyable conference and rec^d
much good instructions from the 1st Presidency &
12 apostles.   <u>Monday 8 Oct 1883.</u>

  I have taken a cold and am nearly sick to
day and my wife Mary Jane is also quite poorly.
being troubled with neuralgia which continued all the week
the weather is also very disagreeable, raining almost continually
and making it disagreeable to get around to do anything out of
doors, but the boys and I managed to get up and pit the
potatoes and ruta bagoes.
  <u>Saturday 13 Oct 1883.</u>
Attended a general priesthood meeting at Logan and had
and excellent meeting, much valuable instruction being given
on the principles of the Gospel. to be adopted by us.

{21}
  <u>Sunday 14th October 1883.</u>
With Bro Smart I went to Logan and held a District Meeting
of the High Priest Quorum and had the Company of Prest W. B.
Preston who gave us some very valuable counsel. I ordained
Bro Ephraim Mickleson a High Priest. and ordained with
Prest Preston (mouth) Bro Ole J. Petersen, also. In the afternoon
attended the Young Mens Mutual improvement Association
conference, and in the Evening I attended a meeting at
Smithfield, Pres^t W. Woodruff preached. I spent the week
following in digging and pitting my roots and vegetables, but
made very slow progress as it was so very stormy and
changeable weather
  <u>Sunday 21 Oct 1883.</u>
With Bro Abel Smart I went to Paradise and held
a district meeting of the H.P. Quorum, quite a number
present from Wellsville, Hyrum, Millville & Paradise, and
we had a good meeting. A recommend was presented
from Millville properly signed and we ordained

Henry Chandler by S. Roskelley	Richard Jessop by Bp Orson Smith	
John C. Hunt	"	Oke Nilson " "
Joseph Humphreys	"	Ola Nilson " "
Hans Olson	"	Charles Eleason " "
James Chantrill	"	

I ate dinner w/ Bp O. Smith and family and atten=
ded afternoon meeting with the saints and spoke about
30 minutes returning Home same Evening traveling 40
miles. And on Monday and Tuesday 22 & 23 October
I fixed up a tent I had bought from the Logan
Temple Suptd and Wednesday I went to Lewiston
and got my tent and Derrik straightened up for
work on Thursday October 26th I again commenced
boring but did not make any headway as the Quicksand would
run in as fast as I could pull it out with the augur. I quit
and came home on Friday 28th October and on Saturday I
commenced digging trees for sale from my nursury so as
to pay up some of my debts &c

Sunday 28th October 1883

Bro Abel Smart and I went to Richmond and met with
the Saints in the Afternoon and occupied 45 minutes on
the necessity of obeying the whole law of God, met with
the members of the High Priests Quorum at 4 O'Clock P.M
and found some of the Wards of this district represented
except Richmond and Smithfield, as the Roads are so very
muddy and bad people cannot travel. Bro Smart and
I returned to Smithfield same night.

Monday Oct 29th I fixed up my sulky Plow and plow
ed most of the afternoon

Tuesday Oct 30th My son William and I planted trees
on my Timber Culture land. And during the week planted out
peas every opportunity between rain storms which were
quite frequent.

On Friday 2nd November 1883

Prest W. Woodruff came to Smithfield from Salt Lake City and
took the liberty of visiting him in the evening and went to
Logan and attended the Quarterly conference of Cache Valley
Stake of Zion. President John Taylor & Joseph F. Smith also

{22}
Prest W. Woodruff with Lorenzo Snow & F. D. Richards, George
Teasdale, M. Thatcher were present and spoke upon the
various duties of the Saints

Sunday 4th November 1883

Attended Logan Quarterly Conference and meeting
at Smithfield at night, I talked a few minutes &
Bp G. L. Farrell & Prest W. Woodruff.– The instructions
given were rich and quite suited to the times and I
passed the week (which was a very stormy one) at the farm as
my sons William and Joseph were getting Wood from the Kanyon.
On Wednesday 7th November I was plowing with Sulky
plow and plow struck a big Rock and the leaver struck me
in my temple and Knocked me off the plow almost senseless,
and on Thursday 8th November I got my horse Tom shod
at Bro Chambers blacksmith shop and I jumped on him
to ride to the farm – he suddenly began bucking throwing me

violently on the ground, striking on the lower end of my back
bone and injuring me so much as to cause me much
pain and annoiance.

      Sunday 11th November 1883.

      With Bro Abel Smart I went to Logan and attended
the High Priests District meeting in the 4th ward school
House, We all enjoyed ourselves much and felt best
ate dinner with Bro W. G. Burton and family and
attended meeting at the Tabernacle. Elder H W Nasbit
preached a most exhaustive discourse on cooperation
and what it has done for the Territory, drove to my
home at Smithfield after night,. roads bad,

      Through the week at my farm repairing tools
and putting a board roof on the house &c preparing
for winter, and killed 2 of my Pigs, weight about 400lb

    <u>Sunday 18 November 1883</u>

      as our High Priests District Meetings at the north and
South end of the Valley are discontinued, I spent the day
at home in Smithfield. Elder James Meikle preached in
the afternoon and Prest W. B. Preston, C. W. Card and Bp
Thos X Smith in the Evening, we visited at Sister Jas Macks
after meeting and administered to her, and Bp Smith
went home and staid with me all night

      Monday 19 November 1883.
started early with son James to go to Logan to school
and worked at farm rest of the week Sold my
sheep to Thomas E Ricks for $126^{00} and sent $50^{00} to
pay balance on M. M. Osborne & Co note at bank at
Logan and also $50^{00} to repay money borrowed from
Bro Sylvester Lowe and $20^{00} for James Boarding to
Sister Tabiatha Ricks.

    <u>Sunday 25 November 1883</u>
Attended High Priest Meeting at Smithfield in the
morning, Ward Meeting in the afternoon, Apostle M
Thatcher preached on the trials & persecutions of
the early reformers, and on Monday

{23}
forenoon wrote some letters and the following week
made a stable under my shed in town, finished the
shed &c. on Saturday 1st December I attended
the monthly Stake priesthood meeting at Logan, the
Presidency of the Stake being absent, but appointment
presided. Prest M Thatcher being present, had a good
meeting.   <u>Sunday 2nd December 1883</u>
Attended meetings at Smithfield and preached in the
better part of the afternoon. In the Evening Elders M F
Cowley of Salt Lake City and Saml Mitten Jr of Wells=
ville preached in the interests of the Y.M.M.I.A.
I finished up my stable &c and hauled hay
from the meadow to pay some debts through the

week. Attended fast meeting on Thursday and assisted
in Blessing 10 or 12 babies and confirming 3 in
the church, also in blessing the oil &c.

Sunday 9th December 1883
Through a misunderstanding Bro Smart was not
able to take me to Logan to the monthly H. P. District
meeting and as I did not learn it until very late
I walked to Logan as I could not get time to go to
my farm to get a team. I found our H.P. meeting
adjourned to the Tabernacle where a Sunday
School Conference was being held. Prest George Q. Cannon
presiding, attended morning and afternoon meetings
and had good meeting. In conversing with Prest W. B.
Preston after meeting he asked me to submit a list
of names for Temple workers when the temple shall be
opened. I worked around home during the week making
improvements during such time as the cold weather would
permit me and I remained at home on Sunday 16 Dec
I went to the ward meeting and spoke a short time to the
Saints in the Evening, and continued making such improvements
necessary during the week. Following week, there is much
stir and agitation all over the United States on the Mormon
question and Political uxsters are aiding Governor Eli H.
Murray (our present governor) to fan the flame of political
excitement against us. I expect to live to see the author
of the accompanying Bill as also other bills now pending
before congress, die in disgrace. I have undertaken to
compile on a large Record book, the names, ages &c
of all the members of the High Priests Quorum of this stake
of Zion, and have been working when the storms would
not permit my working out doors in getting the names of my
dead relatives on sheets ready for Baptism in the temple
font   Sunday 23 December 1883.
With my son William I visited Benson Ward, and
talked to the saints about 3/4 of an hour in the afternoon
on the ordinances necessary for the redemption of the dead
and held a meeting of the members of the H.P Quorum after
ward, all expressed themselves that were present and spend
to feel well in the work, attended Seventy meetings at home
(Smithfield)   Monday 24 December 1883
Went to Elders dance by invitation of the presidency of it in
the Evening. – had a select party and had a good time &c.

{24}
25 December 1883. Christmas Day
all my family gathered at the farm and ate dinner
and enjoyed ourselves in each others company until a late
hour in the Evening. It was a wet, stormy Christmas day
Bro Hillyard was with us and seemed to enjoy himself well
I spent the remainder of the week gathering and writing up
the names and genealogies of the High Priests Quorum in

our new Quorum record book

Sunday December 30th 1883.

Went to the 2 ward meetings in Smithfield

Tuesday 1st January 1884

most of my family and a few friends met at my home in town and had an excellent dinner and I enjoyed the society of my family and thanked my heavenly father for the family and friends he had blessed me with.

Wednesday 2nd Jan 1884.

I went to Bro Hugh Roberts and wrote lists of his and his wife's relatives to be baptized for, and also to be endowed as some had been baptized for and sealed at the Endowment House Salt Lake City. and attended the Stake Priesthood meeting on Saturday 5 Jan 1884, and spoke some time to the Bps about giving the necessary instructions to young people going to get their endowments preparing suitable clothing &c and giving advice to all such persons.

Sunday 6 January 1884.

I took my wife Mary Jane to visit Sister Hyde at Hyde Park and saw little Don. I attended meeting in the Afternoon and spoke to the saints 90 minutes on the Temple ordinances took supper with Bp Daines and went home in the Evening.

Monday 7 January 1884

I attended a High Priests meeting at Hyde Park. Good attendance, all spoke—felt well—a young man a Bro Grant came into the Meeting and after listening to the remarks and testimonies of the Bretheren he got up and acknowlged his past waywardness and said he would try and do better in the future. Bro Abel Smart also spoke he took the minutes of the meeting went home same evening good sleighing. And fixed up a work bench and gathered up my carpenter tool in the Old House in town and did a lot of odd jobs repairing furniture &c

Sunday 13 January 1884

Bro Able Smart and I went to Logan and Held a district meeting at Logan in the Large Room of the Tabernacle we had a large number of High Priests from various parts of the Stake and altho the Room was Cold. We had a good meeting and took part in the Exercises also Bro Chas. O. Card of the Stake presidency, went to ~~Richmond~~ Smithfield and attended meeting in the Evening.

Monday 14 January 1884

Attended meeting at the School house and was elected a Director of the Smithfield Ecclestical ward for the ensuing 2 years. And afterwards rode to Logan and commenced to settle Tithing with the Bishops. Settled and made out the Tithing papers for Clarkston, Clifton, Coveville, and part of

{25}

the Oxford settlement, but no settlement having been made between the present and late Bishop I was sent by Church

Agent Wm B. Preston to make the settlement between them
on Thursday 17 January 1884. I proceeded at once
with Bishop Lewis to Oxford and completed the settlement
by Friday noon and hired Bro John Boyce to take me
to Clifton and Riverdale to Settle tithing with the people
of that ward. as night overtook me I stayed at my
old friend's house Brother and Sister William Gibbons and
had a splendid Visit with them and on

   Saturday 19 January 1884.
we went to Riverdale and I opened up a new book for
Settling Tithing with the people of the War. I settled
with about 1/2 the ward and hitched up the team and
started for Weston, but night overtook us and we put
up with Bro Peter Pool at Dayton, and I slept with Bro
Bro [sic] Joseph Thomas son of Harrison A Thomas of Smithfield
and proceeded Sunday morning 20 January to Weston and
attended Sabbath School and spoke 1/2 an hour to the chil=
dren, Bro Brice and Bro Abel Stuart also spoke to the chil=
dren who listened very attentively. I attended the afternoon
ward meeting, also a High Priests meeting afterwards
at dinner with Bp. A. A. Allen and then with Bro Abel
Stuart (who had come from Smithfield to take me) started for
Clarkston arriving at 6 O'clock. And met my councillor
Bro Frank Gunnell with Bp. H. Hughes and Jas G. Willie of
Mendon. They had preached in the forenoon and we all
went to the Evening meeting Bp Hughes occupied 35 min
=utes. F Gunnell 25 and I talked 40 minutes on the
Marriage principle as revealed to the Latter day Saints

   on Monday 21 January 1884,
Bro A Smart and I traveled to Smithfield getting there
at one P.M. and I spent the rest of the day visiting my
family, and on Tuesday I went to Logan Tithing office
and settled up the Oxford ward tithing for year 1883.
and remained in Logan till Friday Evening settling tithing
with the Bishops of the Wards by invitation I went to my
home in Smithfield (as my son William came to Logan with a team
and sleigh after me and James my son also went home with
us) and with my wives Mary and Mary Jane attended a dance
got up by the Relief Society and had a good time, my sons
William and Joseph also attended with my daughter Mary.

   Saturday 26 January 1884.
I took my team and went to Logan and did a days
work in the Tithing Office and returned home in the Evening
Bro Robert L. Fishburn rode to Smithfield with me, I found
my wife Margaret quite sick. with Cold and Vomiting and
Feaser.

   Sunday 27 January 1884
  Margaret is a little better today, as I sent for
Sister Alice D[anes?] to doctor her, and her treatment seemed
to do good and stop the vomiting. I attended the afternoon
meeting and heard my old Councillor and present Councillor
George Barber relate his late experience in England as

he has just returned on Wednesday last from his visit
to that country to get the means left by his Mother.

{26}
I also by invitation of Bp. G L. Farrell occupied a portion
of the afternoon, relating my experience during my last
mission to England. I stayed at home (at the farm during
the Evening Visiting with my wife Mary and Children.
Monday 28th January 1884.
My Son William took my son James & Bro R. Fishburn and
myself to Logan in the little green Sleigh. and I worked
there all the week till Saturday in Settling up the
Tithing a/cs.   ### Friday 1 Feby 1884.
This evening my wife Mary Jane came to Logan with
Bros Austin F. Merrill and some of the family of his
brothers and attended a surprise party of friends visiting
Bro and Sister Stratton of the 2nd ward Logan and we
went with them and enjoyed ourselves in Visiting, Singing
and dancing with quite a number of my old London
Conference Saints till a late hour. and with my wife
Mary Jane stayed at Bro Thomas E Ricks at night.
Saturday 2nd Feby 1884.
Our Quarterly Conference of the Cache Valley Stake of
Zion commenced, I was the 1st speaker called upon
to report the condition of the High Priests Quorum and
the Bishops reported their wards. The afternoon was
occupied by the Bretheren from Salt Lake City. I went
home at night and again went to Logan on
Sunday 3rd Feby 1884.
At the Close of the afternoon meeting I went to Bro
Prestons. and presented recommends from Mendon, Prov=
-idence, Smithfield, Bannock, Mink Creek, and
Franklin Wards. for some Bretheren to become mem=
bers of the High Priests Quorum to Prests Preston and
John Taylor. after which I met with apostle F D
Richards and gave him all my papers I had brought
from St George about the Records and other Matter
about the Temple and its affairs, as he wanted
such information as I had. I slept with Bp. Gunn
=ell at Bro Thos E Rick's, after spending a pleasant
Evening's conversation with Patriarch Zebedee Coltron
from Spanish Fork, Utah County.
Monday 4 Feby 1884.
By invitations of Bro F.D. Richards I went through the
Temple with the Presidency and apostles and had a
good view of all of it, some changes were suggested
by President Taylor and W. Woodruff, after which I
went to the Logan Tithing Office and worked over the
Richmond Sheet and accounts, and then went home
to Smithfield riding with Bro Wm D Hendricks and
attended a dance of the 70's at the old school

House,, Bro's Thomas E Ricks was this ~~offer~~

{27}
day ordained President of the Snake River Stake
of Zion and William D. Hendricks was ordained
President of ~~Mound Valley~~ /Oneida\ Stake of Zion. the 1st
named by Prest John Taylor and W D. Hendricks by
Prest George Q. Cannon. I rode to Smithfield the same
afternoon and in the Evening attended a meeting of the
17th Quorum of 70s and on Complimentary Invitation with
my wives Mary and Mary Jane attended a pic-nic ball
got up by the Quorum in the Smithfield Ward Meeting
House and had a good party and visit with friends,
     on Tuesday 5 Feby 1884.
I returned to Logan and worked during the week in
the Tithing office as usual. till Saturday 9th Feby
I returned home and found Sister Sarah Rigby and Bro
George Rigby and his Wife and William Rigby's wife Sarah
at my house. My Wife Margaret proved to be in Labor
with Child and about 9 P.M. I went for sister Alice
Duan the Midwife and about 25 minutes to 6 on
the morning of Sunday 10th Feby 1884 my wife
Margaret was delivered of a child, a girl, sound
and whole for which blessing we all feel to thank
our heavenly father. , the weather Very Cold, at 9 a.m.
Bro A. Smart my Quorum Clerk and I started for Logan
to hold District Meeting of High Priest Quorum Meeting
Quite a number present. and had a good meeting. I
ordained Bros Thomas Stirland and Jacob Zollinger of
Providence and Bro F. Theurer ordained Bro Charles
S. Crabtree at my Request High Priests. after meeting
we ate dinner at Sister T Ricks and thence to Smithfield
and I slept part of the Afternoon and Evening so as to be
ready to wait upon my wife Margaret through the night,
which I did.   Monday 11 Feby 1884.
An Exceedingly stormy day I rode to Logan and
worked at the Tithing Office till the following Saturday
during the week I handed Prest W.B. Preston a list
of names from Various parts of the Valley and rec=
=ommending them as persons I believed would make good Temple Hands.
     Sunday 17th 1884.
with Bro Abel Smart went to Hyrum and held
district High Priest meeting in their large school
Room. Bro. W. Maughan from Wellsville and Bp
George O. Pitkin from Millville and Bp Molen from
Hyrum, and my councillor Francis Gunnell was
present and we had an excellent good meeting,
took dinner with Bp Molen and attended the
ward afternoon Meeting and after the saints had
partaken of the sacrament the Bps and F. Gunnell
and I occupied the time. I spoke 35 minutes on a

variety of subjects and encouraged the saints by good
and well doing. returned to Smithfield same night

{28}
and on Monday 18 Feby I went to Logan to continue my
labors in the Tithing office, and, succeeded pretty well in
our labours through the week.
   On Thursday Afternoon 21st Feby with Bp
George L. Farrell, Elder James H. Martineau and the Clerk of
of [sic] the Construction of the Temple Elder James A. Leishman I
visited and went through the Temple at Logan and was
highly gratified to see the Building in so forward a state.
The seats are nearly all made and ready for paining and
several of the rooms are new being painted the last coat of
paint. on Friday afternoon 22nd Feby I assisted
to finish up the Tithing Settlement of Cache Valley Stake of
Zion the sum of $102.903^{11} was paid by 3248 Tithe Payers
an average of $31.68 1/5 to each tithe payer. after which I went to
Messrs Smith and Stratford's the Printing Establishment and
got some certificate of Membership for the members of the
High Priests Quorum which I had printed, also some
certificates of membership for bretheren removing. After
which I left with Sister Tabitha Ricks and order on Logan
Tithing Office for Vegetables $12^{00} Butter and Eggs $6^{30} cash
$2^{20} and an order on Z.C.M.I Logan Branch $3^{50} total $24^{00}
My team having arrived from Smithfield I rode home and
am thankful to record that through the blessings of my heavenly
father my family are all well in health. I spent Saturday
with my three sons James. William and Joseph visiting the ditches
leading to my farm and making preparations for the melting
snows of Spring, and on Sunday 24 Feby 1884 With Ben A
Smart and Francis Sharp I attended ward meeting at
Richmond and heard a good discourse from the lips of
our venerable President of Seventies Milo Andrews and
I followed him for 35 minutes, After which meeting I held
a District High Priests Meeting according to previous ap=
=pointment, and our meeting was a good one. The following
Bretheren were ordained upon proper Recommends. Viz=
Shelden B. Cutler of Franklin by S. Roskelley, mouth
Abednego Wilkinson   " " "
Edmund Buckley   " Bp Nahum Porter "
William C. Parkinson " " " "
William T. Bonnett   " " Bp W. L. Skidmore "
Rode home and attended a meeting of the Saints at
Smithfield. Elder W. E. Sloan of Salt Lake lectured on
Utah-her past, Present and future.
   Monday 25th Feb 1884.
I worked at my carpenters bench repairing various articles
for my family, and followed it up nearly all week as the
weather was squally and very boisterous and would not per=
mit of out door work to any extent. Through the week my

daughter Rebecca was taken sick and was confined to her bed
And my wife Margaret was also suffering with gathered breast
on Right side, and several of the children were afflicted with
bad coughs. Saturday 1st Mch 1884.
　　　I attended the monthly Priesthood Meeting.

{29}
　　　Sunday 2st March 1884. ordained 3 H.P. at Logan
I visited and attended the High Priests meeting of Smithfield Ward
Bro Francis Sharp, had a good meeting- quite a number spoke
I also occupied about 1/2 and hour on general topics and enjoyed a
good flow of the Holy Spirit much to my satisfaction and Joy. I passed
the week when the weather was fine in trimming and scraping my
fruit trees and in the shop when it was bad weather
　　　Sunday 9th March 1884.
with Bro Abel Smart I went to Logan to attend the District
Meeting of the High Priests Quorum- It rained all day and the
roads were very bad, had an excellent meeting- many
present and had a good meeting—Apostle Moses Thatcher
spoke on the Duties and offices of the Priesthood, and gave
some good instruction. Bro E. D. Carpenter spoke on the powers
and duties of the High Priesthood. Bro N. C. Edlefsen spoke
on the Duties of the Various offices of the Aaronic Priesthood
and after meeting I went home to Smithfield in a rainstorm
and attended a ward meeting at Smithfield in the Evening.
And I preached all evening, during the day at Logan
Bro. Charles O. Card, the Superintendent of the construction of
the Logan Temple invited me to come to Logan and assist in
a plan to fix the Carpets—screens and other matters in
the arrangements of the Temple
　　　Monday 10th March 1884.
My daughter Mary's birthday, 14 years old, I took all my
family to the farm and ate supper, and enjoyed ourselves.
　　　Tuesday 11 March 1884.
I went to Logan and consulted with Bro C. O. Card, the Supt.
and T.O. Angell Jr., the Architect, about things necessary for the Temple
to fit it up Properly and Wednesday. with Bro. Angell I
Measured all the Rooms to be carpeted and wrote a bill for
the carpet for the Building The totals are as follows
　　　　1st class Carpet 703 yds.　\ I also made out in writing
　　　　2nd class　　"　258　"　　| a number of suggestions about
　　　　Home Made "　2264 "　　| the seating. and many other
　　　　　　Total　3225 yards / things pertaining to the Temple
addressed to Supt C. O. Card and he took the same to Salt
Lake City to submit to the Temple Committee of the Apostles and
the Church Presidency.　　　Thursday. 13th March 1884.
Got all the Carpet on hand measured up and the lower rooms
all fixed to commence to cut and lay it down, and had
Bro James A. Leishman the clerk of the Logan Temple write to
Sister Libby Benson the president of Cache Valley Stake Relief
Society to furnish a few Sisters to sew up carpet for the Temple Rooms.

I slept in the Temple office on a Cott bedstead made on purpose for
me by Brother White, feeling thankful I had the privilege to labor in
preparing the Temple of God for the Endowment of his Saints.

Friday 14 March 1884.

I hurried the workmen out of the Washing rooms on the North
side of the Temple basement and about 10 Oclock the following named
sisters came to work. Clara Bench Jeppsen, Amanda Eliason
Benson, Anne Andersen Frank, Martha Eulan Reese.
Mary Ann French Farnes, Anna Martha /Johnson\ Henstrom, all from
Logan 1st Ward, and proceeded at once to Cut and sew
Home Made Carpet for the washing rooms, and Bro
Tollifson of Hyrum helped me to clean the Rooms and

{30}
pat down the carpets, and arrange the seats in the 2nd
and third rooms going west on the north side, this was the
1st work done and these were the 1st sisters who worked
in the building to fit it up, and I laid the 1st carpets.

Saturday 15 March 1884.

The following named Sisters of the 2nd Ward Logan came to help
sew carpet at the temple. Emily McNeil Ballard, Susan
Jane Jolly Smith, Kate Tarbott Irvine, Elizabeth Evans Hayball,
Barbara L. Olsen Larsen, Margaret R. Griffith Thaine
Eliza A Perry Benson. Carrie Benson. And we made
and Laid 4 carpets on the ~~north~~ South side of the House
in the Wash rooms also the west Room on the north side
Making 7 Rooms covered in 2 days, of which work we feel
proud, My wife Mary and son Joseph came to Logan
today to see the Temple and I had the pleasure of escort=
=ing them around the building, after which I went home
to Smithfield with my family.

Sunday 16 March.

I attended High Priests meeting at Smithfield. heard
several of the bretheren speak among them Bro Geo Barber
my councillor, after which I gave some instructions on
various topics of interest to the members of the Quorum.

Monday 17 Mch.

A Stormy day- worked in my shop, fixing double trees

Tuesday 18th March.

My wife Margaret and her Sister Lavina went to Newton
with my son Joseph, my son returned next day with the
Team. Roads very muddy. I worked scraping trees and
preparing for spring in Lot in town, till Thursday 20th
a Very stormy day. I was reading nearly all day.

Friday 21st Mch 1884.

I took the team and went to Logan on Temple Business
Bro Chas O. Card the Supt. of Construction made a
formal Request that I take charge of the fitting
up and Laying Carpets of the Temple. I returned home
in the Evening with my son James. from school.

Saturday 22nd Mch 1884.

My Sons James. William and Joseph and I repaired and Washed and greased a set of Harness, got 2 tuyer set on wheels of Light wagon and I painted one of the wheels. and went to the farm at night.

Sunday 23rd March 1884.

The Roads are so very muddy that it seems next to impossible to get around—hence I remained at home today—and attended meetings of the Saints afternoon and evening, and also visited my daughter Rebecca who has been quite sick for some time past with heavy cold and miscarriage.
{31}

Monday 24th 1884

Went to Logan Early in the morning with my sons James who was going to school and William who desired to go through the Temple, I worked at the Temple all day getting ready for our Sisters to work on

Tuesday 25th 1884.

I had prepared the curtains for the Wash Rooms and the following named Sisters came to sew on them.
Sister Elizth Golliaher Benson
Elizth Louisa Wildon Crowther   \   These women cut
Mary Nebeker Farr. | and made some
Elizth John Dunn Townsend | of the Curtains for
Lucy Smith Cardon 4 Wd.   /   the Wash Rooms but
Catherine Tarbet Irvine.   left others unfinished.

Wednesday 26th 1884.

The following named Sisters came to the Temple today to help. Viz Caroline Hobbs Watterson 5 Logan Wd \ These sisters
Sarah Jane Apperly Tarbet   "   " | finished the
Ingar Catherine Mortensend Johnson   "   " | Curtains that
Catherine Mary Holden Hurst   4   " | were commenced
Ann Spanton Andrews   3   "   / on Yesterday
The following named sisters worked sewing Carpets
Mary Knight Benson Logan 1st Ward
Aurelia Hawkins Hurst " 4th "
Eliza Foresman Smith   " 2nd "
The following named Sisters worked cleaning Rooms.
Rebecca Williams Eames   Logan 3rd Wd
Lucy Cook McNeil   "   "   "
Edith Benson   "   1   "
Lorenze Gresle Petersen   "   4   "
Mary Gresle   "   "   "
The sisters finished up the Carpet for the Wash Rooms and also Cleaned the council Room, Garden and Telestial Rooms, doing a heavy day's work. And Keeping me very buisy preparing Material for them.

Thursday 27th 1884.

The following Sisters came to work at the Temple to sew carpet.

Ann Spanton Andrews
for Harriet Pitkin Robinson Robbins Logan 4th Ward
Mary Ross Henderson " 5 "
Pricilla Payne Jacobs " " "
Elizabeth Augusta Legan Wicklund " " "
Elizabeth Barr Archibald " " "
Martha Morgan Burriss " " "
Margaret Farrer Gledhill " " "
May Mortensen Olsen " " "
         over

{32}
  Thursday 27 Mch 1884. continued.
  The following Sisters cleaned up and scrubbed the floors of the 4 Upper Towers in the West Towers and one of the Rooms of the sam Tower, and the Crea Room also.
Josephine Christensen   Logan 5th Ward
Rosina Furgusen   "   "
Eliza Nelson   "   "
Alma Berger Holt.   "   "
Annie Anderson   "   "
Catherine Hendersen Ellis "   "
  Friday 28 march 1884.
Not having any amount of carpet on hand we did not have any Sisters here today to sew but I Bro Jas Hendersen and I carried the Benches down stairs and completed the lower rooms as much as possible, and the afternoon we laid and tacked down the carpet on the Upper Room of West Tower making a splendid Job of it. Saturday 29 March 1884.
  Measured up Rooms and prepared work for the Sisters for Monday next.– some carpet came in and I measured and gave credit for it and went to priesthood (monthly) meeting. and heard some good instruction from the Stake Presidency on temporal affairs. After meeting went again to the Temple and laid off more work for Monday. and rode to Hyde Park with Bp R. Daines and walked to my farm found folks all well. James left School in Logan today, and went home to attend to putting in our crop Sunday 30 March 1884.
I called my Sons James, William and Joseph together this morning and told them I had been reques= =ted to fit up the Logan Temple for work and I may never have another opportunity of the kind in my life there and if they would put in the crop to the best of their ability I would attend to the Temple matter, and they should be blessed in their labors. They divided the work of the farm and nursery and gardens, James & Joseph taking the farm and teams and William the Gardens & nursery. Attended the

Ward High Priests meeting in forenoon and preached
to the Bretheren, and Ward Meeting in the afternoon
and sunday school Union in the Evening and was
much entertained with songs—dialogues &c &c.
James Roskelley was called by Bp G. L. Farrell
to be 2nd assistant to Sth Layton Sunday School
Sup.<u>Monday 31st March 1884</u>
Rode to Logan in my Buggie Joseph driving the
Team. I found a number of the sisters had been
waiting on me for more work. which I soon gave
them. Sewing Carpet. The following named Sisters

{33}
put in all day sewing carpet. viz
Emma Barber Pike   1st Ward Logan
Catherine White Thomas Leishman   "   "   "
Ann John Smith   2   "   "
Barbara Jenzina Dorothea Olsen Larsen   "   "
Emeline Eliza Painter James   "   "
Ann Roberts Hopkins   2nd   "   "
Emma Gedleston Smith   "   "   "
Eliza Cole Hawkes   "   "   "
Matilda Sarah Farnes Smith   "   "   "
Mary Griffiths Ledingham   "   "   "
Mary Ann Barham Farmes   "   "   "
Rosina King Morrell   "   "   "
Selina Johnson Morrell   "   "   "

[*written vertically, right margin:* Elizabeth S. Danton Palmer]

<u>Tuesday 1st day of April 1884</u>
The following named sisters came to the
Temple and sewed to day.
    Mary Wakins Williams   Logan 3rd Ward
    Margaret Rowland Merrell   "   "
    Sarah Jane Williams   "   "
    Clara Christina Jensen Larson   "   "
    Ruth James Parry   "   "
    Mary Parry Rowland   "   "
    Mary Bird Farrell Birdins   2nd Wd
    Susan Ellen Johnson Martineau 1st   "
    Thomas Moore of Richmond
    Robt Angus Bain of Smithfield
we laid off he carpet on the 2nd Room down of
the west tower, all in 1st tower Room in East
tower.

<u>Wednesday 2nd April 1884.</u>
The following named Sisters came to the Temple to help
us sew carpet today
    Tobiatha Hendricks Ricks and 6 others from the
4th Ward. and we laid the carpet in the 1st Room
from the bottom in the East tower.

<u>Thursday 3rd April 1884.</u>

Had 4 Sisters sewing and 5 Cleaning found that the
Carpet we laid yesterday was so poor it could not
stretch so we took it up again and laid it in the
north west dressing Room and it seemed to do better.

Friday 4th Apl 1884.
Bros Moore R A Bair Robt Anderson and I laid the
Carpet in the South East Dressing Room also fixed the
Benches there and in the North West Dressing Room and
in the Afternoon fixed down the carpet that was made
in the Creation Room. finishing up all we could do to it
on   Saturday 5 April 1884.
and we fixed up several little jobs that had been
left undone and I then rode home to Smithfield with
Bros William Ainscough and Littlefield.

{34}
Sunday 6 April 1884.
attended Meeting of Saints in the afternoon and
heard Bro George Barber talk after which I followed
him for near 40 minutes on Marriage and the fashion
of the day, also the duty of children to their Parents.
after meeting Bro Preston D. Moorehead called on me
and I gave him some drawings made by Thomas Angell,
architect of Logan Temple, for some articles to be made
for the Temple at Logan. Spent the Evening at my
farm with my wife Mary and family.

Monday 7 April 1884.
Got up early in the Morning and planted peas and onions and
set out in Boxes Cabbage, Tomatoes & Cauliflower &c and went
to the Temple with Bro Ainscough who hauled some Trees down for
me. I made out plans for 53 Door Mats for the Temple
to send to the Settlement to get them made.

Tuesday 8 April 1884.
I laid off a carpet for the lowest Room in the west Tower
and had it made up. also a carpet for the Top Room
in the East tower. We had 9 sisters working today
sewing on carpets and got along very well, Maggie came
from Newton

Wednesday 9 April 1884.
I got 18 Fruit Trees from Bro John Jacobs @ 9$\underline{00}$. I paid him
an order on Z.C.M.I for 4\underline{00}$ and rode to Smithfield in a
team going to Franklin and at once set to work planting
trees at the farm and did not quit till dark.

Thusday 10 April 1884
I planted tree seeds before breakfast and afterward
went to town and planted trees till train time at 12.13
when I took the train for Logan and worked in the
Temple in the afternoon.

Friday 11 April 1884.
Worked fixing and laying carpet and did so on Saturday till
train time when I went home to Smithfield and trimmed

goosbery trees till night, went to my farm and visited
my famil in the Evening.
Sunday 13 April 1884.
With Bro Abel Smart I rode to Logan and attended a
District Meeting of the High Priests Quorum and had a splendid
meeting – Prest Wm B. Preston was present and spoke about
his recent promotion to the office of Presiding Bishop of the
church and gave us good instruction on quite a number
of topics. I remained in Logan all night attending
a Lecture by Elder Jas A Leishman on the Lives of the
Early Reformers,
Monday 14 April 1884
I worked in the Temple at the Carpets and had 16 of
the Sisters Sewing on them also. My wife Maggie came
from Smithfield and worked in the Temple. all week
with me.

{35}
Saturday 19 Apl 1884
After doing a day's work I went home to Smithfield with
Bro Ainscough and took my wife Maggie & baby.
Sunday 20 April 1884
Attended meeting of the Saints and spent the Evening at
my farm with my family. and on Monday 21st April
I rode to Logan with my son Joseph and I got a
span of horses from Bro Card it being a Temple
team. and I have hired them for 10 days. My son
Joseph went home with the Horses at noon. And I
worked at laying the carpets &c all week till
Friday Afternoon when I took the train with Bro Robert A
Bair and went home to Smithfield, and examined the
labor of my sons on the farm &c, and find they are doing
well putting in Crops. I put in seeds in my gardens
Saturday 26th April 1884
took my wife Margaret to the farm and got all
the help I could from my family and cut and planted
potatoes at the farm but had to buy 10 Bu of seed
potatoes from William Douglass. I put peas in the garden
in town, ### Sunday 27th 1884.
attended High Priests meeting at Smithfield in the Morning,
and Saints meeting in the Afternoon, and visited my
family at the farm in the Evening, and received a letter
from Supt C.O. Card of the Temple asking me to come back
to the Temple as soon as I can push along the work,
Monday 28 April 1884.
Put in some peas and other things at the farm garden
and assisted to plant balance of crop of Potatoes.
After which I took my team and got some furniture
for the Temple from Bro Preston T. Morehead and took
my wife Margaret & son Joseph and Bro Robert Bair
to Logan to the Temple. I also took the Horses I had

hired from the Temple back again. And as I had
rented a room from Bp Thos X Smith in Logan I took
my wife Margaret and babe there, and spent the
latter part of the day at the Temple preparing for
the work of Tuesday 29 April 1884, and spent
the week in arranging seats, making and laying down carpets
&c till Saturday 3 May 1884. I went home to Smithfield
late in the afternoon with Bro G. L. Farrell and attended a
~~High Priests~~ Meeting of the Saints also visited my daughter
Rebecca, on the Sunday 4 May 1884.
On Monday I went to Logan again to continue work on
the temple.   Tuesday 5 May 1884. Bro T Hillyard brought me
2 hansom cedar trees for temple uses. I replanted them imm
=ediately and put them in place. Bro Hillyard and Wives &
Mathew & Sister went through the rooms of the Building. I was
[ ] every thing in place through the week, and on Friday 9th
May, with Bro Jas Leishman I went to R. R. Depot and saw Bro
Jos F. Smith as he was on his way to Bear Lake to attend the
Quarterly Conference of that Stake. ate dinner with him at a
restaurant and chatted about temple matters generally.
Saturday 10 May 1884.   After closing my labors at the
Temple for the week I borrowed a temple team and buggy
and with Bro Robt Bair went to Smithfield and talked to

{36}
my family, and left home again on Sunday morning
and attended High Priest Quorum Meeting at Logan at
1/2 past 10 A.M. And had good exercises and class,
also attended afternoon Meeting at Logan Tabernacle
and held meeting and heard Bro F. D. Richards preach
an excellent sermon, also attended Ward meeting
in the Evening and talked about 40 minutes,
twined 1 cow in the herd at home today.
         Monday 12th May 1884.
Turned all the cows (5) and 1 Bull in the
herd today. for the season.
         Wednesday 13 May 1884.
I set my Wife Margaret and Sister Benson and Elizth G.
Benson and Lucy B. Cardon to making the Vails
for Logan temple after I cut them out. In the
afternoon Prests Taylor, & Cannon, Woodruff, Apostles
E. Snow, L. Snow, A. Carrington, M Thatcher H J Grant and
J. W. Taylor, and Councillor Wells, also Prests McAllister
L. J. Nuttall, and several others were present, and went
through the temple, and seemed well pleased in every
Particular so far as the building and its fixtures were con[ ]
=ted although we had much to do yet to complete the buil
=ding   Thursday 14 May 1884
Today our Record books arrived having been furnished
by the trustee-in-Trust of the Church. 78 Record and
Index Books, also Stationary &c for the use of the temple,

and I placed them in our cupboard made for the purpose
they are a handsome set of Records and books. I kept everybody
around me busy making and putting down carpet
and cleaning-dusting and making the rooms ready for
the work designed, till 10 o'clock on
<u>Saturday Morning 17 May 1884</u>
at which time thousands of people had gathered at
the gates of the Temple Block seeking an Entrance to
the Dedicatory Services. I had had the entire charge
of and arranging of the Stands and large Rooms &c
of the Temple, and when the doors were opened and the
flood of people entered showing their tickets to the
door Keeper at the Entrance, it looked almost like
a sea of heads coming into the doorways, at 1/2 past
10 OClock Prest John Taylor called the attention of the
congregation at ~~1/2 past 10 Oclock~~ and the proceedings
of the dedication are about as contained in the following
report. I occupied the third stand on the Melchizedek side
of the House as president of the High Priests Quorum of the
Cache Valley Stake of Zion with my councillors. Bro
Gunnell and George Barber also Bro Elias Morris of the
Presidency of Salt Lake Stake of the High Priests Quorum
and Bro John Kelly Prest of the High Priests Quorum of Box
Elder Stake and John Stukie Prest of Bear Lake Stake
High Priests Quorum were also present, in the [---]
stand during the 3 days of Dedication, we had a glor

{37}
ious time and one long to be remembered by the Saints
who were privelaged to be present, and altho I was almost
worn out with working in fixing and preparing the building
for the Dedication services also also for the uses designed when
fully completed, I rejoiced much under the influence that
prevailed in the building during the Exercises. My wives.
Mary, Mary Jane and Maggie attended the dedication on Sunday,
and my sons Samuel, James, William and Joseph attended
the Mondays meeting being a repetition of the services.
   [*clipping pasted to page:* "Conference and Dedication of the Temple," *Utah Journal*, 21 May
                                                                                1884, p.2]

{38}
On Saturday, Sunday and Monday, May 17th, 18 & 19th
the days of the dedication I was at work till time of the
meetings and from then close till night.
      <u>Monday 19th May 1884.</u>
While at work arranging the building for work on the
21st, I was summoned by Telephone and a carriage sent for
me to Apostle Moses Thatcher's where Prests Taylor, Cannon
J.F. Smith and all the twelve save B. Young, F. M. Lyman and
John H. Smith, also several of the brethren from various

parts of the Territory were present, and the following named persons
were selected by Vote of all present to fill the offices opposite
their names in the Temple at Logan.
Samuel Roskelley for Recorder, and his wife Margaret for worker
John Crouther for Engineer
William McNeil for Janitor
N.C. Edlefsen for worker
O. N Lilenquist and wife Christina
Thos Work and Wife Susanna.
George T. Baugh
John Oice and wife Mary Ann
Charles Dun and wife Letitia
Charles Hubbard and wife Mary Ann
Robert Bair
Thomas Morrell and wife Selina Jr
Elizabeth J. Townsend.
On the Evening of the same day Bro Chas O
Card and I with the consent of Prest John Taylor called
upon the following named persona to Labor in the temple.

Abel Smart	Elizth Golkier Benson
Thomas X. Smith	Lucy Smith Cardon
Thomas B. Cardon	Elizabeth L. Crowther
John Jacobs	Martha Rowland
Thomas McNeil	Emma Pike
George Barber	Harriett Parry
Robert Henderson	

<u>Tuesday 20th May 1884.</u>

Prest Taylor and party came to the temple and
Examined the water arrangements and all other things he
wished so as to see that all was ready for the work
of tomorrow, and the carpet having arrived by the Express
train in the afternoon. With Bro Robert A Baird went to work
at 20 minutes to 6. P.M and by 8 O'Clock next morning I had the
celestial f[l]oor nearly covered with the carpet altho' it was not
sewn together but it met the approval of Prest John Taylor as it
was.

<u>Wednesday 21 May 1886.</u>

A company of Saints met for Baptisms and Endowments
and at 25 minutes past 8 the following named brethren
assembled in the East rooms. East of Garden and blessed 12
bottles of oil for annointing purposes Prest J F Smith E Snow
H J Grant D H. Wells. A M. Cannon. Patriarch John Smith
Apostles Erastus Snow mouth. And afterward the

{39}
same brethren blessed 6 Bottles of oil for 2nd anointing,
then going into the font room shortly afterwards, I met
Prest Taylor and the councillors and most of the members
of the 12. when Prest Taylor said to me we have Just
elected Bro Marriner W. Merrill president of this temple and
want you to vote too so I put up my hand and voted,

the and the brethren then went into the Garden and at
20 minutes past 9 A.M. Bro Merrill was set apart
to preside over the Logan Temple. by Prest John Taylor
being mouth. Assisted by his councillors and the members
of the 12 apostles. And then Prest Taylor requested
me to sit on the same seat Bro Merrill had just been
sitting on to be ordained and /at\ the same persons laid their
hands on me and Prest George Q Cannon being mouth
set me apart for Recorded for this Temple and blessed
me with great blessings among them the gifts of interpre
tation and deserving the temple of the Saints and reading as
understanding obscure writing and genealogy and then
we commenced work. 51 were baptized for the dead & living
59 were Endowed 1 person ordained Elder, and 9 persons
received 2nd Anointing. Among the number Endowed
was my son James whos Record was the first taken in
the house for Endowments, after the labors of the
day was over the Presidency expressed themselves well
satisfied. David H. Cannon of St George Baptized.

Confirmers
Prest John Taylor 1 Prest Geo Q Cannon 1 Thomas Moore 18
Chas O. Dunn 31

   Witnesses
   Frederick Smith Chas O. Card and Orson Smith
   Recorders at Font L. J. Nuttall & S. Roskelley.

	Endowments	Living	Dead	
Males		21	5 = 26 \	
Females		22.	9. = 31 / 57.	

   Ordinations.

Elders	Living	Dead		
	1	5. = 6		6

   Sealings.
   Prest John Taylor. Prest Geo Q. Cannon. D.H. Wells

| Living | 2 | – | 19. = 21 \ |
| Dead | – | 8 | – = 8 / 29 |

Sealings Children to Parents
   Prest George Q Cannon
Dead   1   1 – 1

   2nd Annointings.
   W. Woodruff J.D.T McA[llister]
    M F   M F
Living 1. 2. 1 1 = 5 \
Dead. 2. 2.   = 4 / 9.

the day has been a Blessed day to us who have
had the previlege to labor in the House set apart for
the performance of the ordinances of the gospel.
We have had a great time and rejoiced much.

{40}
   Thursday 22 May 1884.
we set to work to day to straighten up out hurried

labor of yesterday and make arrangements for giving
Baptisms and Endowments for Living and dead on
tomorrow. About 10 OClock Prest John Taylor and his
councilors and members of the 12 came into the Temple
and looked through number of the rooms and at 20 M
past 10 O'clock the following named persons came into the
recorders office where I was writing at the table
Prests John Taylor, Geo Q Cannon, Jos F. Smith, Lorenzo Snow
Wilford Woodruff, F D Richards, M. Thatcher, George Teasdale,
Danl H. Wells, John D. T. McAllister, Angus M. Cannon,
L. J. Nuttall, David Cannon, M. W. Merrill, S. Roskelley
and Thos Morrell. ~~and~~ Bp Wm B. Preston, Chas O. Card, Erastus
Snow and George W. Thatcher came in during the time
Prest Taylor was talking.   Prest Taylor turned
to me as I was sitting writing and said, I want you
recorders to place on the Records of the temple, that the Lord
is well pleased and has accepted this house and our
labors in its dedication, also the labors of this people
in its building and beautifying, and whatever Saints
may feel to place into it to ornament and Embellish
it will also be accepted. I state this as the word of
the Lord and the Lord will continue to reveal unto
us every principle that shall be necessary for our
guidance in the future in all matters pertaining
to our labors both spiritually and temporally. -
He afterwards said God accepts us if we will do
his will and He will sustain us and no power
shall have power to do us any harm or injure us.
I feel to bless you brethren present in the name of
Israels God and your families shall be blessed
and God will raise you up and lift you on high,
I feel like shouting Hallelujah, Hallelujah, Hallelujah
for the Lord God Omnipotent reigneth. Glory to God
for his kingdom and people shall triumph in the name
of Israels God.   The spirit and influence that
filled the Room brought conviction to the minds and hearts of
all present that the words of President Taylor were true and faith
ful. The presidency and twelve left for Salt Lake City
by the Midday train.

      <u>Friday 23rd May</u>

We gave Endowments today after baptisms, as follows,
Baptisms 7. Endowments 36. Ordinations 1. Sealings 11.

      <u>Saturday 24 May.</u>

I spent the day getting things in their places and starting
my temple books aright. And my son James came to Logan
with a team and took me home in the Evening. My family
gathered at my house in town and we partook of supper
together. As my son James expected to start on his mis
=sion to the Southern States tomorrow.

{41}

<u>Sunday 25th May 1884.</u>
I got my Son James's Satchel with his clothes. Books &c
and packed them up and with many of the family and
friends went to the Railway station and waited for the
Train which was nearly 4 hours late because of washout
by the road. My son left at 3.45 P.M. with the God
blessings of myself and many others. I went to the farm
and spent the Evening tired out and started from home
Early on <u>Monday Morning for Logan.</u> reaching here in
time to take Record for Baptisms on the Tuesdays
my son James was to day ordained a 70 by Pres W.
Woodruff in this Historian's office Salt Lake City and
set apart as a missionary to the Southern States.

<u>Tuesday 27th 1884.</u> Baptismal day
we baptized today. for Renewal of Covenants ~~10~~ 10
          " Restoration of Health ~~14~~ 17
          " for the dead ---------- 214

<u>Wednesday 28th 1884.</u>
Gave Endowments today Living 27 Dead 47 = Total 74
Sealings 26, Children to Parents 6. 2nd Anointings 1.

<u>Thursday 29th 1884.</u>
Gave Endowments today Living 10. Dead 35 = Total 45.
Ordinations 16. Sealings 17.

<u>Friday 30th 1884.</u>
Gave Endowments to day Living 23 Dead 34. Total 57.
Ordinations 10. Sealings 22. Baptisms Health 2. Dead 3.

<u>Saturday 31st May 1884.</u>
Sealing Children to Parents Living 1. Dead 2.
After the temple work was over I went home with Bro Marion
Kerr of Richmond and found my family all well.

<u>Sunday 1st June 1884</u>
with Bro Abel Smart and Francis Sharp I went to Richmond
and held High Priest District Meeting and had a good time
and returned home, and attended ward meeting at
Smithfield, Bros O S Ormsby and George Barber Jr preached

<u>Monday 2nd June 1884.</u>
took my team to Logan. Bro Abel Smart and Thos Moore
went along. took record and made up Register for month
of May. I hired Bro Marinus Anderson at one
Dollar per day. Commencing with today. 1/3 cash 2/3 Store OD

<u>Tuesday 3 June 1884.</u>
Baptismal Day. 1st Baptisms   5 \
      Ren of Covenants   13 | 515
      for Health   21 |
      Dead   476/
I was recorder for most of the above and Confirmed 27.

<u>Wednesday 4th June 1884</u>
Endowments Liv 33. Dead 70 = 103
Ordinations   Dead 26 = 26
Sealings   Liv 13   Dead 22 = 35
Chil to Parants   6

Thursday 5 June 1884.

Endowments Liv 15   Dead 50 = 65
Ordinations   "   1   "   22 = 23
Sealings   "   7   "   14 = 21
Chil to Parants   11

{42}

Thursday 5 June 1884 continued

In the Evening I went to meeting in the basement of the Logan Taber-
=nacle and was present when C. O Card. Stake president of Cache
Valley called Bro A L Schankey as Bishop of the 6th ward of Logan
also Bro Israel Smith as Bishop of 7th Ward. Logan, and I assisted
in setting apart Bro Joseph E. Willson as 2nd Councillor to Bp B M. Lewis
of Logan 1st Ward, also Bp Schankey, and I was mouth in ordaining Bro.
Niels P. Lundeloff 1st Councillor to Bp Smith of 7th ward and assisted
to set apart Bishop Smith and his 2nd Councillor. Bp Schankey's 2
Councillors were set apart on the occasion by Prest C O. Card
and his Councillor M. W. Merrill also Prests John D. T. McAllister and
Samuel Roskelley set the above named persons apart.

Friday 6 Jun 1884
                Liv   Dead
Endowments   15.   56 = 71
Ordinations   –   27 = 27
Sealings   8.   20 = 28
Adoptions   1   1

Saturday 7 Jun 1884.

I copied some Sealing Ceremonies in the morning for Prest M. W Merrill
and then attended the Priesthood meeting in the Tabernacle of the
Stake, and afterward went home to Smithfield and looked around the
Garden to see what had been done and what needed doing.

Sunday 8 Jun 1884.

I came to Logan and attended the High Priests District Meeting at
the Tabernacle and had a splendid good time. Subjects spoke
upon were Celestial Marriage and the new and Everlasting cov-
=enant., I went to Smithfield in the afternoon and spent the
Evening at the farm

Monday 9 June 1884.

Went to Logan in the morning with Bro Abel Smart and with
him and James Leishman I took record all day and was
tired when night came.

Tuesday 10 June 1884.

we had a full house. for Baptisms.
                      Male   Female
for 1st Baptism   5.   4 = 9   \
 " Ren of Cov   21.   39. = 60 |
 " Health   13.   27. = 40 | 943.
 " Dead   448.   386 = 834 /

I confirmed 136. My Son Samuel was baptized for 30
and Joseph for. 26 My daughter Rebecca for . 3 Mary for 5
and Sarah for 15 All my Kindred dead.

         Children sealed to Parents.
Living   1 \ 5.   Adoptions ---- 2.
Dead   4 /
         Wednesday 11 June 1884
                Living Dead
Endowments   30.   81. = 111
Ordinations   ---   31 = 31
Sealings   14   31 = 45
Chil to Parents   2 = 2
Adoptions   1 = 1

{43}
        Thursday 12 Jun 1884.
                Living Dead
Endowments   15.   91. — 106
Ordinations   1.   33. = 34.
Sealings   6.   36. = 42.
        Friday 13 June 1884.
                Living Dead
Endowments   3.   77. = 80
Ordinations   31. = 31.
Sealings   2.   24. = 26
Children to Parents 1   – = 1.
2nd Anointing   1   1 = 2

this Evening I attended the 1st High Council trial that ever
sat on hearing the evidence of the living against dead
for the goodness of a dead man and determine if his live
wife and family should be sealed to him. Prest George Q
Cannon and apostle Franklin D. Richards sat with the coun=
=cil and hear the Evidence.
        Saturday 14 June 1884.
I wrote all the forenoon at the temple and attended a
council of Prest Taylor, Geo Q Cannon, F. D Richards M Thatcher
Bp Preston, and others at Bp Prestons house at which meeting
the council decided to pay me $1,500.00 a year for my services
at the temple as Recorder. The pay to be from the tithing office.
I rode home to Smithfield the same Evening with Bro M W Merrill
and Visited my family
        Sunday 15 Jun 1884.
I went to the farm and looked at the growing crop and
was very thankful it looked so well. Then took my team
and with my son William rode to Logan and attended
meeting at the Tabernacle and heard the apostles and
Presidency give some Valuable instructions to both old
and young.. I remained in Logan all night was very sick
with a very high fevers.
        Monday 16 June 1884.
since better this morning and went to the Temple about
8 Oclock and superintended taking the record for
baptisms on Tuesday 17 June 1884.
on Monday we Anointed 1M 2 females = 3.

Tuesday 17 June 1884.

	Male	Female	
1st Baptisms	5.	3. = 8 \	
Ren of Covenants	22.	29. 51.	
Health	8.	28. 36.	934
Dead	447.	392. 839 /	

and went home in the evening with Bro Jas. S. Lower to Visit my wife Mary Jane who I had heard was sick. With neuralgia and found her much better.

Wednesday 18 June 1884

	Living	Dead	
Endowments	12.	107. = 119	
Ordinations	--.	39. = 39.	
Sealings	11.	39.	50.
Child to Parents	4.	3.	7.
Adoptions	1	–	1.
Baptized Renew of Cov	2 females	2.	

{44}

Thursday 19 June 1884.

	Liv	Dead	
Endowments	3.	105. = 108.	
Ordinations	--	39 = 39.	
Sealings	1.	4 = 5.	
Child to Parents			
Adoptions	1.	–	1

Friday 20 June 1884.

	Liv	Dead	
Endowments	2.	71. = 73	
Ordinations	--.	39 -- 30	
Sealings	2.	31. -- 33	
Child to Parents	1	–	1
Baptized for Ren of Cov	2	–	2

After the days work was through in the Temple I went home to Smith field with Bro Merrill and found the folks as well as usual, the boys had just got the 20 acres of fall wheat watered.

Saturday 21st June 1884.

Prests C O Card & Orson Smith also Prest J D T McAllister and Bp A H Cannon came to Smithfield to preach and hold meeting at 1/2 past 10 A.M. and 1/2 past 2 P.M. and gave us some good talk. I took the last 2 named brethren to dinner with me on green peas and fresh beef,. which they enjoyed. I visited the farm at evening.

Sunday 22nd June 1884.

With Bro Abel Smart I visited Hyrum and took bro S. Lower along from Logan, had a good district meeting of the H.P. Quorum. All seemed to feel well, returned in the Evening to Logan.

Monday 23rd June 1884.

I was at my post at the temple taking record for Baptisms as tomorrow.

Tuesday. 24 June 1884.

Baptized	Male	Female		
1st Baptisms		1. = 1	\	
Ren of Covenants	6	24 = 30.		
for Health	3	14. = 17		666
" Dead	362	256 =618	/	

I went home to Smithfield this Evening with Bro Abel Smart and brought a team and my wife Mary Jane to Logan on   Wednesday 25 June 1884.
on which day I had the pleasure of having my wife Mary Jane anointed to me in the Temple. Bro David A. Cannon being Mouth and Bro J D T McAllister held horn, and I was the recorder Bro M W. Merrill was also present. This makes all the wives I have had sealed to me in their life also anointed to me. We gave

	Living	Dead.	
Endowments	15.	96.	= 111.
Ordinations	--.	34	= 34
Sealings	6.	26.	= 32
Child to Parents	8	2	= 10
2nd Antg.	1		1.

Thursday 26 June 1884.

	Living	Dead	
Endowments	8.	110.	= 118.
Ordinations		41	= 41.
Sealings	5.	26.	= 32.
Child to Parents	4	6	= 10.

{45}

Friday 27 June 1884.

	L.	Dead.	
Endowments	4.	98.	= 102.
Ordinations	--.	38	= 38.
Sealings	1	. 31.	= 32.
Child to Parents	19 –	16	= 35.
2nd Anointings	3.	—	3.

Saturday 28 June 1884
after attending to the Usual business of the day I found an opportunity of going to Smithfield with Bro Peter Neilsen and found my family all well and the boys had Just finished the watering of the crops the first time and were preparing to plow and water the Corn.

Sunday Morning 29 June 1884.
My son William and I went to the meadow, and I found it most covered with water from 1 to 6 inches deep. – after I got back home again some parties called on me about temple work.– I attended meeting of the ward and the family went to my daughter Rebecca's for supper and then with abel Stuart I rode to Logan.

Monday Morning 30th June 1884.

Took record for Baptisms for tomorrow and took record for
2nd anointing   Living

[folded tabular report pasted on the page]

Register of Logan Temple Ordinance Work June 1884																	
Baptisms								Endowments				Ordin =ations	Sealings		Children to Parents		Adoptions		2nd Anointings			
First		Renl. of Cov.		Health		Dead		Living		Dead		Living	Dead	Living	Dead	Living	Dead	Living	Dead	Living		Dead	
M	F	M	F	M	F	M	F	M	F	M	F											M	F	M	F
11	12	56	108	31	83	1504	1203	63	92	404	608	2	391	78	343	50	43	3	3	2	9	1	1
23				164				114				2767				155				1102		393	421		93		6		11		2	
Total 3068														1167				393	421		93		6		13			

Samuel Roskelley
Recorder

{46}

Tuesday 1st July 1884.

My son William was baptized for 28 of our dead Relations & friends
" daughter Rebecca " "   " 9 ---------------
"   "   Mary   " "   " 7 – --------------
"   "   Catherine " " " 14 - ---------------
"   "   Hannah " "   " 7 ---------------

and nothing of moment transpired through the week except
the increase of the word in a natural way. And I will give a
a sinopsis of the amount of work done monthly hereafter.

on Saturday 5 July 1884.

I rode to Smithfield last Evening and Visited with
my family who were celebrating the 4th July, and I also
took part in the Evenings Entertainment, spent the
night at the farm and went to the Priesthood Meeting on
Saturday July 15h. returning home again in the Evening.

Sunday 6 July 1884

Spent the day with my family, at Smithfield, and
rode to Logan Sunday Evening with Brother Abel Smart.

Monday 7 July 1884.

Took record for Tuesdays baptisms and on

Tuesday 8 July 1884

Called names for Baptism at the font all day till
20 minutes to 9 in the Evening baptized 1290 persons.

saturday 12 July 1884.

We have done the largest weeks work since the Temple
was opened, on Thursday we had to turn away a
number as the building would not accommodate them
for Endowments for the dead. Went to Smithfield to night

sunday 13 July 1884.

I went to Logan and attended a High Priests Quorum

meeting at 10'O'Clock. had a good time and afterwards
went to Hyde Park and held meeting preaching to the
people on Temple Matters, here saw my grandson
Don and was met by my wife Mary, and daughter
Rebecca and her husband. Afterward went home to Smith
=field and on Monday 14 July 1884.
again went to Logan to continue my work in the
Temple without any change in the Programme till

<u>Saturday 19 July 1884.</u>
I went to Smithfield and Visited my nursery and
rested and slept for it seemed as though I was tired out
body and mind. and stayed at home on

<u>Sunday 20 July 1884.</u>
and Visited with my family and went to see my dau
=ghter Rebecca and found her sick and administered to her
returning to Logan Monday 21 July 1884 to continue
my Labors in Gods Holy Temple.

{47}

<u>Saturday 26 July 1884.</u>
I attended the usual routine of work the past week
altho not crowded as much as for some weeks previous.
And today attended a priesthood meeting of the stake.
After which I went home to Smithfield.

<u>Sunday 27 July 1884.</u>
with Bro George Barber and Brother Abel Smart I went to
Richmond and held District meeting in the forenoon and
after dinner returned to Smithfield and spent the afternoon
and Evening with my family. and returned to Logan on

<u>Monday 28 July 1884.</u>
The usual routine of Business was gone through for
the balance of the week and on Saturday Issued the
monthly bulletin of work done for the month of July. as follows
[folded tabular report pasted on the page]

Register of Logan Temple Ordinance work July 1884.																		
Baptisms								Endowments		Ordin=ations	Sealings		Children to Parents		Adoptions		2nd Anointings			
First		Renl. of Cov.		Health		Dead		Living	Dead		Living	Dead	Living	Dead	Living	Dead	Living		Dead	
M	F	M	F	M	F	M	F	M	F	M	F								M	F	M	F
4	4	102	131	55	129	2124	1979	65	91	665	1114	3	644	81	540	151	95	1	5	8	2	3
8		233		184		4103		156	1779	647	621		246		1		13		5	
4528								1935		647	621		246		1		18			
Samuel Roskelley Recorder																		

{48}

<u>Saturday 2nd August 1884.</u>
I went home to Smithfield and in the Evening went to the farm to visit my family there and on Sunday Morning I went to the meadow to see about cutting the Hay. And hauling it after which I went to Logan and at 10Oclock Bro Jas A Leishman and my wife Margaret and I went to Millville and held a meeting of the High Priests Quorum. And had a good meeting returning to Logan in the Evening.

Passed the week at the Temple as usual. untill Saturday 9 August 1884. I went to Smithfield and Visited my family Returning to Logan

Sunday <u>10 August 1884</u> and held a meeting of the High Priests Quorum and had an excellent time with the members thereof returning to Smithfield the Same Evening. <u>Monday 11 August 1884</u> I went to Logan and resumed my labors in the best of all houses "The Temple of the Lord" remaining the rest of the week, until

<u>Saturday 16 August 1884.</u> when I went again to my home in Smithfield and enjoyed a short visit with my family. <u>Sunday 17 August,</u> with Bro Abel Smart I went to the Church farm and with Bro Orson Smith of the presidency of the Stake I held a meeting in a new school and meeting house being part of the College farm and part of the Millville ward. Bp Geo O. Pitkin was present and several of the Leading Elders. I was requested to go there by Prest C O. Card to assist at the Dedication. we held meeting at 1/2 past 10 A M and 1/2 past two. At the latter meeting I was mouth in dedicating the New House to the Lord for meetings, Schools and recreative purposes. We returned to Smithfield the same evening.

<u>Monday 18 August 1884</u>
My wife Mary Jane sent for me and on my arrival at home in Smithfield I found her blessed with a fine bright large girl baby born about 5M to 5A.M. I rode to Logan with my son Samuel and his intended wife ~~Alice~~ Agnes Elizabeth Thyberg, they both rec^d their Endowments and were sealed this day in the Temple at Logan by the President Marriner Wood Merrill. I went to Smithfield the same Evening and took my wife Maggie to wait on my wife Mary Jane retur-
=ning again on Thursday morning. My son Joseph rec^d a letter on Monday /last\ stating that my son James was shot in the Arm in Tennessee.

[*folded clipping pasted at bottom of page*]

ALMOST ANOTHER MARTYRDOM.
Elder James Roskelley of Smithfield
Shot and Wounded.

From Brother Samuel Roskelley of
[S]mithfield, now engaged in laboring in
[the] Temple, we learn the particulars of
[a] recent missi[onary] experience of his

son James, who is now laboring in Ten-
[*remainder torn away*]

{49}
passed the remainder of the week at the Temple as usual.
and went home again on Friday Evening, Coming again to the
Temple on Sunday August 24. 1884 and doing some work
for Prest John Taylor and Stayed through the day to the Logan
Meeting in the Large Tabernacle, where a commemoration services
were held Commemorating the Death by a Cruel Mob the Elders
John F. Gibbs and William S. Berry.   I worked as usual
through the week with nothing of Importance transpiring and
went home again on Friday night 29 August 1884. remaining
till Monday Morning 1st September 1884. when I again resumed
my work at the Temple. I took away my cows out of the cow
Herd today and turned them into the field as I com=
=menced Hauling grain from the Upper field or bench land
today.
[*folded tabular report pasted on the sheet in the middle of the page*]

Register of Logan Temple Ordinance work for august 1884																	
Baptisms								Endowments				Ordin =ations		Sealings		Children to Parents		Adoptions		Second Anointings			
First		Renl. of Cov.		Health		Dead		Living		Dead		Living	Dead	Living	Dead	Living	Dead	Living	Dead	Living		Dead	
M	F	M	F	M	F	M	F	M	F	M	F									M	F	M	F
3	1	40	53	37	111	1156	1491	23	45	540	1007	5	517	46	455	112	101	5	2	3	10		1
4		93		148		2647		68		1547		522		501		213		7		13		1	
2891								1615				522		501		213		7		14			
Samuel Roskelley Recorder																	

Wednesday 3 September 1884.
I went to Smithfield tonight and had a Visit with my
family—MyWife Mary Jane improving and baby as well, thanks
be to our Heavenly Father, the giver of all good, and returned to
the Temple Thursday 4 September. Prest Geo Q Cannon
spent the day with us and expressed himself well pleased
with the organization of the House. And its affairs. I
went home to Smithfield on ~~Friday Evening~~ Saturday Evening after
attending the Priesthood Meeting for the Stake on Saturday
morning and remained home on Sunday 7th September 1884.
It was a Very Rainey time and unfit to be out of doors, Just
as I was going to Meeting. I was surprised to see Prest W. Woodruff
and wife Sarah drop into my house and spend the Afternoon and get
dinner &c we had a very pleasant chat. Prest Woodruff and I blessed my
wife Mary Janes Monday 8th September 1884.
baby calling it Florence
I again Returned to the Temple at Logan and took a portion

of the record for Baptism on Tuesday and spent the week as
usual at my work recording, returning to Smithfield on
Thursday Evening and spending the night and going home again
on Saturday Afternoon. 13 Sep 1884.. and found all
my family usually well. wife Mary Jane and her babe
doing well. Spent the Sunday at home. Going to the saints
afternoon meeting and ~~back~~ found it converted into the dual
dual purpose of Sacramental and funeral services through the
death of Young Brother Horatio Merrill. who was accidentally
shot while taking his gun from his wagon. Bp G L Farrell
called on me to preach the funeral sermon which I responded
to. on Monday morning I again Resumed my labors in the
Temple. and on Wednesday Morning 17 Sep 1884

{50}
My wife Margaret came down and as before went to board
with Bp Thos X. Smiths family, staying till Friday night when
she went home and on Saturday 20 Sep 1884 my team
came down and I took to Smithfield Bro & Sister Joseph Hall
and their daughter Millie.

   Sunday 21 Sep <u>1884</u>. and Francis Sharp
With Bros Jos Hall and Abel Smart /and Francis Sharp\ I left Smithfield at 1/2 past
8AM. and overtook Bros Thos Duce and Niels Christiansen of
Hyde Park at the Junction of the Hyde Park Lane with the
main road and proceeded to Clarkston. Stopping on the way
at Newton and Visiting and talking to the Sunday Schools and
after taking dinner at the House of Bro W F. Rigby I proceeded
to Clarkston and found my Councillor Bro Francis Gunnell there
with a number of the representatives of the High Priests from
several settlements, we had a most excellent meeting
commencing at 1/2 past 2 oclock. returning to Smithfield
the same night after dark.

   Monday 22 Sep 1884.
I returned to Logan and resumed my labors as usual and
went home again during the week to see the family. Maggie came
down Wednesday and went home again Friday and I returned home
on Saturday 27 September 1884.

   <u>Sunday 28th September 1884.</u>
With Bro Abel Smart I went to Hyde Park and attended a
meeting of the High Priests of the Hyde Park ward and had
a good time with them returning home so as to attend to
afternoon meeting of the Saints at Smithfield. and afterwards
attended a meeting of the High Priests of Smithfield
Ward. returning to Logan with wife Maggie again on Mon
day to resume my work in the Temple.
[folded tabular report pasted on the page]

Register of Logan Temple Ordinance work for September 1884																	
Baptisms								Endowments				Ordin=ations		Sealings		Children to Parents		Adoptions		Second Anointings			
First		Renl. of Cov.		Health		Dead		Living		Dead		Living	Dead	Living	Dead	Living	Dead	Living	Dead	Living				Dead	
M	F	M	F	M	F	M	F	M	F	M	F									M	F	M	F
5	1	31	41	54	66	1422	1670	41	56	498	1018	3	483	52	414	125	91	2		9	14		4
6		72		120		3092		97		1516		486		466		216		2		23		4	
3290								1613				486		466		216		2		27			
Samuel Roskelley Recorder.																	

{51}
on Friday 3 October we were permitted to close the temple so
as to attend the General Conference in Salt Lake City, which was
a boon to me. I returned to Smithfield with my wife Maggie
this Evening and fixed up quite a number of little things on
Saturday and took the Train at 4 A M. on

<u>Sunday Morning Oct 5 1884.</u>
arriving at Salt Lake City at 10 OClock proceeded immediately
to the Tabernacle to meeting and attended every meeting
until Conference Closed on Tuesday noon, 7 Oct 1884.
I ~~took~~ stayed at Bro Edward Kings nights and ate supper
and breakfast there each day during my stay and also found
~~started~~ a man named George Roskelly from Corn
=wall England. I am satisfied from his build &c he is a
distant relative. started home at 4.40 p m Tuesday
7 Oct 1884. arriving at Smithfield a little after 11P.M.
same Evening. and found my wife Mary Jane suffering much
with fellon on her right hand thumb, spent balance of week
at home. Threshing and fixing up things one way and another.

<u>Sunday 12 October 1884.</u>
With Bro Abel Smart, Thomas Duce and others from Smithfield went to
Richmond and held a High Priests District Meeting and had a Very
good meeting. good subjects good talk and good feeling.

<u>Monday 13 Oct 1882.</u> [sic]
Took wife Maggie and returned to Logan, and also took son
William to go to the School at B.Y. College, and had a Very
hard weeks work at the Temple. a great number of Strangers
at the Temple. and all seemed satisfied with their work and
Labor in the House of the Lord. returned to Smithfield on Friday
night Passenger train and Spent Saturday looking around my
Premises and fixing up some things that were dilapidated.

<u>Sunday 19 October 1884.</u>
I spent the day at home with my family, ate supper with my
daughter Rebecca and returned to Logan on Monday morning
to resume my labor in the House of the Lord. and found a

host of people from he various parts of the Territory and
other places and had the hardest weeks work yet done by
The temple hands. went home on Saturday to Smithfield and
spent Sunday with my family. Attending Quarterly Conference
at Smithfield of the Young Mens Mutual Improvement Association
and had a good time generally. returning to Logan on Monday
morning. 27 October 1884. and on Tuesday Evening I rented
Bp Preston's House on the Logan River Bottoms up the Hollow and
received the Key from him I agreed to feed out the Hay
he had there to his cattle this winter as payment for the
rent of the house he agreed to let me keep a team
and a cow at the place and I to feed as many stock
at my place at Smithfield, as I kept at his place,
My boys moved a stove and some other things on Thursday
Evening 30 Oct 1884 and took my wife Maggie to Smithfield
at night where she packed up her goods and came
down to Logan with Joseph on Friday morning and moved
her goods to the House we had rented. and I spent the
most of the day Saturday in fixing up the house for my
wife Maggie and making her as comfortable as the

{52}
circumstances will permit.
Saturday and Sunday november 1&2nd was Quarterly
Conference of Cache Valley Stake and we had the pleas
of
[folded tabular report pasted on the page]

Register of Logan Temple Ordinance work for October 1884																			
Baptisms								Endowments				Ordin=ations		Sealings				Children to Parents		Adoptions		2nd Anointings			
First		Renl. of Cov.		Health		Dead		Living		Dead		Living	Dead	Living	Dead	Living	Dead	Living	Dead	Living				Dead	
M	F	M	F	M	F	M	F	M	F	M	F									M	F	M	F
3	2	28	34	26	47	1312	1255	93	127	521	916	3	503	111	464	185	169	4	1	5	15	1	5
5		62		73		2567		220		1437		506		575			354			5			20			6	
2707								1657				506		575				354			5		26			
Samuel Roskelley Recorder																			

of the Company of Apostles W. Woodruff & Geo Teasdale from
Salt Lake City and had Excellent meeting, we also had the
pleasure of the company of Apostle George Teasdale in the
Temple during the week, he assisted me at the font
and in taking names on Tuesday. Wednesday and Thursday
     Sunday 9 November 1884
Went to Logan and held District High Priests Meeting
and had the Company of apostle M. Thatcher who spoke
to us on the political situation.
     Sunday 16 Nov 1884

was at home with my family at Smithfield and
came to Logan on Monday to commence my labors
in the Temple for the Week.
   Friday 21 Nov 1884.
I started to Smithfield this Evening and spent Saturday at
home with my family—My son Samuel Sowed 17 acres of
Rye on the lately broke up land, south of the house,
and the Boys Harrowed it in.
   Sunday 23 November 1884.
I returned to Logan with my wife Margaret, and her
sister Lavina and sister Annie Barker. Also my
sons William and Joseph.
   Monday 24 November 1884
My son Joseph started to School at B Y. College
and I continued my labors at the Temple as usual
during the week going to Smithfield on Friday Evening and
moving Stoves and fixing things generally at the House in
town. Sunday 30 November 1884.
Bro Abel Smart and I started from Smithfield with Bro
Stuarts Team and came to Hyde Park and Bro Thomas
Duce hitched up his team and Buggy and took Bro
Smart and I to Hyrum to the District Meeting and we
had quite a good meeting. and the representation of the
High priests was as good as usual on such occasions

{53}
I returned to ~~Smithfield~~ /Logan\ in the Evening and prepared for the
Labor of Monday. and followed the Usual avocations in the
temple during the week. going home on Friday Evening and
returning to Logan again on the Sunday Evening untill
   Monday 15 Dec 1884.
[folded tabular report pasted on the page]

Register of Logan Temple Ordinance Work for November 1884.																	
Baptisms								Endowments				Ordinations	Sealings		Children to Parents		Adoptions		Second Anointings	
First		Renl. of Cov.		Health		Dead		Living		Dead		Living	Dead	Living	Dead	Living	Dead	Living	Dead	Living		Dead	
M	F	M	F	M	F	M	F	M	F	M	F											M	F	M	F
3	5	36	51	27	92	1590	1389	77	109	628	998	6	64	97	448	156	184	1		4	6		3
8		87		119		2979		186		1621		620		545		340		1		10		3	
3193								1812				620		545		340		1		13		
Samuel Roskelley Recorder																	

when I again resumed my labors in the Temple,
our companies were not very large as the Roads are almost
Impassable for mud and Slush.

Sunday 21st December 1884

Bro Geo Barber and myself started from Smithfield to attend a High Priest District Meeting at Clarkston, but on our arrival at Newton we learned that the roads were impassable on a/c of Snowing & blowing blizzards that frequent Clarkston in the Winter. Consequently we stopped and held meeting at Newton and returned to Smithfield at night and as the Temple had Closed on Friday the 19th inst until Monday 29th of Dec. I remained at home enjoying the company and society of my family during the Christmas Holidays, on the Wednesday Evening I and my wives attended a Picnic party at Bro Mouritzens House and had a good time of Enjoyment. but the weather was so disagreeable that we would not get out any where with any degree of satisfaction, but I had my family together several times during the week and spent a very pleasant week.

Sunday 28th December 1884.

I returned to Logan with my wife Maggie to prepare for the duties of the Coming week at the Temple of the God. Oh how I am blessed of God in being priveleged to Labor in his house! O God, may I always be found in the paths of truth and live for the right and have integrity for God and his Saints.

Monday 29th December 1884.

Commenced again to work in the Temple taking the record for baptisms for tomorrow.

Tuesday 30th Dec 1884.

My Sons William and Joseph took 5 animals of Bro Wm B. Preston to winter at my farm in lieu of 1 Cow and 2 Horses I am Keeping at his place in Logan.

Thursday 1. January 1885.

This is my Birthday I am 48 Years Old today and am very thankful for the life and health my family and

{54}

I enjoy. And above all that I have a name and a standing among the Saints of God. I spent my day at work in the Temple. among the rest of my labors in making out my annual report of labor performed for year Ending 31 Dec 1884. a copy of of which I have herewith added.

[folded tabular report pasted on the page]

Register of Logan Temple Ordinance Work for December 1884																	
Baptisms								Endowments				Ordinations	Sealings		Children to Parents		Adoptions		2nd Anointings			
First		Renl. of Cov.		Health		Dead		Living		Dead			Living	Dead	Living	Dead	Living	Dead	Living	Dead	Living		Dead	
M	F	M	F	M	F	M	F	M	F	M	F									M	F	M	F
3	13	25	30	20	44	1485	1237	76	106	416	552		409	97	271	102	66	1			3		
16				55				64				2722				182				968	409	368		168		1		3		
2857									1150					409	368		168		1		3		
Samuel Roskelley Recorder																	

[I re]ceived from the Trustees of the BY College an invitation to be present at the dedication of the new buil =ding but was so engaged at the Temple I could not go but with my wife Margaret attended the dance in the Evening and had a good time.

The work of God is rolling onward and meeting with much opposition, but few are being baptized in the Gentile world and the U S. Judges are doing their best to overawe us as saints. They have sent out 200 spies as U S. deputy marshalls to watch those they suspect where and with whom they sleep so they may inform on them and get a reward from the court of $250.00 if they can fasten a conviction upon any one of Gods Servants but God is at the Helm and will bring the Saints off Triumphantly..

<u>Sunday 4 Jan 1885.</u>
Spent Sunday at Home with my family at Smithfield. And had the pleasure of the Company of Prest W. Woodruff all day. he ate Dinner with us, and we had a very enjoyable chat. Prest Woodruff preached afternoon and Evening to the Saints at Smithfield and gave some Very interesting discourses. I bore testimony in the Evening.

<u>Monday 5 Jan 1885.</u>
I resumed my labors in the Temple and had the pleasure of the Company of Prest W. Woodruff and wife staying in my home in Logan all night. They did some work in the Temple on Tuesday 6 jan 1884, Lavina Rigby commenced boarding with me on Saturday 3 Jan 1885. I went home to Smithfield on Saturday 10th January and on Sunday 11 Jan 1885. in Company with elders Abel Smart and Thomas Duce went to Lewiston and held meeting with the Saints as a District meeting of the High Priests Quorum. we had represen =tatives from Smithfield, Richmond. Coveville, and Lewiston and

all spoke well and enjoyed the meeting. took dinner with
Hyram A. Watson and family. and returned to Smithfield
same Evening.

{55}

Monday 12 January 1885

with my son William returned to Logan – I to work at the
Temple and he to go to School.
[folded tabular report pasted on the page]

Register of Logan Temple Ordinance Work to Dec 31st 1884.																							
Baptisms								Endowments				Ordinations		Sealings		Children to Parents		Adoptions		Second Anointings			
First		Renewal of Cov.		Health		Dead		Living		Dead		Living	Dead	Living	Dead	Living	Dead	Living	Dead	Living		Dead	
M	F	M	F	M	F	M	F	M	F	M	F									M	F	M	F
32	38	326	454	256	590	10829	10514	497	699	3731	6291	23	3614	619	2983	884	756	16	7	30	69	6	19
70		780		846		21343		119		10022		3637		3602		1640		23		99		25	
23039								11218				3637		3602		1640		23		124			

Samuel Roskelley   Recorder

our Companies at the Temple not being so large
enables us to do considerable copying up of the Records.
I went home on Saturday Evening and Remained till

Sunday 18 January 1885.

Returning that day to Logan in time to attend the afternoon
meeting at the Logan Tabernacle. Elder B H. Roberts, the assistant
President of the Southern Mission delivered a lecture on the Constitutional
Rights of the Polygamists of Utah. a very able discourse, In the
Evening my councillors and I met with the Saints at Providence, and
talked to them. returning to Logan at night, we appointed Bro
Wm Smith to look after the High Priests at Providence,
During the following week I received the following letter from
one of the Church architects in Salt Lake City. Which I an=
=swered in due from giving my views based on experience,
[folded letter pasted on page:]

Salt Lake City, Jan. 20,
Samuel Roskelley, Esq:
  Dear Bro.:
    I am
working on plans em
-bracing an entire change
in the interior of this
Temple, as the old plan
made over thirty years ago
is, of course, not up to modern
development in the production
of Temples

Please answer the following
questions and oblige.
Which rooms do you use
for dressing in connection
with font room.
Where do the people leave
their clothing who enter
[verso]
for endowments and
where do they find them
after they are through,
At what points would

you have extra water
closets-if any.
Where would you prefer
to have the Presidents
private room, and where
the clerks room.
How many washing rooms
are necessary, Also please
state any weak points

which you have found
in the Logan Temple.
Please answer at your
earliest convenience
and oblige
    Your bro in the Truth
        T. O. Angell Jr.
P.S. Please find enclosed envelope
        T.O.A. Jr.

[*diary text*]
and spent the weeks at my usual business at
the Temple Going to Smithfield the last of the week
and Remaining at Home over Sunday I preached to
the Saints at Smithfield on Sunday afternoon 25 Jan
1885. returning to Logan on Sunday Evening and
worked as usual at my business in the Temple
through the week till
      Saturday 31 January 1885.
Quarterly conference of the Stake Commenced and we
had a splendid good time altho none by the local
bretheren were present except on Sunday afternoon when
Apostle Moses Thatcher appeared on the Stand and
addressed the Congregation for about an hour on

{56}
"The present situation of the Saints" subject as we are to
the violent persequtins we are now labor under, he
gave a Vivid description of the persequtions of the Saints
are laboring under at the Hands of the U.S. officials
and pictured what would be among the people of the
United States when the Reaction took place.
[*folded tabular report pasted on the page*]

Register of Logan Temple Ordinance Work for January 1885.																			
Baptisms								Endowments				Ordin-ations		Sealings		Children to Parents		Adoptions		Second Anointings			
First		Renl. of Cov.		Health		Dead		Living		Dead		Living	Dead	Living	Dead	Living	Dead	Living	Dead	Living		Dead	
M	F	M	F	M	F	M	F	M	F	M	F									M	F	M	F
4	3	24	30	5	44	1146	853	56	71	595	?		589	69	300	65	49	3			2	1	
7		54		49		1994		127		1281		589		369		117		3		2	1		
2109								1408				589		369		117		3		3			
Samuel Roskelley Recorder																			

As usual I resumed my labors at the Temple on Monday morning 2 Feby and continued all the week we are having good companies all week for Endowments and Sealings. On Saturday 7 Feby 1885. attended Priesthood meeting in the forenoon. and went to Smithfield in the afternoon and on Monday 9 Feby again resumed my labors at the Temple going home again on Saturday 14th inst and again spent the next week at my usual Temple work as usual

Sunday 21 Feby 1885.

I designed going to Clarkston to visit the High Priest today but the bad state of the roads prevents me from going. and I returned to Logan in the Evening and attended the usual routine of Temple Labors during the week. last week and this we are having the largest companies we ever had by the Temple for Endowments. on 19th Feb we Endowed 200 persons

Sunday 28 Feby 1885.

Today is spring like and very pleasant overhead but soft and shushy under foot and bad gitting around. I came home on Friday Evening last and the boys and I greased up a set of harness on Saturday, I returned to Logan in the Afternoon and in the Evening I attended the 4th ward Logan Meeting and spoke to the saints for about 30 Minutes,

Monday 1st March 1885.

[*folded tabular report tipped on the page*]

Register of Logan Temple Ordinance work for Feby 1885																			
Baptisms						Endowments				Ordinations	Sealings		Children to Parents		Adoptions		2nd Anointings		
First		Renl. of Cov.		Health		Dead		Living		Dead		Living	Dead	Living	Dead	Living	Dead	Living		Dead	
M	F	M	F	M	F	M	F	M	F	M	F									M	F	M	F
10	4	49	36	21	56	1899	1522	40	61	1003	1040	3	992	56	523	103	110			1		1	2
14		85		77		3421		101		2043		995		579		213				1		3	
3597						2144						995		579		213				4			
Samuel Roskelley Recorder																							

{57}

<u>Monday 1st March 1885</u>

I today took the record of 10 male and 10 female Lamanites for baptisms and it took me all day as the Language had to be written for I much question if the names of the dead Indians were ever before written, thus the work of the Lord is commenced amongst that people, these Lamanites were baptized on

<u>Tuesday 2nd March 1885.</u>

and they continued the work of Endowments Wednesday. Thursday and friday. much to their gratification.

<u>Friday 6 March 1885.</u>

Sister Lavina Rigby went home with her brother William after attending school and staying at my house to board for 9 weeks. after going to the Temple <u>Saturday 7 March 1885.</u> I learned that parties in Smithfield had given information to the U.S. officials of my family relations and the probabilities were that papers would be prepared for my arrest. I sent Maggie my wife to notify the family at home and I remained in the Temple all day and night till I learned from some of my friends that no warrant had been issued against me. but I deemed it best to be cautious and Keep myself close for the present as "Discretion is the better part of Valor" and Deputy marshalls are making arrests and dragging the families of many of our Bretheren before the court to testify against their Husbands and father.

<u>Wednesday 11 March 1885.</u>

My wife, Mary Jane came ~~came~~ from Smithfield to be endowed for a few of my friends ~~in Smithfield~~ and remained till friday Evening when I took her home.

<u>Friday 13 March 1885.</u>

Brother Merrill (prest of the Temple) of his own accord has this day released my wife Margaret from labor in the Temple as a worker and as President of No 5 Room. She has been ~~with~~ associated with the Temple labor for 11 months having commenced

14 Apl 1884 in helping me to put down carpets and make
curtains and other things for the use of the Endowments &c.

Saturday 14 March 1885.

At home on my farm, I planted Cabbage and Tomatoes in
Boxes and spent most of the day at home and returned to
Logan in the afternoon and Visited the 5 Ward meeting at
night and preached, continuing my labors as usual in the
Temple through the week and again going to Smithfield on
Saturday arranging about my farming and gardening
on   Sunday 22 Mch 1885.
in Company with My Councillor Geo Barber and Bro
Thomas Duce. Also I invited Bro Lorenzo Hatch and Bro
Benj^m Richie and went to Clarkston to hold a
District meeting of the High Priests Quorum, in

{58}
passing through Newton Called at Bro Rigby's and
visited him and the High Priests of Newton to
attend out meeting at Clarkston., in consequence
of Mud and bad roads we had to walk some
distance, but we got there on time and had a
splendid good meeting, for the spirit of the Lord
was poured out, and we enjoyed ourselves several
of our Bretheren from Arizona and other Points
who had been looked upon as outcasts in the Eyes of the
Law were present. Spent the week at my usual labor
in the Temple, taking every precaution especially providing
for any surprise of Deputy Martials on the 27th.
Spent Saturday night at farm. Returning to Logan
on Sunday. 29th Mch 1885.

Tuesday. 31st Mch 1885.

Bp Prestons sons came and got away the
stock I had been feeding all winer, and I agreed
to pay him $6^{00} per month for the house and garden
for the Season

[*folded tabular report pasted on the page*]

Register of Logan Temple Ordinance Work for March 1885																									
Baptisms								Endowments				Ordinations		Sealings		Children to Parents		Adoptions		Second Anointings			
First		Renewal of Cov.		Health		Dead		Living		Dead		Living	Dead	Living	Dead	Living	Dead	Living	Dead	Living				Dead	
M	F	M	F	M	F	M	F	M	F	M	F									M	F			M	F
4	7	86	97	29	93	2254	2096	60	101	803	1030	6	784	93	546	184	151			2	3				1
11				183				122				4350				161				1833		790		639		335				6				
4666																1994				790		639		335				6				
Samuel Roskelley Recorder																										

Friday 3 Apr 1885.

As the Annual Conference is to be held in Logan and deputy marshalls are abundant in town today it has been deemed wise to Close up the temple on last Evening and not do any work for a few days and have also secured our Records in case of a search for them by persons who have no authority from the proper Source and during conference deemed it wisdom to go visiting friends instead going to Conference as I did not desire to be found if wanted by a deputy marshall.

Saturday 11 April Spent at Smithfield, on farm putting in trees on the Qr section and finish planting 20 thousand cuttings and many small trees also and they have all been watered since by Bro Anderson who with Joseph Saxton

{59}
and Bro McCarthy have put in all the cuttings named – I also sowed ~~ruta baga~~ mangoe_Wor-tzels, and on Monday 13th 1885. it rained nice and continued to do so for several days, the boys finished sowing wheat yesterday Friday 10th having put in about 32 acres of wheat. Spent the week as usual at Logan Temple in my calling and on Friday Evening went home and on Sunday 19th Apl with Bro Geo Barber and others went to Richmond and held meeting with the High Priests Quorum of the district—having a good meeting and a number of the High Priests present, Returned home same Evening and learned that my Brother in law had given himself up to the officers of the law on a charge of Polygamy. and the officers had taken him to Oxford for an Examination, this course of Bro William D. Hen=

=dricks causes me to feel bad, as I think it an
unwise move

    Monday 20th April. 1885

Went to Logan and prosecuted my labors for the week
in the Temple, spending

    Sunday 26 Apl 1885 at Smithfield

with my family—going to afternoon Ward Meeting and
listen to Bro William Paxman Pres of Juab Stake
who with many others are keeping out of the way of
the officers, this is my first time of going to the
meeting in Smithfield for months as I had learned
that the officers would like to have me in their
care. but I feel better in the discharge of my
duty as an Elder of Israel than under their
Jurisdiction so I will Keep out of the way as long
as I possibly can with Gods help.

    Attended to my duties as usual at the
Temple during the week

[*folded tabular report pasted on the page*]

Register of Logan Temple Ordinance Work for April 1885

Baptisms								Endowments				Ordin=ations		Sealings		Children to Parents		Adoptions		Second Anointings			
First		Renewal of Cov.		Health		Dead		Living		Dead		Living	Dead	Living	Dead	Living	Dead	Living	Dead	Living		Dead	
M	F	M	F	M	F	M	F	M	F	M	F									M	F	M	F
3	3	31	35	11	45	979	1138	67	100	589	903		577	90	401	138	93			5			
6		66		56		2117		167		1490		577		491		231				5			
2245								1657				577		491		231				5			

Samuel Roskelley   Recorder

{60}

    <u>Saturday 2 May 1885.</u>

attended Quarterly Conference of this Stake and
Reported my Quorum and on Sunday 3 May
1885 I acted Stake Clerk Bro Leishman being sick
and unable to attend, passed the week as usual
at my Post in the Temple in which I take much
pleasure, went home on Friday Evening 8 May and
worked at my garden on Saturday also on

    Sunday 10 May 1885.

I attended a meeting of the Logan District of the
High Priests Quorum at the Logan Tabernacle and
had a good representation from the settlements
of the District and Good Reports which was very
satisfactory to me.

    I spent the week at the Temple
as usual Returning to Smithfield on <u>Saturday 16 May</u>

and feeling that Bro M. Anderson my hired man is a
spy on my family and his associates apostates, I told
him he had better work for Some one else from this
date.   Sunday 17 May 1885.
I returned to Logan and in the Evening got some
more Records from the deposit to the Temple and on
Monday 18 returned my labors in the Temple.
Continuing through the week as usual. untill
            Saturday 23 May 1885
I went to Smithfield getting there about 2 P.M. and in the
afternoon with the boys I put up 36 Rods of 4 Wire fence
between the Grave Yard and and [sic] Bro Sharps Corner South.
Making a good job of it.
            Sunday 24 May 1885
With Bro Abel Smart I started from Smithfield and
called at Hyde Park for Bro Thomas Duce and went
to Wellsville and held a meeting of the members of the
High Priest Quorum for the South end of the Valley
and had a good representation from the wards
of the district. and had a good meeting. I returned to
Logan same evening, proceeding to my usual labors
in the Temple the following week, and having learned that
Bro Robt Thornley had cut down my wire fence I went
to Smithfield on Saturday Evening and took up a labor
with Bro Thornley trying to show him the wrong he had
done but he was persistant in the matter and said
he would do it again. On Sunday morning

{61}
31 May I took with me Elders Thos Mather and James Meikle
and went to Robt Thornley and after near 2 hours of talk
succeeded in getting him to say he would fix up any
fence as he found it, with this understanding I left
him and came to Logan.
[folded tabular report tipped on the page]

Register of Logan Temple Ordinance Work for May 1885																	
Baptisms								Endowments				Ordinations	Sealings		Children to Parents		Adoptions		Second Anointings			
First		Renewal of Cov.		Health		Dead		Living		Dead		Living	Dead	Living	Dead	Living	Dead	Living	Dead	Living		Dead	
M	F	M	F	M	F	M	F	M	F	M	F									M	F	M	F
2		21	28	29	63	1858	1610	36	57	861	1168	2	853	51	610	128	165			3			1
2		49		92		3468		93		2029		855		661		293				4			
3611								2122				855		661		293				4			

Samuel Roskelley   Recorder

and resumed my usual labor in the Lords House which

I deem a great privelage to occupy a position in.- the
weeks labor has not been so heavy for the time being as
usual, I returned home on ~~Wed~~ Thursday Evening
taking Maggy with me to Smithfield for a ride and
taking her back to Logan again next Morning.

Saturday 6 June 1885.

I attended stake priesthood meeting and had a
good time as the bretheren who spoke were influence
by the good spirit of God. went to Smithfield
in the Evening with Maggy and the babe, the weather
is very cold for the season of year Beans and all
tender Vegetation is cut off and will have to
be replanted.

Sunday 7 June 1885

attended Local meeting of the High Priests of the
Smithfield Ward at the City Hall at 8 A.M.
And the Ward Meeting in the Afternoon. Bro David
Weeks and Bp Farrell occupied the time in discoursing
on who are and who are not fit candidates to go
to the Temple.   Monday 8 June 1885
I returned to Logan to resume my labors in the Temple
Early in the morning, and continued through week as
usual.

{62}

Saturday 13th June. 1885. I returned to Smithfield and
found the family all well as usual- I remained over
Sunday at Smithfield. and attended Sunday Afternoon
meeting, returning to Logan on Monday 15 June and
resuming my Labors in the Temple-- went home again
on Tuesday Evening as my boys William and Joseph
had put up a wire fence enclosing the land below
the farm house, and I hired a young man to break up
some of the land, returned to Logan again on
Wednesday Morning. 17 June
Saturday 20 June 1885.   I went home to Smithfield
and on Sunday 21st June 1885. In company. with my
wife Mary Jane and Several of the Bretheren I went to Newton,
and held meeting of the Western district of the High Priests
Quorum and had a splendid good visit and meeting
with the Quorum and the people returning home in the Evening
to Smithfield, and on Monday Returned to Logan to
resume my work in the Temple of the Lord.

on Tuesday 16 June the Water first reached
my land east of my farm through the Upper Logan
Canal. which is a source of great rejoicing to me,
to Know that the water will run through from Logan.

Saturday 27 June 1885.

I returned to Smithfield and remained till Sunday Evening
when I again returned to Logan to resume my temple
work.

[folded tabular report tipped on the page]

Register of Logan Temple Ordinance Work for June 1885

Baptisms								Endowments				Ordinations		Sealings		Children to Parents		Adoptions		Second Anointings			
First		Renewal of Cov.		Health		Dead		Living		Dead		Living	Dead	Living	Dead	Living	Dead	Living	Dead	Living		Dead	
M	F	M	F	M	F	M	F	M	F	M	F									M	F	M	F
	1	22	24	28	81	1594	1797	48	69	622	930	2	613	59	405	185	117			1	3		
1		46		109		3391		117		1552		615		464		302				4			
3547								1669				615		44		302				4			

Samuel Roskelley   Recorder.

{63}

<u>Friday 3 July 1885</u>
I returned to Smithfield in the Evening and spent next
day looking around my farm and advising with my sons
about the work of caring for the crops &c and Spent Sunday
5th July at home, attended meeting at the Ward meeting house
and visiting my family
<u>Monday 6 July</u> 1885
Resumed my labors in the Temple. Continuing all week
at my usual Labor, and Returning to Smithfield on
Saturday 11 July 1885. and on <u>Sunday 12th July 1885</u>
I took my wife Mary and visited the High Priests at
Hyde Park, attended meeting in the afternoon and had
the pleasure of the Company of Sister Eliza R. Snow Smith
and a number of her associates of the Relief Society and
Young ladies Mutuals, together with a number of the
High Priests from other wards.
<u>Monday 12 July 1885.</u>
Resumed labor in the Temple for the week till
<u>Saturday 18 July 1885.</u>
I returned to Smithfield and on Sunday 19 July 1885.
In connexion with Bros Barber, Smart Duce Sharp and
Many others from the Settlements we held a High Priest
district meeting at Lewiston at 1 P.M. and had a good
meeting, with the saints of Lewiston Ward which seemed
to be appreciated.
<u>Monday 20 July 1885.</u>
as usual found me at my post in the temple, and
performing my usual Labor therein through the week
<u>Friday July 24 July 1885</u>. we rec^d a Telegram
from Salt Lake that in consequence of the death
of General Grant on the 23rd all gatherings of
the saints as a festive or Joyous character be
suspended and flags be placed at 1/2 mast
in all the settlements."

Sunday 26 July 1885

At home in Smithfield and attended the
funeral of Bro Henry Watts who had visited
the Temple on the previous Tuesday and had his
Children sealed to him, and I had remarked at the time
that I should not be surprised if he did not live
a week. and sure enough he did not live a week,
I spoke at the funeral.

Monday 27 July 1885.

found me at my post at the Temple to take record
for Baptism as usual. and continued all
the week at my usual work

{64}

Saturday 1 August 1885.

To day attended the stake Quarterly Conference at the
Tabernacle which was well attended by the local priesthood
none of the General Authorities being present.

Sunday 2 Aug 1885.

attended Conference and gave report of Condition of
High Priests Quorum of the Stake. and heard some
good teachings by the local bretheren.

Thursday 6 August 1885

We have Very light Companies in the Temple this week
the lightest we have ever had since the Temple opened,
and this morning we held fast meeting and was
favored with a testimony from Sister Eliza R. Snow,
Smith, and our good Sister Nancy Clark spoke in
Tongues, and all present seemed to Enjoy themselves
singing before prayer was today introduced as part
of our Exercises and Prest M W Merrill told us he
designed to make it part of our Exercised hereafter

Friday 7 August 1885

Went home this Evening to Smithfield and on Saturday
8 August I went over the farm on the bench and
over the Garden, and in the Afternoon went
with the boys to the Meadow and loaded 2 loads
of hay and took it home finishing up our haying
on the Meadow for the season,

Sunday 9 August 1885.

Attended a Priesthood meeting in the Logan Taberna
cle being called as a General Meeting for the High
Priests Quorum and had a good meeting. The
Quorum was well represented from the various
parts of the County, and all the bretheren seemed
to feel well.

[*folded tabular report tipped on the page*]

Register of Logan Temple Ordinance Work of July 1885																	
Baptisms								Endowments				Ordinations		Sealings		Children to Parents		Adoptions		Second Anointings			
First		Renewal of Cov.		Health		Dead		Living		Dead		Living	Dead	Living	Dead	Living	Dead	Living	Dead	Living		Dead	
M	F	M	F	M	F	M	F	M	F	M	F											M	F	M	F
	1	11	10	11	38	1066	1559	46	58	657	1055	4	647	68	454	154	98			1	7		1
1		21		48		2625		104		1712		651		522		252				8		1	
2695								1816				651		522		252				9			
Samuel Roskelley Recorder																	

{65}

      Monday 10 August 1885
I resumed by labors in the Temple.
Nothing of note transpiring till
      Saturday 22 August 1885
I attended the 1st Meeting of Invited pupils to
the Sientific Class in the Temple. My wife
Margaret was also among the persons invited
and I was present on the occasion and we had
a good time in meeting.
      Sunday 23 August 1885.
drove from Smithfield to Logan in an open
Buggy through a Heavy Rain and got wet through
Changed Clothing, and with Bro ~~Abel Smart~~ Thomas
Duce rode to Hyrum and attended a High Priest
district meeting. and had a good time returning
to Logan in the Evening and resuming my
labors in the Temple on Monday 24 Aug 1885
at which labor I continued until Saturday 5 Sep 1885.
[folded tabular report tipped on the page]

Register of Logan Temple Ordinance Work for August 1885																	
Baptisms								Endowments				Ordinations		Sealings		Children to Parents		Adoptions		Second Anointings			
First		Renewal of Cov.		Health		Dead		Living		Dead		Living	Dead	Living	Dead	Living	Dead	Living	Dead	Living		Dead	
M	F	M	F	M	F	M	F	M	F	M	F											M	F	M	F
		5	4	6	13	783	1292	24	33	215	320	1	212	31	113	47	33						
		9		19		2075		57		535		213		144		80							
2103								592				213		144		80							
																	Samuel Roskelley Recorder							

Resuming my labors in the Temple untill
20 September 1885 (Sunday) on which day in Company

with Elder Thos Duce and Bro Hymas of Hyde Park
we held a District Meeting at Clarkston with a good
Representation from the wards of the district, I took my
wife Margaret with me to Newton to visit her relation
and resuming my labors in the Temple again on
Monday 21 Sep 1885. Commenced threshing on Saturday
19th and the machine broke down on the Monday and we
finished threshing on Tuesday Evening 22 Sep having threshed
724 Bu Wheat. 298 Bu Oats and 240 Bu Rye,
one third of which went to the boys William and
Joseph.

{66}
        1 Nov 1885
Nothing of note transpired untill the Conference
of the Church convened at Logan 6 October 1885. as a number
of Deputy marshalls were in town desiring to pick up such
prey as they could lay their hands upon I did not
attend all the conference meetings, but those I did
attend I enjoyed Very much and I also much Enjoyed
the company of the Brethren who Visited the Temple, and
I continued my temple labor without cessation,
occasionally Visiting my family at home untill our
stake Quarterly Conference /1 Nov. 1885\ which I attended,
[*folded tabular report pasted on the page*]

Register of Logan Temple Ordinance Work for September 1885																			
Baptisms								Endowments				Ordinations		Sealings		Children to Parents		Adoptions		Second Anointings			
First		Renewal of Cov.		Health		Dead		Living		Dead		Living	Dead	Living	Dead	Living	Dead	Living	Dead	Living				Dead	
M	F	M	F	M	F	M	F	M	F	M	F											M	F	M	F
		6	14	24	37	1477	1974	65	78	387	604	1		386		73	279	120	97	10		1	6		
		20		61		3451		143		991		387		352		217		10		7		
3532						1134						387		352		217		10		7			

Samuel Roskelley   Recorder

    8 November 1885.
With my Councillor George Barber held a district Meeting
of the High Priest Quorum at Logan and had a good
meeting almost all the wards were represented and had
a good programme. Prests C. O Card and Orson Smith were
present and president Card spoke to us for some length
of time and in connexion with Bro Orson Smith I was
appointed to Preach in the 2nd Ward School house in Logan
[*folded tabular report pasted on the page*]

Register of Logan Temple Ordinance Work for October 1885																		
Baptisms								Endowments				Ordinations		Sealings		Children to Parents		Adoptions		Second Anointings	
First		Renewal of Cov.		Health		Dead		Living		Dead		Living	Dead	Living	Dead	Living	Dead	Living	Dead	Living		Dead	
M	F	M	F	M	F	M	F	M	F	M	F									M	F	M	F
	1	13	12	11	52	1150	1455	114	135	526	834	1	527	132	361	119	127	2	1	1	3	1	3
1		25		63		2605		249		1360		528		493		326		3		8			
2694								1609				528		493		326		3		8	
Samuel Roskelley Recorder																		

{67}
Continued my work in the Temple through the week
and on Saturday <u>14 November 1885</u> Attended and preached
the funeral Sermon of Sister Cordelia Ainscough Thompson the
wife of Bro ~~William~~ Thomas William Thompson of Smithfield
who has now lost every member of his family by death 3 Chi=
=dren and finally his wife.
      <u>Sunday 15th November 1885</u>
Came to Logan and preached in the 7th Ward School
house in the Evening. resuming my usual labors in
the Temple on Monday the 16th inst untill
<u>Saturday 21 November 1885</u> I was at home at my farm
and recd word in haste to get out of the way and secure my family
which I did in a very hurried manner and on my way to secure
myself I met Prest M. W Merrill and we both took steps in a
direction to secure ourselves. remaining in seclusion for a
few days till we learned more favorable news. Continued
my usual work till <u>Saturday 28 November 1885</u> and
went home again to Smithfield the roads being exceedingly
muddy and staid till Sunday afternoon the 29th then returned
to Logan and attended my labors in the Temple as usual until
[*folded tabular report pasted on the page*]

Register of Logan Temple Ordinance Work for November 1885																	
Baptisms								Endowments				Ordinations		Sealings		Children to Parents		Adoptions		Second Anointings			
First		Renewal of Cov.		Health		Dead		Living		Dead		Living	Dead	Living	Dead	Living	Dead	Living	Dead	Living		Dead	
M	F	M	F	M	F	M	F	M	F	M	F										M	F	M	F
–	–	7	10	16	56	1142	1331	95	117	524	757	1		514		118	445	159	119	3	1	5	2	4
		17				72				2473				212				1281		515		563		278		3		6		6	
2562								1493						515		563		278		3		12			

Samuel Roskelley   Recorder

Friday evening 4 Dec I went home again to Smithfield remaining until Sunday Evening 6 Dec. after attending meeting in the afternoon and partaking of the Sacrament with the Saints in Smithfield meeting house and Speaking to the Saints for about 20 Minutes on the spirit of the times. Returned to Logan to persue my usual labors in the Temple at Logan.

<u>Friday evening 11 Dec 1885.</u> again went to Smithfield to visit my family and remained at Logan and was engaged during the Sunday afternoon. and bal of week till Friday 18 Dec 1885 Returned to Smithfield and visited my family, found Bro Camper my hired man had been kicked by one of my horses and he was unable to work, and I had to keep my son Joseph out of school to chop the wood &c untill Bro Camper gets better,

{68}
<u>Sunday 20 December 1885</u>   With Abel Smart /and F. Sharp\ I left Smith=field about 1/2 past Eight A.M. and passing through Hyde park took in Elder Thos Duce and proceeded to Newton (a very Cold day) arriving at Newton, Visited Sunday School and talked a Short time to the School. Took dinner at Bp Rigby's and in the afternoon attended District Meeting of the High Priest Quorum, had a good turnout from the settlements in the district and had a good time. The spirit of God was poured out upon all present.

<u>Monday 21 Dec 1885</u> Resumed my labors in the Temple and had my prayers for a special blessing answered to my souls Joy and Satisfaction for which I feel grateful to My heavenly father in granting my request in so short a space of time, /in giving me my wife Maud and another companion.\ Continued work till Wednesday evening and with my wife Margaret went home to Smithfield and Visited with my families there. as the Temple was shut up for the rest of the week for Christmas. holidays but the weather proved Very unpropitious for it rained & Snowed alternately all

through the Christmas time and the roads were horable.

<u>Friday 25 Dec 1885</u> I spent the day at the farm with my wives Mary and Mary Jane. and their Children and Father and Mother Roberts. Maggie had gone to Newton to spend the Christmas and I returned to Logan on <u>Sunday afternoon 27 Dec 1885</u>. resuming my Temple labors for the week.   our baptisms being light on Tuesday I borrowed Bro Cards Team and carriage and went to Newton and brought my wife Margaret and her sister Lavinia to Logan with me. and as our companies were very light on Wednesday and Thursday Bro Merrill concluded to Close on Thursday Evening and give the Workers a holiday on <u>Friday 1 Jan 1886.</u> My Son Joseph Came with my buggy and took me to Smithfield where I had invited Stake President Card and his family and all my children and Gd Children. and Sons and Sons in law Daughter & daughters in law to partake of my birthday dinner on my 49th birthday. There sat down to dinner 16 of my children, 4 G^d children 4 Wives (1 Son (James) being on a mission and 4 grand children being absent) 2 Sons in law 3 daughters in law (My Eldest child and the youngest sat at the same table) Prest C O Card and 2 wives. Also bro Thos Hillyard and wife & Don C. Hyde and 2 daughters in law making 25 persons of my own family and a total of 33 persons in all. We ate drank (water) sang songs, spoke to each other. danced to music made by my own family, , and had a Splendid time till midnight. when we retired for the night, , I returned to Logan so as to be present at my meetings on Saturday <u>2 January 1886</u>

{69}
[folded tabular report pasted on the page]

Register of Logan Temple Ordinance Work for the year ending 31st Dec. 1886.

Mon.	Baptisms First		Renewal of Cov.		Health		Dead		Endowments Living		Dead		Ordinations Living	Dead	Sealings Living	Dead	Children to Parents Living	Dead	Adoptions Living	Dead	Second Anointings Living		Dead	
	M.	F.	M.	F.	M.	F.	M.	F.	M.	F.	M.	F.									M.	F.	M.	F.
Jan	4	3	24	30	5	44	1146	853	56	71	598	683										2	1	
Feb	10	4	49	36	21	56	1899	1522	40	61	1603	1040	3	589	69	300	68	49	3			1		3
Mar	4	7	86	97	29	93	2254	2096	60	101	803	1030	6	992	56	523	103	110			2	3		1
Apl	3	3	31	35	11	45	979	1138	67	100	587	903		784	93	546	184	151				5		
May	2		21	28	29	63	1858	1610	36	57	861	1168	2	577	90	401	138	93				3		1
June		1	22	24	28	81	1594	1797	48	69	622	930	2	853	51	610	128	165			1	3		
July		1	11	10	10	38	1066	1559	46	58	657	1055	4	613	59	405	188	117			1	7		1
Aug			5	4	6	13	793	1292	24	33	215	32-	1	647	68	454	154	98						
Sep			6	14	24	37	1477	1974	65	78	387	604	1	212	31	113	47	33	10		1	6		
Oct		1	13	12	11	52	1150	1458	114	135	526	834	1	386	73	279	120	97	2	1	1	3		5
Nov			7	10	16	56	1142	1331	95	117	524	757	1	527	132	311	199	127		3	1	5	1	4
Dec			14	11	16	25	1354	1353	96	131	362	440	2	514	118	445	159	119	2	2			2	3
Total	23	20	289	311	216	663	16,762	17,980	747	1,011	7,145	9,654	23	3358	134	250	84	59	17	6	7	38	4	16
	43		600		809		34,682		1,758		16,709		23	7052	974	4687	1569	1218	23		45		20	
					36,134						18,467		7,075	7,075	5,661	5,661	2,787	2,787	23		65			

Samuel Roskelley   Recorder

{69 con't}
I studied at the Temple a lecture written by Elder Charles
W. Nibley and I read it to the Students at the School of Science
in the afternoon as Bro Nibley was not present, and I
returned to Smithfield Saturday evening and visited at the
house in town as most of my family were visiting each
other there since the 1st inst.

Sunday 3rd Jan 1886. by invitation With my wives
Mary, Mary Jane, Maggie Dined with Bro and Sister Mary Ann
Hillyard, his wife Rebecca (my daughter) also being
present, and I returned to Logan with my wife
Margaret and Sons William and Joseph in the afternoon,

Monday 4 Jan 1885 resumed my labors in
the Temple for the week. labor not very heavy. Roads
very bad for travel.

Saturday. 9 January, 1886. I went to Smithfield
and spent the day with Bro Abel Smart the Clk of the
High Priest Quorum, apointing and sending out letters
of instruction to members of the Quorum authorizing
them to act as special visiting teachers &c.

Sunday 10 January 1886. With Elders Abel Smart
and Thomas Duce we visited Providence Ward
and held meeting in the afternoon and had a
good time, returning to Logan at night.

Monday 11 January 1886. Resumed my labors
at the Temple for the week.

Saturday 16 January 1886. Went to Smithfield
and visited my family and on Sunday 17th Bro
Thomas Duce and I went to Lewiston to hold a District
Meeting, through lack of understanding each others
programme the Seventies had a meeting also appoin
=nted. but Kindly gave way for our appointment
and we had a good time. I gave the 70s about 1/2
the time. returned to Smithfield same night and
met my wife Mary at her Mother's and I took
supper there and afterward went to hear Elder
B. H Roberts lecture to the YM. M I.A., at the
Smithfield meeting house, and afterwards with my
son William went to Logan and on
Monday 18th resumed my labors in the Temple

{70}
Saturday 23 January 1886. Went to Smithfield
and Visited with my family and returned to Logan
Sunday 24th and resumed by labors in the Temple
again on Monday 25th 1886. and continuing untill

Saturday morning 30 January. I attended the
/monthly\ ~~quarterly~~ Priesthood meeting for the Stake and heard some
good instructions by members of the Presidency & others &
in the afternoon I attended the School of the Temple hears
a lecture delivered by Bro John C. Carlisle on Science

and afternoon returned home to Smithfield and spent
the night.   Sunday 31 January. 1886.
With my son Joseph went to Logan and Met Elder Thos
Duce and with him went to Millville and held a meeting of
the High Priests Quorum, several bretheren from other settle
=ments being present, had a good meeting, and returned
to Logan in the Evening and met my wives, who had
come together at my request to arrange our family
matters to prepare for future Events..
[folded tabular report pasted on the page]

Register of Logan Temple Ordinance Work for January 1886																	
Baptisms								Endowments				Ordinations		Sealings		Children to Parents		Adoptions		Second Anointings			
First		Renewal of Cov.		Health		Dead		Living				Dead		Living	Dead	Living	Dead	Living	Dead	Living	Dead	Living		Dead	
M	F	M	F	M	F	M	F	M	F	M	F									M	F	M	F
4	2	10	6	9	24	1265	1367	61	76	448	560	2	442	80	322	77	51	2	1	2	7	1	2
6		16		33		2632		137				1008		444		402		128		2	1	9		3	
2687								1145				444		402		128		3		12			
Samuel Roskelley Recorder																	

and continued my labors in the Temple through
the week as usual.
Saturday and Sunday 16th & 7th of Feby 1886 attended the
conference of this stake of Zion, had the company of the apostle
John Henry Smith and Heber J Grant, had an excellent
Conference,
 Wednesday 10th Feby 1886. my wife Maggie was deliv
=ered of a fine Son at 5M to 9 A.M mother & child
doing well.
 Saturday 13th Feby. I went to Smithfield in the
morning and the weather was so cold and blustry
I could not do anything out of doors, I remained at
the farm all day.
 Sunday 14 Feby 1886. came to Logan and
attended an excellent meeting of the High Priests
Quorum Quarterly Conference in the Logan Tabernacle
at 2 P.M. most of the Wards of the Stake were
represented, and a good Spirit prevailed, while in
meeting heard that the marshalls had arrest Prest

{71}
George Q. Cannon at Humbolt, Nevada, which
news proved true, I continued my labors in the Temple
as usual through the week and on
Sunday 21st Feby 1886   Held a District High Priest
meeint of the South District in the Hyrum Tabernacle
and had a splendid good meeting. Elder Geo

Barber A Smart. T. Duce and Bro Hymas from
Hyde Park accompanied me, returned to my home
in Logan in the Evening. and persued the usual
labors of the week at the Temple.
Friday 26th Feby 1886. by the invitation of Prest C O.
Card the Stake president I started with him and Sister
Zina D. H. Smith and Sister E. L. Crowther at 1/2 past
4 P.M. on a visit the Settlements West side of Bear
River, arriving at Newton in time for an Evening meeting
sister Smith and Crowther Prest Card & myself spoke
and had a good time. house well filled. stayed
over night at Bro Rigbys
Saturday 27 Feb 1886. The 4 persons in company
proceeded to Visit Trenton to hold meeting but on
arrival found that no appointment had been
given to the people as the notice failed to get to
the Bishop. so after dinner we returned to
Clarkston, and held meeting in the Evening, the
4 of us spoke as usual to good audience,
Sunday 28 Feb 1886 We held meeting at
10 am and at 2 P.M. having good meetings and
at 1/2 past four P.M. started for Newton, and arrived
in time to hold meeting at 7. OClock. a full house.
I spoke about 70 ~~hrs~~ minutes on Celestial Marriage
and had good liberty sister Zina testified that
She knew Emma Smith gave the Prophet ~~y~~ young
girls placing their hands in his. Prest C O Card
also occupied a short time. stayed at Bro Rigby's
Monday 1 March the company returned to Logan
and I persued my usual labors in the Temple,
for the week
[*folded tabular report pasted on the page*]

Register of Logan Temple Ordinance Work for Febr. 1886.

Baptisms							Endowments				Ordinations		Sealings		Children to Parents		Adoptions		Second Anointings			
First		Renewal of Cov.		Health		Dead		Living		Dead		Living	Dead	Living	Dead	Living	Dead	Living	Dead	Living		Dead	
M	F	M	F	M	F	M	F	M	F	M	F									M	F	M	F
1	2	18	23	15	20	1614	1434	54	74	599	676	12	592	69	417	68	48	1		9	21	1	11
3		41		35		3048		128		1278		604		486		116		1		30		12	
3127								1406				604		486		116		1		42			
Samuel Roskelley Recorder																							

{72}
Tuesday 4 Mch 1886 I received by mail the
following   Salt Lake City 3 Mch 1886
Samuel Roskelley Esq

Logan Utah
Dear Brother,
I have been informed that "Uncle Sam" wants you in the near future; perhaps you may Know of this but I thought I would give you the benefit of my information. I understand that Rigby, Ricks, and Donaldsen of the Snake River Country are also wanted I cannot understand how this is, as they live in Idaho but their names came to me in connexion with yours will you do me the favor in case they are liable to be indicted in the 1st district court of Utah, to write a note to each of them telling them to look out.
With kind regards I remain
Your friend and brother
H. J Grant.

Friday Evening 5 Mch 1886 I went home to my farm and visited my family there returning to the Priesthood meeting in Logan in the Morning Saturday 6 Mch 1886. and at 2. P.M attended a Lecture given by Elder J Z Stewart at the School in the Temple, and after Sch returned to Smithfield and staid thro the night Sunday 7 Mch 1886. I had a heavy chill last night while in bed and afterwards suffered much with head ache. But having an appointment at Newton for a high Priests District Meeting I arose Early and altho weak through sickness I proceededed to Hyde Park and then left my buggy. Going to Newton with Elders Thos Duce and Abel Stuart, Hold meeting in Newton for the District House crowded full, and after meeting return went to the home of Sister Christine Funk and admin=istered to her. and then returned through a snow storm to Logan by way of Hyde Park. the roads have been very bad and it took me till very late to get home. Monday 8th March 1886 Prest C. O. Card has been my guest last night as he has several times of late and I today resume my Temple labors for the week Wednesday 10 March 1886 My son William and Miss Margaret Ann Wildman were today married in the Temple by Prest M W. Merrill
Saturdy 13th Mch 1886 I went to Smithfield and

{73}
Enjoyed a visit with my family at the farm and in town.
Sunday 14 March 1886 I left home early in the morning and got to Logan over Bad roads and took dinner at Logan and then proceeded with Prest C. O. Card and Elder Joseph H. Wilson to Providence and held meeting with the saints. I spoke abt 40 minutes on the Principles of the Gospel and their preached returning to Logan. With Prest C.O. Card visited the Saints in the Logan 7th ward and preached to them a short time

and was followed by Prest C. O Card, and attended to my
duties as Recorder of the Temple during the week following
visiting my family at Smithfield Saturday 20 Mch 1886.
and again returning to Logan <u>Sunday Morning 21 Mch 1886</u>
and spent the afternoon in the Temple copying 2nd Antg Record
and had the great Pleasure of having my wife Sarah M. B.
antd to me. Prest M. W. M. officiating, and on sunday 22nd
Mch resumed my temple labors.   <u>Wednesday 24 Mch 1886</u>
Took Wife Maggie and her Companion Miss Burton also
her sister Lavina to Smithfield to Stay for a while with
my family and visit for a few days, I returned to
Logan the same night, and stayed till Saturday 27
Mch when I went to Smithfield and visited my
family returning to Logan Sunday afternoon 28 March
and with Prest. C. O. Card Visited 1st Ward Logan and
preached 50 minutes, on the duties of Saints. followed
by Prest C. O Card, and on Monday 29 Mch I again
resumed my duties at the Temple
Thursday 1 Apl 1886. Fast meeting held at the
Temple. a splendid meeting. Old Sister Curtis spoke in
Tongues and the interpretation was given by another Sister
and Bro Stephen C. Perry, as follows, The Lord is well pleased with
the Labors of the saints in the temple, also with the admnistra
=tors and the Enemies of the saints should not have power to
enter this building for the spirt of fear should enter them
if they came for the purpose of Entering this building
with unholy desire.
[*folded tabular report pasted on the page*]

Register of Logan Temple Ordinance Work for March 1886.																		
Baptisms								Endowments				Ordinations		Sealings		Children to Parents		Adoptions		Second Anointings	
First		Renewal of Cov.		Health		Dead		Living		Dead		Living	Dead	Living	Dead	Living	Dead	Living	Dead	Living	Dead
M	F	M	F	M	F	M	F	M	F	M	F									M	F	M	F
	2	22	16	26	39	2383	1942	60	83	737	801	2	732	84	521	153	127	1	3		2		
2		38		65		4325		143		1538		734		605		280		4		2			
4430								1681				734		605		280		4		2			

Samuel Roskelley   Recorder

{74}
<u>Saturday 3 April 1886.</u> attended the Monthly
Priesthood meeting of the stake, and had an excellent
meeting much good instruction given by several of
the leading Elders, and in the afternoon attended
the School at the Temple and heard an excellent
lecture: delivered by Apostle Moses Thatcher. At
the Close of the meeting the temple closed till the 12th

of the month and I gave my Keys to the Janitor by
request of Bro Merrill, without any reasons assigned
I went to smithfield same night.

Sunday 4 April 1886 I attended meeting at Smithfield
and preached about one hour, my councillor Bro Barber
occupied the bal of the time, and I worked the bal
of the week putting in some garden at the farm and
town with the aid of bro Schiffman and replaced a
number of dead fruit trees and set out many Rasp
=berry and current trees, & other shrubs and did a lot
of other work, and whitewashed the rooms of the house
my family occupy at Logan.

Sunday 11 April 1886. I took my horse and buggy and
went to Logan with wife Mary in the Morning. And attended
meeting of the saints at the Tabernacle and heard the
Epistle of the 1st Presidency of the Church read to the Saints
-it is a very able document, and on

Monday 12 April 1886 I resumed my labors at the
Temple again much to my satisfaction, continuing
all week and on Saturday 17th Apl I went to Smithfield to
see my family.

[*folded tabular report pasted on the page*]

Register of Logan Temple Ordinance Work for Apl. 1886																		
Baptisms								Endowments				Ordinations		Sealings		Children to Parents		Adoptions		Second Anointings			
First		Renewal of Cov.		Health		Dead		Living		Dead		Living	Dead	Living	Dead	Living	Dead	Living	Dead	Living				Dead	
M	F	M	F	M	F	M	F	M	F	M	F											M	F	M	F
	1	6	6	12	25	888	921	68	80	349	629		345	66	313	143	85	1		1	6	2	1
1		12		37		1809		148		978		345		379		230		1		7		3	
1859								1126				345		379		230		1		10			

Samuel Roskelley   Recorder

{75}

Continuing to follows the same routine of labors the
the remainder of the month of April and on
Sunday 25 April, I attended and presided over
a High Priest District Quorum Meeting at Logan and
had a very good meeting, the speakers all spoke
with spirit. continuing my labors thru the week in the
Temple

Saturday 1 May 1886. Quarterly Conference for Cache
stake of Zion Commenced and continued through the
sunday, apostles F. D. Richards.. M Thatcher and J H. Smith
favored the conference with their company. and gave
much good instruction, resuming my labors that the
week as usual in the Temple.

Saturday 8 May 1886. I went up to Smithfield to visit
my family and on Sunday 9 May Bro Barber and
I went to Richmond and Held a District meeting of the
High Priests Quorum, having a good time as usual
and all seemed to Enjoy themselves in the meeting.
During the Week we got word that a raid was
planned on the settlements of Cache Valley by the Deputy
marshalls and many of the bretheren were notified and
must all left home for a few nights, the marshalls
did appear at Wellsville and took 2 of the Bretheren
at day light in the Morning Bs Minnerly and Smith',
they are the first arrested in Cache Valley Stake
quite a number of residences were searched but
the marshalls could not find as much prey
as they hoped for and again returned to Ogden
Saturday 15 May 1886. I went home to Smithfield
my wives Mary Jane & Maggy went to Newton
to Visit Aunt Sarah and the family of their
Father,   Sunday 16 May. Stayed at my farm
with wife Mary returning to Logan Sunday Evening
Enjoyed the Society of my wife there
Monday 17 May 1886 assisted Prest C.O. Card
to set apart Sara Maud Burton as 1st
Councillor to Sister Jane E. Molens President of
the Primary Associations Cache Valley Stake
this was done before breakfast. He give her a good
blessing and many precious promises,
Continued my labors in the Temple thro' the week and
went to Smithfield Friday Evening 21 May 1886, returning to
Logan Saturday Morning 22nd May. and did some
work in the Temple, and started for Newton in the afternoon
arriving about 1/2 past 6.P.M. staying all night
at Br Rigby's with some of my family.
Sunday morning 23 May. with wife Mary Jane I
went to Clarkston and attended the Sabbath School Union
morning and afternoon, Sister Maud had been there
with Sister Morlen attending a Primary Conference that
day previous and stayed over to attend the SS.
Union today and rode to Newton with me & getting
my wife Margaret & her Sister Lavina and arrived

{76}
at Logan about 1/2 past 8 P.M.
Resumed my labors in the Temple as
usual. on Monday Morning 24 May 1886. and
continuing the week at the usual work, going to Smithfield
Saturday afternoon 29 May 1886 and Kept in Exile
untill Sunday Evening when I returned to Logan resu
=ming my labor in the Temple as usual untill
Saturday 5 June 1886. in the forenoon attended a
priesthood meeting of the Stake, and in the afternoon

attended the Lecture at the Temple class, and going
to Smithfield in the Evening,

<u>Sunday 6 June 1886</u> Went to Hyde Park and met Bro
Duce and Bro Abel Smart and went to Clarkston
and held meeting of the High Priests for the district having
a good meeting; returning to Hyde Park and met Prest
C. O Card and with him preached to the Saints in the
Evening meeting, and going to my home in Smithfield
afterwards.

[folded tabular report pasted end-to-end on the page]

Register of Logan Temple Ordinance Work for May 1886.																	
Baptisms								Endowments				Ordinations	Sealings		Children to Parents		Adoptions		Second Anointings			
First		Renewal of Cov.		Health		Dead		Living		Dead			Living	Dead	Living	Dead	Living	Dead	Living	Dead	Living		Dead	
M	F	M	F	M	F	M	F	M	F	M	F									M	F	M	F
2	1	13	8	20	57	1596 ~~1609~~	1913	50	73	603	927		595	54	406	187	117	1	9	3	8	4	5
3		21		77		3509		123		1530			460		304		10		11	9		
3610									1653						595	460		304		10		20			
Samuel Roskelley Recorder																							

Register of Logan Temple Ordinance Work for June 1886.																	
Baptisms								Endowments				Ordinations	Sealings		Children to Parents		Adoptions		Second Anointings			
First		Renewal of Cov.		Health		Dead		Living		Dead			Living	Dead	Living	Dead	Living	Dead	Living	Dead	Living		Dead	
M	F	M	F	M	F	M	F	M	F	M	F									M	F	M	F
	1	13	18	29	64	1743	2265	63	89	627	1004	2	618	71	434	182	136	4	73	6	15	3	9
1		31		93		4008		152		1631			620		505		318		77		21	12
4133									1783						620	505		318		77		33			
Samuel Roskelley Recorder																							

{77}
<u>Monday 7 June 1886</u> Returned to Logan and resumed
my temple Labor as usual, nothing of note transpired
but trying to keep out of the way of deputies who
occasionally visit this part of the country seeking whom
they may arrest. I am thankful that my heavenly father
has thus far preserved me and Kept me from their grasp
<u>Sunday 27 June 1886</u> with Bro Abel Smart I Visited
the members of our Quorum in Paradise holding a
meeting at 11 O'Clock, and attended a meeting of
the Saints in the afternoon at 2 OClock returning

to Logan in the Evening and resuming my usual
labors in the Temple,
Friday 2nd July 1886. Went to Smithfield and Visited my
family. remaining over Sunday Held meeting with the
members of the Quorum at 8 oclock in the A. M.
and attended meeting with the Saints at 2 P. M. and
spoke about 30 minutes in the bowery to the saints.
returning to Logan again on Monday morning Early
attended to my labors in the Temple during the
week and on
Sunday 11 July 1886. with Bro Abel Smart I went
to Lewiston and held a district meeting of the
Quorum having a good time, returning to Logan
on Monday morning Early and attended to my duties
as usual in the Temple. Sister Eliza Rhees came
up and was adopted to me as a child on the
Thursday. 15th inst. and on Friday 16th inst
went home to Smithfield remaining till Monday
morning 19 July 1886 when I again resumed my labors
in the Temple, for the week
[*remainder of the page crossed out by five vertical strokes*]
<u>Sunday 25 July 1886.</u> Held a district Quorum Meeting
in the Logan Tabernacle at 2 P. M. Elder Jas A Leishman
gave a discourse on the redemption of the dead and Elder
George Goddard gave a sermon on Sabbath Schools, the audience
seemed quite Entertained, and Enjoyed the meeting
<u>Monday 26 July 1886.</u> Deputy Marshalls arrested Prest C.
O. Card this morning and as the train started which he
and the deputy was on to go to Ogden. Bro C. jumped the
train and by a previously arranged plan got on on a horse
and made good his Escape. He is now taking care of
himself, I attended to my usual duties thro' the
week at the temple,
<u>Friday 30 Jul 1886</u> Temple closed for work this Evening
and quite a number of regrets were expressed by many of
the saints,
<u>Saturday 31 July 1886</u> With the clerks I worked putting
our Record books in good shape as possible and stowing
them away during vacation, and went to smithfield

{78}
Friday Evening 22 July 1886 I took my wife Maggie
to smithfield to put up some fruit, &c and I
arranged for sister sarah Maud and Selina
Burton to be at Smithfield to Spend the 24th
with my family
Saturday 24 July 1886 Pioneer day, attended the
celebration at Smithfield in the Bowery, lots of
people present but no Quire, no Brass band or
Procession, some speeches, I talked about 15
minutes and spent the bal of the day with my

dear family and had a splendid Visit, and
on Sunday morning 25 July 1886. I went to Logan
and held a District Meeting of the High
Priests Quorum in the Tabernacle at 2. P M.
Elders Jas A Leishman and George Goddard
spoke very good, I ordained Br. P. W. Cook an
old acquaintance a High Priest., had a good
meeting. And on Monday 26 July 1886, in a
few hours after commencing our Temple labors
word came that Prest C O Card was arrested
on the usual charge of Cohabitation, which
cast a gloom over all of us. But we heard
in the afternoon that he jumped off the Train
and Escaped. All of which is true, I contin=
=ued my labors in the Temple during the week
until.

Friday 30th July 1886 The Temple closed this Evening
for a month and many regrets were expressed by a number
of the saints who had been laboring there

Saturday 31 July 1886. I worked all day placing the
records in a good shape and put them away for the
vacation, and went to smithfield for a months rest.

Sunday 1st August 1886 at the farm with Mary and
Mary Jane and the small children rumours of deputies were
current and I thought it prudent to Keep quiet.
Spent the week laying a foundation for my Granary at
the farm and on Saturday morning 7 August 1886. I
went to Logan and attended Stake Quarterly Conference
none of the Stake presidency were present but High Councillors
Alain Crockett, the stand was very empty.
Apostle H. J Grant and Elder John Morgan occupied the
forenoon and several of the Bishops and I occupied the
afternoon, Attended Priesthood meetings in the Evening at
which Prest C. O. Card. And M. W. Merrill were present

Sunday 8th August.. 1886. Deputies in town. I remained
at home all day writing, my family went to meeting,
and Enjoyed themselves, and I spent the month of
August mostly out on my farm at Smithfield in
building a Granary and preparing a place to store
my Grain &c. on Sunday 22 August 1886

{79}
With My Councillor Geo Barber and Elders Abel Smart and
Thomas Duce. held a District Meeting of the High Priest Quorum
at Hyrum and returned to Logan at night,

Monday 30th August 1886 resumed my labors
at the Temple and recorded quite a number of Names
for Baptism tomorrow. Everybody feeling good that the
Temple is again open

[folded tabular report pasted on the page]

Register of Logan Temple Ordinance Work for July 1886																	
Baptisms								Endowments				Ordinations		Sealings		Children to Parents		Adoptions		Second Anointings			
First		Renewal of Cov.		Health		Dead		Living		Dead		Living	Dead	Living	Dead	Living	Dead	Living	Dead	Living		Dead	
M	F	M	F	M	F	M	F	M	F	M	F									M	F	M	F
		5	8	21	57	1897	1575	52	81	594	983	1	585	49	349	154	151	4		8	11	3	7
		13		78		3472		133		1577		586		398		305		4		19		10	
3563								1710				586		398		305		4		29			
Samuel Roskelley Recorder																							

<u>Tuesday 31st August 1886</u> resumed work as usual in the Temple this morning, but in a few moments I was called in council with the president over a letter just received from the proper authorities to Keep the Temple shut up and giving some general instruction in case of a raid by deputy marshals and advising all the workers to leave the Temple and get out of the way for a few days, all of which I tried to comply with by packing up all the books & records, papers &c of the Temple in Boxes and they were securely put out of the way. by other persons <u>Thursday 2nd September 1806.</u> with my son William I moved part of my furniture as the house I have been occupy=ing is sold to another party and I have to find a new home. Friday 3 Sep 1886. finished moving and took wife Maggie and her children to Smithfield and I exiled myself in my farm.

Sunday 5 Sep 1886. with Bros Smart and Duce I Visited Clarkston and held District Meeting of the High priests Quorum and had the poorest meeting I have ever attended in that capacity as the Bp's Son Richard had died the same day and the saints had gathered to do all they could to add comfort to the grief stricken family. returned to Smithfield Same evening and continued in Exile till <u>Sunday 12 sep 1886.</u> I took Maggie and the children to Logan and occupied aunt Zina' house for the time being till the house I have rented is ready.

<u>Monday 13th September 1886</u> commenced work once more in the Temple much to my Joy and Satisfaction but on <u>Wednesday 15 september</u> the commissioners court was opened in Logan and the Deputy Marshalls commenced hunting subject we learned that 10 bench warrants were issued at once – one for me – as Goodwin the commissioner Knows me well., some of the temple hands narrowly Escaped the hands of the deputies and consequently quit Temple work., I have slept away from home from some time and have not had much comfort with my dear family.

{80}

<u>17 Sep 1886</u> I went to my farm at Smithfield
this Evening and finished My Granary on Saturday and
remained in Exile all day sunday returning to Logan
with Maud on Sunday Evg. after dark, and went
to work in the Temple Monday Morning as usual to watch
=ful & prayerful. For these are sealgy times as the
deputies are watching Every corner to pick up
somebody,, The boys Threshed and had [blank] Bu Wheat
[blank] Bu Oats [blank] Bu Rye. on Friday morning 24
my son James came to the Temple having returned
from his mission to the southern states. I was glad
to see him once more at home but he is Physica
=lly used up, he Visited me all day and on Sat
The Boys moved my goods to the New Rented house
of Sister Lane's. Commencing on Friday and finish
=ing on Saturday the <u>24 & 25 Sep</u> the marshalls are
now very villigent in hunting after their Victims and
I find it best to be very secretive as to my stopping
places. Visiting my family but seldom and that at
night, as I find by so doing I can better keep
out of the way of the deputy marshals and do my
duty at the Temple. sundays is the longest day
in the week as I have to visit the neighbors and
stay in the house free from observation. several
of our bretheren have been arrested and put into
bonds in this stake and the Marshalls are hun
=ting more Victims, which makes me very cautious
and I do not see anybody but my family except
persons coming to the Temple. how long this will
last I do not Know but pray God to be with and
preserve me and help me to be faithful to him and
to his cause to the End of my days. Amen.
      I continued my labors is the Temple by observing to
Keep my own councils as to my sleeping place – not
leaving the Temple till after dark and getting there long
before daylight. Making it long days to do business,
feeling that the Lord is blessing me in permitting me to
remain unmolested by my enimies, and this passed
the month of October.
30 October (Saturday) My Wife Mary Jane had
a beautiful son born this morning at 20 minutes
to 5 I had arranged for suitable persons to wait upon
her as I could not be present, but I spent the
succeeding night with her and am thankful the
Lord had blessed me with another son to my heretage
5 October (Friday) Went to Smithfield after night and a
little before midnight blessed my son and called him John
Henry after one of my Brothers (John) and one of Mary
[folded tabular report pasted between the pages 80–81]

Register of Logan Temple Ordinance Work for Aug & Sep 1886.

August.

Baptisms								Endowments				Ordinations		Sealings		Children to Parents		Adoptions		Second Anointings			
First		Renewal of Cov.		Health		Dead		Living		Dead		Living	Dead	Living	Dead	Living	Dead	Living	Dead	Living		Dead	
M	F	M	F	M	F	M	F	M	F	M	F									M	F	M	F
-	-	-	-	-	-	-	-	-	-	-	-	-	-	-	1	-	-	-	-	1	1	1	
														1						2		2	
																				3			

September.

Baptisms								Endowments				Ordinations		Sealings		Children to Parents		Adoptions		Second Anointings			
First		Renewal of Cov.		Health		Dead		Living		Dead		Living	Dead	Living	Dead	Living	Dead	Living	Dead	Living		Dead	
M	F	M	F	M	F	M	F	M	F	M	F									M	F	M	F
-	-	1	7	5	35	838	987	38	71	198	365	-	196	51	134	83	65	-	-	2	5	1	2
		8		40		1825		109		563		196		185		148				7		3	
187								672				196		185		148				10			

Samuel Roskelley   Recorder

{81}
[folded tabular report pasted on the page]

Register of Logan Temple Ordinance Work for October 1886.

Baptisms								Endowments				Ordinations		Sealings		Children to Parents		Adoptions		Second Anointings			
First		Renewal of Cov.		Health		Dead		Living		Dead		Living	Dead	Living	Dead	Living	Dead	Living	Dead	Living		Dead	
M	F	M	F	M	F	M	F	M	F	M	F									M	F	M	F
	1	7	8	22	52	1345	1614	111 ~~108~~	144	437	666	4	434	127	307 ~~288~~	189	125			3	11	5	4
1		15		74		2959		255		1103		438		434		314				14		9	
3049								1358				438		434		314				23			

Samuel Roskelley   Recorder

Janes Brothers (Henry) I had much of the spirit
of the Lord upon me and and [sic] pronounced Many
great blessings upon the Boy baby for my heart was
full. I being an Exile. hiding from the officers
of the Law and can only Visit my family at
night when none but the Eye of the Lord is

upon me, but I rejoice that my issue is
not cut off but I can see my dear family
once in a while. and continued to labor in the
House of the Lord days and hiding among my
friends nights.

On Friday Evening 12 Nov 1886 by an arrangement
I succeeded in moving Sarah M. to Smithfield and
am thankful in safety.
Sunday 21 Nov. Send Bro Sharp to Preside and my
son James to clerk at H.Priest Quorum District Meeting
at Wellsville and I held meeting with most
of my family at the farm in the afternoon, and had
a good time visiting and talking to them on the
principles of the Gospel and continued the same
practices as much as possible as circumstances
would permit, through the month of November and Dec.
Generally Visiting my family in Logan about twice
a week and those at Smithfield once a week
and at night so as to be safe, altho' I feel
that I run a good many risks to accomplish it
but I feel grateful for Gods protecting care.
[*folded tabular report pasted on the page*]

Register of Logan Temple Ordinance Work for November 1886.																		
Baptisms								Endowments				Ordinations		Sealings		Children to Parents		Adoptions		Second Anointings			
First		Renewal of Cov.		Health		Dead		Living		Dead		Living	Dead	Living	Dead	Living	Dead	Living	Dead	Living		Dead	
M	F	M	F	M	F	M	F	M	F	M	F											M	F	M	F
	1	9	13	15	43	1342	1866	91	107	503	719	5	499	92	314	167	113		2	4	7	3	6
1		22		58		3208		198		1222		504		406		280		2		11		9	
3289								1420				504		406		280		2		20			
Samuel Roskelley Recorder																		

{82}
<u>Friday 24 Dec 1886.</u> Nothing unusual has transpired
of late but the capture of some of our Brethern by the
Marshals in my usual disguise I am able to get around a
little nights, went to Smithfield in the Evening.
<u>Saturday 25 Dec 1886.</u> Christmas Day. spent it at my
hiding place in Smithfield and spent the Evening with
Mary Jane and my family where we ate Supper together
rejoicing in the privilege, returned to Logan Sunday Eve
=ning and continued labor in the Temple till Thursday
night, Temple closed Friday and I stayed at my
hiding place all day – went to Smithfield at night
and took Maud, stayed at the farm all night and
left for my Hiding place Early in the morning, on

Saturday 1 January 1887. I am 50 years old today
and thank the Lord for his goodness to me. I went
to the farm about noon under disguise, and met
my wives and some of my children (8 under 7 years
old) and spend the bal of the day and Evening with
them. When we sat down to dinner I read the
following Poem I had hastily composed,
This blessed New Year and My Grand Jubilee
and I offer my thanks to my Father above
For this blessing he grants ~~me~~ to be with those I love
To hear their Kind greetings, and see their sweet smiles
To feel their devotion amidst all of our trials
and Know that the troubles and sorrows we're passed
Has bound our heart closer Knowing that we are blessed
To feel we are one in both spirit and faith
and can Kneel and ask blessings on aged and youth
no feeling of Anger or malice is held
Toward those ~~we should~~ /that we\ love as part of ourself
To Know we're bound by the Gospels blest ties
By seal of the Priesthood that rules in the skies
By annointings most sacred which brings hearts to blend
In ~~the~~ Everlasting Covenant, a bond without End.
I'm thankful my God my benefactor has given
These dear ones to me to help make a heaven
God grant my Dear Wives and our children too.
May be faithful always and to his Kingdom true.
Following is a recapitulation of the years work in
the House of the Lord and better tells the amount
of my labor than I can write it. as no part

{83}

it has been performed by I have had a hand in it some way.

[folded tabular report pasted on the page]

Register of Logan Temple Ordinance Work for the year ending 31st Dec. 1886.

Mon.	Baptisms First		Baptisms Renewal of Cov.		Baptisms Health		Baptisms Dead		Endowments Living		Endowments Dead		Ordinations Living	Ordinations Dead	Sealings Living	Sealings Dead	Children to Parents Living	Children to Parents Dead	Adoptions Living	Adoptions Dead	Second Anointings Living		Second Anointings Dead	
	M.	F.	M.	F.	M.	F.	M.	F.	M.	F.	M.	F.									M.	F.	M.	F.
Jan.	4	2	10	6	9	24	1265	1367	61	76	448	560	2	422	80	320	77	51	2	1	2	7	1	2
Feb.	1	2	18	23	15	20	1614	1434	54	74	599	679	12	592	69	417	68	48	2	–	9	21	1	11
Mar.	–	2	22	16	26	39	2383	1942	60	83	737	801	2	732	84	521	153	127	1	3	–	2	–	–
Apl.	–	1	6	6	12	25	888	921	68	80	349	629	–	345	66	313	145	85	1	–	1	6	2	1
May	2	1	13	8	20	57	1596	1913	50	73	603	927	–	595	54	406	187	117	1	9	3	8	4	5
June	–	1	13	18	29	64	1743	2265	63	89	627	1004	2	618	71	434	182	136	4	73	6	15	3	9
July	–	–	5	8	21	57	1897	1575	52	81	594	983	1	585	49	349	154	151	4	–	8	11	3	7
Aug.	–	–	–	–	–	–	–	–	–	–	–	–	–	–	–	1	–	–	–	–	1	1	1	–
Sep.	–	–	1	7	5	35	838	987	38	71	198	365	–	196	51	134	83	65	–	–	2	5	1	2
Oct.	–	1	7	8	22	52	1345	1614	111	144	437	666	4	434	127	307	194	126	–	–	3	11	5	4
Nov.	–	1	9	13	15	43	1342	1866	91	107	503	719	5	499	92	314	167	113	–	2	4	7	3	6
Dec.	–	–	9	9	10	20	1389	992	87	100	389	468	2	380	88	247	42	31	–	–	1	3	–	1
	7	11	113	122	184	436	16300	16876	735	978	5484	7801	30	5418	831	3765	1452	1050	14	88	40	97	24	48
	18		235		620		33,176		1713		13285		5448		4596		2502		102		137		72	
	34,049								14,998				5448		4596		2502		102		209			

Samuel Roskelley   Recorder

{83 con't}
In reference to my "lines" the following Verses
were handed to me as expressing the feelings of my
family toward me.
   "A Birthday "Tribute"
To Samuel Roskelley on his 50th Birthday 1 January 1887.
 We feel to say "welcome" dear Husband at home,
 on this ~~thy~~ /your\ glad birthday and Kno thou /you\ art free.
From those who would seek thee /you\, or cause thee /you\ to roam
<u>amongst strangers</u> where none of thy /your\ loved ones can be
our hearts say God bless you! and long may you live
Be a comfort and blessing to those that you love.
And Keep you from men who Know they can't give
<u>a spirit</u> so ~~honorable~~ noble send down from above,
our Father has called thee /you\ to labor on Earth.
That you may prepare for thyself /yourself\ a reward
He has watched and has guided thy /your\ footsteps from birth
<u>Therefore b</u>e thou faithful and true to his word
Thy /Your\ trials have been sore in the days that are past
But if thou /you\ art faithful and true to the End
Your suffering will ease your pleasures will last
<u>When God f</u>or your spirit his angels will Send
The blessings that now are awaiting for you
Will cause you to marvel and Shed tears of joy
For thou /you\ has/ve\ been faithful to God thy /your\ life through
He will make thy /your\ heart glad unmixed with alloy

{84}
Thou /You\ art/e\ fifty years old on this New Years day
and may "years" more be added is the wish of /your wives\
and your children to teach them the way
<u>That they may</u> live true and virtuous lives
a Patriarch and Priest ~~thou wast~~ /you are\ ordained to be
In Heaven out home Ere this Earth it was framed
With wives and a numerous posterity
<u>That will love</u>/,\ ~~thee~~, cherish and honor thy name
Some of your loved ones have passed on before you
To that life beyond, and are waiting you there
Rejoicing in hope, When Earths work is finished
<u>You'll Join</u> them and in their full happiness Share
Your family now living feel always to bless you
For counsels imparted in days that are past
May we Ever be worthy the Love and the Blessings
<u>Your are wil</u>ling to give us, While life it shall last
May they walk in the path of their father has taken
Being faithful and true to God and his works
May they always be firm their faith never Shaken
<u>Ever true t</u>o their duties never Known as Shirk
O Father protect our Loved one we pray thee
From those who would seek his life to destroy
From those who'd deprive him from seeing his /loved ones\

His wives and his friends, his girls and his boys
>   Maud Burton Roskelley, in behalf
>   of the family,

{85}
[*top of the page blank*]
1887 The month of January passed off with its usual labors
and cares, and our temple work Kept up remarkable well
as the following record shows
[*folded tabular report pasted on the page*]

Register of Logan Temple Ordinance Work for January 1887																	
Baptisms								Endowments				Ordinations		Sealings		Children to Parents		Adoptions		Second Anointings			
First		Renewal of Cov.		Health		Dead		Living		Dead		Living	Dead	Living	Dead	Living	Dead	Living	Dead	Living		Dead	
M	F	M	F	M	F	M	F	M	F	M	F									M	F	M	F
	2	2	4	9	17	1366	1011	51	75	583	631	2	577	56	373	60	49	–	–	6	7	1	3
2		6		26		2377		126		1214		589		429		109		--		13		4	
2411								1340				579		429		109		–		17			
Samuel Roskelley Recorder.																							

1887 February quarterly conference found apostles
F. D. Richards and J H. Smith visiting with us – they paid
a visit at the Temple and we enjoyed it.
<u>On Thursday</u> <u>10 Feby</u> the County Sherriff left at
my wife Mary's house a summons from the 1st district
Court of Utah. for me to appear and defend myself
in an action brought by Zions Savings Band to recover
pay on a promissory note for $1000⁰⁰ that I had borrowed and
used by the directors of ~~Zions~~ Logan and Smithfield Canal
Company – in answer thereto I sent the following letter
to B H. Schettler the Cashier.. Logan Utah 15 Feb 1887.
B. H Schettler Esq \
Zions Savings Bank | Dear sir
Salt Lake City Utah/   I am in receipt of
papers issued at your instance by 1st district Court
asking judgement against me on promissory note held
by you as agent of "Zions Savings Bank"
        for Bal of Letter See back of Book a copy
of the Letter marked "L."

{86}
[*folded tabular report pasted on the page*]

Register of Logan Temple Ordinance Work for February 1887																							
Baptisms								Endowments				Ordinations		Sealings		Children to Parents		Adoptions		Second Anointings			
First		Renewal of Cov.		Health		Dead		Living		Dead		Living	Dead	Living	Dead	Living	Dead	Living	Dead	Living				Dead	
M	F	M	F	M	F	M	F	M	F	M	F									M	F	M	F
–	–	8	11	8	17	1056	1214	33	43	386	425	1	381	35	225	53	27	1	2	2	4	2	1
–		19		25		2270		76		809		382		260		80		3		6			3	
2314								885				382		260		80		3		9			

Samuel Roskelley   Recorder

The month of Feby passed rapidly, the Temple work Kept up its usual interest and the U.S. offi= =cials seemed to vie with each other in doing their work of capturing all they could. On thursday 24th Maud gave birth to a beautiful girl,

Friday 4th March 1887 I rec'd a letter requesting me to come home as baby was sick with Cold. —on arrival I saw it was lung fever blessed the babe and gave it the name of Maude Ellen. - I commenced fasting and pleading with the Lord for the life of the child, but notwithstanding all my efforts and pleadings the Lord saw fit to call it hence Sunday Evening 6th March 1887 about 1/2 past 7 O'Clock.. this was a sad blow to us all, as we were in exile and obliged to do every thing tho' others but we got the little lifeless corpse laid away comfortably and can only say "God gave and God hath taken away and blessed be his holy name forever.

Monday 7 Mch 1887. was the first working day since ~~the~~ I have not been at my post for 3 years, but com = = menced my labor again on Tuesday 8 March 1887 Nothing of unusual interest transpired with me until Saturday 26 March I received the information that my son Samuels babe Hugh Roskelley died that morning leaving heart stricken parents and a great many symp =athizers, I did not attend the funeral as I did not deem it prudent for any but my choicest friends to Know my whereabouts.

on Tuesday Morning 29th Mch 1887 a most remarkable circumstance took place – one I shall never forget to be grateful to my heavenly father for his overruling hand in delivering me from. I had spent the Evening from 8 to 10 o'clock at the house of Br & Sister Townsend and went to the Widows to sleep but my mind was uneasy for some cause and I could not rest, I heard the clock strike Every 1/2 hour through the night and at 3 O'Clock I got out of bed and dres =sed in the dark so that a light should not attract any one who may be passing at that unusual hour, I left the

house as the clock struck 1/2 past 3. A.M. Taking my usual
route by Bro Prestons lots for the Temple. I had prayed
before getting out of bed but before leaving the house I had
again Knelt and asked the Lord to preserve me in

{87}
going to the Temple and preserve me from the hands
of wicked men, When I got to the foot bridge
across the Logan & Hyde Park Canal, on the South
side of the Street I discovered dark objects at the ~~the~~
corner of the fence on the S. E corner of the Benson Block
and in crossing the bridge I discovered that it was men
and some had pipes in their mouths smoking, my heart
"jumped in my mouth" in a second and as quick as
lightening I though. I'm caught now sure, What shall I
do? go back, or continue up the hill, or run, or what
? and as I got to the End of the bridge (east,) the thought
came to me. <u>Make</u> s<u>traight</u> <u>for</u> <u>them</u> and go on,
I felt sure they were marshalls but I followed the
promptings of the spirit within and the moment I
received it I turned straight for them, they had
by this time changed position to the East side of
the corner where they could see me, but be more
out of my sight, I had my axe on my left arm and
pipe in my mouth and found 5 men, 3 with their backs
against the fence looking East and 2 standing a few
feet east of them and looking west. I walked between
the 5 with my hand over my pipe as it had
nothing in it– 3 of them were very scrutinizing and
suppose seeing my poor garb thought I was not
the kind they wanted. as I passed the last 2 men I
bawled out "good evening gentlemen" in a coarse tone
of Voice and they answered me good evening, I thought
I heard them whispering after I past a couple of rods,
so I stopped and struck a match on my right
thigh ~~as though~~ and held it to my pipe as though
in the act of lighting my pipe but I could not hear
this conversation, I walked on again 2 or 3 rods
and stopped and lit another match thinking that
some of them would follow me, but I made my
way into the middle of the road and continued 2
blocks till I got to sister Margaret P.W. Youngs house
where I crawled through the fence and watched to
see if they followed me, but not seeing anyone
I went and Knocked and gained admittance till
day light when I got sister Margaret to go to,
the Temple to see if the coast was clear. finding
it was I went to the temple in day light for
the first time for months, –When I stopped
the second time and lit a match the suggestion
came to me "They are watching for Bro Jas Leishman"

which proved to be true for in seeing Bro James

{88}
Lishman I learned that they had been searching his
houses between 1 and 2 O'Clock and had also searched
another house for him without success and had
seemingly come straight from raiding these houses
to the place I found them Bro Larson afterward
saw them near the fence at Bro Prestons Corner. And
they were no doubt all night raiding and
watching to catch some one. They looked like so
many demonds to me, and the feeling I had when
going toward them and while passing them was
simply awful, I feel that this was a direct inter=
=position of my heavenly father in causing these men
to not lay their hands on me when in their power
to do so. I never thought of fear while passing thro'
it but after getting to the Temple, every time I would
think of it it would almost make my blood turn
cold.

[folded tabular report pasted on the page]

Register of Logan Temple Ordinance Work for March 1887																							
Baptisms								Endowments				Ordinations		Sealings		Children to Parents		Adoptions		Second Anointings			
First		Renewal of Cov.		Health		Dead		Living		Dead		Living	Dead	Living	Dead	Living	Dead	Living	Dead	Living		Dead	
M	F	M	F	M	F	M	F	M	F	M	F									M	F	M	F
-	1	6	7	10	30	1327	1416	67	96	439	590	-	436	75	276	60	20	1	2	1	3	1	3
1		13		40		2743		163		1029		436		351		80		3		4		4	
2797								1192				436		351		80		3		8			
Samuel Roskelley Recorder.																							

<u>Friday 1st Apl</u> 1887. closed our work for the
week and it was announced that the Temple would
be closed during Conference the coming Week..
<u>Saturday 2 Apl 1887</u> attended school at the Temple
Bro Z Stewart lectured on Theology, and after the lecture
I assumed my disguise and walked to Smithfield, I
was very tired on my arrival as I had faced a heavy
wind from the north, spent Sunday most of the day
alone at the farm. altho bright overhead it was a
cold raw day and I did not feel well, which
feeling continued until Tuesday I was received to my
son Samuels and Bro Bair called in with my family
to Doctor me as I was growing rapidly worse, this
continued until Friday night 8 Oct when I got so
uneasy fearing some one would find out my whereabouts
my family took me out of bed at my request put me in

a wagon and moved me nearly 4 blocks to a place of
greater safety, where I was carefully nursed by my family
and friends until <u>Sunday Evening 10 Apl 1887.</u> when
I was helped into a wagon and took to Logan and stayed
at the house of a valued friend with Maud until
<u>Tuesday Morning 12th Apl 1887.</u> I walked some distance
to the temple before daylight and resumed my

{89}
labors much to my satisfaction, and with a heart
full of gratitude to god. for it has been a series
of miricals that has given me power to do as
I have done through my sickness. I worked through
the month as usual, nothing of note transpired till
Monday 25 Apl. Wife Mary came from Smithfield and
took Maud to Smithfield and the next day Joseph
took her to Mendon and put her on the train for
Evanston to Visit her Father and 2 Sisters that
are residing there. her health has been much
impaired and we thought the change of air
and surroundings would do her good and help
her health. the balance of April Month passed
off without any change in the programme for the
marshalls were in the Valley. and as viligant as ever

[folded tabular report pasted on the page]

Register of Logan Temple Ordinance Work for Apl. 1887																				
Baptisms								Endowments				Ordinations		Sealings		Children to Parents		Adoptions		Second Anointings			
First		Renewal of Cov.		Health		Dead		Living		Dead		Living	Dead	Living	Dead	Living	Dead	Living	Dead	Living		Dead	
M	F	M	F	M	F	M	F	M	F	M	F								M	F	M	F
–	–	6	10	8	16	318	347	39	48	182	296	1	180	37	135	45	19	2	–	–	–	–
—		16		24		665		87		478		181		172		64		2		—		—	
705								565				181		172		64		2		—			

Samuel Roskelley   Recorder.

The month of May gave us a little more
chance to breath as the marshals were attending the
court. at Ogden part of the time but were in the Valley
looking up witnesses and occasionally dropping on
some one who had been thrown off their guard, and
spotters were plentiful and active, so we had
to be very careful in our visits. During the Month
Prest John Taylor sent Bp John Winder and a man from
Zions Saving Bank to investigate the condition of
the Logan and Smithfield Canal Co and I had
an opportunity to lay before them the state I was
in because of the failure of the company to get

the water in and through the ditch to my farm
this is what I had long desired and came in good
place
[folded tabular report pasted on the page]

Register of Logan Temple Ordinance Work for May 1887.																				
Baptisms								Endowments				Ordinations	Sealings			Children to Parents		Adoptions		Second Anointings
First		Renewal of Cov.		Health		Dead		Living		Dead		Living	Dead	Living	Dead	Living	Dead	Living	Dead	Living	Dead
M	F	M	F	M	F	M	F	M	F	M	F									M	F	M	F
–	1	5	4	22	41	1389	1201	45	55	429	670	1	426	43	353	63	47	1		4	8	3	15
1		9		63		2590		100		1099		427		396		110		1		12		18	
2663								1199				427	396			110		1		30			
Samuel Roskelley Recorder.																							

{90}
the Month of June with its Labors passed with
an occasional breeze made by the marshals in
hunting after our bretheren and friends, the
appointment of Mr. Peters as District Attorney for
the Territory witnessed a little change for the better
Early in June my Wife Maggie hired to go
up Logan Kanyon and cook for Bro Thomas Hill=
=yard and his crew of hands at Coles Saw Mill
and with her Children started for the Kanyon
Wednesday 8 June. this left me alone in Logan
without any family and it proved very lone=
some but we though it might prove for
[folded tabular report pasted on the page]

Register of Logan Temple Ordinance Work for June 1887																							
Baptisms								Endowments				Ordinations	Sealings			Children to Parents		Adoptions		Second Anointings			
First		Renewal of Cov.		Health		Dead		Living		Dead		Living	Dead	Living	Dead	Living	Dead	Living	Dead	Living	Dead		
M	F	M	F	M	F	M	F	M	F	M	F									M	F	M	F
–	–	4	11	13	35	1048	1355	60	78	422	797	3	421	63	347	131	90	1		10	15	3	13
–		15		48		2403		138		1219		424		410		221		1		25		16	
2466								1357				424	410			221		1		41			
Samuel Roskelley Recorder																							

the best good as it seemed impossible
for me to Visit them with any degree of
satisfaction, always being in jopardy and
looking to be caught by marshals I would
generally go home to Smithfield on Friday

evenings and remain till Sunday Evenings
but it always proved a long week to be
away from ones family and loved ones but
I felt it was much better than being in
Prison and guarded by black legs and
associated with wicked men.
During the latter part of June Measures

{91}
were entered into to frame a state constitution
and ask for admission into the Union. as a
soverine state and comities were formed and
worked with a will to accomplish the tasks they
undertook in the matter. the convention met and
framed a constitution ending their general labors
Thursday 7 July 1887. We hope the constitution
framed will be accepted.
On Friday 1st July. With Mary (my Wife) and
my son Joseph I left Logan at 2. P.M and
arrived at Coles saw mill at 1/2 past 10 P.M. finding
Maggie and her children all well and in
the best of spirits and feelings.
[folded tabular report pasted on the page]

Register of Logan Temple Ordinance Work for June 1887 [sic]																		
Baptisms								Endowments				Ordinations		Sealings		Children to Parents		Adoptions		Second Anointings			
First		Renewal of Cov.		Health		Dead		Living		Dead		Living	Dead	Living	Dead	Living	Dead	Living	Dead	Living				Dead	
M	F	M	F	M	F	M	F	M	F	M	F											M	F	M	F
–	–	4	11	13	35	1048	1355	60	78	422	797	3	421	63	347	131	90	1		10	15	3	13
—		15		48		2403		138		1219		424		410		221		1			25		16	
2466								1357				424		410		221		1			41			
Samuel Roskelley Recorder																		

We stayed at camp till Sunday 3rd July
at 4 O'Clock and returned home same night
after a very enjoyable trip – pleasant in Many
ways, and continued my work in the Temple
as usual through the month of July, having
moderately good companies and all working
harmoniously.
2 July. (Friday) I left the temple at 2 O'Clock and
rode ~~home~~ to Hyde Park, with Bro A Toolson and got a
horse and rode home horseback, and the same afternoon
I had the pleasure of meeting my wife Maud who came
home from Evanston leaving the train at Mendon, and
about 8 O'Clock (quite unexpectedly) P.M. my wife
Maggie and children Emma and Ord came from the

Logan Kanyon and I was very pleased to see and
meet them again and Enjoy their society. until
Tuesday morning 26 July 1887, at about 1/2 past

{92}
2 I started with My wife Maud for Logan to resume my
labors in the Temple.
    <u>Tuesday 26th July 1887.</u> Today brought us the
sad tidings of the death of Prest John Taylor which took
place yesterday (Monday) 25 July 1887 at 5 minutes past
8 P.M caused by dropsey, superinduced by close
confinement and lack of exercise. this is a sad
blow to us all at this critical time. the people passing
through the ordeals they are.
<u>Friday 29th July 1887</u> Funeral services were held in
the large tabernacle Salt Lake City over the remains
of Prest John Taylor commencing at 12 noon. appropriate services
were also held in the Temple commencing at 1/2 Past Eight
before Endowments were given. and appropriate rem =
=arks were made by the brethren present.
[folded tabular report pasted on the page]

Register of Logan Temple Ordinance Work for July 1887																		
Baptisms								Endowments				Ordinations		Sealings		Children to Parents		Adoptions		Second Anointings			
First		Renewal of Cov.		Health		Dead		Living		Dead		Living	Dead	Living	Dead	Living	Dead	Living	Dead	Living		Dead	
M	F	M	F	M	F	M	F	M	F	M	F									M	F	M	F
–	–	5	3	9	51	1226	1170	44	64	326	693	–	326	47	222	102	39	–	–	1	4	1	1
—		8		66		2396		108		1019		326		269		141		–	--	5		2	
2470								1127				326		269		141		–		7			
Samuel Roskelley Recorder																		

    Peace and quiet prevailed during the remaining
few days of July and during august. I continued at
my usual labors in the temple uninterrupted on
    <u>Friday 26 August</u> 1887. My wife Mary and son
James and I went up Logan Kanyon and made a visit
to my wife Maggie and children, found the baby Ora
quite sick with whooping cough and teething stayed
till sunday 1.O.'Clock and had an enjoyable time with
my wives. returned to smithfield same night
<u>Monday 29 August 1887.</u> took shortly after day
light with crawp and coldness in my bowels which
was very severe, my family. Mary and Maud did all
they could and I got relief in a few hours. And retu =
= rned to Logan and resumed my labor on the
Evening of same day.

{93}
[folded tabular report pasted on the page]

Register of Logan Temple Ordinance Work for August 1887																									
Baptisms								Endowments				Ordinations		Sealings		Children to Parents		Adoptions		Second Anointings			
First		Renewal of Cov.		Health		Dead		Living		Dead		Living	Dead	Living	Dead	Living	Dead	Living	Dead	Living		Dead	
M	F	M	F	M	F	M	F	M	F	M	F									M	F	M	F
–	–	1	3	8	32	916	1079	28	51	180	419	1	178	37	163	23	38	–	–	4	5		1
—		4		40		1945		79		599		179		200		61		–	–	9		1	
2039								678				179		200		61		—		10			
Samuel Roskelley Recorder																									

Saturday 3rd September 1887. Had the pleasure of
a short visit with Elder D. H. Wells. Who continued
to work with us in the Temple untill 30 Sep during
which time we had many good chats together and
I received much information from him,

1st October. Saturday. Lecture today in the school
by Bro John E. Carlise, subject. Light and Electricity
            Temple closed today today till the 10th Oct
Which was treated very well /\ went home at night with
wife Maud in the buggy and remained at the farm during
sunday, and on
Monday 3 October 1887. My son Joseph and I started
at 6 O'clock for the Coles Mills at the head of Logan
Kanyon to visit my wife Maggie arriving at 1/2 past
6 P.M. and found her preparing to go home, I rem =
=ained with her and helped to fix things ready to
haul home, and started early Friday morning
7 Oct 1887. Arriving at the farm the same night
found all well, and I remained with them till
Monday morning 10th Oct   Son James took me to
Logan in the buggy, arriving before day break.
and continued at my labors in the Temple this the month
without going out door day or night most of the time ~~on~~
except to go home on Saturday night to get a
change of clothing &c. the Deps were very active
and scarcely a day passed without their taking
some good man as a Victim of their Hate and
malice under the disguise and color of law

[folded tabular report pasted on the page]

Register of Logan Temple Ordinance Work for October 1887																								
Baptisms								Endowments				Ordinations		Sealings		Children to Parents		Adoptions		Second Anointings			
First		Renewal of Cov.		Health		Dead		Living		Dead		Living	Dead	Living	Dead	Living	Dead	Living	Dead	Living		Dead	
M	F	M	F	M	F	M	F	M	F	M	F									M	F	M	F
–	1	1	2	16	32	954	549	79	86	280	398	4	279	77	245	115	54		48	3	7	1	4
1		3		48		1503		165		678		283		322		169		48		10		5	
1555								843				283		322		169		48		15			
Samuel Roskelley Recorder.																								

3rd & 4th Maggie moved into the south part of Mary Jane's House and Maud moved into the west room of Sister J— house, for winter quarters.

{94}
1887.
Nov 4&5. Maggie moved into the South part of Mary Jane's house and Maude move into the West part of sister J— house for Winter Quarters.
*Nov 11 <u>Friday</u> Went to Smithfield at night and found all well ,at home.
Nov 11 <u>Saturday</u> spent the day at Mary Janes putting glass in the broken windows and spent sunday at the farm with some of the family – some being at Logan to the confer= ence of the stake. Continued to my Temple labors thro' the week as usual. and Went home to Smithfield. Again on Friday Evening <u>18th November 1887</u> and saw most of the family, and on Saturday 19th helped Maud put down her carpet and arranged her furniture at her rented room at sister J's house. remaining at Smithfield till Monday morning. when I resumed my labor again in the temple, going home again on Saturday Evening <u>Nov 16th 1887</u>. and returning to Logan again on Sunday 27th after dark and bringing Maud with me to Logan to Visit my friends..   during the last few weeks Prest Daniel H. Wells has been working for his dead in the Temple and I have spent Evenings in a most agreeable manner in conversation with him
~~Friday~~
[folded tabular report pasted on the page]

Register of Logan Temple Ordinance Work for November 1887																	
Baptisms								Endowments				Ordinations	Sealings		Children to Parents		Adoptions		Second Anointings			
First		Renewal of Cov.		Health		Dead		Living		Dead		Living	Dead	Living	Dead	Living	Dead	Living	Dead	Living		Dead	
M	F	M	F	M	F	M	F	M	F	M	F											M	F	M	F
1	2	14	16	20	69	1261	1212	81	101	499	723	5	488	83	369	110	109	1	1	4	6	-	1
3		30		89		2473		182		1222		493	452		219		2		10		1	
2595								1404				493	452		219		2		11			

Samuel Roskelley   Recorder

Saturday 3rd December 1887. Maude left for a
Visit to her cousins at Evanston. Wyo, this morning
abt 4 O'clock going by train. from Logan

*Sunday 6 Nov 1887 I took Mary Jane and Maud
in Bro Duce's Buggy and went to Lewiston
and held a meeting with the Bishop and some
of the bretheren and ordained 8 young men
High Priests assisted by the acting Bishop
Wm Wadups and Bro Duce.

[*folded tabular report inserted loosely between pages 94–95*]

Register of Logan Temple Ordinance Work for Sep. 1887																	
Baptisms								Endowments				Ordinations	Sealings		Children to Parents		Adoptions		Second Anointings			
First		Renewal of Cov.		Health		Dead		Living		Dead		Living	Dead	Living	Dead	Living	Dead	Living	Dead	Living		Dead	
M	F	M	F	M	F	M	F	M	F	M	F											M	F	M	F
	1	2	6	13	44	1401	893	57	81	295	579	1	291	63	234	63	67	-	-	2	4	2	11
1		8		57		2294		138		874		292	297		130		—		6		13	
2360								1012				292	297		130		—		19			

Samuel Roskelley   Recorder

{95}
Saturday 3 Dec. attend the lecture at the
Temple by Bro Joseph E. Taylor. on Priesthood
and enjoyed it much and went to Smithfield
saturday Evening (/on\foot) and stayed till Sunday
night. Maggie bringing me down and taking her
sister Lavina back (to stay the week) on Monday
Morning. doing same way on Saturday 10th and 17th
hiding up in my hiding place at Smithfield but having the

company of some members of my family while there. spent the month as usual during my labor in the Temple.

Bro Wm. F. Rigby was arrested on Monday 12 Dec at his home in Newton by Deputy Street and assisted by Com= =missioner Goodwin on the charge of Unlawful Cohabitation and on Friday 23 Dec was sentenced by Judge Hender= =son to Imprisonment in the Pen for 6 months and fine.

Friday 23rd Dec 1887 Went home at night, my daughter Mary meeting me with the buggie, and spent the Saturday 24th at my hiding place and in the Evening went to my house in town and stayed till Monday Morning 26th Dec my Wives Mary, Mary Jane, and Maggie with their children were Present and all ate dinner together my daughter Rebecca and her husband Thos Hillyard also being present, Monday 26 Dec 1887. My son Joseph took me to Logan and before daylight and the companies were lighter than usual through the week.

[folded tabular report pasted on the page]

{95 con't}

Register of Logan Temple Ordinance Work for the year ending Dec. 1887.

Month	Baptisms								Endowments				Ordinations		Sealings		Children to Parents		Adoptions		Second Anointings			
	First		Renewal of Cov.		Health		Dead		Living		Dead		Living	Dead	Living	Dead	Living	Dead	Living	Dead	Living		Dead	
	M.	F.	M.	F.	M.	F.	M.	F.	M.	F.	M.	F.									M.	F.	M.	F.
Jan.	–	2	2	6	12	28	1918	1352	51	75	583	631	2	577	56	373	60	49	–	–	6	7	1	3
Feb	–	–	8	4	8	17	1056	1314	33	43	386	423	1	381	35	225	53	27	1	2	2	4	2	1
Mar.	–	6	6	7	10	30	1327	1416	67	96	459	590	–	436	75	276	60	20	1	2	1	3	1	3
Apl	–	–	6	10	8	16	318	347	39	48	182	296	1	180	37	135	45	19	2	–	–	–	–	–
May	–	1	5	4	22	31	1389	1201	45	55	429	670	1	420	43	353	63	41	1	–	4	8	3	15
June	–	–	4	11	13	35	1048	1355	60	78	422	797	3	421	63	347	131	90	1	–	10	16	4	13
July	–	–	5	3	9	57	1226	1170	44	64	326	693	–	320	47	222	102	39	–	–	1	4	1	1
Aug.	–	–	1	3	8	32	916	1079	28	51	180	419	1	178	37	163	23	38	–	–	4	5	–	1
Sep	–	1	2	6	13	44	1401	893	57	81	295	579	1	291	63	234	63	67	–	–	2	4	2	11
Oct.	–	1	1	2	16	32	954	549	79	86	280	298	4	279	77	245	115	54	–	48	3	7	1	4
Nov.	1	2	14	16	20	69	1261	1212	81	101	499	723	5	488	83	369	110	109	1	1	4	6	–	1
Dec.	1	–	7	10	2	20	644	392	80	95	319	389	–	314	92	191	28	30	–	–	1	1	–	2
	2	8	61	89	121	421	13548	12,180	664	873	4340	6568	19	4297	708	3133	853	589	7	53	38	65	15	55
	10		150		562		35,638		1,537		10,848		4,316	4,316	3,841	3,841	1,442	1,442	60	60	103		70	
	26,360								12,385												173			

Samuel Roskelley Recorder

{96}
1887
29 Dec Friday. My Daughter Mary Meeting me
with the Buggie outside of Logan where I had walked
to I rode home and got supper and went to my
hiding place with Wife Mary Jane and stayed there
Saturday 31st writing up sister Margaret P W. Youngs
record for the Peirce's family and My wife Mary
came in the evening and staid with me till I went
to the farm with her before daylight on
Sunday 1st January 1888.

      I here write my thanksgiving to my
heavenly father for his goodness to me and mine
through the past year. notwithstanding the many
narrow Escapes I have had I have been protected
and blessed and his care has been over me for
good for which I praise his name and trust
his blessings will be over me in the future as
in the past. I pray for the redemption of
Zion and the freedom of the People of God
that Zion and her people may be free. I ask
it in the name of Jesus Christ amen.

{unlined leaf recto}
[blank]

{unlined leaf verso}
 pr Tabitha Ricks
Mdse on Logan Branch 3.50
       order on T Office
Veg 12^{00} Butt 6^{30} – 18.30
Cash   2.2[ ]
                    34.0[ ]

{back pastedown}
[blank]

                [end of journal 5; end of transcript]

Journal [6]

1 January 1888 – 24 November 1901

{cover—ink has been rubbed out of the leather}
Samuel Roskelley's diary
Commencing 1st January 1888.
Closed [rubbed] 1887.

{free front end leaf recto}
[*folded tabular report pasted on the page*]

Register of Logan Temple Ordinance Work for Jan. 1888																		
Baptisms								Endowments				Ordinations		Sealings		Children to Parents		Adoptions		Second Anointings			
First		Renewal of Cov.		Health		Dead		Living		Dead		Living	Dead	Living	Dead	Living	Dead	Living	Dead	Living		Dead	
M	F	M	F	M	F	M	F	M	F	M	F											M	F	M	F
–	–	10	8	2	8	637	240	47	51	200	258	1	197	52	116	8	10	—	—	–	1	1	2
—		18		10		877		98		458		198		168		18		–		1		3	
905								556				198		168		18		–		4			
Samuel Roskelley Recorder																		

{free front end leaf verso}
[*blank*]

{page 1}
Sunday 1 Jan 1888. Before daylight I left my hiding
place with wife Mary and got to the farm just as day broke
and after breakfast sent a team for my wife Mary Jane & children
from town to come and spend My 51st Birthday at the
farm. Maggie and her children were at Newton visiting her
fathers family, her father being in the Penetentiary for
concience sake. And Maud was in Evanston Visiting her

Samuel Roskelley papers, MS 65, Utah State Univ. Special Collections. Line-by-line transcription by page numbers. Page numbers were added to recto pages of the manuscript to simplify matching the transcription to the document. They are given in this transcription between braces.

relatives and nursing a sick woman. Mary provided an Excellent
Dinner and we that were present enjoyed it. In the afternoon my
son James brought my mail- among the rest was a beautiful
White silk Handkerchief sent by Mail from Evanston from Maud
and a beautiful linen Handkerchief from Maggie also a
nice white shirt from my son Joseph all of which I prize very
highly. after spending the day with my loved ones, romping
and playing with the children I went to Logan in the evening with
My son William and resumed my duties in the House of the Lord.
Saturday 7th Jan. Lecture by Bro Wm Apperly. and I went home
at night with son James. returning Sunday night awful
cold and continued so for near 2 weeks – Could hardly bear
to work in the temple it is so cold, companies very light. –
arrests still going on through the Valley.
Saturday 14th Jan. Mary & Mary Jane came to Logan for
me and I stayed at my hiding place till Sunday
night the women bought some coats while at Logan and
Maggie came from Newton and went home to Smithfield
with us after dark-Very Cold-I drove the team. came
to Logan Sunday Evening-Very cold--.
Wednesday 18th Had quite an accident thro the Upper
tank in West tower overflowing which Kept several of us
busy for hours carrying bucks, tubs, pans &c to catch the
water which leaked through 3 floors and damaged
things considerably.
Saturday 21st Jan. went home with Joseph and stayed
in town with Mary Jane & Maggie till Sunday night and
came to Logan with James.
Tuesday 24th Jan Had quite a scare this Evening as
the Roof leaked badly and the water run down through
several floors but did not do much damage to the
Temple other than spot the carpets
28th Jan Saturday. My son James came to Logan and
got a Load of Coal for the family and I rode home with
him after night, the deputy Marshals are very active
Now, there are 4 stationed in Logan. Mary Met me at
my stopping place and remained all night with me. And
Maggie came and staid with me Sunday. till abt 5 O'Clock
when James came with a Sleigh and I covered up with a
Quilt in the Bottom of it and went to the Farm and visited
and ate supper with my sons Hiram and his wife, William
and his wife, and My wives Mary and Maggie and their
children. at 1/2 past 8 OClock William took me

{2}
    1888.
to Logan to attend to my labors there and Joseph to go to school
<u>Saturday 4th Feb 1888</u>. Went home and visited my usual hiding
place and M. Jane stayed all night with me. Ora being sick
Maggie did not come to see me till Sunday eveig when I went
to the farm and then to Logan and persued my usual Vocation

through the week going home again on Friday 11th Feb 1888.
and stayed at my hiding place that night and next day alone
as Ora was sick and Mary had company, but on Saturday
evening I went to Mary Janes & Maggies and found them giving
Ora a sweat – he was quite sick – after which I administered
to him and he dropped off to sleep – sleeping all night. I stayed
there all day Sunday it being Maggies birth day, I enjoyed it with
her – Mary Jane at Logan to conference. I came to Logan
at night, and continued my labors thro the week as usual.
Thursday 17 Feb My Wife Maud returned from Evanston
Where she had been for several weeks on a visit. I went home
Friday night and went to my hiding place and visited with my
Wife Maud Saturday & Sunday, returning to Logan on
Sunday Night and followed my work in the Temple as usual
Saturday 25 Feb 1888. My son Joseph took me home with a team he
had brought for me and I stayed at my usual hiding place with Maud
and Maggie returning to the Temple Monday morning 26 Dec 1888.
The week previous my sons James & William & daughter Rebecca were
taking Endowments for our near kin and Willie & Rebecca did
the sealings so all the work that I have any knowledge of has now
been done.
Thursday 1 Mch 1888. Fast Day – at our usual fast meeting a good
Spirit was manifest – all felt well, Sister Nancy Clark spoke in
tongues and Sister Z. D. Young interpreted to the edification of all
present

[folded tabular report pasted on the page]

Register of Logan Temple Ordinance Work for Feb. 1888																			
Baptisms								Endowments				Ordinations		Sealings		Children to Parents		Adoptions		Second Anointings			
First		Renewal of Cov.		Health		Dead		Living		Dead		Living	Dead	Living	Dead	Living	Dead	Living	Dead	Living				Dead	
M	F	M	F	M	F	M	F	M	F	M	F											M	F	M	F
–	–	11	10	9	14	1434	899	55	59	378	486	2	377	58	270	27	32	3	1	4	4	1	7
–		21		23		2333		114		864		379		328		59		4		8		8	
2377								978				379		328		59		4		16			
Samuel Roskelley Recorder																			

and a general time of rejoicing with those present took place
on Friday 2 Mch 1888 I went home with my son William,
after visiting the farm I went to town and found my wife Mary
Jane sick with neuraligia. I stayed for a few hours and
then visited Maggie after which I went to my hiding place
finding Maud there and stayed till Saturday Evening when
I went again to Mary Janes & Maggies and found Lavina
Card there with her baby. Mary Jane very sick, I
stayed with her till about 3'O'clock next morning when I
went to my hiding place again and stayed till Sunday

{3}
night, when I went to the Farm with Maud and proceeded

to Logan with my son Willie and resumed my labors as
usual in the Temple for the week.
Saturday 10th Mch 1888 My daughter Mary met me at the out
skirts of Logan and I rode home with her in the buggy. Found the
family pretty well except Mary Jane who was quite poorly. I stayed
at my usual hiding place through Sunday, Joseph bringing
me to Logan in the evening, the weather being better
we did a good weeks work in the Temple, and was much
rejoiced on <u>Friday 16 March</u> to have the pleasure of a
Visit from our esteemed apostle George Q Cannon,
I enjoyed a feast with him, I went home with my son
Joseph Saturday night <u>17 Mch</u> Visited the farm and
in town and before day went to the farm Spending Sunday
18 Mch 1888, there. had my wives and 16 children and 1 gd da
and 1 daughter in law. held meeting. all spoke and bore
testimony of the divinity of Gods work and I spoke at some
length, exhorting all to faithfulness and diligence, and
called James on a mission to attend to the farm and
provide for the wants of the family in my absence, we
had an excellent meeting, all felt well, partook of
dinner together and rejoiced in each others society,
my son Joseph bringing me to Logan after dark to resume
my labors in the Holy Temple
Friday 23 Mch 1888. My son William came for me and I went home
with him stopping at my usual hiding place through the night
with Maud after visiting my families in ~~town~~ town, and with
Maud going to the farm Early in the morning (Sunday) remaining
there all day, son James took me to Logan in the Evening,
where I resumed my labors for the week commencing Monday
morning.
Saturday 31st Mch 1888. Attended Lecture and took minutes as
Bro Jas A Leishman was at home waiting upon a sick wife,
Bro L. O. Littlefield lectured on the "Land of Zion," went
home with James, and stayed at my hiding place after
going to see my dear ones in town. Maggie came to
my stopping place and took dinner and stayed the
afternoon with Maud and I, and had a good visit, and we
all enjoyed ourselves. In the Evening I went to Visit sister
Sarah Woodruff and administered to her daughter Mary
who was sick with cold, and then went to farm and stayed
with Mary till 4 O'clock Monday Morning, when Judie
brought me to Logan and Maud came also to see her
folks, and visit them for a few days
      Wednesday 4 Apl 1888. Temple closed for Conference this
Evening and I went to Smithfield
[*folded tabular report pasted on the page*]

Register of Logan Temple Ordinance Work for March 1888																	
Baptisms								Endowments				Ordinations		Sealings		Children to Parents		Adoptions		Second Anointings			
First		Renewal of Cov.		Health		Dead		Living		Dead		Living	Dead	Living	Dead	Living	Dead	Living	Dead	Living		Dead	
M	F	M	F	M	F	M	F	M	F	M	F									M	F	M	F
1	1	4	7	8	24	782	907	38	58	356	545	1	352	43	233	27	31	7	4	–	1	–	6
2		11		32		1689		96		901		353		276		58		11		1		6	
1734								997				353		276		58		11		7			
Samuel Roskelley Recorder																							

{4}
With my son James, Met Hiram at the farm and
arranged for my wife Mary to go to Conference with him
they started Thursday morning 5th Apl 1888. I stayed at
the farm days except Sunday 8th Apl (when I stayed
at my hiding place alone all day) till Monday Evening
9th Apl 1888 when my son James took me to Logan and
I commenced work in the Temple Tuesday morning.
10th Apl. our work through the month being light I
generally managed to go home Friday evenings and return
on Sunday nights the deputies very vigilent and getting
all they possibly can but God be thanked I have the
privelage of laboring in his house and occasionally seeing
my loved ones at home.
[*folded tabular report pasted on the page*]

Register of Logan Temple Ordinance Work for May 1888																	
Baptisms								Endowments				Ordinations		Sealings		Children to Parents		Adoptions		Second Anointings			
First		Renewal of Cov.		Health		Dead		Living		Dead		Living	Dead	Living	Dead	Living	Dead	Living	Dead	Living		Dead	
M	F	M	F	M	F	M	F	M	F	M	F									M	F	M	F
3	–	1	7	10	30	1456	1394	41	53	285	490	1	280	41	193	66	61	–	–	3	5	2	4
3		8		40		2850		94		775		281		234		127		–		8		6	
2901								869				281		234		127		–		14			
Samuel Roskelley Recorder																							

During the month of May I persued the same course
of going home on Friday or Saturday nights and returning
again to my labors in the Temple on Sunday night.
nothing of any particular interest transpired except
that on Tuesday 15 May Marshall Dyer and his attorney
Parley Williams with their short hand reporter visited
the Valley and made a formal demand for the Church
Property Viz. Tithing property, Tabernacle and Square
and Visited the Temple enquiring for the Temple com-
-mittee but did not make any attempt to enter the

building which was closed at the time as it was after hours.

[folded tabular report pasted on the page]

Register of Logan Temple Ordinance Work for Apl. 1888															
Baptisms								Endowments				Ordinations	Sealings		Children to Parents		Adoptions		Second Anointings	
First		Renewal of Cov.		Health		Dead		Living		Dead		Living	Dead	Living	Dead	Living	Dead	Living	Dead	Living	Dead
M	F	M	F	M	F	M	F	M	F	M	F									M	F	M	F
–	–	5	5	2	4	516	381	36	39	114	231	3	114	37	71	38	14	–	–	3	4	–	11
–		10		16		897		75		345		117	108	42		—		7	11
923								420				117	108	42		—		18	

Samuel Roskelley   Recorder

[on back of above tabulation]
15 May 1888
Marshall Dyer & Parly Willies
Visited the Temple grounds

{5}
The Month of June passed much the same as May
I Visited Home and my loved ones as often as I possibly
could. we had the company of some of our leading
brethren occasionally and it was quite refreshing
to the spirit, to see them and hear them talk.
James my son was called and ordained one of
The Presidents of the Quorum of Seventies on 10th
June, S. B Young being mouth, our work still continues
with the blessings of god and is on the increase.

[folded tabular report pasted on the page]

Register of Logan Temple Ordinance Work for June 1888															
Baptisms								Endowments				Ordinations	Sealings		Children to Parents		Adoptions		Second Anointings	
First		Renewal of Cov.		Health		Dead		Living		Dead		Living	Dead	Living	Dead	Living	Dead	Living	Dead	Living	Dead
M	F	M	F	M	F	M	F	M	F	M	F									M	F	M	F
1	1	4	–	11	33	1109	1210	24	45	389	745	—	399	29	261	57	53	5	2	6	14	1	17
2		4		44		2319		69		1134		399	290	110		7		20	18
2369								1203				399	290	110		7		38	

Samuel Roskelley   Recorder

1st July. Thomas Hillyard was arrested today after
being shot at by the deputy. sunday as it was, and
appeared before the Commissioner at Logan an put under Bonds of
$1000.00 and my daughter Rebecca (his wife) $200.00 to appear
before the Grand Jury in Ogden next November - work con
-tinued in the Temple till Friday 13 July when the Temple closed
for a month for renovation and cleaning. I went to Smithfield
at night with wife Maggie, and on

Sunday Morning 15 July 1888 I started with Wife Mary and her
children Richard & Drusie also Maggie and her children Emma
and ora for Bear Lake Valley to Visit Mary's aged parents
and her Brother John and sister Margaret, stopping at
Worm Creek and visited my nieces Janett Kelsey and Elizabeth
Hendrickson and getting dinner with them. Camped about
9 O'clock P.M. by a willow fence about 2 ½ miles from
the fort of the Bear Lake dug way.

Monday 16 July 1888. Started about 6 a.m. and arrived
at John Roberts about 3 O'clock P M after a very pleasant
ride through the Kanyon after a hard walk and pull
up the dug way Road over the mountain, meeting my
wife Mary's father and mother and was made welcome
by them and the family.

Tuesday 17 July 1888 My Brother in law John Roberts hitched
up his team on my buggy and took myself and family to see
Paris and its improvements. called as avid and saw
abell Smart and wife Emma, called at and visited
sister Margaret Morgan and family till night when
we returned to the house of Father and Mother Roberts
except my wife Mary who stayed all night with her
sister Margaret at Liberty.

Wednesday 18 July 1888. My wife Mary came to her pare[nts]
and at 1/2 past one P M I hitched my team and started

{6}
for home by way of Paris, Bloomington, St Charles, to Garden
City, where I arrived about 8 P. M. stopping at the home &
receiving the hospitality of sister Ann Eliza Howland Cook
after taking care of my team I borrowed a boat and took
those of my family present riding on the Lake, Bear
Lake was as smooth as a sea of Glass. not a ripple
on its surface, returned to sister Cooks. took supper
and retired to bed at a late hour.

Thursday 19 July 1888 started up Garden City Kanyon
about 8 a m, and nooned at the old U O saw mill
site in Logan Kanyon. Maggie was afflicted with sick
head ache – and I took a long nooning to let her sleep a
little while, started down the Kanyon about 2 O'clock , had
traveled about 8 miles when it came up a heavy rain
and thunder storm, having no cover on our buggy we
were exposed to the storm and were badly drenched,
for at least an hour or more. I had expected to camp over
night in Logan Kanyon but the storm changed my program
and I drove through to Smithfield arriving about midnight
found the family well as usual, nothing of unusual interest
had transpired during my absence. – stayed at the farm
on Friday 20 July till evening when I went to Logan to
appear before the stake High Council to answer a charge
preferred by Bro W. F Rigby against me and the Brothers
Vannoy for not paying certain debts due to the credit

-ors of the firm of Vannoy & Company – the complaint having
first been laid before the Presidency of the church and
prefered to the High Council of this stake, after investi-
-gation the council found no cause for such action on
Bro Rigbys part and desired the members of the late firm
of Vannoy & Co to get together and fix the business
among ourselves. I spent the time till Sunday 29th July
around home doing what I could to comfort & bless my
family. and Sunday Evening 29 July Mary took me to
Logan and I commenced my work of Copying on Monday
morning feeling glad to get back again to my usual
work and place in the Temple of God. My assistant
came to work (Bro Leishman) on Tuesday Morning so I
had company till the Temple opened again.
on Saturday 4 Aug 1888. I went home in the
Evening with My wife Mary and visited the family
returning on Monday Morning shortly after day
light. Maggie bringing me down, worked thru
the week at copying and returned home on
<u>Friday Evening 10 aug 1888.</u> after Visiting my folks
in town. went to the farm before day light and
soon found my wife M sick I hastily put a
Horse in the buggy and sent her to a place of

{7}
safety, and I went a foot.
      Saturday 11 Aug 1888. My wife Maud gave birth
to a son at 12.20 standard mountain time,
and I thank my heavenly father that he has given
us another beautiful child to be a comfort and blessing
to us, its parents. I stayed with M. Keeping my
wife Maggie company till Sunday evening when I
went to Logan and resumed my labors in the House
of the Lord.
[*folded tabular report pasted on the page*]

Register of Logan Temple Ordinance Work for July 1888																			
Baptisms								Endowments				Ordinations		Sealings		Children to Parents		Adoptions		Second Anointings			
First		Renewal of Cov.		Health		Dead		Living		Dead		Living	Dead	Living	Dead	Living	Dead	Living	Dead	Living				Dead	
M	F	M	F	M	F	M	F	M	F	M	F											M	F	M	F
2	2	4	4	8	20	399	613	23	31	138	273	–	136	25	117	41	18	–	–	–	–	–	–
4		8		28		1012		54		411		136		142		59		–		–		
1052								465				136		142		59		–		—			

Samuel Roskelley   Recorder

Saturday 18 August. I went to Smithfield with
wife Mary and about ½ past 10 O'Clock P.M.
with my son James blessed my son lately born
and called its name Marriner. Mother &

child doing well. Stayed with them during
Sabbath and returned to Logan on the Sunday
Evening resumed my labors again in the House
of the Lord. The Temple opened for work on
Monday 13th Aug 1888 and my time was well occu-
-pied in the labors thereof during the rest of the
month of August.

[folded tabular report pasted on the page]

Register of Logan Temple Ordinance Work for Aug. 1888

Baptisms								Endowments				Ordinations		Sealings		Children to Parents		Adoptions		Second Anointings			
First		Renewal of Cov.		Health		Dead		Living		Dead		Living	Dead	Living	Dead	Living	Dead	Living	Dead	Living		Dead	
M	F	M	F	M	F	M	F	M	F	M	F									M	F	M	F
1	1	3	3	12	28	665	791	36	45	229	364	1	225	35	165	55	44	1	—	1	3	—	2
2		6		40		1456		81		593		226		200		99		1		4		2	
1504								674				226		200		99		1		6			

Samuel Roskelley   Recorder

[folded tabular report pasted on the page]

Register of Logan Temple Ordinance Work for Sep. 1888

Baptisms								Endowments				Ordinations		Sealings		Children to Parents		Adoptions		Second Anointings			
First		Renewal of Cov.		Health		Dead		Living		Dead		Living	Dead	Living	Dead	Living	Dead	Living	Dead	Living		Dead	
M	F	M	F	M	F	M	F	M	F	M	F									M	F	M	F
—	1	6	3	17	50	1163	1218	48	73	398	617	3	391	56	273	94	94	—	1	3	5	3	8
1		9		67		2381		121		1015		396		329		188		1		8		11	
2458								1136				396		329		199		1		19			

Samuel Roskelley   Recorder

During the Month of september nothing of
Unusual interest transpired although the Deputies
Were Very active in Cache County and on
The 17th inst Pres. Geo Q Cannon gave himself up
to the U S. Marshall in the morning appeared in
court – plead guilty to 2 Charges of Unlawful
Cohabitation and was sentenced to pay a fine
of $450.00 and sent to the Penn for 175 days,
all transpiring in one day.

{8}
[unidentified clipping, possibly from the Utah Journal]
Pardons in Utah.
Washington, Sept. 14—In answer
to the resolution, introduced by Delegate DuBoise, calling for information respecting convictions and par-
don for polygamy, the Attorney Gen-

eral has replied in a communication, in which he says that under the provisions of the anti-poligamy law of 1882 and its amendments there have been in the Territory of Utah 470 convictions for polygamy, adultery and unlawful cohabitation, in which fines were imposed, and thirty convictions where the sentence was imprisonment without fine, making in total for the Territory of 500. in Idaho there was a total of 87 cases. There have been 14 pardons granted by the President to persons convicted under the above mentioned acts, which were generally made upon the recommendation of the court and Territorial officials on the grounds of old age, ignorance of the law and extreme poverty. There was 1 conviction in Utah in 1875, 1 in 1881, 4 in 1884, 55 in 1885, 132 in 1886, 220 in 1887 and 105 1888. Fines to the amount of $48,209 have been collected and a forfeiture or $25,000.

[*diary text*]

Friday

Oct 5 Temple closed for work last Evening to give those that wish a chance to go to Conference, and this Evening I got to Smithfield and go to Mary Janes Early Saturday morning 6 Oct and stay there all day. fixing up what I Could in the house without being observed, in the Evening, My son Williams came and I blessed agnes' babe calling it William Leonard afterward went to ~~the farm~~ my stopping place for the night and went to the farm next morning before day, Staying & visiting there all day. and going to Logan at night.

<u>Monday 8 Oct 1888</u>. Resumed usual labor in the House of the Lord and continued till Friday evening 12 Oct 1888. at which time I went to Smithfield and found my wife Mary Jane in labor but it passed off and she rested somewhat Easy – I resumed my usual labor again in the house of the Lord <u>Monday 15 Oct 1888</u> On the Wednesday night following about midnight I was woke up. I found my Son James had come after me as my Wife, Mary Jane was very sick with Labor pains but my previous days work had been so heavy and varied I had not been able to close it up or make out the bulletin and the papers were lying on the desk promiscuously in such a shape I alone could straighten them out so I declined going — fearing my work in the Temple would be misplaced so I could not put it together. this circumstance never had occurred but

2 or 3 times before in my recollection and I hope never will
ever again—I spent the night in supplicating my Heavenly
father to Bless and aid my Dear Wife Which he did, for
on Thursday morning at ½ past 5 we were blessed with
another son. being My 12th boy. and 11th child under 9 yrs old
10 of whom are living now. He was born Thursday morning
18 Oct 1888 at ½ past 5 A.M. I went home on Friday Evening
19th Oct to Comfort my wife and family. returning to Logan
again to Sunday Evening 21 Oct. 1888. and continued my

{9}
Usual labors in the House of the Lord thro' the week. I again
went to Smithfield on Friday Evening 26th Oct 1888 and found
my wives Maggie and Maud at Mary Janes. I blessed the baby
giving the name of George at the request of its Mother Mary Jane
After her Brother George. Stayed all night with Maggie and
on Saturday 19th I sawed wood in the House the Children could saw
it in lengths and bring it to me. At night I went and stayed
with Maud. Mary brought me to Logan Sunday night 28.
Oct 1888. to resume my labors in the House of the Lord.
Saturday 3 Nov 1888. My son James took me Home it
rained & snowed all night and the next day Sunday 4 Nov
and some of my family attended the Quarterly Conference
at Logan in consequence of the storm, but on Monday
Morning 5 Nov my Wife Mary & daughter Mary and Son
James & I started a little after 5 oclock in the Morning
from my farm for Logan arriving at the temple
soon after 7.a.m. I resumed my Temple labor and
my family attended the Quarterly Conference.
[folded tabular report pasted on the page]

Register of Logan Temple Ordinance Work for October 1888																			
Baptisms								Endowments				Ordinations		Sealings		Children to Parents		Adoptions		Second Anointings			
First		Renewal of Cov.		Health		Dead		Living		Dead		Living	Dead	Living	Dead	Living	Dead	Living	Dead	Living				Dead	
M	F	M	F	M	F	M	F	M	F	M	F									M	F	M	F
–	1	11	14	19	57	1100	970	81	95	425	603	4	415	92	283	194	122	1	1	2	7	2	–
1		25		76		2070		176		1028		419		375		316		2		9		2	
2172								1204				419		375		316		2		11			
Samuel Roskelley Recorder																			

Saturday 10 Nov 1888. James was at Logan most of
the day and borrowed $250⁰⁰ from Thatcher Bros for 3 months
at 1¼ per cent per month. I sent $100⁰⁰ East for a Fanning
Mill and a horse power and feed Mill. and in
the Evening I went to Smithfield with him and had
a short Visit with the Family and went to the farm
before day light—staying there through Sunday 11th Nov
having the company of my Wives Mary, Maggie & Maud
also Daughter Rebecca and her Husband Thomas

Hillyard. Maggie and Catherine brought me down
also Rhoda Burton came with with [sic] us after Visiting
her sister Maud for the past week.

Monday 12 Nov 1888. I resumed my labor in the House
of the Lord. My Wife Maggie moved to Logan to
live with her sister Lavina Card through the winter
I visited her Tuesday Evening 13th Nov.

Thursday 15th James Came to Logan to arrange for
a place to board while going to school, his prejudice
prevented him from boarding with His Auntie Maggie
he preferred to stay with strangers. I can sympathize
with Men who are so unfortunate as to loose the
mother of children by death. it seems that the
more my wives do for my sons the less my sons like
to do for them which is a source of annoyance to me and
I would desire it otherwise.

{10}

James quit work at the farm on Wednesday 14 Nov 1888
Thursday he went to Logan, Friday fix the will & attended
a dance. Saturday it rained all day, and he starts to
school Monday 19 Nov 1888.

Friday 16 Nov My wife Mary Came for me and I went
home with her and spent the day Saturday at the farm
also part of Sunday, returning to Logan Sunday Evening
with wife Maggie and Visited her again on Tuesday
evening. learned of the death of my most Esteemed sister
and friend sister Nancy Areta Porter Clark. who died of
Pneumonia at the House of her son in Cassia County Idaho
on Tuesday 13th inst and was buried on the 18th at
Farmington, I had Known her a number of years
but who has worked for the past 3 years in the Temple
at Logan and we have been on the most intimate
terms since then and I formed the highest opinion
of her as a Latter day saint.

Monday 19th Nov 1888. Bro Camper comenced to
work for me at $25⁰⁰ per Month. Moving into my old
Log house in town for the winter

Saturday 24 Nov 1888. Went home to Smithfield
and stayed till Sunday Evening. Maud came to Logan
with Mary to visit her folks and stay with them for
a short time,

30 Nov (Friday) Wife Mary Came for me and I enjoyed
the ride home, went to see Mary Jane at night and
also the children, I shall be thankful indeed
when I can go and see my family and stay as I
may wish without fear. God hasten the day I pray
Continually for there is no comfort or pleasure now
stealing through the streets and over fences like one
was a criminal of the blackest diye. returned
to Logan Sunday Evening, 2 Dec. 1888 and passed

the week pleasantly as I spent 2 Evenings with those
I loved as members of my family. John Roberts
(Marys Brother) arrived from Bear Lake on Sunday
to go with Mary to do Temple work, through the
week for their dead Kindred. I came to Logan
and returned again with Mary to Smithfield 7 Dec
Maggie and Children going with me.
[*folded tabular report pasted on the page*]

Register of Logan Temple Ordinance Work for Nov. 1888.																			
Baptisms								Endowments				Ordinations		Sealings		Children to Parents		Adoptions		Second Anointings			
First		Renewal of Cov.		Health		Dead		Living		Dead		Living	Dead	Living	Dead	Living	Dead	Living	Dead	Living		Dead	
M	F	M	F	M	F	M	F	M	F	M	F									M	F	M	F
1	1	4	5	11	35	1041	875	82	91	359	611	2	353	77	305	70	66	–	–	6	7	2	9
2		9		46		1916		173		970		355		382		136		—		13		11	
1973								1143				355		382		136		—		24			
Samuel Roskelley Recorder																			

{11}
My Fanning Mill, Horse Power and Feed
Chopper had arrived from the East and on Saturday
8th Dec My son James and I set it together, they
worked quite satisfactory and with care will do
us good service for years to come, we cleaned up
some grain and chopped some feed for the Horses
and hogs. I worked at the farm on Saturday and
remained all day Sunday Visiting my family,
return with Maggie to Logan in the Evening. Visiting
her & Maud through the Week, going to Smithfield with
Mary on Friday Evening 14th Dec. worked with my sons
Cleaning wheat Saturday, stayed at the farm this Sunday Visiting
my son Hyrum who had returned from the north and on
Sunday Evening my daughters Mary and Catherine took me to Logan
to resume my labors in the Temple, When at smithfield I Visited
my Wife Mary Jane and found our babe George quite sick with
Cold. I blessed it feeling it would get better, I learned through
the week the was quite sick.
Friday 21st Dec. It being Very dark in the Evening I visited My
wife Maud who was stopping at her parents in Logan during
Christmas, returning to the Temple again and resuming my
labors there during Saturday, My wife Mary came for me in the
Evening and I rode home with her, and went to see my wife
Mary Jane and our Children, the babe was quite sick yet with
cough and cold. but I think considerable better than when I
was at home last, I stayed during the night and most of the
day Sunday, going to the farm Sunday afternoon in the
buggie under cover of some hay. My daughters Mary and
Catherine took me to Logan , it rained all the way and the

roads were very bad and very dark.
Monday 24th Dec 1888. Took record for baptism in the morning
and baptized in the afternoon, and in the evening went home to Smith-
-field with my son James, remaining at the farm during the night
25 Dec 1888 about 11 Oclock rode to Mary Janes family. had
a good well prepared dinner. which all seemed to enjoy.
Bros Thomas Kelsey and Bro Thos Hillyard called during the
day and spent a few hours with me quite agreeably.
rode to Logan in the Evening with Bro Camper to resume
my labors in the house of the Lord.
Wednesday 27 Dec 1888. by Previous appointment Met
with apostle Moses Thatcher at his house in the Evening.
And tendered my resignation as Prest of H.P. Quorum
Cache Valley Stake, as I had been in Exile so long and
there were no prospects at present of any change and I
felt I was only in the way of some one who might do good
in looking after the Quorums My Councillors were also
in Exile and could do nothing. Bro Moses refused to accept
my resignation, but advised me to select 2 good men
who were footloose as temporary councilors and set

{12}
them to work with the Quorum, until the Cloud
rolled by and peace came to use again.
  I also talked to him about giving myself up to the
officers of the law and submitting myself for trial—
but he thought this very unwise at present and thought
it best for me to continue my labors in the temple
and get along with family and other affairs as best
I could until changes took place that would prove
more favorable for the saints.
Friday 28 Dec 1888. My daughter Mary Came with a
team and I took my wives, Maggy & Maud with their children
to the farm to spend New Years, I worked Saturday in
cleaning wheat with my son James, and Bro Camper, and
Sunday spent Visiting with the family at the farm. My wife
Maggie & daughter Catherine brought me to Logan Sunday
Evening. Took Record for Baptisms and baptized on Monday
at the Temple had a very light Company. and went to
Smithfield in the Evening with my daughter Mary. but
the buggie runner broke down and I had to leave the
buggie and My daughter rode the horse home and
I took it afoot. while the rough frozen ground with
but littler snow made quite unpleasant Walking,
I slept at the farm.
       1 Jan 1889.
O God, I thank thee in the name of Jesus Christ thy son
for the Many blessings bestowed on me through the past year.
for the blessing of health and children being born to
me and that I have with my family been blessed and
preserved from the hands of Marshalls and spies

while Visiting My loved ones and traveling to & from
my homes to care for those thou has given me. I thank
the for the Gospel and all the blessings connected there=
=with and may the spirit of Unity remain with my family
for Ever, and in thine own due time give me and mine
the privelage of association together without fear of moles=
=tation or annoyance from the wicked. and in thine own
way deliver me and mine from financial Embarrisment
and give us all that is necessary for our support
and comfort, but above all may the spirit of thy holy
Gospel ever be and abide with us, I thank thee for the
privelage of laboring in thy holy Temple and that mine
Eyes have seen thy salvation manifested therein in
salvation for the living and redemption for the dead.
May thy blessings and the Guidance of the holy
Ghost remain with us the coming year to guide
us safely to thy salvation. I ask it in the name
of Jesus Christ thy son. Amen.

My Wives Mary, Maggie & Maud were at
the farm and I sent for Mary Jane form town, and all
Enjoyed ourselves singing and conversing together,

{13}
about noon my son Hyram came with Wife Vina and
her children also my sons James & William came.
they reported Samuel Very sick in the afternoon
Bros Thos Hillyard came, we all had a sumptuous
dinner—setting 3 tables, so all could eat. I was
only sorry that for fear of suspicion that I was at
home I could not invite all my daughters=in
law to partake of our Hospitality, as it was, I
had 4 wives, 19 children, 6 G^d children, 1 son in law
1 daughter in law to dinner. And in the afternoon I
read a portion of my history that I have lately been
writing and compiling. After dark I rode to my son
Samuels house and administered to him with sons
Hiram & William after which my son William took me
to Logan. Wednesday 2 Jan 1889. resumed my
labors in the Temple of God, continuing until
Friday Evening 4 Jan 1889. I rode to Smithfeld with
My daughter Mary. the weather very cold and
has been for several days past, quite uncom=
=fortable in the temple.
{continues next page}

{13 con't}
[folded tabular report pasted on the page]

Register of Logan Temple Ordinance Work for the yr. 1888

Mon.	Baptisms									Endowments				Ordinations		Sealings		Children to Parents		Adoptions		Second Anointings			
	First		Renewal of Cov.		Health		Dead			Living		Dead		Living	Dead	Living	Dead	Living	Dead	Living	Dead	Living		Dead	
	M.	F.	M.	F.	M.	F.	M.	F.		M.	F.	M.	F.									M.	F.	M.	F.
Jan	–	–	10	8	2	8	637	240		47	51	200	258	1	197	52	116	8	10	–	–	–	1	1	2
Feb	–	1	11	10	9	14	1434	899		55	59	378	486	2	377	58	270	27	32	3	1	4	4	1	7
Mar	1	–	4	7	8	24	782	907		38	58	356	545	1	352	43	233	27	31	7	4	–	1	–	6
Apl	–	–	5	5	2	14	516	381		36	39	114	231	3	114	37	71	28	14	–	–	3	4	–	11
May	3	–	1	7	10	30	1456	1394		41	53	285	490	1	280	41	193	60	61	–	–	3	5	2	4
June	1	1	4		11	33	1109	1210		24	45	389	745	–	399	29	261	57	53	5	2	6	14	1	17
July	2	2	4	4	8	20	399	613		23	31	138	273		136	25	117	41	10	–	–	–	–	–	–
Aug	1	1	3	3	12	28	665	791		36	45	229	364	1	225	35	165	55	44	1	–	1	3	–	2
Sep	–	1	6	3	17	50	1163	1218		48	73	398	617	5	391	56	273	94	94	–	1	3	5	3	8
Oct	–	1	11	14	19	57	1100	970		81	95	425	603	4	415	92	283	194	120	1	1	2	7	2	–
Nov	1	1	4	5	11	35	1041	875		82	91	359	611	2	353	97	305	70	66	–	–	6	7	2	9
Dec	1	4	4	9	11	20	465	625		57	66	197	329	1	197	61	148	22	23	1	–	1	3	1	2
	10	12	67	75	120	333	10767	10123		568	706	3468	5552	21	3436	606	2435	689	568	15	9	28	54	13	68
	22		142		453		20890			1274		9020		3457		3041		1,257		27		83		81	
							21,507			10,294				3,457		3,041		1257		27		164			

Samuel Roskelley   Recorder

{13 con't}
Saturday. Spent the day cleaning wheat
at the farm, staid at my hiding place with
M thro' the night and with her went to my dau=
=ghter's before daylight and spent the day under
the Happiest Circumstances altho in Exile,
My wives were all there and some of my children &
grand children, and out visit was a pleasant one.
we had an Excellent dinner and. at night I went
to Logan in company with son James to my usual
Labors in the Temple I have felt for a month past and
said to some of the family that a change of some
sort was at our door. I did not know what it
was. On Tuesday Evening 8 Jan 1889 I left the
Temple about 1/4 to 7 to visit sister Ricks and learn
if she had heard anything of my son Samuel at
smithfield who is lying sick at Smithfield
It is possible some one saw me leave the
Temple and saw me go to sister Ricks as I had
been there but a short time when the deputy
Marshall Hudsons came into the house and asked

{14}
for me. I was so disguised on the street that I
am sure no one Knew me, so some one that Knew
me must have been with the deputy and pointed me
out by looking thro' the window. after reading the
warrat of arrest I put on my hat and walked to
the commissioners office with the Deputy my son James
accompanying me and was put under $1000.00 bonds
A. J. Bowker & B. F. Riter (a gentile) signed the bonds &
I was notified to appear at 2p.m. next day with
Mary. Mary Jane, Maggie. James & Daughter Mary
as witnesses for whom I agreed to be responsible
without bonds, My son James borrowed a team from
Bro Robert Roberts and we went to smithfield arriv=
=ing at midnight. I visited each of my family & told
them what to prepare for, as I was satisfied as to the
charge that was designed to be alleged under the one
mentioned. Viz—adultery with Mary Jane as she had
a child 2 months old, arrived at Logan with Son
James about 4 o'clock a.m. and took a short nap
before commencing work in the Temple – did my usual
work under difficulties as the workers & visitors had
learned that I was arrested and they poured much
sympathy in my ears for which I felt grateful, every body
I met seemed to feel bad – I visited W. W. Maughan and
engaged him to plead for me as attorney at law. I told
my case to him. but he had no faith in my being dis=
=charged, but thought I would be held under bonds,
to appear before the grand Jury at Ogden. I told him I did

not believe a word of it for I felt my time had come
to be out among the saints. I left the Temple at 1/2
past one after committing my case to the lord in his
Holy House, Every one I met told me they had pray-
=ed to the Lord, for my release, I felt like a child in
my feelings and if Father wanted me to go to the Pen
I felt all right about it, I went to the County
Court House and with my attorney walked to the
commissioners office at 2 P M, and found my family
had arrived, the witnesses were examined and
criticized but their testimony was so straight in my
favor that my attorney asked for my discharge
for lack of evidence, to convict, which was done
without quibble, Friends on every hand shook me
by the hand and Congratulated me on my deliverance
which seemed a mystery to all but my heavenly
father & myself. the rejoicing among the Temple
workers the next morning was unbounded, and many
a heart full of gratitude was poured out to the father

{15}
of mercies for his overruling Kindness in giving me my
freedom,
Thursday 10th Jan. Bro M. W. Merrill came from Richmond
today and reported that the U.S. deputy Marshalls had
arrested him at home today – this caused another
streak of gloom to overshadow up, not Knowing what
might be the outcome, but we trust in the Lord
Saturday 12 Jan I went with Bro M. W. Merrill to the Commis=
=sioners Office at 10 O'Clock meeting his family there and
gave them such advice as I could under the circumstan=
=ces which cheered them up and made them feel better,
as in my case the evidence Elicited from the witnesses
was so straight that the attorney Bro James T. Hammond
asked for the discharge of Bro Merrill which was done
and Bro Merrill went off rejoicing in the Lord I retu=
=rned to the Temple to my usual Work and in the Eveing
rode home with my son Hiram, after Visiting at the Farm
a few hours. I went to see M[aud] and Stayed all night with
her returning to the farm in the Morning Early. and staying
till 1/2 past one P.M. then went with wives Mary & Maggie
to town to Mary Janes and from there to meeting. a larger
congregation had assembled Expecting to see and hear Bro
Angus M. Cannon. but he had gone to Salt Lake City and
I occupied the afternoon talking to the Saints and had good
freedom in so doing. After Meeting I returned to the
farm and at night had M[aud] moved up to the farm also
and I returned to Logan with son William.
Tuesday. 15 Jan 1889. Bro M. W. Merrill was summonsed
before the grand Jury sitting at Ogden but we do not Know
in what case he will be required to testify.. I attended

the High Priests Meeting at Logan Tabernacle last Evening
(Monday) for the first time for about 2 years & 8 months
and had a good meeting, and many congratulated me
on being a free man once more.
Thursday 17th Jan. Prest Merrill returned from Ogden having
answered such Questions as the grand Jury prest to him,
I attended a meeting of the people at Providence in the Evening in
Company with Pres William Walker a good spirit prevailed
I talked about 1 hour and returned to Logan to the Temple
Friday 18 Jan 1889. Went home in the Evening with my
daughter Rebecca & son James. stayed at the farm all
night and helped clean up wheat the next day with the fan
mill, and went to town in the Evening calling on Sister Sarah
Woodruff and chatting some time with her and her son Newton..
stayed at Mary Janes till all night having a good romp
with the children and learning that the Z saving Bank
were about to sell my farm to satisfy the mortgage they
hold on my property in favor of the Logan & Smithfield Canal
Company I started for Salt Lake City at 6.25 P.M. staying
over night at Ogden and arriving at Salt Lake at 11.30 a.m.
Interviewed the Presiding Bishopric and the bank authorities
and had a good talk with Prest W. Woodruff at the

{16}
Gardo House. and had good chat also with Bro John L
Nuttall also Prest F D Richards. – finally got my arrange=
=ments made with the bank manager so they would not
   I also paid up the interest on my note to October 1888
sell my farm /\ and returned home to Logan Wednesday
Evenings train arriving at the Temple Thursday Morning abt
4.30 A.M. a Very Cold night. I stayed 1 night at Salt
Lake City with Bro T. C Griggs and one night with Bro J H.
Moyle the Supt of Construction of the Salt Lake Temple
and had a good visit with both parties. .Bp Preston
treated me exceptionally Kind, being much interested in my
affairs with the Canal Company. continued my labors at the
Temple till Saturday night when I went home to Smithfield and
settled my tithing with Bro Sharp the clerk paying
for the year 1888, and arranged with Bro Sharp to make
a new Mortgage on My farm favor of Zions Saving bank
left for the farm the same night and staid with M., and Kept
in Exile Sunday 27 Jan 1889. to comfort and cheer my loved
ones who are also in Exile, and Sunday night I came
to Logan Mary Js bringing me with a grist for the Mill,
Monday 28 Jan I spent the Evening with Maggie and our chil=
=dren and staid the night, also spent the night of Wednesd=
=ay 30th Jan at the same place and with Gods help and blessing
I shall see my loved ones and stay with them as often as
I possably can, James my son went to Smithfield and got
the Mortgage and note from Bro F Sharp and brought it to
me and I filed it with the County recorder to be recorded

at 1/2 past 10 Thursday 31 Jan 1889. and get his Rec^t
for it and sent the note and Receipt for mortgage to
the Bank (to B. H. Schuttler) on Friday, morning and in
the Evening went to smithfield to see my loved ones..
[*folded tabular report pasted on the page*]

Register of Logan Temple Ordinance Work for Jan. 1889																							
Baptisms								Endowments				Ordinations		Sealings		Children to Parents		Adoptions		Second Anointings			
First		Renewal of Cov.		Health		Dead		Living		Dead		Living	Dead	Living	Dead	Living	Dead	Living	Dead	Living				Dead	
M	F	M	F	M	F	M	F	M	F	M	F									M	F	M	F
2	–	7	3	12	14	679	392	43	52	359	428	1	356	50	247	27	29	–	1	3	9	4	3
2		10		26		1071		95		787		357		297		56		1		12				7	
1109								882				357		297		56		1		19			
Samuel Roskelley Recorder																							

Saturday 2nd Feb 1889. At the Farm with my sons
James & William cleaning (Fanning) wheat and sold
Enough to Thos Richardson at 80cts to pay for the last
note on our McCormick Harvester of $93^{00} due on
15th last Nov. went to town at night and stayed at
Mary Janes and on Sunday morning 3rd Feb rode to
Logan with Bert. Barber and attended the Cache Stake
Quarterly Conference and was greeted by almost every
one I met as I have not attended a conference of
the saints since august 1886, it seemed a long time
while going through it, but a very short time to look
back upon the Exile I have undergone, the meetings
were well attended, 5 meetings were held and good
instructions given by Bro Moses Thatcher Bp Preston
and other Elders. I had to privelage of talking 20
minutes – all seemed to Enjoy a good spirit. &
feeling. I stayed all night with Maggie.

{17}
5 Feb 1889. Tuesday. Resumed work in the Temple
a good days baptisms, and the following days we had
good companies for Ordinance work, went home on Friday
Evening 8th Feb 1889. Maggie and the children going with me
stayed at the farm cleaning up some wheat & lucern seed on
Saturday 9th Feb. going to town late in the Evening and remain
all night with Mary Jane and the children.
Sunday 10th Feb 1889. Bro Thos Duce called for me at 9 a.m.
And we went to Lewiston, called at Viney's and got dinner
and went to meeting at 1. P.M. several Bishops from
other Settlements came. to the High Priests meeting and we
had a most Excellent meeting – a time of rejoicing so many
were present that had been Under Ground and through
the courts &c and Bro Duce had been to prison for his
Religion,. At 4. P.M we started to Richmond and held

meeting at 7 P.M. With a full congregation Bro Duce and I
occupied the time, the congregation were very quiet altho--.
Composed mostly of young people. I returned to Smithfield
to my farm at night, and with wife Maggie and her
children returned to Logan on Monday morning and
resumed my Temple Labors,
Monday Evening 11th Feb. I visited and stayed with
Maggie all night and Wednesday Evening 13 Feb
I visited Maggie & children and Wife Maud and
stayed with the latter all night. Going to smithfield
on Friday Evening 15th Feb with Bro Merrill and Visited and
stayed at the farm thro the night and during saturday
fixing up the place, and at night I went to town
and Visited wife Mary Jane and family and stayed
over night.
Sunday 17th Feby 1889. went to Hyde Park with my
team and met Bro Thos Duce and went to Newton
and changed teams and Bro Benson of Newton took
us to Clarkston, ate dinner with Bp. Jardine
and went to afternoon meeting. Bro Duce & I prea
=ched. a good spirit prevailed, after meeting went
to Newton and ate supper with Sister Betsey
Griffin whose husband is in the Pen, went to.
meeting a good attentive Congregation. and Bro Duce
and I preached he 40 and I 50 minutes. after which
we came to Hyde Park arriving at 11.P.M. Slept at
Bro Duce's. Monday 18th Feb after Breakfast Bro
Duce brought me to Logan, having spent a pleasant
time with the saints, and resumed my labors in the house
of the Lord, on Monday Evening I visited my Wife Maggie &
children and stayed all night, also on Wednesday Evening and
on Thursday Evening 21 Feb I went to Hyde Park with Bro
J. W. D Hurren and met Bp Daines who had just returned
home from Canada and had given himself up to the

{18}
officers of the law—been tried and acquitted.
He and I walked into the Meeting House together.
which was filled with people the Bp had not
been to meeting there since I had about 3 1/2 years
since and the people seemed glad to see us,
Bp Daines talked a few moments and I followed
about 65 minutes on Temple work, a good spirit
prevailed. I remained at Hyde Park all night
and went to Logan on Friday Morning with Elder
Sud Lamb. resuming my labors in the House of
the Lord. and going to Smithfield at night and worked
thro' the day saturday and returned to Logan at night
staying saturday night. Sunday & sunday night
with Maggie & Maud and our children, and had a
good visit, with them. resuming my labors in

the Temple on Monday morning, Visiting the wives
above named thro' the week and on
Saturday 2 Mch 1880. attended the Priesthood
meeting of the stake and spoke about 30 minutes
on the times we live in" and in the afternoon I
attended the school at the Temple,. and heard a lecture
by Elder C. F Nibley. on the necessity of Leaders.
going to smithfield with my daughter mary in
the Evening and traded my nursery with my son
Samuel, giving him lots 1.2 3.1a Block 27 Plat a
smithfield survey for his Railway outfit now
in Washington Territory. Consisting of 6 Head of Horses
[folded tabular report pasted on the page]

Register of Logan Temple Ordinance Work for Feb. 1889																
Baptisms								Endowments				Ordinations	Sealings		Children to Parents		Adoptions		Second Anointings			
First		Renewal of Cov.		Health		Dead		Living		Dead		Living	Dead	Living	Dead	Living	Dead	Living	Dead	Living		Dead	
M	F	M	F	M	F	M	F	M	F	M	F									M	F	M	F
3	1	6	8	15	28	1441	1111	33	39	422	467	1	421	37	289	26	32	1	-	-	1	1	1
4		14		43		2552		72		889		422	326		58		1		1		2	
2613								961					326		58		1		3			
Samuel Roskelley Recorder																

{19}
Viz Foll, & blue, Charley & Poley, Cheap & Barney one of
the horses now belongs to me, 3 sets of Harness, 2. 5th
chains, crotch.Chain & stretchers chain, 1 Wagon with a
rack on and 1 wagon with a bed on, 2 tents, 2 tongue
scrapers, 1 slush scraper, 1 Wheel scraper, 3 pairs
doubletree. 3 neck yokes, 1 lightining saw & other
tools &c.
I also rented my son James the farm, tools &
horses &c for the season, giving him 2/3 of all he
raises for 1/3 the grain put into my binns & 1/3 the
Hay put into the stack, staid in town with
Mary Jane all night and during sunday 3 Mch
went to the ward meeting preached about 70 mints
to an attentive audience, going to the farm at night
and staying till Monday Morning when Bro Camper
took James & I to Logan, I resumed my temple
labors & Visited my wives in Logan at night..
Thursday 8 Mch. Bro Jas A. Leishman my
assistant recorder at the Temple went home
in the evening. Deputy Marshall Whetstone called
at his house in the evening found him there and
arrested him, put him under bonds to appear
at Ogden on Saturday 9th Mch. he left the Temple

Friday morning to go off on the train so as to
get to Ogden in time. I went to Smithfield in the
Evening, and staid at the farm all night and laid the
foundation of the Shed for the fanning mill and feed mill
with James [Juchan] and Bro Campter went to town in the
Evening and staid all night with Mary Jane and on
Sunday 10th Mch I attended meeting at Smithfield and
returned to Logan in the Evening resuming my labors in the
Temple Monday 11th Mch until Friday 15 Mch when
I took my wife Maggie and Children to Smithfield
to live this summer. or as long as I may be permitted
returning to Logan again on
Monday Morning 18th Mch 1889. and resuming my work in
the temple. during the week my wife Maggie and my
daughter in law Maggie fitted up the parlor in my
wife Mary Janes house for a millinery shop and
opened out with a small stock of goods for Sale on
<u>Monday 25th Mch 1889</u>. while I resumed my Temple
labor that day after being home to see the family,
during the week, I arranged with the bank of
Thatcher Bros & Co to borrow $200.00 to put into the
Logan, Hyde Park and Smithfield Canal Co. as Stock
the notes are dated 30 Mch 1889.

{20}
agreeing to pay 1% per Month. one hundred to be
paid in one year, one hundred to be paid in 2 ys.
Went home Friday and worked at farm Saturday
and had wives and all the small children at the
farm on Sunday 30 Mch thankful to have the
privelage to meet them together. Returned to Logan
sunday Evening 31st Mch my daughters Mary, Hannah
and Libby bringing me down. during the week I
learned the dreaful news that my son Hiram
lost his little Son Glenn thro falling into a well
and drowning at the R.R. Camp in Washington
Territory.
Thursday 4 Apr Temple closed this Evening till
Wednesday 10th Apl for Conference, during the
past week my wife Maud Moved from Sister Juchans
to my wife Mary Jane's in town, where she expects to
stay for a season
[*folded tabular report pasted on the page*]

Register of Logan Temple Ordinance Work for Mach 1889																	
Baptisms								Endowments				Ordinations	Sealings		Children to Parents		Adoptions		Second Anointings			
First		Renewal of Cov.		Health		Dead		Living		Dead		Living	Dead	Living	Dead	Living	Dead	Living	Dead	Living		Dead	
M	F	M	F	M	F	M	F	M	F	M	F											M	F	M	F
2	3	9	9	11	45	1504	1235	43	55	397	569	—	408	46	292	56	18	—	—	8	13	1	8
5		18		56		2739		98		966		408	338	74		—		21		9	
2818								1064				408	338		74		—		30			

Samuel Roskelley   Recorder

Bro Camper (my hired man) came for me and I went to the farm with him ~~to the farm~~ and shortly went to town and staid the night with wife Maud, returning to the farm before day light, and worked making cutting for tree patch and setting out some bushes of carrots and other fruits, returning to town again. in the Evening and staying with Mary Jane.

saturday 6 apl I helped set up Maud's stove &c and took 11.30 A M Train for Salt Lake City to attend Conference arriving at 5.30 P.M went to Walter Beaties & stopped during the Conference with Auna Zina, at 7.30 attended priesthood Meeting at the Tabernacle, and had a good meeting 8 of the Apostles present.

Sunday 7th Apl. Attended meeting at Tabernacle which was full to overflowing in the afternoon a first Presidency was Voted for. Consisting of W Woodruff President. George Q Cannon ,& Jos F Smith Councillors, which leaves 9 of the 12 with Lorenzo Snow President of the 12 apostles, voting was done by Quorum, and not a contrary Vote out of abt 10 to 12 Thousand persons. In the Evening attended a Sunday school meeting, and heard good reports

Monday. Bro Lyman was released from the pen this morning and took his seat on the stand with the apostles. And preached in the afternoon, the meetings were good and every body felt well seemingly

{21}
I left the City at 5 P.M. arriving at Smithfield at 10.40 and proceeded to the farm after calling on the folks in town, stayed with Mary..

Tuesday 9th Apl. worked trimming Bushes, and grafting some trees at the farm. Maggie and the children came up and I stayed with her, and she took me to Logan Wednesday Morning 10th Apl. ~~our~~ Our labors commen =ced in the Temple, we baptized a few and then gave Endowments, but the Company was very light, but we continued our labors thro' the week, and sat Evening Maggie came for me and took me to Smithfield, Returning again to Logan Monday Morning 15 Apl 1889.

and worked as usual at my Labors in the Temple during
the week till Friday Evening when I went home to Smithfield and
was engaged most of Saturday 20th Apl in trying to secure
my rights from the Mayor of smithfield City and the
Directors of the Logan & Smithfield Canal Company in getting
pay for the Canal and the land the Canal runs
through belonging to me, attended Meeting in smithfield
ward and a High Priest Meeting afterward, and afterward
went to the farm and stayed all night going to Logan
early Monday morning taking the little buggie with me
to get a new set of wheels &c for which I advanced $15.00
cash to C Lundberg & Co., and that Evening I commenced
to work making BeeHives at Bro Cooks, following my labor
at the temple thro' the week as usual went to smithfield on
Friday Evening 26 Apl 1889. and on saturday 27th one of
my Hives of Bees swarmed and it took all forenoon to take
care of ~~of~~ the new colony and in the afternoon I went
with Bro Sharp who I had engaged to measure that
portions ~~lengths~~ of the Logan & Smithfield Canal I had made
some years since and found from Jensens Hollow to S.
Lows Corner 226 Rods. From there to my wire fence 143 Rods.
and from there to where it crosses under my fence into Bro
Petersons land 123 rods. from Jensons Hollow to Dry Kanyon
wash is 369 Rods which is the work I did the first season
I worked on the ditch went to town in the Evening and staid all
night started with son James and Bro S. Low for Bro T
Duces at Hyde Park and thence to Paradise and
attended sabbath school at 10. and a High Priest
Meeting form 10.30 till 12 M. thence to Hyrum attending
Meeting at 2. and H P. Meeting at 4. P.M. ate supper
and thence to Millville, held meeting at 8.30 and then
returned to Logan and slept at the temple,
Monday 29th Apl. Sent $6.00 to A. I Root for 7lbs
foundation 60 glass tumblers, and gleanings for 1
year, also $15.00 to Simons Bro Salt Lake for
Maggie to apply on bills. returning to smithfield at
night
Tuesday 30 Apl 1889. This day being set apart as a
Holiday for the nation being the centennial of the
Inauguration of Washington the 1st President the U.S.

{22}
I remained at the farm and work at my Bee Hives.
returning to Logan Wednesday morning 1 May and resumed
my Labors at the Temple.
[*folded tabular report pasted on the page*]

Register of Logan Temple Ordinance Work for April 1889																							
Baptisms								Endowments				Ordinations		Sealings		Children to Parents		Adoptions		Second Anointings			
First		Renewal of Cov.		Health		Dead		Living		Dead		Living	Dead	Living	Dead	Living	Dead	Living	Dead	Living		Dead	
M	F	M	F	M	F	M	F	M	F	M	F									M	F	M	F
1	–	8	11	9	23	934	855	35	46	167	297	2	167	42	153	48	44	–	–	2	2	1	1
1		19		32		1789		81		464		169		195		92		–		4		2	
1841								545				169		195		92		—		6			

Samuel Roskelley
Recorder

I found the Following letter awaiting me at the
Temple and according to instructions I found a
suitable place and reported to the President by
the mail

[*letter pasted on page and since removed, now inserted as follows*]

<u>Strictly Private</u>   Brigham City Utah April 29 / [---]

Samuel Roskelly

Dear Brother

I expect to be in Logan
next Saturday to Attend to Conference And I have chosen
you to Engage a room for me somewhere not far from the
Temple or Tabernacle which I can privately occupy at
night while I can I meet with Sarah in the will
want to attend Conference it has been 5 years since
I have been in Logan or Smithfield as soon
as you can get this accomplished drop me a line
so I can tell Sarah where to go on low to do in
the Matter I do not expect to confine myself to that
room to get my meals merely to have a place of
resort at Night We are having a good Conference
here G Q C Symour B Young & myself address
the Saints yesterday & last night

Your Brother

W Woodruff

Address W Woodruff Box B Salt Lake City

[*diary text*]

Friday Evening 3 May 1888. [*sic*] I went to Smithfield
with my daughter Mary, and remained through
the night with Mary Jane.

Saturday 4th May. I arranged and sent sister
Woodruff to Logan with Bro. F. Sharp and then
followed her with another team. after introducing
her to the persons I desired her to stop with
I went to Priesthood Meeting. Bro M. Thatcher &
Geo O Pitkin occupied the time. Moses Preached
on consecrating all our lands to some individuals
to prevent our selling them for money, at 1. P.M.
went to the Logan Depot with Hundreds of others

and the S.S. Children to greet Prest W. Woodruff
and the 3 apostles with him. returned to the Temple
to Priesthood Meeting (Lecture) by L.O. Littlefield
and at Evening went to Bro Moses Thatcher's and
was entertained by Prest Woodruff till late when
I took him & sister Woodruff to their stopping
Place for the night after chatting with him for a
short time I retired for the night, at my usual
sleeping place.
Sunday 5 May 1889. At 1/2 past nine I was at Bro
Woodruff's stopping place and Escorted him to the
Tabernacle, repeating the same programme in the
Evening & the following morning and on
Monday Evening 6th May I obtained the privelage
of my Wives Maggie & Maud and their children
Visiting with Prest Woodruff. Apostle Moses

{23}
Thatcher taking Prest Woodruff & I with his team
to where my wives & children were had agreed
to meet him. He blessed them, and told Ora
that he should be an Elder and preach the
Gospel, and blessed Emma telling her she
should be a woman and become a mother
in Israel,.. and had quite a Visit with the Women
Tusday 7th May 1880. resumed my labors in the
house of the Lord. Visiting my Wife Maud
nights as circumstances permit.
Friday 10th by request of Prest M W. Merrill I
took one of our Record Books to Salt Lake City
and got the Work done and visited with Prests
Geo Q Cannon and Jos F. Smith, returning to Ogden
Saturday Evening – stayed with Bro Jos Hall and
family and arrived at Smithfield at 11am. on
Sunday 12 May. and attended meeting at the Ward
house. returning to Logan Monday Morning
13 May 2ith my wife Maggie resuming my
labors in the temple thro the week and making
bee Hives during the Evenings and Visiting my
wife Maud thro' the nights returned to Smithfield
Friday 17th May – worked at Bee Hives during the
Saturday and on Sunday 19th Had My wives
and children together at the farm Except Maud
and held meeting partaking of the Sacrament.
Wife Maggie came to Logan with me on
Monday Morning, passed the usual labor of
the Week returning to smithfield Friday
24 May taking Maud and babe to the farm
spent Saturday making hives, and attending the
meeting on sunday at Smithfield Ward.
daughter Mary brought me to Logan on

Monday Morning 27th May 1889. to resume my
usual Labors in the Temple till Friday 31st May
I went home to Smithfield and worked at the
farm during Saturday, and attended Ward Meeting
on Sunday 2nd June, returned to Logan Monday Morning
and persued my usual labors at the Temple during the

[folded tabular report pasted on the page]

Register of Logan Temple Ordinance Work for May 1889

Baptisms								Endowments				Ordinations	Sealings	Children to Parents		Adoptions		Second Anointings			
First		Renewal of Cov.		Health		Dead		Living		Dead		Living	Dead	Living	Dead	Living	Dead	Living		Dead	
M	F	M	F	M	F	M	F	M	F	M	F							M	F	M	F
–	2	11	12	16	34	1608	1947	66	76	375	639	–	375	63	272	78	57	4	2	5	11	1	7
2		23		50		3555		142		1014		375	335	135		6		16		8	
3630								1156				375	335	135		6		24			

Samuel Roskelley   Recorder

{24}
week till Friday night where I went home to the farm
and arranged for my Wife Mary Jane to
take her children to Newton on a visit before the
Haying season commenced. she started Sunday
Morning 9th June and I remained with my wife Maud
who is still in Exile and spent the day Very pleas-
=antly with her. returning again to Logan on Monday
morning 10th June 1889. continuing my labors in the
Temple during the Week. Shipped a car load of
Wheat to Hussler &c Co at Salt Lake City on Sunday
9th from Smithfield. Went Home to the farm on
Wednesday 12th June quite sick but returned to the
Temple in time for work Thursday Morning, but went
home again on Saturday by train and chopped wood
and watered garden during the day and on
Sunday Morning with Bro sharp went to Hyde Park
taking my son Richard with me. and with Bros Duce
Sharp and Bp Daines went to Newton and met
with the saints Sunday afternoon and afterward met
the members of the H. P Quorum from Clarkston.
Trenton, & Newton, and had a good little meeting,
Returning to smithfield by way of Hyde Park,
Monday 16th Jun 1889. My wife Maggie took me
to Logan and I returned again to the Farm on
Tuesday Evening, going to Logan Early Wednesday
morning with my daughter Mary. and going to the
farm again on Friday Evening and thence to town
and staid over night with M. Chopped wood and
did business with several till noon when I went
to the farm and worked on some new hives till

night went to ~~the~~ town again and staid with MJ.
got up early and got team & buggy ready for Maggy
and Maud to go to Newton, and then I went
to Hyde Park and with Bro Duce went to Visit
Mendon. took dinner at Bp Hughes and thence
went to saints Meeting Bro Duce & I occupied the
time and afterward held a short meeting with
the High Priests of the Ward. returned to the farm
in the Evening and came to Logan Monday Morning
with daughter Mary. went to the farm again on
Wednesday 26 June with son James. and staid all
night with Mary. Returning to Logan Monday
morning and saw the Watermaster of the L.HP.&Smithfd
Canal who promised me water each week on Friday
night to Sunday for the farm garden & Tree patch

{25}
continued labor in the temple & Evenings making Bee
hives at Cooks place till Friday night 28 June 1889.
When I went to Providence and brought some strawberries
and took home to the family.
Saturday & Sunday 29 & 30 June I was watering
the Tree patch and garden at the farm most of the
time
<u>Monday 1 July 1889</u>. Daughter Mary took me to
Logan Early in the morning and I rec^d word from
US Commissioner CC Goodwin that he would
like to see me. I called on him in the Evening
and he told me he had rec^d word thro his
deputy that I had 2 wives living under one
roof and as a personal friend he would
advise me to separate them. Protesting my
ignorance & innsence I left him feeling
that I was an innocent man.
[folded tabular report pasted on the page]

Register of Logan Temple Ordinance Work for June 1889																		
Baptisms								Endowments				Ordinations		Sealings		Children to Parents		Adoptions		Second Anointings			
First		Renewal of Cov.		Health		Dead		Living		Dead		Living	Dead	Living	Dead	Living	Dead	Living	Dead	Living				Dead	
M	F	M	F	M	F	M	F	M	F	M	F									M	F	M	F
-	2	3	7	15	38	1245	1937	34	59	319	512	2	315	47	215	74	53	1	-	2	4	2	3
2		10		53		3182		93		831		317		262		127		1		6		5	
3247								924				317		262		127		1		11			
Samuel Roskelley Recorder																		

Tuesday Evening 2 July 1889 Went to Smithfield in the
Evening and returned to Logan again in the morning and in
the Evening of 3rd July went again to the farm and staid
over night.

4 July Thursday Temple being Closed for the day I watered
a little and afterwards got Wives and children
together and all had a sumptuous dinner. thankful
for the many blessing we possessed. and prayed for
the return of Blessings we were now deprived of
I made swings under the trees and helped to
swing the children.
Friday 5th July 1889. Hannah took me to Logan
and labored in the Temple and on
Saturday 6th July returned to Smithfield spending
the time as much as possible among my trees to
Keep them alive as water is very, scarce and
attending to my duties at the temple.
Friday 19th July Temple Closed for 5 weeks for the
purpose of cleaning and to make repairs &c
and I went home to Smithfield, and spent my
time pulling weeds, Watering at the farm and
the lots in town and doing some carpenter
work needed, but the sun was so hot it would
overcome me and I would have to seek the
shade and lie down to rest pretty often.
1st August. Thursday got word that Prest
W. Woodruff was in Logan and I went and

{26}
[folded tabular report pasted on the page]

Register of Logan Temple Ordinance Work for July 1889																	
Baptisms								Endowments				Ordinations	Sealings	Children to Parents	Adoptions	Second Anointings					
First		Renewal of Cov.		Health		Dead		Living		Dead		Living	Dead	Living	Dead	Living	Dead	Living	Dead	Living		Dead	
M	F	M	F	M	F	M	F	M	F	M	F									M	F	M	F
–	2	6	6	9	46	1032	1678	38	44	230	423	2	225	35	197	85	87	2	2	3	8	1	5
2		12		55		2710		82		653		227		232		172		4		11		6	
2779								735				227		232		172		4		17		
Temple closed 19th July 1889.														Samuel Roskelley Recorder								

1889.
Visited with him at apostle Moses Thatchers – he
was very free with me and asked me to arrange
matters as I had done for him and his wife at the
previous Quarterly Conference of this stake.
Friday 2nd August Pres. W. Woodruff & Cannon visited the
Temple and attended to some work for the living and
dead. After which I went home.
Saturday 3 august. Quarterly Conference commen-
-ced with 2 of the 1st Presidency and 2 apostles on
the stand. Conference continued also Sunday 4th my
wife Maud was dropped without any reason
assigned being yet an undergrounder. My coun=

=cillors F. Gunnell and Geo Barber were also
released, both being absent. and Thos Duce of Hyde
Park and Joseph Morrell of Logan voted in as
1st and 2nd Councillors to me. we had an Excellent
conference.
Tuesday 6th August 1889. Met with acting President
of stake Pitkin and my councillor Elect and
I set apart Thos Duce and prest Pitkin set apart
Jos Morrell.
Saturday 10th august with my wife Maggie & her
children I left Smithfield in the afternoon
and came to Logan. And got maud and her babe
and went to Wellsville staying all night at
Martha Eckersleys. Attended sunday school
with my councillors Sunday morning and meeting
of the Members of the Quorum at one oclock
and afternoon meeting of the saints at 2 P.M.
then hitched up my carriage and drove to Mantua
and took supper at Fro Hallings and afterwards
drove to Bro C. H. Rhees's at Pleasant View
remaining thence till Tuesday morning. Leaving
my wife Maud there and bringing Maggie back
to smithfield where I arrived at 10 P.M on
Tuesday Evening having success fully made the
trip and visited my friends the Rheese family,
which had long been contemplated. After this
I worked around home watering budding
and trimming trees & etc. My Wife Maggie
was taken very sick Tuesday 20 August
and continued so for some time.
Sunday 25th august my son James took me

{27}
to Logan to resume my labor in the Temple on the
following day Monday 26th august. where I contin-
=ued till Saturday I went to Smithfield, with
Maggie My son William & Wife. remained at
Home during the sunday staying with Mary Jane
and Maggie.
Monday 2 sep 1889. My daughter Mary came
with me to Logan and I remained during the week.
Had the company of Prest Jos F Smith and enjoyed
it very much. went home Friday Evening with my
wife Maggie. And stayed over Sunday. Returning again
Monday morning 9th sep 1889. .
[*folded tabular report pasted on the page*]

Samuel Roskelley

Register of Logan Temple Ordinance Work for August 1889.																				
Baptisms								Endowments				Ordinations		Sealings		Children to Parents		Adoptions		Second Anointings	
First		Renewal of Cov.		Health		Dead		Living		Dead		Living	Dead	Living	Dead	Living	Dead	Living	Dead	Living	Dead
M	F	M	F	M	F	M	F	M	F	M	F									M	F	M	F
–	–	1	1	7	20	326	439	11	15	65	112	–	64	11	45	7	5	3	20	1	4	–	–
—		2		27		765		26		177		64	56		12		23		5		—		
794								203				64	56		12		23		5				

Temple opened august 26th 1889   Samuel Roskelley   Recorder

staying the week and having a full house.
Friday 13th sep Returned home in the evening with Daughter
Mary and stayed at the farm next day loosening bud strings
on trees I had budded, went to town at night and
sunday 14th sep went to Clarkston and held meeting with
members of H P. Quorum at 1Oclock and at 2 met with
the saints Bro Duce & I occupied most of the time.
returned to Smithfield at night and found My
fellow missionary Joseph C. Bentley and had a good
Visit with him. he stayed at Maggies and I
took him to Logan Monday Morning. I continued
my labors at Temple during the week and returned
to Smithfield Friday Evening 20th Sep 1889.
Continuing my usual labors till the Evening of
3 October 1889. when I went to Smithfield and stayed over
night. and on Thursday morning started at 10.30 for the
City to Conference, met my son James & wives Maggie
and Maud, went to the Theatre one night and
spent the balance of time in meetings till Monday
afternoon, when I returned to Logan to resume my
labors in the Temple. Bro J. C Griggs and family
were very kind to me also sister Jay and P. W Young
gave me much Kindness at the Lion House during
our stay at the City.
Went to Smithfield Friday Evening 11th Oct. 1889.
[*folded tabular report pasted on the page*]

Register of Logan Temple Ordinance Work for Sept. 1889																							
Baptisms								Endowments				Ordinations		Sealings		Children to Parents		Adoptions		Second Anointings			
First		Renewal of Cov.		Health		Dead		Living		Dead		Living	Dead	Living	Dead	Living	Dead	Living	Dead	Living		Dead	
M	F	M	F	M	F	M	F	M	F	M	F									M	F	M	F
-	-	9	5	21	49	1341	1639	59	91	390	630	4	316	69	398	122	93	1	9	7	15	2	4
– –		14		70		2980		150		1020		390	467		215		10		22		6		
3064								1170				390	467		215		10		28				

Samuel Roskelley   Recorder

{28}
[folded tabular report pasted on the page]

Register of Logan Temple Ordinance Work from 21st May 1884 to 1st Oct. 1889

Mon.	Baptisms									Endowments				Ordinations		Sealings		Children to Parents		Adoptions		Second Anointings			
	First		Renewal of Cov.		Health		Dead		Living		Dead		Living	Dead	Living	Dead	Living	Dead	Living	Dead	Living		Dead	
	M.	F.	M.	F.	M.	F.	M.	F.	M.	F.	M.	F.									M.	F.	M.	F.
1884	32	38	326	454	256	590	10829	10514	497	699	3731	6291	23	3614	619	2983	884	756	16	7	30	69	6	19
1885	23	20	289	311	206	603	16702	17980	747	1011	7145	4564	23	7052	974	4687	1569	1218	17	6	7	38	4	16
1886	7	11	113	122	184	436	16302	16886	735	978	5484	7801	30	5418	831	3765	1452	1050	14	88	40	97	24	48
1887	2	8	61	89	141	421	13458	12180	664	873	4340	6508	19	4297	708	3133	853	589	7	53	38	65	15	55
1888	10	12	67	75	120	333	10767	10123	568	706	3468	5552	21	3436	606	2435	689	568	18	9	29	54	13	68
Oct.1. 1889	8	20	60	62	115	297	10110	11233	362	477	2724	4077	12	2717	400	2108	523	418	12	34	31	67	13	32
	82	99	916	1113	1022	2,680	78,168	78,916	3,673	4,744	16,892	39,793	128	26,534	4,138	19,111	5970	4599	84	197	175	390	75	238
	181		2,092		3,702		157,084		8,317		66,685		26,662	26,652	19,549	19,549	10,569	10,569	281	281	565		313	
	162,996									75,002												878			

Samuel Roskelley Recorder

{28 con't}

1889. Saturday 12 Oct. spent the day fixing glass and
repairing the windows at Mary Janes. and on
Sunday 13th at Home. apostle M Thatcher preached at
the new meeting house.
Monday 14th Oct. I returned to Logan and resumed my
usual. Labors at the Temple for the week and went
to smithfield again Friday Evening 18 Oct taking a stove
for Mary Mary Jane and took Saturday 19th to put
it up in its place.
Sunday 20 Oct. Went to Hyrum with my Councillors to
a district meeting of the members of the Quorum. and
had a good meeting I spoke 20 minutes and went back
to Logan and Continued my labors thro' the week till
Saturday morning 26 Oct. I got up at 4' o'clock and walked
to Smithfield and worked at the farm putting a shed
over some of my Bees.
Sunday 17th Oct Remained at Home attended meeting &
preached abt 40 minutes in the new meeting house,
Monday 28th My Daughter Mary took me to Logan to
continue my labors in the Temple which I did till
Friday 1 November The past week by the order
of Prest W. Woodruff a room has been set apart and
furnished with bedstead &c and nice carpet for
my use. all of which I appreciate. I went home
with my wife Maggie, in the Evenings, returning again
to Logan saturday morning to attend the Priesthood meeting
and Temple Lecture. Returning with Wife Maggie
to Farm in the Evening, going to town and back the
same Evening and to Logan Sunday to attend Confer
=ence of the stake, also attended the Conference on
Monday, and continued my Labors in the Temple
during the Week. . learned that my little boy
Marriner was Very sick at Evanston. Where my
wife Maud was stopping. I pray God to hear our
prayers in his behalf and heal him up.
Friday 8th Nov. I proved up on my timber culture
Entry with F. Sharp and J.J. Juchan as witnesses,
and went home with Daughter Mary in the
Evening
[folded tabular report pasted on the page]

Register of Logan Temple Ordinance Work for October 1889																		
Baptisms								Endowments				Ordinations		Sealings		Children to Parents		Adoptions		Second Anointings	
First		Renewal of Cov.		Health		Dead		Living		Dead		Living	Dead	Living	Dead	Living	Dead	Living	Dead	Living		Dead	
M	F	M	F	M	F	M	F	M	F	M	F											M	F	M	F
–	–	8	12	11	37	837	1765	83	95	373	553	9	369	76	259	116	75	2	3	8	8	-	8
---		20		48		2602		178		926		378		335		191		5		16	8
2670								1104				378		335		191		5		24	
Samuel Roskelley Recorder																		

{29}
Continued my labors during the month of November
as is usual in the house of the Lord. on the 9th
with Bro Duce I visited the H. Priests of Lewiston,
and Preached to them and the saints a short time
in the afternoon. Visited my Daughter in law
Viney and I blessed her twin boy Cyril and Bro
Thomas Duce blessed the other twin Cyrus.
Sunday 1 Dec 1889. With Elder Thos Duce I visited the
High Priests of Newton, with the saints in the
afternoon meeting, and had a good meeting. My councilor
Joseph Morrell preached most of the afternoon. Bro Duce
and I followed a short time. Bro Morrell & I returned
to Logan and attended Evening Meeting, heard Bro
B. H. Roberts Lecture on the Calling & Ministry of the
70s Continued my labors in the Temple during the
week and returned home Friday Evening 6 Dec 1889.
[*folded tabular report pasted on the page*]

Register of Logan Temple Ordinance Work for Nov. 1889.																		
Baptisms								Endowments				Ordinations		Sealings		Children to Parents		Adoptions		Second Anointings	
First		Renewal of Cov.		Health		Dead		Living		Dead		Living	Dead	Living	Dead	Living	Dead	Living	Dead	Living		Dead	
M	F	M	F	M	F	M	F	M	F	M	F											M	F	M	F
2	1	2	–	16	30	641	1061	55	67	356	570	2	354	62	241	46	50	1	–	7	9	1	8
2		2		46		1702		122		926		356		303		96		1		16	9
1753								1048				356		303		96		1		25	
Samuel Roskelley Recorder																		

Returning to Logan again Monday Morning 9th
Dec, attending the Meeting at Smithfield on the
Sunday, and resumed my usual labors at the
Temple for 2 weeks till Friday Evening 20th Dec 1880.
the Temple closed and I went to Smithfield.
~~Remaining till Monday Dec 23rd and returning~~
~~to Logan on the train. took Record for Baptism~~

~~and Tuesday 14th Dec attended the Baptism and [ ]
Evening~~ remaining there till
Thursday morning 26th Dec 1889. and returned to
Logan on the train. resuming my usual labors
* till Friday Evening, when I again went to
Smithfield.
25 Dec 1889. I spent at the farm. with
Mary and Mary Jane and Maggie and their
children, having an Excellent dinner and a
good time visiting. Maud was not with us
altho' she returned from Evanston to Logan on
the sunday previous. having been absent since
the 10th August. Visiting her friends at Evanston.
Wyoming.
Monday 30 Dec 1889. Returned to Logan and res=
=umed my labor in the Temple
Friday 27 Dec. At the instigation of My
father-in-law Br. W. F. Rigby, I had been notified

{30}
to appear before the High Council of Cache Valley
stake on the friday previous 20 Dec. to answer to
certain charges in connexion with the firm of
Vannoy and Co. but as none of the Vannoys
were Present the case was postponed till the
27th. as the Vannoys were not present because of
sickness, the Council voted that I should do
all I could to bring about a settlement of the case
by getting the parties together and also obtain the
Books of the Company so as to make a settlement
before 1st Mch or Report to the Council at that
date ready for the investigation because of
having failed to bring about a settlement among
the parties.
31st Dec 1889. after baptisms the Temple
closed till Thursday 2nd Jan 1890. and I took
the train and went to Smithfield.
1 Jan 1890.(Wednesday) spent the day at
Mary Janes, with Mary. Mary Jane. Maggie
and their Children and at 3 P.M Maud and her
babe came in having come from Logan on the
Freight train. with my son Joseph, we had
and Excellent dinner and Enjoyed the Visit
together in chatting and good cheer.

{continues next page}

[30 con't]

Register of Logan Temple Ordinance Work for the year 1889.

Mon.	Baptisms									Endowments				Ordinations		Sealings		Children to Parents		Adoptions		Second Anointings			
	First		Renewal of Cov.		Health		Dead		Living		Dead		Living	Dead	Living	Dead	Living	Dead	Living	Dead	Living		Dead	
	M.	F.	M.	F.	M.	F.	M.	F.	M.	F.	M.	F.									M.	F.	M.	F.
Jan	2	–	7	3	12	14	679	392	43	52	359	428	1		50	247	27	29		1	3	9	4	3
Feb	3	1	6	8	15	28	1441	1111	33	39	422	467	1	356	37	284		32	1	–	–	1	1	1
Mar	2	3	9	9	11	45	1504	1235	43	55	397	569	–	421	46	292	56	18	–	–	8	13	1	8
Apl	1	–	8	11	9	23	934	855	35	46	167	297	2	408	42	153	48	44	–	–	2	2	1	1
May	–	2	22	12	16	34	1609	1947	66	76	375	639	–	167	63	272	78	57	4	2	5	11	1	7
June	–	2	4	7	15	38	1241	1937	34	59	319	512	2	3\75	47	215	74	53	–	–	2	4	2	3
July	–	2	7	6	9	46	1032	1678	38	44	230	424	2	315	35	197	85	87	2	2	3	8	1	5
Aug	–	–	1	1	7	20	320	439	11	15	65	112	–	225	11	45	7	5	3	20	1	4	–	–
Sep	–	–	9	5	21	49	1341	1639	59	91	390	630	4	64	69	398	122	93	1	9	7	15	2	4
Oct	–	–	8	12	11	37	837	1765	83	95	373	553	9	386	76	259	116	75	2	3	8	8	–	8
Nov	2	1	2	–	16	30	641	1061	55	67	356	570	2	369	62	241	46	50	1		7	9	1	8
Dec	1	–	4	4	10	27	1266	1037	49	56	270	451	2	354	55	206	44	33	4		1	1	–	–
	11	11	74	78	152	391	12,854	13,096	349	695	3723	5651	25	265	593	2814	729	578	19	39	47	85	14	48
	22		132		543		27,951		1244		9374			3708		3407		1307		56	132		62	
	28667								10618				3733	3733		3,407		1,307		56	194			

Samuel Roskelley
Recorder

Thursday 2 Jan 1890. I returned to Logan by the Early morning train and remained over saturday attending the Stake Priesthood meeting., and the Temple Lecture in the afternoon. and went to Smithfield in the Evening my son Williams wife Maggie desired to sell her interest in the millinary Business that she hold with my wife Maggie, my wife and I took stock on Saturday night 4th Jan and I subsequently bought her share continuing the business under the same firm name as before.

{31 *continues next page*}

{31}
[folded tabular report pasted on the page]

Totals of Ordnance Work in Logan, Manti and St. George Temples, from commencement to 31st December 1889.

	Baptisms				Endowments		Ordinations		Sealings		Children to Parents		Adoptions		2nd Anointings	
	First	Ren. of Cov.	Health	Dead	Living	Dead	Living	Dead	Living	Dead	Living	Dead	Living	Dead	Living	Dead
Logan	185	2059	3,833	163,691	8.722	69,258	141	27,525	4,331	19,817	6,176	4,759	91	200	599	330
Manti	57	1646	5,845	71,793	1,635	26,347	62	10,682	73	9,315	2,459	2,235	230	2,318	333	143
St. George	365	687	2,567	241,230	5160	98,422	1134	37,750	2,722	32,355	3,532	3,684	480	5432	1185	1222
	667	4392	12,245	482714	15,517	194,027	1,337	75,957	7,784	61,487	12,167	10,678	801	7958	2167	1695
Gd. Totals	499,958				208,544		77,294		69,271		22,845		8751		3812	

[on verso of same sheet]

Register of Ordinance Work performed during the year ending Dec. 31. 1890

	Baptisms				Endowments		Ordinations		Sealings		Children to Parents		Adoptions		Second Anointings	
	First	Ren. of Cov.	Health	Dead	Living	Dead	Living	Dead	Living	Dead	Living	Dead	Living	Dead	Living	Dead
Logan	22	152	543	27950	1244	9374	25	3708	593	2814	729	578	19	37	132	62
Manti	38	811	3328	39541	855	16968	41	7000	410	6233	1418	1307	146	1635	168	64
St. George	58	50	81	10315	157	3577	23	1334	87	660	70	116	10	214	11	19
	118	1013	3952	77806	2256	28919	89	12042	1090	9707	2217	2001	175	1886	311	145
Gd. Totals	82889				32175		12131		10797		4218		2061		456	

{31 con't}
January passed as usual so far as my labor
is concerned. James Horse "Bones" died with the
Fierey and my old cow spot died also of old age
the snow averaged 2 ½ feet deep at the farm on
the 18th Jan. I had been staying in town over
night Friday night and called on my daughter
Rebecca before day in the Saturday and administered
to her she being sick with rheumatism, I then
waded through the snow from Knee to waste
deep to the farm and tired myself out, and
when getting on a shed roof to shovel the snow
off I fell and hurt myself on a post and it
made me sick for a week altho' I went to the
Temple and did my work as usual, Coal has
been Very scarce and we have been only able to get
a ton or two at a time for the past week as the
R R has been blocaded with snow.
I returned to Smithfield Friday 24th Jan.
and Visited with my family. going to the ward meeting
and returned to Logan to persue my usual labors
in the Temple Monday 27th January. our coal
for heading the Building was nearly gone and
after taking the record for baptisms when we may have
coal again Prest Merrill concluded to close the
Temple for a week. and I retuned to Smithfield. and worked cleaning up Lucern seed
and fixing up a number of things for the family
Sunday 2nd Feb 1890. attended the stake
Quarterly Conference Apostles. M Thatcher and
F. M Lyman with Bp O.F Whitney with other
Visitors present and we had some excellent
teaching
[folded tabular report pasted on the page]

Register of Logan Temple Ordinance Work for January 1890																			
Baptisms								Endowments				Ordinations	Sealings		Children to Parents		Adoptions		Second Anointings			
First		Renewal of Cov.		Health		Dead		Living		Dead		Living	Dead	Living	Dead	Living	Dead	Living	Dead	Living			Dead	
M	F	M	F	M	F	M	F	M	F	M	F									M	F	M	F
–	4	5	11	4	10	1188	621	34	40	251	326	1	251	33	149	21	12	–	–	1	3	1	4
4		16		14		1809		74		577		252		182		33		—		4			5		
1843								651				252		182		33		—		9			
Samuel Roskelley Recorder																			

{32}
Monday 3 Feby 1890. again attended the Quarterly
Conference and was well repaid with rich instruct
=tions. after the afternoon meeting recd word

thro the Telegraph line that the Supreme Court
of the US. Had rendered a decision today that
the Idaho test oath (which took the franchise
from every person who claims to be a member of
the Mormon Church) is constitutional this
sweeping away at once all liberties & privelages
of citizenship for members of our church,
in the Evening Bp O.F. Whitney delivered a Very
able Lecture to a large audience on Zion &
her Redeption. and apostle M. Thatcher after-
-ward said that the Revelation in the Book of
Doc & Cov where the Lord says he will raise up
a man like unto Moses to deliver his people
form Bondage &c refers to the prophet Joseph
Smith as that Man to Deliver the Saints.
Tuesday 4th Feb 1890. Commenced our labor
in the Temple again having obtained a car load
of coal. and worked till Friday Evening 7 Feb
when I returned to Smithfield. and found a P O O
from James Hymas Bear Lake on the Wintering of the
cattle in our possession.
Saturday Fanned up some wheat at the farm.
Sunday 9th Feb attended meeting and heard Bp G L
Farrell Preach he having lately returned from Canada
Monday 10th Returned to Logan by the Early Morning
train and Continued my work in the House of the
Lord. thro' the Week. Visiting my wife Maud who was
staying at Logan.
Friday 14 Feb again went home to smithfield, and
trimmed trees at the farm. and met Prest C. O Card
at my house in town in the Evening.
Sunday 16th attended meeting and again heard Bp
G L. Farrell preach.
Monday 17 Returned to Logan on Early train and
as usual spent the week at the Temple and returned
home again friday Evening.
Saturday 22nd Feb 1890. Fanned wheat to sell &
got very tired.
Sunday. 23rd James Returned from Salt Lake City
and I listened to the home Missionaries preach &

{33}
[folded tabular report pasted on the page]

Register of Logan Temple Ordinance Work for February 1890																	
Baptisms								Endowments				Ordinations		Sealings		Children to Parents		Adoptions		Second Anointings			
First		Renewal of Cov.		Health		Dead		Living		Dead		Living	Dead	Living	Dead	Living	Dead	Living	Dead	Living		Dead	
M	F	M	F	M	F	M	F	M	F	M	F											M	F	M	F
4	2	13	15	9	14	1779	1164	39	42	417	482	–	415	43	283	39	33	-	-	1	2	-	-
6		28		23		2943		81		899		415		326		71		–		3			
3000								980				415		326		72		–		3			

Samuel Roskelley   Recorder

Bro Thos Duce made some remarks I presented Bro E R. Miles Jr for Teacher of the Members of H.P. in the Smith==field Ward in place of Bro F. Sharp deceased.

Monday 24th Feb Returned to Logan on the Early train and attended my usual work till Friday night. when I again returned to Smithfield.

Saturday 1st Mch 1890. Went to Logan and attended the Priesthood Meeting, but was excused from the Temple Lecture but rode to smithfield on a bed of coal with my son James

Tusday 2 Mch 1890. attended meeting at Smithfield and preached a short time, returned to Logan by the Early train Monday morning 3rd Mch 1890. and continued my usual labors thro' the week. returning to smithfield on Friday Evening 7 Mch 1890. My wife Maud and babe with me. Road Very bad.

Saturday 8 Mch. I trimmed trees all day in town.

Sunday 9 Mch 1890. attended High Priest Meeting at the City Hall in morning and set apart E. R Miles Jr to preside as teacher over the H.P. at Smithfield in place of Bro F Sharp (deceased). also assisted to Reordain Bro John Plowman. as he was dissatisfied with his previous ordination under the hands of Bro J. T. Cantwell. attended meeting. heard the Home Missionaries preach. (Bro S. Mitten & Liljenquist).

Monday 10th Mch 1890. took Early train for Logan and resumed my usual labors at the Temple. and in the Evening attended the H Priest meeting in the basement of the Tabernacle ordained 2 of the Bretheren H. Priests & assisted to ordain 3 others. My daugther Mary's 20 ys old

Tuesday 11th Mch. My son Joseph was baptized for my Brother John Joseph Roskelley in the Temple. (see my Temple & family Reord.). and labored as usual in the Temple thro the week, and returned to Smithfield on Friday Evening 14th Mch. 1890. and found my wife Maud sick in Bed also my wife Mary Jane and also learned that my wife Mary was sick in Bed at the farm, I waited on the

sick during Saturday & Sunday and during the
nights also and left them all a little better on
Monday Morning 17 Mch. I took the Early train
for Logan and returned to smithfield by the 10.10
P.M Train on Tuesday. Visiting the folks at town
and then walking to the farm thro' the snow & mud
to see my wife Mary – found her a little better

{34}
and able to sit up to have her bed made,
I walked back to town again and rested a few
hours returning to Logan by the Early train to
resume my labors in the Temple. continuing
till Friday Evening 21 Mch 1890. when I again.
Returned to. Smithfield. Finding my wives some
better. Saturday 22 Mch 1890. Bro Wm F. Rigby came to my
house for a days since and to day we went to Richmond to
meet the Vannoy's to try & settle up our business affairs, but
could not find them altho the notice of meeting had
been understood for some time previous, so we retur-
=ned to smithfield in the Evening. I stayed at Smithfield
with my family during the sabbath attend meeting in the
afternoon, and on Monday morning returned to Logan
on the Early train. And resumed my labors for the week
Sunday 23 Mch 1890. W.T. Vannoy & his sons Wm D. came
from Richmond and with Bro W. F Rigby & I talked over
our business concluding to send to Bro Ricks and
ask him to call at Blackfoot and see if our Books
are there & get them if possible..
Tuesday 25 Mch 1890. I took the late Evening train
and went to Smithfield to see Prest C. O. Card start
for Canada. he having been stopping with his wife
Vina at my house for a few days. I returned to
Logan again on the Early train Wednesday morning
not having had. Much rest. And returned again to ~~Logan~~
Smithfield with my daughter Mary on Friday Evening
28 Mch. 1890. and finding strangers at the farm I went
to town and stayed with Maud. And saturday I went
to the Farm over the Hill, and put Bro Mathison
to work grubbing &c he having commenced to work for me
this day. I did some grafting and cutting off trees and
Returned to town Sunday 30 Mch 1890. and attended the
afternoon meeting at the school House,
Monday 31 Mch Returned to Logan on the Early
train and resumed my labor in the Temple till
Wednesday Evening 2nd apl. when the Temple closed
for Conference and I went to Smithfield with my
son James

[34 con't; folded tabular report pasted on the page]

Register of Logan Temple Ordinance Work for March 1890																			
Baptisms								Endowments				Ordinations		Sealings		Children to Parents		Adoptions		Second Anointings			
First		Renewal of Cov.		Health		Dead		Living		Dead		Living	Dead	Living	Dead	Living	Dead	Living	Dead	Living		Dead	
M	F	M	F	M	F	M	F	M	F	M	F									M	F	M	F
–	1	16	10	2	22	1375	1525	47	48	395	514	4	394	47	214	43	28	–	–	1	2		
1		26		24		2,900		95		909		398		261		71		–		3			
2,951								1,004				398		261		71		–		3			
Samuel Roskelley Recorder																			

{35}
Thursday & Friday 3&4 apl 1809 Worked at the farm
cutting cuttings for planting & putting out fruit trees &c
Bro Mathiason planted cuttings.
Saturday 5 apl. Worked in town planting fruit and
some shade trees on Maggie's lot.
Sunday 6 apl. At home all day with the folks
and spent afternoon with Maud as I felt quite
poorly,, but on Monday resumed my tree planting
altho not at all well.
Tuesday 8 apl took the Early train for Logan
and continued my labors in the Temple during the
week. returned to Smithfield on Friday Evening
with. Daughter Mary and remained at home
saturday & sunday and attended Ward Meeting taking
Early train Monday 14th apl 1890 for Logan to resume,
my Temple Labors. Working thereall week and
returning to Smitfield again Friday Evening 18th apl 180.
and planted peas and some small garden truck at
Mary Janes & Maggies & put up a little wire fence between
Bro Farrell & I.
Sunday 29th apl. With Bro Duce I Visited the High
Priests at Lewiston and held meeting with them at 9-30 am.
and had a good meeting feeling first class. Returning it rained and
we got quite a wetting, which caused me to stay at home
the rest of the day,
I returned to Logan by the Early train Monday Morning
21 apl 1890. I returned home to the Farm and worked all
day putting in some garden and looking after my trees &c.
Sunday 29 May 1890. I. attended the meeting at the School House
and preached most of the time on the relative value of civil
officers and the offices of the Holy Priesthood.
Monday 28 apl 1890. returned to Logan by Early train
continuing my labors as usual in the Temple thro the week
Friday 2 May I recd the following from Prest Woodruff.
[folded tabular report pasted on the page]

Register of Logan Temple Ordinance Work for April 1890																	
Baptisms								Endowments				Ordinations		Sealings		Children to Parents		Adoptions		Second Anointings			
First		Renewal of Cov.		Health		Dead		Living		Dead		Living	Dead	Living	Dead	Living	Dead	Living	Dead	Living		Dead	
M	F	M	F	M	F	M	F	M	F	M	F									M	F	M	F
2	2	9	12	16	36	1053	1538	45	59	218	373	2	214	47	176	55	53	–	1	1	3	1	1
4		21		52		2591		104		591		216		223		108		1		4		2	
2668								695				216		223		108		1		6			
Samuel Roskelley Recorder																		

[folded letter pasted on the page]

<u>Strictly Private to yourself</u>
   SLCity May 1/90
Samuel Roskelley
  Dear Brother
      George Q
and myself now expect to be
in Logan on Saturday night
to attend the Conference Now I hve
a Sister S in Smithfield who
would like to see me I wish you
would call upon that Sister and
make arrangements for S to stop
etc as before and you will do
me a favor caution is the word
we shall write to Brother Merrill
to [---] him of our [---]
  As ever your Brother
      L Allen

{36}
and in accordance with the instruction I made
the arrangements as desired. going to Smithfield in the
Evening of Friday 2nd May 1890 with my daughter Mary
and staying at the farm over saturday. Doing some
plowing – preparing to water my fruit trees &c. it rained
very much thro the afternoon but my son James
brought me to Logan in the Evening and I met Prest
Woodruff and had a good visit with him. And staid
with my wife Maud thro' the night and ate breakfast
with her
Sunday 4th May 1890 at 1/2 past 9 a m went to the stopping
place of Prest Woodruff and chatted with him till meeting
time and he took my arm, going to meeting together,
I was called upon the open the Conference with prayer,
we had some excellent preaching from Prests L Snow
& W. Woodruff thro' the day. Prest W & I going to Dr. O. C.
Hormsbys to dinner alone.. In the Evening Prest Woodruff

told me he disapproved of Bp Farrell's preaching that a
Bp had a right to nominate the officers of all organ=
izations, political, or spiritual in his ward
he also said it had been his intention to organize
this stake permanently at this Visit with Bro Geo O.
Pitkin as president but he found such an opposition
to Bro Pitkin that he wanted a meeting with Bro
L. Snow and M W. Merrill in the Morning and he
wanted me to be present at the meeting to talk
over the situation. I notified the apostles of
the meeting.
Monday 5 May. at the meeting with the apostles
it was decided to let the present temporary stake
presidency remain till next. Conference in
august, Prest Woodruff told me he would in
the near future appoint some one to preside in the
Logan Temple as he expected apostle M W Merrill
to travel among the people in persuance to his
calling as an apostle and he would only be at
the Temple occasionally – The meetings today have
been full of interest to the saints. Much Valuable
instruction given by Prests Woodruff & Sno.
after meeting Prest Woodruff came to the Temple
and attended to some adoptions with Bro Francis Sharp
who had requested to be adopted to Bro Woodruff
telling me his wishes before he (Sharp) did. I have
now had it attended to. In the Evening Prest W.
apostle Merrill & I enjoyed a chat all alone during
which chat I learned from Prest W's lips more than

{37}
I ever dreamed of about the affairs of the church and,
its present leaders & the situation of men & things
connected therewith. Oh Lord My God preserve me
I pray thee in the name of Jesus Christ thy son from ever
turning my back on the Church or its officers or
raising my voice against the Lords anointed but
Keep me in the faith of the Gospel and always give
me Eyes to see and power to follow and advocate
the truth of Heaven. Amen
My wife Maggie was in Logan and I slept with her
at the House of a friend.
Tuesday 6 May 1890. Took record and called at
the font. going. At night to see my wife Maud.
8th May. (Thursday) I sent $275.00 to Salt Lake City to
Zions Savings Bank to pay interest due and apply
some on the principle.
Friday 9th May. I returned to Smithfield in the
Evening and stayed at the farm on Saturday planting
potatoes &c and in the Evening I went to town and
helped plow a patch for potatoes and garden,

Sunday 10 May 1890. With my sons James & Joseph I
I went to Lewiston and Visited my son Hiram's Wives
Lavina & Addie and their children. Returning in
the Evening to Smithfield and attended the Conjoint
session of the Y.M & Y.L.M.I. A,. My wife being president
of the last named association, the Home Missionary
doing most of the talking.
Monday Morning 12 May I returned to Logan on the
Early morning train and resumed my labor in the
Lords house. We had quite an amount of Record to
take:
Wednesday 14th May 1890.. I took the 12 O'clock
train for smithfield and attended the funeral ser=
=vices of Bro Thos. W. Thompson. I spoke about an
hour. Elders Geo Barber and Bp Farrell also
spoke a short time
Learning from pretty reliable sources that the
marshalls we gathering all the Evidence they
could to make me and my wife trouble because
she Maggie had her ship in Mary Janes House
I spoke to Bp Farrell about it when he professed
to let her occupy his front room in his dwelling
house. free of rent, so as to save. me any
trouble or annoyance from the officers of the law.
Maggie went and looked at the place and
concluded she would move there.

{38}
Thursday 15 May 1890. I took early train to Logan
resuming my usual labors in the Temple.
Friday 16 May I returned in the Evening to Smithfield
and worked around home on Saturday
Sunday 18th went to Hyde park and with My Councillors
held meeting at 12.N with the H. Priests. Going to Bro Duce
to dinner then attended meeting with the saints in the
afternoon. My councillors & myself spoke. Occupying the
whole meeting – returned to Smithfield and remained till
Monday morning 19th may Went to Logan on the Train
and resumed my temple labor. till Friday 23rd May
I returned home with my daughter Mary. taking some
provisions with us Bro Duce & I went to Richmond one
Sunday 25th May. Held meeting with the members of the
Quorum at 10 a.m. And then went to Coveville and
held meeting with the Sunday School then preached
to the saints in the afternoon meeting and held meeting
with members of H. P. Quorum afterwards. Returned to
smithfield in the Evening. And came to Logan in the
buggy Monday 26 May 1890 resuming usual labor
in the Temple till Friday 30 may. Making out usual
monthly report and going home to Smithfield. in the Evening.
Sunday 1 June 1890. attended meeting at Smithfield

heard Home Missionaries A Crockett & N C Edlefsen preach
and bore testimony myself to their preaching. Returning
to Logan Monday 2nd May. and continuing till
Friday 6th May 1889. [sic] Went at night to Smithfield.
And worked in town on Saturday in the Garden
Sunday 8th June Met Bro Duce at Hyde Park
and with him went to Hyrum to attend. The
ward conference Morning and afternoon, holding
a meeting with members of the H.P. Quorum between
the meetings, Returning to Logan in the Evening
and staying at the house of my friends with my
wife and child. Returning to the Temple
Monday. Morning and Resuming the Duties of my
Calling.
[*folded tabular report pasted on the page*]

Register of Logan Temple Ordinance Work for May 1890																	
Baptisms								Endowments				Ordinations		Sealings		Children to Parents		Adoptions		Second Anointings			
First		Renewal of Cov.		Health		Dead		Living				Dead				Living	Dead	Living	Dead	Living	Dead	Living	Dead	Living		Dead	
M	F	M	F	M	F	M	F	M	F	M	F									M	F	M	F
1	1	10	7	17	39	1054	1500	45	52	378	649	1	377	47	274	59	30	2	1	4	10	4	8
2		17		56		2,554		97		1,027		378		321		89		3		14		12	
2,629								1,124				378		321		89		3		26			
Samuel Roskelley Recorder																							

Register of Logan Temple Ordinance /Work\ for June 1890.																							
Baptisms								Endowments				Ordinations		Sealings		Children to Parents		Adoptions		Second Anointings			
First		Renewal of Cov.		Health		Dead		Living				Dead				Living	Dead	Living	Dead	Living	Dead	Living	Dead	Living		Dead	
M	F	M	F	M	F	M	F	M	F	M	F									M	F	M	F
3	2	12	10	19	61	1460	1621	47	64	524	909	1	520	50	433	107	84	3	1	2	4	2	4
5		22		80		3081		111		1433		521		483		191		4		6		6	
3,188								1544				521		483		191		4		12			
Samuel Roskelley Recorder																							

{39}
Continued my labors as usual until
Sunday 29th July with my Councillors Bro Thos Duce I Visited
Clarkston and held meeting with the Members of the
High Priest Quorum in the forenoon and afterwards
returned to Newton and held meeting with the saints
and then with the Members of the Quorum. returning
to Smithfield same Evening.
Monday 30th June. 1890 Rode to Logan with buggy
and resumed my labors for the week as usual

Temple Closed on Thursday 3 July and I went home
and went to farm Early Friday Morning and got all
the folks there and ate dinner together after which I
went to town and with my son James went to Bro
Merrills farm at Richmond to see a Hay stacker.
Sunday 6 July. at Smithfield and attended a
ward Conference. the Stake authorities were present
and we had a good meeting. resumed my duties at
the Temple on Monday 7 July. 1890 and on
Thursday 10 July 1890 I took the Early morning train for
Ogden arriving there at 9.15 found the train from California
had already arrived and I could find no tidings of
my cousin Walter Thomas Hansford and his wife. so I
stayed with Bro Jos Hall and family thro' the day
and in the Evening my son James came from home,
Friday 11 July 1890. I with my son James met my
Cousin W. T. Hansford and his wife on arrival of the
California train and I walked around Ogden for
a few moments- then took the train for Salt
Lake City. where I took them to the Valley
House and I stayed at Bp Geo H Taylors. We
had an Excellent Visit. I introduced them to
President Geo Q Cannon. Bps. Preston. Winder &
and many other. prominent men. Visited the
Temple building. Tabernacle. Gardo House &
Salt Lake. Camp Douglass. Liberty Park and
other places of note. and on Sunday Visited the
14 Ward Sunday school and the meeting in the
afternoon at the Tabernacle. They expressed
themselves Well pleased and much gratified
with their Visit. My son & I left them for
smithfield at 5 P.Mm Sunday 13 July 1890 these
are the 1st relatives I ever had Visit me.
at my Mountain home. and I highly appreciate
it. I returned to the Temple on Sunday evening
my son accompanying me on his way to Smithfield.
Friday 18th July. I packed up books and papers.

{40}
and put them in a safe place and took leave of
the Holy House of God for a season as the temple
was closed for renovation & repairs for 5 weeks.
Thursday 24 July. 1890. Altho a celebration
was in progress in smithfield. I had promised
Bro M Thatcher I would attend the celebration at Logan
which I did and had a good visit, returning to
Smithfield same Evening and put in all my spare
time on fixing to build Marys house at the farm.
Saturday 2 August 1890 at logan to attend the
Stake Quarterly Conference. Prest Woodruff, GQ Cannon
L snow. M Thatcher present at meeting. and I had some

Excellent advice although but few saints present in the Evening I made up my monthly register of Temple work for July.

Sunday 3 august. House crowded full and the speakers quite spirited – a stake presidency of Orson smith, simpson M. Molen & Isaac Smith were sustained for Cache Stake. and ordained by Geo Q Cannon. L. Snow & FD. Richards in the order named. Bro C. O Card was honorably released to preside over the LDS colony in Canada. after afternoon meeting the Bretheren & Logan Choir drove to smithfield and held meeting Prest Geo Q Cannon & W. Woodruff preached. after which Pres Woodruff. C.O. Card & Orson Smith came to my house for supper and Prest Woodruff staid and slept at my house. getting up at 5 o'clock a.m. on the morning of

Monday 4th august. getting breakfast and with Prest Geo Q Cannon . & F. D Richards took train a few minutes past 6 a.m. for Salt Lake City after an agreeable Visit to Cache Stake. I worked in my lot in town during the day and went to Prov= =idence in the evening to buy a long pole for stacking Hay returning by Hyde Park to see and administer to my daughter Rebecca. and finding her Very sick and without sufficient help I returned to Smithfield and procured assistance and returned to Hyde Park with Sister M Gutkie and then went back to the farm. going to bed I had quite a chill. about 2 a.m. a messenger from my daughter Rebecca brought word that she was worse. My son James went with the messenger. I followed on the morning of

{41}

Tuesday 5th Aug 1890 reaching my daughter about 9. a.m found her Very sick. I found the desease (childbed fever) was working up into her bowels and Vitals and after administering to her she seemed easier and talked with me for a short time about her feelings. And circum= =stances, but a rapid change came over her and she sank to rest. breathing her last 5 minutes past 11 a m. she leaves a beautiful babe who was born 4th July 1890. I went to Smithfield soon as I could and arranged for suitable clothing and at 11 PM with Wives Mary & Mary Jane and sons samuel James & Joseph . I went to Hyde Park with a casket and clothing and with the help of the good Sisters of that place prepared her for burial taking her to Smithfield and placing

her in her own home till the funeral.
Sister Mary Ann Hillyard and Sister Elizabeth
Hillyard Raymond were very Kind in preparing
clothing & doing all they could for the deceased
Thursday 7 Aug 1890. The funeral took place
at 4 P.M at the new tabernacle at Smithfield.
Many relatives from Logan. Richmond and
Lewiston & swan Lake attended the funeral
Bros Mathias Cowley. Bp M Lewis & Hyrum Ricks
& Bp Geo L. Farrell were the speakers.. she was
laid to rest, beside her babe Dorris and the
Grave dedicated to God by Brigham Hendricks
(her Cousin) the same Evening Bro Hillyard
and my wives Mary & Maud and I went to Hyde
Park and got the babe as we had learned
that the marshals were in smithfield & Hyde
Park the same day Enquiring about me. But
we hid Maud and the babe till saturday
night the 9th when Bro Hillyard and I took
her and the babe and my daughter Mary
to Lewiston to stay with Lib Harris for a few
weeks. I stayed there over sunday. Returning
to Smithfield Sunday Evening in a rain storm.
[*folded tabular report pasted on the page*]

Register of Logan Temple Ordinance Work for July 1890																	
Baptisms								Endowments				Ordinations		Sealings		Children to Parents		Adoptions		Second Anointings			
First		Renewal of Cov.		Health		Dead		Living		Dead		Living	Dead	Living	Dead	Living	Dead	Living	Dead	Living		Dead	
M	F	M	F	M	F	M	F	M	F	M	F									M	F	M	F
	1	10	12	26	44	1240	1221	36	45	404	646	2	401	33	291	102	94	5	5	13	23	6	6
1		22		70		2,461		81		1050		403		324		196		10		36		12	
2,554								1,131				403		324		196		10		48			
Samuel Roskelley Recorder																							

{42}

Monday 11th aug 1890. I resumed work on the frame
of Mary's new house at the farm and continued working
at it with my little boys Richard and Wilford till
Saturday Evening 23 august. spending sunday at the
farm with the Exiles who had returned form
Lewiston on Wednesday night the 20th. The babe
was very sick for a few days and I felt quite
anxious about it it looked so bad. but in the
mercy of God it recovered with much care and
nursing.
Monday 25th august found me at my post in the
Temple and we had quite a number of names
to record for baptisms on the following day, and the

weeks work was unusually heavy for the season of
the year.
Friday 29 aug 1890. I went to smithfield and spent
Saturday 30 aug 1890 at the Farm working at the
new house. and we went to town at night, spending
Sunday 31 aug in town with the family as I was
sick and not able to go out. I returned to the
Temple Monday Morning altho not feeling well
Bro Robt Meikle died this morning, 1st sep.
and I helped the boys at the farm to raise and
fix the Horse fork for a long Pole to put Hay
into a stack.
Wednesday 3 september 1890. I attended bro
Robt Meikle's funeral at Smithfield and
preached the funeral sermon at the request of
his survivors and returned to Logan in the
morning to attend to my usual Labor. Till
Friday Evening 5 sep 1890 when I returned to
Smithfield, and working on Mary's new house
during the saturdays following as much as
I possably could to get the foundation of
the work along.
[folded tabular reports pasted end-to-end on the page]

Register of Logan Temple Ordinance Work for August 1890.

Baptisms								Endowments				Ordinations		Sealings		Children to Parents		Adoptions		Second Anointings			
First		Renewal of Cov.		Health		Dead		Living		Dead		Living	Dead	Living	Dead	Living	Dead	Living	Dead	Living		Dead	
M	F	M	F	M	F	M	F	M	F	M	F									M	F	M	F
1	1	1	3	3	9	373	271	14	20	73	131	–	71	15	55	21	25	–	–	1	1	–	–
2		5		12		644		34		204		71		70		46		–		2		–	
663								238				71		70		46		–		2			
Samuel Roskelley Recorder																							

Register of Logan Temple Ordinance Work for September 1890

Baptisms								Endowments				Ordinations		Sealings		Children to Parents		Adoptions		Second Anointings			
First		Renewal of Cov.		Health		Dead		Living		Dead		Living	Dead	Living	Dead	Living	Dead	Living	Dead	Living		Dead	
M	F	M	F	M	F	M	F	M	F	M	F									M	F	M	F
2	3	21	24	26	90	2280	2436	58	84	511	805	1	509	64	353	107	94	–	1	8	16	6	7
5		45		116		4716		142		1376		510		417		201		1		24		13	
4,882								1,518				510		417		201		1		37			
Samuel Roskelley Recorder																							

Register of Logan Temple Ordinance Work for October 1890																			
Baptisms								Endowments				Ordinations		Sealings		Children to Parents		Adoptions		Second Anointings			
First		Renewal of Cov.		Health		Dead		Living		Dead		Living	Dead	Living	Dead	Living	Dead	Living	Dead	Living		Dead	
M	F	M	F	M	F	M	F	M	F	M	F	Living	Dead	Living	Dead	Living	Dead	Living	Dead	M	F	M	F
–	–	10	16	18	57	1128	1069	108	122	490	805	9	485	113	425	153	116	8	13	11	13	6	10
		26		75		2197		230		1295		494		538		269		21		24		16	
2,298								1,525				494		538		269		21		40			
Samuel Roskelley Recorder																				

{43}
Continuing my labors in the Temple as usual.
during the week. and going home on Friday Evenings.
Thursday 18 september 1890 was an Eventful
day for my son James. he received Endowments for
my Brother John Joseph Roskelley and was ordained
by me for his Uncle and also took Miss Francis
Annie Emery to wife – we rode to smithfield
after the ceremony and partook of a bountiful
repast prepared by my family who assembled
at the farm to do honor to the occasion. I returned
to Logan in the Morning to continue my labors in
the Temple doing so till
Thursday 2nd October 1890 the Temple closed
for Conference . My sons James & Joseph went
to Conference but I worked painting my new house
at the farm, as fast as the Rustic was put up
resuming work at the Temple on
Thursday morning 9th Oct 1890. and continued till
Friday Evening 10 Oct 1890.
Saturday. Attended priesthood meeting in the forenoon
and went home in the afternoon to Smithfield remaining
till Monday Morning.   I learned that my son Joseph
had received a notice calling him on a
mission to New Zealand. I am thankful to
have boys who are though Enough of to be sent
on Missions to preach the Gospel.
Monday 13 Oct 1890. Returned to my labors in the
Temple. continuing till Friday
Sunday 19th Oct. With Bro Duce Visited Newton and
Clarkston in the Interests of the High Priests Quorum
having a good visit with each body. returning to
my labor in the Temple on Monday Morning.
I returned to Smithfield on Friday Evening 24 Oct and
worked on my wife Mary's new house on Saturday.
Sunday 26th October with my little boys Richard and
Wilford I attended the stake conference at Franklin
and heard good teachings by Prest Geo Q Cannon

apostle M W. Merrill & others. returned to smithfield
in the Evening and returned to Logan to resume my
Temple labors on Monday Morning 27 Oct.
Sunday 2 Nov 1890 I attended Cache Quarterly stake
Conference. apostles L Snow. F D Richards. MW Merrill
with Jacob Gates and C.D. Fjeldsted preached and a
good spirit prevailed. resumed my temple labors
on Monday during intermission of Conference

{44}
1890
Friday 7 Nov Went home in the Evening, and next day with
my sons James & Joseph cleaned wheat to raise money to
help Joseph on his mission to New Zealand.
Sunday 9 Nov. Attended meeting at Smithfield and heard
High Councillors John Jacobs & Wm Sanders (Home Mission
=aries Preach.). spent most of the day with my son Joseph.
Monday 10 November 1890. my son Joseph Started on
his mission to New Zealand with his Companion
Robert Gilbert Meikle. going to Salt Lake City first
to be set apart. and Expecting to sail from San Franciso
on Saturday 15 Nov. Quite a number of persons
met the young missionaries at the Depot and many
were the Kindly words with "God Bless you" said to
them on leaving, the train starting south at 12 Minutes
past 1. P.M.. attended my usual labors in the
Temple during the week and went Home on Friday
Evening 14th Nov and worked fanning Wheat and
fixing new stands for Bees.
Sunday 16 Nov.. Son James and I visited Lewiston
and held meeting with the members of the High
Priest Quorum, and received 6 new members
I ordained 2, Bp. Lewis 2. Bro [blank] 1. and I
authorized the Bp to ordain Bro Dopp and
report to me. Visited Hirams family and ret=
=urned to smithfield.
         Spent the Week in the Temple as usual and
returned home on Friday Evening. 21 Nov. 1890
Spent Sunday at Home. attending meeting. Bro R S.
Collett preached, Returned to Logan Monday Morning
and continued my usual labors thro the week, till
Friday Night, when I returned to Smithfield
and spent Saturday fixing the Roof my Big
House in town. and attended the funeral of Bro
Jenson Ellen Merrill's father and on
Sunday 30 Nov. attended meeting at Coveville and
met with the High Priests of the ward afterwards
and had a good little meeting, returning home
in [the Evening]

[44 con't; folded tabular report pasted on the page]

Register of Logan Temple Ordinance Work for Nov. 1890																	
Baptisms								Endowments			Ordinations		Sealings		Children to Parents		Adoptions		Second Anointings			
First		Renewal of Cov.		Health		Dead		Living		Dead		Living	Dead	Living	Dead	Living	Dead	Living	Dead	Living		Dead	
M	F	M	F	M	F	M	F	M	F	M	F									M	F	M	F
–	2	16	14	17	51	1154	1110	87	94	480	746	5	477	90	343	98	48	5	8	5	10	–	2
2		30		68		2,264		181		1,226		482		433		146		13		15		2
2,364								1,407			482		433		146		13		17			
Samuel Roskelley Recorder																								

{45}
1890.
 Spent the month of December much the same as
November, on Sunday 14th Visited Richmond with my
councillors Bro Duce and Morrell and held meeting
with the Members of the Quorum residing in that ward
and afterward met with the saints in their sacrament
meeting. And. My councillors talked to the saints and
I also occupied a portion of the time.
On Sunday 28th Dec I took the Early train from Smithf-
and rode to Hot Springs and met bro Job Hall and Bro.
Greenwell who took me to Pleasant View where I spent
a few Hours visiting Bro Rhees's family in connexion with
the persons mentioned, Went to meeting at the ward
meeting house and by invitation of the Bishop (Wade)
I occupied about an hour and a Quarter. talking
mostly to the young people. afterward went to the
house of Bro E Ellis and had a good visit with
the family – administered to their daughter the
wife of Bro W. Elisha Cragun who has a cancer on
her breast. returned home to Logan by the Evening
train. and continued my work in the temple. next week
Thursday 25 Dec, after spending the night at the
farm with my wife Mary on the 24th I fixed and
went to town. My wifes Mary Jane & Maggie had fixed
dinner for all the family and we set down to an Excellent
repast and enjoyed the Evening with the family except
Maud who was at Logan Visiting her parents.
Monday 29 Dec 1890 Commenced work at the Temple
as usual and continued till Wednesday Evening when
the Temple Closed and I went to Smithfield finding my
children Emma & George sick with some Kind of fever.
and their mothers nearly worn our nursing them.

Samuel Roskelley

[45 con't; folded tabular report pasted on the page]

Register of Logan Temple Ordinance Work for December 1890																			
Baptisms								Endowments				Ordinations		Sealings		Children to Parents		Adoptions		Second Anointings			
First		Renewal of Cov.		Health		Dead		Living		Dead		Living	Dead	Living	Dead	Living	Dead	Living	Dead	Living		Dead	
M	F	M	F	M	F	M	F	M	F	M	F									M	F	M	F
1	2	12	11	17	29	686	988	65	72	324	470	1	324	73	180	43	27	–	–	2	1	–	1
5		23		46		1,674		137		794		325		253		70		—		3		1	
1,748								931				325		253		70		—		4			

Samuel Roskelley   Recorder

{46}
1891. 1st Jan. another Eventful year has passed
away.. and I am grateful circumstances as as [sic] well
with me and mine. Altho' sickness among my chil=
=dren prevents any gathering of my family as is usual on
this my Birth day, the weather is beautiful for winter
no snow having fallen so far this winter. temple is
closed till Monday 5 Jan 1891.
Monday 5 Jan Returned to Logan to continue my labors in
the Temple after spending the sabbath at home in Smithfd
with my councillors, attending High Priest meeting in the
morning and ordaining Wm Ainscough and James Burgess
and attending the sacrament meeting in the afternoon
Friday 9 Jan. Returned again to Smithfield and went
to the farm staying part of next day,
Sunday 11 Jan. Mary had provided a feast and invited
Mary Jane & Maggie with the Children and myself to
spend the afternoon which I did, returning to
Logan the next Monday Morning Early train. Maud
still at Logan with her people.
Friday 16 Jan 1891.. I returned to Smithfield. and worked

{continues next page}

{46 con't}
[folded tabular report pasted on the page]

Register of Ordinance Work performed during the year ending Dec. 31. 1890

	Baptisms				Endowments		Ordinations		Sealings		Children to Parents		Adoptions		Second Anointings	
	First	Ren. of Cov.	Health	Dead	Living	Dead	Living	Dead	Living	Dead	Living	Dead	Living	Dead	Living	Dead
Logan Temple	37	281	636	29,834	1,367	11,381	27	4,438	655	3,176	848	644	23	30	138	69
Manti Temple	91	579	2,415	31,139	760	13,652	31	5,641	379	6,073	922	816	108	1,696	93	61
St. George Temple	49	73	102	3,452	137	3,759	17	1497	66	1,103	70	72	13	201	40	47
	177	933	3,153	65,425	2,264	28,192	75	11,576	1,100	9,352	1,840	1,632	143	1,927	271	177
Totals	69,688				31,056		11,651		10,452		3,472		2,070		448	

Ordinance Work performed in Logan, Manti and St. George Temples to 31st Dec. 1890

	Baptisms				Endowments		Ordinations		Sealings		Children to Parents		Adoptions		Second Anointings	
	First	Ren. of Cov.	Health	Dead	Living	Dead	Living	Dead	Living	Dead	Living	Dead	Living	Dead	Living	Dead
Logan Temple	222	2,340	4,469	193,525	10,089	80,639	168	31,963	4,986	22,933	7.024	5,403	114	230	737	399
Manti Temple	148	2,225	8,200	103,932	2,395	39,999	93	16,323	1,110	14,388	3,381	3,151	337	4,014	426	204
St. George Temple	414	760	2,669	250,682	5,297	102,181	1,151	39,247	2,788	33,458	3,602	3756	483	5,633	1225	1269
	784	5,321	15,398	548,139	17,781	222,819	1,412	87,533	8,884	70,839	16,007	12,310	944	9877	2388	1872
Totals	569,646				240,600		88,945		79,723		26,317		10,821		4,260	

{47}
painting on the Windows of the new House on the following
day Saturday – and also settled my tithing
sunday 18 Jan 1891. attended meeting in the forenoon
of the High Priests in Smithfield and talked to them
a while. also attended Sacrament Meeting in the
afternoon and occupied the whole time talking to
the saints.. also attended meeting in the Evening an
listened to a discourse form Prest Orson Smith
and afterward returned to Logan on train
Wife Maud has been quite sick with pain
in her head and other parts of her system.
Attended to my usual routine of labor in the
Temple thro the week and returned to Smithfield
on Friday Evening 23 Jan 1891.
saturday 24 Jan. Bro Jensen commenced working,
for me for 1 year. Recd 1st letter from son Jodie. [sic]
Sunday 25th Jan 1891. attended meeting as
usual at Smithfield and took train for
Logan in the Evening. remaining at my Post during the
week and returning to Smithfield ~~Saturday~~ Friday Evening 30 Jan
worked around home during the saturday and on
Sunday 1st Feb 1891. Went to Logan to attend the Quarterly
Conference of Cache Stake. in a blinding & cold Snow
storm remaining over at Logan till. Wednesday Evening
4th Feb when my son William came for me and took
Maud home,
Friday 6 Feb 1891. Wife Mary Jane came with Sarah to
Logan to get teeth pulled and I rode home with them.
but felt quite unwell being full of feaver with pains
[folded tabular report pasted on the page]

Register of Logan Temple Ordinance Work for January 1891

Baptisms								Endowments				Ordinations		Sealings		Children to Parents		Adoptions		Second Anointings			
First		Renewal of Cov.		Health		Dead		Living		Dead		Living	Dead	Living	Dead	Living	Dead	Living	Dead	Living		Dead	
M	F	M	F	M	F	M	F	M	F	M	F									M	F	M	F
3	4	7	7	11	26	904	761	43	53	378	455	–	375	48	207	26	26	2	1	3	2	2	3
7		14		37		1,665		96		833		375		255		52		3		5		5	
1,723								929				375		255		52		3		10			

Samuel Roskelley   Recorder

And aches all thro my body but I visited the farm
and stayed part of the day saturday attending to matters
there, but after going to town I took to my bed remaining
till monday morning doing all I could to aleviate my
suffering, the ride in the sleigh seemed to do me good
and I felt better but when night came on my feaver
increased and from then till I left the Temple on
Thursday afternoon I Kept getting gradually worse.
Prest Merrill sent me home with his team and

sleigh but every jolt in the road seemed to shake me

{48}
to pieces. I went to Bed immediately on my
arrival at home and laid there helpless with
Pneumonia & La Grippe for over 3 weeks with the
best care my dear family could give me day and night
my sufferings no one can describe during the time
and for 2 weeks nothing would relieve the pain in
my head but the administration of the Elders; I recov=
=ered very slowly but on
Monday 16th Mch 1891 I ventured to go to the Temple
and was welcomed by all.
[folded tabular report pasted on the page]

Register of Logan Temple Ordinance Work for February 1891																		
Baptisms								Endowments				Ordinations	Sealings		Children to Parents		Adoptions		Second Anointings		
First		Renewal of Cov.		Health		Dead		Living		Dead		Living	Dead	Living	Dead	Living	Dead	Living	Dead	Living		Dead	
M	F	M	F	M	F	M	F	M	F	M	F									M	F	M	F
1	2	13	17	10	16	1023	328	41	42	446	446	3	445	39	199	26	28	5	2	1	2	2	2
3		30		26		1351		83		892		448		238		54		7		3		4	
1410								975				448		238		54		7		7		
Samuel Roskelley Recorder																		

Found I was not strong but managed to Keep
at work most of the time till
Friday 20 Mch when I went home but housed
up again till Monday 23rd Mch when I again
went to the Temple and resumed my Labors. returned
to smithfield on the 27th and the weather was
so rough I remained in doors till Monday
30th Mch when I again went to the Temple
to resume my labors
/Thursday\ 2 Apl 1891. Temple Closed tonight for Conference
and I went to smithfield and worked at the farm
and in town fixing up things for spring work. as the
weather was to changeable for me to go to the
Conference Tuesday 7 apl. Wife Maud Confined with a girl
Wednesday 8 apl. Temple opened and I was on hand
for duty, till Friday 10th apl 1891.. when I went home
to Smithfield, and returned to Temple again on
the following Monday 13th – returned to Smithfield
again on Wednesday 15th and in the Evening I blessed
my little girl babe calling it Clara, after
one of my wife Maud's Sisters who had been Very
Kind to her. during her Exile . spent the remainder
of the Month in a similar Manner.. My health not
being good I. could not travel and meet with
the members of the High Priests Quorum as I
felt that it would be too much exposure for me

{49}

1st May 1891 The following letter explains itself
and I arranged for the sister mentioned and met
Prest Woodruff and did all I could to make his
stay in Logan as agreeable as possible for
which he expressed his gratitude & thanks and
blessed me in the name of the Lord.
attended Conference 3&4 of May 1891 of the Cache
stake of Zion and we had an extra good
time with Prest Woodruff and 3 of the apostles
present.. my wife Maud with her children
came to Logan on Friday 1st May to stay with
her parents a while..
I continued to labor as usual in the house
of the Lord, going home Friday Evenings as
usual. And on Sunday May 30th Bro Thos
Duce and I Visited Clarkston and had a
good meeting in the morning and talked
to the High Priests in the afternoon met
with the saints and talked to them a
good influence prevailed both meetings
attended to my usual labors thro the week.
Monday. 1st June Maud thought some one
was watching her and picked up hurried
ly and left her Mothers going to O. Bluemell's
and stayed till Tuesday Morning 9th June when
Maggie took her to Hyde Park. I bought
a cart so as to run around with and
commenced to go home nights. and found my
health improved by so doing.
Friday 12 June 1891. I went to the farm at Smith
=field. In the Evening and on Sunday I drove
to Newton and held meeting with the saints
of that ward and afterward with the members
of the High Priests Quorum. Returning to Logan on
Monday Morning and going to Smithfield each
Evening thro' the week.
Sunday 21st June with my councilors I went
south leaving Bro Joseph Morrell to hold meeting at
Hyrum and Bro Duce & I went on to Paradise
and Held meeting at 10-30 with the members of
the Quorum and w with the saints and had
a good visit returning to Smithfield my wife
Maggie being quite Sick. I went to Visit my
wife Maud and children at Hyde Park at
night. And Logan on Monday 22nd

{50}
attending to my duties in the Temple. till
Friday 23rd June when I was summoned to meet
Bro W F Rigby before the Presidency of Cache Valley

stake on a/c of his previous charge against me
on the High Council Minutes. As usual it was
postponed till the following tuesday when Bro W^m
T. Vannoy met with us and each made a
statement before the Prest of Stake Orson Smith
and his councillor Isaac Smith. Bp T. X Smith
and James Quayle being also present, but nothing
was arrived at as a conclusion of this miser=
=able affair, until we could hear from the Young
Vannoys,
I visited the High priest at Wellsville with
Bro Duce in July and had a good attendance
and meeting – also a good meeting in the afternoon
with the Saints, Temple closed on. 17 July till 8 aug
Saturday 1&2 aug attended quarterly Conference
of Cache Valley Stake and had good teachings from
apostles F. D. Richards, M. Thatcher, M W. Merrill &
A. H. Cannon. Political excitement runs high
and it is creating quite a division among our
people.
10th Aug 1891.. I am more than astonished to
day as receiving a letter from my son Joseph
from sanfrancisco learning that he is on his
way home from his missionary labors in New Zealand
17 au. I have been at home a month painting
the Kitchen part of Marys new house, fixing fences
and repairing gates. Watering, pulling Weeds, and
repairing my 2 Wagons and painting them.
and return to Logan this Evening to the Temple
to resume my labors tomorrow morning. The work
of the Temple is resumed by the saints with much
Energy and interest. It is astonishing where the people
come from, for we are quite crowded, I continued
my Labors in the Temple during August and September
going home nights and returning in the morning.
Mary Moved into the New House on the 15th
august and seemed to Enjoy the change.
Things passed as usual with myself and family
Except the Team started to run away and ran over

{51}
Richard Knocking him down but he escaped without
any serious injury, and freddie was coming to the
~~Black~~ Temple from the Blacksmith shop in Logan and
a drunken fellow ran into the cart and tipped it
over and hurt him by Knocking him out and bruising
him bad. Wilford was going to the field for the cows
and the mare stumbled – he fell off cutting his head
bad, and Ora got Kicked with a Colt on the side of
his face & head on 27th aug making it necessary
to send for a Doctor to sew it up.

on Monday 14 sep apostle a. Lund came to the
Temple and I had the pleasure of showing him over
the building and afterwards accompanying him to the
Agricultural College – he being the framer of the bill
to Establish the Institution was shown much respect
by Prof sanborne the Principal.. I had a good visit
with the apostle.
Sunday 20 sep with Bro Duce Visited the bretheren
of the HPriests at Clarkston at 10.30 and attended the
saints meeting at Newton at 2P.M and HP. Meeting
at 4.P.M. returning to smithfield at night,
Maggie moved her goods back to Mary Janes
house form Bp Farrells, on the 18th sep. and
helped to fix up the place with Stove and pipe &c and
make it Comfortable.
Sunday 27 Sep 1891. attended H.P. Meeting at Smith=
=field and ordained & assisted to ordain 7 Bretheren
who were recommended from the Elders Quorum'
Bro Thos Duce was with me and assisted I
sent Bro Duce to attend Meeting in 2nd Ward
Logan at night and call on Bro Jos Morrell
to assist in ordaining some bretheren
who had been recommended form the Elders
of that ward. I attended meeting at Smithfd
Elder C.D. Fjelsted of the 1st Presidency of the
70s Preached and I followed. him. Continued
my labors in the Temple during the week, as
usual.
[*folded tabular report pasted on the page*]

Register of Logan Temple Ordinance Work for August 1891																			
Baptisms								Endowments				Ordinations		Sealings		Children to Parents		Adoptions		Second Anointings			
First		Renewal of Cov.		Health		Dead		Living		Dead		Living	Dead	Living	Dead	Living	Dead	Living	Dead	Living		Dead	
M	F	M	F	M	F	M	F	M	F	M	F									M	F	M	F
–	1	7	4	9	36	503	600	26	27	163	309	4	163	22	103	17	20	2	44	2	4	1	1
1		11		45		1103		53		472		167		125		37		46		6		2	
1,160								525				167		126		37		46		8			
Samuel Roskelley Recorder																			

[51 con't]

Register of Logan Temple Ordinance Work for September 1891

Baptisms								Endowments				Ordinations		Sealings		Children to Parents		Adoptions		Second Anointings			
First		Renewal of Cov.		Health		Dead		Living		Dead		Living	Dead	Living	Dead	Living	Dead	Living	Dead	Living		Dead	
M	F	M	F	M	F	M	F	M	F	M	F									M	F	M	F
2	1	14	11	15	72	1294	1858	71	81	487	723	5	484	68	313	114	100	5	14	7	18	10	15
3		25		87		3,152		152		1210		489		381		214		19		25		25	
3,267								1,362				489		381		214		19		50			

Samuel Roskelley   Recorder

{52}
after completing my labors for the week. with my
wife Mary Jane I took train at Smithfield on
Sunday 4th October for Salt Lake to attend Conference
spending 3 days and getting the good of all the
meetings of the conference – morning afternoon &
Evening, returning to smithfield ~~Wednesday~~ /Tuesday\
Evening. 6 Oct.,
Wednesday & Thursday – with the boys I dug my
potatoes at the farm and put them in the
cellar,, & Friday & Satuday did odd jobs
of repairing wagons &c.
Sunday 11th Oct felt quite under the weather
with cold & did not go to meeting, but rested
in bed. resuming my work at the Temple
on Monday 12th oct and had a heavy Weeks
work.
Thursday Evening I made arrangements with Bro
N Kimball of the Coop W&M Compy to get
a press drill for $85^{00} commencing the payment
therefore in Jan 1882 of 15^{00} and ten dollars each
month afterward till paid. .
Sunday 18th October With my councillor I went South and I visited
the Bretheren of the HP. Quorum at Hyrum and set them right
on the Question of the Jurisdiction of the Quorum over
its members and how far its authority extends. And
where the Bp's authority comes. in..
Elder Duce went to Paradise and Visited the brethen
there and straightened up Bro Gibbs the Teacher
who had been drinking and disgraced himself.
Returned to Smithfield at night and to Logan next
morning (Monday) going to & from Logan to my
home at Smithfield each day.
Sunday 25 Oct 1891. Went with Bro Duce
to Franklin to attend Oneida Stake Conference
apostle M F Lyman preached some stiff
doctrine. Said the Lords will is that we (LDS)

obey the law of the land, casing many
hearts to flutter and feel dispondent. Returned
to Smithfeild at night and Logan on
Monday Morning 26 Oct 1891. and contin
=uing at the Temple thro' the week. only going
home twice thro' the week.

[folded tabular report pasted on the page; duplicates prior page]

Register of Logan Temple Ordinance Work for September 1891																			
Baptisms								Endowments				Ordinations		Sealings		Children to Parents		Adoptions		Second Anointings			
First		Renewal of Cov.		Health		Dead		Living		Dead		Living	Dead	Living	Dead	Living	Dead	Living	Dead	Living		Dead	
M	F	M	F	M	F	M	F	M	F	M	F									M	F	M	F
2	1	14	11	15	72	1294	1858	71	81	487	723	5	484	68	313	114	100	5	14	7	18	10	15
3		25		87		3,152		152		1210		489		381		214		19		25		25	
3,267								1,362				489		381		214		19		50			
Samuel Roskelley Recorder																			

[Loose between pages but pasted together in corner:]

Register of Logan Temple Ordinance Work for October 1891																			
Baptisms								Endowments				Ordinations		Sealings		Children to Parents		Adoptions		Second Anointings			
First		Renewal of Cov.		Health		Dead		Living		Dead		Living	Dead	Living	Dead	Living	Dead	Living	Dead	Living		Dead	
M	F	M	F	M	F	M	F	M	F	M	F									M	F	M	F
–	1	8	12	18	48	1,150	1,224	74	91	463	585	5	459	80	304	180	115	2	6	3	11	7	5
1		20		66		2,374		165		1,048		464		384		295		8		14		12	
2,461								1,213				464		384		295		8		26			
Samuel Roskelley Recorder																			

Register of Logan Temple Ordinance Work for November 1891																			
Baptisms								Endowments				Ordinations		Sealings		Children to Parents		Adoptions		Second Anointings			
First		Renewal of Cov.		Health		Dead		Living		Dead		Living	Dead	Living	Dead	Living	Dead	Living	Dead	Living		Dead	
M	F	M	F	M	F	M	F	M	F	M	F									M	F	M	F
2	2	11	14	21	46	1,131	1,043	73	86	537	661	3	537	77	385	64	61	2	2	19	23	5	13
4		25		67		2,174		159		1,198		540		462		125		4		42		18	
2,270								1,357				540		462		125		4		60			
Samuel Roskelley Recorder																			

[loose con't]

Register of Logan Temple Ordinance Work for Dec. 1891

Baptisms								Endowments				Ordinations		Sealings		Children to Parents		Adoptions		Second Anointings			
First		Renewal of Cov.		Health		Dead		Living		Dead		Living	Dead	Living	Dead	Living	Dead	Living	Dead	Living		Dead	
M	F	M	F	M	F	M	F	M	F	M	F									M	F	M	F
3	3	11	17	8	32	1,036	1,034	80	89	407	527	—	406	91	270	58	42	1	10	10	14	7	8
6		28		40		2,070		169		934		406		361		100		11		24		15	
2,144								1,103				406		361		100		11		39			

Samuel Roskelley   Recorder

{53}

<u>Sunday 1 Nov 1891.</u> Quarterly Conference of Cache Valley
stake commenced with the first Presidency of the Church
all present. They occupied all the time during the 3
meetings of the day and 1 meeting on Monday 2nd Nov.
an Excellent spirit prevailed altho Prest Woodruff said
The Lord had asked him to ask the saints if it is not
best for them to cease the practice of plural marriage
and thus save our Temples & untold suffering among the
members of the Church because of the stringent laws
of the land now in force., during this month Bro Duce
and I visited the High Priests at Lewiston. Richmond and
Coveville also attended the meetings at Smithfield on
several occasions. Continuing my usual Labors at the Temple
through the month.
December 1891. During this month. I only attended one meeting
of the members of the Quorum at Hyde Park as the
weather was quite unpropitious. found all working well
at Hyde Park, with the members of the Quorum.
Thurday 24 Dec. The Temple closed till the 4th Jan1892
I went to smithfield and on
<u>Friday 25th Dec</u> my wives and all my small children
who were at Home ate Dinner and Supper at my wife.
Mary Jane's and we had quite an enjoyable time together.
I did what I could to make the folks comfortable
while at home as the weather proved uncomfortably cold
during the Holidays.
Friday 1st Jan 1892. I am 55 years old today
and I praise God my Heavenly Father for all his
mercies and blessings to me for he has been exceedingly
Kind in preserving my life, and giving me the privelages
and blessings I possess. My wives, Children and Grand
Children assembled at the farm where my wife Mary and
her girls had prepared Dinner and about 40 sat at dinner
and Enjoyed a dance together afterward, interspersed with
singing &c. I had not danced for 6 years till tonight.
Saturday 2Jan1892. Attended the Priesthood meeting at
Logan. Apostle Moses Thatcher addressed us, on current topics

sunday 3 Jan 1892 attended High Priests Meeting at Smithfield
and talked to the Bretheren urging them to live lives as
saints of god. Also attended sunday afternoon meeting and
talked to the people about. doing their duty during the
coming year,
Monday 4 Jan 1892. Commenced my labors again
in the House of the Lord and made up my years <u>accts</u>
of Labor performed in this. Manti and St Georges
Temples. and forwarded a copy to the Presidency of
the Church 12 apostles and several Leading men.

{54}
<u>1892</u>.
10 Jan With Bro Duce I visited Paradise and held
a lengthy meeting with the bretheren of the High
Priests Quorum and all seemed satisfied
with their lot and place and started out in
the New year by asking each others forgiveness
for all past offences. Came to Millville
in the afternoon and held meeting with the

{continues next page}

{54 con't}
High Priests of that ward a good feeling prevailed and we had a season of rejoicing. It was a bitter cold day and the cold seemed to pierce the marrow of our bones,
[folded tabulation pasted on page]

Register of Ordinance work performed during the year ending Dec. 31.st 1891

	Baptisms					Endowments		Ordinations		Sealings		Children to Parents		Adoptions		Second Anointings	
	First	Ren. of Cov.	Health	Dead	Living	Dead	Living	Dead	Living	Dead	Living	Dead	Living	Dead	Living	Dead
Logan Temple	43	324	671	24,349	1,351	11,697	26	4,934	652	3,126	822	664	30	114	232	128
Manti do	85	609	1,964	22,068	783	11,039	32	4,841	503	3,840	829	676	47	898	90	48
St. George do	51	75	85	2,200	121	3,784	13	1600	73	1,479	60	58	9	153	25	27
Totals	179	918	2,720	48617	2955	26,520	71	11,375	1,128	8,445	1711	1398	86	1165	347	203
Gd. Total	52,434					28,775		11,446		9,573		3,109		1,251		550	

Ordinance work performed in Logan, Manti and St. George Temples to 31st Dec. 1891

	Baptisms					Endowments		Ordinations		Sealings		Children to Parents		Adoptions		Second Anointings	
	First	Ren. of Cov.	Health	Dead	Living	Dead	Living	Dead	Living	Dead	Living	Dead	Living	Dead	Living	Dead
Logan Temple	265	2,574	5,140	217,814	1140	92,336	194	36,897	5,638	25,119	7,846	6,067	144	344	969	627
Manti do	233	2,834	10,224	126,000	3,178	41,038	125	21164	1,513	18,228	4,210	3827	384	4,912	516	252
St. George do	465	835	2,754	252,882	5,418	105,965	1,164	40,847	2,861	34,937	3,662	3,814	502	5,716	1250	1296
Totals	963	6,243	18,118	59,6756	20036	24,339	1483	98,808	10,012	79,284	15,718	13,708	1030	11,042	2735	2070
Gnd. Total	622,080					269,375		100,391		89296		29426		12,072		4810	

{54 con't}
[*diary text*]
Friday 15 jan 1892. With Bro Duce We wrote to all the presiding teachers, thro the stake to send us the names of two or 3 High priests from which we could select some missionaries to visit all the members of the Quorum and continued my usual routine of labors in and out of the Temple till
Sunday 31 Jan 1982. attended Stake Quarterly Conference at Logan, apostles F M Lyman & MWMerrill present and gave some good teachings for the occasion. attended meeting also Monday 1st Feb. and on Tuesday sent out letters of appoint =ment and instructions to Persons in Each Ward in the Stake of which the accompanying is a copy.
[*folded letter pasted on the page*]

      Logan City. Utah January 26th 1892
        Elder

Dear Brother. Your name has been suggested and accepted and you are appointed to labor with Elder [*blank*] of [*blank*] to visit all the members of the High Priests Quorum residing in [*blank*] Ward and in [*blank*] Ward as circumstances may permit, and we pray that the spirit of this appointment may accompany you to aid in building up and strengthening the faith and stimula ting good desires in the hearts of the members of the Quorum you may visit. Encouraging all to faithfulness in the performance of every known duty – such as family and secret prayer. Payment of Tithes and Offerings, sustaining Gods chosen servants called to preside in all the departments of the Church. by faith words and works. to live exemplary lives before /wives\ children and friends. Speaking no evil. but having charity for all. and seeking to approximate to the Saviors teachings as near as possible.
To love our neighbors as ourselves. faithfully attending Sacrament Fast and Quorum meetings. as God has commanded his Saints to meet together often. that our hearts may not grow cold toward each other. and the world of the Lord.
A written report fro yourself and companion showing the condition of those you visit. and addressed to George F. Stratton Logan will be appreciated by your fellow laborers.

    Samuel Roskelley \ Of the Presidency of High
    Thomas Duce / Priests Quorum. Cache
          Valley Stake

George F. Stratton
 Secy

{55}
[folded tabular report pasted on the page]

Register of Logan Temple Ordinance Work for January/92																	
Baptisms								Endowments				Ordinations		Sealings		Children to Parents		Adoptions		Second Anointings			
First		Renewal of Cov.		Health		Dead		Living		Dead		Living	Dead	Living	Dead	Living	Dead	Living	Dead	Living		Dead	
M	F	M	F	M	F	M	F	M	F	M	F											M	F	M	F
1	2	11	8	6	14	658	574	25	27	393	449	1	392	30	229	29	20	1	1	5	8	3	8
3		19		20		1232		52		842		393		259		49		2		13		11	
1274								894				393		259		49		2		24			
Samuel Roskelley Recorder																								

During the month of February the Weather and roads were in such a condition that I did not travel, but thought it to be prudent to remain at home on the sabbath days.

Sunday 6 Mch. Should have been the smithfield Ward annual Conference but the Dipthera having broke out the week previous, it was deemed wise to discontinue schools, meetings and in fact all public gatherings. so I attended the Hyde Park ward conference and took part in the Exercises. A good spirit seemed to prevail ..

[folded tabular report pasted on the page]

Register of Logan Temple Ordinance Work for February 1892.																	
Baptisms								Endowments				Ordinations		Sealings		Children to Parents		Adoptions		Second Anointings			
First		Renewal of Cov.		Health		Dead		Living		Dead		Living	Dead	Living	Dead	Living	Dead	Living	Dead	Living		Dead	
M	F	M	F	M	F	M	F	M	F	M	F											M	F	M	F
7	6	16	13	6	23	863	314	37	46	470	475	1	470	44	244	29	21	5	10	4	7	1	5
13		29		29		1177		83		945		471		288		50		15		12		6	
1,248								1,028				471		288		50		15		18			
Samuel Roskelley Recorder																								

The month of March was Cold and Wet Making the roads awful so I Kept at home on the sabbath and attended my usual temple labors.

Apl. I could not consistantly go to Conference my Means was so short, but learned that all who attended felt well at the laying of the cap stone of the Temple. during the month I took part in the political issues in the smithfield City Election and assisted to organize a Republican club and I might say piloted the party to victory at the Polls on 2 May 1892. I feel glad that the party got there with a majority of from 9 to 14 votes – but much bitterness has been exhibited by the other Party especially against myself and the candidates

for office. and some nasty letters have been
published in the Journal (a Democratic Sheet)
Sunday 8th and Monday 9th May 1892 attended the
Quarterly Conference of Cache Valley Stake at
Logan. Prests Woodruff & Cannon were there
and occupied most of the time in giving good
advice & counsel to the saints.

{56}
and I had pleasure of Eating dinner with them
at the Temple on Monday of Conference, and had
a good visit.– Continued at my usual labor
in the Temple – the companys are unusually light.
Sunday 15 May I visited the High Priests in Lewiston Ward
and held meeting with them. Also attended the Saints
Sacrament Meeting. Having a good Visit – my son
Joseph went with me.
Sunday 22 May   Visited the Newton Ward and found
a Sabbath School Jubilee in Session – many present
form Clarkston & Trenton Wards, I held a High
Priests meeting and attended the Jubilee also
returning to Smithfield in the Evening.
[folded tabular report pasted on the page]

Register of Logan Temple Ordinance Work for March 1892.															
Baptisms								Endowments				Ordinations		Sealings		Children to Parents		Adoptions		Second Anointings			
First		Renewal of Cov.		Health		Dead		Living		Dead		Living	Dead	Living	Dead	Living	Dead	Living	Dead	Living		Dead	
M	F	M	F	M	F	M	F	M	F	M	F											M	F	M	F
3	5	12	13	16	35	934	661	53	53	527	612	1	527	47	409	55	32	–	–	3	6	1	3
8		25		51		1595		106		1139		528		456		87		—		9		4	
1,679								1,245				528		456		87		—		13			
Samuel Roskelley Recorder																									

Register of Logan Temple Ordinance Work for apl 1892															
Baptisms								Endowments				Ordinations		Sealings		Children to Parents		Adoptions		Second Anointings			
First		Renewal of Cov.		Health		Dead		Living		Dead		Living	Dead	Living	Dead	Living	Dead	Living	Dead	Living		Dead	
M	F	M	F	M	F	M	F	M	F	M	F											M	F	M	F
–	–	10	7	7	15	375	347	27	20	23	278	2	233	24	165	29	17	–	2	3	3	2	4
—		17		22		722		47		511		235		189		46		2		6		6	
762								558				235		189		46		2		12			
Samuel Roskelley Recorder																									

Sunday 30th May 1892. Attended S.S. Union at
Smithfield thro' the day and continued the
week at the Temple as usual in my calling as

Recorder.

Sunday 5 June 1892. I took my little daughter
Emma as far as Newton, and I went on the Clarkston
and held a High Priest Meeting at 11 oclock, all
present spoke and a good spirit prevailed. I
afterward occupied the time in the afternoon Meeting
speaking to the saints on the different ordinances
revealled to the saints for their salvation, and the redem
=ption of the dead. Returned to Smithfield at night
12 June 1892. I had arranged to go to Coveville tody
but was prevented thro' being sick with a very severe
attact of Indigestion which prostrated me for
several days. but I got back to the Temple

{57}
to work again on the Monday

Friday 17 May 1892 I preached the funeral sermon
of sister Hannah Tregale Burton (the Mother of
Maud, my wife) at the Basement of Logan Tabernacle
being a few days over 40 years since I drank
a glass of wine at their wedding. I also went to
the grave yard, and dedicated the grave and its
contents to the Lord. Praying that no disturbing
Eliments might affect the body. or the Grave till
the morning of the resurecction. It was a Very impres=
=sive funeral, a great concourse of people gathered to
pay their respects to the departed one.

Saturday 18th June I worked on Wife Maggies shanty
and went to the farm at night and stayed till
meeting time, sunday. – went to Meeting and talked
about 1/2 and hour and returned to the farm till
Evening. Came to Logan on Monday Morning and
continued at work in the Temple till Friday Evening
24 June 1892. when my wife Maud went Home to
Smithfield with me. Continued this manner of
Proceedings till the Temple closed for renovation on
Friday 22 July when I went home and with my
little boys I pulled weeds out of the gardens.
watered the gardens. built wife Maggies Shanty
and Painted some wood work for the family
and did numerous other Jobs to Keep things
in some Kind of – shape. during my vacation

Monday 22 aug 1892. with my little boys I
repaired fences at the farm and in the
meadow and turned the Cows here to
pasture.

Tuesday 23 August 1892. commced work again
in the Lords House. and Continued to go home nights and return
to my work in the Mornings sometimes travelling with a buggy
and sometimes with a cart, nothing of unusual interest
transpired. during the remainder of august and

Samuel Roskelley

[*57 con't; folded tabular reports pasted on the page in a stack*]

Register of Logan Temple Ordinance Work for May 1892

Baptisms								Endowments				Ordinations		Sealings		Children to Parents		Adoptions		Second Anointings			
First		Renewal of Cov.		Health		Dead		Living		Dead		Living	Dead	Living	Dead	Living	Dead	Living	Dead	Living		Dead	
M	F	M	F	M	F	M	F	M	F	M	F									M	F	M	F
4	4	8	8	3	49	652	569	33	34	244	394	2	244	32	130	37	40	1	5	6	7	2	7
		16		62		1221		67		638		246		162		77		6		13		9	
1,307								705				246		162		77		6		22			

Samuel Roskelley   Recorder

Register of Logan Temple Ordinance Work for June 1892

Baptisms								Endowments				Ordinations		Sealings		Children to Parents		Adoptions		Second Anointings			
First		Renewal of Cov.		Health		Dead		Living		Dead		Living	Dead	Living	Dead	Living	Dead	Living	Dead	Living		Dead	
M	F	M	F	M	F	M	F	M	F	M	F									M	F	M	F
1	3	5	14	17	47	853	653	49	67	411	709	1	407	65	321	81	66	2	2	5	11	4	7
4		19		64		1506		116		1120		408		386		147		4		16		11	
1593								1236				408		386		147		4		27			

Samuel Roskelley   Recorder

Register of Logan Temple Ordinance Work for July 1892.

Baptisms								Endowments				Ordinations		Sealings		Children to Parents		Adoptions		Second Anointings			
First		Renewal of Cov.		Health		Dead		Living		Dead		Living	Dead	Living	Dead	Living	Dead	Living	Dead	Living		Dead	
M	F	M	F	M	F	M	F	M	F	M	F									M	F	M	F
1	2	11	5	9	30	371	433	23	28	216	420	–	215	24	229	37	29	1	–	5	9	1	2
3		17		39		804		51		636		215		253		66		1		14		3	
862								687				215		253		66		1		17			

Register of Logan Temple Ordinance Work for August 1892

1	2	9	7	2	31	260	395	15	13	81	143	–	81	13	68	14	12	–	–	9	13	2	9
3		16		33		655		28		224		81		81		26		—		22		11	
707								252				81		81		26		—		33			

Samuel Roskelley   Recorder

Journal 6, 1888–1901

[57 con't]

Baptisms								Endowments				Ordinations		Sealings		Children to Parents		Adoptions		Second Anointings			
First		Renewal of Cov.		Health		Dead		Living		Dead		Living	Dead	Living	Dead	Living	Dead	Living	Dead	Living		Dead	
M	F	M	F	M	F	M	F	M	F	M	F									M	F	M	F
8	5	7	10	16	68	563	523	60	72	303	523	—	301	74	169	67	71	5	9	9	22	11	12
13		17		84		1,080		132		826		311		243		138		14		31		23	
1,200								958				301		243		138		14		54			

Register of Logan Temple Ordinance Work for Sep. 1892

Samuel Roskelley   Recorder

{58}
1892 during the fall and winter during the
winter I sold to Bro J. Z. Stewart nearly 200 acres
of Land south of my farm at Smithfield for money
to pay up Zion's savings Bank on the note they
held against me on a/c of the Logan and Smithfield
Canal Company. Also the note held by Bro David
James against me on a/c of the Vannoy & Co
which was a very great relief to me, my son
James gave up the farm and I assumed the
responsibility of running it myself. Putting
in about 50 acres of fall wheat in the field below
the house, I also rented the land on the upper
bench to Bro Wm Watson for 1/4 of what he could
raise on it. I agreeing to do 1/2 of the water
ditching for the water for it.

    Christmas and New year was spent Very
pleasantly, with my family, Wm Watson Jr
worked for me all winter taking care of the stock
and doing the chores, Maud moved to Logan in
January and I stayed there and with my children
Catherine & Sarah (who were attending School) when the
weather was Very severe.,
The Logan Temple Closed Friday 31st Mch for Conference
and Dedication /Salt Lake Temple\ I received an Invitation to attend
the 1st dedication services and went to Salt Lake
City on Tuesday Morning 4th apl 1893. attended
the Conference in the afternoon and all day on
5th april and also attended the 1st dedication
services at the temple (after going thro' the Temple)
at 10 aM. On the morning of the 6th april, the
magnificence and grandure of the house I can
never describe – I dont believe pen can write
it – and the spirit of the meeting was equally
grand and sublime. Prest Woodruff seemed to
have unusual strength and his councillors Bro
Cannon and Smith with the 12 sat in their seats
and seemed clothed in Gods Power.

on Friday 7th apl. I was invited with my
councillors to sit in the stand and represent
the Presidency of the High Priest Quorum
I did so at the afternoon meeting with
My Councillor Thos Duce. and Alvin Crockett rep-
=resenting my councillor Bro Jos Morrell who
was absent. My wives Mary. Maggie and Maud were
present at the meeting. also my son James and his wife —
as at the previous Meeting the spirit of God was
poured out to an overwhelming Extent and it was a

{59}
7 apl 1893
time of feasting and reflection seldom witnessed by me
in my history in the Church if ever before. those that spoke
seemed filled with the power of God showing what a
deliverance the Lord had wrought in behalf of his
saints, for a few short years before the temple and
grounds were in the hands of the government officer
with little prospect of Ever passing back into the hands
of the Saints again but God overruled so his
saints now posses and have finished this sacred
Edifice and offered it to the Lord and the whole
Congregation Voted that they felt the Lord had
accepted the Offering at the hands of his saints
(This was also done at the Meeting on the 6th).
a feeling of Love. Dilligence and faithfulness together
of forgiveness and charity went from these meetings
throughout the Church that I never before saw or felt.
Sunday 30 april 1893, The Quarterly Conference of
the Cache stake of Zion Commenced Bright Young
presiding – with apostles J.H. Smith and M W Merrill.
Present– It was the best Quarterly Conference I ever
attended, the saints were filled with humility and
the remarks of the apostles were inspiring to those
who were desirous of being saints indeed. at the
Evening session the apostles were called home to
salt Lake because of the sickness of Prest Woodruff
and Monday 1st May apostle M W. Merrill was the
leading spirit of the conference and we had 2
delightful meetings. I continued my labors
at the Temple as usual.

[59 con't; folded tabular report pasted on the page in a stack]

Register of Logan Temple Ordinance Work for October 1892.																				
Baptisms								Endowments				Ordinations		Sealings		Children to Parents		Adoptions		Second Anointings			
First		Renewal of Cov.		Health		Dead		Living		Dead		Living	Dead	Living	Dead	Living	Dead	Living	Dead	Living		Dead	
M	F	M	F	M	F	M	F	M	F	M	F									M	F	M	F
–	5	5	7	7	18	331	391	57	59	173	293	5	172	56	145	55	28	1	–	13	16	–	1
5		12		25		722		116		466		177		201		83		1		29		1	
764								582				177		201		83		1		30			
Samuel Roskelley Recorder																				

Register of Logan Temple Ordinance Work for Nov. 1892																				
Baptisms								Endowments				Ordinations		Sealings		Children to Parents		Adoptions		Second Anointings			
First		Renewal of Cov.		Health		Dead		Living		Dead		Living	Dead	Living	Dead	Living	Dead	Living	Dead	Living		Dead	
M	F	M	F	M	F	M	F	M	F	M	F									M	F	M	F
7	3	14	9	22	45	708	644	100	94	380	471	5	380	95	201	116	5	2	18	5	11	1	1
10		23		67		1352		194		851		385		296		171		20		16		2	
1452								1045				385		296		171		20		18			
Samuel Roskelley Recorder																				

{continues next page}

{59 con't}
[folded tabulation pasted on page]

Register of Ordinance work performed during the year ending Dec. 31st 1892

	Baptisms					Endowments		Ordinations		Sealings		Children to Parents		Adoptions		Second Anointings	
	First	Ren. of Cov.	Health	Dead	Living	Dead	Living	Dead	Living	Dead	Living	Dead	Living	Dead	Living	Dead
Logan Temple	76	228	513	12,518	1,105	8,767	19	3,675	561	2,478	571	407	18	47	198	93
Manti do	83	626	1,657	20,342	757	9,158	43	3,862	391	3,374	588	437	35	721	129	60
St. George do	51	49	75	6,157	108	3,105	16	1,421	55	945	33	48	9	272	21	32
	210	903	2,245	39,017	1,804	21,030	78	8,058	1007	6,797	1,192	892	62	1040	348	185
Gd. Total for 1892	42,375					22,970		9,036		7,804		2,084		1,102		533	

Ordinance work performed in Logan, Manti and St. George Temples to 31st Dec. 1892

	Baptisms					Endowments		Ordinations		Sealings		Children to Parents		Adoptions		Second Anointings	
	First	Ren. of Cov.	Health	Dead	Living	Dead	Living	Dead	Living	Dead	Living	Dead	Living	Dead	Living	Dead
Logan Temple	341	2,802	5,653	230,392	12,545	101,103	213	40,573	6,199	28,597	8,417	6,474	162	391	1,167	620
Manti do	316	3,460	12,071	146,342	3,905	60,196	168	25026	1,904	21,602	4,798	4,264	419	5,633	645	312
St. George do	516	884	2,829	259,039	5,526	109,070	1,170	42268	2,916	35,892	3,695	3,862	511	6,058	1,271	1,328
	1,173	7,146	20,553	655,773	21,976	270,369	1551	107,867	11019	86,091	16,910	14,600	1,092	12,082	3083	2260
Gnd. Total	664,645					292,345		109,418		Xx,110		31,510		13,174		5,343	

{continues next page}

{59 con't}

Register of Logan Temple Ordinance Work for January 1893

Baptisms								Endowments				Ordinations	Sealings		Children to Parents		Adoptions		Second Anointings			
First		Renewal of Cov.		Health		Dead		Living		Dead		Living	Dead	Living	Dead	Living	Dead	Living	Dead	Living		Dead	
M	F	M	F	M	F	M	F	M	F	M	F									M	F	M	F
–	5	10	15	10	23	435	314	37	40	284	248	1	283	43	134	30	11	–	–	5	5	–	–
5		25		33		749		77		532		284	177		41		---		10		–		
812								609				284	177		41		---		10				

Samuel Roskelley   Recorder

Register of Logan Temple Ordinance Work for February 1893

Baptisms								Endowments				Ordinations	Sealings		Children to Parents		Adoptions		Second Anointings			
First		Renewal of Cov.		Health		Dead		Living		Dead		Living	Dead	Living	Dead	Living	Dead	Living	Dead	Living		Dead	
M	F	M	F	M	F	M	F	M	F	M	F									M	F	M	F
7	3	18	8	8	27	481	509	56	51	435	329	1	435	47	156	34	16	1	2	2	1		1
10		26		35		990		107		764		436	203		50		3		3		1		

Samuel Roskelley   Recorder

Register of Logan Temple Ordinance Work for March 1893

Baptisms								Endowments				Ordinations	Sealings		Children to Parents		Adoptions		Second Anointings			
First		Renewal of Cov.		Health		Dead		Living		Dead		Living	Dead	Living	Dead	Living	Dead	Living	Dead	Living		Dead	
M	F	M	F	M	F	M	F	M	F	M	F									M	F	M	F
7	9	22	23	2	25	838	433	56	57	647	613	1	646	55	407	77	38	–	–	4	5	–	–
16		45		27		1271		113		1260		647	462		115		---		9		---		
1359								1373				647	462		115		---		9				

Samuel Roskelley   Recorder

{60}
sunday 21st May 1893. With Bro Thos Duce I visited the
Members of the High Priests Quorum at Clarkston and
had a good turn out and a good meeting, a good
spirit prevailed. Bro Duce and I occupied the time,
at 2 p.M. attended the saints meeting at Newton
at which Bro Duce and I spoke again after
which we held a High Priest Meeting and I
spoke followed by Bro Duce and Bp Griffin ,
we all felt well at these meetings. as we
tried to point out the duties of the High Priests
Sunday 4 June 1893. With Bro Thos Duce I visited the

members of the HP. Quorum at Mendon at 1/2 past
11 a m and had a good meeting 10 members Present
and all expressed their feelings – and seemed to
feel Well.   attend the afternoon Meeting
and Bro Duce & I occupied most of the time
discoursing upon the topics of the day.
[double line across the page]
Sunday 11 June 1893 With Bro Thos Duce I visited the
members of the Quorum at Hyrum at 10 a.m. And
had a good Meeting – the bretheren seem to feel
well generally – we added 13 new members to
the Quorum by ordination – they having been
properly recommended and Endowed.
[line across the page]
Sunday 2 July With Bro Thos Duce I visited
Lewiston and met disappointment as only 2
member of the Quorum came to meet with
us and as we had another appointment at
Coveville We pushed on and attended the
sunday school and the sacrament meeting
and held a H. Priest meeting afterwards
and enjoyed ourselves well
[double line across the page]
Saturday 1 July 1893. attended Priesthood (Stake) Meeting
and after meeting Prest Orson Smith called on me to
sit with Bp Larsen of 7th Logan Ward on a case
at Smithfield between Bro Bain and Bp Farrell
Bro Bain having preferred a charge against Bp
Farrell for refusing a settlement and other
matters.   Bp Larsen and one of his Council
=lors & I sat on the Case from 0 p.M till 1.20
A.M and finally got the parties to settle it
themselves.

{61}
21 July 1893. Friday. Temple closed for renovation &c
and I went home needing rest but the rest I got
was hard work out of doors. during the Vacation I
fixed up my binder. To cut my grain but found
it too short to cut with a binder. so I took a
trip to Deweyville and hired a Bro Marble
to come with Header and Cut it for 100lbs on
the acre to put it into the stack. also had
the Theshing done 70 acres turned off 491 Bu
Wheat. 11 acres oats a total loss, I built
a good shed and covered it for my stock
and Horses at the farm, Made a good Hay rack
and threshed my grain. Put up 2 stackers for
stacking hay. Fixed up my meadow fence,
and cut and Hauled and stacked my meadow
hay – part at the farm and part in town. Kept

the lots & gardens watered and fixed up Hay
rake, and plows, and did quite an amount
of plowing on the field Just cut.
[line half across the page]
22 July 1893. Temple opened – work light – which
gave a good chance to Copy.
[line half across the page]
3rd Sep 1893. Attended the funeral and spoke of
Elder Lyman O. Littlefield. it was quite
a large gathering.
[line half across the page]
4 Sep 1893 (Monday) I Excused myself from the
Temple as I found the deps were on my
track. spotters having been seen several times
after night around Mary's house at the farm,
and as Maud was living there I though best
to move her into Idaho– so I took train
and went to Preston and rented 2 rooms from
Bro & Sister Porter at 5$\underline{00}$ per Month for Maud
and her Children.
[line half across the page]
5 Sep 1893. I went to the AC College and paid
Jas E Hyde the Secty 20\underline{00}$ Entrance fee for
Cassie Haniah. Sarah & Libby, for the year.
[line half]
6 Sep Wednesday the Girls Moved to Logan to the
room I had rented from Sister Johnson.
[line across the page]
7 Sep Thursday — The Girls started to School

{62}
1893

9 sep Saturday — Loaded up Mauds Household goods
and sent William Watson with them to Preston
to the house I had rented for her.
[line]
10 Sep 1893 Sunday—I took Maud and the children
in the big Buggy with some of her household
goods to Preston – Came back to Smithfield
next day.
[line across the page]
Oct 10 1893 I did not go to Conference as Money was
so scarce I could not get any for fare_I
worked around home and fixed up a lazy
saw at the farm to run by Horse power to
saw firewood (Pine) to save the boys labor.
and when the Temple reopened on today the
companys were quite small.
[line across the page]
With Bro Duce I held quite a number of High Priests
Meetings thro' the wards of the stake during the summer

and Fall.
[line across the page]
[folded tabular report pasted on the page torn away, now missing]
[folded tabular reports pasted on the page in a stack]

Register of Logan Temple Ordinance Work for May 1893

Baptisms								Endowments				Ordinations		Sealings		Children to Parents		Adoptions		Second Anointings			
First		Renewal of Cov.		Health		Dead		Living		Dead		Living	Dead	Living	Dead	Living	Dead	Living	Dead	Living		Dead	
M	F	M	F	M	F	M	F	M	F	M	F									M	F	M	F
9	6	5	10	13	23	690	483	33	32	204	328	–	203	35	98	63	31	–	–	3	3	1	2
15		15		36		1173		65		532		203		133		94		—		6		3	
1,239								597				203		133		94		—		9			

Samuel Roskelley   Recorder

Register of Logan Temple Ordinance Work for June 1893

Baptisms								Endowments				Ordinations		Sealings		Children to Parents		Adoptions		Second Anointings			
First		Renewal of Cov.		Health		Dead		Living		Dead		Living	Dead	Living	Dead	Living	Dead	Living	Dead	Living		Dead	
M	F	M	F	M	F	M	F	M	F	M	F									M	F	M	F
3	1	10	9	10	36	605	635	28	29	259	479	2	256	31	133	42	24	–	25	1	4	1	–
4		19		46		1,240		57		738		258		164		66		25		5		1	
1,309								795				258		164		66		25		6			

Samuel Roskelley   Recorder

Register of Logan Temple Ordinance Work for July ending 21st 1893

Baptisms								Endowments				Ordinations		Sealings		Children to Parents		Adoptions		Second Anointings			
First		Renewal of Cov.		Health		Dead		Living		Dead		Living	Dead	Living	Dead	Living	Dead	Living	Dead	Living		Dead	
M	F	M	F	M	F	M	F	M	F	M	F									M	F	M	F
3	3	1	2	3	16	190	234	3	9	149	276	–	148	7	71	17	16	–	–	–	–	–	–
6		3		19		424		12		425		148		78		33		—		—			
452								437				148		78		33		—		—			

Samuel Roskelley   Recorder

Register of Logan Temple Ordinance Work for 22d to 31st aug. 1893

Baptisms								Endowments				Ordinations		Sealings		Children to Parents		Adoptions		Second Anointings			
First		Renewal of Cov.		Health		Dead		Living		Dead		Living	Dead	Living	Dead	Living	Dead	Living	Dead	Living		Dead	
M	F	M	F	M	F	M	F	M	F	M	F									M	F	M	F
–	2	2	1	6	9	165	118	6	7	62	76	1	62	8	21	3	4	–	–	3	2		1
2		3		15		283		13		138		63		29		7		—		5		1	
303								151				63		29		7		—		6			

Samuel Roskelley   Recorder

[62 con't]

Register of Logan Temple Ordinance Work for September 1893

Baptisms								Endowments				Ordinations		Sealings		Children to Parents		Adoptions		Second Anointings			
First		Renewal of Cov.		Health		Dead		Living		Dead		Living	Dead	Living	Dead	Living	Dead	Living	Dead	Living		Dead	
M	F	M	F	M	F	M	F	M	F	M	F									M	F	M	F
6	2	5	7	6	28	307	337	23	27	205	286	1	203	24	75	33	24	–	2	1	1	–	–
8		12		34		644		50		491		204		99		57		2		2		–	
698								541				204		99		57		2		2			

Samuel Roskelley   Recorder

Register of Logan Temple Ordinance Work for October 1893.

Baptisms								Endowments				Ordinations		Sealings		Children to Parents		Adoptions		Second Anointings			
First		Renewal of Cov.		Health		Dead		Living		Dead		Living	Dead	Living	Dead	Living	Dead	Living	Dead	Living		Dead	
M	F	M	F	M	F	M	F	M	F	M	F									M	F	M	F
4	7	4	5	10	24	393	534	20	21	123	191	2	122	23	92	28	17	–	–	2	3	–	–
11		9		34		927		41		314		124		115		45		—		5		–	
981								355				124		115		45		—		5			

Samuel Roskelley   Recorder

and the weeks and months fled past as
tho' they were on Wings, my son James had
a very severe sick spell with Typhoyd Feaver in
Salt Lake City late in the fall and his wife went
from my farm where she and her Children had
been living during the fruit season, to the City
to wait on him. I furnished my son William
with seed grain to put in on his own land
and also on James Broke land at Weston,
after which William came to Smithfield to
Live for the Winter. and get Employment so
as to get means to live on. I tried to Visit

{63}
my wife Maud at Preston as often as once
a week during the fall and Early winter.
The Temple closed on Friday 22 Dec 1893 for
Christmas. and reopened on the 27th for one
day only till the 2 day of Jan 1894
my Wives and Children (except Maud and her
children) met at Mary Janes on Christmas day
and took dinner together.
27th Dec 1893. My wife Maud gave birth to
a boy baby– on Thursday the 28th my wife
Maggie and I went to Preston and stayed all

night with Maud, returning next Evening and
bringing Marriner to stay with aunt Maggie
for a few days– I bargained today for a
horse from Daniel K Green for Buggie uses
named Dan _ to pay him in T.O scrip $10.00 each
month on 3 Feb 3. Mch. 3 apl. 3 May 3 Jun3 1894. I got
the horse Saturday 30 Dec. 1893.
1st Jan 1894—My 57th Birth day – Mary invited
us all to the Farm to spend the day. all at home
attended. Except wife May and Children who were at Preston
Idaho, also sons James. Samuel. William & Joseph & families were
not present. . all present seemed to Enjoy themselves. My Wife
Maggie and children Emma & Ora started to Salt Lake
City saturday 13th Jan 1894 as my wife wished to go and
nurse a couple of friends during their Confinement and
The friends were Plural U.G.'s I consented and she
and her two Children spent the winter in Salt Lake
City until I went to the april Conference and Brought
her and our children with me.

   Nothing of importance transpired out of the usual
line of Events during the summer. The temple work
absorbed all my time except during Vacation from
Friday 13th July until Tuesday 21st august. during
which time I built a hay barn in town & &
did my harvesting and Cut and hauled my
meadow hay. During the fall the work in
the Temple became very slack and Companies
for baptism and Endowments very light, which
gave us a good opportunity to copy up our work,
I did not attend the October Conference
as money was too scarce with me.

{64}
1894
10th Dec To day stake President Orson Smith called
on me and stated that several Bishops through
the stake had expressed a desire to organize a
prayer Circle and had asked him to appoint some
one to help them to do so– said his councillors &
himself had canvassed the matter and
had concluded to ask me to attend to that
important matter—meeting with those who
desired and giving them such instructions, as
may be necessary to Effect an organization
and start them right and in a proper way.
I gave him assurance I would do all I
could in this matter.

   Christmas and New Year passed off as
usual with seeing the Children pleased and
the usual gatherings of the family—spring came
in Very tardy and I had to rely on the little

boys to help on the farm as I was unable to
hire to any Extent. In Feby I was Elected a
Director of the Logan H.P and Smithfield Canal Co
and afterward the President – This increasing my
labor and travel as I had to make frequent
trips to the Canal to see things were all right,
as also to carry on my usual Visiting of the
Members of the High Priest Quorum in the
Various Wards of the stake making my life
a Very active and busy one.
1895. 5 May   Bro Jos Morrell & I Visited Richmond
and ordained 12 High Priests after a meeting
with the Members of the Quorum.
19 May   I Visited Newton and held meeting with
the members of the Quorum,   Bro Jos Morrell
Visited Providence. and held meeting with
the Quorum. and in connexion with my
Councillors – visited nearly all the Wards
and held Meeting with the members of
the Quorum.
16th July. My Wife Mary Jane gave birth at
5.15 a.m to a girl baby and at 5.20 a.m
gave birth to a boy baby – she had a hard
struggle but the children were more than
a compensation for the great cost..

{65}
1895
19 July Temple Closed for renovation till 29th august
next – during Vacation I labored helping my
boys on the farm. getting up hay from Meadow
filling Bar in town cutting hauling & Threshing the
dry farm fall grain from below the old house
which was Threshed 8th & 9th aug – and
and yielded 1600 Bu Wheat. Also harvested
hauled and threshed the Wheat from the 33
acres of north Bench and 5 acres of
oats – Threshed on 26th august and
yielded 396 Bu Wheat and 101 Bu oats
Making a total threshed 1996 Bu Wheat
    <u>101 "</u> oats
    2097
for which I feel deeply grateful to my
heavenly father for so good a crop .
18th Aug Elder T Duce and I Visited Newton
and ordained Hyrum Curtis an High Priest
he being recommended from the 70s T. Duce mouth
[line across the page]
27 Aug. Temple opened and I continued my
labors there as usual as Recorder,
8th september With Bro Duce Visited Benson

Ward and organized the High Priests there
I set apart Bro Charles Reese to preside
over them. giving him the necessary instructions
how to organize and Report his labors
15 sep – With Elder T. Duce Visited the
Greenville Ward and designed organizing a
Branch of the Quorum but the Bishop being
absent we postponed such an organization
for the present,
Temple Closed on 27th sep and I worked
at farm putting up wire fence on line
north of Old house, to protect my corn
till Thursday 3rd Oct when I took 3.20 PM,
train for Conference arriving at Salt Lake
about 8 P.M. met wife Maggie & daughters
Hannah at station going to Bro stonemans
and stayed nights during conference on
4.5.6 Oct. also attended the great Welch
gathering of musical people held in the

{66}
      1895
great Tabernacle which was filled to its utmost
capacity on Friday & Saturday Evenings the 4&5
of Oct – The singing was grand – The conference was
grand, sunday 6 Oct. Wife Maggie. Daughter
Hannah & I was escorted thro' Salt Lake Temple
rom top to Bototm by Elder W. Woodruff Jr., by
permission of Prest L snow who had previously
given me the permission to go and take with me
who I might deem proper – it is truly a most
magnificent sight and I shall long remember
it and the feelings it. produces. I took
the 4-45 P.M train from salt Lake arriving
at Smithfield about 9.3.0 P.M.
8th Oct 1895 Resumed my labors in the
Temple at Logan taking record for Baptisms
for the dead.,– I had the pleasure of 1/2 an
hours conversation with President Lorenzo Snow.
The conversation was very free between us and
after discussing some Temple affairs the conver
=sation drifted on the present Conditions of the
saints in political & Religous matters generally
together with the worldly applause now given to
this people.. I said What does this all mean
? said he This is our Boon, but you watch
the future—there will be a great apostacy and
you will be surprised to see those standing in
respectable and high places go overboard and
apostatize. I was much impressed with the
Earnestness with which he spoke. after ward

– 332 –

in closing the Conversation he said, you Know
I don't talk to may the way I have to you.
27th Oct 1895. Bro Duce and I called a special
meeting of the High Priests in smithfield and addressed
them in the Tabernacle after afternoon services,
and ordained 8. to the office of High Priest –
2 that were recommended not being present.
Sunday 3 Nov 1895 attended Quarterly Conference in
Logan, apostles H.J. Grant. J W Taylor. M W. Merrill
were present also apostle M Thatcher attended
the sunday services and spoke at the forenoon
meeting for some 30 Minutes – he looks the

{67}
picture of ill health.
Sunday Nov. 10 – 1895 With my daughter Cassie & wife
Maggie I attended the Y.L. M I. Conference at Logan
and was well repaid. Sister [blank] Jensen Snow and
Zina W. Card were present and took a leading part
giving good instructions to both Old and Young that
were present – home industries. Training of the head
and heart in the proper direction., how & who to
marry for time & Eternity. and Kindred subjects
were well discussed.
Continued my labors throughout November and December
in the Temple as usual. Christmas & New Years
day we were closed and I was at home with my
family on those days. – Maggie was at Newton
with her folks on New Years – Maud was at Logan
with her father & sister Rhoda.. I spent the days
generally in town and Visited the farm..
1896 our work increased Very Rapidly during Jan^y
in the Temple, altho the Reports for 1895 were
quite interesting as the following figures will
show

{continues next page}

{67 con't}
[folded tabulation pasted on page]

Register of Ordinance work performed during the Year Ending 31st December 1895

Name of Temple	Baptisms				Endowments		Ordinations		Sealings		Children to Parents		Adoptions		Second Anointings	
	First	Ren. of Cov.	Health	Dead	Living	Dead	Living	Dead	Living	Dead	Living	Dead	Living	Dead	Living	Dead
In Logan Temple	135	166	421	14,411	583	7,715	16	3,310	278	2,022	641	1,213	–	–	54	27
Manti Temple	146	231	226	6704	391	6,136	25	2,595	200	2,355	431	2,459	–	1	58	45
St. George Temple	59	44	69	3,814	172	3,413	13	1,625	97	1,138	84	621	–	–	12	14
Salt Lake	–	–	985	36,174	1461	21,337	20	8,631	644	5,625	1,644	5,954	–	22	260	131
	340	441	1,704	61,103	2,607	38,601	74	16,161	1,219	11,140	2,799	10,247	15	23	384	217
Gd. Total	63588				41,208		16,235		12,359		13,046		38		801	

Totals of all Ordinance Work performed in Logan, Manti and St. George and Salt Lake Temples to 31st Dec. 1895

Name of Temple	Baptisms				Endowments		Ordinations		Sealings		Children to Parents		Adoptions		Second Anointings	
	First	Ren. of Cov.	Health	Dead	Living	Dead	Living	Dead	Living	Dead	Living	Dead	Living	Dead	Living	Dead
Logan	706	3,327	6,768	26,2126	14,407	12,2708	260	49,737	7,128	33,724	9,926	8,989	168	421	1325	681
Manti	677	4,344	13,144	170,622	5,115	80,222	235	33739	2,545	28,325	5,897	10,339	443	6,086	808	403
St. George	678	1,022	3020	269,521	5,932	118,898	1,214	46,748	3,146	38,874	3,860	4,748	516	6,160	1313	1389
Salt Lake	1	34	2612	98,723	4,405	56,874	31	22,371	1,798	15,080	4,618	12,565	62	632	815	402
	2,062	8727	25,544	800,992	29,499	378,702	1740	152,595	14,617	116,003	24,301	36,621	1,189	13,299	4,261	2875
Gd. Totals	837,325				408,201		154,335		130,620		60,922		14,488		7136	

Samuel Roskelley, Recorder of Logan Temple

{68}
1896 Jan My Labors in the Temple and seeing after the Wants
of the family Kept me quite Busy,, thro the month, and I
Visited several wards in the interest of the HP Qum.
[line across the page]
11 Feb The meeting of the stockholders of the Logan HP &
smithfield Canal Co accepted the reports for the past
year. Colds – coughs and some other sickness among
the children & family continued some time .
My son Joseph came down from Rexburg and Visited
several days, Visiting among the family
Maud lived all winter with her father, Keeping
house for him,
Mch Very blustry and bad roads – unsettled every
thing in the shape of work – Richard sick and now
able to attend school. Most of the Month
Apl – I did not attend Conference – Cash too scarce
at home working fixing [---] for plowing &c
21st apl sister Zina made me a present of 54 Rods
of land in Lot 3 Block 11 Plat C Logan City survey
in Consideration of what I had done on the
Huntingdon Record for the dead. Maud rented
a 2 Roomed house in 6 Ward to live this summer
On the 2st apl. from Bro Du[text obscured by slip pasted on page]n a
mission to southern states.
[slip text]
> 26th apl 1896. With my councillor Bro Thos Duce I organized the
> High Priests of Avon Ward With Alma O. Jackson as Presiding
> Teacher. and also held meeting with the High Priests in Paradise
> Ward have good spirited meetings at both places.
> I afterward set Bro Jackson apart for his office
> in Bro Morrell's store assisted by Bro Morrell.

[diary text]
May – The weather so Very unsettled our work
on the farm badly retarded, and but little progress
made cropping. I succeeded however with hired help to
put in some 40 acres of lucern ~~seed~~ for seed on
the bench and break up some 16 or 18 acres of sage
brush land. and clear it off – sowing late grains.
Spending nearly all my earnings on fixing the farm
in a better shape to make it more profitable. if
possible, when the boys quit school they worked
on the farm..
June – We put in Corn & potatoes the Early part
of the month and cleaned out our Waterditches
and put in the last of our grain in the ground
I worked in the temple all the time.
July 3. Temple closed today till 1st sep – on trying
to work out of doors. I found it very hard on my
body and could stand it but a few hours at
a time – I suffered Very much in trying to help
the boys a little in the fields but I stuck to

{69}
it as best I could and Visited many of the
Wards of the stake in the interest of the High Priests
Quorum on the sabbath days.
August This Month I past thro' a much similar
ordeal s last month. But the boys &
I got the Hay cut and Hauled, and most of our
grain Cut and some hauled & stacked.
Sep 1st Temple opened today – and we Recorders
had a letter read to us by Prest M W. Merrill requiring
us to put in a full weeks time in the temple at
our labor, as heretofore I had the privelage of
staying home on saturdays to see to my family
and attend to my business affairs at home.
Sep 16.17. Threshed. My son James taking Charge
It being the first part of my crop, we threshed
296.Bu Oats, 944 Bu Wheat, which I am
Exceedingly thankful to my heavenly father for
Sep 18th Friday. it commenced to blow from the East
and increased to fearful Violence thro' the night
lasting till about 4 in the Morning of the 19th
I was up much of the night, as I was fearful
lest it might blow the house to pieces in
Town – it stripped the orchards of fruit. and
denuded the trees of leaves broke off and
stewed the ground with Many large. Limbs
from the shade trees and tore up by the
roots some of my largest and oldest Balm
of Gilead and Box Elder shade trees, on the
East side Walk. some of them over 30 years
old. We had hired cut some 7 or 8 acres of
seed Lucern and the wind came and blew
it all away. And also destroyed scores of
Trees at the farm and about 5 acres of Wheat and
as many Oats that was standing ready for the harvest
destroying some hundreds of Bushel of Grain. For me
October – Cash too scarce to attend the Conference, but
I got the folks together, and dug some of my potatoes
and gathered up several loads of Excellent squash
all the latter part of the month was cold. raining
and prevented much being done on the farm, I
had no hired help. Every thing went at loose Ends
at my homes,
11th November. My Daughter Hannah Roskelley

{70}
1896 \ was sealed to a young man named Henry R
Nov / Newbold by apostle M W. Merrill in the Logan
Temple after receiving their Endowments the same day.
supper was partaken at the farm, most of the family
was present together with a few invited friends and

a very pleasant Evening spent together.
during the summer and fall I spent sundays in
Visiting the organizations of the High priests Quorum
through the Valley and frequently Visited the saints
meetings sunday afternoons.
The Temple closed during the Christmas & New Year holidays
Christmas was spent Very agreeably the most of the family
coming together at My Wife Mary Janes house and having
a cleaning up of the Christmas Eve spree. For my folks
had got a Christmas tree and Maggie & Maud had
trimmed it with a present for every one in the family
some of my grown daughters helping them and on
Christmas Eve all the family were invited and
unknown to the children, the Room were the tree was
all lit up with Candles and the rich presents was
suddenly opened and Oh! What a sight! and such
Joy! All seemed to enjoy it hughly — for a few day
sister Zina Young the President of all the Relief Societies
of the Church came and spent a few days with
the family. – after attending the meeting of the saints at
the Tabernacle. Most of my family met at, Mary Janes.
with sister Zina on sunday Evening.
27th Dec 1886. and we had a delightful time together
we sand Oh my father & other hymns and aunt Zina spoke
to us – giving us her testimony to the principle of Celestial
order of Marriage &c.
<u>1st January 1897– My 60th Birthday</u> – as the whole
family had had so much meeting & reunion during the Christmas
holidays—I though we could afford to spent New Years day
Quietly, and I could get off and take comfort in my Meditations
I therefore went up to my farm to Visit my family living there
(Mary & children) – I had Just got comfortably settled down with
a book in my hand when my wives Maggie & Mary Jane
with their Children and most of my other Children drove
up to the door in sleds with wraps and food and
such Comforts as the season demanded, coming into the
house the first I heard was "<u>Surprise</u>". Sounded in
my Ears and it was a Veritable Surprise for I had
not dreamed of such a thing, my other children
came later on – Table set – and such a Table – loaded
with the good things of life to over flowing – My heart
and house was full – full of gratitude for the good
feelings shown, and for Gods mercies & blessings

{71}
1897. in permitting me to see and Enjoy them with my
dear ones, The Evening was spent in singing & playing
till all were satisfied, and retired
      Following is the results of the Years work in all
the Temples – with all work to date in all the Temples
now Running for Ordinance work

{71 con't}
[folded tabulation pasted on page]

Register of Ordinance work performed during the year ending 31st Dec. 1896

Name of Temple	Baptisms				Endowments		Ordinations		Sealings		Children to Parents		Adoptions		Second Anointings	
	First	Ren. of Cov.	Health	Dead	Living	Dead	Living	Dead	Living	Dead	Living	Dead	Living	Dead	Living	Dead
Logan Temple	135	157	329	14,108	620	7,233	20	2980	291	1,124	390	1,037	–	–	66	30
Manti Temple	175	109	233	7,289	418	6,476	23	2704	108	1,972	445	1,598	–	8	152	75
St. George Temple	66	34	66	3,962	138	4,255	5	1,894	68	1,469	79	596	–	2	11	13
Salt Lake	–	–	843	34,287	1,469	18,728	19	7,496	630	4,746	1,281	4,202	6	6	180	104
	379	300	1,471	59646	2,645	36,692	67	15,074	1,197	9,311	2,195	7,433	6	16	409	222
Gd. Total	61,796				39,337		15,141		10,508		9,628		22		631	

Totals of all Ordinance Work performed in Logan, Manti and St. George and Salt Lake Temples to 31st Dec. 1896

In Logan \ Temple /	Baptisms				Endowments		Ordinations		Sealings		Children to Parents		Adoptions		Second Anointings	
	First	Ren. of Cov.	Health	Dead	Living	Dead	Living	Dead	Living	Dead	Living	Dead	Living	Dead	Living	Dead
Logan	841	3,684	7,097	276,234	15,019	129,949	280	52,717	7,419	34,848	10,316	10,026	168	421	1,391	711
Manti	855	4,453	13,377	177,911	5,533	86,698	258	36,443	2,753	30,297	6,342	11,937	443	6,094	960	478
St. George	746	1,056	3,086	273,483	6,070	123,153	1,219	48,642	3,214	40343	3,939	5,344	516	6,102	1,324	1402
Salt Lake	1	34	3,455	133,010	5,514	875,602	50	29,867	2,428	18,826	5,899	15,747	68	638	995	506
	2,441	9,027	27,015	860,638	32,136	415,402	1,807	167,669	15,184	125,134	26,498	44,054	1,195	13,315	4,670	3,097
Gnd. Total	899,121				447,538		169,476		141,128		70,550		14,510		7767	

Samuel Roskelley, Recorder of Logan Temple

{71 con't}
1897
8 Feb   at the Meeting of Logan. H.Park & S. Canal Co I was reElected
a Director of the company and at the meeting of the
Directors on the 16th W. W Crookston was Elected Prest
and I was elected Vice Prest to serve 2 years.
7 apl* I attended Meeting of High Priests at smithfield and had
several of the bretheren talk after which I occupied abt
3/4 of an hour on the privelages of men holding the
High Priesthood and the results of faithful labors
in that ministry and calling .
1st May To day I commenced work for a new house
and home for my wife Maggie . My son Joseph
digging the foundation. Bro Rutcain was hired
to put in the foundation and Bro C Craigan to
superintend the Carpenter work.
8 May Bro Thos & I Visited the High Priests in Mendon
Ward and Held Meeting with them at the house
of Bro Jaspar Lemmond – ordained 3 new Members
Bro H. Huges and 2 others. returned home
during the afternoon as the water was very high
and danger of Bridges being swept away.
15 May Attended conjoint conference of Y.M & Y L.
of Cache Valley stake – held it in Logan tabernacle –
Alumina Taylor, Susa Y Gates & other Visitors –
had good spirited meetings
22 May I attended meeting of the High Priests of
Clarkston Ward at the Tithing office Clarkston
most of the members present Warned the Brethren
against neglect of duties and opportunities and
urged all to fulfil their part of all duties
assigned them in Every calling of life.
attended. afternoon sacrament meeting and
occupied a short time in talking and Explaining
the preparation necessary for Temple work.

{72}
1897
29 May attended Meeting at Benson Ward with the saints
Elder T. Duce met me there. High Councillors Geo
O. Pitkin and Chas Robins were there as Home
Missionaries and preached – Elder Duce & I occupied
a few minutes each. held a meeting afterward
with the Members of H.P. Quorum, and advised
the holding of Regular Meetings and come together
promptly that all may be Edified. I ordained
John Reese on a proper Recomend a High

---

* Samuel presents the entries for 1 May and 7 Apr in order but reversed the entry dates in the original journal, marking them himself to correct their placement. The transcript presents the dates as he corrected them.

Priest. After Voting by the people and the
Members of the Quorum.
13 June I requested Elder Thos Duce to Visit the
stirling Ward and ordain 2 of the bretheren
who had be recommended by the High Council
I visited. The Newton Ward and met
the missionaries of the Y.M.M. Elders
Bullen & Merrill. I talked a short time
also in the afternoon meeting. Held a
High Priest's meeting afterwards and
several of the bretheren spoke well. I
occupied about 20 minutes Encouraging
the Bretheren to faithfulness.
27 June attended the Ward Meeting at Hyde Park
and related Experience of Signers of the Declaration
of Independence Visiting Prest Woodruff after the
opening of the St George Temple at St George showing
and testifying to the communication of persons from
the spirit world to saints on Earth, but Very remarkable
manifestations.
4 July. Prest Orson Smith handed me recommend for Elder C.H
Larsen of Newton to be ordained a High Priest as he
had recently been sustained before he ward as
the Councillor to Bp William Griffin so I went to
Newton and attended the Ward fast meeting and
after duly laying the Matter before the saints they
Voted to sustain Bro Larsen to be ordained a
High Priest I thereupon ordained him. Assisted
by Bp. W. H. Griffin. . A High Priest.
Friday | 16 July Temple closed to day till 14 Sep for Cleaning &
repairs &c and all the Temple hands drawing
salaries were notified by Prest Merrill that
we would be released till the date of opening
as a month's salary would be appreciated to purchase
wood for the Temple – This by the approval of the
Presidency of the Church
I continued my labors sabath's in Visiting the
Various Wards organizations of the High Priest
ordaining some on recomends issued by

{73}
the Bps & Endorsed by High Council of stake and
this labor has been persistently Kept up by me and
my councilors during summer and fall.
    my crop turned out better than it had done
for some years past and prices were much better
also. Enabling me to free myself from most
of my financial obligations – beside placing my
farm in a better shape than it had ever been
in before, for profit as I had good teams
and outfit to run it to better advantage.

1897 The winter found me with my family in a
little better circumstances – Maggie's house
finished and occupied and Mary Jane's house
fixed over a little and in a better shape.
and all the children at School. My Wife
Maud living in the 7th Ward Logan and
blessed with another babe – born 28 Dec 1897
and named Gilbert. the middle name of
his Mothers father.. Winter proved long and Very
tedious tho' not very severe.

1st Jan. My Birthday. 61 years old today. Where
1898 has the time gone? My family met at my
wife sarah were with us. We had a very
Enjoyable time till the small hours of morning
bade us take leave of Each other for the time
being.
spring found me with more wheat sown than
usual having something over 100 acres in wheat
and about 6 acres oats for myself & boys, we
also have a large quantity of Lucerne – the
spring rains being very favorable for the sprouting
of seeds of all Kinds
I made several trips to various settle=
=ments to Visit the Bretheren during the spring,
and my friend Bro N.C. Edlefsen the Vice President
of the Logan Temple died on 5th Feby 1898 of
Kidney disease. and on the 23 Feb 1898. Elders
Thomas Morgan and James Quale were set apart
assistants to Prest M.W. Merrill of the Logan Temples
Temple Closed for renovation on 15 July 1898 and reopened
29 My 1898. during the Vacation I worked with my boys
in Hay and harvest fields also Weeding. Watering garden
and doing some carpenter work. in town on

{74}
1898   Maggies shanty & putting roof on lean to Mary
Aug   Janes barn.   Thursday 16 aug I took team &
my Wives mary & Maggie also sister Stoneman
of salt Lake and Visited my son in law Bro
Thos Hillyard and my daughter Mary. at the
sawmill at Lago in Gentile Valley Idaho
returning to Smithfield on the Friday following
29 Aug I met Bro JA Leishman my assistant at
Logan Temple and commenced our labors
therein by taking record for baptisms for the
Dead.
16 sep 1898   Gave note for 100.00 Cash to Jos E Cowley for 6 months
1t 10% interest. Visited Clarkston & Newton, Hyde
Park and smithfield Quorum organizations during
September & October, and had good meetings
about the middle of September Bro Thos Duce

who has been my 1st Councillor for many years
moved to Canada taking his 1st wife and most
of her family, he requested not to be released
as he may desire to come back and resume
his position, but I doubt it.

Sunday   I took Wife Mary and went to Visit my boys James
27 Nov 1898   and William at their farms west of Weston in
Idaho – Remained over night with Willie and he took
me on Monday and showed me some land he had
in his Charge for sale – which I may buy some
time, visited with the Boys and their families
and came home again on Monday. 28 nov

Sunday   I visited Hyrum High Priests Meeting at
20 Nov 1898   10 OClock and found a number of Bretheren in
attendance. had a very good meeting the Bp &
his Councillors there. Ordained 3 bretheren who
had been Recommended. and named 6 mem
=bers of the Quorum – 4 from Hyrum & 2 from
Wellsville as missionaries to Visit the Quorum
Meetings during the winter, at Hyrum, Wellsville
Mendon. College, Millville, Paradise, Avon and
Stirling. appointing Elder John G. Wilson to
arrange their Visits and look after the labors.

Wednesday   Prest M. W. Merrill Called me into his office
30th Nov   in the Temple to lay hands on Elder James Henry
1898.   Martineau when he ordained and set apart
Bro Martineau a patriarch in the church of
Jesus Christ of Latter-day-Saints. I wrote a
certificate of the ordination signing it as
Recorder of the Logan Temple and as s witness of
the ordination.

{75}
1898
30 Nov. I set in motion a Chore of 6 missionaries – 4
from Logan and 2 from Hyde Park to Visit Logan,
Providence, Benson. Hyde Park and Greenville under
the charge of Elder Chas B. Robbins of Logan.
I pray that they may accomplish much good..
I spent Christmas & New Year's at Smithfield with
my family Very Quietly, my 62nd birth day. Oh!
how time flies!
1899
15 Jan I went to Newton with Wife Mary Jane – a cold time
had the twins with us. organized a missionary Chore
of 4 from Newton and 2 from Clarkston to Visit Newton
Clarkston and Trenton members of the High Priests Qur–
staid to sacrament meeting and talked to saints,
15 Feby 1899. Received word from stake President Orson
Smith that Elder John Peter Gunnarson of the Logan
5th Ward was very sick and Bro Smith desired me

to go and ordain him a High Priest. I took Bp Hyde
of the 5th Ward along and ordained the man – he died
about 2 Hours after.
In the afternoon same day I attended Stockholders
meeting Logan ~~Richmond~~ & Hyde Park & Smithfield Canal Co
and was Elected Director of that Company for 2 years, and
at a meeting of the Directors Elect on Thursday 16th
I was Elected Prest of the Company for 2 years. This
being the 2 term of my Presidency of the Company, with
an interval of 2 years between. It took me all my spare
time to arrange to for the missionaries throughout the stake
Visiting the Various Wards in the interest of the Quorium.
13th Mch 1899. I attended the meeting at the members
of the Quorum at Logan and talked to the Bretheren
relative to their duties – to themselves – their families
the Church and their God. . 17 names were recommended
for ordination, presented, and Voted upon to be ordained
and received as members of the Quorum. 14 were
present and Voted upon. Bros T. Morgan. L R. Martineau
E Carlisle, C. B. Robbins & Bp Larsen assisting me
and taking part in ordaining them.
The Day before (Sunday) 12th March I attended
a meeting of the High Priests at Smithfield, and
Voted in Bro Thomas M. Kelsey and I ordained him a
member of the Quorum.
April 4th Temple Closed to night for Conference and I spent
3 days at home in the lots putting in garden and fixing
trees & bushes for the folks and took train and
went to Conference on Saturday 8th with wife Maggie
stopping off at Ogden and staying over night

{76}
1899 with Halls folks, attended the Conference
on sunday and Monday went to state Land Office
and paid $25^{89} for land in Logan Kanyon
covering pat of Logan, HP & smithfield Canal
buying it for the use of said Canal.
Tuesday 11th Returned to Logan with train &
resuming my labors in Logan Temple
Sunday 31 May. Quarterly Conference of Cache Stake
Commenced at Smithfield Prest O. Smith presiding
councillor S M Molen present also, councillor Issac
smith sick could not attend. Apostles M W Merrill
& Anton H. Lund on the stand.
Monday 1 May. Conference continued, had some
good instructions, from apostles & other. Congregation
small because of Very bad weather. And horse cold.
7th May with Bro Morrell, Visited High Priests at
Hyrum. Winter missionaries of the Quorum from
Hyrum & Wellsville and Presiding Teacher H. W.
Jackson form Paradise also met with us. all

spoke and felt good. released winter Missionaries
with Vote of thanks – ordained 7 from Hyrm
& 1 from Paradise. Bro E. R. Miles Junr took me from
Smithfield to Hyrum & return.

21st May took wife Maggie to Newton. attended Saints
afternoon Ward Meeting spoke a short time, held
meeting with High Priests afterward a good spirit
prevailed – Winter missionaries reported, had had
a good time in their labors. I did not release them
as I felt they had not completed their labors,

4th June attended fast meeting at Smithfield
and assisted as usual when at home in blessing the
babies. I blessed my daughter Hanna's babe with
some others as it fell to my turn to do so.

3 June at the monthly Priesthood meeting today I
was appointed to organize prayer circles in the
wards of the stake whenever the Bps had a place
prepared for such purposes.

9 June I borrowed 50.00 from Thatcher Bros Bank
for 60 days – payable 9th august.

11 June. I attended High Priests Meeting at
smithfield Many Questions discussed as to
proper Methods of ordination & administration

{77}
1899
and blessing children &c. attended the
saints afternoon meeting and rested the
rest of the day as my lungs were quite bad

Friday 28th July. With my wife Mary Jane, and sons James
Richard. Wilford, Frederick & child. Martin I started from
smithfield at 12.30. P.M with 3 Loaded teams and my one
horse buggy for my newly acquired lands at Blue
springs, arriving there the next day. saturday, about
1.30 P.M. and immediately set to work hunting
corners of the Quarter sections I had purchased from
Orson smith and his wives. during the following week
Wilford plowed (broke) about 8 acres and Fred & I
put up a shed with posts 12 & 14 ft and covered
it with a shingle roof. Returning again to
smithfield on Friday the 4 Aug. a very heavy
rain storm poured down upon us nearly the
whole of the day. My sons James & Richard
did not remain long with us, leaving us on Monday
morning the 31 July.

Sunday & Monday 6 & 7 aug Quarterly Conference
of Cache stake held at Logan – Prests L Snow, Jos F
smith apostles Lyman – F D. Richards, Merrill & Cowley
present Law of tithing the main question laid
before the saints. James V. Allen came to me and offered
as the manager of the Farmers Union Mill to Either Buy or

take on Deposit all the old wheat I had . altho at a low
figure if I sold 45^{cts} it is 5 cts above Market Price and
I considered it as a God send to me as I had some debts
pressing and other matters I needed some money very
bad to attend to.
3rd sep sunday fast Meeting bore my testamony & also
prayed in public for the recovery to health of Bro Mose Jr
who is now on a mission to the southern states.
Monday
4th Sep. Logan Temple opened and I was on hand
to do my part took record of some 112 persons to
be baptized for.
Friday 8 september. My boys Wilford, Ora & Henry with
hired man Nephi Pierson also Bro Thos Kelsey to cook
for them started with 10 head of horses & 4 Wagons
to Blue springs to break & harrow & burn sage
brush taking a supply of food & feed and a load
of slabs for various purposes
Sunday 10th sep. With Elder saul Lamb of Hyde Park
I went to Paradise and held Meeting with the members
of the Quorum 9 Present out of 14. had a Very interesting
time and took dinner with Bro H.C. Jackson.
attended the afternoon meeting of the saints and spoke
abt 30 minutes. on temple work. Tithing & Kindred subjects
after meeting called the members of the Melchisidic

{78}
together and spoke of necessity of having a prayer circle
being organized in the ward. bretheren responded I
thought quite admirably.
The weather proved quite unfavorable for our farming
and much of our work had to be laid over time and again
27 sep 1899. I paid E R Miles Junr agent for the Hand[?]
Man Wm Q. Owens $550^{00} for his house and 4 lots in the N E part
of smithfield City and had the Deed made in favor of my wife
Sarah Maud Burton Roskelley. So I thank my heavenly
father that each of my Wives & families have a house
and home that they can Call their own and I trust
they will live long to appreciate and Enjoy them.
9 Oct 1899. The Boys with Wife Mary Jane went to blue creek
to finish plowing & sowing grain but weather proved so unfavorable
they accomplished by little in 10 days sowed about 20 acres
30 Oct My sons Richard &. Wilford. Henry with Bro Thos
Kelsey again went to my Blue Creek farm to finish up
the sowing for the season – cleared up about 10 acres &
sowed about 46 acres making a total of Plowing &
clearing & sowing of about 66 acres for the season and
I pray Gods blessings upon it for it has been quite
a drag to get that much accomplished with the work
at home..
29th & 30th Oct Cache Quarterly Conference at Logan

with Prest L. Snow & apostles F. M Lyman. J. H Smith & M
W. Merrill & other Visitors. Prest Orson Smith also had
returned from alaska and now resigned his position
as president of Cache stake of Zion. Prest L snow
nominated apostle M W. Merrill to succeed Orson smith
as president of Cache stake of Zion with Jos Morrell
and Isaac smith as councillors. <u>Unanimous Vote</u>
this leaves me without councillors as Bro Duce my
late 1st Councillor is now 1st Councillor to Prest C
O. Card of Alberta stake Canada. and Jos Morrell
is now 1st Councillor to Prest M W. Merrill of Cache
stake, asked who I wanted for Councillors I named
Elders Wm Brigham Parkinson and Willard Done.
<u>Sunday 12th Nov</u> 1899. Went to Newton with Bro W. B.
Parkinson and held meetings with the High Priests a
12.M added bro Ledingham to the Missionary list of
High Priests. For that district on West of Bear River
and asked the same persons to continue their
labors tho the winter. all agreed to do so *Bro WB
Parkinson and I gave some instructions on the
force of Example. returned to smithfield thro' bad
roads and Logan Temple next morning
*I ordained 2 bretheren who were Recommended

{79}
viz Peter Petersen and Hans C. Hansen in the
saints meeting in the afternoon
<u>Wednesday 22 Nov</u> 1899. Elder Wm B. Parkinson was
set apart as my 1st Councillor by apostle M W. Merrill
assisted by his councillors Jose Morrell & G Smith & S Roskelley
in the little office in the Temple. Bro Merrill gave him a
blessing in connexion with it.
<u>Sunday 25 Nov</u> 1899. I met with the High Priests at Smithfield
this morning and listened to some of them relate some of
their Experience. Several asked what was a tithing? the
Bishop of the ward being present – I referred the question
to him – he said he paid 1 tenth of all he raised
without counting out the seed cost of hired help &
threshers &c. In my remarks I stated I thought
the Bishop had given the most liberal view and
construction that could be placed on the wording of
the revelation – I thought the revelation needed
no interpretation as it Explained itself. One tenth
of all our interests or Increase annually
<u>Wednesday 29th Nov</u> Bro Richard McNeil quit
working for me after being in my Employ for over
<u>3 years</u>. he is a good hand, and I have
trusted almost all my farm matters to him
<u>Thursday 30th Nov</u> <u>Thanksgiving day</u>. Temple being
closed I remained at smithfield – ate dinner
with Mary. at farm and her family.

Sunday 3rd Dec 1899 With my councillors Bro
W. B. Parkinson and Willard Doan went to Mill=
=ville as Bro samuel Holt the presiding teacher had
moved to Logan. we Expected to put in a new
Presiding teacher, but failed as the High priests
had not been notified of our coming and had
no meeting as a quorum, we however met with
the sunday school and talked to them a short time
also met with the General priesthood meeting of
the ward and urged the importance of a Prayer
Circle meeting. we also attended the afternoon
saints meeting (fast Meeting) and the 3 of us with
a Return Missionary (Young Bro Pitkin) occupied
the time. and the saints seemed interested,
at the suggestion of Bishop Rasche I called
upon a Brother Olsen to be a Temple
Missionary to copy records for the Winter
and the saints Voted to sustain him.
Wednesday 6th at the meeting of the stake presidency

{80}
here in the Temple. Elder Willard Done was ~~set apart~~ ordained a High Priest and set apart as my
2nd councillor to preside over the High Priest Quorum
Cache Valley stake of Zion by apostle M W. Merrill,
sunday 10 Dec 1899. Prest M W. Merrill and councillors Visited
smithfield ward so I remained at home to Visit with them
Bro Jos Morrell stayed with me..
sunday 17 Dec 1899. With my Councillors Visited Hurum
High Priests and had a good turn out and good
spiritual feast. The 3 of us occupied the time
of the meeting and the bretheren seemed pleased,
are also attended the afternoon saints meeting.
and had an interesting meeting – I advocated
the preparation of a room for a prayer Circle.
at both meetings;
sunday 17th Dec 1899. My Councillors & I Visited Hyde Park
attending the saints meeting in the afternoon and occupying the
whole of the time afterward holding a meeting of members of
the Quorum, with some members of other Quorums present
my councillors & I spoke on the duties & obligations of the
High Priests and Exhorted them to do what is required in
the spirit of the Gospel. Spent the Christmas at
smithfield with my family as the weather was cold I
could do no outside work, and had to be satisfied to
remain in doors most of the time
1st January 1900. My 63 birthday I spent the
forenoon at smithfield with the family and took my wife
Maggie to Logan with her Children in the afternoon & we
spent the night at Mauds, I going to resume my labors
at the temple on Tuesday 2nd January 1900.

14th Jan 1900. I took my wife Maggie and went to
Wellsville. My councillors had arranged to meet me there
but Bro Parkinson's little boy was so sick he could
not come and this threw out Bro Done also. I attended
H.P meeting in the forenoon with the bretheren from
Wellsville & 4 from stirling, the Good spirit met with
us and we had cause to be glad.
Attended the saints meeting in the afternoon and
preached to the saints. Temple Work. and returned to
Logan in the Evening.
Friday 19th Jan 1900. Prest Merrill received a telegram
from Prest snow requesting him to close the temple
until further notice, we learned afterward that
the small pox had made its appearance in so many
places that Prest snow had closed the salt Lake
Temple on the Wednesday previous and Manti on
the same day as Logan. I took part of the day

{81}
saturday 20th Jan to fix up and put away books
papers &c going to smithfield in the afternoon. And
devoting the time the following three weeks to repairing
washing & greasing harness when it was storming,
and when fine weather I was out of doors trimming
up Raspberries, currants &c in the Garden I also
devoted some few days to the interests of the
Upper Canal Company of which as its President
I sought to promote.
Sunday 4th Feby 1900 My Councillors & I attended a
meeting of the members of the Quorum at smithfied
had a good turn out and good meeting I advocated
Establishing a Prayer Circle in the Ward.
Sunday 11 Feby 1900. attended saints meeting at
Richmond – 2 Home Missionaries, stake councillor
Isaac Smith, and one Return Missionary and
Prest & apostle M W. Merrill occupied the time of the afternoon
services, afterward the High Priests met in the Vestry and
were addressed by My Councillor Willard Doan and
myself among other things I advocated organizing a
Prayer Circle. Elder Parkinson had been to Richmond
in the Morning but had Returned to Logan by train in
consequence of being sick.
Monday 12 Feby 1900 Temple Reopened. I spent the
forenoon in arranging papers & books and taking record
for Baptism tomorrow. and in the afternoon I attended
and presided over the annual Meeting of the L. HP & S
Canal Co. at the 5 Ward Meeting house Vestry.
and made the annual Report to the stockholders
Sunday 25th Feb 1900. Went to Newton by request of Prest
M W. Merrill and dedicated an upper room of the
Vestry of the Meeting house for the use of a Prayer

Circle. At 12.30 and attended saints meeting at 2
P.M. afterwards went to the Vestry Room again
with the Ward Bishoprick and 6 High Priests and
2 seventies besides myself. Clothed and instructed
all present in the way to use the signs of the Holy
Priesthood and showed them how to offer the
signes & Pray to the father. returned to smithfield
in the evening – Roads Very bad
Thursday 1st Mch. I went to Thatchers Bank and
borrowed $150.00 for 50 days and paid it to bro Orson smith
on a/c of the bonus for the 400 acres of Land at Blue Creek
leaving me in debt to him 50 dollars yet due.
Saturday 3 Mch. I let Samuel Nielson have 8 of my best
calves and 3-2 year old steers & two year old bull

{82}
1900 \ 12 head in all which he will sell with his cattle the
3 Mch/ first opportunity and get me the cash for them
Sunday \ With My Councillors Parkinson and Doan went to
4th Mch / the 2nd Logan Ward and there I dedicated the upper
room of the Vestry for the uses of a Prayer Circle and
afterward drilled the Bretheren in the offering up the
signs of the Holy Priesthood, and organized a
prayer Circle after the manner observed in the
Temple of the Lord. Showing there how to use the
sighs and Offer Prayer & Consecrate the oil
spent the balance of the day with my wife Maud
and family who have been quite sick,
having had a miscarriage and is quite feeble
yet.
Thursday 17 May. My sons Wilford, Fred, Ora & Henry started
to Blue spring farm to herd stock off the grain &
get the grain harrowed – as word was sent to us that
there was a good stand of wheat but Cattle were Eatg
it all off
Sunday 20th May. Bro W. Doan came to Smithfield and preachd
the funeral discourse of my Grand daughter Eva
Willie's daughter who died the satiday night previous
about 2.45 a m. consoling remarks were made to
an appreciative audience. commencing at 11.15
a m.   Bro Doan & I then took team for
Benson Ward. Holding meeting with the saints.
Bro Done & I occupying the time. I called a
meeting of the Melchisedic Priesthood after
the afternoon meeting and urged the necessity
of organizing a prayer circle in the ward and
showed up the Benefits therefrom after which
I called a High Priests meeting 7 Present
found things. So far as meetings are concerned
Very unsatisfactory – had held no meetings for
2 months. and the spirit of meeting seemed

dying out. Bro Doan & I urged the
necessity of holding regular & lively meetings
at least once a month. Retuned to Smithf^d
Monday 21. Thos Kelsey started to my farm in a cart
with my Wick horse, to cook for the Boys there
about 2 P.M. my sons James. Richard &
Fred with son in law Wm Watson started to
Blue spring farm to survey and locate the
corners and get out posts and prepare to
fence the farm.
Sunday 27 May. Pres^t M W. Merrill notified me on
Friday last that the Stake Presidency had
decided at their late meeting that day to ask

{83}
me to go and preside at the Ward conference of Trenton
Ward – this stake. I had invited my councillor Bro W. Doan
and together we started from Smithfield at 7.30 am. Arriving
at Bp Binghams in Trenton about 10.30. Meeting commenced
at their White Brick School House at 12 noon. had reports
from several Ward organizations. And ajourned for 1 hour.
ate dinner at the Bishops. and commenced meeting again at
2.15. heard the report of the rest of the ward organizations
and Voted to sustain the officers <u>all unanimous</u>
and Elder Doan & I arrived at Smithfield at 7.30
P.M. Very Tired. Called upon and administered to
Bro Colemans Child.
<u>Friday 25th May</u> My son James arrived from Blue
springs having surveyed and laid off the lines of
the farm and got the corners located. He brought
5 head horses home with him.
Monday 28th May. Went to the Temple was called upon
to administer to Bro Hall. Just across the street
north of the Temple, he was very sick
also Bro Perks the Watermaster of L.HP & S Canal Co
called & told me that the Hurcules Power Company
had blasted some rock from their Excavation
about our canal and it had fallen into our
canal impeding the flow of water. Bro Perks & I
went to their office and saw the superintendent
Mr Bacon and the overseer of the work and
they agreed to take out the obstructions today.
Wednesday 30th May   Having been disappointed in obtaining Wire
to fence with. at Blue Springs Expecting it for several days
past. I today sent Bro R^d McNiel with provisions for the
boys there and learn of their Welfare, as the Temple
was Closed today – I took the opportunity to spray my
orchards as far as I could do so, and in the afternoon
all the family at home met at the grave yard and
placed flowers on the graves of our loved ones including
Bro Thos Kelseys wives as he is at Blue springs now

cooking for my Boys.
Thursday 31 May. Bro McNeil returned from Blue
springs about 5 P.M. bringing sons Ora & Henry home
to go to School till it closes for the season..
Sunday 3 June. At the Request of Bp N. Woodruff I addressed
a congregation of the Melchesedic Priesthood of Smithfield
Ward who had been called together after the Fast meeting
on the Subject of organizing a Prayer Circle. Elders Willard
Done also addressed the same audience on the same

{84}
1900
3 June subject.
7 June My sons Richard, Fred also Bros Kelsey & W. Watson
returned from Blue springs. having finished the fences
as far as possible. So the stock can be kept off the
land. The boys however say the grain is nearly
all ate off by plundering stock.
17 June Elder W Done & I went to Avon to attend the
ward conference being appointed by Prest Merrill
two meetings were held at which fairly good
reports were given of the Various Ward organ=
=izations. we were well received and had a
good time generally. some of the High Priests of
Paradise accompanied us to Avon. we came
back to Paradise about 5 oclock and sister
Bessie Jackson treated us to all the strawberries
and cream & Bread & butter we could Eat.
19th June I paid the last $50.00 to attorney W. W. Mayhew
for Bro Orson smith for the land at Blue springs
(see Receipt) this completes all that I agreed
to Pay as Bonus to the smith family for
the land.
1st July Sunday. Having invited Bp Newton Woodruff of Smithfield to
1900   to accompany me to day, we went to Logan 3rd Ward and
met Bp Yeats with his invited Bretheren at the Vestry
of the Meeting house at 8. a m. after preliminary
Exercises, we proceeded to their upper Room in the Vestry
and I took charge and organized a Prayer Circle
I invited Elder Joseph E. Cowley who was a temple worker
and was present to talk on the Question before us,
and I followed with remarks suitable to the occasion
I rededicated the room for holding prayer Circle
and Elected the Bishop as the President and his
councillors as assistants, also a Secty, the Bretheren
seemed well satisfied.
at 12 noon Elder Woodruff & I met with the
bretheren of the Priesthood at the 2nd Ward Meeting
House Vestry and by stake President M. W Merrill
request, previous made to me, I received the late
Bp H W. Ballard's resignation as Prest of the Prayer

Circle thus dissolving the organization, I then
reorganized it by Electing the Present Bp A Anderson
as President with his councillors. Worley & Ballard
as assistants. with Bro smith as secty Elder Jos E
Cowley present from the 3rd Ward by my invitation
then drilled the Bretheren thoroughly, so they could
act united by, making appropriate remarks upon
the subject, I followed with a few suggestions.

{85}
and called on Bro s. G. spillman (a Temple worker)
to open with prayer, I formed the circle and I led
with prayer. a number of questions were asked and
answered. And a profitable time Enjoyed.
Bp N Woodruff & I returned to smithfield in time to
attend most of the afternoon fast meeting in the Smithfd
meeting hous.
Sunday \ I attended meeting at Smithfield Elders A M Cannon
8 July / of salt Lake and Cache Home Missionaries Pitkin &
J Z. Stewart Jr were the Speakers, after Meeting Elder Cannon &
I visited Sister L. O Littlefield and related some of our Early
Experiences in the Church.
13 Aug 1900 With my wife Maggie and sons Richard. Wilford.
Henry & Fred started Monday noon for our Ranch at Blue
springs with Lumber. Provisions & Hay and 4 teams. Arrived there
at 5 oclock tuesday Evening. and pitched tent &c formed
that all our Labor putting in Crop the fall of 1899 had been
Entirely destroyed by the stock before we got our
fence up. this last spring. So Wilford went to using the
Disk Harrow but failed to make any impression as
the ground was so hard. and had to be replowed,
so he plowed. Richard hauled rock sand & clay
for a foundation of House. Fred. Henry & I dug the
trench and went to making foundation good and solid
we worked faithfully and built up a good substantial
log house. rock foundation & shingle Roof and got
home again Thursday Evening 29 Aug 1900..
Thursday 30th aug 1900 Commenced threshing. I had a little over
2000 Bu of Wheat. Oats & Barley – all told. and my boys Rd & Wilford
had a little over 400 Bu in Smithfield of which I got 2/5.
finished up threshing on Saturday Evening. And the following
Tuesday Morning 4th sep 1900 I resumed my labor in
the House of the Lord in Logan.
Friday 21st Sep 1900 I started my wife Mary Jane. Wilford
Richard, Fred & Henry to Blue springs Ranch with 4 teams
of our own and a team I hired from Jacob Watson at
the rate of 50cts per day in Church pay for Each day
used.
4th October (Thursday) Temple Closed this Evening for the
Gen Conference. And Friday with the little boys I
dug and pitted potatoes from my wife Mauds lot, and

the boys continued all during the conference.
Saturday 6th Oct with my boy Marriner I went to
my Ranch at Blue springs to visit my family
there and take provisions to them found they had
got along with the flowing & sowing quite well.
& Returned home to smithfield Sunday 7th Oct

{86}
1900 and resumed potatoe digging. We had a
little over 130 Bu on Mauds lot. Left abt
30 bu for Maud. Pitted 25 Bu for Maggie
and pitted abt 45 bu for Mary Jane. And
sold bal to Niles at 1$\underline{35}$ per cwt.
Wednesday 10th Oct My Wife Mary Jane and
sons Richard. Wilford & Fred came home from
Blue springs with teams & outfit having put
in about 60 acres of wheat in good shape
Wednesday \ Commenced again in the Temple.
10 Oct 1900/
Sunday \ With Bro Saul Lamb of Hyde Park went to Clarkson
14 Oct 1900/ and held meeting at 11 oclock with the High Priests
10 present, all in the Ward at home. Bro Lamb and I occupied
the time, (those present said profitably) the Lord be praised
if good was done for he did it, we came down to Newton
and attended the Saints afternoon Sunday sacrament Meeting
and Bro Pitkin & Davis of the High Council missionaries also Elder
Hendrickson & Langton of the Board of Y. M M I. A. was
present leaving but little time for Bro Lamb and I. returned.
To smithfield same night.
<u>4 Nov</u> 1900 attended fast Meeting at Smithfield and assist
the Bishoprick in blessing the children (babies)
11th Nov Expecting a Visit from my councillor Willard Done from
Salt Lake City to day I attended meeting with the High Priests
in smithfield, but Bro Done did not come – I addressed
the Bretheren. for a short time, my son Martin sick with
some pains in his stomach – which afterward developed
into Putrid Sore throad and for days was quite bad
<u>12th Nov</u> /Monday\ I hired Anthon Sorensen for the winter at 12$\underline{00}$ per month
and board, and put him to work at the farm. My son Martin
slowly recovered from his sudden attack of Sickness.
19th Nov. The storm made roads Very bad as a
horse had to wallow thro' mud Knee deep
20th Nov. Tuesday. I concluded to stay in Logan nights
and quite traveling nights and mornings. Prest Merrill
gave me permission to sleep and board in the Temple
during the bad weather, which I gladly accepted. I ate
supper with my daughter Drusie Tuesday & Wednesday and
commenced boarding at Temple Thursday Evening 22 Nov
<u>22nd November 1900</u>. I bought from Bp William Hyde the
north 1/2 of N.W. 12 Sec [blank] in Blue Creek Valley with the
proviso that he (Hyde) retain the right to continue

building a Reservoir on the Land in Company with
Fred Turner. giving me the right of 1/3 interest in the
Dam and Reservoir.
Saturday 1st Dec 1900. I sent the 1st payment to the Land
office (State) for the 2 Quarter sections I had made no
payments previously upon, one of which – the N. W. Q^r is
contains the 80 ac above mentioned I recently bought

{87}
1900 from William Hyde,
Sunday 9th Dec 1900. With my wife Maud I went to Benson
Ward to Visit the members of the H.P Quorum. I
found the funeral Services being held over the remains
of one of Bro & Sister ~~Caesh~~ Cash's Children who had
died of Typhoid feaver, and I offered a few consoling
remarks. The whole of the ward nearly had turned
out to the funeral and desired to go to the Burial at
Hyde Park so I did not hold a meeting..
Friday 14th Dec. The Very fine altho Very foggy weather has
dried up the land so well I have ventured to sow
(by hand) about 20 acres of fall grain on the South
12 of the 55. and finished harrowing it today my
~~Sunda~~ Daughter Florence has been sick with Rhumatism
for 2 or 3 Weekes past and we have been doing all
we could to help her. The school of the town have
been closed for 2 weeks, and the children have
all been home but much sickness has prevailed
through the town with small pox and many other
deseases.. now my daughter Florence is Broken out
with what resembles the small pox. Some 8 or 9
postules on her face & neck.
Saturday 15 Dec 1900 My Wife Mary Jane's family & home is put
under Quarintene and city Marshall Bert Merrill
put up a danger flag., Bro W F Rigby has been in Logan
several Weeks very sick – general break down of the
whole system,– and the Doctors here dont help him
that I can see.
Sunday   \
16 Dec 1900 / According to Previous appointment I went to Hyde
Park to hold meeting with the High Priests after the usual
afternoon Services. I found on arrival there that the usual
afternoon Meeting had been quite short and the Bretheren
had nearly all gone home, consequently I held no
meetings as I had expected.
21st Dec Temple Closed today till 2nd January 1901
25 Dec Christmas day. I Visited around among the family
spending a little time with Each except Mary Jane &
her Children who was Quarintined – but I went there
several times during the day and talked to them
through the Window. taking such things to make
them Comfortable as I could obtain. The weather is

quite Cold – but no snow – roads dusty. and
much sickness. spent the few days at home
fixing up many things needed for comfort.
Sunday 30 Dec. Maggie & I spent Visiting her sick father at
Logan, as we thought it a charitable act and time
well spent
Tuesday 1st Jan 1901. spent the day Visiting the family going
from place to place – at dinner with Mary &
her Children. Mary Jane still quarentined

{88}
1901
Wednesday 2 Jan I sent $77^{40} in a check to the State Land
office salt Lake City. Annual payments for the 3
Q^r sections of Land at Blue Creek.
Temple opened again today.
Sunday   \ attended High Priest Meeting at Smithfield in
6 Jan 1901 / forenoon – many bretheren bore their testamony to the
gospel truth attended fall meeting afternoon
and assisted in blessing Children.
13 Jan 1901. Sunday. Went to Richmond and attended Saints after=
noon Sacrament meeting. Spoke fairly good, congre=
=gation about 20 minutes. Held a high priests
meeting afterwards – had several bretheren express
their feelings – I also occupied about 20 minutes
in Exhorting the bretheren to faithfulness and good
works.
Tuesday 15th Jan 1901. The Smithfield City officers took
away the Quarantine flag form my wife Mary
Janes House as there remained no symptoms of
small pos. this caused much Joy to my family.
Sunday 20th Jan With my wife Mary Jane went to Logan and stayed
4 hours with her father – talking and singing for him to Comfort
and solace him in his affliction & pain. – he seemed to appre=
=ciate my coming. returned to Smithfield at night. And
resumed Labor at Temple in the morning.
Sunday 27 Jan 1901 attended Quarterly Conference of Cache stake of
&   Zion. I suppose for last time as it was announced
Monday 28   that the stake would soon be divided. Apostles
Teasdale. Merrill & Cowley all Spoke. Bro Merrill only
attended 1 day he was sick Monday and did not get
out. apostle Teasdale attended meeting at Smithfield
Monday Evening and preached to the people. he stayed
over night at Maggies house.
a danger flag was put up at Mary's home to day
because Richard had Exposed himself to the
small pox – so they have to suffer Quarintine.
Tuesday 29 Jan 1901. By Request of Bp J C. Larsen of
the 7th Ward Logan I went with him and
ordained Jens Martin Nielsen of the 7th Ward
a High Priest. he was Recommended about a

year ago but thro' sickness could not attend
the meeting to be ordained.
Sunday 3 Feb 1901 I invited Bp J D Wright of Hyrum and
Elder E R Miles Jr of smithfield to go with me to the
2nd Ward Logan. Prest M W. Merrill had requested
me to go there and dedicate a new Vestry room to
their meeting house for a prayer circle Room. A
large number of Bretheren from that ward was
present and the Holy spirit was present giving us
much Joy in our Meeting. I gave much instruction
on manner of Prayer order to be observed, and
manner of Keeping record of such meetings and the

{89}
wording of anointing Sick and sealing annointing &c &c
cautioned them against repetitions.
Sunday 10 Feb 1901. Went to Lewiston – met with High
Priests & 13 bretheren who had been recommended
for ordination – after some catacizing remarks
and all had expressed their feelings in shout – I took
Bp W H Lewis & Bro Waddups to assist and ordained
those recommended instructing all present in
working of an ordination to any Quorum of
Priesthood from Deacon to High Priest. My talk
seemed to touch the Bretheren and gave them
new thoughts on the subjects that were object
lessons to them. I love this ministry and
to teach others how to minister according to
Gods plan as far as I have been instructed.
Tuesday 12th Feby – Bro W F Rigby still very sick at
Lavina Cards. I happened there when Lawyer
W W Mayhew was there and saw Bo Rigby
sign his will and other papers with my specks
on his Eyes, and I was the 1st Witness to
sign his papers as a witness that I saw him
do so. It looks as tho' his time is short
in mortality. .
13 Mch 1901 (Wednesday) at 5.45 this Morning My
Esteemed colaborer and friend Wm F. Rigby passed
away from the mortal career to the great
beyond – he died at his daughters home in
Logan (Mrs Lavinia Card) and on Thursday
(next day) was removed to his old home Newton
where his wives sarah and Lizzie are living
also some of his sons.
16th Mch 1901 (saturday) My Wives Mary Jane &
Maggie, (daughters of Bro Rigby) also my wife
Mary Roberts with the Children of the 1st 2 named
& I went to Newton and attended the funeral
Services were held at the Meeting house a large
congregation assembled and were addressed by

Prest Thos E Ricks of the Bannock stake (to whom
Bro Rigby was 2st Councillor) and others of
the Bretheren of his old associates. Much,
was said commendable of the life and devotion
1901 \ of the Deceased to the Work of God.
Apl 5/ Went from Logan to Salt Lake City to attend the Genl
Conference of the church. Attended meetings, and also
the priesthood meeting on the Monday, and received much
precious instruction, and returned home again on

{90}
1901   Tuesday Morning. Going direct to the Temple and
Sunday   Continuing my labors there.
21 apr   With my Councillor Willard Done went to Hyrum and
attended meeting of High Priests in forenoon and with Bro
Done Encouraged the bretheren to do their full duties
and stayed and talked to the saints in the afternoon
the weather & Roads being so bad I could not get
Apl   \ out much during the month.
28&29 / Quarterly Conference of Cache stake, held at Logan
apostles young Merrill. Cowley. Woodruff & Clauson present
on Motion Cache stake was divided , in 3 stakes
the Northern stake with Head Quarters at Richmond
Middle stake with head Quarters at Logan and the
southern stake with head Quarters at Hyrum. .
Joseph Morrell my former councillor chosen President
of Middle or Cache stake with Isaac smith
and Willard Maughan Councillors.
30 Apl Meetings were held at Richmond and the
former Bp of Lewiston Wm H. Lewis sustained as
president with Alma Merrill and B. A.
Hendricks as councillors, Meetings were
also held at Hyrum. and William s Parkinson
sustained as president. no other officers were
chosen that day. as smithfield Ward now
belongs to the northern stake, or Benson stake
I will become identified hereafter with that
stake of Zion. I do not yet know in what
Official Capacity, altho apostle M W. Merrill
said today he wanted I should labor there
as a stake officer
Sunday I attended meeting with the High Priests of Smithfd
12 May to finish up the Business of the old stake by ordaining
those what had been recommended. I ordained the
following named persons. Viz. Noah Jenkinson
Jens Peter Turesen. John August Petersen James Cantwell
High Priests.– there were others recommended by
they were not present. alto notified.
In the afternoon went to Hyde Park and met with
the High Priests of that ward and by appointment
Met Elders E. W. smith the newly appointed president

of the H.P. Quorum of the Center or Cache stake
I took charge of the Meeting until I ordained
the following named Bretheren who were properly
recommended. Viz. George seamons, Jacob

{91}
ashcraft, anders Christensen, Troles Jorgansen,
I gave some instructions to the members of the Quorum
present and then turned the charge of the Meeting over
to President smith as Hyde Park Ward now belongs
to the center or Cache stake. The bretheren voted
me a Vote of thanks for past services.
       With my wife Mary Jane I—
Sunday Went to Clarkston according to appointment.
19 May to finish up our old stake business, I held
recommends and ordained the following named
bretheren. Viz James M. archibald. William
H. Clark. William sparks. John Zougg, Joseph
stewart, John E. Godgrey, Hans Jensen
Joseph E Myler and Bengt Ravsteen and
after the afternoon meeting I went with
the Bishop John Jardine and ordained
Frederick Holton who was confined to his
home thro' sickness. I then returned to
smithfield and resumed my labor on
Monday in the Temple at Logan.
Friday \ I sent Elder W^m G Burton $25^{00} to day by
17 May / mail to go into Cornwall and hunt up
Geaneological Record for me. some of this
money had been contributed by my wife Maggie
and her Children also my son James .
Sunday With My Wife Mary Jane I went to Clarkston and
19th May spent the day and attended High Priest Quorum Meeting in the
forenoon and issued High Priest Certificates to all the
Bretheren living there. and ordained (myself) the following
named Bretheren High Priests, having received their
recommends properly Endorsed, Bengt M Ravsten
Jos W. Stewart, W^m H Clark, James M. archibald
W^m sparks, hans Jensen, Jos E Myler, John E Godfrey
Fred^k Holton, spent the afternoon in saints meeting
and occupied a portion of the time speaking to the
saints. returned to Smithfield in the Evening.
Sunday attended High Priest meeting at Smithfield in the
26 May forenoon and ordained Bro Jens C Petersen a High Priest
as he was not Present at the former meeting when the
others were ordained. I also addressed the Bretheren
present on the duties pertaining to our priesthood
in sustaining those placed to Preside over us,
being quite poorly did not go to afternoon
meeting of saints, but Kept my bed – resumed my
labor Monday Morning in the Temple .

{92}
Wednesday \ Received a communication from Elder Geo Reynolds
29 May 1901/ Box B asking addressed E^d Roskelley which I
supposed was ment for my son Richard. Asking
if he could take a mission to northern States.
Richard at my suggestion wrote to apostle Grant
that if he desired – he R^d would go with him to
Japan.
Sunday
2nd June With Wife Maggie went to Newton. and attended the
Prayer Circle meting with the Bretheren and had
a good time. offered a few suggestions to improve
the conditions.   attended fast meeting in the
afternoon and spoke 40 minutes . Urging the
young people to obtain a testimony for themselves
afterward met with High Priests and Exhorted
them to dilligence & faithfulness, and issued
Certificates of ordination to all present.
Returned home to smithfield in Evening.
16 June Went to Logan 5 Ward Meeting House and Met with
Sunday the Bishoprick and a number of the Priesthood who
had been invited by them and after I had dedicated
the /upper\ Room of the Vestry I organized a Prayer Circle
and gave necessary instructions relative to its being
conducted in future.
23 June
Sunday. Went to Clarkston & picked up Elder C H Larsen at
his home in Newton to go along (as he was a Temple Worker)
and drive to Bro David Buttars home abt 1 1/2 miles
north of Clarkston. and found 16 Men there waiting for
me .– I dedicated a room. upstairs. and gave
the necessary instructions and organized a Prayer
circle for the Clarkston ward, had an Excellent
spirit with us. ate dinner with Bro & Sister
Buttars. then went to Newton to afternoon
Meeting and talked to Saints 20 minutes and
returned home, to Smithfield. Tired

[vertically, in margin]
    * 16 June, My son Richard
    married Hilda Marie
    Johnson of Logan.
    See My Temple Record
        S.R.

[diary text]
4 July 1901. Went to Depot with some of the boys and got an
organ – took it to Mary Janes and set it up
while she was at meeting. Making a surprize
on her. Worked on Hay rack bal of day
7 July. Sunday. attended a Meeting of Bishoprick & Elders of
1st Logan Ward. in Vestry of Tabernacle at 12 noon
and organized a Prayer Circle. 19 Present. Elder [James]
Quayle being present I had him assist me and do

some of the talking. a good spirit prevailed &
all seemed to appreciate the situation exp=
ressing satisfaction with my Visit

{93}
Sunday continued In the afternoon returned home and after
a short rest in town, went to my farm and ate
dinner with wife Mary & family & a few others
including son Richard & wife & my wife Maggie.
as son Richard starts tomorrow to go to Salt Lake
City and thence East on a Mission to the Eastern
states he desired me to give him a blessing.
Which I did – My wife Maggie being scribe.
My health was very poor all spring. and continued
so the summer.
Friday
26 July   Temple Closed for Renovation and Repairs till
1901   sep 4th next. during vacation I fixed up
2 pairs wagon Trucks – having sent for the Wheels
from the East, and fitted Hay racks on them
making it much Easier for my boys to load
hay on them and to do farm work.
Sunday 4 aug. attended 1st Conference of the Benson stake
at Lewiston with My wives Maggie & Maud. I
was sustained as Prest of High Priest Quorum
for the stake during the afternoon sessions and
was set apart in the Vestry of the meeting house
after the close of the afternoon meeting by
apostles Cowley & Clawson.. apostle Cowley being
mouth. And Oh What a Blessing he gave me!
he asked the privelage of Blessing me of the
Bretheren who was laying on hands with him
setting apart the stake officers but it was
not his turn to be mouth in my case hence
his begging the privelage of setting me apart
his blessing was so far reaching that it
brought tears to my Eyes that the Lord had
not forgotten me.
Monday 5 aug   I again attended Conference at Lewiston
apostle Clawson presiding as apostle Cowley
had gone home – My wife Maud with me,
she was sustained as 1st Councillor to
Sister Ellen J. Merrill in the Presidency of
the stake Relief society. (<u>but I afterwards
learned that sister Merrill declined acting in
that Position</u>.) Wife Maud was set apart to the
office of 1st Councillor by Prest W. H Lewis,
My Wife Maggie was also sustained as
1st Councillor to stake Prest Mina M Pond
of the Y. L. M. I. A. and set apart later on

{94}
1901 My Councillors James B. Jardine and W^m H
Roskelley were sustained at afternoon Session
of Conference and set apart later on.
Sunday
18 Aug I organized a Prayer Circle for Lewiston Ward
with 22 Members Bp Waddups President and his
councillors assistants. Prest W. H. Lewis & his
councillors present and took part in Exercises
at their request I first Dedicated the Room for
Prayer Circle purposes then organized and gave
instructions. and then dedicated the building
and grounds and appurtinances to God for
tithing purposes, a attended afternoon
services of the Ward and spoke to the saints
about 20 minutes, at the Close of the Meeting
We retired to the Vestry and at the request of
Prest W. H. Lewis. I was mouth in setting apart
my wife Maggie 1st Con in Y.LMIA. Of the
Benson stake. the stake presidency having their
hands on her head with me.

My 1st Councillor Jas B. Jardine was set
apart by Prest W. H Lewis. & councillors he
being mouth.
Sunday
25 aug I attended the 1st Conference of Hyrum stake
at Hyrum.. Prest W. C Parkinson Presiding
apostles J. H. smith and M W. Merrill present
No officers called that day but Excellent remarks
made by many speakers.
Sunday In salt lake City attending funeral of my
1st sep beloved friend sister Zina D Young returning home
Monday Morning
Monday I ordained my son William H Roskelley a
2nd sep High Priest and afterward gave him a
fathers blessing, at the house of my wife
Mary at the farm.
Monday /&2nd\
& Tuesday 3rd sep Threshed our Grain had in all
  260 Bu Barley.
  222 1/2 " oats
  824^{35} " Wheat
  200^{lbs} Lucerne seed
Wednesday
4 sep Commenced my usual Labor in Logan Temple
and met many old tried friends. Prest Merrill
had gone with Elder Geo Reynolds to the Big horn
settlements to hold conference.

{95}
1901
Sunday 8sep   Met with the Prayer Circle at Clarkston
at 8am. remaining 2 1/2 Hours giving it instructions.
then with My councillor Jas B Jardine met the High
Priests of Newton at 6 P.M. released bro anderson
who had been presiding teacher for years, but had
grown very deaf, and Elected Bro H. C Larsen
and I set him apart, attended saints afternoon
sacrament meeting and talked about 40 M.
after which I attended their Prayer Circle and
gave instructions for about an hour & half.
returning home same Evening with Wife Maggie
who was with me on a Visit to Newton
Sunday
15 sep 1901 By previous arrangement my Councillors J.B Jardine & W^m
H Roskelley. met at my house in Smithfield and went to the
meeting of the High Priests at the City Hall at 10 a m. a
number of the Bretheren were present as I desired to
reorganize this Smithfield members of the Quorum I at
once conferred with 1st Cou to Bishop Bro s Nelson who told
me that the Bishop was a Bro Jos Richardsons he having lost
his babe by death this morning I sent my Councillor Jardine
with Bp's councillor S Nelson to see and advise with the
Bp. about retaining Bro E.R. Miles Jr as the presiding
Teacher of the High Priests of smithfield Ward. Returning
the Bishop to N Woodruff with them he told me in the
presense of S Nelson & W. H Roskelley , he could not
sustain Bro. Miles giving his reasons. and I then
proposed to refer the whole matter to Prest W. H Lewis
for his suggestions how to act. again going into
meeting of High Priests. I motioned to accept
Thos Mather & W. H. Roskelley as members of the
High Priests Quorum. as they had been ordained
High Priests to fill offices in the stake, all voted
unanimous. but in consequence of the Bishopric not
being willing to sustain Bro Miles & did nothing
about the Reorganization. My councillors talked
and I occupied some time outlining our desires
in starting a good Record for the Benson stake
High Priests Quorum. after this meeting my
Councillors & I met at my house and discussed
the question of a secretary for the Quorum. we
settled on Elder Hans T. Petersen. Having
received permission from Prest W. H. Lewis at the
last stake Priesthood meeting to appoint a
suitable person and ordain them a High
Priest if they did not already hold that office

{96}
15 sep
continued
1901

as Bro Peterson was not a High Priest and
had not been Consulted, my Councillors went
to see him at his home – tell him our desires
and learn his feeling regarding it he came
back to my house with my Councillors when I
Explained the nature of the call and the duties
that would be required of him. – with some
hesetancy he accepted. I had previously asked
Bp Woodruff what standing Bro Petersen had in
the Ward – he answered 1st Class – We then
went to Ward Meeting when I told the Bp that
Bro Petersen had accepted the call from us
to the Sectyship of the Quorum – and asked
that he present the name for ordination
for the saints to Vote upon it – he did so
and the Vote was unanimous. After the
Ward Meeting My Councillors, Bp. Woodruff
and his Councillor S Nelson with Myself & Bro
Petersen met again at my house when I
ordained Bro Hans J. Petersen a High Priest
and afterward set him apart as secty of
the High Priests Quorum of Benson stake of
Zion
Sunday
22nd sep   I took Bro H. J. Petersen with me to Cove and there
met my Councillors. Bro Yeates was also there from
Clarkston. attended the sunday school & the saints
sacrament meeting. we also addressed the saints
after which we held a High Priest Meeting 5 present
out of 10 talked some and organized them
calling Bro James C Allen as Presiding Teacher
as he was not Present we could not set him
apart. After getting dinner we got home about
6 P. M having had a profitable Visit.
Sunday   With Elder Morgan and my wife Mary Jane I Visited
29 sep   Wellsville and organized a Prayer Circle, Prest Wm Parkinson
and his Councillor Geo O Pitkin were present, I was mouth
in the dedication of the Room. and gave appropriate
instructions aSsisted by Bro T. Morgan to the 25
persons present, we held a long session to Thoroughly
impress those present and enable them to be capable
hereafter to go ahead with the good work. I was
also mouth in prayer in the Circle. a good spirit
prevailed and all seemed satisfied,
attended afternoon fast meeting services and I was
asked to speak – I did so for a few minutes only
as there were others to speak Viz. Prest Wm Parkinson
& Geo O Pitkin. Elder. T Morgan. we had a good
Meeting many of the saints spoke bearing testimony
of the work of God.

{97}
12 Oct 1901   Attended Stake priesthood meeting at Richmond.
Saturday   Prest Lewis & Councillors Presiding. I addressed them abt
15 minutes. Local Matters principally discussed.
At the Request of Prest Lewis the Prsidency & I set
My son Wm Roskelley apart. 2nd Councillor in
the presidency of the High Priests Quorum. I being
mouth also set Bro [blank] Allen apart presiding
teacher of the High Priests at Coveville.
Sunday \   Met with the High priests at Lewiston with my
13 Oct   /   Councillors. Prest Lewis of the Stake presidency
also Present. Bro Allen the presiding teacher
resizned and Bro Joseph Pond was sustained for
the future presiding officer. I occupied most of
the time of the meeting showing the nature of the
important Calling & responsabilities of a High Priest
had an important meeting.
Councillors & I met with saints in afternoon
sacrament meeting. I talked by request for
abt 45 minutes. Principally on Prest L Snows
life & works this being his funeral day.
took dinner with Prest W. H. Lewis and then
Home
Sunday
27th Oct   With my son William attended the Cache stake
quarterly Conference at Logan and heard the apostles
Cowley talk.
Saturday \   With Wife Maud attended special Conference at
3rd Nov   /   Lewiston to vote on lately Elected Presidency
of Church also the officers sustained to fill the
Vacancies in apostle & Presiding Bishopric.
Saturday
9 Nov 1901   Went to Salt Lake to attend special General
Conference of the Church.
Sunday
10 Nov 1901   attended Conference at Big Tabernacle.
Prest Jos F smith preached forenoon giving some
advanced ideas as to the authority and position
of the Patriarch of the church. And other matters
of importance.
The afternoon services were Very impressive
the church Voted by Quorums on Each of the
General authorities of the Church and all were
unanimously sustained.
in the Evening attended 16 Ward meeting Prest
Jos F smith Preached sermon on growth & develop
ment of Church from organization till now

{98}
giving causes in the spreading of the people. My son James
was also present, I shook hands with Prest smith at the

close of meeting.

Monday 11th Nov. 1901   spent part of forenoon with Bro
C. W. Penrose at Deseret News office. had a good
Visit and inspected their type setting Machine
and also the printing Machines it is Wonderful
spent Most of the afternoon with Recorder John Nichols
in Salt Lake Temple. and came to Ogden with
son James in the Evening. Stayed with Jos Hall
and family over night having a good Visit
Tuesday 12 Nov came to Logan and to the Temple at
noon & home to smithfield in Evening – found my
family all out from under the Quarintine and
again Enjoying health which I am thankful to
my heavenly father for.
Sunday 24th /&25\ Nov 1901. Benson state Quarterly Conference at
& Monday. Richmond. Apostles John H. Smith, M W Merrill & M F Cowley
present. . My wife Maud was Released form her position as
1st Councillor to president of Relief society as the President
resigned for cause – and others were appointed.
The usual routine of Conference was attended to. I
was called upon to report of H P. Quorum to start
with. other reports followed. Apostles gave good
teachings on needed topics – principally the
looking after & teaching the young boys & young men
in the lesser priesthood Quorums and promoting each
in Acordance with Merit and advising 70s not
to increase their Quorums without good reasons. For so
doing. but letter Elders be instructed & Educated in
their Elders Quorum Meetings and become qualified
to fill missions and any labor thro' diligence &
faithfulness as Elders

[end of journal 6; end of transcript]

Journal [7]

1 December 1901 – 10 October 1910

{front pastedown}
[blank]

{endleaf recto}
[blank]

{endleaf verso}
[blank]

{three leaves cut out at the gutter}

{page 1}
1st Dec ~~30th November~~ 1901
Sunday
1st Dec
~~30 Nov~~ 1901. Myself and councillors met at the
                                                 house of
my Wife Mary Jane this day, also our Quorum
                                        Secty. Bro Petersen,
and we thoroughly discussed the condition and
                                            circumstance
of the Quorum and we decided to invite the
                                           Presiding
teachers of the Quorum in the Wards of the stake,
to the stake priesthood meeting on Saturday next

the 7th inst and there lay before them a plan to
organize a Prayer circle as soon as Convenient
and set a time for meeting to become acquainted
with Each other and pray together that we may
get the spirit of our Calling &c &c, we afterward
attended the ward fast meeting in Smithfield, and I
took the opportunity to bear my testimony to the
                                               truth
of the Latter-day work.
Saturday 7th Dec with Wife Maggie ~~attend~~ /went\
                                               to
Lewiston and I attended the Priesthood meeting
and my wife the Y.L.M.I.A Meeting. . I afterward
called the High Priest Quorum teachers together
                                             and
canvased the Question to having a Prayer circle
                                             meeting
at Lewiston all voted to have one to-morrow
                                             sunday
at the Lewiston Tithing Office.
Sunday 8th Dec 1901. With son William drove to
                                             Lewiston
and met with their regular Prayer Circle at 9. a m.
by Request of Bp Waddup I took the charge.
and corrected some Errors. &c but had a good
meeting.

Samuel Roskelley papers, MS 65, Utah State Univ. Special Collections. The volume was microfilmed in September 1954 by the Utah Genealogical Society; microfilm now available as MS 8239, Church History Library, Salt Lake City. The microfilm was digitized ca.2014. This version is a line-by-line transcription of the manuscript. Page numbers were added to recto (right hand) pages of the volume to simplify matching the transcription to the document. They are given in this transcription between braces. The numbers *do not* relate to digital-file image numbers.

at 11. A.M the teachers of the H.P. Quorum
from the Wards of the stake met. Clothed and had
instruction from me about the formation of a
Prayer circle.. and we united in Prayer, my late
Councillor Willard Dove Offered Prayer. Afterward
I talked of the necessity of our getting together
and nearer to Each other and it was
arranged to meet again in a similar way
2nd sunday in Feby next. Elder Dove and my
present Councillor Jas Jardine talked on the
advisability of preparing studies for the
meetings of the High Priests in the wards—it
was decided that we take up the study
of Church History from the Manual of the

{2}
1901
Y.M.M.I.A published in 1899.
attended meeting of Lewiston Ward in the
afternoon. Elder W. Done, my son William
and I talked to the saints
Sunday 15th remained at home – not feeling well
had a heavy cold on my lungs.
Friday 20th December The Temple Closed this
 Evening
for holidays until 6th January next. and Saturday
21st I was paying debts. & arranging for material
for a shed for the Cows, for the folks in town
Sunday 22 Dec. with wife Maggie son William &
H.T. Petersen went to Newton., to meet with the
High Priests. According to a previous arrangement
my Councillor J.B. Jardine also met us there at

11 a.m. I took the High Priests present, who Voted
to sustain the Church with its present organization
Jos F. smith as its head. with all the authorities,
 general
& local as now organized, and made a roll,
read the names of them and Voted to sustain Each
other as Members of the High Priests Quorum of
the Benson stake of the C. of J.C. Of L.D S. thus
 starting
the organization. other High Priests lived in the
ward but not being present they were not received
as members until they presented themselves,
4 persons presented a recommend for ordination
and agreeing to sustain the the church as its
present organized and do their duty as High
Priests. they were ordained. I being mouth in
ordaining Jonas N Beck, Councillors Jardine,
Roskelley & secty Petersen talked about the use

and adoption of the Y.M.M Manual for 1899-1900
as a text book and advised its study &
adoption in regular course, and urged that
meetings be held Every 2 weeks, or twice Each
month. at least for the study of the principles
in the Church History contained in the Manuel.
we attended the afternoon services of the
saints – being Memorial services of the
Birth of the Prophet Joseph smith. with others
speakers (who gave some Historical data)
I followed giving reference to doctrines that

{3}
had been given to the saints & the world by
the Prophet Jos smith and the Evidences that
the Father & the son were 2 separate persons,
returned home in the Evening.
Monday 23rd Dec I was getting the material
 together
and Commenced work roofing the corrall shed
on Mary Jane's lot to Make the Cows Comfort=
able and dry. worked tuesday same way
Wednesday 25 Dec Christmas day. spent it
in Visiting around among my wives & children
ate dinner with Maud and went to the
farm and Visited with my family there also
and continued balance of the week at the
corrall shed in town with all the boys
I could get to work at it.
Sunday 29th Dec. It being Holliday time I did
not go out in the settlements to Visit the High
Priests.
Monday 30th Dec working at shed.
Tuesday 31st "   do   do
Wednesday 1st Jan 1902. My birth day. 65
years old. And I thank my heavenly father
for his protecting care. Especially that I am
still in the Gospel and all my family
are members of the Church of J C of LD. Saints
I received many congratulations from the
members of my family and others..
Maud invited Mary Jane & Maggie to her home
and we all ate an Excellent dinner & supper
together. with thankful hearts. Oh. how few
families there remains now in the Celestial order
of marriage, in all this ward of some 1500 in-
=habitants only 6 families that I know of are now
living in that order of marriage, and it almost
seems refreshing to shake hands with a man or
woman. That sticks to that principle.
Wm F. Rigby is at my farm with some of my

boys driving for a flowing well. A long needed commodity.
By letter from my son Richard from Pittsburg Penn. I learn he is doing well and writes Encouraging letters home. God bless him in his labors.

{4}
1902
we finished the Roof of the shed in town Saturday 4th Jan 1902. and made a good Job of it. –
Sunday 5th Jan. by Previous appointment my son William H. and secty H T. Petersen and myself met with the High Priests in smithfield for Reorganization in the
[written vertically in the margin]
  *Elder E R Miles Jr sustained as Teacher Benson stake /\ nearly all the High Priests residing in the ward present. the names of those present was read and a motion made that the names read be accepted members of the H.P. Quorum of the Benson stake of Zion. objections was raised by Bp Councillor S Nelson to some who were present because they Visited saloons those objected to promised to do better in future, and were accepted ..
Sunday self and Councillors & Bro Petersen our secty met by appointment with the High Pirests at Newton and Reorganized as part of the H P. Quorum of the Benson stake of
                                            Zion
Elder C H Larsen was Chosen and set apart as Presiding Teacher ___ Bretheren were recom=mended and ordained High Priests.
Sunday 19 Jan 1902 self and Councillor W. H.
                                            Roskelley,
met with the High Priests at Coveville, and organized the bretheren as part of the H P. Quorum of the Benson stake Elder [blank] Allen was sustained as Presiding teacher and Bro Alma Hendricks as clerk
17 Jan 1902. I assisted Prest NWMerrill to ordain Robert Baxter of Wellsville a High Priest and set
                                            him
apart a Patriarch of the Church. Having officiated about a year ago in like capacity in Elder J H. Martineau's case of Mexico.
Sunday 2 Feby 1902. My step son H A Watson called on me and we talked for a length of time as I had not seen him for 10 years – as he has been wandering thru Idaho. Oregon & Washington States for some time. My son William and

{5}
Secty Petersen met with the High Priests of our Smithfield Ward to day and heard the Manual Exercise, which they say was good.
Sunday 9 Feb 1902. according to appointment my Councillors. Secty and the Presiding Teachers of the High Priests Quorum met in Prayer Circle at the Lewiston Tithing office and had a most delightful time. Each Reported the Condition and feelings of the bretheren they presided over and how they Conducted their meetings. Newton & Trenton were not represented.
Sunday 16 Feb 1902. Councillors /Bro Jardine
                                            &\ W.H. Roskelley
and Secty Petersen and I met with the members of the H.P. Quorum at Richmond. Wallace K Burnham resigned in consequence of being a stake high councillor and being on home missionary list. Bro Frank – the Bps Councillor was chosen and set apart by Councillor (Stake) Alma Merrill to preside over the High Priests in Richmond ward our Meeting seemed to give satisfaction.
Sunday & Monday 23 & 24 Mch attended
                                            Quarterly
Conference Benson stake held at Smithfield Stake Councillor Hendricks & wife stayed with my wife Maggie, had good meetings and a good spirit prompted the speakers.
Sunday 2 Mch 1902 with Son W. H. R & secty
                                            Petersen
attended H.P. Meeting at Smithfield heard Manual Exercises and with others offered suggestions and had a good visit.
Saturday 8th March Located and had Wm Watson dig out a spring in skunk hollow on my farm and found a good flow of water. with my boys Henry. Ora & Marriner made a box for a tank 4x8 feet, and partially sunk it to cover the springs so as to protect the springs from falling Earth &c
Tuesday 11th March. In accordance with previous arrangements I sent 100^{\underline{50}}$ to Elder John H. Petersen in Rotterdam Holland.

{6}
11 Mch 1902.
through a draft from Thatcher bank for Bro
Petersen to send me a good man to work
for me this coming year.
Sunday
16 Mch 1902. sunday my son & councillor William H.
and secty Petersen & met at at My Wife Maggies
and talked with Bro W^m F Rigby about his
indifference
to his position and calling in the priesthood.
Showed what
was Expected of him and how he should magnify
his
calling, he promised better . Acknowledging his
neglect
also attended H P. Quorum Meeting in smithfield
had good attendance – good spirit – listened to
Manuel Exercises which were farely well rendered
considering all things. Meeting in afternoon. And
visiting with my family – took midnight train for
Logan. as Roads were so very. very bad.
Sunday
30 Mch 1902 with son William met with High
Priests
again. listened to Manual Exercises at Smithfed
farely well rendered, attended afternoon sacrament
Meeting – fast day and blessed my grnd child
my daughter sarah's babe, naming it William
Kenneth Watson.
Sunday 6 apl did not go out all day. in bed
sick with neuralgia & high fever. in the Evening
Bro Wm Chambers & my son William came and
administered
to me and I go Ease and Comfort right away &
went
to sleep thanking my heavenly father for his
Kindness
to me. the Roads still very bad.
Sunday 13 apl With son William, went to Newton
and
there held our stake High Priests Prayer
Circle, Compound of Presidency & secty and the
Presiding
Teachers of the Quorum in the wards. all present
but Bro Funk of Richmond. I changed the order
of Presidency as Requested by Prest M W. Merrill
by Placing my 2nd Councillor on my right instead
of being my 2nd man on my left. we had a
good meeting.
Met also with High Priests of Newton. Elder C. H.
Larsen our Presiding Teacher – leaving for
Denmark
in a few days. was honorably released and Elder
Wm F. Rigby Voted to take his place. I was mouth
in setting him apart. all business was done to the

{7}
satisfaction of all present seemingly.
stayed to the saints afternoon meeting and
spoke about 30 Minutes relating experiences,
and returned home in Evening.
Thursday 17th apl The man I sent to Holland for
Bro Jouce de Haan arrived in smithfield. I
had him drive team Reeling grain land part of
the Evening.
The weather so rainy and Roads so cut up
and my health so poor. I did not do any
Visiting personally but rested on the sabbath days
having my Councillors & secty travel and do
the business of the Quorum till
Sunday 25 May = with My wife Maud I attended
the stake Conference at Lewiston and had
a very profitable time listening to the remarks
of the bretheren & also the singing, apostle Cowley
spoke sunday afternoon with great force & power.
and all seemed to enjoy it. .Prest Merrill
was present at afternoon services and requested
me to go to the Temple on Monday to see to its
business – consequently I did not attend the
Conference on that day.
Sunday 1st June 1902. With my Councillors met
with the Clarkston Ward Prayer Circle at
the House of Bro David Butters at 9 a M. and
arranged the order of the Presidency of the
circle as desired by apostle Merrill
Met with the presiding teachers of the H. P.
Quorum. Of the stake at 10 a.m. Held Prayer
Circle with them and afterward had a
meeting with them receiving Reports &c of
work being done by the Quorum. . .
met with Clarkston High Priests at 11.30
aM. and heard reports of Progress Made
by the bretheren all present seemed to feel
well in the Gospel.
At 2 P.M. Met in fast meeting with the
saints and spoke to them on the object
of the fasting, and many other matters of
interest to Latter-day saints. Returned
home in a drenching rain storm.
8th June 1902. my son being at his ranch
Plowing and my other councillor J Jardine so

distant. I Visited Coveville Ward alone

{8}
[circled:] 8 June 1901 found bretheren all feeling well with Exception of 2 who had failed to come to Meeting all present bore good faithful testemony and I gave them all the Encouragement I could
sunday 22 June, attended Quarterly Conference at Hyrum. Spoke 25 Minutes comparing present with past conditions.. listened to Prest A H Lund and Jos F smith preach Excellent discourses in the afternoon.
1st July Tuesday. My Boys finished putting up 1st stack of Hay for the season East of grave yard, same night storm arose and blew off top of stack. Scattering it badly – Jos [Debaum/Delsaver] fell off stack spraining his ankle.
Saturday \ With Wife Maggie. Went to Lewiston
5 July 1902 / to Priesthood Meeting. returning in the afternoon and got derrick from south field to the farm
Sunday \ By request of Presidency of stake my
6 July / son William and I went to Clarkston and reorganized their Prayer Circle Placing the new Bp John Ravsten at the head with his Councillors as his assistants. and reconstructed the Entire list. [blank] also met with the High Priests. at 11. a. M. discussed the propriety of making a change in the Presiding teacher but finally thought best to retain the old one Thos Griffin. . got home in time to attend fast meeting. and bore my testimony. to the saints in smithfield
    Visited Prayer Circle at Lewiston and made change in order of Presidency standing at the alter in Circle.
also held meeting with the High Priests of the ward. My son William also present recd reports and admitted some new members or old members Just wok up and had good meeting.
15 aug 1902 took midnight train for st Anthony Idaho. arriving there Saturday (with My daughter Emma who was with me) abt 1.30. met at

{9}
the depot my son Joseph – going to his home with

him Visiting his Wife and child & himself and on
Sunday morning 17th aug. Joseph & wife & child myself & daughter Emma started to Marysville 18 Miles distant, arriving abt 1.30. ate dinner with Bro Eli Harriss & wife my niece Libby & family. attended saints sacrament meeting and I talked an hour & ten minutes on Temple work, and matters connected with ordinance work in and out of Temples. after meeting met with a number of my old friends as Bro Eli Harris'es and Visited Ann Bainbridge Wife of my nephew the late James Bainbridge – and spent the night at Harris'es left in Morning. Calling on my Bro in law Joseph Hendricks & wife Sariah. and Visited my son Joseph's farm, thence to st anthony, ate dinner. and went over the Egin bench and saw the beautiful farm over the great stretch of Country stayed over night with my Br in law Joseph Rigby of Egin Ward and next day to Rexburg Visiting the President of stake Bro Bassett – sister Ricks & daughter. Bro anderson – my stepson's Children & lots of others. took train at 3.30 and started home. arriving at Smithfield Tuesday 19 aug.
sunday 14 sep with Bro H T. Petersen Visited Coveville and met with the High Priests. had a good meeting. receiving 1 New Member. who had failed to put in an appearance before at our Meetings since the new organization.
Monday 15th at Home threshing the 2nd time making a total of 908 Bu Wheat 130 Bu Oats 87 Bu Barley, also put up some Lucerne on stack
Traded my Pet mare to son Wilford for his Bird horse. and sold my

{10}
1902
imported Bull to Alma hillyard for $50.00 $16.00 I owed him & 34.00 Cash.
I did not attend General Conference this october as my health was poor and I wanted to look to the labor of my sons at home.
Sunday 12 Oct. I attended High Priests meeting at Smithfield. 2 presented themselves for ordina= =ation – previously recommended – I ordained Bro

John Kelsey. and samuel Nelson by my request ordained solyman s. Merrill.
9 Nov 1902 With Wife Maggie & son William my Councillor I visited Clarkston – met with the High Priests. all 3 of the Presidency Present and all talked – prastable & to the point, and the bretheren all seemed satisfied.
after dinner went to Tenton & visited the High Priests, attended afternoon sacrament meeting afterward with wife Maggie attended Young Ladies Meeting and. my wife organ ized a branch of the Y.L M.I.I. Trenton Ward at Request of Bishop Bingham I set sister Merrill apart as President
23 & 24 Nov attended Benson stake Conference apostle M.W. Merrill and M. F Cowley Present had good meetings and much good instruction sunday 30 nov: Took wife Maggie to Newton and I attended High Priest special meeting 10 out of 19 Present. 3 sick. 3 absent from home. The bretheren all Expressed themselves about the manual Exercises and the majority wished to continue the lessons .
21st Dec sunday. Son & Councillor William H. R. also secty H. T. Petersen met at my house at 9 a.m. And after devotional Exercises advised together about interests of the Quorum and agreed to recommend to members to take 1/2 of the manual Lesson Each Meeting and Each alternate meeting give 1/2 of meeting to Missionaries that may be appointed – and /at\ the next meeting

{11}
1/2 the time to testimony bearing.
At the Close of our Meeting went to the regular H.Priest Meeting of the Smithfield Ward.
spent the usual Holidays with the folk Visiting with the family – Wife Mary Jane quite sick having met with mishap, from which it took much time to recover. also surveyed & leveled a line for water pipes from my Reservoir at farm to my town property – Each place – also from main line to town to Mary's house. it proved to have on Main line 120 ft 8 tenths fall to george Merrills corner. From bottom of Reservoir.
Saturday \ Took Wife Maggie to Lewiston 3rd Jan 1903/ to her Y L Meeting and I attended stake Priesthood Meeting. I spoke on Temple work and [blank]
[blank line]

Tuesday 6 Jan 1903 Resumed Temple work
Sunday 4th Jan 1903 Went to Clarkston – Willie & H T. Petersen also were there – attended Prayer Circle at 10 a.m; and Had a good time also attended a H.P. Meeting at 12.30 arranged for the new Program and Voted for it – I talked to the Members for abt 35 minues showing the advan= =tages of all doing their duty.
The spring and summer past away in the usual manner and in august my daughter Emma and I went to Marysville Idaho to Visit my son Joseph and Wife & Uncle Joe Hendricks & family and Eli Harris & family – while there I found that James Bainbridges wife ann Lewis Bainbridge had in her possession Grand ma Hendrick's written history and also some Items of work performed by her and her sons in the salt Lake Endowment house Of Baptisms & sealings for the dead of the Hendricks family. She lived in Marysville. I went to see her and she consented to let me have the book. Much of it had been written

{12}
by her deceased husband James Bangridge and also by Grandma herself..
I got the book – brought it home and it is now in the possession of my son James.

omitted 28 Mch 1903
By previous invitation my family met at my Wife's home at the farm and Celebrated the 50th Anniversary of my leaving Liverpool as an Emigrant on the 28th March 1853. we had a grand time of it 63 of my family present and took supper together The following Committees acted.
    on General Program
    S Roskelley Jr
    Mary Roskelley Jr
    Sarah Roskelley Watson
      on Invitation
Wm H Roskelley, Mary Jane R Roskelley
Drusilla Roskelley   ora Roskelley
   Florence Roskelley
   on Reception.
Wilford Roskelley   Catherine Roskelley
Libby Roskelley Watson   Henry Roskelley
William Watson   Fred K Roskelley

on Entertainment
Mary Roberts Roskelley   Maggie Rigby Roskelley
Hannah Roskelley Newbold   Jacob Watson
    Henry Newbold
    on Music
S. Maud. Burton Roskelley   William H Roskelley
    Emma Roskelley

{13}
    28 March 1903
    on Finance
S Roskelley Jr   Jas Roskelley
William H Roskelley   Wilford Roskelley
In september 1903. the 11 national Irrig=
=ation Congress sat for deliberation in
Ogden Utah for 3 days and I with
my wife Maud were Honored with seats
as Delegates from Logan. Hyde Park
and smithfield Canal Co. I also received
a fine badge as a delegate and also
1 badge as a pioneer 50 Year
Irrigator. a gift in Each case from
the Congress, I feel proud of these
badges
    11th
    ~~14~~ June 1904
I turned the water from the settling
box into the Reservoir. And in a
few minutes it flowed thro the
pipet and was seen at the house,
it was a book indeed. But unfor=
=tunately in two days afterward the
reservoir gave way and was partially
destroyed. also on 11 June 1904
Richard , Ora, Henry and I went to
the Pilkington Bridge across out
Birch Kanyon ditch and put a
Weir in the ditch a little distance
above the bridge after the pattern
approved by the Irrigation Engineer
of the a.c College – the Water that
flowed over the Weir measured
4 feet 2ide by 5 9/8in deep on top
of the metal Weir.
    14 July 1904
Thursday Eve Went to my Daughter Libby's
Watson and with the father blessed the

{14}
    14 July 1904

twin Babies naming one (the Eldest)
William R Watson and the youngest
Wilford J Watson. I was mouth in both
cases
Spent the Usual summer Vacation from the
Temple at home with the family Enjoying them and
fixing up their homes to make them Comfortable
and also helping the boys put up the hay and
grain . Thresh &c.
The Usual General Conference of the church
I attended in Salt Lake City and Prest Jos F
smith called on Prest J.D.T. McAllister to Repres=
=ent the Manti Temple and its labors also –
myself to represent the Logan Temple and
its labors. And Prest David H. Cannon to
represent the st George Temple and its labors
but I cannot understand Why I was called
upon to be the Representative of Logan Temple
in such an important gathering and before
the General Conference of the Church. It was
the first time in my life I ever spoke to
the Great Tabernacle and before a General
Conference of the Church. As I am only the
Recorder of Logan Temple.
The Usual Holliday festivities were
Celebrated by my family in a quiet way
at the homes of my family. and thus past
my 68th birth day.
my labors in the Temple and in the Ministry
as president of the High priests Quorum has
Kept me so busy that I scarce have
visit with my family so
after talking the situation over with
Prest M. W. Merrill he suggested that
I resign from the President of the
Quorum of which I had been president
for some 24 years. I did so and following
is the acceptance of my resignation

[*three leaves cut out at the gutter*]

{15}
[*pasted on page*]
    May 4 1905
    President Samuel Roskelley
    Smithfield Utah
    Dear Brother
    As per your request we have accep-
ted your resignation as President of the
High Priest's Quorum knowing of your ardu

ous labors.
 We appreciate very much your past labors in the Quorum and the grand success you have made with the same, and trust you will be blessed in all your duties and labors in the future and you have been in your labors in the past in the quorum
  With Kind personal regards
   we remain your bretheren in the Gospel
    W^m H Lewis
    Alma Merrill
    BA Hendricks
     Stake Presidency

[*diary text*]

<u>Sunday 14 May 1905</u> I attended the Benson stake Conference held at Lewiston. Apostle Hyrum M. Smith and Elder Rulon S Wells were present .. The Presidency of the High Priests Quorum Viz. Samuel Roskelley. James B Jardine and William Hendricks Roskelley were released by Vote of thanks honorably – but it was found afterward that some complications arose in tehmid of the apostle about the persons named for our successors and I was requested by the stake presidency to con= =tinue my labors with my councillors in looking after the Quorum until complications were all straightened out and successors duly installed

sunday 21 May 1905. attended a High Priest meeting at Lewiston – good attendance and with my councillors Bro JB Jardine addressed the bretheren – all expressed sorrow to part with us as presidency after laboring together so many years my son and councillor W^m H R. was sick at home and could not attend the Meeting.

<u>Sunday 28 May 1905</u>. With my son and Councillor William H. Roskelley and sect Petersen met with the High Priests at Covevill and had a good meting all felt well but Expressed regrets we were to not enjoy each others company longer because of my release. Sickness in the ward caused the Meetings for some time to be discontinued.

<u>Sunday 4th June 1905</u> With Councillor W H R and secty Petersen held meeting with High Priests in Clarkston. My Councillor bro J B Jardine was also present, we had a thoroughly Enjoyable meeting – large majority of the Bretheren were present – all the presidency spoke also the Bishop and Councillors – we also attended fast meeting services in the afternoon and I occupied considerable time. Taking to the saints which they seemed to Enjoy

{16}

<u>Sunday 11th June 1905</u> With Councillor W. H Roskelley and secty Petersen attended High Priests meeting at Richmond. Listening to part of their class Exercises of Manual lesson and with my bretheren addressed the High Priests present on the Discipline of the Church. and order of Church Government in the 2 Grades of Priesthood. Explaining many points not given in manual.

<u>Sunday 18 June 1905</u> With son William H Ros =kelly and secty Petersen went to Lewiston and organized a 2nd Prayer Circle of 20 persons. 5 High Priests 8 seventies 7 Elders with Bro Rawlins President. B. Pond and A Hyer assistants for Presidency. had a genuine good itme also took my wife Maud to attend a stake board Meeting of the Relief society.

Sunday 25 June 1905. With son and Councillor W^m H roskelley attended High Priests meeting at Coveville – nearly all the High Priests of the ward Present and expressed kindley feelings for our past labors with them and feelingly bade us Gods blessing.

<u>Sunday 2nd July 1905</u>. With Elder Thos Morgan of the Temple attended the prayer circle meeting in the 2nd ward Logan and gave some Valuable instructions that have come to ussince their Circle was organized. We had a Very nice quiet peacefulspirit and pleasant Visit with the Bretheren there who Expressed themselves as well satisfied with our Visit. And I trust good will come out of it

With my councillors and secretary I visited all the High Preist Quorum Organizations of the stake between the May and august quarterly Conferences /of the stake\ and many regrets were Expressed by the bretheren became of our resignation of the Presidency of the Quorum.

Sunday 13 august 1905 – 2nd day's session of the Benson Stake Conference held at Richmond. Apostle John Henry smith made a short speech about the duties of Patriarchs in the Church and stated that he felt impressed by the spirit of the Lord that it was the mind of the Lord that William D Hendricks and Samuel Roskelley

{17}
be called and ordained Patriarch in the Church and empowered to bless the saints – that he Knew– that we Knew nothing about it, but he had counselled with his fellow apostle M W Merrill and also the stake presidency who had given their hearty consent. Putting it to the vote of the assembled saints – they Voted unanimously for which apostle smith thanked them for their confidence an united sustinance.
Elder Wm D. Hendricks and myself were invited to the Vestry of the meeting house and there ordained by apostle John Henry smith assisted by Patriarch Lorenzo H Hatch who was present. Thankful to God for his Kindness and Mercy shown to me in crowing me with this blessing after so many years of roil and labor in the ministry I feel I am more than paid for all my toil.
Sunday 1 Oct 1905 With my wife Maud went to Lewiston to fill a previous appointment. And met most of the Members of the late President Wm H. Lewis's family. Bp Wm Waddoups of Lewiston and 1st High Councillor of the stake Harvey M. Rawlins also being present – I talked to the family about being being united and feeling for Each others interests == following in the footsteps of their father and doing all in their power to accomplish their Temple work begun in his life time. All seemed deeply interested and impresesd with my words – after which I gave 2 wives and 6 of the Eldest Children a Patriarchal blessing also a fathers blessing as their fathers were dead The spirit of God was poured out upon us and we felt its influence quit manifest.
Friday 6th October 1905. Went to salt Lake City with morning train to attend General Conference of the Church. Attended all meetings except 1st Morning. And had a good spiritual feast Made my home with wives Mary Jane and Maggie at Bro & sister stoneman's who treated us Royally.

{18}
retuned home on Monday Evening.
Tuesday 10th October 1905. Resumed my labors in the Logan Temple. and continued till 22nd Dec when the Temple closed for 1 week till 2 Jan 1906 I have ministered in my patriarchal colling on several occasions during the latter part of the year in giving blessings spent Christmas, most all day at the farm with my wife Mary and her family – all the living children being present. and spent my time between Christmas and New Years day Visiting my dear ones, even my family and took comfort in their Company
1st January 1906 My 69th birth day. spent the day with wives Mary. Mary Jane Maggie and Maud at wife Mauds home my son Joseph and his wife and babe were also present. ate dinner together and had a good Visit gave Wife Mary a Patriarchal and fathers blessing. at twilight we all left Mauds together except Mary Jane who had preceeded us to Maggies home. When we arrived there What a sight and a surprise Greeted me, without any previous Knowledge my folks had arranged for all my smaller children and a number of my grand children to be at Maggies home where they filled the Kitchen. Standing in rows. the smallest totts in front and larger behind till it looked like a small sea of faces. And on my entering the door they all shouted surprise Grand-pa and then commenced to sing an appropriate song, about 50 were present of my family – this scene was followed with songs and recitations &c until all seemed satisfied, when they all sat on seats and floor and ate lunch of cake sandwiches. pie. nuts & Candy &c. indulging in Merry rivalry to the fullest extent I was asked to talk which I did an related some of my Early history and

{19}
Experiences comming into the church. Thus

past as pleasant birthday as I ever Knew
for this birthday I was a Patriarch not
only of my family but by gift of God thro'
ordination by his Royal priesthood.
O! What a contrast between to night
and the 16 Oct 1853 when I landed on
~~Emigration~~ 16th Ward square in Salt Lake
City, a boy without money or friends. Clothed
in rags – with no means of support but
my hands and owned nothing but a
Testimony of the Gospel and its divinity
and the devine mission of the prophet
Joseph Smith. owing the Church for my
Emigration something over $90.00 and it run=
=ing on interest. Oh! My! has not God
been good to me! I praise him Every
Breath I draw, for I owe it all to him.
Sunday 14 Jan 1906 With my son James I visited
Lewiston by invitation of the Bishop Andrew Hyer
together with the stake presidency and I
reorganized the 2nd Prayer Circle by Electing
the present Bishop Bro Hyer as President
and his councillors as assistants leaving the
1st Circle to be presided over by the former
Bishop but now Councillor in stake presidency
William Waddoups. we had a good time all
day – returning home late in the Evening.
Tuesday 6 Feb 1906 Apostle and President
M W. Merrill died at his residence to day the
Ending of a Very useful and active life, he
leaves 8 living wives and a large posterity.
and his works follow him.
Saturday 10 Feb 1906. with Members of my
family attended the funeral services and
(took part therein) of apostle M W Merrill.
Prest A H Lund presiding accompanied by 5
Members of the 12 apostles. I had a long and
pleasant interview with Prest Lund, at his
request. About our Temple affairs (Logan Temple,
and he advised one relative to its affairs
generally. which gave me much satisfaction

{20}
Wednesday 28th Feb /1906\ a Messenger form the
Church presidency visited me and brought
instructions relative to our Temple affairs
and gave Elder Thurgan and Myself some
General instructions:
Sunday 4th Mch 1806. Had all Records of Logan
Temple removed so if necessary I could sware
I did [not] Know where they are. this seemed a

necessary precaution as times are precarious
more ways than one. and I hope not to be
caught napping. Bro Thos Morgan is
overseeing the general affairs of the Temple
Since the death of Prest M W Merrill
In answer to a brief report by me of the
way things are being conducted in the Temple
I received the following reply.
[letter once pasted on page has been removed and is no
                                    longer present]
In Consequence of the bad roads the past
3 weeks and lack of hay at my stable at
Logan I and my boys Ora. Henry and Marr=
=iner have stayed in Logan from Monday
Morning to Friday Evening – doing our
traveling on the Train.
and I had to continue to do the same
till the Temple closed for Conference the 4th
day of april
My son Henry having completed his mission
=ary Course at the B.Y. College Quit school
and went home on Friday 30th March 1906
not having received any call from Box B.
he does no Know if he is wanted in the

{21}
missionary field at present.
Friday 6th April 1906 Took train for Salt Lake
City and attended General Conference also the
Priesthood Meetings and delighted with all the
proceedings Except to lear that apostle John
W. Taylor and Mathias F. Cowley has sent in their
resignations as members of the 12 apostles and
Prest M F Lyman stated that the quorum had accep
-ted the resignations as these men were not in
                                    harmony
with them – It is a matter of deep regret as they
                                    seemed
tobe good faithful – dilligent workers. 3 new
                                    apostles
were Voted in to fill up the quorum in place of the
2 Just named and M.W. Merrill who died 6 Feb
                                    1906.
the men chosen and Voted were Geo F. Richards
Orson F. Whitney and David O McKay, also
Elder Charles N Hart was Elected to fill the
Vacancy in the 1st Council of the 70 in place of
Daniel C. Fjeldsted who died during the winter
1905-6. I stayed at stonemans' nights – gave
Bro & sister Stonemand and Bp Warren smith
and sister Thomas each a Patriarchal Blessing

Came home Monday night and went to the
Temple Tuesday Morning at its opening:
during my absence my son James ~~James~~
sold all my surplus stock which helped
me to free myself from Encumbrances
financially, for which I am thankful to
my heavenly father.
Sunday 22 apl 1906 attended Smithfield High Priest
Meeting and took part in the Manual Exercises under
the class Leader samuel Nelson. The President of he
Quorum also 1st Councillor & secty Viz. Bro skidmore,
Burnham and Morrison were present. The two former
spoke for a Very short time only. it seemed funny
for me not to have anything to say as Bro skidmores
ways are not like mine in meeting and
ordination matters: perhaps we shall see alike
later on.
Sunday 19 and 20 May attended Quarterly Confer=
=ence of Benson stake held at Richmond old hall
apostles George a smith and Geo M. Richards present
whos remarks were general in their nature. Had
some good Meetings Reports &c. I had the privelage
of talking a few moments before the close of the

{22}
20th May 1906
sunday afternoon Meeting.
Sunday 3rd June 1906 . with wife Maud attended
funeral services of Prest Jos Morrell of Cache stake,
and the largest Funeral I ever attended in Logan
The Priesthood Quorums and officers of auxillary
organizations met at his home and marched
2 abrest before the hearse containing the casket
to the tabernacle, apostle C W. Penrose spoke
fine on the object of our Existence here on the
Earth and our previous and future Estates and
made Mormonism of more than usual importance
to all interested. Elder seymour B. Young also
spoke splendid on the life and character of
our "Jo Morrell', Oh My! how my old
associates & fellow laborers are passing away
I almost feel lonesome.
Friday 15th June 1906. We have learned by the
newspaper that Prest Wm Budge of the Bear Lake

stake was released from the Presidency of that
stake on Sunday last as he had been appointed to
Preside over Logan Temple – this is the first
official announcement we heard. But to day
Prest Wm Budge came to the Temple and after
being closeted with Elder Thos Morgan for
some time – we learned that he was Expecting
to move to Logan and assume charge of the
Temple after the august vacation.
20 July 1906. Temple closed for Renovation and
Repairs which was badly needed..
During the Vacation the weather was quite
hot and I was unable to do much out of doors
but my son John Henry received a missionary call
to go to Japan and I had to get the money together
to send him away. He left home on the Evening
of 3rd aug. his Brothers James and Ora went with
him to Cache Junction where he met Elder Dan
Woodland who had been to Japan before and
returned to settle up his dead fathers Estate
and was now Returning to fill his mission
He proceeded by rail to seattle in the State

{23}
1906
of Washington and sailed for Japan on the
7th august 1906. his Mother and I had been
with him to salt Lake city and I had the
privelage of assisting Elder seymour B. Young
and George Reynolds of the fisr Presidency of
the seventies in setting him apart for his
mission. Elder S.B. Young being Mouth. It
Cost $120.00 for transportation and 50.00
for Expenses when landing in Japan.
Our Lucern Harvest was greatly injured
by heavy rains and the wheat stacks also.
As the rain when through the stacks and
much of the Grain sprouted making it
unsalable, our Blue Creek land raised
a fairly good Crop of Rye but I could get
no one to cut it and it went back into the
ground save what Grants Horses ate. So
the years harvest was very poor indeed.
but I thank God that he provided us as
a family with food and Rayment. and shelter.
Monday 3rd sep 1906 Temple opened today
and I was at my post With Prest William
Budge Presising.. it seems quite a change
from the last administration, but all seemed
to move very well and the work rolls on as
usual. one man step aside and another

takes his place and our Heavenly father controlls all to the accomplishment of his purposes.
25 sep 1906 We rented 2 rooms over Jos Newbolds store on Main Street and Moved into them on the 18th the day school started but boys commenced school 25th sep, The fall and winter proved Wet and Very bad for getting around to do any outdoor work of any Kind and the public roads were almost impassable all winter
1st Jan 1907. My Birth day (70) proved a more pleasant day than usual and I took comfort in Visiting my family and seeking to comfort them all I could during the Vacation from the temple during the holidays

{24}
our Means for Extras was quite limited thro the winter because of the Crop failure and we had to curtail our Expenses as much as possible consequently we had no family gathering as had been usual years previous,
I am thankful the Lord has spared my life to be enable to get around as do as much as I am able to, and I trust I may continue to be useful yet many years to be a benefit to some –
Roads are Very bad all spring and I have been obliged to say in Logan many nights because of it. and it is not pleasant to Keep batch.
10th apl 1907 With Maggie I attended the General Conference in salt Lake City and had a good visit – as nothing could be done at home – the Weather is so unpropitious and roads so bad
sunday 12 May 1907. We have had a few fine days and I was induced to make and appointment to go to paradise to day and organize a prayer Circle. a Rain storm with snow set in yesterday making the roads Very bad again but I came to Logan and took up Elder Thos Morgan and went to Paradise through storm and mud and made the organization returning by way of Logan and taking up sister Lillie M Paull and taking her to smithfield to have a visit with my folks over night
saturday 15th June 1907. With my wife Maud I started with 1 horse and buggy with provisions &c for my boys Ora, Marriner and George at our Blue Spring Ranch – found Mauds nephew & wife at Garland and ate dinner with them arriving at our place at 6–30 P.M found all well & remained over sunday returning again Monday leaving there at 9 a.M. arriving at smithfield

{25}
at 7 P.M. finding all well at home
   The Boys had done some plowing on the land formerly plowed but Weather Conditions had prevented much being done as they had been there 8 days previous.
Thursday 20th June I started Wife Maggie with son Lorenzo and daughter Margie to the Blue spring Ranch with with span of horses (Doll and —) to help plow, also I hired Jake Watsons horse and sent along to take the place of my smallest horse now there (Kit) so Lorenzo could ride it home. Maggie & Margie was Expecting to stay as long as the boys remained there plowing and burning the sage Brush .
Sunday 23rd June 1907 With Wife Mary Jane went to Newton and attended 2 sessions of High Priests Conference – attendance small but had good meetings
learned of the Death of Jonas N Beck an old time resident and neighbour of the Rigby family at Newton
I Knew him and his father before him when I lived in the 19th Ward salt Lake City in 1858-59-60 as they were neibors to the Hendricks folks.
Monday 24 June 1907 – Lorenzo Returned from Blue Creek and brought letters stating all all well and progressing with the plowing.
~~Saturday 14th~~ having finished the Harvesting and threshing at home during aug, the Temple opened 3 sep 1907 and I was on hand as usual – but found things had gone wrong with Bro Jas A Leishman – he seemed to an Extent to have lost his balance and so nervous that he could do nothing at the work in the Temple.
Saturday 14th sep 1907. With Wife Mary Jane started to Blue Creek at 6am and got there about 4 P.M and found all well.
the boys Ora. Marriner. Lorenzo & Marnie having gone 2 days before .. to level the land and put in the Grain.

{26}
sunday 15th sep 1907. Went over all the land and saw how it looked. I left the springs about 11.30 and arrived at home in smithfield 8.30. resuming my labors in the Temple next morning as usual
saturday 21st sep 1907 Took Wife Maud and daughter Margie in Buggie and I started for farm on Blue Creek – wife Maud stayed at Garland to Visit her nephew Charles Blumell and his family and Margie & I went [ ] to our Blue Creek Property – found all well the Boys doing well arriving about 6.P.M. Gald to see wife Mary Jane and my 4 Children Ora Marriner. Lorenzo & Marney. stayed till Sunday 10–30 – Came to Garland alone – ate dinner and with Wife Maud Came back to Smithfield arriving about 8.30 P.M. The Boys Commenced sowing grain on Wednesday 18th about 3 P.M and had about 30 of the 80 acres sowed and the land was being put in pretty good shape – resumed labors in pretty goo Temple Monday Morning 23 sep 1907. Bro Leishman no better but Bedfast as usual
3 Oct 1907. With Wife maggie went to the Genl Conference at salt Lake City as the Boys Ora and Marriner wished to go to school – and ora had started – we rented 2 West Rooms over Bp Jos Newbolds store which Were comfortable The Temple was only open the first two days of October as the workmen were putting in a new heating boiler and new smoke stack. Close also during the month of November and opened for work 4th Dec 1907 – this rest for me was a good one and gave one the opportunity to be with my family altho' I could not do much because my boys were all at school. but the time passed pleasantly with my family, during
December I was not Well. Traveling home nights did not agree with me and I took a succession of Colds

{27}
25. Dec 1907. Christmas day spent with Mary and her Children & /her\ sister Elizabeth at the farm but was too sick to Enjoy it. so in the afternoon Went to town and to Bed at Maggies and did not get up again till Monday 7th Jan 1908. Everybody thought me too sick to get up again for some time but through the blessings of God and his priesthood I got onto my feet and went to the Temple on Tuesday and assisted with the work to be done. The Baptisms, Endowments and other ordinance Work has been quite Heavy since last October and promises to Keep so for some time yet as we have a number of German and switzerland people who have large records and are Hiring much work done for their Relatives and friends.
<u>Wednesday 8 april 1908</u> Altho I have been so much afficted all winter that it has seemed a cross to move and get about, I have Kept going and coming to the Temple, Except when the weather has been very severe when I have stayed in
Logan with my Boys at their Rooms, as it was sometimes convenient for some of my family to come from home and they stay over night with me. The Grippe never let up seemingly all winter and spring all the left side of my head being affected and inactive – my left Ear useless, and I seemed in Every way demoralized I attended the General Conference with wife Maggie and by getting a good seat near the stand heard with my right Ear most of the proceedings and speeches of the Conference The special Priesthood meeting was of great interest to me and instructions of a special nature on Matters of Church discipline were treated upon with much care.
Our Companies at the Temple have Kept up remarkably well and wehave had lots of work to do.
Sunday 17th May 1908. Went with wife Maggie to Lewiston and reorganized a Prayer Circle naming it by request of Bp Andrew

{28}
L Hyer. Lewiston 1st Ward Prayer Circle with 21 Members returning home immediately after, much fategued in body. And resuming my labor the next day at the Temple.
Friday 9th april 1909 – With my son William H. Roskelley took train for St Anthony. Idaho. On a Visit
to son Joseph & wife and our many Relatives who live there, and in the Rexburg Coungry, thus, filling up the Vacation from the Temple during the General Conference which I attended at

Salt Lake City – Had a splendid opportunity to Visit with son & family and Uncle Joseph S. Hendricks & family also Viney Watson & a number of her & Husband children living at Rexbug also sister Tabitha Ricks & her Children. I returned home in time for Temple work Tuesday 13 apr 1909.
Sunday 9th May 1909. With My Wife Mary I took small Buggy, and son James took team, and took my son Samuel and part of his family, also my wife Maud to Richmond and attended the funeral services of my Brother-in-law Patriarch William D Hendricks who died Thursday 5 May 1909 at Lewiston – The funeral was held in the Richmond new Tabernacle and it was filled with Relatives & friends – Everything went off well – a number of speakers testified to the good work and faithfulness of the patriarch and held him in high Esteem. His only Brother Joseph S. Hendricks and myself were among the speakers as I had Known him since the the spring of 1855, and was acquainted with his labors and Efforts to do Good. he leaves 5 living Wives and a numerous posterity – among them some Very prominent sons who are worthy representatives of the Hendricks family and of the Church they are Members of – The casket and floral offerings were grand, representing the Banking and milling associations he was connected with in Logan and other places.

{29}
Saturday 15 May 1909. With my wife Maggie also Bro Wm G. Burton & son Marnie started to Blue Creek Encountered a heavy rain storm from Bear River to top of Newton Divide making road quite heavy and altho we had 2 teams & outfits it was quite difficult traveling, arriving at our place away after night and very dark, found my hands. William Draper & Hans Hansen well. Also sons Richard and Wilford well – the latter two are working their own farms and it is refreshing to see the splendid feed and the Excellent manner the land is cultivated and the Grain coming up so nicely Thanks to God for his Kindness., altho' it runs me in debt Badly I feel Justified in Breaking more land and bringing it under Cultivation for future use while I have plenty of team to do it with having purchased 10 head of horses from Bro Kelsey and his son last fall I have now the power to move in the matter of team labor. I took Bro Burton out of cook for the boys for a month or so, so the boys working for me can devote all their time to the team work. I will have to borrow money to get thro' till the crop comes off in the fall. there is however good prospect on 50 of the 80 acres sown to Wheat last fall
sunday 13th June 1909 Today sold to son William H. Roskelley for $5000.00 my Blue Creek possessions consisting of 3 Quarter sections of land with Log house on Condition of $1000.00 being paid 1st Oct next and $1000.00 Each succeeding fall 1st Oct till all is paid
sunday 27th June 1909 With Wife Maud went to Clarkston a long promised Visit attended their prayer Circle meeting at 9 a m. gave 3 patriarchal blessings, attended sunday school – ate dinner at Bro Shumway's with his family and gave one of his daughters a blessing – went to afternoon meeting and met Prest of stake alma Merrill. and with him occupied time of Meeting. again went to the tithing office and gave 3 more Blessings and returned home at 10 oclock night being a day well spent.
Monday & Tuesday 28 & 29th June – took a spell of stomach trouble and suffered much for a time .

{30}
saturday 16th July 1909
Quarterly Conference commenced to day at Smithfield Prest M F. Lyman and Jos McMurrin Vistors from Salt Lake – our Tabernacle was full of People and we had much good fatherly talk along the line of doing good while we have opportunity in Mortality as it is a Very short period but so very important in its bearing upon the Eternities to come. Bro McMurrin gave some Excellent gospel discourse well suited to the times and circumstances we are now in. I had a private conversation with President R.M.

Lyman .. Explained to him Ora's Circumstances and Views regarding further Education and he advised me to send him to the University of Utah to take out a degree before going East to attend one of the Universities, for final work, he gave me some Very pointed. Views about the calling & Labors of a Patriarch in the Church and was quite sevier in some of his Expressions on those that hid their calling under a bushel and did not magnify it to the benefit of the saints and themselves and said he and the authorities of the Church had quit ordaining new to that office unless they felt assured the parties ordained would magnify their Calling.. he also stated to me that he intended to investigate all rumors of persons being sealed as plural cases, in Logan Temple. /or any where Else\ bring them to light. And if any are found to have been sealed within the past 5 years to see that they are cut off the church, to gether with those that sealed them

sunday 6th Feb 1910. Learning my son Ora was sick in Salt Lake and his mother had gone to waite upon him I took train this morning to go and see him. Getting there OK. I found stonemans' place in the 18th Ward and afterward Maggie My Wife and Ora came. Ora having recovered his health Enough to come and see me. Spent the night at Stonemans with wife & son and the Evening had the Company of Bro and sister sherwood (Charles) and had a splendid visit with them all. which they seemed to Enjoy as well as us as Visitors

{31}
Monday 7th Feb 1910
Went to Visit the Commissioners who had been appointed by Governor spry to take the names and official applications of all the men an surviving widows of men who had served at any time in fighting or guarding Indians in their depridations on the White people since the settlement of the state and found out what information would be needed for me to file an application in my own case. I then went to meet the train to get Robert Thornley and William

Douglass by previous arrangement had agreed to come from Smithfield to Salt Lake City be witnesses for me to testify that I was in the Military Organization and had been Employed in Indian Raids years ago. I had given these two men $5.00 Each to pay their fair and provide food &c to go to Salt Lake City, and they were true to their promise and came on the train bringing with them widows of David Weekes and John Kelsey who were in the war with the Indians on the 23 July 1860 when the Indians Killed Ira Merrill on the bench above smithfield we ate dinner at a Restaurant and then went to the Commissioners office and I gave my sworn statement as to the part I took in the trying to head off the Indians when they Killed Ira Merrill. And the two witnesses Verified my statement, after which I went to the place (Simons Bros) where Maggie was buying hats &c for her millinary store, we then were met by my son Ora and went to the University of Utah and going through the building viewing the many interesting specimens & devices and apparatus for the students to study the lessons They were seeking to get, met and was introduced to Dr Merrill, and Prof Lyman of the University of Utah and had Conversation with him as to the future of Ora's labors and both advised me to Keep him in school there until he had

{32}
obtained his Diploma and was graduated from there went to Ora's stopping place Prof Driggs treated us Very Kindly and his wife made a good supper for us. which we much Enjoyed. I stayed there with Wife & Ora and held conversation with Prof Driggs & wife until bet time and went to Wm stonemans to sleep –   Tuesday 8th Feb 1910
I forgot to record yesterday. I gave Robt Thornley $5.00 to add to the $10.00 to pay Expenses of himself && Wm Douglass to salt Lake City as Witnesses for me this Tuesday Morning I went to the Historians Office and saw Secty Jos F. smith Jr. Visited the Library of

Samuel Roskelley

the Genealogical & Historical society in same
building and there found some record of Roskill's
of Cornwall Eng. The country where my people had
lived and died. Except my father's family and
the assistant recorder Miss Cameron agreed to
get all the record of the Roskilly's from the
records and forward to Logan to me also
I found Roskell's and arranged to get them
also as I believe this an abbreviation of their
name.– went from there to the Temple and
had an Interview with Bro Madson on some
important matters and also Recorders McAllister
and Christensen and Visited the Font Room &c
met several of the Quorum of ~~the~~ apostles &
many of the Presidents of stakes who all
greeted me with much Earnestness and
cordiality. And when going from the Temple
met and received a hearty shak of the hand
from our dear leaders Prest Jos F. smith
Prest A. H Lund and apostle John H. smith
while at the Temple learned several
important items pertaining to Temple Work
which were of Value to me. from there
proceeded to the Train with Wife Maggie
and went to Ogden, and Visited Maggies
Brother in law and her sister. (Bro & sister Jacobs)
and then took train for home or rather I to
Logan and Maggie to smithfield.

{33}
Wednesday 9th Feb 1910
Today the people of Cache stake commenced their
annual Visit to the Temple for 1 Week or more
as they could arrange, the 1st & 2nd Wards are
to furnish their Quoto this week and we
had 195 for Endowments today with an
average of sealing & Children to Parents
Saturday 12 Feb 1910 I sent East to Waterloo Iowa
to the William Galloway Co for a Manure spreader, and
sent a check for 69$\underline{^{00}}$ to pay for. Check on Smithfield
Bank
9th March 1910 My sons James. William and
Richard looked through our Records and found
that I samuel Roskelley had since the Temple opened
for ordinance Work 21 May 1884 up to and including
9th March 1910 Ordained proxies for dead men
16.196 persons for the Dead to the office of Elder,
and 71 living persons to the office of Elder,
<u>2nd april 1910</u>. Today I was officially
served with a summoned by City Marshall
Emil Petersen with a warrant to appear
before Justice of Peace samuel Nelson and
answer the charge of tieing my horse to
my fence on my sidewalk at my wife
Maud's. the result as follows, after hearing
the complaint made by the Marshall read
I pleaded guilty to tieing the Horse to the.
Fence because the road was so Exceedingly
muddy and I only had one neighbor living
beyond me and I though to hurt no one
by my action not Knowing such ordinance
was on the statue Books prohibiting going
on the sidewalk; Justice Samuel Nelson
fined me 5$\underline{^{00}}$ for the offence or 5 days in
the City Jail, and as I did not have the
money I was Locked up in the City Jail
in a filthy place 16 feet one way by
4 ft 6 1/2 inches the other. One window so
closed, I could not open it and the cement
floor so wet and fithly and the closet
so further it was utterly unfit for any

{34}
1910
human being to be incarcarated and Kept
in such a filthy Hole. My sons and many
friends learning of my Confinement came to
my rescue before night and paid the
fine (which I did not design to pay) thus
liberating me and the Boys & George
Merrill came and with the Marshall
assisted me home in a Buggy.
31st March 1910 from 9th to 31st March I have
ordained 96 proxies to the Office of Elder for the
Dead.
16th and 17th April 1910 Attended Quarterly Conference
of Benson stake held at Smithfield Tabernacle
apostle Hyrum M smith and Prest of seventies
James H. Hart were Present and delivered
some Exellent discourses.
Sunday 24th apl by appointment went ~~to~~
Clarkston – tookWife Maud. attended Prayer
Circle and also Visited sunday school and
with Prest alma Merrill and his Bro alonzo
the High Councillor Visited the afternoon
meeting and talked awhile on Temple Work
and during the day gave 6 Patriarchal

Blessings
During the Month of apl I carried
on my usual Labors in the Temple and attended
to many home affairs also as
my health had somewhat improved
I ordained 82 proxies to the Office of
Elders for the dead during the month
and during the month of May I ordained
101 Proxies for the dead to the office of
Elder in the Church of Christ.
During the month of June I ordained
117 Proxies for the Dead to the Office of Elder
in the Church of Christ

{35}
1910
During the month of July I ordained 109 proxies to the
office of Elder for the Dead and
During the month of september I ordained 97 proxies to
the office of Elder for the Dead
attended the Genl Conference at salt Lake City
with wives
Maggie &Maud and had much delight in hearing
the Teaching
of the Bretheren and also the singing of the noted
Quire
Everything went off splendid and a most Excellent
spirit
prevailed. Prest Jos F smith was very emphatic in
denouncing
those who had assumed the authority to perform
Plural
Marriages since the Manifesto issued by Prest W.
Woodruff
and stated his position before the people of the
world in
consequence of these breaches of trust. it seems
also
that fashon pride has obtained great sway in salt
Lake
City for some of the ladies dresses were ridiculous
and
unbecoming as Latter-day-saints – The funerals of
sister Bathsheba Smith the wife of the late apostle
and President Geo a smith and President of the
Whole Church Relief Societies was held a week
before Conference. Also sister Lucy Walker Kimball
Smith's funeral was held a few days previous to the
Conference – I had Known both of these good
women a long time sister Lucy was the wife of the
Prophet Joseph Smith sealed to him in Nauvoo and
she
has been devoted to his interests
saturday. 15 Oct 1910. With my wife Maud I
attended
the Benson stake Conference held at Richmond
also attended same Conference on sunday 16th Oct
at same place, the Visitors from salt Lake were
apostle Jos F. Smith Jr and Elder Edgar Young
of the 1st Presidents of 70's.

[*remainder of volume blank*]

[*end of journal 7; end of transcript*]

"A Faith Promoting Incident"

ca.1888

THE GOOD OLD days we used to enjoy in the [18]50's should never be forgotten, said William Hopeful, who had just got up from the table of his hospitable friend, John Humphries, who resides in the thrifty town of [blank] in one of our Border Stakes of Zion. And as the sentence closed, Sister Humphries, rising from the table invited her husband's guest to occupy the parlor where she had made a nice fire in the stove and prepared to make the guest comfortable as long as he wished to stay under her husband's roof. For she had heard her husband often speak of his friend, William Hopeful, as being one of his youthful companions in the [blank] Branch of the Church in England, not many years after the sound of the voice of the message of Salvation had been heard by the people of that country. She had heard also that her husband and Brother Hopeful joined the church and had taken their district to deliver tracts at the homes of the people, and had also been ordained to the priesthood about the same time and were afterwards chosen by the Counsel of the Branch to go on Sundays to the adjacent village and preach to the people "outdoors". And she had also learned that when her husband (then a young man) had by his industry and economy secured enough means to come to Zion with the £10.00 Company, which at that time came by way of New Orleans, Keokuck, and the overland journey across Iowa and the Great Plains, that the Local Church Authorities had told Brother Hopeful they had learned that his parents and relatives had turned against him because he had embraced Mormonism against their wishes and were embittered against him because he would advocate Bible truths which they could not gainsay or disprove. Consequently, they had turned him out doors, but if he would get ready he could have the privilege of going to Zion by the perpetual emigration Fund and that probably he might cross the sea in the same ship with Brother Humphries, which he did. But on arriving at the frontier they were placed in different companies to cross the plains and on arriving in the valleys had located quite a distance from each other, consequently had not seen each other for years. But their former love for each other had not ceased to burn in their hearts and the occasional mention of Brother Hopeful's name in the newspaper as a missionary or some other useful position in the church would be the cause for a repetition by her husband of some incident in the early career of the two, now gray-haired men. These little circumstances Sister Humphries was familiar with relative to the history of the two men. And now that the cruel Edmunds Tucker Law was being enforced by the heartless, prejudiced and vindictive Governmental Officers it had caused

---

Manuscript presently unlocated; transcribed ca.1945 by Lula Mortensen. Transcript published in *The Roskelley Family Record* 5, no.1–2 (September, December 1955): 85–88, 89–92.

Brother Hopeful to leave his happy home and God-fearing families in the care of Him who suffereth not a Sparrow to fall to the ground unnoticed, and go into exile, where ever the Spirit would lead him, to find friends, rest and repose to his spirit and body, after being hunted and searched for by the merciless Minions of the law at his home and places of residence, For she had heard that he had obeyed the Celestial law and bad families "like flocks" and she realized that with her keen, shrude, penetrating power, she could with such a guest in her house, be soon enabled to determine the caliber of the man she had heard so much of and determined in her own mind the difference in her own husband and his friend, for though her husband like herself, had been prompt in attending meetings, paying their tithes and offerings, relieving the wants of the poor, and held offices of trust and responsibility in the ward where they reside, still they had never seen the time when they felt they had enough around them to justify him in taking another wife or maintaining another family, or that the blessings of another family would be worth the sacrifice of the little Heavenly world they possessed. Hence they had never contended earnestly for a testimony from the Lord concerning that doctrine, but now that Brother Hopeful being driven into exile had become their guest she hoped seeing he was a polygamist to show him how nice and comfortable they lived in their quiet home. blessed with the comforts and good things of life, with no anxiety about Deputy Marshalls or fear of being dragged before packed juries of the "Open Venire" kind or be "found guilty" without evidence—and condemned, fined and sent to prison because "you are reputed to have another wife" and up to date no wandering exile, for conscience sake, had called to ask of them a resting place for a few days and seek retirement to write letters of council, advice and good cheer to the loved ones at home, and to tell mothers how to do and ask them to instill into the minds of the children—old and young—that" father says" if all—mothers and children—will pray earnestly to God in faith three times a day for him to escape the hands of the wicked officers that he will not be captured—except it be the design of God that he should go to prison—to tell the boys what to do to forward the work and to make their mas comfortable and as happy as possible under the circumstances.

When the two men were seated in the parlor the good Mrs. Humphries with her daughter soon cleared off the table and arranged the dishes in their proper places and entering the parlor found the two men engaged in earnest conversation. Recounting some of the scenes of their boyhood days and reminding each other of events that transpired in their early history. Elder Hopeful relating the circumstances of his first meeting with the Saints, his lingering at the close of the meeting around the doorway wondering at the strange actions of the Saints in their handshaking and manifestation of love and good feelings for each other—of the feeling that went through him when Elder [blank], the Branch President, came to him and putting his right hand on his head said, "I prophesy in the name of the Lord that you will yet become a Mormon Elder and preach the Gospel in its fullness. Also the circumstances connected with their baptism into the church. The persons' names that were in the boat that carried them across the river to the place of baptism. The singing of "How glorious will be the Morning" by Elders and sisters. So and so of them feeling on coming out of the water and the feelings of joy that sprang up in their hearts on the return trip knowing that their sins were remitted and that God had accepted them as His sons through obedience to the law of Baptism.

When Mrs. Humphries and her daughters were comfortably seated with a little lace work in their hands, for Sister H. prided herself on her industrious habits, Brother Humphries turned to her saying, "Now, wife we have often talked about Brother Hopeful and the experience he was getting, for you know he had filled foreign missions, also a number of home missions something you know I have never done since I came to the Country, and be being a polygamist in practice as well as faith, can perhaps give us some items of his experience that will be valuable to us in our future lives. "Yes," said Sister Humphries, "I should like to hear Brother Hopeful relate some of his experiences and especially what testimony he received concerning the principle of Celestial marriage, for I'd like to know what there is to induce a man in his church to take the responsibility of more than one family on his shoulders and have to work so hard to maintain them, and especially in these hard times when it's almost worth a man's life to marry more than one wife. For it is found out that both him and his families have to suffer. He to go to prison for a series of years and be confined with the worst class of men living, and the family to be debarred of his companionship and assistance and be deprived of many comforts they might otherwise enjoy.

"Well," said Brother Hopeful, "You have asked me some important questions which I shall be pleased to answer—I trust to your satisfaction. I said when rising from your table a short time since, the good old days we used to enjoy in the 50's should never be forgotten because of the peace and harmony that prevailed in all the settlements of the Saints throughout the Territory. Almost everyone you met was a Brother or Sister and a friend because they were all baptized with one baptism into one faith—forsaking Babylon and her institutions. We left homes and kindred to come to Zion and walk in the ways of the Lord. You know a drunken person was a thing unknown until Stephens' Army quartered in Salt Lake City in the winter of and prostitution in any form was unheard of until a certain Judge brought a nude woman and sat her on the judicial bench beside him in Fillmore and from that time to this, crime of every kind has been introduced by those who have come into the Territory professing Christianity, until unlike the days I referred to in the 50's when everybody in a settlement went to bed at night and without a door being locked or a window barred—no police or Constable necessary to keep the peace and the man with one or more families would call his families around him morning and night and all kneeling before the Lord offer their sacred devotions for blessings past, for further grace to pursue the journey of life and that as they forgave, so might they be forgiven. Today the leaders and trusted men amongst the Saints are hunted like felons of the deepest dye—their wives and children whom they love as themselves are hounded, insulted and abused by persons in the garb of men calling themselves officers of the law—but to my subject—you asked me to relate some of my experiences and especially what testimony I had received concerning the principle of Celestial Marriage, to which I will say that my testimonies of the Divinity of God's work in the earth are so abundant that I should have to deny my own existence to deny the many and varied testimonies God has favored me with. For the prophecy of Elder, the President of the Branch where your husband and I became members of the Church through the ordinance of Baptism, etc., has been fulfilled to the letter for I have filled several missions delegated with authority to preach the Gospel both in our territory and among the nations and God has made manifest His power in my behalf on many occasions through prayer and fasting on my part and has always come to my aid when I have put my trust in Him, and I have been in many strange places in the course of my experience in this church. The present ordeal we are passing through confirms my faith for our Heavenly Father will not put us in possession of a crown and kingdom only as we prove ourselves worthy of such blessings. The Savior said as recorded by Mark "Whosoever therefore shall be ashamed of me and of my words in this adulterous and sinful generation, of him also shall the Son of Man be ashamed when He cometh in the glory of his Father with the Holy Angels". As I understood his language, if we refuse to obey the principles of Salvation he has revealed to our understanding we virtually deny Him. The principle of Celestial, commonly called Plural marriage, was very repugnant to my feelings when I first heard it, shortly after embracing the Gospel, but the spirit of the Lord induced me to restrain my feelings and lay my views of the question on the shelf for the time being, I was not prepared to judge the matter only from notions framed and built upon sectarian ideas of Morality. But after coming to the mountains and reading the revelation on the subject carefully and prayerfully the same spirit that gave me a testimony of the divinity of the work after I was baptized and confirmed a member of the church, rested upon me and by its influence I knew that revelation was also true and that in the language of the revelation "no one can reject this covenant and be permitted to enter into my Glory"—"And he that receiveth a fullness thereof, must and shall abide the law, or he shall be damned saith the Lord God". Also I read, "For they are given unto him to multiply and replenish the earth, according to my commandment and to fulfill the promise which was given by my Father before the foundation of the world: and for their exaltation in the eternal worlds, that they may bear the souls of men; for herein is the work of my Father continued, that He may be glorified". On reading this, I began asking myself some serious questions, Am I doing right to remain unmarried with these things so plainly set forth? And as the Father is glorified, and the female is exalted in the eternal worlds by bearing the souls of men, then if the glory of woman is her offspring. will not two or more women with offspring add to a man's glory more than one can possibly do? These and many other questions presented themselves to my mind until with the assistance of the Holy Spirit I became thoroughly convinced of the truth of the principle and resolved to obey it. But thinking that perhaps a little experience in seeing the workings of the principle in some family or organization I laid the matter before the Lord and sought and obtained employment from a man who was a well-known polygamist [Brigham Young] and after a few months service I received his consent to board with his family and remained in his employ for nearly two and a half years during which time I became so much attached to his family that it seemed like home because of the harmony and good feeling that prevailed amongst them. But I was not doing my duty—I was a drone so far as the principle of Celestial Marriage is concerned and the Lord took steps to change my position in life. I was too dilatory in living up to the laws I was acquainted with and God saw fit through his servants to call me on a mission to Europe and get me out of my comfortable situation and well beaten path and give me an experience of another kind. I filled the mission assigned me to the best of my ability and I believe to the entire satisfaction of the presiding officers of the Mission, presiding as I did over one of the Welch Conferences nearly all the time I was in the mission and returning home with the missionary company at the time the Buchanan Army were en route for Utah. And witnessed the hand of God in guiding and protecting his servants on their return to their families and friends in these valleys. Soon after the return of the Saints from the Southern part of the territory to their homes in the North, I married, poor as I was. And in a short time afterwards I made the acquaintance of another young lady and married her also, convinced as I was that it was my duty—for nothing but duty would have induced me to take another wife—as my wife and home was the nearest to Heaven I bad ever got up to that date. With this action came the experience common to men who, having watched others under, as they think, similar circumstances, fancy they have obtained in the family I had watched so closely would not fit in my case and I was nonplussed—confused—I had fancied I was prepared for almost any emergency but experience proved I had reckoned without '"Mine Host." I had overestimated my ability and strength and the Lord wanted to let me feel my nothingness when his help was withdrawn from me, for it seemed that the Heavens were as brass over my head—and the spirit of supplication that I used to enjoy In my devotions before the Lord had fled. While I was tempted and tried almost beyond endurance, and the adversary would whisper in my ear when I attempted to pray, '"What's the use of your praying, the Lord will not hear your prayers for you have destroyed your once happy home by your own acts?" And people that had been my best friends and knew my former circumstances shunned me, this alone almost killed my sensitive spirit. But I had not forgotten the Lord, nor His many mercies to me and I resolved to fast and pray until I got that same spirit back that gave me a testimony of the divinity of the principle. I fasted and prayed several days—the cloud and gloom gradually withdrew and the power of the adversary was broken—and God heard my prayers—the same spirit I had before possessed came back and I rejoiced in the Lord, but I did not feel like the same man. I no longer had that confidence and strength in my own ability that I before possessed for God had taught me that from Him alone came my strength and to him alone must I look for help and support and He gave me power to get my wives together and calm their feelings and teach them how to live and cultivate a spirit of love for each other—Oh, what joy I felt at that meeting.

For the Spirt of the Lord was poured our upon us—we fell upon each other's necks and wept tears of sorrow for *our* follies—of joy for the return of happiness. We forgave each other trespasses and we all knelt down and gave thanks to God for the reconciliation, I learned through this circumstance that I must govern myself better and live nearer to God than I had ever done and this I tried to do. In a few years I was called by God's servants to fill another mission to Great Britain with a request [and] respond to the call at an early date. I did to but not without some personal sacrifice, feeling that "Sacrifice calls forth the blessings of Heaven. Filling my mission to the best of my ability, most of the time president of an important conference in England. After being honorably released I was given charge of a large company of Saints on my return home to the Mountains. I found on arriving that family and friends met me with a warm welcome but my family during my absence had become somewhat indebted and I was promptly requested to meet these obligations. My health was not the best at the time and I felt somewhat disheartened because of my circumstances until I met Brother [blank] who offered me employment at a fair salary by which means I could help my family and pay up my indebtedness. I accepted his offer with gladness—after I had been there employed some little time I was standing on the main road to the town of [blank] enjoying a pleasant conversation with my employer when some of my relatives and friends came along, meeting me quite unexpectedly, and giving me a warm welcome—among them was a young lady whom I had been quite well acquainted with before going on my late mission and on seeing her something seemed to suggest to me that I ought to ask her to be my wife.

It was but the thought of a moment, but it sank deep in my mind, and I felt that all the blood in my body came to my face in a moment, but after they had gone away my employer and I had resumed conversation, my thoughts were not upon the conversation with him but upon the feeling that came over me when I saw the young lady mentioned, and later in the day in reflecting on the questions—my poverty, the condition of my family and their necessities, came before me and I resolved to banish the thought from my heart of marrying any more in this life and the feeling left me.

But a short time afterwards I chanced to get into company of some friends among whom was this same young lady before mentioned, and as my eye caught hers the impression and feeling came over me that I had before received and I felt there must be a providence about it in some manner, but again after mature reflection I felt justified in saying to myself—I am both too poor and too old to again marry and will not entertain the idea, For I consider in looking over my past life and I have done pretty well, much more than many of the Elders of Israel of similar standing in the church. And why should I seek to excel and take more on my shoulder than I have ability to provide for? And why bring the principle into disrepute because I have perhaps an opportunity of getting another wife? I thought No. I will not. If I provide for those I have I am doing well, and I will not have the care and responsibility of another family for I have enough to care for.

It was evening and I went to bed contemplating the thoughts and feelings that were in my mind through the past day—and justifying myself in my resolutions.

I fell asleep and dreamed I had ended my earthly career, or in other words, I was dead and was ushered into the presence of my Heavenly Father. I knew Him well. His face and person I was quite familiar with and He greeted me by saying, "Well, my son, you have finished up your mission on Earth and returned home, have you?" I answered respectfully, "Yes Sir." at the same time wondering if He would accept my earthly career and bid me welcome.

He continued, "I suppose you think you have done pretty well, at least as well as the majority who have been your associates on the earth?" This inspired in me a little confidence and I answered, "Yes Sir, I think so," Said He, "You have been successful In retaining the Faith of the Gospel in your heart and preaching it to others and in filling the positions of responsibility and trust that have been given you—setting examples for good among your associates, haven't you?" Said I, "I think so, considering my surroundings. At the same time a feeling of satisfaction and assurance of His approval came over me that is easier felt than described. For I began to feel with all my sins and weaknesses, my general course of life would receive His approval, for He asked me many questions in a manner that l could answer in the affirmative and take pleasure that I could live but said He, "How is it about your family that I gave you—why did you not take my handmaiden that My spirit prompted you to take to wife and also others that were yours by my gift if you had reached out your hand to have received my blessings?

Why did you repudiate the suggestions of my spirit and cut yourself short of that glory and exaltation you might have attained to? I felt at once where I was and I pled that poverty and a lack of faith I had thought a sufficient cause for not taking to wife the person He mentioned "But," said He, "Can you recollect a time in your experience when you were in too straightened circumstances and you called upon Me for assistance but I gave it to you? And have you ever lacked for anything you really needed when you were in the line of duty, and have I not answered your prayers on land and on the sea?

To all of which questions I could not but with shamefacedness answer that He had given me all these blessings—"and yet"—continued He, "with all these evidences before you and the promptings of My Spirit to guide you, you made a firm resolve that you would not marry any more, and dried up the faith that had been placed in your heart of reliance upon me."

Said He, "Look." And He waved His hand and I looked and saw this same young woman with a beautiful family of children with her. Said He, "These might have been yours if you had listened to the repeated promptings of My Spirit. And also these"—pointing to other women and children that I knew well, "but you cut off your increase and the experience you would have gained with them by saying in your heart, 'I will not accept the suggestions of the Spirit,' and you sinned against me by refusing to obey My law when you had opportunity and the way was opened for you to do so. In all your future life you might have been associated with these, my servants and handmaidens if you had observed my counsels," and He again waived his hand and I saw a number of Brethren with their wives and children, beautiful and lovely beyond description. Many of whom I had been intimately acquainted and associated with on the earth, "but now your future associates will be these, "and He waved His hand again and I saw a number of persons I had been acquainted with in the church on earth and they looked, so small physically and mentally so diminutive—for though I recognized them to be the same persons I had previously known, I wondered what had befallen them to make them so lilliputian in stature and mind.

I shuddered and especially so when Father said "And I have no assurance to give you that you can retain the family you now seem to have and enjoy." Although I had much experience before this I never knew what mental suffering was to the extent l then felt and I hope never again to pass through experiences and feel the same as I felt at that time and a few weeks afterwards. I asked if there was no chance for repentance—but was answered that my opportunity for repentance had been given me on the earth if I had been willing to accept them that I had stopped my own increase and growth—through repudiating the suggestions and promptings of the Holy Spirit.

I awoke but I could hardly realize I was still mortal and with mortality on the earth. It was but a dream, it was true, but Oh! the vivid recollection of my condition in that dream was terrible. For many days and nights following I knew no peace. l besought the Lord with earnestness in fasting and prayer that I might be forgiven for the thoughts I had entertained and for my action in refusing to obey the promptings of the Spirit.

Did the Lord hear my prayers? Yes, He did, for my repentance was sincere and l assure you I lost no time after I felt the Lord had given me an opportunity of repenting, in going to the girl and proposing to marry her, and as an evidence that my offering was accepted to Him, He blessed me with her and I now have a beautiful family of children by her and a better wife no man can wish to possess. Did the Lord open up my way to provide for my growing family? Yes, I received ability to provide for them and to meet my obligations satisfactory, which gave me another testimony that God hears and answers prayer and supplication and taught me to rely upon My Heavenly father for guidance day by day.

Well," said Sister Humphries, "If I could have such testimonies as that from the Lord I should not mind my husband having another wife—you know we have plenty around us to support another if we could only find the right one—but I think there is so much risk in getting one that is genial, you know," and she sat back in her easy chair with an air of self-confidence that such a suitable person could not be found.

"That is not a hard matter when the Lord is consulted," said Brother Hopeful, "and as you asked me what testimonies I have received concerning the principle of Celestial Marriage. I will give you a few more items of my experience. A few years since, it was suggested to me by a man of competent authority, that it was now a good time to show to the Lord my faith in the law of Celestial Marriage by taking another wife—for said he, "There are circumstances that existed during the 50's before the Poland bill passed the Congress, that will not do so under present circumstances." I felt that this suggestion was binding—that I could not ignore it and be justified with the recollection of my dream before my mind.

So I pondered upon the matter, asking myself who shall I ask to be my wife in these critical times? I resolved to fast and ask the Lord about it for if it was right, who could show me where to go and who to ask better than He who knows the hearts of all His children? I did fast and pray earnestly that he would show me who to solicit to become my wife. For several weeks I continued my supplication, when He showed me in the vision of my mind the complete bust of a young lady with whom I had but a very slight acquaintance. I became satisfied in my own mind, but the question arose, how will my family look upon it Will they accept her as a member of the family upon my say so? For although I had every evidence to believe my family had all confidence in me as a husband and father, yet I felt that if it was right, I should add another wife to my household, those I already had would be deeply interested in the matter, for my present family enjoyed each other's company and society, knowing each other's weaknesses and each other's virtues and to bung in an uncongenial associate would be perhaps disastrous to the whole family, and inasmuch as this is God's work, He is as able to give my wives a testimony and show them who He wishes me to have as to show me.

At the same time I felt I was willing to do my part inasmuch as He had shown me what to do, so the first opportunity I had, I told each wife privately what was required at my hands and asked them if they were willing to give me their faith, prayers and blessing in complying with the requirement, to which they each assented, asking in each case, "Who do you intend getting?" I answered their question by asking, "Who would you suggest?" and asking further that each fast and pray to God to show them who He desired me to have, and suggesting that we take plenty of time to plead with the Lord regarding so momentous a question and after I thought they had sufficient time to learn the will of the Lord on the question, I ventured to ask the result of their fasting, prayer and pleadings.

Their answers were, "Yes, I know who it is for the face of a person was shown me while at prayer, but I only know part of her name and it seems as though I have known her all my life yet I have never seen her but few times."

Another said, "Yes, my eyes were directed to a person in meeting on Sunday and it seemed impossible for me to take them from her for something seemed to say, "That is the person you are looking for, and you will become better acquainted." Though they had never met to know each other, she was able to tell me her name. Here was the goodness of God displayed in answer to prayer and my bean melted within me with gratitude. I was slightly acquainted with the person and had spoken to her but few times, but relying upon the Lord I consulted and gained consent of the parents and after a brief interview with her in which I advised that she do as I had done, go to the Lord and accept His counsel. She took time to consider and the next time we met she gave me a favorable answer for she said the satisfaction she had received from the Lord in answer to prayer and fasting, gave convincing proof that it was a right step and she bad never received such evidence concerning any person who had proposed marriage to her before.

These, my friends, are some of the outlines of evidence I have received in favor of Celestial Marriage—the Hand of the Lord has been quite as manifest in the details as in the outlines and I believe it to be the privilege and duty of every Elder in the church to whom the law of Celestial Marriage shall come, to seek the mind of the Lord and obey that law in connection with all other laws of the Gospel—and if they would, our fair daughters would become the honored wives of men having faith in God and Gospel ordinances and would not seek the companionship of the ungodly and those who know not God and observe not His laws. And I am satisfied that many Elders of Israel will be held at least partially responsible for so many of our young women marrying outside of the church.

"Well, "said Sister Humphries, "I never saw things in that light before and I am resolved if my husband is willing to take your plan and go and ask the Lord about this matter and with His blessing we will try and follow your example.

"I am very thankful the Lord has prompted you to come to see us for this has been a pleasurable and I trust profitable evening to us."

A Visit from the Spirit World

[*missing first sheet (2 pages)*]
be right to do so. I desisted in my efforts when thus so gently rebuked—and said to me "Well Sammy, you are pretty sick ain't you?" I answered "Yes, and I should like to know how it is going to terminate, for I am getting tired of being as I am." Said he, "I need some help in the position I am in and have permission to call either you, Frank Gunnell, Liney Farrell, or brother Olsen to come and help me and I have come to learn what your financial condition is so as to know if you can be spared better than any of the other boys I have named. What is your condition and how are your families situated?" I told him as near as possible my situation and how my families would be left if I was to person called for. I asked what he thought of the situation? Raising his head from a seemingly thoughtful position he replied, "I don't know, we'll see pretty soon." And bidding me good night he was gone in the twinkling of an eye. Before long I began to recover and rapidly gained health and strength and was soon able to resume my labors. As the winter approached and the time drew near for the settling of tithing at Logan I received a message from brother G. L. Farrell that he was very sick and desired me to come and see him. The question flashed through my mind at once, "I wonder if he is the victim?" I felt that I had no faith for him, if I went to see him, as brother Maughn's words had left so deep an impression on my mind, but feeling that I should deeply regret it should he pass away without my seeing him, I went to visit and administered to him. Although without faith on my part as all I could do was to ask the Lord if it was His will that he should be healed up, which seemed almost improbable as his head was very much swollen and a perfect mass of erysipelas scabs, he could talk it is true but his tongue was very thick, consequently he talked with difficulty. I parted with him with very strange feelings but hoped for the best, but I did not say a word to him nor had I told anyone up to this time of brother Peter Maughan's visit to me. Time rolled around and brother Farrell got better which I was very thankful for.

We met as usual in the following winter to make the tithing settlement except brother C. L. Olsen who had been employed as bookkeeper by elder Moses Thatcher, the manager of the Logan Branch Z.C.M.I.A. We had nearly got through the work of making up the general accounts when Bro. Francis Gunnell went home with an attack of rheumatism. I thought perhaps a day or two nursing would release him of his aches and pains but in a few days we learned he had sent for a doctor and the doctor pronounced the case a very bad one of acute rheumatism, and unless the patient could get immediate relief he thought the case would go hard. Reports brought us the assurance that he was at death's door and could not live much longer unless relief came from some unexpected source as the doctor declared he was hopeless and could do nothing for him but administer drugs to allay pain. I was all the time

---

Manuscript presently unlocated, but transcribed by Lula Mortensen ca.1945. Mortensen's transcript was published in *The Roskelley Organ* 1, no.? (1955): 31–32, from which this publication is taken.

asking myself, shall I see Frank again in the flesh? Is it possible he is the victim? He is the 3rd person attacked out of the 4 whose names were mentioned, I wonder how it will go with him? But I afterwards learned that a sudden change came over him during the worst of his sickness and he rapidly recovered. I did not have an opportunity of conversing with him upon the subject till the next winter when we met as usual in the old Logan Tithing office—made sacred to us by the many pleasant hours spent together and telling each other of the bits of our history now and again.

We had completed a long days work—it was near midnight. He and I were alone and preparing to go to bed in a little back room of the office and I brought up the subject of his sickness of the previous spring. "Ha!" said he, "a funny thing happened which I have said little about to anyone outside of my family. But I'll tell you how I came to get around so quick after the doctor and everybody else had given me up to die. You know I was awful sick. I wanted to die and get out of my misery. The doctor had left medicine to be given me every so often to kill the pain but I could not tell any difference before or after I had taken it and I had taken so much of one thing and another I had got sick of it and lost all faith in its doing me any good. Well, one night about 12 o'clock my watchers had gone in another room to get something to eat and prepare for a nights siege with me. I was lying as still as I could for pain, pondering over the situation and wondering what would be the outcome. I silently asked the Lord if my time had come to take me out of my misery but if it had not come to give me ease and restore me to health that I might do my duty in the Church and to my family. All of a sudden in comes Peter Maughan and after him came his 1st wife and my 1st wife. Said he, 'Well Frank you are pretty sick ain't you?' 'Yes' said I, 'I am, can't you do nothing to ease a fellow's pain?' 'Well,' said he, 'We'll see. In the course of 1/2 or 3/4 of an hour. We are now going to hold a council on your case and we'll know more about it very soon whether its best to have you stay or come with us.' After so saying he led the way and all three went off without saying goodnight or anything. Well in less than an hour I was as easy as could be. And from that time rapidly recovered."

The recital of brother Gunnell's experience thrilled me from head to foot, brought fresh to my mind my experience with brother Maughan and I related it to him before I slept because his experience corroberated with mine. He was quite surprised to know I had kept it from him so long and knowing as I did his situation. But said he, perhaps the thing has blowed over and we ain't wanted on the other side now. The matter partially passed from my mind for a little over a year. In the spring of 18__ I met bishop Liljenquist on the street in Logan. He enquired if I knew brother Olsen was sick and asked me to go and administer to him. I did so, although brother Maughan's visit came afresh to my mind and I was almost hoping against hope, as he was the last of the four mentioned and the others had passed through a spell of sickness. I visited Logan again in a few days and learned brother Olsen was dead. I attended the funeral and related the circumstance of Bro. Maughan's visit to me some time before.

Afterword

So, there you have it, all of grandfather Roskelley's autobiographical reminiscences and his diaries—his personal writings. As this transcription goes to press, all three of Samuel's autobiographical writings and two of the manuscript diaries remain at large, lost somewhere in the family (I hope). When this transcript comes to your hands, if you have Journals 1 or 3, or family documents, correspondence, or photographs, please consider ensuring they do not remain in your hands, lost to history. One is only genuinely a caretaker of family history when the charges are rendered safely permanent and accessible to all descendants. Hoarding things is seriously uncool.

www.ingramcontent.com/pod-product-compliance
Lightning Source LLC
Chambersburg PA
CBHW080117020526
44112CB00037B/2764